Vinson Brown

THE
Amateur
NATURALIST'S
HANDBOOK

A SPECTRUM BOOK

PRENTICE-HALL, INC., *Englewood Cliffs, N.J. 07632*

Library of Congress Cataloging in Publication Data

BROWN, VINSON, 1912-   The amateur naturalist's handbook.

(A Spectrum Book)
Bibliography: p.
Includes index.
1.—Nature, study.   I.–Title.
QH53.B785   1980   574   80-15354
ISBN 0-13-023739-6
ISBN 0-13-023721-3 (pbk.)

To my wife, Barbara,
a light in my life and a fulfiller of dreams,
and to all who open their eyes and ears and minds
to the marvels of nature.

Editorial/production supervision and interior design by Donald Chanfrau
Cover design by Judith Kazdym Leeds
Manufacturing buyer: Cathie Lenard

A SPECTRUM BOOK

10 9 8 7 6 5 4

Printed in the United States of America

PRENTICE-HALL INTERNATIONAL, INC., *London*
PRENTICE-HALL OF AUSTRALIA PTY. LIMITED, *Sydney*
PRENTICE-HALL OF CANADA, LTD., *Toronto*
PRENTICE-HALL OF INDIA PRIVATE LIMITED, *New Delhi*
PRENTICE-HALL OF JAPAN, *Tokyo*
PRENTICE-HALL OF SOUTHEAST ASIA PTE. LTD., *Singapore*
WHITEHALL BOOKS LIMITED, *Wellington, New Zealand*

Contents

9
Beginning Ecology   91

II
THE STUDENT NATURALIST   99

10
Thinking out a Problem   101

11
Animal Study   106

12
Plant Study   140

13
Study of Rocks and Minerals 157

14
Climate Study 181

15
The Student Ecologist 203

16
Continuing the Trail of the Naturalist 217

III
THE ADVANCED NATURALIST 225

17
The Classification and Special Study of Animals 227

23
Conclusion: The Crossroads 381

Preface

A great deal has happened in the scientific world, and especially in our understandings of the relationships of people to life on this planet, since this book was first published by Little, Brown in 1948. Although the book was successful enough to go through fourteen printings, the need for an improvement today was very great and I am grateful to Prentice-Hall, Inc., the present publisher, for the opportunity to do this revision.

Today the amateur naturalist must be warned that our human experience with nature since 1948 teaches us to approach the making of collections of animals and plants with the greatest caution because of the upset balance of life so often produced in recent years by predatory and exploitative humans. Pollutions and other destructions of natural environments have gone on apace, but today we are more aware of the danger these pose, not only to animal and plant life, but to our own species and to the whole beauty and harmony of this planet. We are beginning to prevent further losses and to spread knowledge so that the degenerative process can be reversed. So, collect specimens only when you feel it is vital to your research and then only with the greatest caution. We generally can collect, without worry, animals and plants that are extremely common, although this should be checked with your nearest college biology department and your nearest Department of Fish and Game office, and you can collect those animals and birds whose freshly killed bodies you find along a highway or elsewhere. (Of course, those who do not wish to collect specimens can still be naturalists by using photos and drawings as your specimens.)

Major additions that appear in this book over the previous one include much more information on the science of ecology and a new chapter on ecology's branch science, ethology, the behavior of life. In the new book, text measurements given are by the metric system, with the old English system in parentheses, because all scientific work in America has gone metric. (A metric conversion chart has been added after the Index for this purpose.) Otherwise changes are minor, but each is made on the basis of improved knowledge. It is hoped that you will find the whole book useful and inspiring and that you will not hesitate to make suggestions for future improvements.

Much thanks to Robin Brickman for her illustrations on habitats. And to Mary Kennan, Editor for Spectrum Books at Prentice-Hall, I owe much gratitude for her excellent assistance, her suggestions, and her wisdom during my writing and researching of this revision.

Preface
to the First Edition

Naturalists usually start in as beginners who have had their curiosity aroused about nature. Some start very young; others not until late in life. Age does not matter in a naturalist; it is the spirit that counts.

This book is for all who like the out-of-doors and would like to know more about the many interesting things they see. It is for those who want to go beyond mere collecting and naming into the land of the true naturalist, that of careful observation, study and experiment; who wish to gain some of the wisdom of workers before them, and who may be numbered among wise workers in time to come.

In looking through this book you will notice that we study all parts of nature—not only animals, for example, but also rocks, plants, and climate.

You may ask "Why not study only what I am interested in, learn a lot about it, and let the rest go?"

One reason is that often you will be just as interested in other parts of nature if you will only try to learn something about them. Also, a wise beginner learns as much as possible in many fields, before choosing the one in which to specialize; because then he or she will know something about the whole of natural science, and its many relations and interactions with his or her specialty.

In this book you will be given suggestions about how to go about your work so that you will learn more and more as you go along, and you will be given information about a number of tools useful in studying nature, many of which you can make yourself. The study of each of the great sections of nature is so arranged that there are things to learn and do for the Beginning, Student, Advanced, and Explorer Naturalist. The Appendix has a series of tests to help you advance, step by step, until you are able to do the work of a true naturalist.

Also, in the Appendix, there is a list of books, or Bibliography, naming those useful to the naturalist, which are arranged according to the fields they cover—as "General Biological Works," "Books on Mammals," "Books on Rocks and Minerals." Throughout this book, mention will be made of other books particularly worthy of study by a naturalist. Turn to the Bibliography in the back for further information on who publishes them and when they were first printed. But remember that many of these books can be found in your local library. Look them up—you will be delighted at the stores of knowledge that you find.

INTRODUCTION

CHAPTER

1

The Trail
of the Naturalist

It is a day just at the beginning of summer, somewhere in North America. We choose early summer for this story not because it is the only good time to study nature, but because then nature comes into full glory and the hum of life is deepest.

We see a land of rolling hills, of meadows rich in green grass, but with here and there a small clump of forest. Flowers blaze their colors in the sunlight, and bees hum straight to them from the distant apiaries of the farm.

The cows by the fence lift their heads from grazing and stare with dull wonderment at a figure that has come through a gate and is now wading through the rich grass. In their well-fed contentment, there is no place for curiosity about the world around them; and soon they lower their heads again to their delicious repast. The being who walks across the field is a different sort of animal. Bulging pockets, a carrying case on the side and a butterfly net in one hand, mark a naturalist. But this is no mere collecting trip. The fields call with a deeper purpose.

The net swings swiftly to catch a darting dragonfly, and the insect buzzes angrily in the green folds of cloth. Yet the act of catching a specimen is only one part of this person's being alive, for the eyes look keenly about and up and down. They see the feathery trails of cirrus clouds high in the blue and mark them for a sign of good weather. The mouse paths through the grass appear like tiny highways of Lilliputians, and a glance catches the flash of a small brown form as it plummets down a half-hidden hole. Stooping to pick up a hard pebble of white chalcedony that a winter freshet laid down in the field, the naturalist glances at other pebbles, which indicate that this is not far from where volcanoes raged a million years ago. By another mouse hole a field cricket is spotted, and when it too disappears down the dark hole it is marked as a "commensal" creature, an uninvited guest who takes advantage of the field mouse's work for shelter from enemies.

Beyond the next hill the walker comes to rocky outcropping, and this is the goal of the hike. On days before, fingers have touched the fine sandstone of the rocks and marked them as pressure-molded sediment of many ages past; but now the naturalist glances at a sheltered spot where a bastion of rock leans outward from the small cliff's side and so forms protection to many of nature's creatures. Here is an ideal spot to study what naturalists call the "ecologic niche." The words simply mean a small section of the world that certain animals and plants have found their most favorable place for living. This "niche" is a favorite spot for spiders, particularly for the clever "sheet web weavers" of the family *Linyphidae*. Their hammocklike webs spread across the rocks' surface and cling here and there to the tips of maidenhair fern or the stalks of red pentstemon flowers.

Our naturalist is not so much interested in the kinds of spiders found here (although in a side case are some small vials of alcohol to collect specimens of each species if necessary) as in the success or lack of success of the different spiders in catching food. The naturalist's problem is to know, in other words, why certain parts of this "niche" are more sought after than others and what spiders are most successful in getting food and why. So now the naturalist takes out a notebook and proceeds to draw on it a sketch (very much like that in Figure 10-1). Each web is lettered as it is found upon the rock for use in reference, and the watcher proceeds to sit down and quietly watch.

The spiders, which scuttled into dark holes and crannies at the first noise, now cautiously begin to come out to points of vantage where they may be able to spring upon any prey caught in their nets. It is like the jungle where the tiger crouches by the water hole waiting for the dainty coming of the antelope. To the fly, joyfully swirling through the summer air, the spider is just as terrible an enemy. Time passes through the noisy summer silence. A crane fly (some call it a "gallinipper") comes clumsily whirring through the air and slaps into one of the sticky webs. The spider rushes out across its trap, sure as a tightrope walker in her natural element. She does not actually attack the crane fly, but first circles her prey; then, seizing the proper moment, throws new silken cords across the struggling fly with dexterous hind feet. When the prey is firmly enmeshed, the spider comes close with a quick dart and makes several bites on the body and head. The crane fly's struggles slowly stop as the poison from the bites takes effect.

This drama of the little world is repeated many times that morning, as the observer patiently watches and each time carefully marks down in the notebook the web that receives its prey. Perhaps A web catches few insects, while C and B and K get very many. The spiders in C, B, and K are large and powerful; they can drive away rivals and get the best places. But the naturalist notes that there is a struggle in choice between the places that are best suited for catching insects and those that are best protected from wind and rain. Newcomers among the spiders that seek to spin webs in this niche must do so on the outer edges, where conditions are not so good. Perhaps in time they gradually force their way in, toward the more favorable middle sections, if they grow large enough and strong enough. Perhaps, if they are too small and their luck is too poor, they move away from this crowded place and seek a less-touched one, much as emigrants leave a crowded mother country to seek their fortunes in a new world. There are many problems for the naturalist to study here, many mornings to watch carefully and patiently, jotting down in the notebook what is observed, before many of these problems are solved.

Now the new naturalist moves home again, with a creased brow and eyes not quite so alert as they were earlier. In that brain, the facts of the day's observations are being grouped into their proper places and a picture of the whole is beginning to form. Why had the little gray spider been able to make its home so successfully in the midst of its larger cousins? Some webs caught no prey at all. So how long could spiders live without food? This is the process of *deduction*, and its result is the building of *hypotheses* (frameworks for ideas) and finally *theories*, the wonderful work of the human brain that has built up our knowledge of the universe to the state where it is today, and that will build it on to yet unimagined heights of knowing in the future.

A butterfly wings by our naturalist, who automatically swings the net to catch it. The naturalist has some similar specimens, so this one goes free, but the naturalist's mind wanders after it and perhaps wonders what interesting things there may be to learn about that single kind of creature. A breeze sways the tall grasses—and the naturalist sees again the infinite wonder of nature and realizes how on all sides lie new worlds to conquer. Even the cows, peacefully chewing their cud by the gate that leads to the milking barn, are worthy of intent study—for, indeed, has not study and experimenting with cows in the past made them the indispensable animal they are to humans today? Before you come back to this scene and the things learned by following the naturalist's trail, you are going to start trekking on a trail of your own. You will make this trail intensely interesting to yourself if you keep your eyes and mind open, and if you are ready and eager to learn. Just keep in mind that exploring the out-of-doors is an adventure, not a task, and you will have the right attitude. At the end of the next seven chapters you will be ready to join our friend of the spider niche again, and this time with a sufficient knowledge and background to better understand. And that, you will surely find, will be fun!

CHAPTER
2

What
Nature Study Is

The study of nature is simply the study of the natural world around us, the rocks, plants, animals, stars, climate, and perhaps even ourselves, since we are a part of nature.

Our understanding of nature has grown very slowly. For long ages, people did not realize that the earth was round; even into the 1800s some great scientists still thought many living creatures (flies, for example) could spring alive and full grown from the earth, or manure, or rotting vegetation, or the waters of the sea.

Today we are surrounded by countless little mysteries of life. Can anyone tell you just how the ladybird beetles come together in great swarms in the fall of the year? No, because they have not studied this phenomenon enough to know. Entomologists (insect students) know the life history of the bee, but can tell us little or nothing of the life histories of countless other interesting insects. A botanist may call a certain flower by name, but it is often unlikely that he or she can tell us very exactly its distribution in the hills, or the special kinds of soil

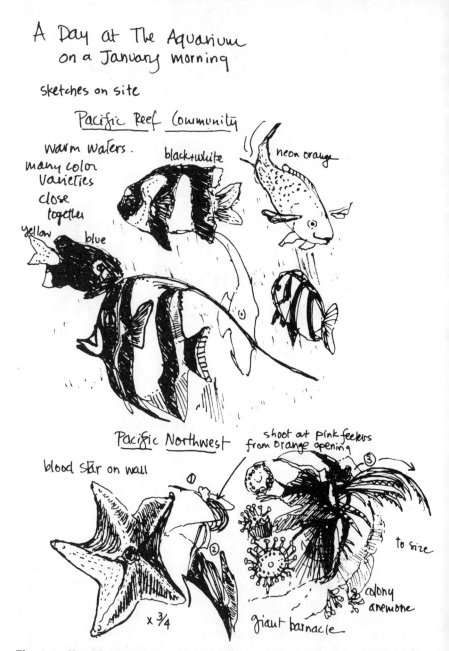

A Day at The Aquarium
on a January morning

sketches on site

Pacific Reef Community

warm waters.
many color
varieties
close
together

yellow   blue

black+white

neon orange

Pacific Northwest

shoot out pink feelers
from orange opening

blood star on wall

①

②

③

to size

colony
anemone

× ¾

giant barnacle

Fig. 2-1. *Sketchbook page from a visit to an aquarium. Drawing offers a focus for study and record taking of animals seen at places such as an aquarium. From Nature Drawing: A Tool For Learning, by Clare Walker Leslie. (Englewood Cliffs, N.J.: Prentice Hall, 1980), p. 127. Used by permission.*

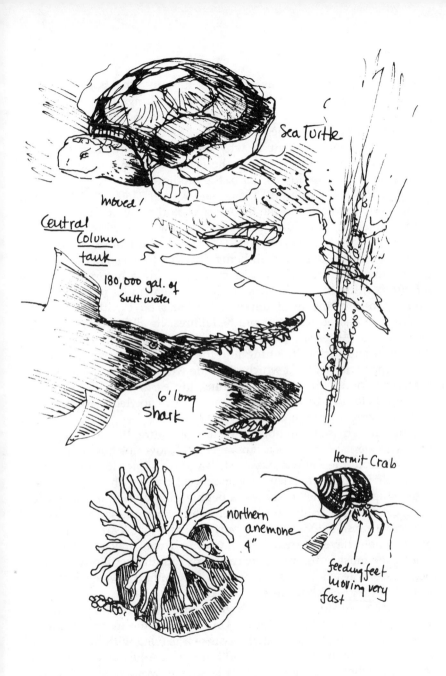

Sea Turtle

moved!

Central
Column
tank

180,000 gal. of
salt water

6' long
shark

Hermit Crab

northern
anemone
4"

feeding feet
moving very
fast

9

it likes, or the plants it usually lives next to. The botanist hasn't studied that yet, because there are too many things to study. All the present naturalists of the world, working night and day, could not in one hundred years even begin to unravel the numerous problems and questions of nature. That is why all of us, perhaps in our own backyards, have a chance to join the march of truth and open up by humble efforts some tiny corner of the unknown.

Let us take an example, CHARLES DARWIN (1809–82), the great naturalist who developed the theory of evolution by natural selection, while wandering in his garden one day saw an earthworm emerge from its burrow. Millions of people have seen earthworms and thought nothing of them—beyond their being dirty creatures, sometimes useful in catching fish. But Darwin was curious, being a naturalist, and he set out to study the earthworm. To his amazement he found that this worm is one of the most important animals on earth! Without the earthworm, half our crops would be failures. Its all important job is to bring air to the earth, to open the pores of the ground by boring through it and eating it, letting into the soil the life-giving, nitrogen-making bacteria, without which plant life would be nearly impossible. If Darwin found this out by watching the earthworm, is it so wise then for us to turn up our noses at the bits of knowledge we may gain from studying nature in our backyards?

True naturalists are humble in the face of nature, because they know the vast extent of their own ignorance. "I know not how others may see it," wrote the famous physicist, ISAAC NEWTON (1642–1727), "but to myself I seem a child who wanders all day on the seashore and gathers up here a shell and there a pebble, colored by the wave, while the great ocean of truth stretches before him, boundless, unexplored!"

Even if your nature study is only the sort that learns again what other people have learned before you, still you may count yourself among the most fortunate of the earth, for countless millions of human beings never learn to be familiar with the animals, plants, rocks, and stars that they see about them every day.

Many people stop short of studying nature because they let the big words of science frighten them. This is the same as the fright that some children get from the dark because it is filled with the unknown. In both cases there is, of course, nothing to fear. Just as with a foreign language, when one uses it a bit, the strange words take on meaning and soon become like old friends.

Zoology, botany, geology, and all their subdivisions are rich with meaning to the naturalist. They are the pathways that break down and make understandable the vast complexity of the natural world. Each such pathway leads to a region of adventurous exploration, the unknown lands of science.

NATURAL SCIENCE DIVISIONS

It is a good idea to get a picture of some of these divisions of natural science, before we turn to the study of any one of them. Below is an outline of some of the many sciences of nature.

BIOLOGY (the study of plants and animals).

ZOOLOGY (the study of animals).
Including such sciences as:
    ENTOMOLOGY (the study of insects).
    ORNITHOLOGY (the study of birds).
    PROTOZOOLOGY (the study of single-celled animals).
    EMBRYOLOGY (the study of embryos—animals before they are born).
    MAMMALOGY (the study of mammals).

BOTANY (the study of plants).
Including such sciences as:
    SYSTEMATIC BOTANY (the study of the classification of plants).
    MYCOLOGY (the study of fungus).
    BACTERIOLOGY (the study of bacteria).

GEOLOGY (the study of rocks).
Including such sciences as:
    PETROLOGY (rocks).
    MINERALOGY (the study of minerals).
    CRYSTALLOGRAPHY (the study of crystals).
    PALEONTOLOGY (the study of fossils).

ASTRONOMY (the study of the heavens).

METEOROLOGY (the study of weather).

SPECIAL SCIENCES
 Including:
    Ecology (the study of the relationships and interactions of life).
    Physiology (the study of the chemical actions of life, movement,
        and functions of animal blood or plant sap, and so on).
    Pathology (the study of diseases).
    Parasitology (the study of parasites, both animals and plants).
    Cytology (the study of cells).
    Anatomy (the study of life structure).
    Genetics (the study of inheritance).

GREAT NATURALISTS

The lives of the great scientists contain strange and interesting tales of
how they got started in their special fields. They also show us how,
while most people go all through their lives blind to the wonder
around them, the person with trained observation picks out the details
that both enrich his or her own life and add to the knowledge of the
whole world.

Jean Lamarck (1744–1829), the famous French naturalist, was confined for many months to a garret in the heart of the great city of Paris,
sick with yellow jaundice. Many people in such a position would have
been bored and miserable, but not Lamarck. As he lay there in that
bare tiny room, alone with the sky that looked in his single window,
he studied the clouds that came and went across the blue. As the long
days passed, through his close observations he made the first scientific
analysis of cloud forms and their meanings. He came to know what
the great billowy cumulus clouds meant in the way of weather and
how the long fingers of cirro-stratus, spreading thinly across the sky,
foretold a storm. Because of this knowledge, Lamarck became the
world's first scientific meteorologist.

In 1745, Carl Linnaeus (1707–78), a graduate of the University of
Lund in Sweden who was interested in nature study, became so
annoyed with the clumsy systems of natural classification in use at
that time that he rushed vigorously into the tremendous task of making
a truly scientific classification of plants and animals. His annoyance
brought forth *Systema Naturae*, a great book that will probably remain

forever the basis of all natural classification. Linnaeus was therefore the first real *systematist* (student of systematic classification) among scientists.

In Austria, during the quiet years of the 1870s, a Catholic abbot, GREGOR MENDEL (1822–84), carefully kept records of the controlled cross-fertilization of certain plants in his monastery gardens. His curious mind, drawn by the appearance of some strange variations in the sweet peas he cultivated in his garden, caused him to isolate these plants in special greenhouses, pollinate them by a small hand brush with chosen pollen, and then carefully record over many years the interesting things that happened from the plant crosses he made. His results were described in an obscure scientific journal of the 1880s and soon forgotten. But some thirty years afterward, their discovery burst like a bombshell on the scientific world and made the *Mendelian laws of inheritance* as true and everlasting as Newton's *laws of gravity*. Mendel was the first true *geneticist* (student of inheritance).

JEAN HENRI FABRE (1823–1915), when only a boy in the French countryside, became interested in the strange antics of insects. His curiosity led him in later years into some of the first intimate studies of the lives of insects that had ever been made. His stories of insect lives will remain forever among the immortal works of science and literature. Bee, wasp, cricket, and ant were all subjects of his detailed study; and he made their jointed-legged, instinct-run lives for the first time seem real.

In the United States, a few decades ago, RAYMOND LEE DITMARS (1876–1942) was a young fellow who collected and studied snakes and lizards to the worry of his family. But young Raymond kept building his collection of living reptiles up to the point where he was trading for and buying specimens from many strange parts of the world. He even had a standing order with the big shipping firms of New York City to turn over to him any snakes that came in with shipments of fruit or other products from the tropics. He not only collected snakes, but began to study their life habits and to keep careful notes on how they acted and what they ate. Raymond Ditmars's early hobby made him a world-famous authority on snakes and other reptiles. People everywhere turned to him for advice and knowledge. Snakes, to him, even as a boy, were a living part of the world worthy of much curiosity and study.

JOHN MUIR (1838–1914), the Scotch-American who explored the nature of the early West, was another person who very early had the outlook of the naturalist. He writes:

When I was a boy in Scotland I was fond of everything that was wild, and all my life I've been growing fonder and fonder of wild places and wild creatures. With red-blooded playmates, wild as myself, I loved to wander in the fields to hear the birds sing, and along the seashore to gaze and wonder at the shells and seaweeds, eels and crabs in the pools among the rocks when the tide was low; and best of all to watch the waves in awful storms thundering on the black headlands and craggy ruins of the old Dunbar castle when the sea and the sky, the waves and the clouds were mingled together as one. *

Many other fine naturalists started in early years to learn about the world's wonders. LOUIS AGASSIZ (1807–73), the famous Swiss-American naturalist and geologist, as a boy caught fishes and put them in a stone drinking fountain to study them. His later studies of fishes were world-renowned. EDWARD D. COPE (1840–97), a great American paleontologist, at seven went with his father on a voyage from Philadelphia to Boston and drew pictures of jellyfish and other marine animals in his diary. DAVID STARR JORDAN (1851–1931), who later became president of Stanford University and a world expert on fishes, at the age of thirteen made up a list of all the plants in his neighborhood and followed this by learning all the constellations of stars in the northern sky.

Sometimes these young naturalists had rather funny experiences. It is said of Charles Darwin that as a boy he was once collecting insects and, having run out of containers to put them in, he carried one precious bug home in his mouth!

Our great naturalist president, THEODORE ROOSEVELT (1858–1919), when a young fellow had a similar experience, only much more embarrassing. He was collecting specimens along the Hudson River with some friends. When he found he had no more room in any of his bulging pockets, which were already crammed with insects, frogs,

* From *The Story of My Boyhood and Youth* by John Muir. Copyright, 1913 by John Muir. Copyright renewed 1940 by Wanda Muir Hanna. Reprinted by permission of Houghton Mifflin Company.

toads, and snakes of all sorts, he stuck the last frog he caught under his hat. But very soon after this, the group met the Honorable Hamilton Fish, then United States Secretary of State, and his very dignified wife. Poor Teddy doffed his hat and lost both his frog and his own dignity! No one seems to know what the lady did.*

Not all those who study nature have the chance or even the desire to become professional naturalists, but many of them may become amateur naturalists. A large part of the world's share of knowledge has been gathered by these same amateurs. Theodore Roosevelt was such an amateur, adding much to our knowledge of big game animals.

Another was THOMAS BELT (1832–78), who, while acting as a mining engineer in Nicaragua, also studied the animals and plants of that interesting tropical country. The book that he wrote from his observations (*A Naturalist in Nicaragua, 1888*) makes stimulating and exciting reading that every beginning naturalist would be wise to read it. OTTO DIENTZ, a businessman of New York City, made his name famous by his spare-time work with beetles. CHRISTIAN GROTH, a well-known jeweler of New York, was another person who had a scientific hobby in his spare time that brought him lasting credit. He became a world authority on swallowtail butterflies.

THREE NATURALISTS
WHO OVERCAME ADVERSITY

Until recently, the prevailing opinion in America and many other places was that blacks of any nationality, American Indians, and women in general were incapable of doing scientific work. Even today such prejudices are strong in some areas despite the fact that modern science shows us that all human beings, regardless of sex or race, have precisely the same kind of blood and nerve cells, and that it is proper training, not sex or race, that allows the mind to develop creatively. The three stories that follow illustrate how two women and a black man became famous scientists and naturalists despite these prejudices and other difficulties.

RACHEL CARSON (1907–1964) was so quiet and unassuming in her

---

* Henry Fairfield Osborn, *Impressions of Great Naturalists* (New York: Scribner's, 1928), pp. 167–68.

youth that only those few who had read her early writings and appreciated their beauty and wisdom guessed that she was due for greatness. Yet even those few would have been surprised to know that she would in time combine a fine writing ability with a wide and deep scientific knowledge. They did not know that already as a girl she had spent many hours carefully watching animals and plants in gardens, fields, and woods until she had developed the quick and seeing eye that reads the hidden stories of nature. She showed this later in her research in laboratories and in the field and in her famous books such as *Under the Sea Wind,* and *The Sea Around Us,* but her greatest quality became evident when some friends brought her some bodies of robins killed by deadly DDT spray, used to protect crops. The agony of dying she saw in the way they had pulled their legs up tightly against their bodies filled her not only with compassion but fighting anger. Alone and looked down upon as a woman, she determined to take on huge corporations and powerful government officials. She led the way for other scientists and naturalists that must continue. Researching carefully she laid bare the subterfuges and blind greed that some huge corporations and even nations allowed to drive them along the paths of poisoning and polluting wide areas of the earth, often ostensibly to save crops. Her book *Silent Spring* thrilled millions with its agonizing cry to stop this evil before it was too late. Her own words speak of her dedication:

> *Now to these people (those who put profits and success in science and industry above life), apparently the balance of nature is something that was repealed as soon as man came on the scene. You might just as well assume that you could repeal the law of gravity! The balance of nature is built of a series of interrelationships between living things, and between living things and their environment. This doesn't mean that we must not attempt to tilt the balance of nature in our favor; but when we do make this attempt we must know what we are doing. We must know the consequences!**

* Philip Sterling, *The Sea and The Earth: The Life of Rachel Carson* (New York: Crowell, 1970), p. 183, with kind permission of the publishers. Originally broadcast April 3, 1963 over the CBS Television Network as part of "CBS Reports: The Silent Spring of Rachel Carson." © CBS Inc. 1963. All rights reserved. Used with permission.

JANE GOODALL (1938–   ) was different from many children. Even as a child she had an overwhelming desire to go to Africa and study the lives of wild animals. Finishing high school, she did not go on at first to college in England where she lived, but got a job as a waitress in her home town of Bournemouth to earn and save the money to go to Africa. At Nairobi in Kenya, she had the good fortune to be introduced to Dr. Louis Leakey, the famous paleontologist who discovered the most ancient bones of humans and man-apes and who was then the curator of the National Museum of Natural History. Sensing immediately that Goodall was a woman with burning curiosity and interest in animals, Dr. Leakey hired her as an assistant and took her with his party of diggers for ancient bones to Oldavai Gorge on the Serengeti Plains in what is now Tanzania. Her true love, however, was not digging for old bones, but studying live animals. When Dr. Leakey found financial backing to send her to investigate the lives of chimpanzees at a special Gombe Stream Chimpanzee Reserve on the eastern shore of Lake Tanganyika, she was thrilled and jumped at the chance.

The primitive conditions of this place, the open hostility of some of the natives, and the extreme shyness of the wild chimpanzees in the savage jungle country where she went to study them gave her a challenge, however, far beyond what Goodall had anticipated. That she rose to this challenge and finally conquered it after two years of mostly fruitless and heartbreaking work tells us that she was one investigator in a million. That she finally came to see the chimpanzees at close hand playing and feeding, no longer afraid of her, was due to a certain attitude toward her work and a feeling for life explained by her in these words:

One day, as I sat near him [one of the large chimpanzees]—, I saw a ripe red palm nut lying on the ground. I picked it up and held it out to him on my open palm. He turned his head away. When I moved my hand, he looked at it, and then at me, and then took the fruit, and at the same time held my hand firmly and gently with his own.

At that moment there was no need of any scientific knowledge to understand his communication of reassurance. The soft pressure of his fingers spoke to me not through my intellect but through a more

*primitive emotional channel: the barrier of untold centuries, which
has grown up during the separate evolution of man and chimpanzee,
was, for those few seconds, broken down.*

It was a reward far beyond my greatest hopes. *

The life of GEORGE WASHINGTON CARVER (c. 1864–1943), in its
success, points out one of the saddest results of prejudice in human
beings—the probably literally millions of other children who have
been stunted in their mental growth and their great potential creativity.
The life of the great black naturalist and agriculturist was filled with
often seemingly insurmountable difficulties, which he had to break
through to realize his tremendous possibilities. As a child he showed
great promise, even though sickly and frail in health, because he
looked at plants with the "seeing eye" of the true naturalist, loved
them, and learned quickly how to treat them well and make them
grow. But, even though a few educated white people saw this in him,
their minds said, "It is impossible for him ever to develop this ability,
since he is the son of a Negro slave."

Carver never saw his parents, although he did have help occasionally
as a boy and youth from kind people, both white and black. But
always they thought the only work he could do was menial. And at
such jobs he did work vigorously to earn money that he spent almost
entirely in ways to further his education. Something drove him forward
in his quest and finally led him in his late twenties to prove to Ames
College of Agriculture in Ames, Iowa, that he could join their student
body and earn his B.S. degree.

George Washington Carver even became a respected teacher at
Ames, but his great opportunity to serve people, especially his own,
came when Booker T. Washington, the famous black founder of Tuskegee Institute in Georgia, called Carver there for the awesome task of
helping to raise American blacks out of the despair and degradation of
slavery and its aftermath. Although Carver worked heroically at this
task, his genius as a naturalist made him work for all people, discov-
ering constantly new ways to use plants for food, healing, and in

---

* Jane van Lawick-Goodall, *In the Shadow of Man* (Boston: Houghton Mifflin, 1971).
© 1971 by Hugo and Jane van-Lawick Goodall. Reprinted by permission of Houghton
Mifflin and Collins Publishers (London).

manufactured products, and finding in the peanut alone more than one hundred such uses, thereby astonishing the world!

Many black boys and girls learned in Dr. Carver's classes how to enlarge their lives and become creators and leaders, but the one who could be his right hand had to show the qualities of a true naturalist. In September 1935, one of many hopefuls stood in the door at Rockefeller Hall on the Tuskegee Campus, eager to assist the master scientist. He was Austin W. Curtis, Jr., a chemistry graduate from Cornell University. But unlike the others who came and gave up after a short while, for Carver was so involved in his creative work that he had little time to show them what to do, young Curtis started to work quietly on his own experiments. He was so industrious and so involved that finally Carver asked him the magic words "What are you doing?" and followed this up shortly with the equally wonderful "Let me know if you need any help!*" From then on the great partnership between Carver and Curtis grew and grew. Curtis did bring his problems to Carver, but he found no easy answers. Carver's piercing questions drove him instead to think deeply, experiment carefully, and try over and over until a satisfactory answer could be found. For those who can find in themselves these qualities of a naturalist, they, too, can become fine scientists even if still amateurs.

To become a professional naturalist takes long and arduous preparation, and there is very little money along the way. Thus the advice of Louis Agassiz' father to his son, when Louis wanted to start immediately to work full-time in science, is still good. The father wrote:

*Let the sciences be the balloon in which you prepare to travel through higher regions, but let medicine and surgery be your parachutes.**

Remember that you can do fine scientific work in your spare time and that it is good to keep such a job as your "parachute" in case it ever becomes impossible to realize fully your dream of becoming a professional naturalist.

* Lawrence Elliott, *George Washington Carver: The Man Who Overcame* (Englewood Cliffs, N.J.: Prentice-Hall, Inc., 1966), by permission of the publishers.

* Osborn, *Impressions*, p. 24.

THINGS TO REMEMBER
IN STUDYING NATURE

1. *Collections are best if they tell a story.* Just a collection for a collection's sake—of unknown rocks, for example—is seldom very valuable. Even if your specimens are labeled with their names, they will still be good only for learning names *(identification)*. But names alone are not worth much unless you know something more about the things that are named—where they are found, who found them, what they were found with, what time of the year, what they looked like when found, and, if an animal, what its food was, and so forth. Knowledge of this sort makes the solid meat of a collection, a collection that will make a scientist say: "Well, here you have something really valuable. Your collection *tells me a story.*"

2. *Written observations and sketches build knowledge far better than trying to keep what you see merely in your head.* You probably remember times when you have said to yourself: "I used to remember what that thing looked like, but I've forgotten now." Suppose you were being asked about some wild animal that you saw about a year ago out in the hills. You would say: "Well, it looked kind of yellow, but it might have been brown, and it sneaked along through some bushes, though maybe it jumped over them. And I'm not sure whether it was as big as a dog or not. And maybe it was tall and thin, though it could have been fat. And it might have had long ears, though maybe not." That *would* be quite a help! We wouldn't know whether you saw a desert fox, a coyote, a badger, a raccoon, or a jack rabbit!

But if you had been a naturalist, you would have written what you saw in your notebook: "It was an animal about three feet long with yellowish fur and short, sharp-pointed ears, and a bushy tail. It had tracks like those of a dog, about as big as a collie's, and I saw it zigzag and sneak along through the brush." If you had written even such brief notes, ten years later a naturalist would look at your old notebook and tell you that you had seen a coyote, and there would be no doubt! Remember, then, that a naturalist keeps notes, and more notes, and still more notes. A lot of them might not be very good, but sooner or later, if he or she has been careful, patient, and alert, there are bound to be some among them that are pure gold!

3. *In nature you rarely find anything that stands by itself, since nearly everything that surrounds it acts upon it.* A rock, for instance, is shaped

by the action of wind and water. Gradually they wear it away in its weakest spots. Once it may have been on a high hill, but now perhaps it lies in a valley because a spring flood brought it there. An animal may kick it with its foot and turn it over, and so on, moving it, breaking it up, wearing it away. Once heat may have formed it down in the earth depths where volcanic fires roar, and then hurled it from the volcano's mouth down to the plain below; or a slow river brought the silt that made it down to the sea, layer on layer until the tremendous pressures of earth and water plus thousands of years of time formed it into a sedimentary rock like shale.

Seek for the reasons back of things if you would be a naturalist. A bird flies into a bush because it has seen a hawk. A man ducks his head low because the sun is shining in his eyes. A deer does not throw its head up suddenly just for amusement. Perhaps its keen nose has caught the scent of a dog down the wind. Some birds have short stout bills because they eat hard seeds; others have long slender bills because they catch and eat small insects deep in the narrow crevices of the tree bark. If you will realize that nothing you see results without cause, and always carefully look for the cause, you will be studying nature as a naturalist does.

4. *Ask questions.* Always ask questions, not only of others, but of yourself. Then don't be contented with just *any* answer; find the *right* one. This book was written to answer many such questions, but remember that in your public library are many books written by great authorities on the different natural sciences that may answer the questions unanswered here.

Remember the real naturalist uses words such as "probably" or "possibly" when answering questions, until he or she is quite sure. This is called the "scientific attitude" and means that the naturalist wants to find the real truth—not what is supposed to be the truth. Last of all, remember that nature gives the best answers to all questions: the answers that can only be found by careful observation and patient study in the out-of-doors.

CHAPTER
3
Ideals
of the Naturalist

Ideals are like good tools, very useful when well kept and used, useless when discarded and forgotten. Four of the best tools of the naturalist are *patience, vigilance, neatness,* and *cooperation.* We might add a fifth, curiosity, but it is really part of *vigilance,* and a sixth, accuracy, but it may be classed as the result of both *patience* and *vigilance.* These, then, are the four watchwords of the naturalist. They need to become a part of you, through long use and through the desire you yourself must have to make them your tools. No one can order or lecture the habit of using them into you; it will only come from your own constant practice. All of the great naturalists lived up to these ideals in varying degrees. Do not be too proud to follow the same road.

1. *Patience.* Being patient means such things as sitting in silence for long periods watching for wild animals, or working on and on without giving up until your job is done; it means also being so patiently careful with your work that the smallest details are strictly accurate. To a naturalist it may mean endless experiments, many of which seem wasted, but which in the end may lead to a great discovery.

Once three students were sitting in a small glade in the hills watching for wild animals. They sat still for about five minutes and then two of them began to fidget. "Why don't the animals show up?" asked one. He began to break sticks in his hands. They made cracking noises in the stillness so that a blue jay scolded him from a treetop, but that was all. "We've been here ten minutes," he finally complained, "and haven't seen a thing! Let's go." Two of the students left, but the third stayed for over an hour.

He became as still as the stones at his feet. Birds came down from the trees to peck at insects on the ground within six feet of him. A lizard scuttled by his hand and a snake slithered after it. Then suddenly a dark form with dark beady eyes appeared among some low bushes. The animal's claws made slight cracklings in the leaves and it moved over the ground in swift lopes up under some small redwood trees. It was all grace and beauty—its muscles acting like steel springs, its dark brown fur gleaming in the light. It found a trail of some creature along the edge of a gully, a rabbit perhaps, put its nose down and swiftly, eagerly bounded away with the twisting movements of a snake, its black eyes sparkling with excitement. It was a mink, possibly the first that had ever been seen in those woods. One observer had caught the true spirit of the naturalist and waited until this rare and beautiful sight became his own.

A young person at our Naturalists' Summer Camp asked for the job of making a checklist of the animals we had seen in that region. In three days the youngster made a list eighteen pages long, all correct. This was done with very little help, setting the example of a patient and accurate worker that every naturalist should be.

2. *Vigilance.* Alertness means the same thing as vigilance. It means being wide awake, on your toes, ready for anything. It also means being prepared for emergencies; and it means that on your field trips you are always ready to notice interesting things around you. In short, it means being more alive. Always be ready to study and seek to understand every least bit of movement in the wild, each flash of color, each whisper of sound, and to watch the shapes of leaf, tree, bird, and rock. A naturalist learns to know a bird first by its color, size, and shape, next by its movements when far away, and last by its call or song when out of sight. This is a marvelous power, but to obtain it takes constant training. Step onto any hillside, grove of trees, or rocky beach, and the wonder that lies around you, hidden in the grass,

beneath the bark, in the rock crannies, under the surface of soil or sand will be beyond your imagining. The vigilant naturalist turns upon it all with fingers and spade, with magnifying glass and forceps, and beneath what may seem lifeless dirt or rock, he or she finds life in all its myriad forms for study and thought. Even in winter the moths and butterflies have their pupae and chrysalids hidden along the bare tree branches, the fur-bearing creatures leave their interesting tracks to tell a story in the snow, and the fish still swim beneath the ice.

In the jungles of Panama a native hunter took me on a long trail through the mountains. In the afternoon when the sun still shone brightly down through the treetops, he told me that it was going to rain soon.

"Come now, Domingo," said I, "it surely isn't going to rain with the sun shining like this."

"Look señor," he answered, "do you see that big blue butterfly up there among the branches?"

"Yes."

"Do its wings shine like mirrors as they did not long ago?"

"No."

"Then know, *amigo,* that when the blue butterfly's wings refuse to shine it means that soon rain will come."

Sure enough, just as Domingo predicted, in a few hours rain came.

When the blue Morpho butterfly's wings stop shining like mirrors in the sunlight, it means the sun has gone behind a thin veil of cirro-stratus clouds, and cirro-stratus clouds usually mean rain is coming. The naturalist must learn to see, in small things that escape the eye of most people, signs of what has passed, what is happening, and what is yet to come.

Vigilance in a sense means curiosity also, and it is the curiosity of the scientist and the explorer that has opened up the world to people. You can rarely be too curious about nature. Keep trying to find the answer to your wonderings. Swiss-born naturalist LOUIS AGASSIZ (1807–73) was so curious that it is said of him that when his wife screamed that there was a snake in her shoe, he shouted back: "What, only one snake, my dear?".

3. *Neatness.* The naturalist needs neatness in both surroundings and mind if work is to be most effective. Neat collections and neat notebooks are more useful to us and to others who may see or use

them. Imagine a naturalist trying to make head or tail out of a notebook you had filled with smudgy scrawlings, without headings or margins. Or imagine the delay if one tried to study, say, your collection of insects and found them all jumbled together in two or three boxes with the names in the wrong places and most of them broken or ruined from crowding. Your notes and collection would probably be completely useless.

It always gives one a deep feeling of pleasure to find an amateur naturalist who has neat collections and notes. At one nature show in a western city, to which many boys and girls brought collections to try for prizes and awards, one eight-year-old had worked with tremendous patience and care to arrange a collection of over one hundred rocks and minerals with neatly typewritten labels and descriptions. We might have expected work as good from a student of fourteen or fifteen, but hardly from such a young child. However, others of varying ages had some excellent displays, including two fine collections of mounted plants; so it could be seen that many young naturalists had caught the true naturalist's spirit of neatness in their work.

4. *Cooperation.* Many naturalists work with another naturalist or a group, but in observing wild life, if one person is noisy, the chances of all to see something interesting are gone.

On July 1, 1858, the scientific world was shaken by a cataclysm. Two great English naturalists, ALFRED RUSSEL WALLACE (1823–1913) and Charles Darwin, had their papers describing the new *theory of evolution* published jointly on that day. Wallace's essay, "On the Tendencies of Varieties to Part Indefinitely from the Original Type," and Darwin's book, *The Origin of the Species by Natural Selection*, were both masterly descriptions of a theory of life that startled and enlightened the world. But perhaps the most remarkable feature of this introduction of a new theory was the cooperation shown by these two great men of science. Instead of each rushing to claim credit for first producing the new idea, both men worked modestly together as one team. The cause of science was immensely helped by this teamwork. A letter of Wallace's in 1860 typified this truly noble spirit of scientific cooperation. He wrote:

I could never have approached the completeness of his (Darwin's) book, its vast accumulation of evidence, its overwhelming argument, and its admirable tone and spirit. I really feel thankful that it has not been left to me to give the theory to the world. Mr. Darwin has created a new science and a new philosophy.*

Wallace was not content only to praise Darwin; he applied himself with great energy to backing up Darwin's facts and figures with his own, gathered through years of careful research.

We shall be wise indeed to learn from Darwin and Wallace this great lesson of cooperation and learn to work with and aid our friends in science.

With these four ideals, you will have the four essential tools of a naturalist. Use them constantly, so that their use becomes second nature. You are neat eventually not because you think about it, but because neatness has become one of your habits in life. You are at last vigilant as a hawk is vigilant who sweeps the land below unceasingly with sharp eyes. Your eyes naturally seek out interesting things about you; your ears naturally hear every sound that might have meaning. You keep patiently working until a job is finished because that seems to you the only thing to do.

If you would care to see how these ideals have helped the great naturalists of the past, read *Green Laurels* by Donald Culross Peattie, which seems to take you into the living green of the forest and jungle where the piercing, searching eyes of these naturalists unraveled the secrets that none had noticed before them.

---

*Osborn, *Impressions*, p. 19.

CHAPTER
4
Nature in the City

City people have a tendency to throw up their hands and say, "How can I find anything of interest to a naturalist in my city!" This is a mistaken attitude, and it is due to not really looking closely at their surroundings. City backyards, parks, botanical gardens, and the pools and ponds often found among them are swarming with more life than most people are aware of. You may not be able to collect animal and plant life in these places because of local laws, but you can certainly watch, photograph, draw, and write notes about whatever you see. WILLIAM BEEBE (1877–1962), the famous naturalist of the New York Zoological Gardens, spent a year studying the wildlife in his city and came up with a good-sized book detailing the thousands of kinds of life he discovered in this huge metropolis.

If you have a microscope or can borrow one, you can study the invisible-to-the-naked-eye life that swarms in most any drop of water taken from a pond or backyard goldfish pool. Many experiments and detailed investigations can be done with such microscopic life (see the

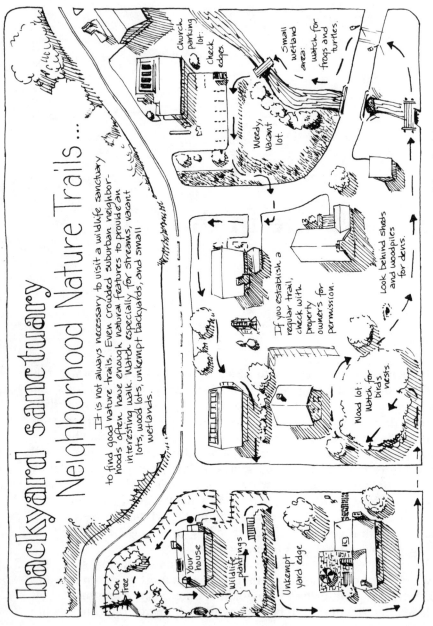

backyard sanctuary

Neighborhood Nature Trails...

It is not always necessary to visit a wildlife sanctuary to find good nature trails. Even crowded suburban neighborhoods often have enough natural features to provide an interesting walk. Watch especially for streams, vacant lots, wood lots, unkempt backyards, and small wetlands.

Church parking lot: check edges.

Small wetland area: watch for frogs and turtles.

Weedy, vacant lot.

If you establish a regular trail, check with property owners for permission.

Look behind sheds and woodpiles for dens.

Wood lot: Watch for birds' nests.

Dan tree

Your house

Wildlife plantings

Unkempt yard edge

Fig. 4-1. *Courtesy of and copyright by the Massachusetts Audubon Society.*

28

Bibliography). At the back of this book are listed experiments and investigations that you, as an amateur naturalist, can carry out. There is at least one such experiment for each chapter that can be done in the city. Numerous others can be devised by using your intelligence and investigative ability.

Cities, even more than the countryside, need to conserve and expand all elements of nature that lie within them. Involve yourself in helping conserve, expand, and make more beautiful the parks and other nature areas of your city. One section of a certain city, for example, was recovered from urban blight and made into a place of beauty by the new people who moved in there combining with older residents to plant as many flowers, vegetables, and other plants in window boxes, on roofs, and anywhere else they could to enhance the beauty and interest of the surroundings. At first they met with indifference and even vandalism of their projects, but gradually attitudes changed as these people persisted in their work of improvement. Finally, all in the neighborhood became proud of what was being done and realized that with more nature and beauty around them, their whole attitude toward life and toward each other changed for the better.

Quetzalcoatl, the famous prophet-king of Tollan, the ancient capital of the Toltecs in Mexico, was said to have turned his city into the most beautiful ever seen on earth by building it with terraces covered with bright flowers and flowering trees and lining the canals with vegetable and flower gardens. Even wild animals and birds were said to enter this city in numbers because they were treated so well by the people in it, and some even went into the homes. Such a city is something not only to dream about, but someday to make a reality!

DIVISION
I
THE BEGINNING NATURALIST

The beginner pauses at the edge of the great valley of nature and gazes with longing eyes across to where the explorer-naturalist stands on the first summit of nature knowledge. With a leap of his or her mind, the beginner would cross that valley to be where the other is; but there is no easy way that leads there. Work is the only way. In these beginning chapters, you will be shown the start of the way.

The explorer-naturalist is our symbol for the student who has successfully and completely studied all the information that is given in this book and has used what he or she has learned to carry out individual projects in natural science. Start at the beginning and work carefully through each section before going on to the next. In this way you will lay the firm groundwork that is necessary for the more advanced study to come.

CHAPTER

5

Animals
and Animal Collecting

Under the name *animal*, naturalists include all living things except plants. Jellyfish, barnacles, birds, cats, dogs, mice, sponges, fish, shellfish, hydras, crabs, insects, worms, single-celled amoebas—all are animals. But between the single-celled plants and the single-celled animals there is in some cases so little difference that it is hard to draw a line and say: "On this side is the animal kingdom, and on that side the plant kingdom." (See Chapters Eleven and Twelve for a full explanation of the differences between plants and animals.)

Animals affect our lives on every side. They furnish a large part of our food—meat, honey, eggs, and milk being a few of the foods they give us. They both fertilize our crops by carrying pollen between the flowers, as numerous insects do, and destroy the same crops by eating the leaves, as other insects do. They give us many bad diseases such as dysentery, malaria, and sleeping sickness. They annoy us without end in the form of flies and mosquitoes. On the other hand, pets such as dogs and cats give us great comfort and enjoyment, while such creatures as birds delight us with their songs. Apparently animals are decidedly important to us.

The two first tasks of the beginning naturalist are to learn how to observe and how to collect. Just becoming familiar with the common animals of your neighboring countryside is a great step forward. To be able to mount and preserve specimens efficiently and neatly is another ability that no naturalist can be without—but be careful to collect lawfully.

OBSERVING ANIMALS

It was the ability of JOHN AUDUBON (1785–1851) the famous painter-naturalist, to observe every small detail about the birds he watched and painted that made his bird pictures the most famous in the world. Into his pictures he put not only the true colors, sizes, and shapes of the birds, but also their characteristic attitudes and habits, even the food they fed upon. Thus his pictures teach a manifold lesson instead of just one. In the same way a naturalist observes not only the size, shape, and color of birds he or she is watching, but also their movements, the food they eat, their calls, the way they fly, their homes, and the kind of environment or surroundings they seek.

For instance, if you carefully watched some cedar waxwings, you would find that these beautifully crested creatures are about the size of large sparrows; that, outside of the mating season, they go in large flocks; that they love to eat many kinds of berries; that they are so exceedingly greedy that they tumble over one another in their haste to get food, often hanging upside down and gobbling berries; and yet that they can be very courteous to one another when food is scarce, passing it around carefully from bird to bird (as some observers have noticed). You would also see that they have a velvety black patch around the eye, small red waxy ends to the feathers in the middle of each wing, and a sharp band of bright yellow across the end of the tail. You would notice perhaps that, when excited, they raise the crest of feathers on the tops of their heads; while when they become afraid these crests fall back flat. You would besides this hear the cedar waxwing make only a soft sibilant note while it hopped around in a treetop, rarely any loud calls or songs. You would look at the feet and see that it belonged to the order *Passeres*, or perching birds, because it had four toes, three forward and one back, all with weakly developed claws, meant for perching, not walking, running, climbing, or killing. Its bill, if you noticed it closely, would appear short and stout for breaking open seeds, but it would also be wide and sharply pointed for good use in catching insects on the wing.

Seeing all these things, you would have a good picture of a cedar waxwing so that thereafter you would not mistake it for any other bird, except perhaps its close cousin the Bohemian waxwing. However, the Bohemian waxwing may be distinguished from the cedar waxwing by the appearance of the black eye patch, which, in the Bohemian, extends up over the head and has a parallel black patch underneath the chin.

As a naturalist you wish to learn about as many different kinds of animals as you can. Wherever possible go with expert naturalists on hikes and have them point out and name the different kinds of creatures for you. Keep lists and notes of what you see. (See the section Collecting Animals, later in this chapter, for information on how to keep a notebook.) If nothing else, take out books on the natural history of your neighborhood from the library and study illustrations and descriptions in regard to the creatures you see. But do not be sure you have found the right name until an expert has checked your observations. Later in this book are lessons on how to classify animals. But before you are ripe for this more serious job, it is a good beginning simply to become familiar on sight with the common animals of your state or province.

Taking Notes

The following are the special things to watch for in observing any animal. Remember each as you watch creatures in nature, and you will have a clear picture in your mind of what you have seen.

1. *Color.* Notice where each kind of color is found and just what area of the animal it covers. Notice particularly the locality of bars, spots, or other peculiar markings. For instance, the common striped skunk has two white stripes up its back that join together at its neck, whereas the little spotted skunk has several broken stripes that do not join together at the neck.

2. *Size.* In a bird compare the size with that of a warbler, a sparrow, a robin, a quail, a crow, a large hawk, judging whether it is a little

smaller or larger or about the same (see Figure 5-1). In an animal compare its size with that of a mouse, a rat, a woodchuck, a raccoon or fox, a coyote, a deer, a bear, a moose, and so on up the size scale. When you can actually measure an animal, do so.

3. *Shape.* In a bird, notice particularly the shape of the bill (see Figure 5-2), the legs, the wings, and the feet. Long legs, for instance, mean a wading bird such as a heron; curved, strong claws mean a bird of prey such as a hawk; a thin, sharp bill means a bird such as a bush tit that eats insects found in cracks in bark; short, blunt wings, such as those of a towhee, mean a bird that lives near the ground and does not fly far. In a mammal look for horns, shape of head, shape of ears, kind of tail, general body form, and other such details. Two big strong teeth in front usually mean a rodent, jumping legs a rabbit or hare, curled horns a mountain sheep, and so on. In insects the shape of the antennae or feelers is often important; a moth for instance has pointed antennae whereas a butterfly has antennae with small knobs on the ends.

4. *Actions.* A good naturalist can often tell a certain animal by its actions alone with little idea of color, size, or shape. Actions are particularly important for identifying some creature seen far away. A jay, for instance, in flying from tree to tree, will rise and dip and rise again in a characteristic wavelike flight. A wren will jerk its short tail around and up in a distinguishing way. A monarch butterfly has a way of flying steadily through the air at a certain altitude that usually shows its difference from other butterfly kinds.

5. *Voices, noise, and other characteristics.* A mule deer has a different way of crashing through brush than the smaller deer species; the time between the crashes is slightly longer. Songs and calls of birds are extremely important in identifying them. The song is often a truer way to tell a warbler, for instance, than is shape, size, color, or actions, since many kinds of warblers look and act alike. Sit still for a long time in a wood or a field and watch and listen. If a wren pops up in a bush near you and starts singing or talking to itself, you are in on the ground floor of knowing that wren. When you hear one again in the countryside, you'll know just who it is without needing to see.

6. *Food.* The type of food plant is often the surest way to tell an insect, particularly the caterpillars of butterflies or moths, as so many kinds will eat only special foods. The caterpillar of the anise swallowtail lives on anise, while the caterpillar of the monarch lives on milkweed. From the droppings of an animal or the disgorged pellets of an owl,

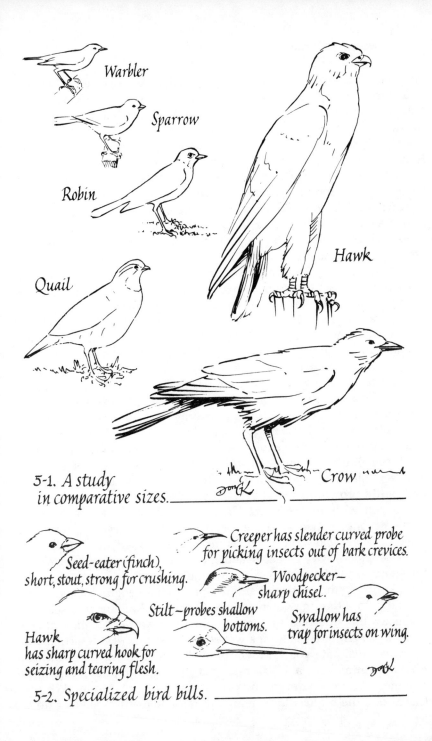

Warbler

Sparrow

Robin

Quail

Hawk

Crow

5-1. A study in comparative sizes.

Seed-eater (finch), short, stout, strong for crushing.

Creeper has slender curved probe for picking insects out of bark crevices.

Woodpecker— sharp chisel.

Stilt—probes shallow bottoms.

Swallow has trap for insects on wing.

Hawk has sharp curved hook for seizing and tearing flesh.

5-2. Specialized bird bills.

you can often tell the kind of creature it is. Berries mixed with hair and bones often mean a wildcat or a mountain lion. Crayfish and fishbones in droppings by the side of a stream are likely to spell otter or coon. The disgorged pellets of a screech owl are smaller and rounder than those of a great horned owl. Birds feeding on flies in the air are likely to be flycatchers if they wheel out from the tip of a branch to catch them, or swallows if they sweep and dash through the air at them without stopping to perch anywhere.

7. *Homes.* Places where animals live are often important in learning their names. Most birds, for instance, have nests that are peculiar to their own kind. The mud-plastered nest of the robin is very familiar. Few people would fail to recognize a beaver's home, while the line of pushed-up earth gives away the secret of the mole. Even small creatures such as mud wasps have their own peculiar way of construction, and the webs of spiders are almost as varied as their kinds.

8. *Time of activity.* Most animals are active only during certain hours of the day. A good way to tell the difference between the little brown bat and the hoary bat, for instance, is that the former comes out in the early evening and goes to bed long before dark, while the latter comes out just as it begins to grow really dark. Certain snakes, such as the racers, hunt during the middle of the day, while others such as the rubber boas come out after their prey only in deep darkness.

9. *Geographic and climatic location.* If you were in the mountains of West Virginia or Vermont and saw a deer, it could be only one possible kind, the Virginian white-tailed deer or *Odocoileus virginianus*. This is a deer of slender build with a tail that is all white on the underside and partly brown on the upper. This deer is found all over the East. But if you were in the Sierra Nevada of California, a deer you saw could be one of two kinds: either the Rocky Mountain mule deer, *Odocoileus hemionus*, or the Columbia black-tailed deer, *Odocoileus columbianus*, which is smaller and more slender and has a black tail. But there would be no Virginia white-tail in the Sierra Nevada. In this way, knowing the particular animals of a given geographic location is a great help in cutting down confusion about what you may see.

Go up the side of a high mountain from warm lowlands to cold, rocky uplands, or cross from a wet coastal belt to a dry desert, and the changes in climate you find will produce equal changes in species or kinds of animals to a 2,000-mile change in geographic location. For instance, in the warm country near the base of Mount Whitney, California, the highest U.S. mountain outside of Alaska, you find the brightly colored purple finch *(Carpodacus purpureus californicus)*, while higher by 2,000 to 3,000 feet is the duller colored and slightly larger Cassin's purple finch *(Carpodacus cassini)*. Still higher and in the region of eternal snows, above 11,000 feet, lives the gray-crowned rosy finch *(Leucosticte tephrocotis tephrocotis)*, whose wings and rump are tinged with pink but whose head is gray. If you should climb Mount Whitney, you would probably be able to tell what finches you were seeing as you climbed simply by the altitude you had reached at each point.

It is very easy to make mistakes about creatures you have seen if you are not very careful. Once I caught sight of what looked like the head of a large animal moving through the waters of the Eel River in California. I rushed back to camp to tell everybody to come quietly and see the otter. When we crept down to the river again, however, it proved to be a small female Merganser duck! Scooting through the shallows in the peculiar lights and shadows cast by the willows, she made me imagine I saw the blunt-nosed head of that big weasel, the otter, who likes to fish in those waters. The laughter at my mistake has made me a lot more careful since.

Sometimes to mistake one animal for another is dangerous. In Yellowstone National Park, four young naturalists sat quietly watching the grizzly bears being fed. We were safe behind a high steel fence, but even so the tremendous power the bears showed when they attacked each other ferociously for special tidbits made one uneasy. A park naturalist warned the onlookers about the grizzlies, saying: "Stay clear of a grizzly; it will probably leave you alone if you stay far enough away, but if you come too near and it thinks you are bothering it, look out! They can cover a hundred yards faster than a racehorse, and a man has mighty little chance to get up a tree in time." I noticed one of my young friends looked rather chastened, and I asked him about it. He replied: "I tried to take a photograph of a bear last evening when you were fixing supper, and I thought it was just a black bear; but now that I see the humps on the shoulders of these grizzlies, I think it was a grizzly that I was trying to take a picture of! And I was about fifty feet away!" (See also chapters on ecology.)

COLLECTING ANIMALS

Making a collection for your own museum or room helps you learn a good deal about the animals you collect. However, we should remember that, today, because of our need to protect and conserve life on this planet, we should collect only if absolutely necessary and only where permissible by law. In Chapter Eleven we describe more difficult animal collecting, which you should leave till later. Carefully study the following directions on collecting and mounting specimens before you start. A naturalist's collection should be so carefully made that it tells a story, not only to the naturalist, but to all who see it.

1. *A collection bag.* Many naturalists take one of these with them on field trips. The best bag is a canvas carrying bag with a leather strap to hang across your shoulder. This should be divided into two compartments. (see Figure 5-3). In one you can carry your nature notebook, while in the other you can carry specimens that you collect on field trips. If you ever collect soft-bodied insects or spiders, you will need to carry with you small glass vials in an upright position in the bag so that the formaldehyde or alcohol they carry will not spill. To do this, sew into the pocket small cloth strips, each in a half circle (see Figure 5-3) so that the vials will be held tightly. Make sure that the cloth fits the vials. All such vials should be numbered so that as you collect specimens in them you can write down in your notebook where they were collected and when, under each number. As:

No. I. *Spiders found under rotten log 6 kilometers up Hunter Creek Canyon, Reno, Nevada, June 14, 1980.*

2. *A killing jar.* To kill insects and other small creatures, it is necessary to have some sort of killing jar. A fairly safe but not always effective poison jar can be made by dropping cotton saturated with either chloroform or ether into the bottom of a small jar and covering this with a round piece of blotting paper cut to fit. The cotton, however, has to be resaturated every time the jar is taken into the field. Gasoline dropped on most insect's heads will soon kill them. Only a small quantity need be carried.

The most effective of the *safe* killing jars (Figure 5-4) is that made from ethyl acetate. Obtain some plaster of Paris and a small bottle of ethyl acetate from your drugstore. Mix the plaster of Paris with water to form a thick cream and pour into the bottom of a small jar, forming a layer about 3.8 centimeters (1 1/2 inches) deep. After the plaster of Paris has hardened, place the jar in an oven and bake until all moisture has left the plaster. Now pour about 2.5 centimeters (1 inch) of ethyl acetate in on top of the plaster of Paris and allow the jar to stand until

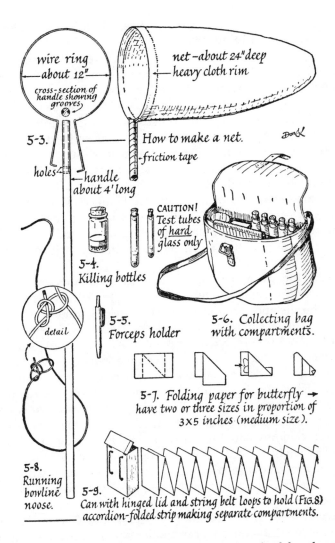

wire ring
—about 12"—
cross-section of
handle showing
grooves

net –about 24" deep
heavy cloth rim

5-3.

How to make a net.   Donal

holes

handle
about 4' long

friction tape

CAUTION!
Test tubes
of *hard*
glass only

5-4.
Killing bottles

detail

5-5.
Forceps holder

5-6. Collecting bag
with compartments.

5-7. Folding paper for butterfly →
have two or three sizes in proportion of
3×5 inches (medium size).

5-8.
Running
bowline
noose.

5-9.
Can with hinged lid and string belt loops to hold (Fig.8)
accordion-folded strip making separate compartments.

as much as possible of the liquid has been absorbed by the plaster. Empty the remainder and allow the jar to dry. Cut out two or three pieces of blotting paper to fit the jar and pack them down on top of the plaster of Paris. Your jar is now ready and will last for many months, killing any insect that is put into it and, best of all, being perfectly safe for you to handle. However, some insects may absorb some of the ethyl acetate into the hairs on their bodies, and this can be cleaned off with a brush dipped in liquid ether.

3. *A net.* This is used for collecting many insects. Get an old broom handle and cut off the broom part. Then take a sharp knife and cut 6 millimeters (1/4 inch) wide and 6 millimeters deep grooves along the sides from the cut-off end of the handle, for 15 centimeters on one side and 16 1/2 centimeters on the other. Bore two 6-millimeter holes through the handle at the end of each groove. Next, get a 107.5-centimeter piece of 6-millimeter wire and bend this in the form of a circle, but with two straight and parallel ends, one 16.5 centimeters long, the other 18.5 centimeters long. Bend the last 13 millimeters of each of these ends toward the other (see Figure 5-5) and place in the parallel grooves on the stick with the 13-millimeter (1/2-inch) bent portions sticking into the holes you bored at the end of the grooves. Now bind the wire tightly to the handle with black friction tape. Such a net will be very solidly made.

To make the cloth part of the net, use bobbinet or green voile (mosquito netting usually tears too easily). With a tape measure, measure the distance around your wire circle. If this is, say, 1 meter (40 inches), cut a square piece of cloth 1 meter wide and about 1.1 meter long. Fold this directly in the middle and, with scissors, cut an even oval end for the net. A sewing machine (not absolutely necessary) should then be used to sew the net edges together, going around twice, if you wish, for double strength. Next get a strip of heavy cheesecloth, 1 meter long and 25 centimeters (10 inches) wide. Fold this twice around the wire and sew it strongly all the way around the loop. Next, carefully sew the net itself onto the cheesecloth, and your new tool is ready for action. Such a net should be strong enough to use not only for catching insects in the air, but also for beating through light herbage and grass, one of the best ways for catching beetles and plant bugs.

4. *Forceps.* Most insects caught in a net must be placed in the poison jar in order to kill them. This can be done with either the fingers or a pair of light *forceps* (another very useful tool of the naturalist). A *forceps holder* can be made out of a piece of tin pipe about 12.5 centimeters (5 inches) long by 13 millimeters (1/2 inch) in diameter. This piece of pipe should be tightly pinched together at one end with a pair of pliers. Then get a thin strip of tin about 5 centimeters (2 inches) long and solder its tips onto the pipe so that the holder may be

carried on the belt (see Figure 5-6). A pair of forceps, either straight or curved, will fit easily into the pipe and, being carried on the belt, will be ready for instant service.

Forceps are also often necessary in the case of wasps or bees, although the best and safest way to kill these dangerous insects once they are in the net is to get them into a corner and then place that section of net entirely within the killing jar, holding the cover over the opening as tightly as you can until the insect becomes unconscious. Once in this state, it can be easily taken out of the net and dropped into the poison jar without fear of its escaping or causing any harm.

There is a trick to catching and killing butterflies in the net that is much quicker than trying to get them into a killing jar and is much easier on their wings as well. This is to fold the net over quickly once you have a butterfly in it, then get the butterfly cornered in some part of the net with its wings folded over its back. This is done by pressing the sides of the net together and so imprisoning the insect. Now take your thumb and forefinger and tightly press the thorax or chest of the butterfly between them, using your thumbnail for extra pressure. Small butterflies are killed instantly; large ones may take from a few seconds to a minute.

5. *Transparent envelopes.* These are to be bought at any large paper supply house. Do no get cellophane bags; use those made of semitransparent paper. Place insects from your killing jar in these envelopes, writing with pen and ink or indelible pencil the date and the location where they were caught. Such specimens can then be carried safely in your collecting bag. Less satisfactory, but nevertheless useful, envelopes can be made by hand out of pices of newspaper or other paper cut to size (as in Figure 5-7). When you get your specimens home, you can mount them right away while they are still soft or you can put them away in a box with mothballs or para-di-chloride of benzine crystals (the best protection against pests) until later. (For what to do about mounting dried insects, see later in this chapter.)

6. *A collecting can.* It should be one that can be hung on the belt. There are two kinds. At most any sporting goods store you can get a "bait can" with small holes in its top. But you can easily make one yourself, by getting a small square tin can with a tight cover, which you can fix for attaching to your belt by boring four small holes in its side, about 4 centimeters apart, and knotting the ends of two pieces of heavy string through these holes (as in Figure 5-8). Punch more holes

in the lid for ventilation. Into this can, live insects, lizards, small snakes, or mice can be placed.

For collecting butterflies, a different sort of can is needed. Get a tobacco tin about 12.5 × 7.5 × 5 centimeters (5 × 3 × 2 inches) in size with an overlapping lid, and solder onto one side of this two strips of tin (or use two strong strings as in Figure 5-8) for use as belt holders. Then get a large sheet of strong oiled tracing paper (such as is used by engineers) and cut this into strips about 7 centimeters wide (to fit the can). Strongly glue these strips together so as to have one long strip of about 9 meters (10 yards), and then fold this every 12 centimeters (4 3/4 inches) so that the whole strip will fit neatly into the box. To each end of the strip glue a piece of cardboard that also will fit closely into the box (see Figure 5-8). With this box at your belt, you have some sixty or more small compartments, into each of which you can drop a butterfly as soon as you catch it, thus saving much valuable time.

7. *A beating net.* This is made in the same way as the net described above except that canvas or unbleached muslin is used instead of green voile and that a stronger, 1 centimeter (3/8 inch) wire is necessary. Another name for it is a "crash net" because you use it to sweep with a crash through strong bushes or tree branches where the ordinary net would soon be torn to shreds. When you have crashed several bushes, lay the net on the ground and gradually push up the contents from the bottom, quickly seizing all insects you wish for your collection in your forceps and dropping them into your poison jar. Or, if you have a large poison jar, you can dump the entire contents of the beating net into the jar and pick over the specimens later when they are all dead. Each such catch should be carefully placed in a separate bag or other container and fully labeled with the date and exact place of capture.

8. *A water net.* For collecting specimens in ponds, rivers, and the sea, a water net can be purchased at almost any pet or sporting goods store. It must, however, have a fine mesh—so that small creatures cannot escape it once within its folds. Bobbinet may be used for the net material, and such a net is easily made at home.

Snakes and lizards require still different tools. First is the *noose,* which is made with a piece of string on the end of a long stick. The string should be about 12 to 15 centimeters (5 to 6 inches) long (a piece of fishline is best), and the noose is best made by tying a running bowline (see Figure 5-9). Keep the noose a little larger than the head of the snake or lizard you wish to catch, then slip it over the creature's head so slowly that it is not frightened, and draw the noose tight. The snake or lizard may then be lifted up and placed in a *reptile bag*, which is any kind of stout bag, such as a flour sack—canvas, of course, is best. Bags are best if they have a draw cord, but a strong string or a rubber band may be used to close the opening. A pair of *scissors* is necessary in collecting poisonous snakes. It is used to snip off the noose string as the reptile is dropped into its bag. *Do not try to handle any poisonous snakes until you have been taught how by an expert.* They are too dangerous for a beginner to experiment with them.

How to trap mammals and birds alive is described in Chapter Eleven. Killing animals and birds for museum specimens is permissible provided you follow the laws of your state in this regard or get from your local fish and game commission a special permit for shooting study skins. But remember to kill only specimens you yourself can mount. *Every naturalist is strongly against all useless killing.*

9. *A light trap.* This is to catch night insects, particularly moths, and can be made out of a box, two sheets of glass, a piece of wire screen, a bright lantern, and a poison jar (see Figure 5-10). The glass is held in place by four strips of wood tacked onto the insides of the box, each at an angle of about forty-five degrees. The two pieces of glass should thus slant inward toward each other, leaving a small 13-millimeter

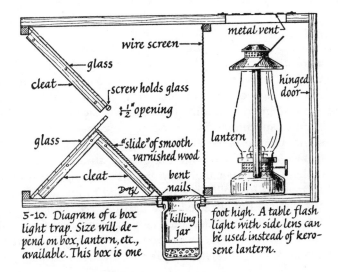

5-10. Diagram of a box light trap. Size will depend on box, lantern, etc., available. This box is one foot high. A table flash light with side lens can be used instead of kerosene lantern.

(1/2-inch) slit between, through which the insects that are attracted to the light can fly and crawl. The rear of the box is made into a hinged door through which the lantern can be slipped to take its place in the back half of the box. Directly above the lantern, a hole about 10.16 centimeters (4 inches) wide must be cut in the top of the box, and over this a piece of tin, punched full of small holes, is tacked. It is through the holes in the tin that the heat from the lantern is allowed to escape. The lantern is shielded from the front half of the box by a square of wire screen. Another hole is made in the bottom of the front half of the box, and this hole should exactly fit the top of the poison jar so that the jar can be held in the hole by means of a small bent nail. In order to make the insects fall more quickly into the open mouth of this jar, clay or some other nonburnable material may be stuffed into the corners of the front half of the box and sloped down toward the jar opening. The box itself may be hung with wires or rope from a tree or barn with the opening from which the light comes faced toward a forest or field. Such a trap will work for you all night long, but will, of course, work best in the wilderness, far from any center of manufactured light. In the morning you can turn the nail to take out the killing jar, and from the jar take your dead insects.

10. *Other tools for night hunts.* A way that many naturalists prefer for catching night insects is to use a *bright light and a sheet,* see Figure 9-10). This allows the more delicate kinds of insects to be placed in separate killing jars, thus preventing their being injured. The sheet is hung up on a wall or between a couple of trees so that it faces some good collecting ground such as a forest or field, and the light is hung up in front of the sheet. The best light is a Coleman gasoline lantern, but a powerful flashlight or a bright kerosene lamp will do. Below this sheet, on a box, have a row of two or more killing jars, at least one reserved for frail insects and another for heavy insects. A separate jar for moths is also good, as moths have fuzzy scales on their wings that often ruin other specimens that brush against them.

Now stand by the sheet with a pair of forceps, and catch your insects as fast as they land on the sheet, attracted by its shining whiteness. Drop each specimen into the jar that is prepared for it.

Another method for collecting moths (good to know because of the many kinds that are not attracted by a light) is *tree sugaring*. To do this get about a gallon of molasses and, as you bring this to a boil, pour into it several bottles of stale beer. Some honey may be added to this and the whole thoroughly stirred. Taking the resultant mixture in a bucket, go out on a summer or late spring night and, with a brush, lay a trail of sweetness on the trunks of the trees. You may also dip rags in the mixture and hang them up on branches. Go back an hour or so later with a flashlight and you will find, gathered here and there at your sweet bait, beautiful creatures of the night. This is one of the most exciting ways to collect moths, since you must approach carefully and noiselessly, or, alarmed by your presence, they will flee like shadows into the darkness.

Scientific and naturalist's equipment may be bought from:

Ward's Natural Science Establishment, 3000 Ridge Road E., Rochester, NY 14622.

Standard Scientific Supply Corporation, 30 Turner Place, Piscataway, NJ 08854.

Ann Arbor Biological Center, 6780 Jackson Road, Ann Arbor, MI 48103.

California Biological Service, 1612 West Glendale Blvd., Glendale, Calif. 91201.

11. *The notebook.* Every naturalist should have a notebook to take on field trips. It should have blank pages so that he or she can make many drawings. The best size is about 10×18 centimeters (4×7 inches). It should be strongly bound and be of good paper so that it won't tear easily and will take either pen or pencil. It should be carried in some kind of pouch or bag (as described earlier in this chapter). Try to keep your notebook as clean as you can. If you wish to be truly careful of your notes, or at least the most important ones, have a second notebook into which you rewrite these notes after each trip. In making notes, write down many details, as these all add to your knowledge of nature. A complete nature note appears in Figure 5-11.

Taking notes like these will train you in the exact observation that is so necessary to the good naturalist. Plan your notes differently if you wish, but arrange them as systematically as you can so that others can best understand what you are trying to tell.

HOW TO MAKE MOUNTED COLLECTIONS

1. *Feathers, small bones, and animal fur or hair.* These may all be mounted in the same way. With a little glue attach them to a white sheet of cardboard or to the page of a scrapbook. Arrange your

NAME: Water Ouzel or Dipper (<u>Cinclus mexicanus unicolor</u>).

DATE: July 10, 1980.   **TIME:** 10 a.m.
PLACE: Waterfall on creek entering south end of Bear
Lake, Rocky Mountain National Park, Colorado.
WEATHER: Sunny and warm; no clouds.

SIZE: Robin size, about 8" long.
SHAPE: A plump bird with short, small wings; sharp
pointed bill of medium length; short pointed tail; feet of a perching bird.
COLOR: Slate-gray in general, darker on the upper
parts, lighter below where the feathers are
often tipped with white; bill black.

GENERAL REMARKS: We found a pair of these birds
nesting in a ledge just below a 20' waterfall.
This ledge is in the form of a crevice
about 6" deep, and in the deepest
part lay cradled the nest made of
green-growing moss, kept constantly
wet by spray from the falls. Four
young birds with wide open
mouths constantly filled the round
opening to this nest. The parents
seemed to take turns feeding them.
Each adult would go to a rock in the creek, dip
or duck its body up and down 3 or 4 times, then
walk into the water where sometimes we could
see them actually flying under the surface. We
saw them bring small crayfish, caddis worms,
dragonfly larvae and other aquatic life to feed
their young, who never seemed to have enough.

WATERFALL

NEST

LEDGE

5-11. Sample page from a naturalist's notebook.

specimens in an orderly fashion and under each write the name, if you know it, the place where it was found, and the date collected. Up above write, for example, FEATHER COLLECTION OF JOHN JONES.

2. *Larger bones.* Place neatly in a box with a small square of adhesive tape attached to each, on which is written the specimen's number. On the top of the box, glue or paste a clean white paper with the same numbers written on it. Opposite each number of the list write the name of the bone, the place and date of collection, and the name of the animal from which it came, as:

No. 5. *Tail bone of a cow. Richmond Point Beach, California. October 18, 1981.*

If you are not sure of a name put a question mark after it.

3. *Sea shells.* Mount and number these in the same way. Don't try to stick such specimens down in any way, as they are more valuable when you can pick them up and study them in your hand.

4. *Insects.* These are more difficult to mount correctly. Soft-bodied insects and spiders should be placed in small glass vials of alcohol or formaldehyde. Alcohol is better provided you can get a high percentage (at least 95 percent pure), but, as this is often difficult to buy, you may substitute formaldehyde. Never put a specimen in a high percentage alcohol at first, as this makes the body hard and brittle. Start with about 70 percent alcohol and work up in stages over three to four days to the 95 percent.

Each vial containing one or more specimens of a single species (kind of animal) should have a label stuck or attached to it on which is written both the common and scientific name when possible. The scientific name of the Devastating Grasshopper, for instance, is *Melanoplus devastator* (the subject of scientific names is taken up with more detail in Chapter Eleven). Underneath the names write the place of collection and the date. If the vial is too small for this, put a number on it; repeat this number, with the information about the specimen written opposite it, under the top of the box in which the vial is kept. Vials, tightly corked and laid away in a cigar box on cotton, will keep the specimens neatly and safely for many years.

5. *Hard-bodied insects.* These are two chief ways to mount these.

(a) *The easiest and most satisfactory way for the beginner is to mount them on smooth cotton under the glass of a riker mount* (see Figure 5-13).

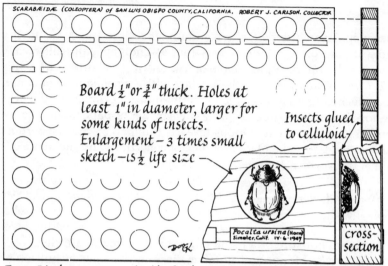

SCARAB/EID/E. (COLEOPTERA) of SAN LUIS OBISPO COUNTY, CALIFORNIA. ROBERT J. CARLSON. COLLECTOR.

Board ½" or ¾" thick. Holes at
least 1" in diameter, larger for
some kinds of insects.
Enlargement – 3 times small
sketch –is ½ life size –

Insects glued
to celluloid

Pocalta ursina (Horn)
Simeler, Calif. IV· 6· 1947

cross-
section

5-12. Display mount – suitable for demonstration or "sample" collection, –
e.g., one or two each of all the orders of insects; one each of the 100-odd chief
families of beetles (if you can get 'em!); all the true bugs of your own yard, etc.

Box ⅝" to 1" deep. Glass to fit exactly
inside cover. Cut cover, leaving enough
to hold glass. Cut cotton neatly from
roll to fit box. Sprinkle moth flakes in
bottom before placing specimens.

5-13. The Riker–another display mount.
glass   pasteboard box
cotton

Better suited than FIG.12 for display of butterflies, moths, dragonflies,
and ideal for life-history displays requiring host plants. (see **5-15**).

Or mount them in separate holes bored into a board (as in Figure 5-12), covering them with transparent celluloid. In the latter case no cotton is used, as the specimens are glued by the legs in a lifelike manner onto the celluloid at the bottom of each hole.

A riker mount is easily made by taking a fairly flat cardboard box and cutting out most of the top (as in Figure 5-13) with a razor or sharp knife. A smooth, even job should be done. Now take your cut top to a hardware store and have them cut you a piece of glass that will exactly fit the box top (or do the same yourself, it you have a glass cutter). Glue this glass tightly into the top by applying glue to both cardboard and glass and putting a heavy weight down on both for several hours. In the bottom half of the box, first put an even layer of cheap cotton batting; then on top of this a thinner, smoother layer of white drugstore cotton. This last should have its top a little above the sides of the box, so that when the top of the box is put over the bottom, the glass in the top will press firmly and evenly on the cotton below.

Insects may now be placed on this cotton under the glass, and each should have a number. On the back of the riker mount, paste a white paper with the numbers and opposite each number the name, location, and date of collection of each specimen carefully printed. When the riker mount can hold no more insects, sprinkle some naphthalene flakes or some crystals of para-di-chloride of benzine on the cotton and seal the open edges of the box with tape. This will permanently keep out the deadly enemy of all insect collections, the Dermestes beetle. Keep such a mount in a dry place and mold also will not bother it.

Insects placed in riker mounts should be put in when they are freshly killed or after they have been relaxed (see next paragraph). This allows one to spread their legs and wings in a lifelike manner. To spread the six legs in a natural way, take a pin and tease each leg out from under the body until all are fully spread. For a collection made in a board with holes bored in it (such as is pictured in Figure 5-12), the leg of each insect should be carefully glued to the celluloid at the bottom of the hole.

To relax insects that have become stiff (most dead insects soon become dry and stiff), get a jar and fill the bottom with either damp sand or a damp rag (sand is better). Then place the insects on top of a piece of paper in the jar or in paper envelopes, screw on the top, and leave them for two days (rarely any longer, as mold may come and spoil them). They will then be relaxed and may be safely mounted.

To spread the wings of butterflies and moths for mounting in a riker mount, get a smooth, soft wood board (white pine, redwood, balsa wood, for instance), or some smooth corrugated cardboard from the side of a packing box. Take the body of the butterfly between your forefinger and thumb (never touch the wing of a butterfly or moth, as you will brush off the delicate scales and possibly ruin a specimen) and turn it with the wings down. Then take a pin—an insect pin (see later in this chapter) is best, though an ordinary pin will do—and stick this at right angles through the thorax (see Figure 5-14A), the thorax being another name for the chest. Hold the butterfly on the pin above the board and gently spread the wings apart with a pencil or, better, another pin, at the same time pressing the insect down upon the board until you can stick the pin into the board and hold the specimen there. In this position the upper part of the wings of the butterfly are next to the board. Now take another pin and place the point just behind the main vein of the forewing. With this as a lever, gently move the wing into such a position that it is at right anles to the body (see Figure 5-14B), and stick the pin through into the board to hold the wing there. Do the same with the other forewing, and then bring up the hind wings so that they just overlap the lower edges of the forewings. Next take two small strips of paper and pin them down tightly over the wings. The pins that were stuck through the wings to hold them down may now be taken out by gently twisting the pinheads between the thumb and forefinger until they easily come out.

The butterfly is left stretched in this way for about five days in some safe dry place. By this time it becomes thoroughly stiff, so that the paper strips can be removed from its wings and the pin twisted up and out of its thorax. The butterfly is now ready to put in the riker mount; to do this take a pair of forceps and pick it up gently by the body, placing it underside down and as neatly as possible on top of

5-14A. *Pinning butterfly for* — B. *Spreading to dry*

the cotton. The glass, when lowered on top of the specimen, will hold it firmly in place.

Some collectors make very interesting mounts by putting in with the butterfly, the egg, the caterpillar, the chrysalid and the food plant of the species (see Figure 5-15). The food plant, of course, is the plant on which the caterpillar lives. The chrysalid is the quiet stage during which the caterpillar makes the wonderful transformation into the butterfly. Such mounts are quite scientific as they show the life history from egg to adult.

Caterpillars may be prepared for mounting by squeezing out the insides just after death. This is done by rolling a round pencil over the body several times, working from the head toward the tail. With the

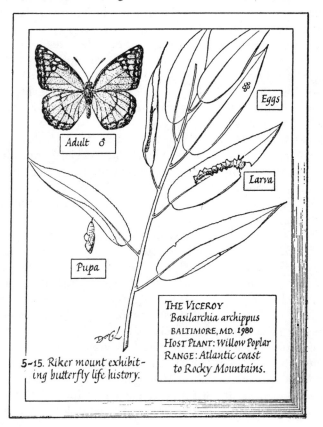

Adult ♂

Eggs

Larva

Pupa

THE VICEROY
Basilarchia archippus
BALTIMORE, MD. 1980
HOST PLANT: *Willow Poplar*
RANGE: *Atlantic coast
to Rocky Mountains.*

5-15. *Riker mount exhibit-
ing butterfly life history.*

insides out, the caterpillar must now be blown back to its former size by hot air. This can be done by taking a large-size medicine dropper and heating it over a gas flame (not too much or it will break). Move the medicine dropper slowly back and forth over the flame for a few moments; then force the hot air into the caterpillar by pushing the point of the medicine dropper into the tail and squeezing the bulb. This may have to be repeated several times. Using great care, after the specimen has been completely inflated, poke small bits of cotton into the body with a toothpick until the shape is secure. Chrysalids usually need no special mounting method, as they will usually dry out just like the adult insect. However, caterpillars or chrysalids may be placed in a small vial full of alcohol or formaldehyde and then placed in the riker mount beside the butterfly. For correct mounting of the food plant in the display, see Chapter Six.

Grasshoppers need only the wings of one side spread, and this may be done in the same way as with butterflies or moths, except that the forewings should not be at right angles, but should be pushed forward a little so that all of the hind wing can be seen (see Figure 5-16). Dragonflies and damselflies are mounted (as shown in Figures 5-17A and B) with the wings widely spread.

(b) *Mounting insects on pins* requires a different technique from that used for riker mounts. The pins needed are special nonrusting insect pins, which can be bought only from scientific equipment houses (see earlier in this chapter). Pins come in sizes all the way from very small, Number 00, to very large, Number 5. Size Number 2 is about average and is the best for most insects.

For mounting most insects (excluding butterflies, moths, grasshoppers, dragonflies, and damselflies) on pins, get a piece of balsa wood or Celotex or Masonite about 30 centimeters (1 foot) square. Nail this onto a wooden frame made to the same size and about 2 centimeters (3/4 inch) thick (see Figure 5-18). On top of this frame tightly tack a thin sheet of cardboard or stiff, strong paper. Take an insect that is either freshly killed or recently relaxed, stick a pin through it in the way shown for the same type of insect in Figure 5-19, then stick the pin through the cardboard or paper of your mounting frame and on into the Masonite (or whatever material you have used) below. The insect should now be about properly placed on the pin (two-thirds of the way up) and its legs can be spread in a natural way on the surface

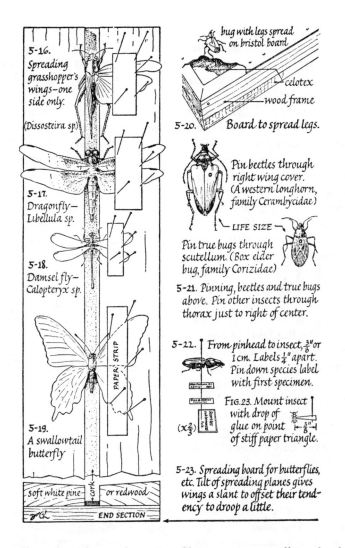

5-16. Spreading grasshopper's wings—one side only.

(Dissosteira sp.)

5-17. Dragonfly— Libellula sp.

5-18. Damsel fly— Calopteryx sp.

PAPER STRIP

5-19. A swallowtail butterfly

soft white pine—cork—or redwood

END SECTION

bug with legs spread on bristol board

celotex

wood frame

5-20. Board to spread legs.

Pin beetles through right wing cover. (A western longhorn, family Cerambycidae)

LIFE SIZE

Pin true bugs through scutellum. (Box elder bug, family Corizidae)

5-21. Pinning, beetles and true bugs above. Pin other insects through thorax just to right of center.

5-22. From pinhead to insect, $\frac{3}{8}$" or 1 cm. Labels $\frac{1}{4}$" apart. Pin down species label with first specimen.

FIG. 23. Mount insect with drop of glue on point of stiff paper triangle.

(x$\frac{2}{3}$)

$\frac{3}{8}$

5-23. Spreading board for butterflies, etc. Tilt of spreading planes gives wings a slant to offset their tendency to droop a little.

of the cardboard with another pin. Change your cardboard when it gets too full of holes.

As shown in Figure 5-19, beetles have their pins stuck through the right wing cover or *elytra;* flies are stuck through slightly to the left of the middle of the *thorax* or chest; bees, wasps, and ants have the pin stuck through the middle of the thorax; grasshoppers, dragonflies, butterflies, and moths also through the thorax; and plant bugs, cicadas, water skaters, assassin bugs, electric light bugs, through the *scutellum*, a small triangle found between the wings and just behind the thorax in these insects.

Butterflies, moths, grasshoppers, and dragonflies, when mounted on pins, need a different kind of mounting board (see Figure 5-20). It is made by taking a 40 cm (16") or 30 cm (1') long strip of Masonite, balsa wood, Celotex, or cork, 5 to 7.5 centimeters (2 to 3 inches) wide, and nailing this onto two strips of some soft wood such as pine or redwood, 40 × 7 centimeters (16 × 2 3/4 inches). A narrow crack, between 6 and 18 millimeters (1/4 and 3/4 inches) wide, is left between these strips to hold the insect's body. The relaxed or fresh butterfly is taken by the thorax between the thumb and forefinger and an insect pin stuck through the thorax from the upper side between the wings and at right angles to the body. When two-thirds of the pin is through the butterfly, the point is stuck into the soft material at the bottom of the crack in the mounting board. The body of the butterfly rests in the upper part of the crack, while the base of the wings should now be parallel with the level of the board tops. By means of a pair of forceps or a pin, the wings can be forced down onto the boards where they are held by means of pins stuck just behind the main wing veins (as in Figure 5-21). The forewings are now moved forward by the use of pins until they are at right angles to the body, and the hind wings brought up so as to come just under the forewings with their upper edges. Next strips of paper are pinned tightly over the wings, the pins in the wings removed by careful thumb and finger twisting, and the butterfly left to dry.

All insects mounted on pins must have labels with them, stuck below the insect body on the pin. The upper label gives the name of the collector (it is placed about 12 to 13 millimeters (1/2 inch)above the pin point). The next label gives the place collected, the date, and the food plant, if known (it is placed about 7 millimeters (1/4 inch) above the pin point). Pinned to the bottom of the specimen box appears a label with the names of the species, the genus, and the common name (as in Figure 5-22). The printing of the words on these labels should be done neatly with a fine drawing pen and India ink. It should be made as small and yet as easily readable as possible. Small blocks with holes through them, one 6 to 7 millimeters (1/4 inch) high and the other 12 to 13 millimeters high, are useful aids in getting labels on quickly at the right heights.

To mount very small insects, too small to be put on a pin, a "point" is used. This is a small triangular pice of cardboard (see Figure 5-23) through which an ordinary insect pin is stuck. At the point of the triangle a drop of glue is placed and to this is attached the tiny insect. This is useful to remember, as tiny insects are just as likely to be valuable to a naturalist as large insects.

Insect boxes, for holding pinned specimens, can be purchased from large science equipment companies (see earlier in this chapter), or made by a good amateur carpenter. These boxes usually have balsa wood bottoms and tight covers to keep out pests. A fair substitute is a cigar box. Fasten a cork, Celotex, Masonite, or balsa wood sheet on the bottom of your box with glue and it will be ready for your pinned insects. Small squares of cork can be used, one for each specimen, instead of a whole sheet. Put similar insects into one box; beetles in one, for instance, and butterflies in another. Label each box on the outside with the name of the kind of insects you have in it.

A unique and beautiful way to mount butterflies or moths is to take the wings alone and make prints of them on cards. A filing card serves very well. Thoroughly wax (candle wax will do) two cards until each shines with wax all over one side. Then place the wings of the butterfly in as natural a manner as possible on one of the waxed cards with half of the wings (on one side) showing their upper sides and the other half showing their undersides. Now carefully place the second card on top of the first card, being sure not to move the wings, and run a hot iron over the two of them several times. When the cards are carefully separated, the wings of the butterfly in the shape of the myriads of tiny scales will be found imprisoned upon the cards. To preserve your specimens from wear, coat each card with colorless shellac or varnish. Write on the back of the card the name of the butterfly and where and when it was collected, as well as any other interesting information. A file of such cards kept in a box and arranged either alphabetically or, better, according to the different families of butterflies, forms a very compact, easily studied butterfly collection and will last a long time.

6. *Soft-bodied creatures.* Specimens from sea and pond, such as sea urchins, shellfish or molluscs, worms, crayfish, frogs, salamanders, and crabs, should be mounted in vials or jars according to size. Fill these jars with formaldehyde or alcohol and label them on the outside

with the names of specimens, and places and dates of their collection. This is about the only way to keep such specimens safely. Snakes and lizards are best kept in this way also, but must have their bellies cut by slits to allow entrance of the preservative.

SKINNING

Skinning animals is not difficult if you take a little time and care in learning how. Start first with a snake. Cut off its head, and then, placing it back down on a board, begin to cut along its middle with a sharp (one-sided) razor or knife, taking care not to cut through into the insides, but merely to cut the skin. When a complete cut is made all along the snake's belly, begin to work the skin back up the sides with your fingers, cutting carefully with your razor where the muscles and sinews hold the skin back. When you finally get your fingers through around the back you can usually slip and tug the skin off as one would a tight coat. The skin may then be spread out on a board and stretched by means of pins (as in Figure 5-24). It is then salted all over to preserve it, the salt being rubbed into the underside of the skin. Before this, however, all remaining bits of meat and fat must be carefully scraped off the skin. This skin will dry as stiff as a board and may then be turned over, tacked onto another board with the snake's outer surface up, and exhibited on the wall of one's room, its name and place and date of capture printed below it.

As the skinning of all large animals is very much the same as that of small ones, the information given here will help you with all kinds of study skins.

1. *To skin and stuff a mouse.* The job of skinning a mouse is a good bit more difficult than that of skinning a snake; so do not be discouraged if your first tries are failures.

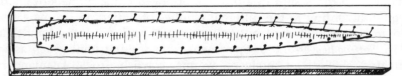

5-24. Snake skin, pinned inside up to board to dry, rubbed with salt.

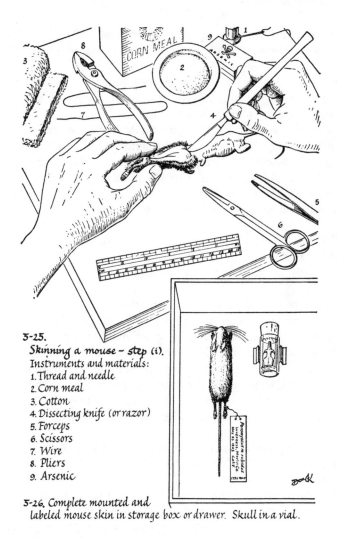

3-25.
Skinning a mouse – step (i).
Instruments and materials:
1. Thread and needle
2. Corn meal
3. Cotton
4. Dissecting knife (or razor)
5. Forceps
6. Scissors
7. Wire
8. Pliers
9. Arsenic

3-26. Complete mounted and
labeled mouse skin in storage box or drawer. Skull in a vial.

Your mouse should be freshly killed, and besides the mouse you should have the following materials (see Figure 5-25): *(1)* some thin white or gray thread and a needle, *(2)* some cornmeal (used for drying up the blood), *(3)* a roll of cotton batting, *(4)* a very sharp knife or one-sided razor, *(5)* a pair of forceps, *(6)* a pair of small sharp scissors, *(7)* about 30 centimeters (1 foot) of 1 1/2-millimeter (1/6-inch) wire, *(8)* a pair of pliers, and (9) some arsenic (alum is safer than arsenic but not so effective). Arsenic will kill any insect pests that may later attack the skin.

Do not use arsenic unless you are positive your hands are free from cuts, and be very careful not to touch your hands to your mouth while using it. Wash hands thoroughly immediately afterward.

Before you start skinning, you should measure the mouse from nose-tip to tail-tip. Measure also the length of the tail, the length of the hind foot, and the exact length of the ears. These measurements should all be written or printed neatly with ink on a small card, 13 × 50 millimeters (1/2 × 2 inches). Also on this card should go the name of the kind of mouse, and where and when it was captured.

#2 *Peromyscus maniculatus gambelii*, Deer Mouse
April 15, 1980. Coos Bay, Oregon.
Total length 16 cm. Tail 5.2 cm. Hind foot 16 mm. Ear 13 mm.

This card is later tied to the leg of the finished specimen with a short string that has been run through two holes poked in the end of the card. Below are the steps to be taken in skinning a mouse.

(a) Place your mouse, back down, on a wide smooth board and cut through the skin of the stomach and directly in the middle with your small scissors. Carefully cut the skin up the middle of the body until you reach the throat. Be careful not to open up the insides. Wherever blood appears, blot it out with the cornmeal, which you should use freely.

(b) From the central opening now cut with your scissors down the middle of each hind leg through the skin and about two-thirds of the way up to the first joint.

(c) With your sharp knife or razor, begin cutting the skin away from around the anus (opening by the tail) so that you can force the skin back with your fingers until your thumb and forefinger can meet around the back of the mouse under the skin. At the same time work the skin toward the back all along the side of the body.

(d) When you have the skin free from the fleshy parts of the hind legs and have worked it down to the first joint, take your scissors and cut through the thigh bone of each hind leg about halfway between the joints. You can then cut the meat off the remaining part of each bone with your scissors until there is little left. Leave these cleaned lower leg bones attached to the skin.

(e) Working now mainly with your fingers, push the skin off the back and away from the anus. Use the razor when muscles interfere until only the tail in the back still has the skin on. You must be very careful not to cut the skin around the tail.

(f) The bony tail must now be pulled right out of its skin, and this job you must do entirely with your fingers, rubbing them along the bone and pushing carefully, while, with the fingers of the other hand, you pull at the tip of the tail. Often the skin will come right off the tail with little trouble, if you will just be patient.

(g) Now the whole back part of the skin is free from the body. Again, with the scissors, make slits down the middle of each foreleg two-thirds of the way to the joint.

(h) Cut the fleshy part of each leg through the middle, halfway between the joints, and then work the skin down the legs with your fingers until you can cut away the meat from the remaining leg bones. You can now, still pushing the skin away from the body with your fingers, have the skin all free save for the head.

(i) On the head you use mainly the sharp razor or knife (see Figure 5-25). Keep pulling the skin back over the head, pushing the skin with your fingers, but wherever it seems stuck cut it carefully free with the knife or razor.

(j) The first thing to watch for on the head is the ears. Only experience will tell you when and where to cut these. They will appear first as small gray lumps, and they must be cut across with the razor as close to the head as you can.

(k) When the ears are free, your next problem is the eyes, which appear as black lumps toward the front of the head. Cut through the film that covers the eyes as far back on the head as you can, and then carefully cut through the eye edges until the skin that is attached to them is free.

(l) Last comes the nose and the lips. You must cut through the fleshy inner part of the lips both upper and lower until at last the skin gives way and comes entirely free from the body.

(m) You can now make a mounted specimen—or "study skin," as naturalists call it. Throw away the body, but keep the head, as later you are going to have to clean out the skull. Take your needle and thread and sew the two lips together, tying with a single knot at their tips.

(n) Take your alum or arsenic, and after most of the flesh has been scraped free, sprinkle and rub the preservative all over the inside of the skin.

(o) Cut a piece of the thin wire about 2.5 centimeters (1 inch) longer than the tail. Around this roll a thin sheet of cotton, moistened slightly with water, until the wire and cotton are about as thick as the original fleshy part of the tail.

(p) Now carefully shove this down into the empty tail-skin, being sure that the end of the wire does not poke through the skin. You may have to take off some of the cotton, if the wire won't go in easily.

(q) Similar but shorter wires are wrapped with cotton for the legs and shoved down the legs between the skin and the bone, in each case with about 13 to 17 millimeters (1/2 to 3/4 inches) of wire sticking out into the body cavity.

(r) Then take a small section of cotton and roll it into a cylinder approximately the same size as the mouse's body. Take your forceps and tightly pinch together one end of the roll, folding it and kneading it with the forceps until you get a hard "nose" of cotton.

(s) Still holding this nose tightly together with the forceps, stick it into the head of the mouse so that "nose" meets nose. Pull the skin up over the cotton so that the cotton is entirely inside.

(t) Take your needle and thread and begin to sew the skin together carefully from the throat down to the tail, taking care to pull the two skin edges together tightly. When the skin is all sewed up, take the specimen in your hands and straighten out the legs and tail in a natural manner and knead the body with your fingers until its shape appears as it did in life. Groom the skin with a small brush until all the hair is lying down and smooth.

(u) Now you must tie to one of the specimen's legs the card mentioned earlier.

(v) Cut the skull free from the body and cut away all meat that you find on the outside of the skull. Clean out the skull by means of a toy plastic spoon or a brain spoon (made by whittling a tiny wooden spoon) dipped again and again into the brain cavity until most of the brain matter is gone.

(w) Dry this cleaned skull in the sun and let ants finish the job of cleaning it; then place it in a small glass bottle or cardboard box with a number that is the same as the number on the card attached to the leg of the mounted specimen. The appearance of the complete mount is shown in Figure 5-26.

If you do all this carefully, you will have a scientific specimen for your collection, and one that might even prove valuable to a working naturalist. It sounds like a lot of trouble, but expert naturalists have trained themselves to skin and mount a mouse in five minutes!

2. *To skin a bird.* This is a somewhat different problem. The job in general is done much as the skinning of the mouse, explained above, with the following differences:

(a) The skin of most birds is more delicate than that of mammals, and thus greater care must be taken in the skinning.

(b) The wing bones and leg bones are cut off from inside the skin, as with the mouse; but the skin must be pushed back from the limbs with much greater care, as it is very much easier to break through at these points.

(c) The tail bone is cut through right next to the skin, leaving only the last joint attached to skin and tailfeathers.

(d) When the limbs and main part of the skin are cut free from the body, cut the skin carefully free from the neck, but do not try to pull the skin off the skull.

(e) The skin is pulled up over the back half of the skull, and this part of the skull is cut off with a sharp knife. This leaves the *forward part of the skull still encased within the face skin and attached to the bill.* (This is important.)

(f) This remainder of the skull attached to the skin is now thoroughly cleaned out with a brain spoon. With a small bird, the eyeballs may be left in, but with a large bird they must be worked out of the skull and replaced with artificial eyes or marbles.

(g) The skull, the limbs, and all deep recesses of the skin are cleaned of flesh and powdered and rubbed with arsenic. Much arsenic is put inside the skull.

(h) Cut a small round stick to fit exactly the length of the bird from inside the skull to the base of the tail. Place this stick in the skull and hold it there with wadded cotton.

(i) With wire, varying in thickness according to the size of the bird, form supports for the legs and wings. The lengths of wire are run down the limbs between the bones and the skin until a firm support is given, and the other end of each wire is attached to the stick in the middle.

(j) One end of the stick is now placed at the tail bone, and the whole stick wrapped with cotton to take the shape of the body of the bird.

(k) The sewn-up bird is brushed and its body and limbs formed in a natural manner; then it is put away in a safe dry place for the skin to harden and preserve the form.

(l) As with the mouse, a label is attached to one foot on which is placed the name, location, date, number, and the measurements of the body, legs, and wings before skinning.

Further information on skinning and stuffing specimens may be obtained from any of the books on taxidermy listed below.

Books on Taxidermy and Museum Exhibitions

Brown, Vinson, *How to Make a Home Nature Museum.* Happy Camp, Calif.: Naturegraph Publishers, 1954.

Grantz, Gerald J., *Home Book of Taxidermy and Tanning.* Harrisburg, Pa.: Stackpole Books, 1970.

Labrie, Jean, *The Amateur Taxidermist.* New York: Hart Publishing, 1972.

Tinsley, Russell, *Taxidermy Guide.* Chicago: Follett Publishing, 1977.

CHAPTER
6

Plants
and Plant Collecting

Plants are all around us; they make up more than two-thirds of our food, and without them there would be too little oxygen in the air for us to live. And yet how few people know much about them! One of the first and most important things the beginning naturalist has to do is to learn the names of the common wild plants of his or her neighborhood. This is not only because of the importance of the plants themselves, but because plants determine more than anything else the kinds and types of animals found near them.

A naturalist friend, Ted Zschokke, gave me my first picture of this relationship between plants and animals. I was staying with him at his laboratory near Palm Springs, California, on the edge of the great Colorado Desert. From this place at nearly sea level, we climbed one day thousands of feet onto the rocky ridges of Mt. San Jacinto, whose summit reaches jaggedly to the region of eternal snow. At 6,000 feet we stopped and looked back down the brushy slopes to a golden sea of desert stretching into the hazy distance.

"Look," said Ted, "you can see that we have climbed through three zones of life (see Figure 11-6). On the floor of the desert is what scientists call the Lower Sonoran Zone. Mesquite is almost the only tree there, and cactus is dominant. Giant scorpions live there, and so do ugly vinegarroons, which are large spiderlike creatures, the desert foxes, and desert jumping rats, and other creatures that only come out in the cool of the night to feed and play. Many of the small creatures down there use the spines of the cactus to protect themselves from their enemies. The larger animals, such as the foxes, make burrows between the stout roots of the mesquite; it gives them protection from people and from the intense heat of the desert sun.

"When we reached an altitude of 1,500 feet," Ted continued, "we entered the Upper Sonoran Zone. Chaparral, a tangle of low thorny shrubs, such as buckbrush, manzanita, chamise, and coffeeberry, takes the place of cactus, and you can also see an occasional Digger pine. Various species of brush mice, rats, and rabbits thrive in this region, and the coyote becomes more numerous; but larger animals are rare, because the dwarf forest of the chaparral not only is too thick for them to pass through easily, but it doesn't furnish enough shelter, food, or water.

"After we climbed to 5,000 feet, we entered the Transition Zone, where we are now. You can see about us stands of yellow pine and white fir, typical trees of this zone, while in the snow we've seen numerous tracks of deer, raccoons, tree squirrels, mink, and other dwellers of the forest. We should also find signs of black bear here, another lover of the mountain forest."

The day was waning and there was no time to go higher. But Ted pointed out for me, up the slope, the Canadian Life Zone—a region of high pine and fir forest; and beyond that, first, the Hudsonian Zone, a region of stunted junipers, low brush, and moss, like the tundra of the Far North; and second, the Boreal or Arctic-Alpine Zone where snow and rocks prevail and life is rare. So we did not see the still different kinds of plants and animals that dwell in these higher regions. But going back over the snow in our downward climb from the mountain, we saw the tracks of a mountain lion. The big round prints were often placed in the middle of our own earlier shoe prints, showing where he had followed us upward from the beginning of the Transition Zone! This lion then was another animal that liked the shelter of those high pines and firs, helping to show again the dependence of animals on the plants that surround them.

Plants are divided into five great classes, with the green algae, seaweed, and single-celled plants in one; the fungi and bacteria in a second; the mosses and liverworts in a third; the ferns in a fourth; and the flowering and cone-bearing plants in a fifth. It is the fifth class that will most concern us and which we see most often, but the other classes are very important and should not be forgotten. We will try to study these great divisions and learn something about the classification of plants in later chapters.

Your first task now is simply to become acquainted with some of the common plants of your neighborhood.

OBSERVING PLANTS

Figure 6-1 shows a complete plant, picturing roots, stem, leaves, flowers, fruit, and seeds. Learn to tell plants by the color, type, and arrangement of their flowers and flower parts; the shape, size, arrangement, and number of their leaves; the feel and appearance of their stems; and the kind of seeds, fruit, roots, and bark they have; using all of these to help you and never depending on one. The books listed in the Bibliography will help you learn the names of many plants, but never be completely sure that you have given the right name to a plant until an experienced naturalist has agreed with you, for it is very easy to be wrong.

Other things worth observing about plants and very helpful in learning to name them are listed below.

1. *Their homes.* This includes the kind of soil they live in and whether they are found on mountains, in valleys, or on plains, or other places; whether they are sheltered by rocks or trees or other plants; whether they are near streams; on the north or south sides of hills, and so forth. Small trees near streams, for instance, are quite likely to be willows, while on the shady damp sides of large rocks we find ferns and other dampness-loving plants. Small-leaved chaparral can stand the sun-scorched hill slopes, while large-leaved plants, like maple and thimbleberry, seek cooler and more shady slopes.

2. *Their growth.* We must see whether they grow thickly together or

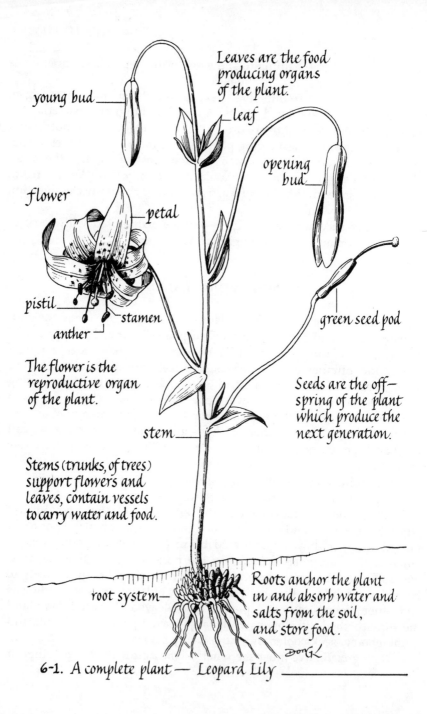

young bud

Leaves are the food producing organs of the plant.

leaf

opening bud

flower

petal

pistil

stamen

anther

green seed pod

The flower is the reproductive organ of the plant.

Seeds are the offspring of the plant which produce the next generation.

stem

Stems (trunks, of trees) support flowers and leaves, contain vessels to carry water and food.

root system

Roots anchor the plant in and absorb water and salts from the soil, and store food.

DonGK

6-1. A complete plant — Leopard Lily

sparsely, whether they are stunted or tall. Some plants, such as ivy and chamise or greasewood, like to grow in thickly populated colonies; others, such as dogwood and certain oaks, seem to do better alone or in small groups.

3. *Their parasites and diseases.* Holes, scars, and mottled bands on leaves or stems show how other plants or animals have been attacking them. Some plants are subject to such attacks; others are not. The live oak tree, for instance, is extremely subject to attacks from the caterpillar of the oak moth, while the scrub oak is practically never attacked by this insect.

4. *Their relations to other plants.* Honeysuckle and poison oak and ivy use other plants to climb on in order to get up to more sunlight. Thimbleberry, snowberry, twinberry, and similar plants seem to need the protection of trees from too much sunlight. The mistletoe gains its sustenance from the sap of trees, particularly oaks, which it parasitizes.

5. *Their relations to animals.* Nearly all plants try to attract animal allies. The yellow color of the buttercup is to attract insects who will come and drink the flower's nectar, aiding in the bearing of pollen between the flowers and thus helping them fertilize each other. Sweet-tasting berries attract animals who eat the berries and then spread the seeds that are hidden in the berries by the droppings the animals make on the ground. Some plants secrete a bitter juice in their leaves, or grow thorns or stinging hairs, all to make animals leave them alone, particularly, of course, animals that would otherwise eat their leaves.

When Carl Linnaeus, the famous systematist and botanist, was a boy, his father used to take him into the garden or the fields and show him the flowers. His father taught him not only the names, but also how the inner and outer parts of the flowers determine those names. Every naturalist needs to follow in the footsteps of Linnaeus if he or she would have a sure base to knowledge of the out-of-doors, but there is no need to rush in hurriedly and then be repelled by the seeming complexity of botanical classification. The natural way to begin is to take a few flowers you really know and look them up in any botanical handbook that tells about them so that you can see how the description in the text applies to the plant that you hold in your hand. Take the genus *Rosa* (rose). If you open up a rose flower and look inside, you will see that the many yellow *stamens* are attached to a thin disc that bears in its middle the many distinct *pistils* (see Figure 6-2). You will see also that the base of this flower is shaped like a cup, and hence it

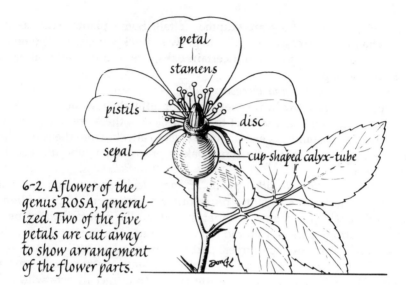

petal

stamens

pistils

disc

sepal

cup-shaped calyx-tube

6-2. A flower of the genus ROSA, generalized. Two of the five petals are cut away to show arrangement of the flower parts.

belongs to a large group of flowers called the *"cup flowers."* Also, rose flowers are usually good-sized, with five white or rose-colored petals, five green *sepals* below them, and they grow on a prickly shrub with net-veined, toothed leaves. All of these characteristics join to make *Rosa* different from any other genus or group of similar species (kinds) of plants. In Chapters Twelve and Eighteen, we begin the close study of plant parts so that you can use this knowledge in classifying plants that you do not know.

COLLECTING PLANTS

In collecting plants, naturalists observe certain common-sense rules. They try not to pick plants near a highway where their absence would take away the beauty that others wish to see. When they find only one or two specimens of a kind of plant, they leave them so that more will grow there. And they never pick any plant that they are neither going to press and mount nor plan to take for some useful purpose, as to do otherwise would be to classify themselves with those who have already disfigured and laid waste large areas of our countryside.

1. *A vasculum, tin box for collecting plants* (see Figure 6-3b). Any

kind of box or bag comes in handy for a beginner, since plants carried in the hand soon wilt. But real naturalists seldom use these because a collector is apt to get into the dangerous habit of collecting plants in a vasculum and then forgetting them so that they uselessly wither away.

2. *A plant press.* Such waste can be avoided if the plant collector carries a plant press (see Figure 6-3a). This not only is handy to put specimens in, in the field, but preserves them by drying and pressing them so that in a few days they may be safely mounted. The simplest plant press is made by getting two flat boards (such as plyboard) about 30 centimeters (1 foot) wide by 45 centimeters (18 inches) long and 7 millimeters (¼ inch) thick. Place between these boards newspaper sheets folded and arranged in twelve-sheet sections so that a plant specimen can be placed between every twelve sheets. Boards and

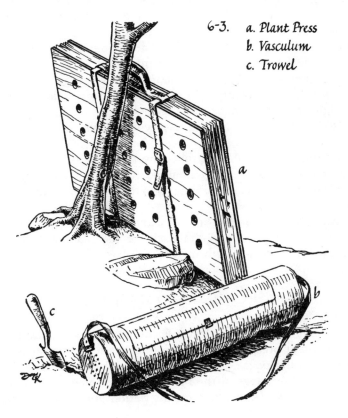

6-3. a. *Plant Press*
b. *Vasculum*
c. *Trowel*

newspaper are then bound together by two canvas straps with buckles, so that the boards press the newspaper tightly together. To allow air to circulate through the press, bore holes in even rows through the boards. An old leather suitcase handle may be tied onto the straps of the press to make easier carrying.

As each specimen is placed between a folded sheet, you should place with it a piece of paper on which is written the place and date of collection and the name, if you know it. Besides this, if you are a careful naturalist, you will number each plant and under the same number in your nature field book write a description of the plant as you saw it when alive, along with an account of its surroundings.

A press full of plants may be carried home and left overnight, but the next day fresh newspaper to surround each plant should be placed in the press. This helps the drying. A more elaborate press can be made by gluing or riveting strips of light hardwood together in the form of a pair of latticework frames. In large cities you can buy gray cardboard blotters, cut to size, that are better than newspaper for drying—they take up less room, are much easier to handle, and dry the plants more quickly. Two separate blotters go around each plant with a single sheet of newspaper, doubled over, holding the plant. The single sheet need not be changed, but change the blotters every day. At the end of five to eight days your plants should be ready for mounting.

One thing to remember in collecting plants is to try to get roots as well as flowers and seeds. A small *trowel* can be carried in a canvas sheath at your side, ready for digging out roots at any time (see Figure 6-3c).

Seeds may be collected in *transparent paper bags* such as those described in Chapter Five, the name of the plant and the date of collection being written with ink on each bag.

PRESSING AND MOUNTING

Leaves brought home for a leaf collection should either be pressed in a regular plant press or placed in a folded newspaper sheet and this put between the pages of a *large and heavy book such as a dictionary.* The place of the leaves in the book should be changed every day for five or more days. At the end of this period you may take the leaves out and mount them with glue on the pages of your nature scrapbook, writing below each its name.

Flowers or whole plants may be pressed, as described, with either press or book and may afterward be mounted with glue on the pages of a scrapbook or a binder filled with botany paper. To hold them on more securely, use strips of transparent tape. Arrange specimens neatly

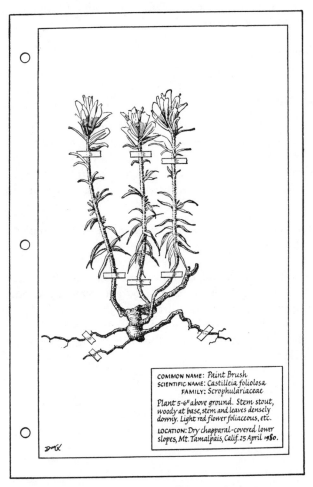

COMMON NAME: *Paint Brush*
SCIENTIFIC NAME: *Castilleia foliolosa*
FAMILY: *Scrophulariaceae*

Plant 5-6" above ground. Stem stout, woody at base, stem and leaves densely downy. Light red flower foliaceous, etc.

LOCATION: *Dry chapparal-covered lower slopes, Mt. Tamalpais, Calif. 25 April 1980.*

6-4. *A page from a botanical collection, or herbarium* ($\times \frac{3}{8}$).

and do not try to crowd too many on a single page. Each plant in a naturalist's collection should have good examples of flowers, stem, leaves, roots, and, if possible, the fruit and seeds. It should have attached to it a numbered label, giving its name, the exact place collected, and the date. (See Figure 6-4 for an illustration of a correctly mounted specimen.) If you are a good naturalist, you will also include details about the surroundings where each plant was found and information regarding its color, size, shape, and arrangement of leaves and flower parts, as below:

Common name: *Common Trillium.*

Scientific name: *Trillium sessile.*

Family: Liliaceae, *or Lily Family.*

A plant about 30 centimeters (1 foot) high with its stout stem supporting three large, broad, sessile (stemless) leaves 5 to 10 centimeters (2 to 4 inches) long with purplish veins, and a purple flower 17 millimeters (¾ inch) high in the center with three petals, three green sepals, six stamens, and three styles attached to a three-celled ovary.

Location: *Damp ground under trees in woods two miles north of Madison, Wisconsin, May, 1, 1980.*

Such a collection should be made and kept neatly and put in some container where the specimens will be protected from both breakage and dampness. A reference library of mounted and named plant specimens will keep your knowledge of the plants of your neighborhood fresh throughout the year, besides being first-class training in nature work.

CHAPTER
7

Rocks and Minerals and Their Collecting

As a boy my first thought of rocks was that they were simply a large mass of rather uninteresting brown and black objects that I had to walk over in the hills. They were just "rocks." I am glad I got over this foolish idea and found out how amazingly interesting rocks are and how many different kinds, each with a different and curious history of its own.

My first "insight" into rocks came when I was fourteen years old. On a hike I met an old man who was breaking out some rocks from a hillside with a small pick.

"Why take so much trouble with that common gray rock? I asked. His sharp eyes looked me scornfully up and down.

"Don't bother me, boy," he said, "if that is the best you can say for this rock."

But I was curious and kept asking. Finally he laid out in the palm of his hand a slab of gray stone that had on it the perfect picture of a fern, exquisite in design.

"Millions of years ago," he said, "this fern lived near here in a world strangely different from that which we see about us now. Giant salamanders ten feet long crawled ponderously through flowerless marshes made of giant ferns and strange leafless plants such as the modern 'horse tails.' This fern I think must have fallen into a slow-moving stream and was carried down and buried in a great mud flat. Centuries of time saw the sinking of the mud flat beneath the sea and there the great pressure of water gradually turned the mud into a rock, 'shale,' that we see here now."

"But how was the picture of the fern preserved?" I asked.

"Well, you see, in the mud there was no air or very little, and it is air that contains the bacteria that cause a plant to decay rapidly. So the fern kept its shape for a long time and only slowly was its place taken by solutions that seeped through the mud and shale, finally leaving this design upon the rock."

Having learned that rocks were interesting after all, I stayed several hours helping the old man search for the story in that "common gray rock." We found the mark of ancient pine needles and part of the fossil of a trilobite, a strange and primitive sea animal of long ago. Who the old man was I do not know to this day; he may have been a famous paleontologist, for he had the piercing eyes and the nimble hands of the scientist.

The rocks beneath our feet not only carry within them the history of the ages, but they also carry the future of human beings. For it is what we do with the rocks that has made and will make much of our success on earth. Iron and steel, aluminum, sulphur, and nitrate all come from rocks, and they have made a good deal of today's civilization. Radium and molybdenum and fluorite may well make tomorrow's.

To study rocks and minerals, you not only need to be interested, but you must develop your powers of observation and alertness. People have stepped over fortunes beneath their feet because they were too blind to see what lay there. Gold in the raw often looks dull and uninteresting. Pitchblende, the extremely valuable ore of radium, looks like the commonest kind of rock. Valuable agates and opals are usually hidden inside clay-colored concretions (round rocks) that most people would carelessly kick out of their path. However, study rocks not only for the hidden treasure you may someday stumble upon, but also for the great amount of interesting knowledge you can gain from them.

Even the commonest rock has a history extending back into the millions of years, involving perhaps great upheavals of the land or the action of fiery volcanoes, and may contain within it in the form of fossils a link in the history of life on earth.

Just what are rocks and minerals? Since minerals are the basis of all rocks, we had better look at them first. A *mineral*, in chemical terms, is any element or compound in solid form. An *element* is one of the basic parts of matter, such as pure iron or copper or oxygen. But oxygen is not a mineral, since it is a gas. A diamond, for instance, is a pure carbon mineral and is thus made up of only one element. A *compound is a combination of elements* locked together chemically so that they cannot be separated save by chemical action. Water, for example, is a compound of oxygen and hydrogen, and these elements can only be separated by a chemical action such as electrolysis where electric charges running between lead poles break the two elements apart and set them free.

Examples of common minerals are: *quartz*, a compound of silicon and oxygen; *pyrite*, a compound of iron and sulphur; *cinnabar*, a compound of mercury and sulphur; *dolomite*, a compound of magnesium, calcium, carbon, and oxygen; and *orthoclase feldspar*, a compound of aluminum, potassium, silicon, and oxygen.

Rocks, on the other hand, are made up of *one or more minerals grouped together* in more or less close association. Rocks may even be defined as including such things as sand, mud, or volcanic ashes, as well as the more solid rocks such as granite and shale. The rocks are divided into three great divisions: (1) *igneous rocks*, those which have solidified by cooling out of a molten magma (liquid rock) such as is found in volcanoes—including granites, basalts, lavas, and similar rocks; (2) *sedimentary rocks*, those which were formed, by pressure or chemical cementation or both, out of loose sediment such as sand, mud, gravel—including sandstone, shale, conglomerate, limestone, and so forth; and (3) *metamorphic rocks*, which originally were once either igneous or sedimentary, but have been changed by the action of heat, pressure, and/or water to something altogether new. Serpentines, schists, gneisses, and marbles are various metamorphic rocks. In Chapter 13 we take up the study of these three great divisions in more detail.

Until you are prepared by further study to tackle the classification of rocks yourself, you must turn for advice on the naming of your rock specimens to people who know them or to the collections of rocks in your nearest museum. But, as with animals and plants, don't be too sure you have the right name until it is checked by an authority.

LOOKING FOR ROCKS AND MINERALS

The most useful tool for the rock and mineral collector is a geology pick, although a good hammer will do in a pinch. With this tool, you can break a rock up and see what the inside is like, and it is inside rocks that the most interesting things are likely to be found. Not only does this breaking up expose to you fresh and unweathered surfaces that will tell you the rock's true nature, but often you run across mineral veins or even the crystals of minerals that were not visible on the worn and dirty outer surface.

Look particularly in the following places:

1. In old quarries where the weathered rock on the surface has been blasted away and the new rock underneath exposed.

2. In cuts made through the hills for roads, or places dug out for bridges and so forth. Here again fresh rock has been exposed.

3. Along dried-up stream beds or where the water is low, you will often find interesting pebbles or bits of rock washed out from some deep-cut layer. In such a place the first gold in California was discovered.

4. In coarse sand on ocean beaches. Valuable minerals are often found in sand, hidden among commoner grains—jasper, rose quartz, opal, and amber, among others.

5. At the openings to mines where much ore and crushed and broken rock have been thrown out onto slag piles. This material, carefully picked over, yeilds valuable finds.

6. On the tops of hills or mountains where the constant weathering often exposes rock layers that are completely covered in the surrounding valleys or plains.

7. Where a stream has cut a deep gash through the earth, it often uncovers many interesting rock layers. Look carefully in such places for good specimens (see Figure 7-1).

8. Near any place where there has been a recent volcanic eruption there

7-1. A river has cut its way through a ridge of tilted sedimentary beds, exposing the edges of rock layers.

are bound to be many interesting volcanic rocks, and near the edge of a formerly red-hot area such as a lava tube there are likely to be some good sections of metamorphic rock, metamorphosed by the heat.

Collecting in such places, you will gradually build up a rock and mineral collection that will tell you much about the vastly interesting history of the earth and the nature of some of the things from which it is made.

MAKING A ROCK COLLECTION

Much of the value of your rock collection depends upon the completeness of the story it tells. It is best to take notes as you collect rocks and minerals, putting a piece of adhesive tape with a number on each specimen. Opposite this number in your field notebook you can then write a description of the exact location where the rock or mineral was found, such as:

7-2. A rock collection fits nicely into a set of shallow drawers. Add partitions.

FELDSPAR ORTHOCLASE
MICROCLINE SiO_2,Al_2O_3,K_2O

QUARTZ - ROCK CRYSTAL
SiO_2

GRANITE
(PRE-CAMBRIAN)
St. Lawrence Co. New York

GABBRO
(PRE-CAMBRIAN)

DIABASE
(PRE-CAMBRIAN)

BASALT
Mt. St. Helens. Wash.

IGNEOUS ROCKS

ROCKS
for

SEDIMENTARY ROCKS

METAMORPHIC ROCKS

No. 18. *Piece of* CINNABAR. *Found at mouth of old quicksilver mine fifteen miles north of Napa, California. Cinnabar is the ore from which quicksilver or mercury is made. It is a compound of mercury and sulphur. Small bits of cinnabar were lying in the mass of slag at the mouth of the mine, though most of this mineral had long ago been used up by the miners. The slag with the cinnabar was mostly a light yellow rock or mud, very crumbly, and apparently made up of considerable clay mineral.* **July 1, 1980.**

Transfer such a description to a card that is to go with your specimen into your museum collection, and, if you will continue this practice, you will be on your way to having a scientific collection. Such a collection would be very valuable in working out a rock and mineral map of your neighborhood.

A beginner's rock collection does not have to be quite this complicated. A useful collection can be made by merely numbering your rocks, as explained above, and then on a card attached to the box holding your collection having the names of the numbered rocks printed opposite their correct numbers (for an example, see Figure 7-2).

CHAPTER
8
Climate

We study climate because it has a tremendous effect on everything that lives, as well as on nonliving things such as rocks, minerals, and dirt. In the desert there are different kinds of animals and plants than on a rainy coast. Everything alive adapts itself to the climate in which it lives. We study clouds because they bring rain, and rain is perhaps the most important part of climate because of the renewal of life it causes.

Climate then is one of the large sections that fit into the puzzle of nature, and it is the business of the naturalist to learn as much as he or she can about each part of that puzzle. The significance and meaning of life in your neighborhood will take on much more interest if you learn to see it in relation to your local climate, and in turn the sky itself will become no longer merely the home of good or bad weather, but a book full of many readings of great curiosity.

The best way to start our inquiry into the nature of climate is to imagine ourselves in outer space and looking at the earth from a distance of about two thousand miles. To see from this position the secrets of climate and weather, we must have the ability to see air currents on the earth's surface, and the distribution and amount of moisture and sunlight, rain, and air pressure.

We see from our point in space that the earth is a great ball slowly turning on its axis from left to right (if our bodies are pointed from north to south, with our heads north). The first great fact to notice is that half of this ball is bathed in light from the sun while the other half is dark with night. The sun is the all-important giver of life, light, and energy, giving these things most to the parts of the earth where its light is most direct (the equator) and least where its light is most at an angle (the polar regions).

From our position far from the earth, we begin to notice many climatic facts or laws. These we can divide into three great divisions: (1) laws referring to *temperature*; (2) laws having to do with *winds*; and (3) laws dealing with *moisture*.*

SOME LAWS OF TEMPERATURE

1. *The sun warms the earth and its atmosphere during the day.* This eternal renewal of warmth is the only barrier between life and the great cold of outer space.

2. *Vertical rays from the sun* (such as those at the equator) *warm the earth more than sun rays at an angle* (as at the poles). The warmth of summer and the cold of winter are an application of this law.

3. *At night the earth's surface is cooled by outward radiation of heat to the overlying air, which is then warmed and so rises and carries the heat off into space.* This losing of heat is the reason for a night getting gradually cooler (see Figure 8-1).

4. *Water vapor and dust in the air slow up the passage of heat so that the drier and thinner the air the more heat reaches the earth, while at the same time there is more rapid cooling of the earth at night and in the shade.* Anybody who has climbed a high mountain on a sunny day, and noticed how up there in the dry thin air it may be quite hot in the sunlight and yet at the same time very cool in the shade, has seen this

*Adapted from S.S. Visher, *Climatic Laws* (New York: AMS Press, Inc., 1977).

8-1. *Cooling of the earth's surface at night. Wavy lines = surface heat. Note gradual straightening (=cooling) and rising, away from sun toward dark (night). Small arrows = cold upper air descending to replace risen warm air.*

law in action. This also explains why hot deserts usually cool off quite noticeably at night.

5. *Water warms less easily and more slowly than land, and cools more slowly.* Because of this, oceans stay comparatively warm long after the continent near them has become very cold, and, in an opposite manner, in summer oceans stay cold after the land near them has become warm. It is because of this that cities near the sea usually have a more even all-year temperature than cities far inland. The sea warms the air near it in winter and cools it in summer. Thus in winter we would see snow spreading far down through the inner parts of continents, while coming more slowly and reluctantly to the seashore.

6. *The temperature of the earth increases until the loss of heat is equaled by the addition of heat.* Watching the earth from our position in space, we notice that each day the greatest heat is likely to be not at noon when the sun is directly overhead, but two or three hours later when there has been more time for the day's heat to accumulate. Through the year the greatest heat is most likely to fall in July or August and not in June in the Northern Hemisphere, even though the sun's light is most direct and the days are longest in June. This is the phenomena known as *temperature lag.*

7. *Rapid lowering warms air while rapid climbing cools it.* It is the cooling climbing currents of air that produce the white fluffy cumulus clouds by condensing the water vapor in the air when the current reaches around four thousand feet. Warm air radiating into space cools and condenses and at night is pulled down to earth by gravity, to be warmed and lifted up again the next day (see Figure 8-2).

SOME LAWS OF WINDS

1. *Cold air usually sinks and crowds under warmer air, thus forcing it to rise.* This is because cold air fills less space and is therefore heavier than warm air. The downward thrust of the cold air is usually the start of a wind. The larger the bulk of hot air rising, the greater the wind that rushes the cold air in under it.

2. *Wind always blows from a place of higher air pressure to a place of lower air pressure, much in the way water runs downhill.* The low-pressure centers are usually formed by the hot air that rises from them, leaving a partial vacuum beneath into which the cooler air from the colder high-pressure centers rushes. *Pressure is simply the weight of the air in the atmosphere.* Few people realize that at sea level the air is pressing on all parts of their bodies with a weight equivalent to about 14.7 pounds per square inch. The reason we don't feel this is that there is an equal pressure inside our bodies pushing against this outside pressure, and thus equalizing it. When we climb swiftly up a mountainside, a singing in our ears soon tells us that the pressure within is greater than that without, and we have to equalize the two pressures again by swallowing.

3. *The direction of winds is changed by the rotation of the earth* (or

8-2. *How a wind starts. Hot air (wavy lines at right) rises from earth, cooling as it rises. Cool upper air sinks downward and finding "vacuum" left by risen hot air, rushes in — creating wind.*

centrifugal force); *to the right* (or clockwise) *in the Northern Hemisphere, and to the left* (contraclockwise) *in the Southern Hemisphere.* This is the reason why a cyclonic storm in the northern latitudes usually has wind from the east in its beginning and wind from the west at its end (see Figure 8-3a). This is also why hurricanes, typhoons, and tornadoes are circular storms. And thus, wind does not usually blow *directly* from a center of high pressure to a center of low pressure, but more or less *curves* toward it.

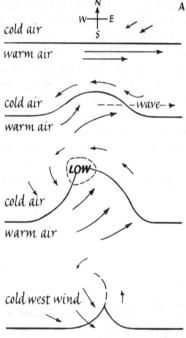

A 1. *A cyclone begins to form along the line of contact between a warm air mass and a cold air mass, just as a whirlpool forms between two opposing currents of water.*

2. *The faster moving warm air is deflected toward NE and pushes into and over the cold mass.*

3. *As the warm bulge pushes farther into the cold mass, the cold air begins to circle southward and wedge under the warm mass from the west. The center of the vortex thus formed is a low pressure area or "low."*

4. *This typical northern hemisphere cyclone (winds blowing counterclockwise around a low) will probably end with the cold west wind overtaking and pinching off the warm bulge.*

(Diagrams above adapted from Wenstrom: WEATHER AND THE OCEAN OF AIR, 1980)

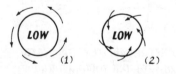

B 1. Winds circle wide around a low over flat country or open water;
2. veer toward center where friction is caused by trees, hills, buildings, etc.

8-3. A. Formation of a cyclonic storm in northern latitudes; and
B. Effect of local conditions on winds around a "low."

4. *Winds are influenced by topography* (features on the surface of the earth) *and surface temperature.* Friction or resistance is set up by trees, houses, hills, and the like, but is cut down where there are plains or open sea. Where there is little friction, as on the sea, winds circulate round and round a center of low pressure; where there is lots of friction, as in hilly, wooded country, they go more directly toward the center of the low (see Figure 8-3b). It can be understood from this how a great forest fire could influence the climate of a region by destroying the trees that held back the wind. Wind usually goes down slopes, follows valleys, goes toward warm regions, and avoids elevations and cold areas.

SOME LAWS OF MOISTURE

1. *Air can hold twice as much moisture with every 18-degree Fahrenheit or 10-degree Celsius increase in temperature.* This explains why a hot day is more likely to be dry than a cool day and why when moisture-saturated air becomes cooled it must deposit some of its moisture (as by rainfall).

2. *Moisture in the atmosphere comes from all moist surfaces, but particularly from the ocean.* However, in the inner parts of continents a much larger share of atmospheric moisture comes from the ground and streams. From our position in space we can see the whole earth having moisture sucked up from it into the air with each rising of the sun, but we see the greatest clouds of moisture rising from the sea.

3. *The rate of evaporation increases with temperature and wind velocity, and with lesser humidity.* We all know how a brisk warm dry wind dries out wet clothes in a very few minutes, while on a "muggy" day with no wind and an overcast sky the same clothes take many hours to dry. On the sea we can watch the water vapor rising most rapidly from those areas where winds whip along the surface of the waves, exposing the water many times to the sucking-up process of dry air.

4. *Atmospheric moisture is carried about chiefly by wind and the upward moving of air, called "convection."* From our viewpoint in space we notice how the cloud masses over the whole surface of the world are constantly being moved about by the winds.

5. *Moisture in the air is "condensed"* (thickened into visible form) *when the air is cooled below the "saturation" or "dew" point.* This is the

cause of clouds and rain. Water vapor itself is usually invisible. The moisture in a clear blue sky is really there, but it is all in the form of invisible vapor until the temperature drops below the dew point. If the air is very dry its dew point is very low; but there is always one time in the day when the temperature is likely to go down to that point, and that is in the dawn. This is why dew (condensed moisture) appears in the early morning, a phenomenon found even in the desert and one of the ways in which desert mammals, birds, and insects manage to get a little water. Clouds are also made of condensed moisture, in their case such small droplets that the rising currents of air (convection currents) keep the collected drops in the sky. But, if these droplets begin to enlarge, because of more moisture condensing, eventually they grow heavy enough to fall—usually in the form of rain. The droplets in the clouds act like tiny mirrors, reflecting the sunlight, and producing the dazzling snowy whiteness we often see in the legions of the sky. This is the same whiteness that is found in powdered glass, even though each tiny piece of glass alone is entirely transparent.

Let us watch, as an example, rain developing over the western margin of North America. From out in space we see the sun's light fall upon the ocean as the world turns. The air is warmed; and since this warm air can hold more moisture than it could when it was cold, evaporation (or turning of moisture into vapor) from the sea's surface increases. We see the warm moisture-laden air rise, more air (cooler) drawn in to take its place, and a wind start up, increasing evaporation again. The wind blows upon the land carrying moisture from the ocean. Wherever the moisture is cooled below the saturation point, we see it form clouds. Soon the wind encounters a mountain range and is forced to rise. The higher the clouds go, the cooler the air gets and the more condensation there is until a drizzle sets in. If the moisture-laden air is cooled still further by rising or by cold currents meeting it or overturning it, we see rain fall out of the clouds until the excess moisture is gone (see Figure 8-4).

And now from our position in space we notice a few last facts. The great ball of the earth shows both oceans and continents. Over the oceans, as we might suspect, we see many more clouds than over the continents. And looking at the land we see that the more mountain ranges that we cross to go away from the sea, the less clouds there are and so the less moisture. So naturally we expect to find the worst

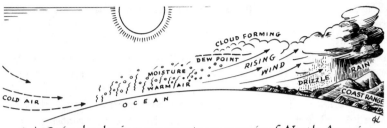

8-4. *Rain developing over western margin of North America.*

deserts far inland behind ranges of mountains that catch the rain before it reaches the desert, and the most humid wet places along the coasts where the ocean rain can fall.

Since it is rain that influences life more than anything else except the sun, we begin to understand now why the study of climate is so important to the naturalist. Study the above laws carefully. They are only the beginning of climate study, but try to apply them to your own neighborhood so that you will be able to understand its own drama of climate and weather.

CLOUDS

Clouds are worth watching. They are the one part of nature that is always changing before your eyes. On the stage of the sky they act out parts that sometimes have grim and sometimes happy meanings for the animals and plants beneath them. A disastrous thunderstorm, a blizzard, a period of long dry fine weather, all these are foretold by the cloud actors in the sky. But the act they put on is so magnificent in itself, so filled with pure beauty and drama, that I have often wondered why so few people pay much attention to clouds. Perhaps it is because these people have not ever tried to learn about clouds so that one type of cloud means no more to them than another. It is the same kind of blindness with which most people look at insects. To them they are all just "bugs," while to the naturalist insects are infinite in their variety, beauty, and interest. But, although insects are difficult to study, clouds are ridiculously easy. You can learn cloud types so quickly and easily that you soon become amazed that you did not tackle the job before.

The beginning naturalist should learn to recognize the three chief types of clouds: *cumulus, cirrus,* and *stratus* (illustrated in Figure 14-2 in the chart of cloud forms).

1. *Cumulus.* These clouds are the true marching "legions of the sky." Large, white, and fluffy, they are variously called "sheep's wool" and "cauliflower" clouds. As explained above, they are formed by convection currents cooling to the condensation points when they reach around 4,000 feet in altitude. They give the effect of plates piled high with ice cream, because of their flat bases, which are caused by the convection currents hitting a line of condensation. *If medium in size and high,* these clouds mean fair weather. *If large, low, and increasing in density,* they often mean rain.

2. *Stratus.* These are usually quite low, flat clouds, such as a sheet of fog lifted no more than 3,000 feet off the ground. Rain seldom falls from stratus clouds even though they may look ominously dark. We often call such clouds "high fog."

3. *Cirrus.* Feather or hairlike clouds high in the sky (averaging 30,000 feet above the earth) are cirrus. These clouds are so high that they are not made up of water droplets but of tiny particles of ice. If cirrus clouds come and then disappear, it means fair weather. If they stay and increase in size, becoming cirrostratus, the outlook is bad.

CHAPTER
9

Beginning Ecology

Ecology is the study of the interrelations of life and of life with inanimate things, of how a bee, for instance, must depend on people for the beehive, on flowers for honey, on weather for the sunshine in which it can work best, and on its own community of bees for protection against enemies and the strength to accomplish large tasks. Today ecology has become a most important science, because it has opened a vast new realm of unexplored study and because it is so important to any real understanding of life on earth.

Humans may be considered to have reached the highest point of ecological relationship. By this is meant that they depend for life, health, and happiness on more things outside themselves than does any other living thing. Metals, minerals, stone, and lumber build their cities, their homes, and all the civilized conveniences that they use. Diseases brought to humans by all sorts of one-celled animals and plants, by worms and by insects, give them ill-health. Thus every time a person catches a cold, the way he or she feels may be caused by a microscopic plant. Animals supply people with meat, eggs, honey, horns, dyes, silk, and a hundred other useful things. Plants clothe them with cotton, feed them with wheat, vegetables, and fruits, and attack them with weeds. People depend upon people for peace, for war, for government, for protection from famines or floods or disease, and for entertainment. The list of all is too long for this book, and all comes under the study of ecology.

What we are interested in here is the general ecology of all life, and the various interrelationships.

TYPES OF ACTION OF CLIMATE ON ANIMALS

1. *Cold climate* forces animals to grow warm fur or feathers, people to put on woolen or fur clothing (Figure 9-1).

2. *Hot climate* forces animals to seek shade and water, lose hair; people to wear sun helmets, or evolve a dark skin and eyes.

3. *High tides* force sea animals of the beach to develop ways to keep

9-1. An animal's adaptation to cold climate. Long, thick, shaggy hair protects the muskox of arctic North America from year-round extreme cold.
(From habitat group, Amer. Mus. Nat. Hist., N.Y.)

themselves moist and so prevent drying out when the tide goes down; they force people to build long docks out to sea and place shore houses on high piles.

4. *Storms* force migrating birds to take roundabout flights to avoid the danger; they force people to build boats very strong.

5. *Snow* forces animals either to develop large feet for snowshoe treading (as in snowshoe rabbits) or to beat hard yards in the snow as the deer do; snow forces people to carry belongings on sleds and toboggans and to use snow plows to keep roads clear.

TYPES OF ACTION OF CLIMATE ON PLANTS

1. *Cold weather* causes plants with big leaves to lose them to prevent the freezing of sap.

2. *Heavy, constant winds* cause plants either to build themselves strong stout trunks and deep roots, or to be pliant so that they easily bow before the wind (as grasses do), thus not risking breakage by resistance.

3. *Dry weather*, as on deserts, causes plants either to develop very deep roots to reach supplies of water in underground streams (as desert palms do), or to develop leaves and stems in which water can be stored for long periods (as the cactus plant does), or to grow very rapidly during the short rains, drop seeds, and then die (as the desert grasses and wild flowers do). (See Figure 9-2 for plant response to dry climate.)

4. *Hot weather* causes plants to develop small leaves (as do scrub oak, manzanita, chamiso, and other plants of the chaparral or dwarf forest of the West). These small leaves hold onto moisture much better than large leaves.

TYPES OF ACTION OF GEOGRAPHY
ON ANIMALS AND PLANTS

1. *Numerous narrow valleys separated by high mountains* may produce quite different species or forms of animals and plants within a short distance, because of their being cut off from one another; or make people in different valleys have different kinds of governments and

Organ-pipe cactus

9-2.
Response of plant life to a dry climate. In the cactus family, stems have taken on the work as well as the green color of leaves. Note in flat middle ground a characteristic of deserts—separation of plants into well-spaced clumps in response to uniform dearth of water.

customs, as did the many small states of ancient Greece, for instance.

2. *Warm ocean currents* may allow animals and plants of temperate climates to live much farther north than usual, as they do in north-western Europe because of the Gulf Stream, a warm-water current of the Atlantic.

3. *Cold ocean currents*, sweeping far up from the Antarctic Ocean, reach the Galápagos Islands on the Equator off the coast of South America and allow cold-weather animals such as penguins and seals to live there.

4. Oceans near land produce fog and rain, which make the coast inhabitable for dampness-loving plants and animals.

TYPES OF ACTION
OF PLANTS ON PLANTS

1. *There is a partnership or "symbiosis" between certain species of algae and fungi to form the interesting lichen* that we see on many trees and rocks. The fungus gathers the food materials from bark and rock that

the algae, with its chlorophyll, uses in the manufacture of food for both of them (see Figure 9-3).

2. *Parasitism*, as when the mistletoe lives off the sap of the oak tree, or the bracket fungus sucks the life out of the elm.

3. *Food production*, as when bacteria decompose animal or vegetable matter and this is later absorbed and used in the manufacture of foods by more highly developed plants.

4. *Support*, as when a tree forms a support for a vine such as the honeysuckle or climbing ivy.

TYPES OF ACTION
OF ANIMAL ON ANIMAL

1. *One animal eats another,* as a mountain lion eats a deer.

2. *Partnership or symbiosis* (internal partnership), as when the one-celled flagellate in the stomach of the termite (white ant) helps the larger animal digest their common food, wood pulp. The flagellate gets

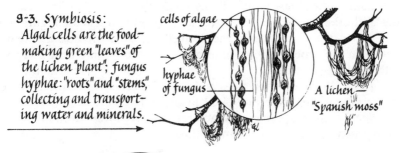

9-3. Symbiosis: Algal cells are the food-making green "leaves" of the lichen "plant"; fungus hyphae: "roots" and "stems," collecting and transporting water and minerals.

cells of algae

hyphae of fungus

A lichen— "Spanish moss"

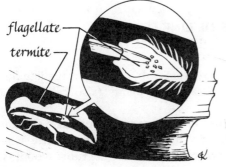

flagellate

termite

9-4. Another case of mutual benefit: in exchange for room and board, the protozoan flagellate chemically converts cellulose into food for both animals.

shelter from the termite, while the termite would die without the flagellate (see Figure 9-4).

3. *External partnership, "commensalism,"* as when the sponge gets transportation by riding on the back of the crab, and the crab is camouflaged from its enemies by the sponge.

4. *Internal parasitism,* as when the ichneumon fly lays its eggs in the back of the living caterpillar, or when people are parasitized in their intestines by the tapeworm.

5. *External parasitism,* as when the leach or tick clings to some animal, bird, or person and sucks its blood.

TYPES OF INTERACTION
OF ANIMALS AND PLANTS

1. *Parasitism,* as when bacteria (tiny plants) enter the bloodstream or tissues of large animals, including humans.

2. *Eating of plants by animals,* as when a horse eats grass, or a person eats spinach.

3. *Eating of animals by plants,* as when the Venus Fly Trap catches flies and other insects in its flower and absorbs them (see Figure 9-5).

4. *Partnership,* as when the unicellular algae inside the worm *Convoluta* are protected by the animal and at the same time supply it with food (see Figure 9-6).

5. *Fertilization,* as when bees and other insects help fertilize flowers by carrying pollen from one plant to another.

6. *Special food supplying,* as when flowers give sweet nectar to insects to get them to come and pollinate them.

TYPES OF LINKAGE
OF MANY ECOLOGIC FACTORS

1. *Sea bird eats mackerel,* mackerel eats crab, crab eats flagellate (kind of one-celled animal), flagellate eats tiny plants (also called a food chain).

2. *Pine-boring beetles bore holes in pine trees;* burrowing wasps use these holes for nests; ichneumon flies and other parasitic wasps parasitize both the burrowing wasps and the beetle grubs; woodpeck-

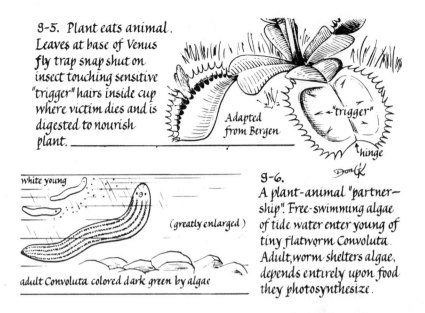

9-5. Plant eats animal. Leaves at base of Venus fly trap snap shut on insect touching sensitive "trigger" hairs inside cup where victim dies and is digested to nourish plant.

Adapted from Bergen

"trigger"

hinge

Don(K

9-6.
A plant-animal "partner-ship". Free-swimming algae of tide water enter young of tiny flatworm Convoluta. Adult worm shelters algae, depends entirely upon food they photosynthesize.

white young

(greatly enlarged)

adult Convoluta colored dark green by algae

ers peck holes in the tree and eat all these various insects; cats and people kill the woodpeckers. On all of these factors depend the number of any one animal (see Figure 9-7).

3. *People burn or cut down a forest;* chaparral or brush comes to take its place; people burn and reburn the chaparral until grass, which fire does not harm so easily, takes the place of both chaparral and trees. This is called the upset balance of life, which happens whenever too much of one thing in nature is destroyed. If people leave the land alone, perhaps time may see the balance swing back, with the grass first supplanted by the chaparral, and finally this giving way to the original trees, whose shade would make it impossible for the sun-loving chaparral to exist successfully.

4. *People destroy the mountain lion and wolves* over wide areas, with the result that the deer become so numerous (as they did in the Kaibab Forest in Arizona) that they eat up all the edible grass and bark in the forest, and then starve into a weakened condition in which bacteria (coming as a disease) attack them and kill them off in large numbers.

5. *People protect cats and let them run wild;* cats kill great numbers of birds that usually eat up insects that harm humans' crops, making it

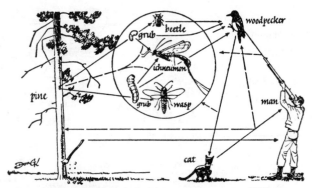

9-7. Linkage of many ecological factors. EXPLANATION: Solid lines connect aggressor and his victim, arrows pointing to beneficiary of action. Broken lines with arrows point to indirect beneficiary of aggression – e.g.: man kills woodpecker; insects benefit. Man kills cat; woodpecker and tree benefit. Note that man gains nothing by killing insect-eating bird, but loses tree to insects.

possible for the crops to be destroyed by the insects that the birds no longer keep under control.

Ecological relationships are so many and varied that it is impossible to go anywhere in nature without finding them. Some very interesting ones can be found in your own backyard.

A good ecological study for a beginner to try is to study the relationships of life within a small area of ground. Mark off your area (not less than 3 square meters, or 10 square feet) with stakes at the corners and run strings between the four stakes. Next, carefully map this area on a large sheet of plain drawing paper, marking down and numbering all the different rocks and plants. The area should be carefully studied over a period of several days to three or four weeks. Watch for all the animals that come and go upon it, to see what influence they have upon each other and the plants. Also carefully check from day to day the effect of any variation in the weather upon the plant and animal life in your area. At the end prepare a chart in which you mark down all the relationships of rocks, earth, plants, people, animals, and climate that you find in this small area. If you have done a careful job, you will be amazed at the number of interesting relationships you will find, and you will be delighted at the far greater insight into the activities of nature that you have gained.

THE STUDENT NATURALIST

The growth of knowledge is like the growth of a tree. At first it is a small plant with few branches, but gradually the branches increase in number and the girth of the tree increases until the tree one day attracts the gaze of humans for its majesty and beauty. Now you who have been beginning naturalists have raised your first small stem of knowledge toward the sky, and you must continue to let this knowledge grow great within you, pushing out the branches into the main pathways of natural science. You will no longer find the going so simple or so easy, but if you will keep the picture before you of the need for growth, you will not let obstacles stop your progress, but you will overcome them with the glad spirit of the explorer who surmounts the ranges of an unknown land.

CHAPTER
10

Thinking out a Problem

In this very short chapter we take up a trail we dropped some pages ago about an amateur naturalist and his or her adventures at a spider niche. We left this seeker wandering home deep in thought, trying to place the facts observed into some kind of intelligent order in his or her mind. Since clarity is a mark of scientific thought, it might be wise for you to go back and read Chapter One again, so that you can remember more clearly the problem with which our friend was faced. You were told at that time, if you studied the chapters directed to the beginning naturalist and applied their principles in actual practice, that you would be ready to understand what our naturalist was about to do. So here, at Chapter Ten, you are ready, it can be assumed, to use your newly developed knowledge to good effect.

To our naturalist, thinking was only the beginning. It was necessary to get more *facts*. Suppose the seeker, after that first day, had written an account on the spider niche. If he or she were an accurate observer and a good writer, an interesting story could be written, but the

101

conclusions could hardly reach very deep without being mainly imagination. And imagination does not stand up as science, or truth, or knowledge!

So our friend goes back to the little cliff and again taking measurements of the spider webs, makes a more careful map (see Figures 10-1 and 10-2). The watcher makes records of the number of catches each spider makes, and from day to day also keeps records of the weather and its changes. Realizing how deeply weather influences the rhythm of life, and that this relationship is part of the problem of spider life, the naturalist wants to find the answers.

GRAPH STUDY

Before many weeks pass, the naturalist comes to some conclusions about all the observations. The main results show on a *graph*, and since a graph is at the same time one of the most interesting and one of the most useful tools of both naturalist and scientist, it will pay us to study what our friend has done.

A graph looks complicated at first glance, but it is very easy to understand once one studies it a little. It is simply a method of measuring phenomena or activity in such a way that we can get a more accurate picture of it than words or figures alone could give us. In the graph shown in Figure 10-3, three kinds of phenomena have been recorded. First, in the lower part of the graph, the *insect catching records of three spiderwebs* of the niche under the cliff are shown by a solid line, a dashed line, and a dotted line. Each web is representative of a different part of the niche. Each line shows how the number of insects caught in that particular web have varied from day to day during a fourteen-day period extending from June 1 to June 14. The second phenomena is the *rainfall* over the same fourteen-day period. (As the rain did not fall every day, it is better to show the amount of fall on separate days by solid columns rather than a continuous line. Thus, on June 1 the column shows that a little over 7.5 millimeters (3/10 inch) of rain fell, while on June 11, 15 millimeters (6/10 inch) fell. Third, on the upper part of the graph is shown the *temperature variation* during the fourteen-day period, the temperature being recorded each day at the time the naturalist was studying the spiderwebs under the cliff. The solid line moves up and down depending on whether the day was hot,

DonGL

(SKETCH FROM THE NATURALIST'S NOTEBOOK)

10-1. "Map" of the spider niche in the rock cliff.

10-2. INSET: Profile of niche showing relative exposure to rain.

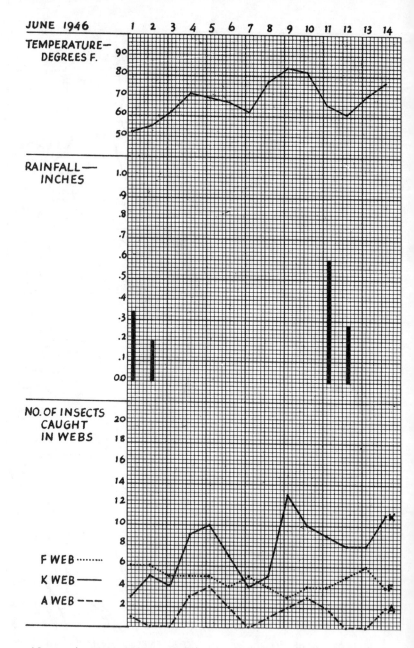

10-3. The naturalist's graph of observations of the spider niche.

warm, or cool. Thus, on June 1 it was fairly cool, being 52 degrees Fahrenheit (usually written 52° F.) or 11 degrees Celsius (11° C).

Now if you study the graph you will see that our naturalist was able to draw the following conclusions from it:

1. "K" web is in the most favorable place, catching the most insects, but this happens mostly during good weather.

2. "K" and "A" webs are strongly influenced by the change in temperature, the number of insects caught being lower the lower the temperature.

3. "A" is in the worst place, catching fewest insects.

4. "K" and "A" webs also seem to be influenced by the rainfall, catching few insects on rainy days; "A" web catching none at all, as probably it got wet on those days.

5. "F" web, because of its sheltered locality, seems to be little influenced by the weather, actually catching more insects on rainy and cool days perhaps because the insects come deep under the cliff on such days to seek shelter from the adverse weather. "F" web would thus have the favored locality, as its food supply would be fairly steady throughout a longer period of the year.

Our naturalist friend has closely observed the spiders in these webs. The spider in "F" web is large and powerful, fully capable of driving intruding spiders away from its favored locality. The spider of "K" web is nearly as large. It too has a good locality. But the "A" web spider is small and weak. Not being able to fight for and hold a good hunting territory, it apparently must take the poor leavings of the outskirts of the spider niche.

What is the picture? Are not weather, shelter, plenitude of food, fighting ability all intimately associated in the lives of these sheet weaving spiders? Although the scientific work involved in this problem is very small compared to what naturalists must usually do, still our naturalist has made a very creditable beginning. The seeker has grasped a problem in nature, applied facts to it, and found answers. If the reader can do as well with the first real natural science problem tackled, he or she can count it as an excellent beginning!

CHAPTER
11
Animal Study

Ideas have lifted the eyes of men and women from the ground and raised them to the stars. What romance is there in the days of the Wild West that is not equaled or surpassed by the drama of human victories and temporary defeats in the struggle for knowledge and the destruction of ignorance? Like lighthouses standing where once were only the swirling mists of the past, great advances in zoology guide human progress out of darkness.

After the first flare of scientific thinking in the land of Greece 2,000 odd years ago, the words of ARISTOTLE, the great Greek naturalist and philosopher, anchored upon the thinking minds of the world like the sacred voice of a scientific god. For 1,000 years or more, Aristotle's writings were almost the only knowledge of natural history in the world! After the year 1500, however, the shackled minds began to break free from their old master and seek new light. Slowly and then more rapidly the great discoveries came.

ROBERT HOOKE (1635–1703), a keen-minded Englishman, left the musty books and sought truth with his own good eyes and a magnifying glass. He discovered the then astounding truth that *all living things are made of cells*. The *cell theory* today is the very anchor of scientific zoology.

The Italian scientist FRANCESCO REDI (c. 1626–97), in 1680, exploded the *theory of spontaneous generation*, the ancient belief that flies spring spontaneously alive from manure or decaying meat, or that worms and similar creatures rise out of rotting vegetation. Other scientists had accepted this belief without question. They were too complacently satisfied to *experiment*. But Redi was not. He put meat in a jar and covered the jar with gauze. If the theory were true, after a while flies would rise from the rotting meat. But no flies came out of the meat; instead flies came from outside and laid their eggs on the gauze above the meat, proving to anyone with sense to see that flies reproduce themselves.

In 1864 LOUIS PASTEUR (1822–95), the great French scientist, clinched Redi's defeat of the spontaneous generation theory by proving through careful study with his microscope that even bacteria reproduce themselves in the same way as other living things.

The year 1628 is another shining landmark. It was the year the English doctor WILLIAM HARVEY (1578–1657) discovered *the circulation of the blood*. We, who think of the blood's circulation as a common fact of life, forget how such an idea once would have been laughed at, or how it might even have led its announcer to the dark torture of the dungeon. Once, people believed the heart was the seat of thought!

In 1806, the French biologist JEAN LAMARCK announced the idea of *evolution*. True, he believed the *theory of the inheritance of acquired characteristics*, or the idea that what an animal develops during its lifetime (a new method of running on its toes, for instance) is inherited by its descendants, a theory that seems to have certain weaknesses. But there was more truth in what Lamarck said than had ever been said before about animal descent. It was one of history's blind moments. No one listened to the quiet Frenchman whose words were so much more important than the fanfare and trumpets of Napoleon's march across Europe. GEORGES CUVIER (1769–1832), the greatest of French anatomists, whose own discoveries of fossil animals in the rocks should have helped rather than hindered the idea of evolution, ridiculed Lamarck and so utterly crushed his ideas with beautiful argument that they sank into obscurity.

The world was ready, in 1859, when Charles Darwin's book *The Origin of Species by Means of Natural Selection* was published (see Figure 11-1); but it was ready with lashing criticism and bitter denunciation from both church leaders and scientists. They felt, and felt rightly, that Darwin's book would upset all the old established ideas of life on earth. Each kind of animal, they believed, was today and always had been exactly as it was at the creation of the world. Darwin saw the animals and plants of the earth engaged in a constant struggle for life, which he called "the survival of the fittest." Life, starting probably as a single cell, has been changed and modified through millions of years by this struggle for existence, and those animals and plants that were best adapted to the fight were selected to live on. By this method all the animals we see on earth today were finally developed.

Opponents claimed the idea was fantastic, but the facts of animal and plant structure, of fossils and of physiology that the anatomists, the paleontologists, and the physiologists had been calmly building through the years, plus the observations of the naturalists on how animals actually struggle for survival, were too much for the strongest opposition. Also, THOMAS HUXLEY (1825–95), an extraordinary orator, thinker, and writer, as well as a fine biologist, so aggressively cham-

11-1. Charles Darwin in middle life — from a little-known portrait in Locy. As a young explorer–naturalist on the 5-year voyage (1831–36) of H.M.S. Beagle, Darwin began the observation and thinking that led to his great theories of evolution.

pioned the theory, and so skillfully defended it, that other scientists were brought over to its ideas almost before they realized what had happened to them. Today the *theory of evolution* is one of the firmest cornerstones to the science of zoology. Now people can see and compare the real relationships between different kinds of living things, according to the stages of the various developments from each group's common beginning.

In more recent times, the laboratory worker has taken over the bulk of scientific zoology. His or her countless experiments on animals and plants under the controlled conditions of the test tube, the glass-sided cage, the microscope, and the section knife (a knife that cuts a very thin slice of animal tissue for use in microscopic slides) have shown much about how these living things tick. A Dutchman, HUGO DE VREIS (1848–1935), the codiscoverer of Mendel's *laws of inheritance* (see Chapter Two), and THOMAS MORGAN (1866–1945), whose work on the inheritance factors in a thousand generations of fruit flies has made him world renowned, have modified Darwin's simpler ideas of evolution. Their discoveries of *genes* (the fundamental and microscopic links of inheritance) and of *mutations* (the strange and sudden changes that occur in these genes in nearly every generation of life, producing new varieties and kinds of animals or plants, some better and some worse adapted for the struggle for existence) have opened new horizons of study, knowledge, and experiment to the scientist.

But the naturalist still has an important place in the scheme, for he or she alone is the one who goes into the wild and studies animals in their natural surroundings. These findings, when checked with those of the pure laboratory worker, lend balance and perspective to the work of zoology. Such men as WILLIAM BEEBE, who studied the life of the sea and the jungle, and Laurence M. Klauber, a great reptile student, combined the two kinds of work in the same lifetimes with excellent results.

THE NATURE OF ANIMAL LIFE

1. *Similarities.* As all animals have some things in common, it is necessary to know in the beginning what these things are—so that later, when we go into the many *differences* between animals, we will

have in our minds a better picture of the animal kingdom as a whole. Below are listed the main similarities:

All animals are made up of cells or a cell.

All animals react to stimuli (touch, light, heat, cold, sound, and so on) if this is properly applied.

All animals must eat food, either vegetable or animal.

All animals burn this food within their bodies to make the energy necessary for movement.

In all animals this burning leaves waste materials that the animal must get rid of, or excrete.

All animals breathe in, or absorb, oxygen and breathe out, or exhale, carbon dioxide and water vapor, the oxygen being used for the burning of food.

2. *The animal cell.* In Figure 11-2 you see examples of many different kinds of animal cells. All animals are made up of cells, some very simple and some very complex. Life shows a variety all the way from

11-2. Examples of typical animal cells.

11-3. The Amoeba, typical animal cell.

the one-celled amoeba to the millions of cells that are found in the human body. The bodies of most animals have many, sometimes hundreds, of different kinds of cells. Nerve cells specialize in being the telephone system of the body. Blood cells specialize in carrying oxygen and food to the other cells, just as dairies and truck farms send their trucks with milk and vegetables into the big cities to help to keep alive the people there. The bloodstream itself is like a garbage collector or sewage system, for it carries away the waste material from the cells throughout the body and passes it through to the kidneys from where it is conducted to the outside. But all these different animal cells have some things in common.

Figure 11-3 shows a typical animal cell, a one-celled animal, the amoeba. This cell is made up of what scientists call *protoplasm*, which is a name for living matter. The protoplasm has two main divisions in the cell, the *cytoplasm*, which is the chief liquid part of the cell, and the *nucleus* (see Figure 11-3). The nucleus apparently acts very much like a brain, for it seems to direct the movements and actions of the whole cell. Into the cell from the outside comes: (1) food (vegetable matter and very tiny one-celled animals in the case of the amoeba); (2) water, which the cell absorbs through its walls; and (3) oxygen, which it needs for burning up the food in order to liberate energy for movement. Water is necessary because more than two thirds of the living matter of protoplasm is made up of water, and this must be constantly replenished (remember how much you drink on a hot day) whenever any is lost or the cell would die.

Food is the fuel that supplies the living dynamo of the cell, giving it power, which in turn gives it movement. Just how this is done not even the wisest scientists are quite sure; so all we can say is that this is what we see happen. The cell moves and by its movement it burns fuel, just as a diesel engine uses up diesel fuel in order to turn around its wheels, or a car burns gasoline. When the fuel (food) is used up, the cell must get some more in order to continue its actions. This used-up fuel, however, is still there in the cell, just as when you burn coal the ashes remain, and the cell must get rid of this useless material. So it forms *vacuoles* or small round spaces in the cell that are filled up gradually by the waste matter of the used-up food. When a vacuole gets big enough, it is pushed over to the side of the cell and then squeezed out through the wall by pressure of the cytoplasm, just as you might take a rubber bulb in your hand and squirt water out through the opening. In this way the cell gets rid of its waste matter.

That is all very easy in the amoeba, but in your own body and that of other large animals (as mentioned above) the bloodstream must come along and carry away separately the waste matter of each of the millions of cells.

3. *Reaction to stimuli.* Heat, light, darkness, sound, cold, chemical changes and probing all affect the animal cell. Touch a single-celled animal with a tiny probe under a microscope and you will see it react by turning as swiftly as it can and going in the opposite direction or by recoiling. Some animals respond to warmth by going toward it; others by going away. The same with cold or light. We all know how the moth is attracted to the candle flame, usually to its eventual sorrow. But most animal reaction to stimuli is for the safekeeping of the animal. You withdraw your hand from a fire to save yourself from getting burned. A deer turns and runs to escape the hunter. When those queer animals the sporozoa suddenly snap into a rigid state and throw a tough shell around themselves because a little nicotinic acid is put in the water with them, they do so to save their lives. In their free state the acid would kill them, but in the spore state they are protected against such dangers by the leathery wall that completely surrounds them. When conditions are again safe, they break out of the spores and become free moving once more (Figure 11-4 shows some of these various reactions).

Cells divide into two to produce new cells. This is the earliest kind of *reproduction.* (True sexual reproduction is caused by the joining of two specialized cells, the egg and the sperm and is found in all the higher forms of animal life. The more advanced books about zoology cover this in more detail than is needed here.) The cells underneath your skin are continually dividing to produce new skin as the old is sloughed off. Single-celled animals seem, at first, to live on forever simply by constantly dividing into two. But scientists have found that there always comes a point in such straight-line reproduction when two cells must come together and fuse, joining the potentialities of each to put new life into the species, this new combined cell then splitting into two again and on and on. (Figure 11-5 shows how these divisions occur.) By some curious trick of development in more complex animals, the simple cells with which they begin life gradually come to produce more and more complex cells, such as blood cells, nerve cells, bone cells, stomach cells, each made for a different function.

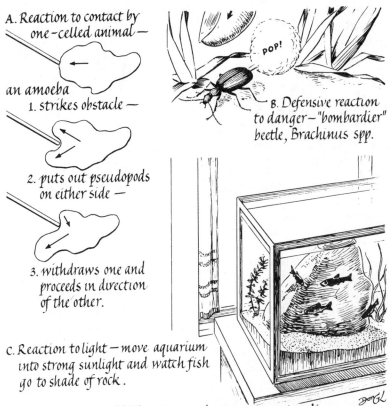

A. Reaction to contact by one-celled animal —

an amoeba
  1. strikes obstacle —

  2. puts out pseudopods on either side —

  3. withdraws one and proceeds in direction of the other.

POP!

B. Defensive reaction to danger — "bombardier" beetle, Brachinus spp.

C. Reaction to light — move aquarium into strong sunlight and watch fish go to shade of rock.

11-4. Reactions of different animals to various stimuli.

If you can get the use of a good microscope, much of this can be seen with your own eyes. The web of a living frog's foot will show you the blood cells coursing on their way through arteries, capillaries, and veins. Some scummy water from a pond will show you a myriad forms of single-celled animals, preying and being preyed on, darting or crawling their way through the world of miniature life. The slides of any naturalist or doctor will show you some of the many kinds of cells with the parts of which they are made stained in different colors so that you can see them clearly. Also, in your public library, the illustrations in the books on zoology will explain to you the nature of the many kinds of cells.

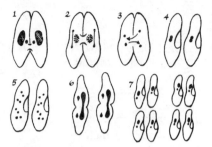

A. Stages in the division
of an Amoeba.

B. Conjugation and binary fission —
the beginnings of "sexual" reproduction are seen in Paramecium.

11-5. Animal cell division and fusion, exemplified by Protozoa.

MAKING YOUR OWN ZOO

The easiest and often the best way to study animals is in captivity, provided you can make their cages natural enough so that they feel almost as much at home as in the wild. For most of us this is only possible with small animals, but field mice and wood rats, snakes, lizards, frogs, and salamanders all offer fascinating chances for study in one's own zoo. An insect zoo is also worth trying and will repay the naturalist who tends it well.

Catching wild animals alive is not so easy, as those who have done it for a living will tell you, but it is a good sport because it calls on all your ingenuity and care. The simplest live trap, and one which will catch not only small mammals such as shrews and mice, but also snakes, lizards, and beetles, can be made by placing a deep, smooth-sided can in a hole in the ground with its top level with the ground (see Figure 11-6). To make this most effective, put four small stones around the trap and on them place a board or a large flat rock. Animals seeking shelter under the board or rock will fall into the trap. But they should never be left there to die of starvation and thirst. Always look at such traps every day and cover them over when you are through with them, as even the smallest of animals suffer hunger and thirst just as we do.

Another simple trap is made by getting an ordinary mouse trap and fastening a coffee can to it with screws (see Figure 11-7), then lashing a wire screen onto the steel rectangle of the trap so that when the trap is set and sprung the mouse is thrown into the can by the screen and held there tightly.

The easiest box trap to make, and probably one of the most effective, is shown in Figure 11-8. The sliding door is kept up by a wire delicately inserted in a small hole cut about 1 inch (2.6 centimeters) from the bottom of the door. The wire lies along the top of the box and has a hook at its farther end, to which is attached a string that goes down through a hole in the upper end of the box, and when the animal grabs the bait (apple, cheese, or lettuce for rats and mice; meat for

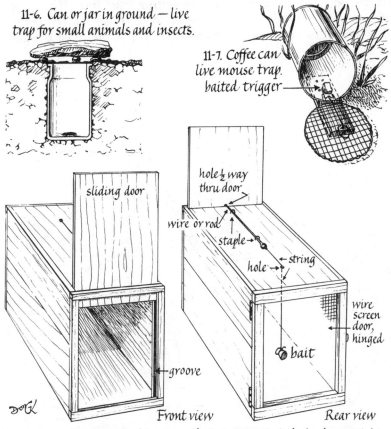

11-6. *Can or jar in ground — live trap for small animals and insects.*

11-7. *Coffee can live mouse trap. baited trigger*

sliding door

hole ½ way thru door

wire or rod

staple

hole ← string

bait

wire screen door, hinged

groove

Front view

Rear view

11-8. *Live box trap. Rod is set at "hair trigger" in hole in door. Slight jerk on bait string pulls rod, drops door. Important: — door must slide very freely in its groove, which can be waxed.*

skunks or weasels) the wire is pulled out of the hole in the door and the door crashes down and imprisons the animal. Care must be taken (by using grease or soap) to see that the door slides easily and also that the bottom edge of the door is protected by a wood or metal strip so that the animal can't get its paw underneath the door and lift up. Heavy wire or screen may be placed over the end opposite the door to give the animal the feeling it can still escape (see also Figure 11-9).

This trap may be varied in size so as to catch all manner of animals from mice to coyotes. But the cleverer animals can never be caught in it unless you use the utmost care in setting your trap. If the trap is partly covered with brush, this helps to disguise its "nonnatural" nature, but it is your own human smell that is the most dangerous

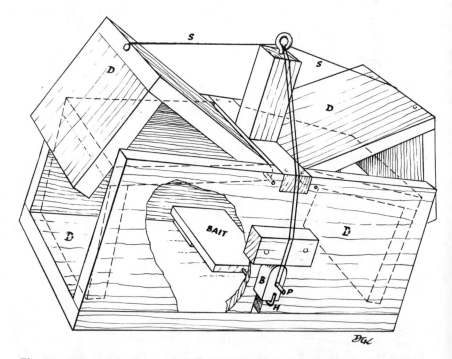

Fig. 11-9. *One of the best live traps for small mammals (adapted from a design by Robert Smith, 1768, by courtesy of Dr. Tracy Storer). Open doors at both ends make animal feel safe inside. From Vinson Brown,* How to Make a Miniature Zoo, *(Boston: Little, Brown, 1957), with permission of the author.*

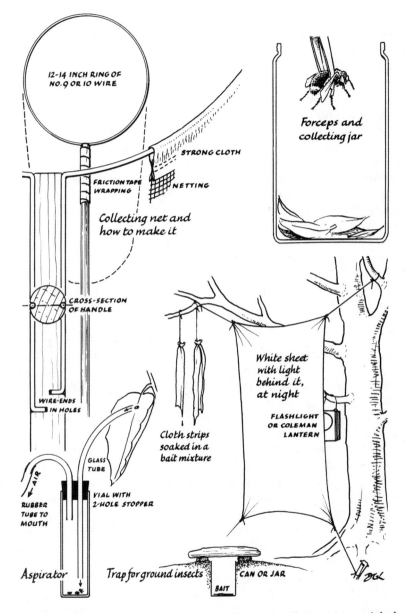

12-14 INCH RING OF NO. 9 OR 10 WIRE

STRONG CLOTH

FRICTION TAPE WRAPPING

NETTING

Collecting net and how to make it

Forceps and collecting jar

CROSS-SECTION OF HANDLE

WIRE-ENDS IN HOLES

White sheet with light behind it, at night

FLASHLIGHT OR COLEMAN LANTERN

Cloth strips soaked in a bait mixture

GLASS TUBE

VIAL WITH 2-HOLE STOPPER

AIR

RUBBER TUBE TO MOUTH

Aspirator *Trap for ground insects* **CAN OR JAR**

BAIT

Fig. 11-10. *Some other tools and traps for collecting small creatures, mainly best for catching them alive. The aspirator is used for catching insects too small to be trapped any other way. From Vinson Brown,* How to Make a Miniature Zoo, *(Boston: Little, Brown, 1957), with permission of the author.*

giveaway. To avoid this, take some strong-smelling plant such as sage or turpentine weed and boil it in a pot of water. Soak a cloth and some gloves in this mixture; then wipe the trap all over with the wet cloth until it smells like the plant, and from that moment until you set the trap, handle it with your gloves. Handle your bait with these same gloves and nothing else. Taking these two precautions, you will get rid of the "human" smell and may even catch the sly fox.

A young naturalist friend has had very hard luck as a skunk catcher, but he still tries. It is not that he doesn't catch the skunks—that is not so difficult—but the trouble seems to be that the skunks catch him! Once I had been told that if a skunk were picked up by its tail it could not fire its odor at you because in order to do this the hind legs had to have traction on the ground. I passed this on to the young naturalist for what it was worth, and he seemed to take the idea quite to heart. Not long after this he met me strongly smelling of skunk and somewhat indignant.

"I thought you said skunks couldn't shoot when they were picked up by the tail?" he testily asked.

"I merely said that that was what I had heard."

"Well, this skunk I picked up sure could shoot. We were out last night along a country road and I saw this big striped skunk running along in front of the car lights. So I hopped out of the car, remembering what you had said, and chased after Mr. Skunk. He couldn't run fast at all; so I ran up quick and grabbed him right up into the air. He didn't have a chance to shoot while he was on the ground, but, boy, did he let me have it when I got him up!"

However, to show that my friend was an experimenter all the way through, skunk or no skunk, this tale is not complete without telling about his experience with a spotted skunk. A year later he decided to see whether a spotted skunk, suddenly encountered on a night hike, would be safe when grabbed by the tail. However, this skunk had other ideas about the matter and started running around a tree in a circle. Not to be daunted, my friend Burne valiantly chased around after it. This hilarious circular motion—hilarious to everybody but Burne and the skunk, who were deadly serious about the matter—continued about three times. Then Burne made a dive for the tail; the skunk let out a squeak and something far more deadly; and both skunk and Burne rapidly parted company, one heading for the brush and the other for the creek!

IMPORTANT THINGS TO REMEMBER
ABOUT KEEPING WILD ANIMALS

1. *They appreciate just as much as you do light, air, room, warmth, food, and water.* It is completely needless to be so cruel as to keep any of these things from them. The best advice to follow is the example of the snake expert Raymond Ditmars, who, when a young fellow, set out to turn a room in his house into a snake room before he ever got any snakes to put in it. He wanted to have cages that the snakes would like and ones that would stay in good condition for a long time. So he made deep wooden trays covered with closely fitting glass tops and with hinged doors in front. Each cage he thoroughly sandpapered to take down all rough edges, and then he varnished them carefully inside and out with several coats. The varnish was to keep moisture from having any effect on the wood and thus to allow the cages to be cleaned out, food and excretions leaving no stains behind. On the floor of each cage he placed a light layer of sand and put a pottery feeding and drinking tray in each cage in such a way that it could be easily filled from outside without danger of the captive escaping. Later he learned to put small electric light globes in the cages so that the snakes would be able to stay warm and active right through the winter. He used every way he could to make his snakes comfortable and happy, with the result that he was able to keep more different kinds of snakes alive in captivity than any other person before him. If you will follow this same technique, you will be able to get some fine results from studying animals you keep in cages. Slovenly, ill-kept cages, on the other hand, spell only unnatural torture for the animals kept in them, with probably early death. Rather than commit this crime against nature, set your animal free.

Figure 11-11 shows the plan of such a small zoo. Plan your own zoo with the same meticulous care for detail, and you will get the same fine results that Raymond Ditmars got. Good books that will give you more detailed information about keeping animals in captivity are *Our Small Native Animals, Their Habits and Care,* by Robert Snedigar, (Dover, 1963) and my book, *How to Make a Miniature Zoo* (Little, Brown, 1957).

2. *Make your cages large and roomy.* A box 60 × 30 millimeters (2 × 1 feet) with wire screen on top will do for a pair of mice, but a raccoon would need a cage as large as 2½ square meters (8 square feet) or

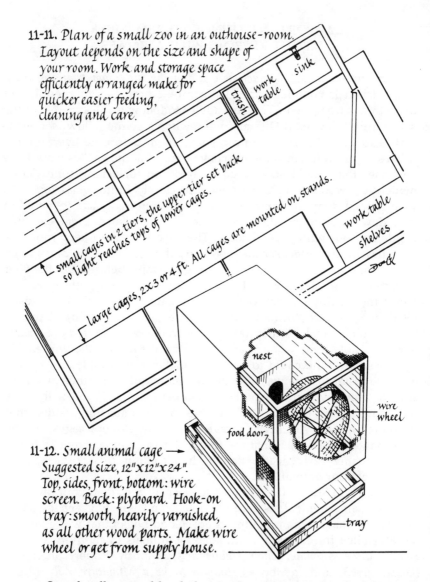

11-11. Plan of a small zoo in an outhouse-room. Layout depends on the size and shape of your room. Work and storage space efficiently arranged make for quicker easier feeding, cleaning and care.

sink

work table

trash

small cages in 2 tiers, the upper tier set back so light reaches tops of lower cages.

large cages, 2x3 or 4 ft. All cages are mounted on stands.

work table

shelves

nest

wire wheel

food door

11-12. Small animal cage → Suggested size, 12"x12"x24". Top, sides, front, bottom: wire screen. Back: plyboard. Hook-on tray: smooth, heavily varnished, as all other wood parts. Make wire wheel or get from supply house.

tray

more. Supply all warm-blooded animals with some kind of material, such as cotton or wool, with which they can make a nest or sleeping place. Then make sure that each day they get water and food. Unless you can make a real pet out of a wild creature, it is not a very good idea to keep one very long. Keep it long enough to study its actions and its habits and then let it go. It will make you feel better to know that your wild creature is free and active in the woods and fields once more.

To mice, rats, and rabbits you can feed raisins, pieces of bread, rolled oats, carrots, and lettuce. Meat eaters, such as raccoons, skunks, foxes, weasels, and wildcats, need meat, of course, and scraps of both meat and fish from the market will do, but make sure such scraps are not tainted (rotting). Remember, though, that most meat eaters will also take and need vegetable food, even cooked vegetables.

3. *Keep cages clean.* Give them a thorough cleansing at least once a week. If you make a cement floor to your cage, have it slope down so that it may be easily washed and the water will drain off. Sandpaper and varnish wooden cages well, put straw or sand on the floor, and put in fresh material at every cleansing. A simple, easily built and easily cleaned cage is diagrammed in Figure 11-12. A detachable floor is hooked on to the upper part of the cage, which is made of strong wire netting and pine (2.5 centimeters, or 1 inch, thick), roofed with shingles. To clean this cage, you merely unhook the floor and carefully lift off the upper portion onto the ground, keeping the animal within the cage. Clean up the floor and replace the upper part back on it when done and lock with the hooks.

Animals such as chipmunks and squirrels need a wheel in which they can run. A wire wheel can be purchased at most pet shops, or simply make one by twisting some wire netting (of fairly large mesh so the animal's claws won't get caught) into a circle and soldering or tying it together. Run spokes of wire across the wheel and solder them onto a wire axle in the middle (see Figure 11-12).

Snakes, lizards, and tortoises like sand and rock in their cages, and glass tops are better than wire screens, as they keep the animals warmer. However, circulation of air must be allowed for by holes or other means. Reptiles may be kept warm and active all winter by putting a small electric light bulb in the cage and keeping it burning during the cold days and nights (see terrariums in Figure 11-13).

Frogs, toads, and salamanders need water in their cages, some kind of bowl or large pan being satisfactory. The pan should have rocks around and in it, and perhaps moss on the rocks to make the place look and feel more natural. These animals need small pieces of meat or flies and other insects for food. They will usually readily take living food, but they often need to have the meat forced down. This must be done very carefully and not too frequently or it will kill them. Take a

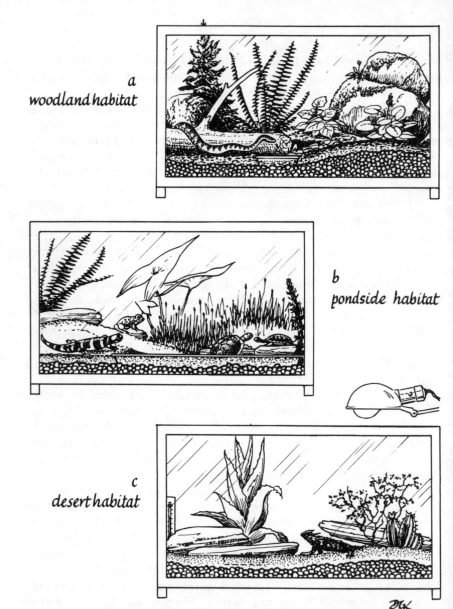

a
woodland habitat

b
pondside habitat

c
desert habitat

Fig. 11-13. *Glass herbariums with habitat backgrounds. These can be made the same as the aquarium shown in Figures 11-16 and 11-17, but can use fewer glass sides if desired. Note lamp always keeps desert habitat warm. From Vinson Brown,* How to Make a Miniature Zoo, *(Boston: Little, Brown, 1957), by permission of the author.*

Fig. 11-14. *How to collect small insects and worms to feed young amphibians or reptiles. Place leaf mold collected in woods or brush in funnel, and heat of light will drive creatures to drop into jar. From Vinson Brown,* How to Make a Miniature Zoo, *(Boston: Little, Brown, 1957), with permission of the author.*

small piece of meat in a pair of forceps, open the toad's mouth and push in the meat, shoving it down farther with gentle taps of the point of a pencil. (For another method of feeding, see Figure 11-14.)

Lizards also eat flies and other insects and will usually take these readily. Small snakes will eat grasshoppers or flies. Large snakes will take living mice, and usually need to be fed about once in two weeks or a month. To force-feed a snake or lizard with meat, you must force small pieces of meat down the gullet farther than with a frog or toad, since they can otherwise throw the meat up. Do this with a pencil, but work slowly and gently. Some snakes refuse to digest forced down food, and these should be fed only live food. Some snakes, particularly rattlesnakes, will go a year without eating. So do not be alarmed by lack of hunger, especially during the winter when cold-blooded creatures like to lie dormant.

Birds, unless they become real pets, should not be kept by anyone who cannot build a large and comfortable cage, as they are likely to be the most unhappy of creatures in captivity. See the Bibliography for a book that will tell you how to raise birds in captivity. It is against the law to capture most birds.

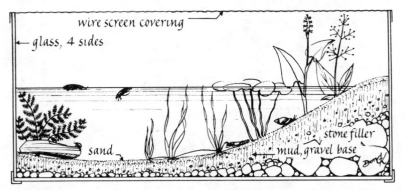

11-15. *An aquarium for water insects should reproduce as far as possible the nature of the pond or shallow stream margin from which plant and insect specimens are taken. Carnivorous insects will, of course, destroy your other stock.* If you can't get a

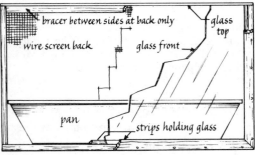

11-16.

large, somewhat shallow glass tank, make a cage with wooden bottom and ends; a wire screen back for air, window-glass top and front for observation; rectangular pan for water, sand, mud and plants.

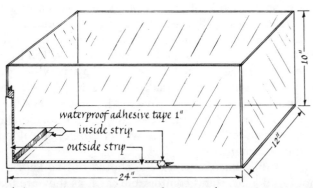

11-17. *Make your own aquarium of window glass and waterproof tape - any size desired, not exceeding dimensions given in diagram. But it is better to give it a wooden framework.*

Insects may be kept in cages also, the size depending on the size and number of the insects. Aquatic insects such as dragonflies need a large cage with water in a metal tray on the bottom with aquatic plants growing in it (see Figures 11-15, 11-16, and 11-17). It is most interest-

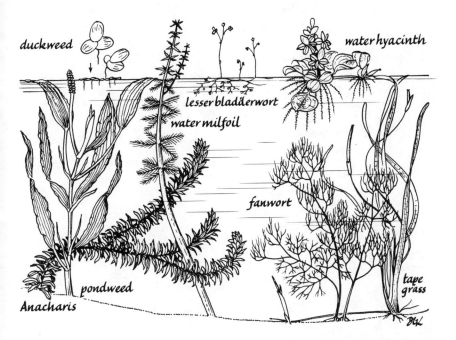

duckweed

water hyacinth

lesser bladderwort

water milfoil

fanwort

tape grass

pondweed

Anacharis

Fig. 11-18. *Useful plants for an aquarium (not drawn to relative scale), obtainable at a pet shop or aquarium store or at a local pond. From Vinson Brown,* How to Make a Miniature Zoo, *Boston: Little, Brown, 1957), with permission of the author.*

ing to watch an insect grow all the way from the egg to the adult, particularly the more complex kinds such as butterflies and wasps and flies. It is wise to remember that in many cases the full-grown insect lives on entirely different food than its larva.

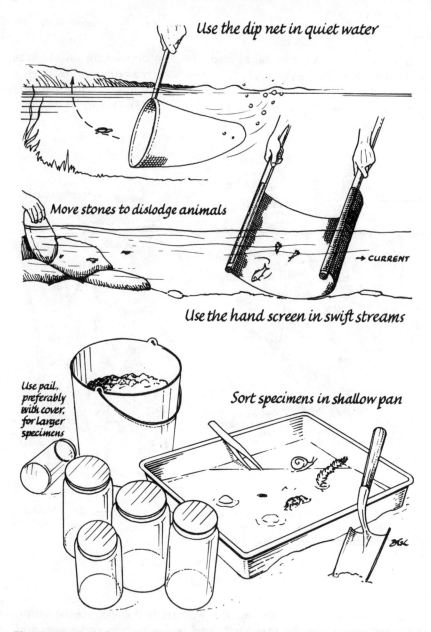

Use the dip net in quiet water

Move stones to dislodge animals

→ CURRENT

Use the hand screen in swift streams

Use pail, preferably with cover, for larger specimens

Sort specimens in shallow pan

Fig. 11-19. *Tools for collecting pond and stream life. From Vinson Brown,* How to Make a Miniature Zoo, *(Boston: Little, Brown, 1957), used by permission of the author.*

HOMES FOR INSECTS

A large jar with holes punched in its cover will do for most insects. For instance, if you find a caterpillar, put it in such a jar along with whatever kind of leaf you found it feeding on. Keep feeding it with these leaves each day, cleaning out the jar of old leaves and dirt every other day or so. Eventually it either weaves itself a cocoon, if it is a moth, or forms itself into a chrysalid, if a butterfly. The butterfly or moth will not eat leaves, but must be fed on sugar water or weak honey. Either hang cloth strips, sweetened with sugar water, on the sides of the cage (which should be much larger for the adult insect) or teach the butterfly or moth to feed out of your hands or out of a small pan by holding it gently in your fingers and touching its proboscis or tongue to the sweet water. If you can get a female and male together in one cage, the result may be eggs, and so there will be more insects to raise.

The simplest way to have an artifical ant colony to study in your home is to take a large jar and fill it with soft black earth, and then find a colony of small black or brown ants. You must dig this colony out with a trowel, keeping a sharp eye out for the queen, who is much larger and fatter than the small workers. When you find her, put her in the jar along with a couple of hundred workers. They will quickly get busy making passageways down into the earth, and if you feed them a little sugar, honey, meat, and bread crumbs each day, they will make their ant town right in your jar. In order to see their passageways under the earth, cover the jar up to the level of the dirt with black cloth or paper and take this off only at rare intervals. When you do take it off, you will see passageways running down right next to the glass, and will be able to watch the ants about their work down underground.

A more elaborate nest for watching the underground work of ants is made by putting two sheets of glass in a frame (see Figure 11-20) and corking up the bottom and top. If you want something interesting to study, put some aphids (also called plant lice and ant cows) in the nest with some leaves of the plants they feed on. If the ants are the right kind, they will tend and milk these cows much as humans do their cows. Other ants put into the nest also will cause some interesting developments.

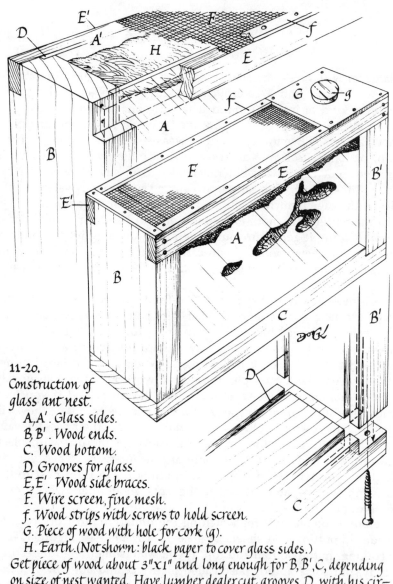

11-20.
Construction of
glass ant nest.
  A,A'. Glass sides.
  B,B'. Wood ends.
  C. Wood bottom.
  D. Grooves for glass.
  E,E'. Wood side braces.
  F. Wire screen, fine mesh.
  f. Wood strips with screws to hold screen.
  G. Piece of wood with hole for cork (g).
  H. Earth. (Not shown: black paper to cover glass sides.)

Get piece of wood about 3"x1" and long enough for B, B',C, depending
on size of nest wanted. Have lumber dealer cut grooves, D, with his circular saw, right width for window glass, which should fit snugly. Put
together entirely with screws so it can be taken apart for cleaning and
changing. Screen admits air. Ants and food are dropped through the
corked hole.

AN AQUARIUM

An *aquarium* is one of the most fascinating of nature projects, and animals in an aquarium are very easy to watch and study. You can, of course, buy an aquarium tank ready made from a pet store or a scientific equipment house (see names listed earlier in this chaper). But it is a good idea to make one yourself. For an average-sized tank, buy at your local hardware store five sheets of glass: two of 25 × 60 centimeters (10 × 24 inches), two of 30 × 25 centimeters (12 × 10 inches), and one 30 × 60 centimeters (12 × 24 inches). Larger or smaller sizes can, of course, be used. Buy some waterproof adhesive tape, and heavily tape your glass parts together inside and out (as shown in Figures 11-16 and 11-17). Next build a wooden frame that will exactly fit the glass tank, and lower the tank into this frame where it will have

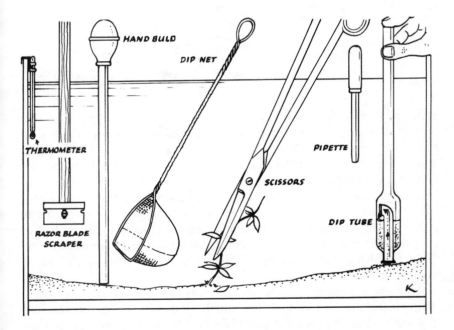

Fig. 11-21. *Tools and instruments used with aquariums. From Vinson Brown,* How to Make a Miniature Zoo, *(Boston: Little, Brown, 1957), by permission of the author.*

11-22. *A balanced aquarium with pond life.*

better protection from breakage. Put a layer of sand and gravel on the bottom of your tank and some rocks on top of this, among which you can place water plants brought from the nearest pond. Fill the tank about three-quarters full of water, and you are now ready to put in fish, frogs, water insects, small turtles, or whatever else you want. For frogs and turtles you need to have the rocks project above the water surface so that they may have places to rest, and you will have to put either a screen or glass top on your aquarium to keep them in. If it is of glass, put rubber or wooden blocks about 6 to 8 millimeters (¼ to ⅜ inch) thick between the glass top and the glass sides so that some air can get in.

Your main problem with an aquarium is to see that it is "balanced." This means that the animal life, which gives off carbon dioxide into the water, must balance the plant life, which gives off oxygen into the water and takes in carbon dioxide (see Figure 11-22). If you have too many animals they will soon fill the water so full of carbon dioxide that they will die. On the other hand, if you have too many plants, the plants will not get enough carbon dioxide. You must, therefore, experiment and see what is the best amount of plant and animal life to have in your aquarium. Since it is much easier to get too many animals than too many plants, be very careful about the number of animals you put in. One very useful animal to have in your aquarium is the common pond snail. It is a scavenger, which means that it goes about eating up all the dead organic (formerly living) matter in the aquarium and thus helps keep the aquarium clean.

You will have to clean your aquarium yourself as soon as the water begins to turn a little green and dirty. Have a tub of fresh water near, and with a little water net (such as is pictured in Figure 11-21), dip into your aquarium and catch and move your animals from the aquarium into the tub. Next take your rocks and plants out of the aquarium and then dump the dirty water out, carefully cleaning all the walls of the tank before you put fresh water in. When the fresh water is in, you may move rocks, plants, and animals back, being sure to handle the animals gently.

To keep your aquarium water fresh in the way it is done in the large public aquariums, you might try this experiment. Get a soccer, basketball, or football bladder and fill it with air at your local service station. Attach a glass or rubber tube to the bladder opening, this tube being partially obstructed with a cork or something similar, past which only a little air can escape at a time. Place the open end of your tube in the aquarium, and the bubbles of air rising from the tube will supply fresh oxygen to the water. A visit to the service station once every day or so should be sufficient. *Blowing up the bladder with your own breath won't do, as your breath is full of carbon dioxide, the very thing you are trying to get rid of.* If you have a hand pump, use it!

OBSERVING ANIMALS IN CAPTIVITY

Just as you keep notes on animals you watch in the wild, so keep notes of the animals you have in captivity. A notebook permanently kept within easy reach in your zoo will be a great help in understanding your captives. Loose leaves are best, as you can keep the names of your specimens alphabetically arranged and correctly spaced. Each day make it a habit to mark down in the notebook anything at all interesting that happens in the cages. (Be sure to give the exact date and the hour of the day with each notation.) In this way you will build up valuable records of the food your animals eat, when they eat it, and how much; and you will notice the times of the day when they are most active. Sit quietly by a cage for ten minutes or more and watch what happens. If you are extremely quiet, soon the animals will go about their business just as if you weren't there and you will begin to learn some of the facts about their lives. Review the hints on observing wild animals described in Chapter Five, and use this information in your notes on both captive and wild animals.

BEGINNING CLASSIFICATION AND ANATOMY OF ANIMALS

In Chapter Two, we spoke about Linnaeus, the great Swedish scientist, and how he took the important step of starting the scientific classification of animals and plants. He used for his classification what is called the system of *binomial nomenclature,* or the use of two words (preferably Latin or Greek) for the name of each kind of animal or plant. Thus the common fence lizard (see Figure 11-23) is called *Sceloporus undulatus* by zoologists. It is perhaps unfortunate that this big improvement by Linnaeus made use of words that are so mysterious and queer to the ordinary person that even to this day the scientific names of animals and plants scare many people away from very deep involvement in natural science. This fear is based on the mistaken idea that anything with a big word connected with it must

11-23. *Fence lizard, Sceloporus.*

be hard to learn. Actually it is much easier to become familiar with scientific nomenclature than to learn the easiest of foreign languages.

But why, you might ask, is it necessary to learn or use these scientific names? It is necessary because common names are different in different languages (whereas Latin is the universal language of scientists all over the world) and because common names are not only so carelessly applied that they are liable to serve for many different animals, but they give no adequate idea of the true position of the animal they name in the animal kingdom. For instance, *Sceloporus undulatus* is called not only a "fence" lizard, but also a "pine" and "swift" lizard. This is likely to be confusing to say the least!

What is the meaning of the double word *Sceloporus undulatus?* It is not necessary to know the exact meaning in Latin of these words. The main thing to know is that the last word, *undulatus,* is the name of the species, or kind of animal. The species is made up of closely similar animals, which inhabit one geographic range and can interbreed. The species *undulatus,* then, is a member of the larger group, or genus, called *Sceloporus.* Other related species belonging to this same genus include *Sceloporus scalaris,* the striped swift, *S. variabilis,* the variable swift, and *S. occidentalis,* the western swift.

The genus *Sceloporus* belongs to a still larger division: the "family," *Iguanidae.* This family includes, among forty-eight different genera (loosely related through some common characteristics), the genus *Iguana,* or the large iguana lizards of tropical America; the genus *Phrynosoma,* or horned "toads" of the western deserts; and the genus *Anolis,* the American "chameleon."

The family *Iguanidae* joins with other families, such as the family *Chamaeleontidae* (chameleons) and the family *Scincidae* (skinks), to make the "suborder" *Sauria,* or lizards.

The two suborders *Sauria* and *Serpentes* (snakes) make the "order" *Squamata,* or lizards and snakes. The order Squamata joins with the orders of *Chelonia,* turtles, and *Crocodilia,* crocodiles and alligators, to make the class *Reptilia,* or reptiles. This class is one among many classes, including *Mammalia,* mammals, and *Aves,* birds, that make up the "subphylum" *Vertebrata,* or vertebrates. The highest division of the animal kingdom is the "phylum," and the subphylum *Vertebrata* fits, with three lesser subphyla, into the phylum *Chordata,* or chordates (animals with a dorsal (upper) nerve column).

The divisions then in ascending scale are:

Species	*undulatus*
Genus	*Sceloporus*
Family	*Iguanidae*
Suborder	*Sauria*
Order	*Squamata*
Class	*Reptilia*
Subphylum	*Vertebrata*
Phylum	*Chordata*

Further divisions that are used when needed by zoologists are *subspecies, race, subgenus, tribe, subfamily, superfamily, superorder, subclass,* and *superclass.* Each of these divisions denotes a special relationship. For instance, all that a superfamily means is that there is a group of families in a given order more closely related than other groups of families in the same order. A subspecies is shown by a third word, such as *Peromyscus polionotus niveiventris,* the Florida beach mouse.

Chapter Seventeen takes up in some detail the classification of animals. Here we want to gain an idea merely of a few of the most important divisions and what there is about the bodies of animals, inside and outside, that puts them in different classifications. These differences are called *anatomical* differences, and it is anatomy that interests us now.

We will take as our typical animals belonging to great divisions of the animal kingdom the earthworm, which belongs to the phylum *Annelida,* or segmented worms; the starfish, which belongs to the phylum *Echinodermata,* or starfish and brittle stars; the snail, belonging to the phylum *Mollusca,* or snails, slugs, shellfish, and octopi and squid; the amoeba, which belongs to the phylum *Protozoa,* or single-celled animals; the grasshopper, belonging to the phylum *Arthropoda,* or jointed-footed animals; and the frog, belonging to the phylum *Chordata.* Figures 11-24, 11-25, and 11-26 show diagrams of the internal anatomy of all these animals, except the snail and the amoeba. (The amoeba is described earlier in this chapter and is pictured in Figure 11-3). If you carefully study these diagrams and then study the chart on the pages following which gives the main differences of these phyla, you will begin to see why zoologists have placed the animals that belong to them in different divisions.

A little exploration into animal anatomy is a naturalist's road to learning. You need to understand how creatures are constructed before you can more fully understand the way they act in life.

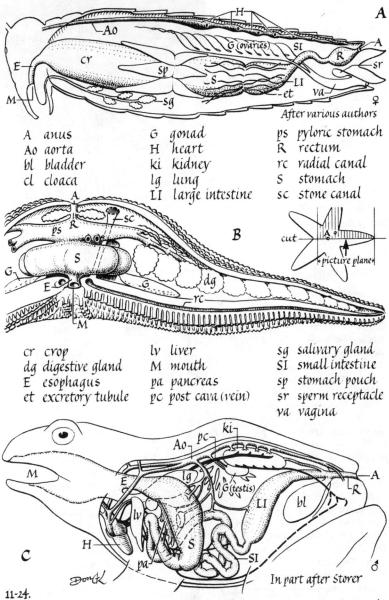

A

Ao

H

G (ovaries)   SI   A

cr   R

E   sr

sp

S

M   LI

sg   et   va
                                        ♀

After various authors

A anus	G gonad	ps pyloric stomach
Ao aorta	H heart	R rectum
bl bladder	ki kidney	rc radial canal
cl cloaca	lg lung	S stomach
	LI large intestine	sc stone canal

A

ps R   sc

S   B   cut   picture plane

G   dg

E   G

rc

M

cr crop	lv liver	sg salivary gland
dg digestive gland	M mouth	SI small intestine
E esophagus	pa pancreas	sp stomach pouch
et excretory tubule	pc post cava (vein)	sr sperm receptacle
		va vagina

ki

Ao   pc

M   lg   G (testis)   A

E   R

LI   bl

lv

S

H   SI

pa

C   ♂

In part after Storer

Don GL

11-24.
  Internal anatomy of (**A**) the Grasshopper, (**B**) the Starfish, and (**C**) the Frog. Diagrams schematic and generalized; digestive tract emphasized by stippling; circulatory system shaded or black.

11-25. *Anatomy of the earthworm. Use bank pins (½") to pin back sidewalls, one in every 5th segment. Septa are membranes between segments. (Simplified. See zoology texts for more complete diagrams.)*

11-26. *(below) Circulatory system of the frog. Schematic, some parts not shown. Liver, etc., drawn as if transparent.*

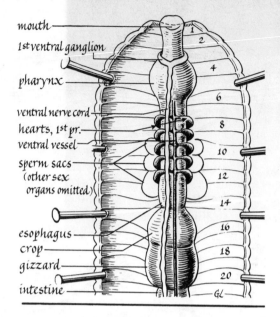

mouth
1st ventral ganglion
pharynx
ventral nerve cord
hearts, 1st pr.
ventral vessel
sperm sacs
(other sex organs omitted)
esophagus
crop
gizzard
intestine

1
2
4
6
8
10
12
14
16
18
20
GL

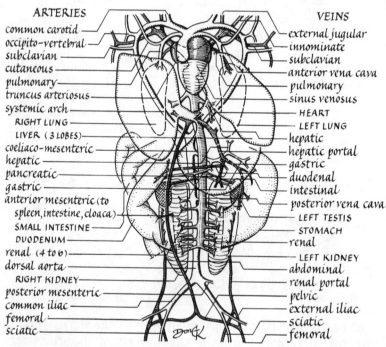

ARTERIES

common carotid
occipito-vertebral
subclavian
cutaneous
pulmonary
truncus arteriosus
systemic arch
RIGHT LUNG
LIVER (3 LOBES)
coeliaco-mesenteric
hepatic
pancreatic
gastric
anterior mesenteric (to spleen, intestine, cloaca)
SMALL INTESTINE
DUODENUM
renal (4 to 6)
dorsal aorta
RIGHT KIDNEY
posterior mesenteric
common iliac
femoral
sciatic

VEINS

external jugular
innominate
subclavian
anterior vena cava
pulmonary
sinus venosus
HEART
LEFT LUNG
hepatic
hepatic portal
gastric
duodenal
intestinal
posterior vena cava
LEFT TESTIS
STOMACH
renal
LEFT KIDNEY
abdominal
renal portal
pelvic
external iliac
sciatic
femoral

DISSECTING

For animal dissection you need three tools:

1. A very sharp knife or scalpel.
2. A pair of small sharp scissors.
3. A pair of forceps.

Place your animal for dissection in a shallow enamel (or tin) dish and on a section of linoleum weighted down with lead. With any of the animals mentioned above, water in the dish, once the animal is opened up, helps keep the internal organs in a natural condition. Warm salt water will keep the heart of a frog beating long after death. We will consider the dissection of the three animals in the chart: the earthworm, the grasshopper, and the frog.

The earthworm should be cut open down the middle of the underside with the scissors. Pin back the side walls of the body as shown in Figure 11-25. Particularly notice the septa (segmental walls), the six divisions of the digestive system, the five pairs of hearts with their dorsal (upper) and ventral (lower) blood vessels, and the ventral nerve chord, which is exactly opposite to that of the vertebrates.

The grasshopper is best studied when freshly killed or after some hours soaking in formaldehyde. Get as large a grasshopper as you can. A small but powerful magnifying glass would be very useful in studying the grasshopper's anatomy. It is best to cut this insect open down the back. Cut off all the legs and wings. Carefully cut through each segment of the outer skeleton with the scissors, starting at the end of the abdomen. Spread the body walls to either side with pins. With your forceps probe and turn to one side or other the different organs.

Notice particularly:

1. Compound eye (made up of many small eye facets).
2. Jointed body segments, so that the body can turn within the armorlike plates.
3. Soft and pliant but very strong muscle fibers extending between body walls.
4. Fore gut, mid gut, and hind gut of the digestive system.
5. Heart with its forward and hind tubes (found just under the back).

6. Network of little breathing tubes (trachea) that extend out from a hole in the side wall of each body segment.
7. Malpighian tubes, which are attached to the hind gut and correspond to human kidneys in their function of excretion of waste products.
8. Small brain in the head with its ventral nerve cord extending along the under part of the body to the end of the abdomen.

For the frog, cut with the scissors from the tail up through the skin of the stomach to the throat. Cut right through the bones of the chest, laying bare the organs of the body cavity. Bathe these under warm salt water. If the frog if freshly killed, the heart should still be beating and you may watch how the heart muscles contract to force out the blood. Pin back the sides of the body and cut away any obstructing muscles with your scalpel. Figure 11-26 shows the blood vascular or circulatory system of the frog. Try to follow the individual arteries (which generally carry oxygen-filled blood from the heart to other parts of the body) and the veins (which carry air-depleted blood back to the heart). Nearly all vertebrate animals have a similar system. The blood leaves the ventricle (the lower chamber of the heart) by the aorta (the main artery) and passes by smaller arteries to the tiny capillaries, where it gives out food and oxygen to the cells. Then it passes on to the veins, which carry it back to the right auricle (one of two upper chambers of the heart). From the right auricle it passes to the ventricle, which pumps it to the lungs where its oxygen is renewed, then back to the left aorta and again to the ventricle. In humans and in other mammals the ventricle has two chambers instead of the single one that is found in amphibians and reptiles.

With your dissecting needles or forceps, turn over the different organs of the frog's body and look for:

1. Right and left lungs, which lie just above and on either side of the heart.
2. Esophagus (the food tube in the throat), the stomach, the small intestine, and the large intestine of the digestive system.
3. Right and left kidneys and the urinary bladder to which they are connected, which all together form the excretory system.
4. Hinged tongue (for catching flies).

5. Reddish liver, which is attached to the stomach and acts upon its contents with digestive juices.
6. Pancreas, which is imbedded in the transparent mesentery (a thin tissue between the stomach and the small intestine) and is attached to and supplies digestive juices for the small intestine.
7. Gall bladder (round whitish globe), which also helps digestion by pouring another digestive juice—bile—through the pancreas and into the small intestine.
8. Nervous system, which appears as a slender white cord inside the protection of the backbone and is attached to and is a part of the brain in the skull. The little bumps, called ganglia, along the nerve chord are the centers of nervous reaction in the frog's body. The nervous system acts as a coordinator or director of all the other parts of the body.

This brief description of anatomy is naturally only the barest introduction to the subject. But it should furnish a springboard for further work, and the interested naturalist can follow much deeper into animal anatomy by studying some of the books listed in the Bibliography at the end of this book.

CHAPTER
12
Plant Study

About 10,000 years ago, humans became interested in growing plants. Their interest, of course, was purely from the angle of food. Wild wheat was a plant from which a mealy bread could be made; why not try to grow more of it? Some early man or woman for the first time took wild plants and tried to cultivate them. Wheat, barley, oats, corn, and many other crops came from that early experimenting. When such food became plentiful, towns and then cities came into being, and thus plants were one of the main factors in the forming of civilization.

A little over 2,000 years ago there lived the first people who looked at the whole plant kingdom with curious eyes. These were Greeks, and the names of two of them have come down to us through the centuries—THEOPHRASTUS and DIOSCORIDES. We do not know what these two looked like, but their writings show keen, inquisitive minds that were not content to look at plants from afar, but must approach them with the eye of the hummingbird who probes the innermost depths of the flower for the secret treasure that lies there. These Greeks

140

started the science of botany; they studied and took notes on all the plants they could and wrote books about them. They looked at plants almost with the eyes of the modern naturalist. But soon came the Dark Ages, and for over 1,000 years the science of botany had few lights.

In the Middle Ages the only interest people seemed to have had in plants was in those that produced food and those that had medicinal value. Strange people, half-doctors, half-magicians, were the only humans of this time that ever wandered in the fields to gather and study plants, and even they were under the spell of the great Greeks, believing that every word the ancient botanists had written was the ultimate truth on plants. To the knight and the squire, the bishop and the queen's lady, the brickmason and the peasant farmer, the world of plants beyond the few that were cultivated meant nothing. Narcissus and lily bloomed in the summer woods; hyacinth and red anemone ran riot with color in the uplands; but none cared, or very few. None saw the wonder of knowledge to be gained from the study of such things, for it is the very essence of ignorance to think that there is nothing new to learn.

But as century followed century, one mind after another began to tear down the curtain of darkness, the first few with timid tugs, and then, as boldness grew, the later with great sweeps that exposed whole new worlds to conquer. Such a vigorous sweeper of past cobwebs was GASPARD BAUHIN, (1560–1624) a man not content with musty books, but eager for the knowledge the green world itself could teach him. His own book, *Prodromus*, in 1623, was probably the first modern botanical work, and in it he introduced the idea of binomial nomenclature. But other men had to build on this suggestion before it was ready. Over 130 years later (1757) Linnaeus (See Figure 12-1) swept it forward in the light of his genius to a permanent place in science.

Linnaeus had the inspiring personality needed to popularize science. He drove people into the out-of-doors to look and study from life itself, and he made it fun. There had to be a Linnaeus, because before he came there were so few who cared to seek knowledge from life. Donald Culross Peattie describes an adventure of Linnaeus (when he was a youth at Upsala University in Sweden) that shows us how rare was his kind.

It was late in April, on one of the first days of early spring, that the old Dean Olaf Celsius, a flower lover and a friend to science, came for

12-1. Linnaeus.
(After old engraving in Locy.)

a stroll in the dilapidated botanical garden. He was presently aware of a young, unknown student sitting on a bench, with flowers in his hand, writing notes upon them in a book. So strange a sight had not been witnessed for many a year. Celsius drew near, and fell into talk with the student.

The answers came back so charged with significant enthusiasm, so knowledgeable of the neglected subject, that the oldster could scarce credit his ears.*

Dean Celsius was so delighted at finding such a kindred spirit that he took Linnaeus into his home and got him a scholarship so that he could continue his studies without nearly starving to death as he had up to that time at the university.

Today modern scientists look for the same kind of eager people, ready to answer the call for the great work in nature that has yet to be done, and in these times of automobiles, television, and space flights, they are still not so easy to find!

As with zoology, botany also needed the touch of Charles Darwin's master hand, and the astonishing discoveries of Gregor Mendel (see Chapter Two) regarding the inheritance of plants, to bring it to full fruit. Until the coming of the theory of evolution, the Linnaean idea of classification had no guiding light to make its families and orders and genera take on vital meaning. Asa Gray (1810–88), a famous professor of botany at Harvard University in the nineteenth century, came along at just the right time to translate the evolutionary theory into the actuality of botanical study in America. His book *Lessons in Botany* remains to this day one of the best introductions to the science of plants ever written. With Gray's push, modern botany came to see the tree of life of the plant kingdom and the place of each kind of plant in that kingdom (see Figure 18-1 for a picture of the evolution of plants).

Luther Burbank (1849–1926) and other great horticulturists or plant raisers of more recent years have used Mendel's laws of inheritance, combined with the new knowledge of evolution, of genes and mutations (see beginning of Chapter Eleven), to produce the most marvelous varieties in plant kinds. Seedless grapes and oranges, diseaseless wheat, giant blackberries and strawberries, all of these are results of a new understanding of nature.

GROWING PLANTS

I remember how hard my partner and I once worked, planting bean seeds on our homestead in the jungles of Panama. Those beans were to be a large part of our diet in the months to come, and we were anxious that they come up right. It was a thrill when the tiny green shoots began to push up through the black soil, each forming two thick little leaves that waved gently in the breeze. We were jealous of the safety of those baby plants. When we found some of them torn up and the footmarks of an agouti (a large rodent that looks like a young pig) among them, we were furious. We lay in wait for the culprit in a blind made of slabs of bark and got him early the next morning when he stuck his black nose out of the jungle and minced along the nearest green row ready for a feast.

The naturalist has this same personal interest in all the plants that grow out of the ground, but his or her interest is greatest, of course, in the things he or she is raising especially for study. The student who would know something about plants must learn about them as they grow upward from the seed and watch closely the stages of their growth. No amount of book study will take the place of this close acquaintance with the real growing plants.

Different plants grow at different speeds. For your first experiment it is wise to take plants that grow fairly rapidly, such as mustard or milkweed or wild clover. Some of these plants start new growths so often during the year that you can get seeds almost any time. You can also save seeds you find in the fall to plant the next spring. Of course, if you have to, you can buy seeds, but why not see what you can find in the wild?

Plant each seed in damp rich soil and then give it plenty of sunlight. Water it a little each day, if the rain won't do this for you, but not too much, as too much water can kill just as well as too much dryness. Then watch it grow (see Figure 12-2)! If you will study your plant carefully each day, you will see some wonderful things. You will see leaves, stem, and flower take shape and form from day to day. If a plant is dicotyledonous, as most of the common wild flowers are, as soon as the first green shoot comes up it forms two small leaves (called cotyledons), which are the first leaves of the plant. In some plants these leaves are thick and fleshy because they carry a lot of food to give the plant a start in life. Later, as the plant grows older, they lose this food to the growing plant and wither away and die. Be sure to watch for this in the plants you study and write down what happens in your notebook.

Some interesting experiments can be done with your plants to see what relation the sun has to their growth. You will notice that, as the plant grows, it seems to stretch out its leaves toward the sun. This is so they will get the maximum amount of light, since light is highly necessary in the manufacture of food by the plant. When the plant reaches out like this, take it and turn it around in the other direction so that the leaves reach away from the sun. If the sun is really so important to the plant, somehow or other the leaves will be brought around to reach for the sun again. Try another experiment. When your plant has several sets of leaves, cut a hole in a piece of cardboard and put the cardboard carefully down over the plant so that the lower two or four leaves are covered. Leave it so for a few days and then take a look at the lower leaves. What differences do you find between them

1 seed, one
split open to show ↑
embryo leaves. 2 root stock
growing downward. 3 stem
arching up to surface. 4 cotyledons above ground, shedding seed
coat; leaves → emerging. 5 leaves
opening on erect stem; cotyledons shriveling. 6 leaves fully developed. 7 flower ↓
8 pod, green seed ←

Don K

12-2. Cycle of development of the bean plant, from seed to seed.

and the ones above the cardboard? What do you think all this has to do with sunlight?

Study the development of the flower of your plant. See how many days it takes to become a complete flower and how many days to turn into seed. Guard one flower with a screen or some cloth in such a way that there is no way for it to get pollen from other plants. Does it produce any seeds?

THE NATURE OF PLANTS

1. *Similarities.* Just as with animals, all plants have some things in common. They are:

1. Plants are made up of one or more cells.
2. Plants have cellulose in their cell walls.
3. Plants inhale oxygen and use it for burning energy, just as animals do, but as plants have no need for rapid movement, they use much less energy than animals.
4. Plants give off large or small amounts of oxygen (mostly in the daytime when they are most active).
5. Plants absorb large or small amounts of carbon dioxide, which they use in the manufacture of food.
6. Most plants manufacture their own food by means of the green chemical substance *chlorophyll* that is found in their cells.

By turning to the beginning of Chapter Eleven, where the general characteristics of animals are given, you can easily see the main differences between the animal and plant kingdoms. However, there is a shady border province between plants and animals, which scientists find hard to classify in one kingdom or the other. The slime molds, for instance, are supposed to be plants, and yet if ever you saw one creeping ghostlike over a damp log you would think it some kind of unearthly animal. Euglena is the name of a strange one-celled animal-plant that has the green coloring matter (chlorophyll) of plants, the mysterious stuff that manufactures food out of air and water and minerals, and yet the Euglena can dart about through the water with the same speed as a real animal, the paramecium. All of us know, also, how much sea sponges and sea anemones look like plants, although they are really animals (see Figure 12-3).

2. *The plant cell.* Except for its wall of cellulose (woody material), this is very similar to the animal cell. It too has its cytoplasm (cellular liquid) surrounding a nucleus. But its internal functions are different (as is shown in the diagram of Figure 12-4a), and there are not nearly so many different kinds of plant cells as there are animal cells (see Figure 12-4b) for some examples of different plants cells). A green plant draws carbon dioxide from the air, water from the ground, and

12-3. Sea Anemone – an animal – not a plant.

light from the sun into its leaves. The plant's chlorophyll then acts as a catalyst or chemical helper and helps turn all of these sources into food. This is the wonderful basis of all life on earth (see Figure 12-5 for a diagram of the way plants manufacture food). Bacteria and the various kinds of fungi, such as toadstools, mushrooms, and so forth, are the big exception to the general rule that a plant is able to manufacture its own food. These strange plants draw their food from live or dead and decaying matter by absorbing the necessary liquids through their cell walls. Hence they have no green chlorophyll.

The cellulose that lies in the wall of the plant cell is the same stuff that we use every day in the form of wood or paper. It is this cellulose that causes plants to have much simpler general features than animals. It is as if one nation invented a wonderful tool that served to feed it, clothe it, shelter it, and carry its individuals from place to place, whereas all other nations had to invent many different ways to do these same things. While animals have experimented in widely varied ways in developing their forms of life, using chiton (insect armor), bone, fur, feathers, and a dozen other materials in the making of their bodies, plants, using their universal tool of cellulose, have been able to live successfully with much less complexity in their makeup. It is cellulose that gives trees the strength to rear their heads and branches hundreds of feet in the air and stand the power of strong winds. It is cellulose also that gives the pliant strength to the weeds and grasses that bow before the same wind.

Plants have carried simplicity into all their structure. Even the most queer-looking plant is hardly more than an unusual combination of

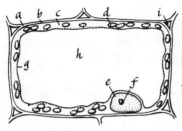

12-4a. Green plant cell. a. cell wall. b. cytoplasmic membrane, passes matter to and from c. cytoplasm. d. chloroplast, food-making body. e. nucleus, life-center of cell. f. nucleolus. g. vacuolar membrane encloses h. vacuole, water solution of salts, sugars, etc. i. intercellular space. (After Fuller.)

12-4b. Plant tissue cells.——→
a. collenchyma, strengthening cells found in stems. b. epidermal cells (beneath outer cutin), protective covering of leaves, stems, roots. c. xylem fibers, strengtheners. (After Fuller.)

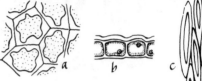

12-5. How a plant manufactures and transports food. Photosynthesis—leaf to left: agents and raw materials; leaf to right: end products.

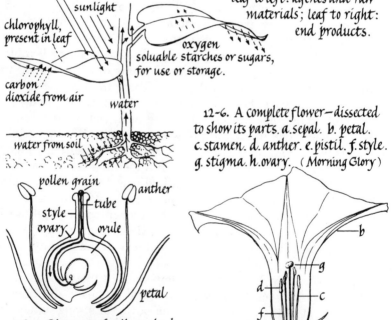

sunlight

chlorophyll, present in leaf

oxygen
soluable starches or sugars, for use or storage.

carbon dioxide from air

water

water from soil

12-6. A complete flower—dissected to show its parts. a. sepal. b. petal. c. stamen. d. anther. e. pistil. f. style. g. stigma. h. ovary. (Morning Glory)

pollen grain

anther

style
ovary

tube

ovule

petal

12-7. Diagram of pollen tube descending style of the pistil to bring male gametes for fusion with the unfertilized ovules.

DonK

(Pistil, e. blacked in for emphasis)

leaves. In the evolution of the plant, scientists tell us that the leaf was once a stem and the petal, sepal, and in fact all the parts of a flower, once leaves. If you will remember this simplicity as you start to learn the names of different plants, you will not be so worried by their seeming complexity, and you will be better able to see the relation of the parts to the whole (see Figure 12-6).

THE PARTS OF A PLANT
AND THEIR FUNCTIONS

In Figure 6-1 you see diagrammed the main parts of a plant. Each has a function. The roots and root hairs gather mineral water solutions from the soil to send up to the leaves, and the roots also act as anchors for the plant. The stem not only holds up the flower head and the leaves, but it acts as a pipe system through which goes water and mineral salts up to the leaves, while food (in the form of sugar) in solution may go down the stem to be stored (as starch) either at its base or in the roots for future use. The leaf, of course, is the manufacturing plant. Here carbon dioxide from the air, water from the soil, and light from the sun are worked together by the chlorophyll to make food (starch), which can be turned into solution (as a sugar) and transported elsewhere in the plant (see Figure 12-5). The flower has the very important function of starting the next generation of plants and thus keeping the species alive through the centuries.

In the dissection of the flower and its parts (see Figure 12-6), we see how nature has taken simple leaves and refashioned them into something entirely different. The sepals are the outermost protection of the flower, and in many plants they look very much like leaves. When the flower is in bud, it is the sepals that cover it over with a protective layer, shielding it from both injury and cold. The petals are the advertisement of the flower. Usually flaming with color, they tell the passing bees and other insects that here is a treasure-trove of honey-dew, ready for eager takers. But, of course, like many things, the honey is not free; the bees pay a toll for every drop. Inside the beautiful petals is the plain reason why the flower wants the insects to come. Here we find the stamens and the sepals, the male and female parts of the flower. The upper part of the stamen is called the anther and it is in this organ that the pollen is stored. Bees and other insects brush against this pollen, catching it among the hairs of their legs, and carry it away with them when they go. Some of the pollen is then deposited on the top of the pistil (the upper part of the pistil is called the style) of a neighboring plant of the same kind.

At the base of the pistil there may be one or more ovaries, and in each ovary there may be one or more ovules. The pollen sends a long tube down the style of the pistil (see Figure 12-7) and in the end of this tube travels the fertilizing (or male) cell. This cell joins with the female (or egg) cell (or the ovule), and from the union there results a fertilized cell, which gradually, by repeated cell division, turns into the seed. The process, as a whole, is called *pollination*. The seed, carried by wind or by birds, falls in time upon the ground, and, if the sun, moisture, and soil are right for germination, starts a new plant.

It is wise to remember that we are talking only of flowering plants, and that cone-bearing trees, ferns, mosses, mushrooms, and algae have other ways of reproducing themselves different from those outlined above. (Chapter 19 discusses these alternate methods of reproduction in plants.)

I. *Types of leaves.* In Figure 12-8 you see pictured the main types of leaves. The earliest form of leaf, as we have said, was little more than a modified stem. A very primitive plant, the horsetail or *Equisetum* has small scalelike leaves, but uses its stem more for the function of leaves. Leaves are either simple or compound. But besides these differences, leaves are also opposite, alternate, or basal.

Leaves are named for their general outline (linear, orbiculate, oblong, cordate, and so on), the form of their apexes (acute, truncate, obtuse, and so on), their types of margins (entire, serrate, dentate, repand, lobed, cleft, and so on), their venation or arrangement of leaf veins (palmately veined, pinnately veined, and parallel veined), their forms of growth (petiolate, perfoliate, connate, sessile, and so on), and their types of compounding (pinnately compound or palmately compound).

Compound leaves are made up of leaflets. These leaflets themselves may show different leaf forms, as serrate, entire, oblong, and so forth. A compound leaf may be two or three times compound, that is with each leaflet subdivided into smaller leaflets, as many of the parsley plants are.

The form and arrangement of the leaves of any plant are often very important in determining just what kind of plant it is, and so should be carefully studied.

2. *Types of stems.* Figure 12-9 shows various kinds of stems. Some

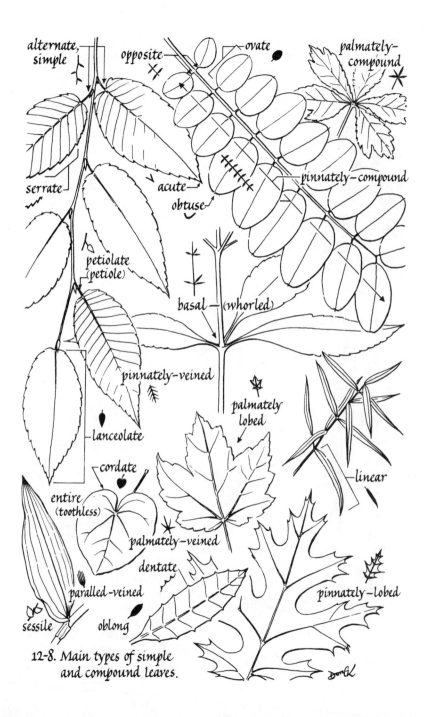

alternate, simple

opposite

ovate

palmately-compound

serrate

acute

obtuse

pinnately-compound

petiolate (petiole)

basal (whorled)

pinnately-veined

palmately lobed

linear

lanceolate

cordate

entire (toothless)

palmately-veined

dentate

parallel-veined

sessile

oblong

pinnately-lobed

12-8. Main types of simple and compound leaves.

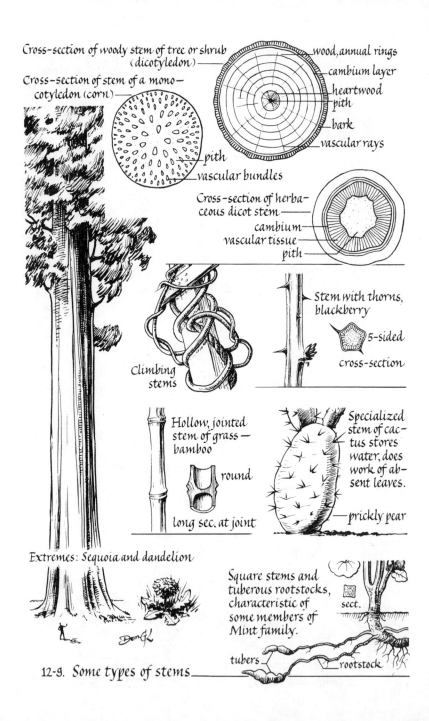

Cross-section of woody stem of tree or shrub (dicotyledon) — wood, annual rings

— cambium layer

— heartwood

— pith

Cross-section of stem of a mono-cotyledon (corn)

— bark

— vascular rays

pith

vascular bundles

Cross-section of herbaceous dicot stem

— cambium

vascular tissue

pith

Climbing stems

Stem with thorns, blackberry

5-sided cross-section

Hollow, jointed stem of grass — bamboo

round

long sec. at joint

Specialized stem of cactus stores water, does work of absent leaves.

— prickly pear

Extremes: Sequoia and dandelion

Square stems and tuberous rootstocks, characteristic of some members of Mint family.

sect.

tubers

rootstock

DonGL

12-3. Some types of stems

plants have practically no stems at all, the dandelion being one example. Others, such as the redwood, are nearly all stem. Some stems are found beneath the ground where they are called "root stocks" and are used for both anchoring the plant and storing the food. The potato is a root stock and not a root as most people think. Stems help a good deal in determining the name of a plant. You can tell a mint by its square stem. The thorns of the blackberry quickly tell this plant apart from poison oak, which otherwise looks very much like it. Plants of the honeysuckle family have trailing and climbing stems with tendrils that help them cling to other plants and to rocks or boards. The covering and content of stems are important also. The stinging hairs of the nettle stem are a painful reminder of the plant's name. The milky juice of the milkweed betrays the type of plant at once. Trees are plants with tall woody stems. Figure 12-9 shows the cross section of a tree with its region of growth next to the bark (cambian layer) and its nearly dead center of heart wood. The two main types of stems are those of the monocotyledonous (with one cotyledon or early leaf) and of the dicotyledonous plants. The former have fibrovascular bundles (woody threads) scattered throughout the stem, while the latter have these bundles formed in more or less regular rings.

3. *Types of roots.* Figure 12-10 shows the main kinds of roots. Roots are usually simpler than stems. Their two main functions are to act as anchors for the plant and to furnish a passageway for water and minerals from the soil. Besides this they often form storage places for food.

4. *Types of flowers.* The main types of flowers are shown in Figure

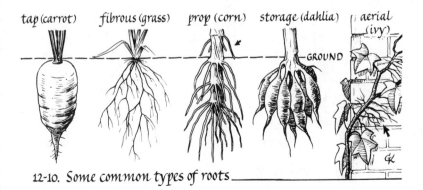

tap (carrot)   fibrous (grass)   prop (corn)   storage (dahlia)   aerial (ivy)

GROUND

12-10. *Some common types of roots*

12-11a. The types of flower arrangement or inflorescence are shown in Figure 12-11b. Flowers are divided into three great divisions: (I) *apetalous,* or with no petals, although sometimes with a petallike perianth of sepals; (2) *choripetalous,* or with petals and sepals, but these not joined together; and (3) *sympetalous,* or with the petals joined together at least at the base. Flowers are formed as they are for a purpose. The pea flower (Figure 12-11a), for instance, allows only certain kinds of insects to get inside its petals; while the snapdragon's honey can only be reached by insects with long tongues or by hummingbirds. By this specialization these flowers make sure that their favored customers return again and again and so carry the pollen to plants of the same species.

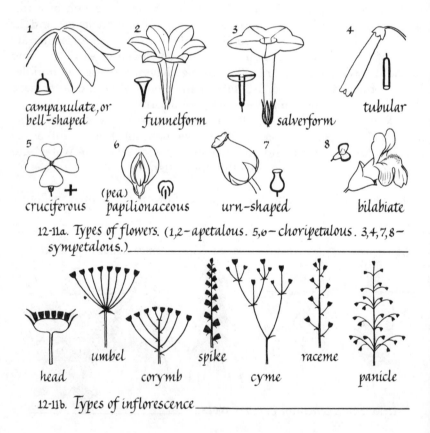

1 campanulate, or bell-shaped
2 funnelform
3 salverform
4 tubular
5 cruciferous
6 (pea) papilionaceous
7 urn-shaped
8 bilabiate

12-11a. Types of flowers. (1,2 – apetalous. 5,6 – choripetalous. 3,4,7,8 – sympetalous.)

head
umbel
corymb
spike
cyme
raceme
panicle

12-11b. Types of inflorescence

All of these flower variations are useful in identification of plants. Study them carefully.

AN EXPERIMENT IN PLANT PHYSIOLOGY

An experiment that will show you how the leaf is actually manufacturing food every day can be made as follows:

1. Take the leaf of a common geranium plant after it has spent a day in the sun, and boil it in water. This kills the protoplasmic parts of the cells and softens and swells the grains of starch.
2. Soak the leaf in strong alcohol for a day or two to get rid of the chlorophyll.
3. Rinse out the alcohol with plenty of water and then place the leaf for ten to fifteen minutes in a 5 to 10 percent solution of iodine.
4. The starch in the leaf, if there is any, will turn blue. You can test the truth of this by mixing cornstarch with the same solution of iodine. It too will turn blue.

In order to see whether or not a leaf manufactures food without sunlight, put your plant in a dark room for two or three days, and then test the leaf for starch. Is it there? How much?

AN INTRODUCTION
TO THE CLASSIFICATION OF PLANTS

As in the animal kingdom, plants have different divisions. The largest division is the subkingdom. Next comes the class, then the order, the family, the tribe, the genus, the subgenus, and last the species (sometimes there is the subspecies).

For an example, let us take *Solidago californica*, the common western goldenrod. The species name is *californica*, and *Solidago* is the genus name. There is besides *Solidago californica* also *Solidago occidentalis*, *S. corymbosa*, and several other species, all members of this one genus of *Solidago*. The genus *Solidago* belongs with other genera to the chicory tribe or the *Cichorieae*. The tribe belongs to the sunflower family, or *Compositae*. This family belongs to the Asters, or order *Asterales*. This order belongs to the subclass *Dicotyledonae*, which includes many other orders, such as the *Rosales*, roses, and *Ranunculales*, buttercups. The subclass belongs to the class *Angiospermae*, or flowering plants, and this class to the subkingdom *Spermatophyta*, or seed plants.

CHAPTER
13

Study
of Rocks
and Minerals

A small native child in the Panama jungle once found a pretty stone in the sand bar of a river. This stone gleamed greenishly in the sunlight, and when he held it up it sparkled with a hundred lights. To the boy it was just a pretty plaything.

Now a shadow fell across the face of the boy, and he looked up to see a tall, leathery faced stranger staring at him. The boy drew back and shivered as if a cold breeze had come from the hills, because the eyes of the man were evil and the light in their depths was greed. The man knew what the boy did not know; the pretty stone was an emerald and it had been cut and fashioned for use in a bracelet by the hands of an Indian craftsman. And the man knew that long before it had been dug from the bottom of a mineshaft 500 miles south in the land of the Chibcha Indians in Colombia and brought by boat and runner to a Doraske Indian cutter of fine gems, who lived on the mountain called Chiriqui.

The stranger traded the boy a watch for the stone and then panned the sand bar for the golden bracelet from which he knew the emerald came. This emerald was a clue on the trail of a great lost treasure! But the whole story is too long to tell here.

What you should know now is that about 300 years ago, people were much like that little boy in their ignorance of the science of geology. People saw boulders standing in wide plains and wondered how they got there, but they did little to find out. They found the skeletons of ancient animals and plants embedded in rock and the remains of seashells high on the sides of mountains, but these findings meant little more than curiosities to them, much as the pretty green stone did to the boy. They did not know or even seek for the reasons back of these things.

This great ignorance was first really broken by JAMES HUTTON (1726–97), an Englishman and the "Father of Geology," whose famous *theory of the earth* proclaimed the until then unheard-of idea that "time, which means everything in our idea, and is often deficient to our schemes, is to nature endless and as nothing." Until then, people had thought the earth was born on October 4, 4004 B.C.; but Hutton saw the childishness of this belief, for he was not content to sit back and theorize, but went out and really studied the story of the earth. For the first time a person actually calculated how long it would take water to wear away stone. Hutton found it would take millions of years for one river to wear out its valley! There was grim humor in Hutton's words: "Time is long." "Long!" Think of this illustration of Darwin's: If you stretched a piece of tape along a wall for 83 feet and 4 inches (25.65 meters) and let that represent 1,000,000 years, then 1/10 of an inch (.25 centimeters) would be 100 years, a longer life than most men live! And yet the earth itself is at least 2,000,000,000 years old.

Geology by the early nineteenth century was still in a state of flux. A great battle raged between two schools of thought. The *plutonists*, represented by Professor JOHN PLAYFAIR (1748–1819) and other followers of James Hutton, took arms against the *neptunists*, represented by Professor ABRAHAM WERNER (1750–1817), a German geologist, and JEAN ANDRÉ DELUC (1727–1817), a Swiss scientist.

The plutonists believed that all rocks had been formed by some kind of volcanic action, in other words were fire rocks, while the neptunists upheld the theory that all rocks had been formed by the sea, or were made in the same way as the rocks that we now call "sedimentary." This battle was complicated by the fact that even though people were beginning to give up the idea that the earth was born in 4004 B.C., they still held to the thought that catastrophes such as the deluge told about in the Bible had periodically overwhelmed the earth, destroying all life there. This fallacious theory was doomed to go down before original and careful investigation of the earth's surface, but it clung on far longer in the minds of people than such wrong theories have any right to do, lasting in geological textbooks even past the midnineteenth century. The reason it had such a strong following was that it made it so easy to explain the strange phenomena that people were now beginning to observe about the earth. If you found a big boulder standing alone on top of a hill, it was easy to say that it had been brought there by the flood of a great deluge. But like many things that are too easy, this theory was wrong.

It took a real genius, SIR CHARLES LYELL (1797–1875), to get down to bedrock and show the facts. He joined the two conflicting theories of the neptunists and the plutonists together by pointing out that there were two chief kinds of rocks in the world, *igneous* or fire rocks and *sedimentary* or deposited rocks, and then he went on to show that between these two was an intermediate rock called *metamorphic*, which was caused by the action of heat and/pressure on the other two.

Look at Lyell's face (Figure 13-1) and you can see that the calm keen mind back of those eyes could not accept an inconsistent world. Geology had to have laws or it would not deserve to be a science. Lyell's crowning glory was in bringing to full fruit the *theory of uniformitarianism*, which had been started by Hutton. "Identical causes," said Lyell, "if the surrounding circumstances are identical, always produce identical results." He also said, "The past must be explained by the present," and he proved it by showing that the factors that are making new rocks today must have worked in the past, because exactly the same kinds of rocks are produced now as then. This broke down the theory of great catastrophes, since catastrophes were no longer needed to explain rock formation. Geology became a science with some stable laws.

It is a dramatic curiosity of scientific history that the two men of the nineteenth century whose minds were most keenly aware of the world about them—who produced two of the most startling scientific theories of all time, and whose influence on geology as well as on the other natural sciences was gigantic—were bitterly at sword's point. The *theory of the glaciers*, the idea of great masses of ice creeping down

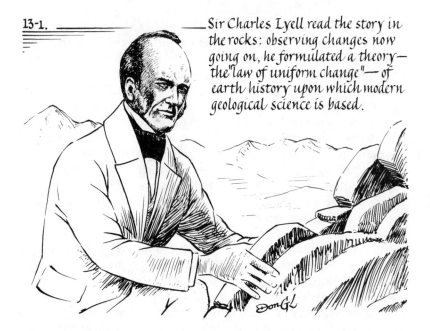

13-1. _____ Sir Charles Lyell read the story in the rocks: observing changes now going on, he formulated a theory—the "law of uniform change"— of earth history upon which modern geological science is based.

over the northern continents to drive the animals and plants southward and carry millions of tons of earth and rock with the moving ice masses, startled the world. Even people in the street talked about this fantastic-sounding idea, while the great scientists lined up in two ominous opposing phalanxes to fight for it and against it. Louis Agassiz (Figure 13-2) was the man with the giant intellect that hatched this theory and battled it through to victory on a wave of mounting facts. Like a hero of old, Agassiz, a brilliant young Swiss, climbed hundreds of the great slopes of the Alps to bring back convincing proof of how glaciers form and how they work down into the valleys from the peaks, carrying everything before them and slowing up only for the heat of the lower altitudes. The finding of glacier-scratched rocks and the terminal moraines of glaciers in lowland valleys throughout North America and Europe proved a past age of glaciers. Sir Charles Lyell, from the height of his great fame, pronounced the theory of Agassiz correct and the roaring of its enemies subsided to a muttering and then to nothing.

13-2. Louis Agassiz, determined to find the truth about glaciers, spent years measuring and recording the movements of the great ice rivers of the Alps. (Hut from actual life sketch.)

Some thirty years later when the glacial theory was secure and Agassiz had moved to America to become its leading naturalist and a professor at Harvard University, a new scientific light broke on the world. Charles Darwin, probably the master naturalist of all time, as modest and retiring as Agassiz was forthright and talkative, so honest that it hurt, so careful and patient that he waited and labored forty years with his great idea so that the world would be ripe for it, came forth with *the theory of evolution based on natural selection.* Where the glacial theory had been a bombshell, the idea of evolution was the explosion of a volcano! And not the least part of the explosion was the roar that came from Harvard. Agassiz, the thinker and the doer, the one man who above all others should have welcomed the thought of evolution, turned it down! Evolution for the first time made the fossils speak. Bones and skeletons found in the ancient clay beds, leaves and flowers caught in the crush of coal deposits, were no longer mere curiosities, but the actual ancestors of modern plants and animals. They traced the history of life down through the layers of rocks until the most ancient rocks showed the most primitive of living things, the one-celled animal-plants of the beginning. See Figure 13-3 for a picture of the vast panorama of the development of life as revealed through the geological study of these rock layers.

The work Agassiz himself did on fossils and glaciers was a monu-

Fig.13-3. *Geological and Life History of North America*
G. = Geological record.   L. = Life record.   N.A. = North America.

ARCHEOZOIC
G. Birth of oceans, atmosphere, continents. History little known, as rocks are much changed since this time.
L. *Age of One-celled Life:* Protozoa and Protophyta. No fossils.

PROTEROZOIC
G. *Laurentian Revolution.* Earliest evidence of glaciation. Much tension in earth's crust due to shrinkage, shown by twisted metamorphic rocks.
L. *Age of Primitive Water-dwelling Life:* small, shell-less invertebrates and plants. No fossils.

PALEOZOIC
Cambrian
G. Sea advances over North America, then gradually withdraws, leaving sediment. A mild revolution (i.e., change in climatic conditions).
L. *Age of Primitive Marine Animals and Plants.* Dominated by trilobites. First shells; some make first fossils.

Ordovician
G. Organisms produce first oil and gas. Sea again advances over most of N.A., but, as it withdraws, Taconic Mts. are built in East.
L. *Age of Marine Invertebrates and Water-dwelling Plants.* Rise of corals, nautilids, and first-known fish.

Silurian

G. Sea advances and retreats twice. Great limestone beds formed by sea animals in middle of N.A.; left by finally retreating sea.

L. First-known land plants; rise of lungfish and scorpions.

Devonian

G. Sea again advances over nearly half of N.A., but gradually withdraws, as volcanic action and folding of earth pushes up Acadian Mts. in East.

L. *Age of Fishes and Primitive Land Plants.* First forests and first amphibia and spiders.

Carboniferous

G. Acadian Mts. continue rising as sea sweeps again and again over much of N.A. Coal beds formed in eastern swamps.

L. Crinoids, blastoids, sharks, and echinoderms dominate seas; fernlike plants create enormous forests; primitive reptiles and insects appear.

Permian

G. *Appalachian Revolution.* Building of Appalachian Mts. combines with worldwide glaciation. Sea advances, but climate arid in South.

L. *Last Age of Amphibians and Ancient Flora.* Rise of conifer forests, insects, and reptiles bring extinction to more ancient life.

MESOZOIC
Triassic

G. As more of N.A. rises from sea, accompanied by volcanic activity in northeast, climate becomes arid.

L. *Age of Reptiles.* Rise of dinosaurs and cycad plants.

Jurassic

G. A long period of erosion, with volcanoes active and sea advancing on Pacific Coast, followed by beginning of Sierra Nevada uplift.

L. *Age of Reptiles and Medieval Flora.* Greatest spread of conifer and cycad forests; first birds and flying reptiles appear.

Comanchean

G. As Sierra Nevada continue to rise, seas spread through middle of N.A. and parts of Pacific Coast.

L. First flowering plants appear. Reptiles still dominant.

Lower Cretaceous

G. Much of N.A. submerged by sea, while great chalk, coal, and sandstone formations are laid down.

L. *Age of Reptiles and Primitive Flowering Plants.* Dinosaurs grow to greatest size. Higher flowering plants and insects appear.

Upper Cretaceous

G. Rockies push up with uplifting of western plateaus and new rising of Appalachians. Climate colder.

L. Dinosaurs die off from overspecialization as primitive mammals appear.

CENOZOIC
Eocene

G. *Laramide Revolution.* Mountains continue to grow, while volcanoes become active in West, but much erosion in high mountains.

L. *Age of Mammals and Flowering Plants.* First monkeys, cereals and fruit. Archaic mammals die out. Tropical plants in North.

Oligocene

G. Much sediment deposited on eastern coast, but volcanoes active in West.
L. Rise of the higher mammals. Specialization and social life in insects grows stronger.

Miocene

G. Much sedimentation and erosion over most of N.A. Tremendous lava plateaus built by crevice eruptions in northwest.
L. Period of the horse. Apes appear and large mammals dominant. Tropical forests retreat from middle N.A.

Pliocene

G. Worldwide elevation of mountains and cooling of climate, as first glaciation begins.
L. Horse and other ungulates dominate grassy plains. Man-ape changing into humans. Redwoods retreat from mountains to Pacific Coast.

Pleistocene

G. *Cascadian Revolution.* Coast Range formed in West as western volcanoes erupt; great Ice Age spreads over N.A.; deserts grow in southwest.
L. Giant mammals mostly die off; earliest red men come to N.A. People learn to live in tribes.

"Psychozoic" I (Present Time)

G. Mountains growing in the West. *Post-glacial Epoch.* Most of North America now above seas.
L. *Age of Man or Age of Reason.* Modern plants and animals; rise of world civilizations.

mental addition to the evidence for evolution, but he was strangely too blind to see it. The fossil fishes he found were an important link in the growing plan of life, but, above all, the theory of the glacial ages was proof positive of the very stresses and strains of nature that were so important a part of Darwin's idea of the "survival of the fittest." Only the fittest animals and plants were able to withstand and live through the terrific rigors of life when ice covered half the earth. Agassiz could not or would not see this. But for all his violent lectures against Darwin's words, neither he nor others could stem the tide of rising facts, and when Sir Charles Lyell, the giant among geologists, put his seal of approval on Darwin's theory, the battle was better than half won. Evolution gave new laws to geology, embedding its work deeper in fact and making of it the live science it was destined to be.

SEDIMENTARY, IGNEOUS, AND METAMORPHIC ROCKS

The next time you pick up a rock, break it open with a hammer and see what you see. If it is so hard that you cannot easily scratch it with a knife, it is likely to be an igneous rock. If you can easily scratch it, then it is probably a sedimentary rock. These two kinds of rock make up the bulk of the earth's crust, with metamorphic rocks forming the small remainder.

1. *Igneous rocks.* These are, as their name implies, "fire" rocks. In the earth's youth they were almost the only rocks, as most of the earth's surface was one roaring volcano. It was water in the form of rain that helped cool this hot surface, and it was water in the work of erosion that broke the igneous rock into small particles and later in seas and oceans turned these particles by pressure into sedimentary rocks.

Figure 13-4 shows the various ways in which igneous rocks are formed. The great molten mass of rocks called *magma* rises toward the surface under the push of pressure from below. This pressure has two causes: (1) since the continents are made of lighter rock material than that under the sea, the continental rocks are squeezed upward by their heavier neighbors, and (2) the gas stored inside the magma is constantly trying to expand to its natural size, and this often produces an explosive upward push. If the magma of red-hot liquid rock breaks through to the surface it forms volcanoes; if not, it remains under the surface rock as a vast underground lake that slowly cools to solid rock.

Here then are the two fundamental ways in which igneous rocks are formed. *Volcanic rocks,* because they contact the air, cool quickly and hence the minerals in them have very little or no time to form crystals. Volcanic rocks are thus either fine grained (with small crystals) like basalt, or glassy (with no crystals) like obsidian. *Granitic rocks,* the other type of igneous rock, cool so slowly underground that the minerals within the magma have a chance slowly to crystallize each mineral into a crystal form all its own. Thus granites and gabbros (dark igneous rock) appear to be formed of large grains or large crystals. Even in such rocks, however, the crystals do not have a chance to take their full form, since there is too much crowding. It is only when some chance appears, such as the forming of an air pocket above some molten magma, that a mineral crystal may find the room necessary to grow into its full form (for more about the crystallization of minerals see later in this chapter).

2. *Sedimentary rocks.* Rocks are sedimentary if they have been laid down in the sea, lakes, streams, or rivers by the action of water, or even on land by the action of wind (the dust storms that formed the loess of central China), or gravity (the falling of rock fragments from cliffs to build up a slowly consolidating debris). Some are formed by water depositing minerals out of solution in such a way that they form a cement locking small or large particles of sand or rock together. Shale, for instance, is formed by layers of mud and clay being pushed together so tightly by their own pressure and that of water that they form into rock. Limestone may be formed either by ocean pressure turning the countless billions of calcareous (lime-built) skeletons and shells of ocean animals into rocks, or by calcite being deposited in caves in the form of stalactites and stalagmites. Figure 13-5 shows some of the various ways in which sedimentary rocks are formed.

3. *Metamorphic rocks.* These are rocks that have been changed from either sedimentary or igneous rocks by heat, pressure, or the chemical action of water solutions. For instance, great heat may partially crystallize limestone so as to turn it into marble. Where does this heat usually come from? It comes from the molten magma beneath the earth's surface, which may push up against a region of sedimentary or older igneous rocks and by its terrific heat change the rock layers near it. The heat, in our example, does not fuse the limestone (if it did the

13-4. How igneous rock formations are made. (Block diagram after Emmons, Thiel, etc.)

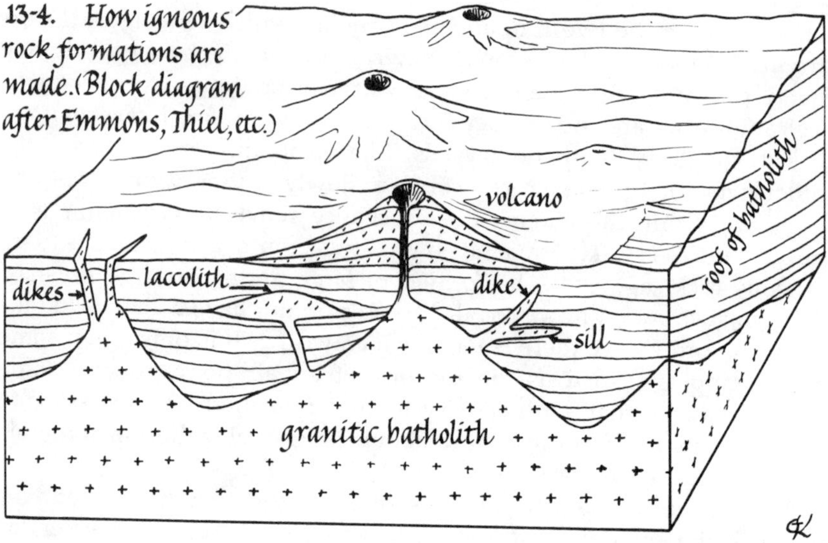

volcano

dikes → laccolith dike

sill

roof of batholith

granitic batholith

limestone would be changed into a molten magma and then into igneous rock when this cooled), but makes a less radical change in the rock's structure, creating a crystalline structure where there was none before. Solutions of minerals in water may change a rock's chemical nature in a different way, producing another kind of metamorphic rock in which one mineral has been taken in solution out of a rock while another has been deposited in its place. This takes place most effectively under heat and pressure, but neither is entirely necessary. Serpentine, for instance, is a rock that has come through two periods of metamorphosis. First it was a shale, and this shale was metamorphosed by heat into a schist, a rock of very thin crystalline bands; then this schist was again metamorphosed by groundwater soaking through it and taking out minerals such as *pyroxene* while leaving the green mineral *serpentine* in its place. Many metamorphic rocks appear striated or banded because the forming crystals have been first softened by the heat and then flattened out by the pressure. If the bands are thin, it is likely to be a *schist*; if thick, it is probably a *gneiss*. The charts on page 170 give a general idea of rock evolution. Figure 13-6 shows the various ways in which metamorphic rocks are formed.

13-5. How sedimentary rock beds are formed — Example: a series of beds is exposed (A) by a river's cutting of its canyon. How may beds have been formed?

Analysis: Suppose a great plain of granitic rock of the earth's crust (B) —

Prevailing wind brings sand from nearby desert. Crust slowly sinks under weight

until a rapid settling brings in sea which deposits silt carried down by rivers.

More settling again sends sea inland. Now instead of silt there is deposition of lime skeletons, in billions, of tiny marine animals. Pressure and cementing action of sea-salts bind sandgrains to make sandstone and silt particles to make shale.

4. *Some lesser rock types and their differences.* The name *conglomerate rock* applies to all rocks made up of large cemented-together parts, such as pebbles cemented together. A *quartzite* may be distinguished from a *sandstone* by its greater hardness and the fact that, when broken, the break cuts right through the grains of sand instead of around them. *Slates* may be distinguished from the common brown, black, and yellow *shales* by their greater hardness (hard to scratch with a knife) and the ease with which they split into thin or thick sheets. *Phyllite* is a rock that breaks into very thin sheets and, different from slate, shows to the eye flakes of mica (silvery and semitransparent). Unlike a *schist*

Chart of Rock Development

Loose Sediment	Sedimentary Rocks	Metamorphic Rocks
GRAVEL	changes to conglomerate	changes to gneiss
SAND	" " sandstone	" " quartzite
MUD	" " shale	" " slate, and this to schist
IMPURE CLAY	" " shale	" " slate or phyllite
SHELLS AND OTHER LIME DEPOSITS	change to limestone	" " marble

	Igneous Rocks	Metamorphic Rocks
	COARSE IGNEOUS ROCKS (granite, gabbro, etc.)	change to gneiss (thick bands)
	FINE IGNEOUS ROCKS (felsite, basalt, etc.)	" " schist (thin bands)

Chart of Crystal Development in Igneous Rocks

Glassy (no crystals; cooled quickly)	Dense (small crystals; cooled slowly)	Grained (large crystals; cooled very slowly)
obsidian	rhyolite	granite
perlite	trachite	syenite
pumice	felsite	diorite
scoria	basalt	gabbro

*Adapted from Loomis's *Field Book of Rocks and Minerals* (G. P. Putnam's Sons, 1925)

(which is made of two or more visible minerals), no other minerals save mica can be seen in phyllite. A drop of hydrochloric acid on *limestone* fizzes, as it does also when put on *marble*, but marble, when looked at through a magnifying glass, shows a crystalline structure that is missing in limestone.

Obsidian is a volcanic glass of usually smooth surface, while *perlite* is a glassy lava that has cracked into ball-like forms with layers like an onion. *Pumice* is a glassy rock filled with tiny holes, while in *scoria* the holes are larger and are irregular in shape. *Rhyolite* is a very fine-grained, light-colored rock, which is so hard, because of the quartz in it, that it cannot be scratched by a knife, whereas the similar *trachite* can barely be scratched. A common name for such light-colored lava

13-6. Some types of metamorphism of rocks.

A. CONTACT. Intrusion of molten magma into limestone, chemically changing it. New rocks formed are combinations of elements present in both magma and invaded rock. Of great effect are gases given off by molten rock.

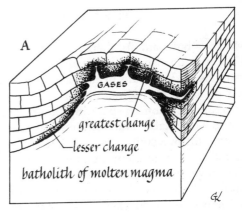

GASES

greatest change

lesser change

batholith of molten magma

P

pressure folds strata, alters rocks

B. DYNAMIC. Pressure and heat caused by great movements of the earth's crust crystallize and make denser the minerals of sedimentary rocks, changing shales to slates, etc.

C. REPLACEMENT. Water dissolves substance (e.g., wood), replaces it, molecule by molecule, with

Petrified forest

minerals in solution, keeping the exact form of the original.

rocks as *trachite, rhyolite,* and *dacite* is *felsite. Basalt* is a dark-colored, fine-grained lava rock, usually too hard to be scratched with a knife. It is extremely common in the western states. *Granite, syenite,* and *diorite* are such similar light-colored and large-grained igneous rocks that it is often difficult to tell them apart, but all are harder than sedimentary rocks, being difficult or impossible to scratch with a knife. Diorite is usually darker than the other two, while syenite, because of its lack of quartz, is softer and therefore more easily scratched than granite. *Gabbro* is a dark-colored, large-grained rock.

THE NATURE OF MINERALS

Minerals have among them the most beautiful of all nonliving things. They include also the most valuable. Who would not be thrilled by the intricate and delicate beauty of a moss agate or a fire opal? Who has not dreamed of finding a hidden treasure of sapphires, rubies, emeralds, and diamonds, sparkling in a pirate's old brass-bound chest? Yet the most valuable and wonderful minerals are the ones on which we have built our civilization. *Iron* is a mineral; so are *lead, zinc, copper,* and *aluminum,* to mention a few of the elemental and metallic minerals that have built our cities and our communications systems, our ships, and our railroads. *Corundum* (aluminum and oxygen) gives us the hard stone we use for sharpening knives; *carnotite* (made of potassium oxide combined with uranium oxide, vanadium oxide, and water) is the chief producer of *radium,* the most valuable metal on earth; and *colemanite* (made of calcium, barium, and oxygen plus water) is today's chief source of *borax,* which is used so much in medicines, colored glazes, enamels, cosmetics, and as a preservative.

These are only a very few of the minerals. Minerals to the naturalist are a part of the natural world. The naturalist is keenly interested in minerals because they help explain many things one sees in that world and because they are part of the beauty and curiosity of nature. A well-kept mineral collection is something to be proud of, and, unlike most collections, it will last practically forever.

CLASSIFICATION OF MINERALS

When next you take up a piece of granite, notice how the crystals are visible as light and dark angular-shaped spots all over the rock. In the beginning each mineral, which is to become part of a rock later, is found in the molten solution of a magma mixed with many other minerals. As the magma cools, it forms into a rock of mixed mineral crystals. Thus granite may be composed of the mineral crystals of feldspar, quartz, and either mica, hornblende, or augite. The quartz crystals will appear white, the mica shining silver or black, the feldspar pinkish white, and the hornblende or augite black.

It is apparently the nature of minerals to form crystals, and each mineral takes on a distinctive crystal shape all its own. This crystal shape would be plain to see if each mineral crystal had room to develop by itself, but this rarely happens, as usually each growing crystal is pushing against and is being pushed by many other crystals, which limit its shape.

Chapter Nineteen takes up seriously the classification of minerals; here we can study a few of the preliminary facts.

1. *Minerals are divided into two great sections—metallic and nonmetallic.* Argentite, for instance, is a metallic mineral because it is a combination of silver and sulphur, the first of which is a metal. *Quartz* is a nonmetallic mineral because it is made of silicon and oxygen, neither of which is a metal.

2. *All mineral crystals are divided into crystal systems.* There are six possible systems of arrangement of crystals, by which is meant that the crystal of every mineral takes a certain geometrical form and there are six of these forms (see Figure 19-1). However, the actual number of variations in appearance of crystals is much greater, as each form may have several variations in shape.

3. *All minerals vary in hardness.* But each kind has a particular degree of hardness, varying from talc, which is very soft, to the diamond, which is the hardest of all minerals. This hardness is very important in classification.

4. *With metallic minerals, the streak is also very important.* This streak is made by rubbing the mineral on a "streak plate" or piece of unglazed porcelain. Although the color of a given mineral may vary, the color of the streak will usually remain the same. This is not so true, however, with the nonmetallic minerals.

5. *Luster*, the appearance of a mineral surface in reflected light; *cleavage*, the way each kind of mineral breaks or cleaves along certain planes of its structure; *specific gravity*, the weight of a mineral compared with the weight of an equal volume of water; and *color*, the natural color of a mineral's surface, are other important characteristics with which we will deal more fully later.

We have seen how the molten magma, which precedes the formation of igneous rocks, is the place where the minerals are first joined into a mass. Later, when the igneous rocks have taken form, these minerals are broken up out of the rocks by the action of water, wind, ice, and other forces. The minerals dissolve into the water (as calcite does), are carried by it in a mixture (as clay is), or simply are swept along mechanically (as sand or gravel are). (See Figure 19-4). In whatever way a mineral is carried, it is later deposited somewhere, most of it in the sea, some in a lake or a river delta, or simply on another part of the land. In its new location it takes part in the building of new rocks; first sedimentary rocks, then metamorphic rocks, if pressure and heat become very great. Sandstone, for example, is usually made of sand grains that have been carried mechanically by a river down to the sea after the breaking up of granite into quartz and feldspar crystals. These tiny crystals are cemented together by a dissolved (and now deposited) mineral (such as silica, calcite, iron oxide, or clay impurities), which itself originally came from some igneous rocks, and the whole is packed by pressure into sandstone. Next, heat or pressure may add to or change the nature of these minerals, producing the metamorphic rock quartzite, in which the sandstone grains are changed or "metamorphized" (softened and partially fused together into a crystalline structure). If there is still more heat the rock will dissolve into a magma and come out, at cooling, as igneous rocks. Thus is the circle completed (see Figures 13-4, 13-5, and 13-6).

A BRIEF HISTORY
OF ROCKS—AND OF LIFE

"Time is long," said James Hutton, and time has had to be long indeed for the titanic and wondrous changes that have happened to the earth. About 3,000,000,000 to 2,000,000,000 years ago, if we had traveled in some super spaceship into the part of the universe inhabited by our medium-sized sun, we would have seen things far different from those that space travelers in a similar ship would see now. Remember that our sun, which drives through space at a speed of about twelve miles a second, was then far away in another part of the universe, and the earth at that time was probably just born.

"Just born," perhaps 1,000,000 years before! Or 10,000,000 . . . But to nature "time is long," and what is a million more or less when compared to billions?

Well, so the earth was just born and only at the start of its remarkable existence. At that time, however, it was only a very hot little ball wrapped in rolling storm clouds, loud with the rumble of volcanoes, the hiss of steam, and the roar of hurricane winds.

The earliest rocks that had a chance to form in that turbulent youth of the earth were igneous rocks, but these rocks had very little time to keep their initial form, for they were immediately and violently attacked by water, steam, and heat. Torrential rains lashed them, and the earth was constantly buckling under them as molten magmas surged upward from below. Consequently the most ancient rocks that we find today, the Archeozoic rocks ("ancient-life rocks"), show the results of this tremendous battering. These are intensely metamorphosed rocks, mostly schists and gneisses, and usually so deep under other layers or rocks that they are exposed only by deep canyons, mines, or quarries.

There are very few signs of life in these rocks (they were made about 1,400,000,000 years ago), but occasionally the very ancient fossils of single-celled animal-plants make their appearance, to show that life began hundreds of millions of years after the earth itself was born. A fossil is simply the rock-preserved imprint of some form of previously existing life (see Figure 13-7 for examples.) Fossils are clear evidence of the evolution of both plant and animal life from very simple forms, such as the algae (pond scum) for plants and the amoeba (Figure 11-3) for animals, up through more and more complex forms, to such modern

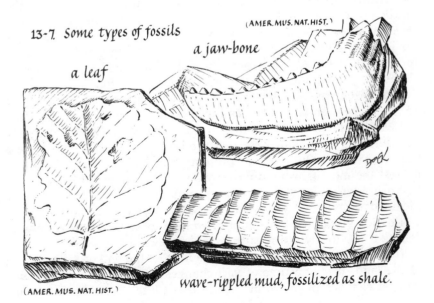

13-7. Some types of fossils

(AMER. MUS. NAT. HIST.)

a jaw-bone

a leaf

(AMER. MUS. NAT. HIST.)

wave-rippled mud, fossilized as shale.

highly evolved plants as the sunflower and the snapdragon, and such complex animals as humans, the horse, and the eagle.

Of course, no one knows exactly how life began on the earth, but it is fairly evident that it appeared first as a very simple single cell. We have noted already how the often very complex chemicals of minerals tend to form crystals, actually seeming to grow in a lifelike way. This tendency of chemicals to take form possibly has something to do with the formation of life. At any rate, probably in some warm shallow sea near one of the polar regions, the conditions became just right for life to appear—and it did. From that beginning, it spread over the earth, first through the seas, then onto the land, and last into the air (see Figure 13-3).

The Proterozoic (former life) era followed the Archeozoic (ancient life) era. In this Proterozoic period the earth became more sedate and not so constantly bursting loose with volcanic eruptions. For the first time large amounts of sedimentary rocks appeared; thousands of peaceful years must have passed for the gradual laying down of sediments. But the earth was still capable of tremendous reversals of policy, and often thousand-foot thicknesses of sedimentary sandstones and shales would be lifted from the ocean floor by underground forces and thrown up into the ridges of new and titanic mountains, the backbones of new continents. Now the history of the earth's surface began to show a certain wavelike progression. Upheavals of the rocks would be followed by long quiescent periods during which the mountains would be gradually worn, through millions of years, down to plains, only to be lifted up again by renewed earth forces. During and right after the time of upheaval there would be much more land surface on the globe than usual, but as the rocks were worn away by water and washed down to the sea, the surface of the oceans would gradually rise, flooding in shallow seas over the land, and there would be less land than usual. Our earth at present seems to be in an era that is nearest the mountain-building extreme. In the Proterozoic period the first primitive multicelled plants and animals of the sea appeared. They included sponges, jellyfish, and seaweeds. Then also came the first worldwide glaciation, a result of lifted land masses and the coming of cold to a previously warm earth.

The Paleozoic (old life) period came next, at the end of a great uplift of the land. It is at a time of vast changes in the earth's surface that parallel changes in the forms of life take place, showing that in the stress and strain of such times only the most hardy and adaptable forms of life manage to live on, and these themselves are forced to mighty changes. It is as if life were a man carrying a big load and fleeing desperately from an angry bear. First one useless weight and then another is thrown from his load, until he runs naked and with none of his power of flight hindered. Only thus may he escape with his life. Life, in time of stress, not only must get rid of useless weight, but may even be forced to change gait and style to meet a danger not known before. In such a way new type animals and plants seem to rise at the beginning of each new age (see Figure 13-3). First shellfish and worms and insects, then fishes and frogs and salamanders rose to success during the Paleozoic times. Club mosses grew as large as trees, and ferns also were gigantic and covered the land with rank forests, but no single flower showed its color anywhere on earth. Out of the vast swamp forests of these times has come the organic rock we call coal, made up of billions of pressed and partially fossilized plants. In the sea thousands of millions of shellfish and other animals who protected themselves with mineral-made armor or skeletons died to make the limestone beds, the radiolarian chert, and the diatomaceous earth we find today.

During the late Paleozoic another great uplift of the land came, followed by a period of worldwide glaciation. Again life was on trial and again new life arose to replace or surpass the old that could not stand the strain. The Paleozoic laid down its layer on layer of rocks on the Proterozoic and Archeozoic below.

But do not think that today we can easily go down through the layers of rocks and point out each age. In only a few rare places is this possible (see Figure 13-8, with its picture of a cross section of the Grand Canyon), for in most places the wearing away of rock by water and its constant redeposition in other places, plus the shifting and bending of rocks by the upheaval of earthquakes, makes the present appearance of the rock very different from a student's ideal.

We can always tell the signs of a past period of great uplift of the rocks by the telltale traces of metamorphism, as where there is an uplift and a bending of rock layers there is always bound to have been heat and pressure, the two greatest causes of metamorphic rocks. During the Paleozoic era, a time of such vast change occurred and is shown today through certain sections of the Appalachian Mountains by the metamorphic rocks that are found there (see Figure 13-9).

13-8. "An abyss in time," Dr. John C. Merriam called the GRAND CANYON in his book THE LIVING PAST (1930).

ERA	PERIOD AND EPOCH	GROUP AND FORMATION	KIND OF ROCK	PREVAILING COLOR	THICKNESS IN FEET
MESOZOIC	TRIASSIC	Shinarump congl.	Conglomerate	Brown	25
		Moenkopi	Shale and sandstone	Red	480
		UNCONFORMITY			
	PERMIAN	Kaibab limestone	Limestone and sandstone	Gray, buff and red	525
PALEOZOIC		Coconino sandstone	Sandstone	Light buff	350
		Hermit shale	Sandy shale	Red	225
		Supai formation	Sandstone and shale with some limestone	Red and gray	825
		UNCONFORMITY			
	CARBONIFEROUS MISS.	Redwall limestone	Limestone	Gray stained red	450 to 500
	DEVONIAN	Temple Butte ls.	Limestone and sandstone	Pale purplish red	0–36
		UNCONFORMITY			
	CAMBRIAN	Muav limestone	Sandy shale and limestone	Gray	100
		Bright Angel shale	Sandy shale	Greenish gray	450 to 650
		Tapeats sandstone	Sandstone	Brown	225
		GREAT UNCONFORMITY			
PROTEROZOIC	ALGONKIAN	Unkar and Chuar groups of Grand Canyon Series	Sandstone and shale with some limestone; contains sheets and dikes of lava	Mostly red	0 to 12000
		GREAT UNCONFORMITY			
	ARCHEAN	Vishnu schist	Schist, granite, and gneiss	Dark gray	Not known

Tonto Group

DIAGRAMMATIC PROFILE

CEDAR MOUNTAIN — SURFACE OF KAIBAB AND COCONINO PLATEAUS — RIM OF GRAND CANYON — Sea deposits with marine shells, etc. — Probably dune sands with tracks of primitive reptiles and amphibians — Foot prints; primitive "evergreens"; fern-like plants; insects; and sun-cracked silts — ESPLANADE — Red flood plain deposits with land animals and plants — Old land surface — Sea deposits with shells, corals, etc. — Fish scales — Sea deposits with shells and seaweeds — Trilobites — TONTO PLATFORM — seaweeds — Shinumo quartzite — Hakatai shale — Base limestone — traces of life — Vishnu — Vishnu schist — Pegmatite — "GRANITE" GORGE — REDRAWN AFTER NATIONAL PARK SERVICE

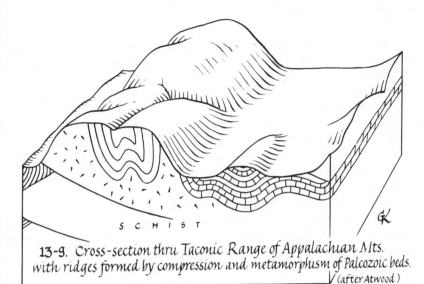

13-3. Cross-section thru Taconic Range of Appalachian Mts. with ridges formed by compression and metamorphism of Paleozoic beds.
(after Atwood)

The Mesozoic (middle life) era, which followed after the Paleozoic, was the golden age of monsters. Giant reptiles or dinosaurs came to rule the earth, but also such important events as the appearance of the first birds, mammals, and flowering plants occurred. Red sandstones and shales as well as new beds of coal were the rule among sedimentary rocks at first, but as the seas gradually began to overrun the lands toward the middle and the end of the era, great deposits of limestone were laid down by the animals of the sea. Most all of North America was then under water, and the Rocky Mountains were unknown giants of the future.

The Cenozoic (recent life) era was born during the fourth of the great upheavals of the earth. The ponderous dinosaurs who had ruled so long vanished as if they were nothing, and the small-haired and feathered creatures, whose warm blood and warm covering allowed them to withstand great cold, became the dominant life on earth. Flowering plants also began to reach their full development, and the ancestors of modern trees reared their leafy heads high in the air. Life became more vibrant and truly alive—for now, for the first time in the history of life, intelligence began to supplant the long-used instinct (most fully developed in the insects) as the dominant way of living. Instinct, with its automatic reactions passed on at birth to new generations, continues to serve life well, but now the higher animals were no longer programmed to cast their newborn guideless on the world. They began instead to rear them and teach them as true parents.

Now also the plants (in their flowering forms) developed protective parenthood. In the flowering plant the seed grows to full size within the body of the mother plant until it is ready to face the dangers of the world with a hard coat and a plentiful supply of food, while in the more ancient and primitive plants thousands of naked spores are cast loose to the winds, the parent plant counting on quantity rather than quality to start the next generation.

After the first great uplift of the rocks at the beginning of the Cenozoic, there was a long period of quiescence during which the mountains everywhere were worn very low by water action. This was followed a little over 1,000,000 years ago by a new period of uplifting of the land. The region of the Grand Canyon of the Colorado, for instance, was raised around 1,800 meters (6,000 feet) at this time, causing the river to start cutting the tremendous canyon we see there now. There was also tremendous volcanic action, and sometimes basaltic lava thousands of feet thick poured out upon the surrounding plains (vast areas of Oregon, Washington, and Idaho are so covered to this day). The late Cenozoic saw the most extensive of all glacial periods when tremendous stretches of North America and Eurasia were covered with ice. The vast glaciers produced their own kind of erosion, cutting out hanging valleys such as those found in Yosemite, pushing before them to new regions vast quantities of dirt and rock (such as are found in New England), and, by the erosion caused by the streams that flowed from them as they melted, producing new river canyons and valleys.

Finally, the Cenozoic era is noteworthy for the appearance of humans, the one animal who has been able to change the appearance of the surface of the earth to a great degree.

Carefully study the chart of earth history (Figure 13-3), and you will begin to understand the wonderful story told by the rocks.

Find out from the director of the United States Geological Survey, Washington, D.C., about maps and publications relating to the geology of your region. If you can get hold of these, they will tell you much about the rocks and minerals of your particular locality. You will be able to go into the country and tell from the appearance and nature of the rocks their position and importance in the history of the earth.

CHAPTER
14

Climate Study

Out of the chamber of the south cometh the storm: and cold out of the north. By the breath of God ice is given: and the breadth of the water is straightened. Yea, he ladeth the thick cloud with moisture; he spreadeth abroad the cloud of his lightning; and it is turned around by his guidance, that they may do whatsoever he commandeth them upon the face of the habitable world.

BOOK OF JOB. XXXVI

We had rounded the northern tip of the island of Luzon, the great northern island of the Philippines, and our freighter, the *Golden Wall*, bucked into the long swells of the South China Sea, headed for Hong Kong. "Sparks," the radioman, passed me where I was scraping paint on the bridge and waved a yellow paper. "You won't be doing that long," he said with a grin. "Typhoon's coming!" Neither Sparks nor

I had ever seen a typhoon, that terrible storm of the Oriental seas, and we looked forward to it as a great adventure. Not so the Norwegian-born captain. He was worried.

When I entered the chart room to sweep it, the captain was bending over a chart moving some pins. "Come here, boy," he said kindly, "and I'll show you what's happening."

He put his finger on the northern half of Luzon and said, "The typhoon's just passed over this part of the island, killing a lot of natives the radio says, and now she's heading directly for us at a speed of about twelve or thirteen knots, two or three knots faster than we can do. Ordinarily we'd head north and get out of her way, but chances are we can make Hong Kong before we get caught and that would save us so much time that we're going to take that chance. A captain one hundred years ago would have had to plow his ship through these seas without knowing where or when a typhoon was going to strike him, but now, thanks to the radio and accurate weather reports from both land stations and ships, we have a good chance to beat or avoid the storm."

"Just what causes a typhoon, sir?" I asked.

"Heat," he replied, "is the main cause. The air becomes so heated in some section of the ocean that it begins to rise much more swiftly than cool air can come in to take its place. This gradually produces a whirling center of suction to which air from all directions is drawn. This center begins to move slowly over the sea, with the whirling winds reaching tremendous speeds of more than a hundred miles an hour and producing the most terrible waves, capable of crushing in the sides of a ship. The typhoon moves generally from south to north because the centrifugal force of the earth draws it toward the North Pole."

"But why do the winds go around the center?"

"That again is because of centrifugal force. Winds to the north of the equator turn to the left or contraclockwise, while those to the south of the equator turn to the right or clockwise. If you move a spoon rapidly through a bucket of water, the whirlpools on the right side of the spoon will go clockwise; those on the left will go contraclockwise. It is the same principle."

He stepped out of the chart house for a minute to scan the sky. It was nearly covered with gray clouds, the higher ones broken up like a horse's mane.

"The wind is blowing from the north now," said the captain.

"But I thought the storm was coming from the south."

"So it is. But look here." He pointed to circular lines he had drawn on a chart of the South China Sea. "The storm is now to our southeast. Since the winds are moving contraclockwise around the storm, that made the winds to the northwest of the storm center where we are blow south. They continue south in a great circle down behind the storm center, swinging completely around it, though all the time approaching it closer and closer. But the center itself is without any wind at all, as there all the air is moving straight up into the sky."

The following morning when I woke in my bunk I could hear the ship groaning through all her steel plates, and the way she heeled and held over, nearly throwing me out of bed, as if the flat of a giant's hand were trying to push her into the sea, was strangely frightening. The wind no longer cried among the mastheads, but roared deeply and violently like a bull goaded beyond all fury. When I came on deck, blast after blast struck my face with needlelike spray, and I saw the forms of men moving ponderously like monsters in the gloom. The air was no longer something you easily moved through; it was a wall that heaved against you and against which you blindly fought, counting inches like hard-fought mountain miles. Never before in my life had I realized what a real thing air was; now I knew! Savage swells of the sea, moving, snow-tipped mountains with the force of a thousand battering rams, rushed endlessly out of the east to send the ship rolling and pitching till green waves poured over the bow and sides and buried the sailors in fighting water as they clung to the lifelines.

How we fought through the storm and escaped it is too long a story to tell here. But if you have caught the feeling of the fateful force of the weather when "out of the chamber of the south cometh the storm," then you will know how sailors have felt on a lashing sea ever since the first of them launched a boat upon the waves.

In the early days of civilization, people thought storms the work of devils or gods, and the small ships of those times went fearfully out upon the sea like cats sneaking into a neighborhood full of savage dogs. Most knowledge of the weather was contained in proverbs such as: "A red sky at night is the shepherd's delight; a red sky in the morning is the shepherd's warning"; or "If the sun goes pale to bed, 'twill rain tomorrow so 'tis said."

The Greeks were the first people to look at the weather with more than a superstitious eye. The greatest of the Greek philosopher-scientists, Aristotle, gathered together all the weather lore and weather knowledge of his time into a part of a book of science called *Meteorologica*. For 1,700 years this was the only book on weather, and perhaps for this reason the science of weather today is called meteorology.

The great discoveries and voyages of the fifteenth and sixteenth centuries made people more conscious of the weather than ever before, but little was done about it by scientists. One exception was the writing of a *Discourse on Winds* by WILLIAM DAMPIER (1652–1715), who was a famous English buccaneer of the Spanish Main. His keen eyes, which sought out each new thing he saw in the lands of America, noticed also many of the interesting features of the trade winds and the hurricanes of the Atlantic and the Caribbean Sea.

It took the genius of ALEXANDER VON HUMBOLDT (1769–1859), one of the greatest of all explorer-naturalists (Figure 14-1), to build up the first worldwide climatic laws. After five years spent exploring South and Central America, the regions of the Caribbean Sea and the Gulf of Mexico, he returned to Paris to write in four magnificent volumes called the *Kosmos* the fruits of his careful observations and thought. Humboldt was the first to map the earth's surface in lines of average equal temperature—*isothermal* lines—by which he obtained a method of comparing the climates of different countries. He also studied the source of the Gulf Stream and noted its warming effect on the climate of Europe, and he was the first to point out the zones of volcanic

14-1.
Young Humboldt, with a new continent ahead—South America!

Baron Alexander von Humboldt (1769-1859) began over 150 years ago observations in the Americas and Asia that made him one of the greatest of all explorer-naturalists and founder of climatology. Compare this quotation from him (1807): "The variations of temperature, of many parts of the earth, depend principally on the character of the bottom of the aërial ocean..." with the title of William H. Wenstrom's book, WEATHER AND THE OCEAN OF AIR (Houghton Mifflin, 1942).

activity that ring the Pacific Ocean and send an offshoot up through the islands of the Caribbean. He studied the origin of tropical storms and noted the way plants and animals were distributed in regard to the climatic conditions that surrounded them.

In 1643 EVANGELISTA TORRICELLI (1608–47) invented the thermometer and barometer by putting columns of mercury inside marked glass tubes, making the first accurate weather instruments. If the temperature were kept constant, the mercury column would record the variation in air pressure in a given locality; if the pressure were kept constant, the mercury, expanding under heat and contracting in cold, would record the temperature.

But stations for the study of weather were for a long time private affairs, kept by a few rich men, and, in spite of the importance of weather to both navigation and agriculture, little was done to develop the science of meteorology. The first meteorological society, founded in London in 1823 with the influence of essayist and historian THOMAS CARLYLE (1795–1881), concentrated on helping the sailor rather than the farmer, as weather on the sea is easier to understand than that on land. It was not until 1872 that weather became an international affair, with most nations agreeing to share their day-by-day weather knowledge so that all could benefit. Careful daily reports from land weather stations plus the reports from ships at sea gradually began to turn meteorology into a science based more on fact and less on theory. But attempts to predict weather more than two or three days ahead with any considerable accuracy have too often failed. For this reason meteorology is still to a large extent an experimental science, strong in explanation of past weather, but somewhat shaky in predictions as to the weather to come. *Climatology,* the study of climate as a whole, however, rests on firmer ground. We have seen (in Chapter Eight) the laws of climate, and many of these are as definite and exact as the astronomer's prediction of the time of the sun's rising each morning.

AIR MASS ANALYSIS

One of the most spectacular advances in weather science in all its history was made in Norway, in the 1940s. A Norwegian, Vilhelm Bjerknes, (1862–1951), brought to meteorology the *theory of air mass analysis.* Actually this new theory made the whole problem of weather a great deal simpler than it had been before.

We have all experienced weather that goes on day after day very much the same. Perhaps it is clear and cold and dry. Smoke rises almost straight up. There are few clouds. You can almost smell that kind of weather. In the State of Illinois, for example, such weather means that a great mass of cold, dry air has come down from Canada and overlies the land. This air mass is called *Polar Canadian.* Then one day toward summer all this suddenly changes. The sky becomes gradually more overcast and the next day a steady rain begins. When the rain has gone, the "feel" of the weather has completely changed. It is hot and muggy. In the afternoon there will likely be thunderstorms. A new air mass has come to overlie Illinois. This air mass is called *Tropical Gulf.*

There is a constant warfare going on in the sky over the United States and Canada between the great tropical air masses and the great polar air masses. The cold heavy air mass from the north presses against and under the hot light air mass from the south. In the winter the polar air mass seems to win for it presses far southward. But in summer the tropical air mass comes up north riding, hot and full of moisture, over the cold air mass. When the polar air mass presses south, it is called an "advancing cold front." Because it presses under the warm air mass, it gives little advance warning. It may appear rather suddenly as a cold northwest wind. When the tropical air mass presses north, it is called an "advancing warm front." Then you see its coming far in advance, first as light cirrus clouds in the sky gradually thickening, then as a thin layer of cirrostratus with its halo around the moon or sun, then as gradually lowering dark rain clouds.

Weather is thus sharply divided into two kinds: (1) *air mass weather*, with the same kind of weather day after day, or (2) *air front weather*, with sharp and sudden changes, usually having strong winds or rain or both. We can see now that a storm is simply a battle in the sky between two opposing air masses. Storms occupy the no man's land between the great rival powers. The heat of summer gives the tropical air mass the fighting power to push northward and overwhelm the polar air masses. The cold of winter gives the polar air mass its chance to pour southward in conquering waves that may bring shivers as far south as a palm leaf hut in Central America.

Let us take a look at the chief American air masses. If we watch for them in the sky, we shall be helped in judging what weather is coming.

We shall better understand the effects of weather on animal and plant life.

1. *Polar Canadian*. This is usually cold and dry air. But it may become changed by contact with the moisture of the Great Lakes into snow and rain storms in the country just south of the lakes. It occurs over the East and Midwest.

2. *Tropical Gulf* or *Tropical Atlantic*. This comes as the typical hot, moisture-laden days of an eastern summer.

3. *Polar Pacific*. This appears as a cool, fairly moist air out of the northwest Pacific. It may bring rain, and in California it is the frequent cause of the masses of fog along the coast. But by rising over the mountains and flowing down their steep eastern sides, it becomes compressed. This compression warms and dries it, producing the warm, dry Chinook winds of the interior of the continent.

4. *Tropical Pacific*. The balmy, sunny days of California are caused by this air mass. It does not have nearly as much moisture in it as does Tropical Gulf.

5. *Polar Atlantic*. A cold, blustery air, often full of rain or snow and the smell of the deep sea.

6. *Tropical Continental*. This air mass comes up out of the hot heart of Mexico and is so dry it causes drought wherever it strikes. It is the cause of the deserts of the Southwest.

7. *Sec Superieur*. This rare air mass is said to come from the region of the Galapagos Islands. When it strikes, it is as if a hot, dry tongue licks down from the sky. All moisture disappears. Farmers fear it.

There is a great deal more to the theory of air mass analysis than we have been able to give here. You can turn to the climate and weather books listed in the Bibliography for further information. For naturalists, the study of air masses opens up new avenues of understanding as the effect of weather on life. They begin to understand what causes the dryness of certain areas, the wetness of others, the coldness that drives animals and birds south or into hibernation. There is a rhythmic cycle to the weather, and it is wise to catch the feel of it.

CLOUDS

Clouds write the message of the weather, good or bad. Since a change in the weather changes the face of all nature, both bringing forth and destroying life, the wise naturalist becomes a lifelong student of the clouds. Since cloud study is one of the most fascinating and easily learned of all nature studies, it becomes far more pleasure than work. Clouds seem to the naturalist like actors on a stage, sometimes friends who bring cheerful news of fine days to come, at other times messengers of the dark rain that lies beyond the horizon.

Study carefully the pictures of the different types of clouds shown in Figure 14-2; then compare them with their descriptions in the outline below in which the vertical location of clouds in the earth's atmosphere is given.*

(a) Detached or rounded forms (chiefly in dry weather).
(b) Widespread or veillike forms (rainy weather).

A. HIGHEST CLOUDS: AVERAGING 9100 METERS (30,000 FEET) ABOVE THE EARTH
   1. Featherlike clouds (cirrus).
   2. Thin sheets (cirrostratus).

B. MIDDLE CLOUDS: 4500 to 7300 METERS (13,000 TO 22,000 FEET) ABOVE THE EARTH
   3. Small balls or flakes, glistening white, arranged in groups, lines, or ripples (cirrocumulus).
   4. Large balls, like white cotton, also in groups, lines or waves (altocumulus).
   5. Thick ashy or blue-gray sheets (altostratus).

C. LOW CLOUDS: UNDER 3200 METERS (10,000 FEET)
   6. Large balls or rolls of gray cloud masses (stratocumulus).
   7. Torn sheets of gray clouds from which rain usually falls (nimbostratus).
   8. Sheets of the fog lifted no more than 3,000 feet off the ground (stratus).
   9. "Scuds" or detached fragments of nimbostratus or cumulonimbus clouds, usually traveling rapidly at low altitudes.
   10. Stratus clouds broken up into shreds by the wind or by mountain tops (fractostratus).

*Adapted from H.H. Clayton, World Weather (New York: Macmillan, 1933).

D. CLOUDS OF THE CLIMBING CURRENTS OF AIR:
1,650 to 8,300 METERS (5,000 TO 25,000 FEET)
ABOVE THE EARTH

11. Piled clouds like huge banks of snow or wool *(cumulus)*.
12. Thundershower clouds, often piling to tremendous heights into the sky and ominously dark below *(cumulonimbus)*.
13. Tattered cloud pieces torn by wind from the top or bottom of cumulus clouds *(fractocumulus)*.

E. UNUSUAL CLOUD FORMS

14. A series of cloud bands or billows with intervening strips of blue sky *(billow clouds)*. (A type of *cirrus* or *cirrocumulus*.)
15. A lens-shaped cloud formed by the upward deflection of air by mountain peaks on their leeward sides *(lenticular cloud)*.
16. A long cloud covering the crest of a long mountain *(crest cloud)*.
17. A white cloud banner floating from a high mountain peak, often made of snow particles *(banner cloud)*.
18. A convex cirruslike cloud forming on the upper surface of a rapidly mounting cumulus cloud *(scarf cloud)*.
19. Wind-blown cirruslike streamers combed out of the tops of cumulonimbus *(false cirrus)*.
20. A cumulus cloud with bumps or sacklike projections extending from its bottom *(mammatocumulus)*.
21. Numerous castlelike forms on the tops of cumulonimbus *(cumulo nimbuscastellatus)*.
22. Funnel-shaped cloud, whirling at a tremendous speed *(tornado)*.

CLOUD WEATHER SIGNS

The following cloud signs tell us about the weather:

1. Cirrostratus clouds usually mean rain is coming. If either the sun or the moon shows a halo, that is a sign of cirrostratus clouds high in the sky.

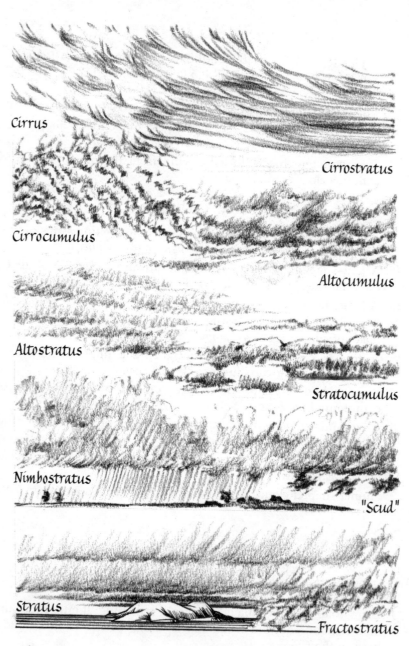

Cirrus

Cirrostratus

Cirrocumulus

Altocumulus

Altostratus

Stratocumulus

Nimbostratus

"Scud"

Stratus

Fractostratus

14-2. Cloud forms: typical examples of main types — drawn

Cumulonimbus

Cumulus

Fractocumulus

from nature and modified from U.S. Weather Bureau photos.

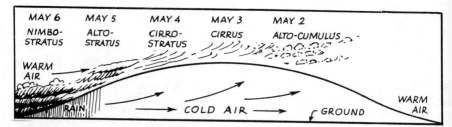

Fig. 14-3. *The coming of a storm. Read signs of its coming from right to left of the drawing. From Vinson Brown,* How to Explore the Secret Worlds of Nature *(Boston: Little, Brown, 1962), with permission of the author.*

2. Cirrus clouds usually mean good weather. Unless they begin to thicken; then they may mean rain.

3. Cumulus clouds also mean good weather. Unless they begin to increase in numbers.

4. The top of a great pile of white clouds far away on the horizon on a summer day. If this comes nearer and grows larger and darker, it means a thunderstorm is coming.

5. Stratus, or fog, usually does not mean rain. But sometimes it gradually thickens into *nimbostratus.*

6. The appearance of increasing stretches of blue between nimbostratus clouds. This usually means the end of a storm.

MAKING YOUR OWN WEATHER STATION

Meteorologists developed weather stations in order to get a picture of weather all over the earth over a period of many years. Only by doing this could the study of weather and climate in general become an exact science. Today amateur meteorologists who are ready to keep careful records of the day-by-day state of the weather in their neighborhood can be very useful to science. The information they gather goes into the tremendous store of weather knowledge that is building up a unified view of the weather and climate of all the earth.

To the naturalist whose primary interest may be animals or plants, developing a weather station may not seem very necessary. This is a mistaken idea. The weather has a tremendous effect on animal and

192

plant life. Many of the habits and instincts of animals and plants turn on the state of the weather in the region where they live. The cactus stores water in its leaves during the short rainy season on the desert so that it will have a supply during the long dry period. The coming of dew in the early dawn is an aid to keeping many animals alive during dry seasons. Rainy weather brings fungi such as toadstools and slime molds into their most active states; it also brings out frogs and salamanders and worms onto the land. Thus the knowledge of how to make and keep a weather station can be of tremendous value to the intelligent naturalist. As a matter of fact so little of this comparative nature work has been done that it is merely the beginning of a tremendously large and fascinating field of scientific study. Just what the effect of the weather is on plant and animal life is worthy of the study of every naturalist.

Making your own weather station is not only useful but fun. Even if you cannot afford to buy many weather instruments, you can still make a weather station. A rain gauge, a thermometer, a wind indicator, and some graph paper can be bought or made very cheaply, and these plus careful daily observation with your eyes and daily records of what you observe are the only basic requirements of an amateur weather station. Below we will discuss the main instruments used by a weather station, but remember that the above are all you need to begin. (See the discussion in Chapter Ten on how to make and use a graph.)

The National Weather Service will give you one requirement of a weather station, amateur or otherwise, and that is a *daily weather map* (see Figure 14-4). Write to the Superintendent of Documents, Washington, D.C., asking for information about a subscription to the daily weather map. This map will be sent to you daily except Sunday if you subscribe. The map not only gives you information about your local weather, but it tells you what is coming from 1610 kilometers (1,000 miles) or more away. It is also useful in that it can take the place of a barometer by giving you the day-to-day atmospheric pressure of your neighborhood. However, in this regard, you must remember that altitude makes a difference in such pressure, and you should inquire of the weather office regarding the variation in pressure of your home from that at sea level (see information about the barometer later in this chapter).

In Figure 14-4 you will see an example of a United States weather map. It is important for the naturalist to be able to read and understand

14-4. Section of weather map of the United States issued by the
WEATHER BUREAU

DAILY WEATHER MAP

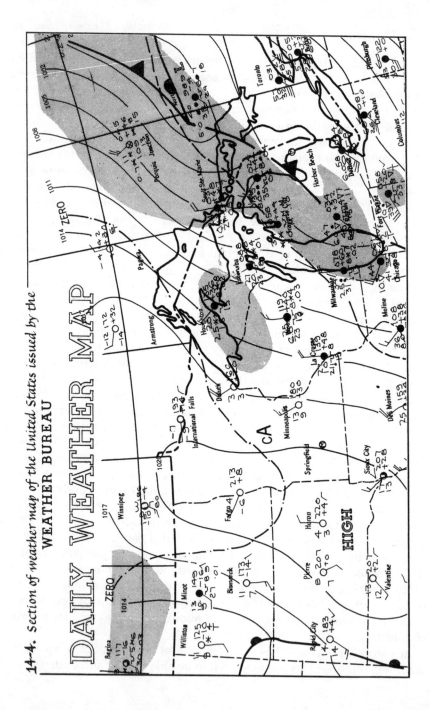

these maps. (Much information on how to read it is given on the map itself.) The first thing to notice is that there are two types of continuous lines on the map, isobars and isotherms. *Isobars* are the indicators of a continuous line of similar air pressure. The numbers on the isobars, 1020, 1023, 1026, and so on, refer to the number of a certain unit of air pressure called the *millibar*—1,000 millibars equals the amount of atmospheric pressure necessary to push a column of mercury in a glass tube 74.5 centimeters (29.53 inches) into the air. For practical purposes all we need to know about the millibar scale is that it shows the difference on the map between areas of high atmospheric pressure where there is usually good weather and areas of low pressure where the weather is liable to be stormy. Anything below about 1,020 millibars of pressure (at sea level) can be classed as low pressure, whereas pressure much higher than this would be classed as high pressure. A low of 990 or below would indicate a well-developed storm, while a hurricane or typhoon would probably produce a terrible low-pressure isobar of around 950 or even lower.

Isotherms are the indicators of a continuous line of similar temperature. These are dashed lines, and such a line marked "freezing" would mean that all along that line the temperature was at about 32° Fahrenheit (0° Celsius) at the hour of the day indicated on the map.

On the map you will notice that there is printed a *Beaufort Scale of Wind Force* and that little arrows on the map indicate the direction and force of the wind. Each barb on an arrow shows a Beaufort unit of wind force, so that an arrow with four barbs, for instance, would show a force of 4 or a wind speed of from 13 to 18 miles an hour. On page 197, is the complete Beaufort scale of wind force with observational equivalents so that the naturalist can intelligently record the force of the wind at his or her weather station each day. Admiral Sir FRANCIS BEAUFORT (1774–1857) introduced this scale of wind force in the middle of the nineteenth century and it has been a useful tool of weather scientists ever since.

A storm wind on the weather map would require an arrow with eleven barbs. It is fortunate that such arrows are rarely marked!

Weather symbols and abbreviations that are used on maps (some only rarely) are given below. These are also useful for your own notes and other records of daily weather conditions at your station. Study them carefully.

⋎ Aurora

O Clear

● Cloudy

Ω Dew

●° Drizzle

∞ Dust-haze

⚹ Dust-storm

≡ Fog

⚡ Gale

∼ Glazed frost

⩳ Ground fog

▲ Hail

⊔ Hoar frost

←• Ice crystals

↲ Lightning

Ⱳ Lunar corona

Ⱳ Lunar halo

⋈ Mirage

≡° Mist

◑ Partly cloudy

⌒ Rainbow

V Rime

☆ or ⑤ Snow

⊞ Snow on ground

⊛ Snow and rain together

↟ Snowdrift

△ Soft hail

◔ Solar corona

⊕ Solar halo

T Thunder

⍦ Thunderstorm

0 Unusual visibility of distant objects

≡⋮ Wet fog

♏ Zodiacal light

Aurora means dawn, usually a clear dawn. *Glazed frost* means frost that has become icy. *Hoar frost* is a frost that is white and fluffy, not icy. *Coronas*, both *lunar* (moon) and *solar* (sun), are rings of light, but they differ from *halos* in that they touch on all sides the disk of sun or moon, while halos form circles of light farther out, much like the rings of Saturn. A *rime* is a light frost. *Zodiacal light* is another name for the aurora borealis, or the mysterious display of northern lights that sweeps the sky during the dark winters of the Far North.

CLOUD NAME ABBREVIATIONS

1. *High clouds:* Cɪ.=cirrus. Cɪ.-sт.=cirrostratus. Cɪ.-cu.=cirrocumulus.

2. *Medium clouds:* A.-cu.=altocumulus. A.-sт.=altostratus. A.-cu.-Cᴀsт.=altocumuluscastellatus.

3. *Low clouds:* Sт.-cu.=stratocumulus. Mᴀ.-cu.=mammatocumulus. cu.=cumulus. Fʀ.-cu.=fractocumulus. Cu.-ɴɪ.=cumulonimbus. Sт.=stratus. Fʀ.-sт.=fractostratus. Lᴇɴт.=lenticular.

Use these abbreviations in your weather notes and save space.

Chart of Wind Force

Name of wind (Beaufort Number)	Kilometers (Miles) per hour		Effects shown on land
CALM (0)	0–1.6	(0–1)	Smoke rises straight up.
LIGHT AIR (1)	1.6–4.8	(1–3)	Smoke slowly drifts to show direction of wind, but wind vanes do not move.
SLIGHT BREEZE (2)	4.8–11.3	(4–7)	Wind felt on face, leaves rustle, wind vanes move.
GENTLE BREEZE (3)	11.3–19.4	(8–12)	Moves leaves and small twigs, extends light flag.
MODERATE BREEZE (4)	19.4–29	(13–18)	Raises dust and loose leaves, small branches are moved.
FRESH BREEZE (5)	29.–38.8	(19–24)	Small trees in leaf begin to sway, whitecaps form on lakes.
STRONG BREEZE (6)	38.8–50	(25–31)	Large branches start moving, wind whistles in telephone wires, hats liable to be blown off.
MODERATE GALE (7)	50–61.4	(32–38)	Whole trees in motion, you have to bow forward to walk in the wind.
GALE (8)	61.4–74.3	(39–46)	Twigs and small branches broken off trees, trees in violent motion.
STRONG GALE (9)	75.8–92	(47–54)	Shingles ripped off roofs, small trees knocked down.
WHOLE GALE (10)	93.6–100	(55–63)	Rare inland, large trees uprooted, walls blown down.
STORM (11)	101.6–120	(64–75)	Very rare, telephone poles and houses knocked down.
HURRICANE (12)	120 + (Greater than 75)		Wind so strong as to be impossible to stand against.

An interesting fact to notice about the direction of the wind on the weather map is that usually it points along the isobars when near a low pressure zone, with the area of low pressure always on its left. This is called *Buys-Ballot's Law* and is based on the contraclockwise motion of wind about a center of low pressure that we have already discussed.

TOOLS

1. *The barometer.* This is one of the weather forecaster's standby instruments. In Figures 14-5A and 14-5B, we see two types of barometers, the sea barometer and the land barometer. Both work on the

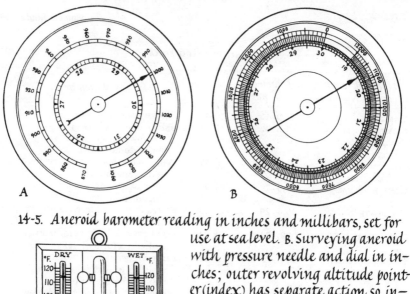

14-5. Aneroid barometer reading in inches and millibars, set for use at sea level. B. Surveying aneroid with pressure needle and dial in inches; outer revolving altitude pointer (index) has separate action so instrument can be set for a fixed altitude. (Dials modified from catalogs.)
← C. Dry and wet bulb thermometers. (You can make your own with 2 ordinary thermometers, muslin wick and water jar.)

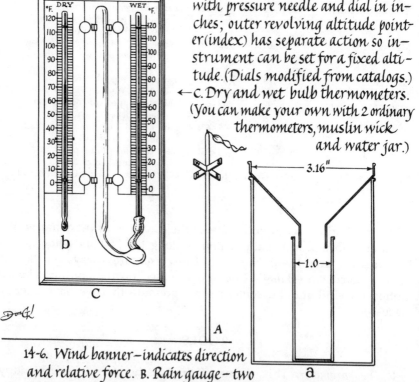

14-6. Wind banner–indicates direction and relative force. B. Rain gauge–two cans, and funnel with mouth 10 times area (3.16 times diameter) of rain-receiving can. Not shown: measuring jar, same diameter as small can, or stick, either one marked off in scale 10"=1.0".

same principle of recording the pressure of the air, but the land barometer is supplied with a scale and a second needle that can be set for any altitude above sea level. While the barometer in general is an indicator of fair and bad weather, this is not always so. Sometimes the needle of the barometer will stay in exactly the same position while a succession of rainy and sunny skies, of wind and calm, come. Many interesting studies could be made with the aid of a barometer on the effect of low and high pressures on animal and plant life. Three or even four observations of the barometer a day is the regular procedure at weather stations. However, the amateur may cut this to two observations, spaced about twelve hours apart. The barometer must be kept indoors in a place where the temperature is as constant as possible, as otherwise the mercury in the barometer expands or contracts too much for the readings to be very exact.

2. *The thermometer.* This should be placed outside in a place where it is protected from both wind and sun to prevent it from being too extreme in its show of temperature. It is more important in taking records from the thermometer to get the warmest and coldest temperatures of the day than it is to get the average, as these extremes of temperature are the ones that have the most effect upon life. One reading of the thermometer as early in the morning as you can, another about two or three o'clock, and a third around nine o'clock at night are the best times.

Most regular weather stations have two thermometers for recording extremes of temperature. One is arranged so that it pushes up a small marker as high as the temperature goes each day and thus gives an accurate measure of the highest temperature reached, while the other pushes a marker down to the lowest temperature reached. Such thermometers have to be set each day in order to get new records. A still further advance is to have a recording machine with a roll of graph paper on a drum where the record of temperature for every minute of the day is marked by pen and ink.

3. *Dry- and wet-bulb thermometers* (Figure 14-5C). These are necessary instruments for anyone wishing to get a record of the amount of moisture in the air and how near the dew or condensation point it is. The wet bulb is covered by a piece of muslin that is kept constantly wet by a dish of water in which part of the cloth hangs. The wet bulb is cooled by the evaporation of water from the muslin, being cooled most on dry days when there is much evaporation and least on damp

days. The difference in temperature between the two thermometers thus shows the amount of humidity in the air. Tables to help you find the percentage of humidity by this method can be obtained from your nearest National Weather Service, and also at some large bookstores. These two thermometers should be kept in a well-protected box mounted out-of-doors on posts. The response of animals and plants to variations in humidity is so great that a daily study of humidity in relation to the reactions of life can often show startling results.

4. *A hygrometer or humidity indicator.* This is used for the same purpose as the dry- and wet-bulb thermometers, but it is based on the contraction and expansion of a human hair and is not so exact in what it records.

5. *A rain gauge.* This is easily made and is very important. Figure 14-6B shows the construction of a gauge out of two cans, a funnel, and a jar marked in centimeters (or inches and fractions of an inch). The jar should be exactly the same size as the can that catches the rain. The whole gauge should be placed in a position where it is both shielded from too much wind and the danger of being knocked down and at the same time is completely in the open. Empty the gauge into the jar and measure the amount of water at a stated hour each day, marking the amount under the proper date in your weather notebook. A simpler rain gauge can be made out of a single wide-mouth jar, which is carefully marked for fractions of an inch or centimeters and is set out on a stand in the yard to receive rain.

6. *A wind indicator.* Your last necessary instrument. A well-constructed weather vane will do, but a banner of some light but stiff cloth, attached by loose rope to a pole (Figure 14-6A) is easier to make and will serve satisfactorily. As indicated in the figures, the base of the pole or axis in each case must be carefully marked with the true directions of the compass. As the needle of a compass does not usually point to the true north, but to the magnetic north, it is necessary in marking out your directions to make allowance for the compass variation in your part of the country. The compass variations for different parts of the United States are shown in Figure 14-7.

The wind indicator should be placed so that it is well above surrounding houses and trees, as otherwise it will not give a very exact indication of wind direction. As with the other weather observations, you should have stated periods of the day for observation of wind direction and force. Use the chart of wind force earlier in this chapter

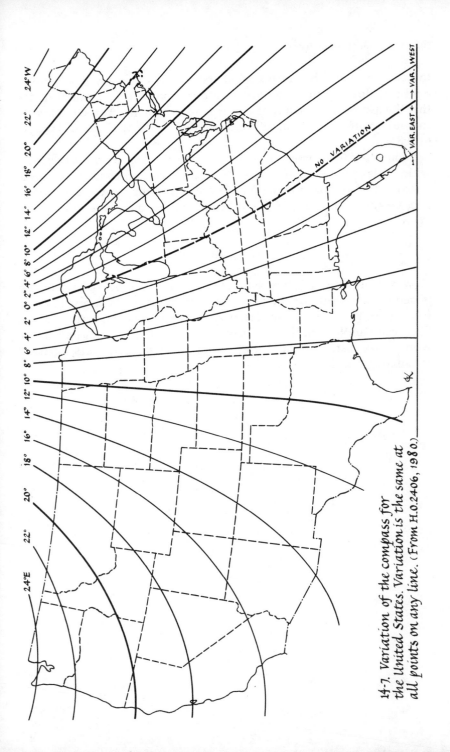

14-7. Variation of the compass for the United States. Variation is the same at all points on any line. (From H.O.2406, 1980.)

to help you mark the correct wind speed. Thus one day your banner might be flowing out in a northwest direction, and you would notice that the leaves and small twigs of trees were moving. You would write in your weather notebook: "Wind from SE, force 3, 12 noon, January 6, 1981."

Some other instruments used by a weather station are the *nethoscope*, which tells the motion of clouds; the *hyetograph*, which records the fall and duration of rain; the *sunshine recorder*; and the *anemograph*, which keeps a constant record of the direction and the amount of wind.

RECORDS

How would your day-by-day records of weather go? (See Chapter Sixteen.) Let us put our notes for a week period into the form of graphs (see Figure 16-1.) In Chapter Ten is an example of a comparative graph. Such comparative studies are becoming more and more a part of the work of the naturalist, and they are as interesting as working out a fascinating puzzle.

CHAPTER
15

The Student Ecologist

Natural history or biology is divided into three major divisions: *anatomy*, the study of the physical structure of animals and plants; *physiology*, the study of the functions and vital processes of organisms or their parts and organs; and *ecology*, the relations of animals and plants to their environment. As far as the amateur naturalist is concerned, ecology is by far the most likely field in which he or she will become involved, although a knowledge of the other two is vital to a well-rounded understanding of ecology. Ecology itself is so complex and so involved that it even includes how the anatomy and physiology of an animal or plant reacts with its environment. It also includes several large divisions, of which *ethology*, the study of animal behavior (see Chapter Twenty-One); *economic ecology*, or how to use our knowledge of ecology to help humankind economically; and *geographic ecology*, the relation of species to different geographic areas, are but a few of the divisions.

Later in this chapter is a simple beginning glossary to some of the more important-to-know ecologic terms and words, which you will need to study and learn carefully in order to understand how to work as an ecologist does. But before examining them, let us take up some beginning studies of ecologic niches, the basic units of ecologic work, and something we have already lightly touched on in Chapters One and Nine. Study the definition of an ecologic niche given in the glossary before you read what follows.

STUDYING A NICHE

The ecologic niche can be a fascinating world to explore and perhaps your first introduction to a genuine discovery of a hitherto unknown secret of nature. There are so many hundreds of thousands of species of animals and plants in this world that naturalists have so far explored the lives and ecologic niches of only a small percentage of them.

It is best to start with a comparatively simple ecologic niche so as to understand it thoroughly. In the first chapter of this book, we studied the niche where sheet-web spiders lived. But only two facets of the ecologic niche were touched on, the relation of favorable food-gathering places and the relation of the localities of the spiders on the cliff space to protection from the weather. But to understand an ecologic niche of one animal species as a whole, we need to study all possible facets.

Let us examine the niche of a water strider, or pond skater as it is also called. This insect, with its four strong rowing legs and its prey-grasping front legs, is especially adapted to live on the surface of the calm water of a pond, lake, or slow-moving stream. The surface film, which is like a very thin transparent skin on top of the water and is somewhat sticky in its action, is actually highly dangerous to most insect-size small land creatures and even to some water creatures if they get connected to it in the wrong way. It traps such insects so they may find it difficult or even impossible to get out of the water once they fall into it. The feet of the water strider, however, are coated with a water-repelling wax that enables these creatures to skate over the water surface somewhat like a human does with ice skates on ice. Ordinarily the water strider is kept on the upper side of the surface film by its wax-coated feet, but if a storm suddenly blows up waves or a rock is thrown to break the surface beside the water strider, it may be dragged under the surface and will drown. This is why captured water striders you are taking home to study in your aquarium should never be carried in jars filled with water. They soon drown.

It is very simple and easy to watch the water strider in the ecologic niche it occupies on top of the water, for it practically never leaves it. However, it can, if frightened badly enough, leap onto the land and run or jump quite nimbly across it to another stretch of water and so to safety. But the water surface is its niche and over this niche it is master in a very effective way, since the major part of its life is spent watching for or grabbing dead or drowning insects that become trapped on the water film or surface. Its eyes are especially adapted to catch the glitter of light that is created by such creatures on the water when they move their legs. The water strider grabs its victim with its strong front legs and thrusts its beak or spearlike proboscis or mouth parts into the insect so it can suck up the body fluids.

But this is only part of the water strider's relations to its environment or ecologic niche, and it is the total picture you need to see. Since it is much better to learn by experience than to be told, following are some questions that you should answer by your own observations and experiments, carefully recording everything you observe in your notebook. What are the relations between the sexes of this species? Usually you can tell the differences between them at the time of mating, and you should write down in your notebook any marks or body shapes that differentiate between them. Does the male or female or both guard a territory on the water surface into which they do not let other water striders enter? If so, how do they do this guarding? Are there any actual fights between individuals on the borderlines between territories, or does just the threat of a fight cause one to run away? (Remember that too much fighting would cause injuries and deaths, which might hurt the species.) What other insects or other creatures are there that live on or immediately under the water surface with whom the water strider comes into conflict? Describe the nature of this conflict and explain its effect on the water strider. How and where do females lay their eggs and how do they protect them from enemies? Do young, newly hatched water striders act exactly like their elders or do they have another way to live? What kinds of insects form the principle food of water striders on the pond where you are watching them? What enemies attack and kill or parasitize water striders and what are their techniques? To observe this, you may need to hide in a blind since birds or mammals will probably be too shy to come near if they see you. How do water striders escape from these creatures and how successful are they? There are other questions you can try to answer about water striders. Keep trying until you can give a fairly complete report on the life and ecologic niche of a water strider.

A plant can be watched even more closely than an animal to study and understand its ecologic niche, and it is wise to start such a study with a plant of limited distribution in one simple ecologic niche, such as a rock-dwelling plant like the rock lettuce. Perhaps the best way to begin to explore and understand the ecologic niche of a plant is to stake out three or four areas, each about 3 meters square, (3 square yards) in your neighborhood where this plant grows and keep careful records of growth, flowering, fruiting, seeds, and seed dispersal in all the areas, plus relations with other plants, population, soil types and conditions, and enemies or parasites that attack these plants, and what defense they have against them. Does either drought or too much water harm these plants in any way? Try to ask as many questions about the plants as you can think of, and then answer them by observation and experiment, putting down the records of your work in your notebook. One of the plants transplanted and placed in a similar ecologic niche in your home garden might also help you to find answers.

Other similar animals or plants to study who have simple ecologic niches include, among animals, the creeper, salamander, meadow mouse or shrew, and such reptiles as sand or rock lizards (see Figure 11-3), plus spiders or insects who dwell in one simple niche, such as the springtails that live in the soil or the orb-weaving spiders in their beautiful and prominent webs. Plants would be rock ferns, water plants on the edges of ponds, and eel grass on the edge of the sea.

A GLOSSARY
OF ECOLOGICAL WORDS AND TERMS

This glossary is only a beginning to the many words and terms that are vital to a basic knowledge of ecology. As you read further in this book you will find some of these words repeated, and you can refer back to this glossary for better understanding. Where necessary, illustrations help your understanding.

Aspection: deals with the yearly cycle of seasonal change and how this affects the activities, composition, and appearance of different animals and plants in a community. The aspects of the yearly cycle are *prevernal* (just before spring), *vernal* (springtime), *aestival* (summer), *serotinal* (the time of late summer flowering), *autumnal* (autumn), and *hiemal* (the coldest part of winter). (See Figure 15-1.)

Association: usually applied to the largest clearly separate divisions of a biome or a natural community, such as the Deciduous Forest Biome of eastern North America. The beech-maple association or the oak-hickory association are two such divisions inside this biome. An association usually has one or

Fig. 15-1. *The red fox varies its diet, especially with the change of the seasons. Although it has the sharp teeth and fierce disposition of the carnivore, it feeds, especially in summer and fall, on many plant products. (Based on Cook and Hamilton.) From Ralph and Mildred Buchsbaum,* Basic Ecology *(Pacific Grove, Calif.: Boxwood Press), with kind permission of the publisher.*

two clearly dominant plants to help distinguish it (see *facies* for a variation in such an association).

Biomass: the complete weight of all the individuals, plant and animal, in a specifically described territory, such as a pond, a deciduous forest of a given area, and so forth. The weight is usually determined by sampling from different sample plots what is found in each and then multiplying by the total area to get a fairly close estimate of the biomass.

Biome: usually defined as the largest community of animals and plants that takes on a distinct character over a large area, for example, the Needlegrass-Antelope Biome or Temperate Grassland of central North America, or the Spruce-Caribou (Northern Coniferous Forest) Biome in the northern part of the continent.

Biota: the complete animal and plant population of an area, as described and listed by species (taxonomically).

Characteristic species: an animal or plant that is usually always associated with a specific community, whether plentifully or less so.

Climax: the final community toward which all earlier communities, in a succession, tend to develop and which becomes the most stable (see *succession*); a climax species is one usually associated with a climax.

Coactions: interactions between individuals and species, generally causing some kind of physical contact (see also *reactions*).

Community: meaning similar to that of a *biota*, but a community gives the feeling of the dynamic interactions of associated individual plants and animals rather than just a taxonomic list of species present. It is better to use the word *community* to describe the total interacting life found in a specific area of naturally associated species than to use such a term as animal community or plant community, since both are always present together. Modern research of such plant and animal communities shows that each can be thrown into severe disharmony and even destroyed when humans interfere with community functions through a lack of wisdom.

Community development: means practically the same as *succession*, as a community develops through a series of stages (a sere) into a climax community.

Cycling of nutrients: in any ecosystem there is a cycling of nutrients (elements and compounds vital to life) through the interactions of plants and animals and of both with the sun, the atmosphere, the water, and the soil (see Figure 15-2). Plants, which are the *producers,* combine solar energy by photosynthesis with nutrients taken from the soil to produce food that is consumed by *primary consumers* (vegetarian animals) to give them energy. The vegetarians are eaten in turn by the *secondary consumers* (predators). All three—plants, and primary and secondary consumers—at death are consumed and decomposed by the *decomposers* (fungi, bacteria, and so on), who then return the nutrients to the soil for another round in the cycle.

Dominants: an example of a dominant plant is the ponderosa pine, which dominates large areas of coniferous forest in the West. The buffalo was once

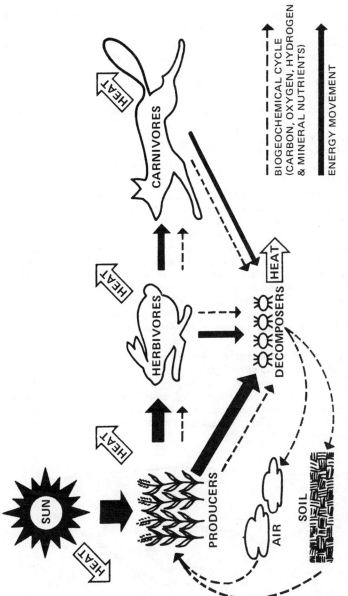

Fig. 15-2. *Cycling of nutrients as energy flow in the closed system. From Osborn Segerberg, Where Have All the Flowers, Fishes, Birds, Trees, Water and Air Gone (New York: David McKay, 1971), with kind permission of the publishers.*

an animal that dominated the Great Plains. But sometimes even a tiny insect can be a dominant, as when the spruce bud moth destroys large areas of spruce trees in the northern coniferous forest.

Ecologic equilibrium: a climax community is usually in ecologic equilibrium, meaning all species are pretty much in balance with each other and no one species is destroying too many of another. It is a dynamic equilibrium, however, with an ebbing and flowing of numbers of different species, but as part of a harmonious whole. Human beings have too often upset this equilibrium and produced erosion, pollution, and other signs of disharmony.

Ecologic niche: the place in its environment to which a species has adapted, or its living space (see Figure 15-3). Sometimes these niches are very tiny, including only one habitat, as with the water strider; sometimes they include many habitats, as with a fox or a mink.

Ecosystem: a combination of a habitat (earth, sky, water) with a plant and animal community. It can include other habitats and other communities as long as it has a somewhat integrated system, as is found in the deciduous forests of eastern North America. Ecosystems can be more or less stable. Denitrifying bacteria lose nitrogen to the atmosphere, but nitrogen-fixing bacteria capture it for the use of plants and animals. When nitrogen is added to the soil in greater quantities than it is lost by plants and animals, the habitat becomes more fertile, and there can be a succession of habitats richer in life (see *succession*). The sun is the great center of energy for the ecosystem, giving heat and life, which plants turn into carbohydrates through photosynthesis, while herbivorous animals, such as deer and

Fig. 15-3. *The desert-crested lizard* (Dipsosaurus dorsalis) *lives in sandy deserts and dunes where its ecologic niche is made up of its burrow, where the temperature is about 95 degrees in summer, and the surface sand and bushes where the temperature may be 108 degrees or more. The lizard usually comes out in the early morning or evening to hunt for insects. From Ralph and Mildred Buchsbaum,* Basic Ecology *(Pacific Grove, Calif.: Boxwood Press), with kind permission of the publishers.*

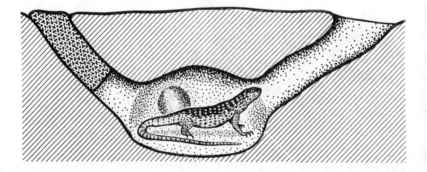

rabbits, convert the leaves, fruits, and seeds of plants into energy by digestion. Such elements and compounds as oxygen, carbon, nitrogen, sulphates, and so on, all vital to life, cycle daily between the habitat and its plants and animals. They appear first in the plants (producers), then in the vegetarians (*primary consumers*), next in the carnivores (*secondary consumers*), and last in the fungi, bacteria, and certain animals who convert dead things, both plants and animals, into energy and also clean up the environment, acting as *decomposers*, transformers or reducers. Energy flows through the ecosystem from the sun and eventually becomes lost to the atmosphere and so must be eternally renewed (see Figure 15-2).

Ecotone: a community that acts as a border or transition between two biomes or other large ecological units, a forest-grassland border, for example.

Faciation: a subdivision community of a climax biome whose species vary in appearance from surrounding areas of the biome.

Facies: similar to a *faciation*, except facies are found mainly as separate parts of communities that are developmental or on the way to becoming part of a climax. Thus the long-leaf pine forest of the Southeast, which is developmental toward the climax oak-hickory forest, might have a facies that would be a group of different trees found inside or on the border of the pine forest.

Flow of energy: the sun throws a tremendous amount of energy at the earth with its sunlight, but about 30 percent of this is reflected back into space, while nearly 70 percent is absorbed by the atmosphere and the earth. Only a tiny 0.1 percent is taken into the plants (producers) and used in photosynthesis, which produces the food eaten by the primary consumers (the herbivores), who become food for the secondary consumers (the carnivores). All three, when they die, may become food for, and be decomposed back into the earth by, the decomposers (fungi, bacteria, and such). This is the flow of energy as shown in the diagram (see Figure 15-2).

Food chains and food webs: a simple food chain occurs when a plant is eaten by a herbivore (rabbit) and then the herbivore is eaten by a carnivore (fox). More complicated food chains happen when four or more links appear in the chain, as when an algae is eaten by a paramecium in a pond, the paramecium is eaten by a rotifer, who is eaten by a small fish, who is eaten by a large fish, who is eaten by an otter (see Figure 15-4). A food web is a combination of the many food chains in a biome, such as a pond (Figure 20-6.) or a broad-leaf forest (see Figure 20-2).

Food pyramid: (see Figure 15-5).

Influence: how one species of animal operates to affect the activities and abundance of other animals.

Influent: major influent (see Figure 15-1) is an animal such as a bear or fox who kills sufficient numbers of other animals to influence their numbers significantly, or a very successful hunting bird such as a horned owl. Another major influent can be a small insect, such as a mosquito, who in vast numbers can drive other animals out of an area. Minor influents have less effect; possibly the largest minor influent is a porcupine.

Fig. 15-4. *Food chain: from one-celled plant to paramecium to rotifer to small fish to large fish to human. From Vinson Brown,* How to Explore the Secret Worlds of Nature *(Boston: Little, Brown & Co., 1962), with permission of the author.*

Life cycles and sensitive periods: understanding the life cycle of an animal or plant is important in the study of ecology. A tree such as a conifer has a comparatively simple life cycle. It simply grows big enough to form male and female cones, with the wind carrying the pollen from the male cones of one tree to the female cones of another tree to produce the seeds of a new generation, and eventually the tree gets old and dies. A broad-leaf tree has a more complicated life cycle, as every year in fall it must lose its leaves and go into a state of suspended animation before spring comes and allows the production of new leaves, plus flowers, fruits, and seeds. Some insects have very complicated life cycles, starting with eggs, followed by larvae, which pupate into a form of suspended animation that protects them through the winter. Then they appear as winged adult insects in the spring by metamorphosis, flying about to find their mates, fertilize the eggs, and then die.

Sensitive periods in life cycles appear when cold or dryness, or rain or snow, or combinations of these produce times in a life cycle when a species is in danger of dying unless it has the proper protection. Thus frogs and toads bury themselves in the mud of ponds and just barely stay alive during a period of long dryness. Insects and crayfish and other arthropods have periods in their lives when they change an old hard exoskeleton for a temporarily soft new one so they can grow. At such times they are vulnerable to enemies and hence have a sensitive period when they must hide until the new exoskeleton grows hard.

Life zones: the main temperature and plant zones on the sides of mountains, especially in the West, but have not been found to be very practical in the East and Midwest (see also Chapters Ten and Fifteen). In western mountains they tie in fairly well with plant and animal communities, with grasslands and lower deserts in California, for example, paralleling the Lower Sonoran Zone; chaparral and oak woodlands with the Upper Sonoran Zone; ponderosa pine forests with the Transition Zone; red fir forests with the Canadian Zone; white-bark pine with the Hudsonian Zone; and various low herbs and dwarf alpine willow with the Arctic-Alpine Zone (see Figures 15-6 and 20-4).

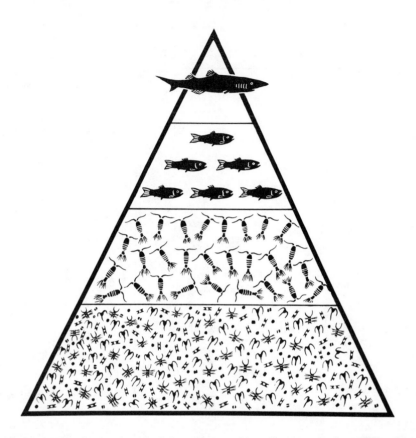

Fig. 15-5. *This food pyramid of sea creatures shows the quantitative relationship between different predators and their food, something that is not shown in a food chain or food web. From Ralph and Mildred Buchsbaum,* Basic Ecology *(Pacific Grove, Calif.: Boxwood Press), with kind permission of the publishers.*

Limiting factor: any factor in a community environment that limits some species from living there or in certain parts of it. Thus the great horned owl limits most species of small owls from hunting in open spaces in woodlands and forests where the great horned is dominant. The small owls have to stay close to thick tree cover for protection.

Master factors and paired factors: a master factor is one that dominates some stage in the life history of a species. For example, a certain plant may flower in early June because the amount of light and heat from the sun is such at this time that it becomes a master factor in triggering flowering. Paired factors occur, for example, when two factors such as temperature and relative humidity become just right for a certain wasp species to come out of its pupal case into the springtime.

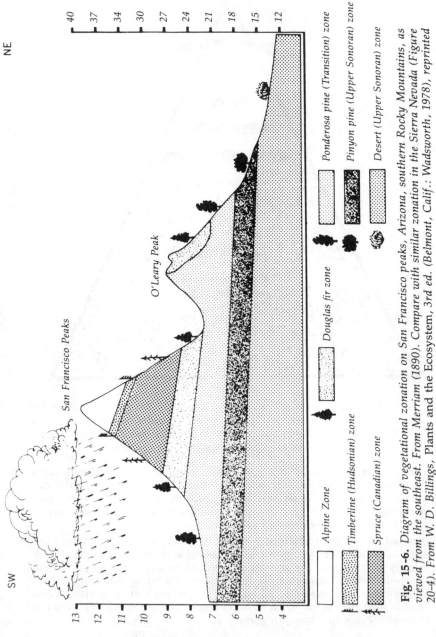

Fig. 15-6. Diagram of vegetational zonation on San Francisco peaks, Arizona, southern Rocky Mountains, as viewed from the southeast. From Merriam (1890). Compare with similar zonation in the Sierra Nevada (Figure 20-4). From W. D. Billings, Plants and the Ecosystem, 3rd ed. (Belmont, Calif.: Wadsworth, 1978), reprinted by permission of the publisher.

Natural communities: another name for *biomes*, as these are the large and medium-sized communities, such as grasslands, northern coniferous forests, and so on that are themselves divided into lesser communities and faciations (see map of North America, Figure 20-1).

Permeants: a name for animals that enter a climax and become part of its faciations or seral stages in their daily or weekly activities.

Population densities and distribution: distribution of the population of any given species of animal or plant depends on the factors that control it, and how these factors control it we can often determine by carefully studying its distribution and population densities. Thus the fact that the fireweed (*Epilobium angustifolium*) springs up over wide areas soon after fires have destroyed forests shows us that it is not limited by climate and that it is limited, as are a number of species of plants of this type, by an early seral stage in the development of a community caused by fire. On the other hand, the snowshoe hare is limited to living in cold and snowy coniferous forest areas where the climate suits its large hind feet, which can travel fast on snow, and its ability to turn white when the snow comes.

Reactions: the way organisms affect their habitats, as when a grizzly bear tears a boulder out of the ground to get at a ground squirrel, or caterpillars destroy a tree by eating all its leaves.

Sere: a succession of plant communities, one replacing another. For example, starting with bare rock and usually ending with a climax forest (a xerosere), or starting with the water of a bare pond and also ending with a climax

Fig. 15-7. *Succession in a lake or pond. From Leon Dorfman,* The Student Biologist Explores Biology *(New York: Richard Rosen Press, 1975), by kind permission.*

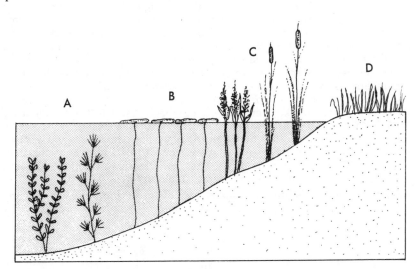

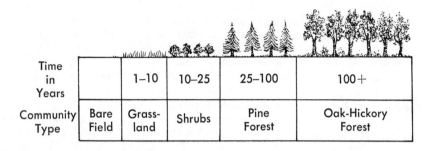

Time in Years		1–10	10–25	25–100	100+
Community Type	Bare Field	Grass-land	Shrubs	Pine Forest	Oak-Hickory Forest

Fig. 15-8. *Succession or successive stages of plant growth starting with an abandoned field in the southeastern United States. From Leon Dorfman,* The Student Biologist Explores Biology *(New York: Richard Rosen Press, 1975), by kind permission.*

forest that has filled in the pond by stages (a hydrosere). Most seres start from a higher point in the chain than bare rock, such as after a fire, flood, or a destruction by people (see *succession*).

Succession of communities (also called a *sere*): since plants long ago first invaded the land, there have been successions of plant communities from the beginning of bare rock up to the great climax forests on land (see Figure 15-8), or from a pond or lake of water without any life in it, perhaps just made by the gouging out of rock by a glacier, up to a pond lined with many kinds of water plants and full of rich fish and other animal life, to the final climax or end of a pond when it becomes so choked with plant life that it turns into land (see Figure 15-7). The kind of succession most commonly seen is the partial succession that happens after a fire or the clear-cutting of a forest by a timber company. In what was originally a spruce fir forest in the Rocky Mountains such a succession would be first grasses, then low shrubs, then large shrubs and small softwood trees like the quaking aspens, then pine trees, and finally the climax spruce-fir forest that may stay in balance for centuries if undisturbed. It should be pointed out, however, that succession is by no means always as simple and direct as described here, since some seres or communities may stay so long, due to the action of fires or other causes, as to become subclimaxes, not giving the true climax a chance to take over. (See ecology books listed in the Bibliography for further details.) Succession also usually includes a change in the animal life going along with the change in the plant life. Thus grassland animals such as jackrabbits give way by succession to tree squirrels as the trees grow, while grassland birds such as meadowlarks are replaced by thrushes, warblers, vireos, and others in a forest community.

Temperature and moisture, light and shade: the major limiting factors in any biome. Study constantly how they act on life.

CHAPTER

16

Continuing the Trail of the Naturalist

"I was wondering," said my beginning naturalist friend, "just what the field mice and the ants and other creatures that live in the ground do during rainy weather and what effect such weather has on their lives."

"I can guess," said I, "but my guess might be way off. Why don't you try to find out the real facts? This would be a scientific problem to solve."

The young naturalist ran off enthusiastically, but was back the next day with a quiet face.

"Well?"

"It's not so easy. It was raining today, and I dug up a few holes of field mice. The mice nests are dug back at an angle from the main tunnels so that the water doesn't get in there, and that seems to be where the mice stay when it rains. The ants are just down deep in the ground usually, under a rock or root. But I guess everybody who has studied these animals knows that. What I think needs to be found out is what long-range effect the weather has on both mice and ants."

"Why don't you find out?"

"That's what isn't so easy. I don't know how to go about it."

"Think of it as a problem. First, what do you want to find out? Write down as many questions as you can think of that need answering; then write down as many ways as you can think of to find the answers. Then come back and tell me what you've got."

My naturalist was back in a few hours with a smiling face.

"It begins to get clear. Here are the questions: (1) Do field mice and ants stay underground completely during rainy weather, or do they sometimes come out for food? (2) What is the difference in their activity during warm and during cold weather? (3) At what point of either wetness or coldness does their activity stop altogether? (4) What combination or what sequence of weather produces the greatest activity? (5) What effect does the humidity of the air have on their activity? (6) What effect does sunlight have on their activity? (7) What effect does wind, its direction and velocity?"

"Wait a minute," I said. "I thought you were just going to find out the effects of rainy weather!"

"I was, but I soon saw that all the effects of weather would have some influence on the animals and so all would have to be studied to find out the true effects of the one."

"Very good, but now how are you going to go about it?"

"First, I must set up a weather station in order to take accurate weather records each day, and then I'm going to take regular daily observations on the field mice and the ant nests during a period of one month. I'll take for study a certain section of tunnels of the field mouse, *Microtus*, that I know, and for my ants I'll take three nearby nests."

"Good enough."

My naturalist didn't hear me, but merely left some dust. There was much activity during the next week getting a weather station in order, so as to start out on April 1 with a whole good month for study. First, the naturalist fixed a tall pole with a banner on it to tell wind direction; then maximum and minimum thermometers. A wet-and-dry-bulb thermometer was too expensive, so a daily humidity record was obtained from the nearby weather bureau. For rainfall, a homemade rain collector and gauge did the job. To tell the force of the wind, the same idea was used as shown in the chart of wind force in Chapter Fourteen. For recording the amount of sunlight, a semiopaque screen was rigged up over a piece of blueprint paper each day. If the sunlight were very strong, the blueprint paper would entirely change its color when put in a chemical bath. If the sunlight were weak, the blueprint paper would keep much of its blue color. In this way, the naturalist could roughly judge the percentage of sunlight in any given day.

My young friend was out in the hills every day about 7:30 A.M. and then again at 4 P.M. to see the mice and ants, always carrying a notebook to make a careful record of everything seen. About the middle of April, I saw two pages of the notebook, which looked something like the samples below.

April 10, 1981

WEATHER RECORD: *rain off and on today, prec. 0.47 inch; sun. 0; rel. hum., morning 93, P.M. 77; wind dir. SE; w.f. 7 (mod. gale); max. temp. 52, min. temp. 42.*

MOUSE RECORD: A.M. *V.Q.* only 1 mouse seen; it ran out of 1 hole and popped down another, seemed quite bedraggled. Water was running into some holes. Dug up hole from which mouse came and found wet nest. Maybe weather forced this mouse to find new quarters.* P.M. *V.Q. No mice seen.*

ANT RECORD. *No activity at all today.*

April 12, 1981

WEATHER RECORD: *clear and sunny today; sun. 100% rel. hum., A.M. 51; P.M. 51; wind dir. N.W.; w.f. 4 (moderate breeze); mx. temp. 75, min. temp. 53.*

MOUSE RECORD: *Tre. activity today; mice constantly in the runways, apparently both visiting each other and foraging for food. Sitting quietly for about 25 minutes, I saw no less than 16 mice pass along a single runway. Saw what seemed to be a fight between a meadow mouse* **(Microtus)** *and a deer mouse* **(Peromyscus maniculatus).** *The meadow mouse chased the deer mouse in and out the little pathways and once or twice they clinched, rolling over and over fighting. The deer mouse ran away. Heard a slight squealing down one hole, and when I opened it up a little, found a mother meadow mouse and about*

---

*V.Q. meant very quiet, and, in the same way, the naturalist used Q. for quiet. Prec. meant precipitation or amount of rain that fell; w.f. meant wind force; and so on. Readers can probably figure out what the other abbreviations mean.

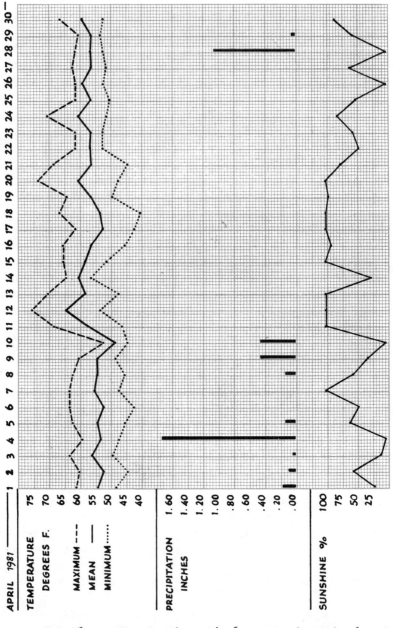

16-1. The amateur naturalist's graph of a month's observation of

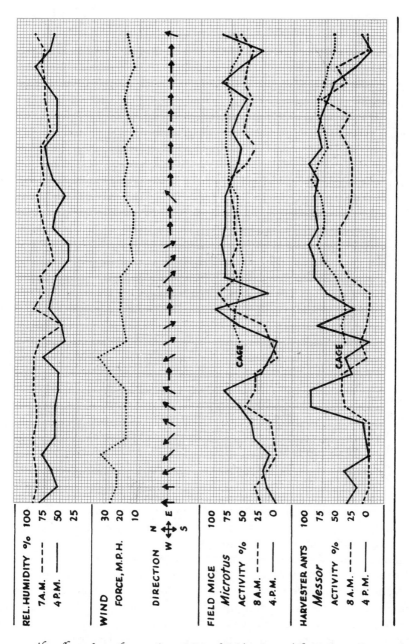

REL. HUMIDITY % 100 75 50 25

7 A.M. – – – –
4 P.M. ————

WIND

FORCE, M.P.H. 30 20 10

DIRECTION

N
W ⟷ E
S

FIELD MICE
Microtus

ACTIVITY % 100 75 50 25 0

8 A.M. – – – –
4 P.M. ————

CAGE

HARVESTER ANTS
Messor

ACTIVITY % 100 75 50 25 0

8 A.M. – – – –
4 P.M. ————

CAGE

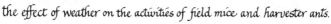

the effect of weather on the activities of field mice and harvester ants.

221

eight hairless, pink-skinned babies that she had brought near the entrance to get some sun.

Ant Record: *Also great activity today. All three ant nests swarmed with ants, most working at clearing away debris brought by the rain, some of which stuff had blocked some of the holes. In the afternoon lines of ants were busy bringing fresh grass blades into the nest; a few brought seeds and pieces of dead last-year's grass. The pieces of green grass were cut very small. All the ants seemed to have a more vibrant life than usual; they moved about much more quickly than on colder days. When I put a red and black ant* (Fusca) *in the nest the black harvester ants* (Messor) *attacked it quickly, although they were much too clumsy to catch the more active red and black. Many ants would stop work for a minute to stand on their four hind legs and scrape their head with their front legs at the same time lifting their bodies slightly toward the sky as if they were getting some sort of enjoyment out of the sunlight and the warmth and purity of the air.*

A few days later I went over to my friend's laboratory and was shown a strange cage in the garden. It was very long and very narrow and one side was made of a strip of glass. This glass, however, was covered with a piece of black cloth. The cage was full of about 20 to 25 centimeters (8 to 10 inches) of dirt. When the cloth was removed, I could see a pair of quivering field mice in an underground nest next to the glass. They both ran away through tunnels that led the length of the glass, but hardly anywhere were they able to get completely out of sight.

"What's the idea?" I asked.

"Well," said my naturalist, "it was a nuisance to have to dig up field mouse nests all the time to see what the mice were doing underground, so I rigged up this contraption to help me watch their underground activities. I've got an ant nest like this, too, for the harvester ants." Nearby was a still stranger device made out of two sheets of glass in a wooden frame, also covered with black cloth, and attached to a wooden platform surrounded by tin walls. This was a homemade ant nest rigged up so that the ants could be watched underground when the cloth was removed and they could also be fed comfortably aboveground on the platform. The black cloth gave the feeling to both the ants and the mice that they were in safe darkness.

"If," said my inventive friend, "I could fix up some kind of light at night that wouldn't bother these creatures, red light for instance, then I could watch their activities and know that they were acting perfectly natural. Do you think it worth trying?"

"Anything like that is worth trying."

The young naturalist by no means gave up the studies of the ants and mice in the field, but now had a check on their activities at home as well. It was such an interesting problem that I am afraid more time was spent watching the ants and mice than anything else! At the end of the month, the naturalist came over with a chart (see Figure 16-1), which shows the results of the project. You will see that this chart really tells a story about life activity, and that, after all, is just about what any naturalist is always trying to do—trying to find out the true story of each of the various activities of nature. Since there is an uncounted number of such stories, the naturalist's work is never ended and probably never will be.

(NOTE: *A good test for amateur naturalists who read this is to turn back to the questions listed at the beginning of this chapter and see what answers you can get out of the completed graph that our naturalist friend made. Remember that* all *the answers can be found in the graph.)*

DIVISION
III

THE ADVANCED NATURALIST

There is something very satisfying about coming to grips with a problem and conquering it. It is similar to the feeling the mountain climber has when finally scaling the high peak that he or she has set as a goal. It is this ability of humans to make goals for themselves and then strive through thick and thin to reach them that, above everything else, sets them apart from the beasts. It is said on good authority that a human can track and run down eventually any other mammal on earth. In the end, because of that unique virtue called "determination," a human can out-tire and out-fight even the grizzly bear or the tiger or the elephant.

In the pages that follow are some big tests of your "determination." It is time to begin to find your goals, to start to bring your work into focus, and to make each thing you do count toward those goals. One goal over which there can be no argument is your first one, and that is to lay a firm groundwork of knowledge. Your other goals are up to you personally. But even to lay that groundwork of knowledge, you have a big task ahead. You have a start, it is true, but the way a naturalist looks at it, this is one goal you never quite reach. The work goes on and on and on. However, it can be guaranteed to make life interesting for all your years.

"Interesting? Why?" you ask.

Out of the past a great naturalist answers that question; a naturalist who, at the age of twenty-one, wrote a book on the fishes of Brazil; who, a little later, climbed more of the Alps than had any other person, to prove the great **theory of the glacial ages;** *who started and personally directed the Museum of Comparative Zoology at Harvard University; who did more to start and spread an interest in nature study in the United States than any man or woman before or since; and whose other numerous activities as a naturalist would each alone be a key to greatness.*

"They gave me but one lifetime," one can hear Louis Agassiz cry, "when I needed ten! Oh, to live again and again, to see the Harvard Museum finished, to search once more for the inner secrets of the mountains, to study life on the teeming Amazon, to study the life beneath the sea and along its shores! I have only done a day's work of the years I want to do; I have learned only a sand grain of the dunes of knowledge there is yet to know."

CHAPTER
17

The Classification and Special Study of Animals

THE ANIMAL KINGDOM

Theodore O. Zschokke, or Ted or Toz as I variously called him, was the first to open my eyes to some of the rare joys of the naturalist. We two young fellows spent a summer together broiling in the 110° heat of the Colorado Desert (in Southern California). Although we were both very poor and our meals together would turn up a good cook's nose, those days were among the richest of our lives. Ted had a neat little laboratory filled with cheap insect boxes, vials, bottles, and small cages, and to this day I cannot smell the odor of formaldehyde or para-di-chloride of benzine crystals without sharply remembering those keen, exciting days and nights in the midst of the desert.

Ted is quite a small man and that summer he was suffering from some of the effects of tropical dysentery, caught in Panama. So he couldn't get around very much, but we found more than enough interesting things to watch and do right around our cabin. Most of the days, of course, it was so hot that we would simply put on swimming trunks and lie in our hammocks with a handy hose near, running water, and there we would carry on tremendous discussions about everything under heaven. But our day would not really begin until evening, for then it was that the desert itself came awake. And how it woke! Coyotes howled and yapped up toward the blue bulk of Mount San Jacinto, and desert foxes gave their shrill, sharp barks among the mesquite bushes. Some evenings we would set up a bright light by the laboratory, and out of the soft darkness would come the strange winged creatures of the night; giant pine beetles of the genus *Prionus;* ichneumon flies, those slender-bodied parasites of the little world; moths with velvet wings; and June bugs, whirring in blindly to bang against the wall. Toads came hopping from the shadows to feast on the dazzled insects, and grasshopper mice darted at incredible speed along the very rim of gloom.

"Each of these creatures," said Ted, "is a bundle of terrifically complex factors. Take that ugly toad crouching by the faucet. About eight hundred million years have made it what it is today. A careful study of the toad's life would tell us many fascinating things about its inheritance. It is a conservative. More virile, adventuresome animals have found more successful ways to live, have spread themselves over a vaster territory, and have learned how to conquer a battery of adverse circumstances. The old toad is much as its ancestor was tens of millions of years ago. It seems to have learned little that is new. But it gets along, because long ago its ancestors discovered two very effective ways of dealing with the dangers of existence, and the toad is satisfied with them. First, if it gets too cold or too dry, it buries as deep as it can in the earth and goes into a kind of stupor, a deathlike life from which very little energy is lost, and from which it is ready to rise when the right conditions for activity return. Second, it is attacked and eaten by few animals because on the back of the toad's neck are glands that secrete an evil-tasting fluid that makes its flesh unpalatable. So it is an ugly, clumsy old creature, easy to catch and destroy, but hardly worth anybody's trouble since it can't be eaten.

"But observe the cunning and skill of the toad's insect collecting. There it sits, apparently hardly more than a brown lump of dirt on the ground, but, when an unsuspecting plant bug buzzes near, its curious hinged tongue unfolds into the air with lightning speed, and the bug is caught on its sticky end to be whisked immediately inside that cavernous mouth. The toad's whole life, conservative or not, is thus an example of marvelous adaptation. It is a machine presenting a thousand phases for study. And yet it is an individual. Watch it jump when compared to that of the toad over there by that mimosa. There *is* a difference. If you look closely, you cannot deny it. The other toad moves less clumsily; its leap is longer. Look at the way they catch flies. See, the one pretends that it is asleep; the other keeps its eyes open. Even these creatures learn from experience; their lives are not all run by instinct, even if they are born without the protection of a mother. And instinct itself, that marvelous aid to living that nature has given to the lesser animals, is it not worthy of earnest study in its own right? What are the instincts of the toad? We talk glibly of its mostly instinctive reaction, but where in the toad do instincts end and habits begin?

Ted's mind probed and searched into the nature of each creature that we saw. I came to believe with him that treasures of knowledge lay waiting all around us for intelligent discovery, in the forms that scuttled through the mimosa clumps, in the eyes that glittered at the end of our flashlight beam, even in the leaves of the cacti where the plants silently struggle to keep the water the rare rain brings them against the fierce pull of the sun. No longer was a beetle simply a "bug"; it was a subject as filled with mystery and meaning as the eyes of the sphinx; every piece of its armored body wove a part of the story from its billion-year past; and the very scent cells of its antennae vied in complexity and interest with the internal design of an ocean liner.

On moonlit evenings we wandered out into a desert where time might have stood still for all the influence humans seem to have had on those cactus thickets and the wavy stretches of wind-blown sand. We would crouch silently by some hillock of mesquite and watch and listen. Then would come the little creatures of the night; jumping mice and rats darting, leaping from hole to hole; bats flitting softly along the tenuous highways of the air; and tiny shrews threading through the grass stems, as fierce and secretive as miniature panthers. We heard the thumping of the jumping rats, drum signals of some underworld, and watched their fights, savage kicking affairs beneath the moon.

"You see," said Ted, "the things that people miss who have never learned to sit quietly in the country dark and patiently wait the coming of life."

Life was indeed rich to the naturalist on those long warm summer evenings in the desert. And life is rich to the naturalist anywhere he or she may go, for the naturalist has the privilege to read, out of all things both small and large, the message and the wisdom of the world. Animals, as we have seen in Chapter Eleven, are divided by zoologists into great divisions, or phyla. It is wise for us at this point to get a bird's-eye view of the animal kingdom as a whole, and for this purpose the outline below, which classifies the kingdom down through phyla and classes, seems the best plan. With a few rare exceptions, any animal you might find on earth will fit somewhere into these great divisions. Because of this, you can use this outline as your beginning key to the animal kingdom. When you find some animal whose position in life puzzles you, turn to this outline and trace it down to its proper classification. You can naturally do this much more easily if you thoroughly familiarize yourself with the chart, particularly becoming well enough acquainted with the phyla so that you can immediately turn to the right one for whatever specimen you have started to classify.

It is wise to remember, however, that this outline is made by humans, and therefore is subject to the mistakes humans sometimes make. For instance, certain classes grade so gradually into other classes that it is difficult to place your finger on the exact dividing line. In others the line of evolution is so confused or still so little known that animals now listed in such classes may be shifted to different classes as knowledge grows. If these facts are remembered, the chart can still be used by a naturalist as a very effective working tool. Later in this chapter we will go somewhat into the subject of "keys" to the finer divisions of animal life, the families, genera, and species. But now, use and study the outline to get a picture of animals as a whole. More than a million different species of animals have been described.

AN OUTLINE OF THE PHYLA AND CLASSES
OF ANIMALS (FIGURES 17-1 TO 17-50)

Sub-kingdom PROTOZOA. One-celled animals.

Phylum SARCODINA. *Amoeba*, etc. Protozoa that move by means of false feet, or pseudopodia.

Phylum MASTIGOPHORA. Protozoa that move by means of flagella, a kind of whipping tail. This phylum includes curious animals (*Euglena*) that could almost be called plants, since they have green chlorophyll and can manufacture their own food.

Phylum SPOROZOA. *Monocystis,* etc. Protozoa without moving parts (flagella, feet, cilia, etc.), but with a spore (round, shell-like) stage in their life cycle. The hard quiet spore stage gives these strange creatures a chance to live through very dry conditions when they otherwise might die.

Phylum CILIATA. *Paramecium,* etc. Protozoa that move by means of cilia (oarlike projections from their cell walls).

Sub-kingdom METAZOA. Many-celled animals.

Phylum PORIFERA. Sponges. Animals with only two cell layers; no appendages (legs, tentacles, etc.).

Class I.
CALCISPONGIAE. Calcareous sponges. *Leucosolenia,* etc. Mostly marine shallow water sponges made up of calcareous (lime) spicules (the bonelike structure that make up the skeleton).

Class II.
HEXACTINALLIDA (or Hylaospongiae). Glass sponges. *Euplectella,* etc. Mostly deep-sea sponges with siliceous (silica, as in quartz) spicules, arranged like six rays.

Class III.
DEMOSPONGIAE. Common sponges. *Tethya, Cliona, Haliclona,* etc. Common sponges, often massive and brightly colored, with complicated canal system connected with small, spherical, flagellate chambers (see Figure 17-7). Spicules siliceous, but rarely with six rays.

Phylum COELENTERATA. Simple water animals with only two cell layers and having nematocysts (small, stinging, explosive barbs) for protection and aggression. Includes jellyfish, sea fans, hydras, sea anemones, etc.

Class I.
HYDROZOA. *Hydra,* etc. Almost all colonial animals. The polyps (stationary tentacle-bearing forms) give rise by budding to free or clinging medusae (tiny jellyfishlike forms) with a velum (mouth) and a nerve ring.

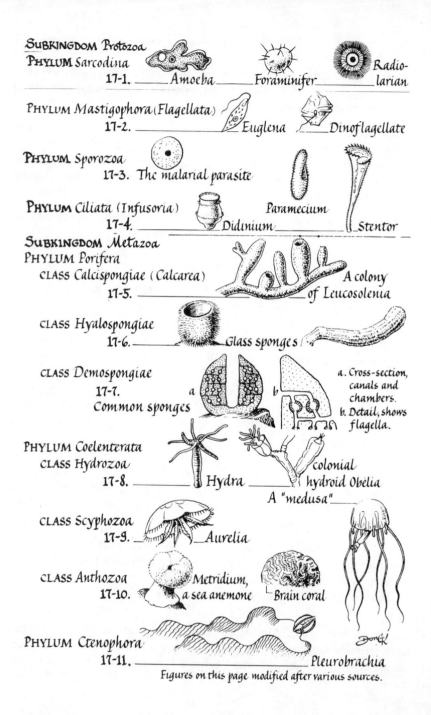

SUBKINGDOM Protozoa
PHYLUM Sarcodina
17-1. _____ Amoeba _____ Foraminifer _____ Radio-larian

PHYLUM Mastigophora (Flagellata)
17-2. _____ Euglena _____ Dinoflagellate

PHYLUM Sporozoa
17-3. The malarial parasite

PHYLUM Ciliata (Infusoria)   Paramecium
17-4. _____ Didinium _____ Stentor

SUBKINGDOM Metazoa
PHYLUM Porifera
  CLASS Calcispongiae (Calcarea)
  17-5. _____ A colony of Leucosolenia

  CLASS Hyalospongiae
  17-6. _____ Glass sponges

  CLASS Demospongiae
  17-7.   a   b   a. Cross-section, canals and chambers.
  Common sponges   b. Detail, shows flagella.

PHYLUM Coelenterata
  CLASS Hydrozoa
  17-8. _____ Hydra _____ colonial hydroid Obelia

                    A "medusa" _____
  CLASS Scyphozoa
  17-9. _____ Aurelia

  CLASS Anthozoa
  17-10. _____ Metridium, a sea anemone _____ Brain coral

PHYLUM Ctenophora
17-11. _____ Pleurobrachia

Figures on this page modified after various sources.

Class II.

SCYPHOZOA. *Aurelia,* etc. Most of the larger jellyfish belong here. The umbrella is notched.

Class III.

ANTHOZOA. *Metridium* (the sea anemone), *Astrangia* (coral polyps), etc. Solitary or colonial coelenterates with a polyp stage but no medusae.

Phylum CTENOPHORA. Comb jellies. Jellylike animals with 8 rows of ciliated swimming plates. No nematocysts. Live in salt water.

Phylum PLATYHELMINTHES. Flatworms. An aceoelomate, which means it has no distinct body cavity. Usually nonsegmented, free-living, or parasitic worms with bodies generally flat in shape; alimentary canal not complete.

Class I.

TURBELLARIA. Mostly free-living (nonparasitic) worms. Body covered with cilia; suckers usually absent. Found under stones in brooks and ponds; some forms marine (in the ocean).

Class II.

TREMATODA. Parasitic worms. No cilia in adult, but a skin is present. Suckers on the lower surface of the body. *Fasciola hepatica* (the liver fluke), etc.

Class III.

CESTODA. Internal parasites of humans and other mammals. Very long, apparently segmented worms. Tapeworms of the genus *Taenia,* etc.

Phylum NEMERTINEA (or Rhynchocoela). Mostly free-living marine worms with flattened bodies. Alimentary canal (intestine) with mouth and anus present; a long proboscis or nose with sheath into which it can be withdrawn. *Prostoma, Lineus,* etc.

Phylum NEMATODA. Nematode worms. Unsegmented round worms, long and slender, with smooth and glistening surfaces. With intestine, but no proboscis. *Turbatrix* (the vinegar eel), *Ascaris, Trichinella* (the trichina parasite of humans and hogs), etc. Abundant wherever there is water.

Phylum ACANTHOCEPHALA. Similar to above, but with a spiny proboscis. The spineheaded worms. In ponds and streams; some marine.

Phylum ROTIFERA. Rotifers or wheel animalcules. Almost microscopic,

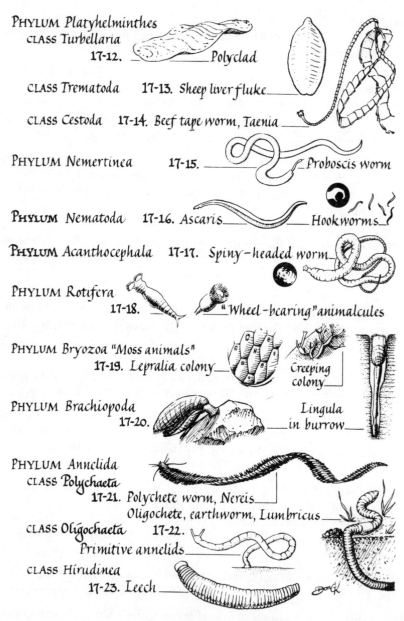

PHYLUM *Platyhelminthes*
 CLASS Turbellaria
  17-12. _____ Polyclad

 CLASS Trematoda   17-13. Sheep liver fluke _____

 CLASS Cestoda   17-14. Beef tape worm, Taenia _____

PHYLUM Nemertinea   17-15. _____ _____ Proboscis worm

PHYLUM Nematoda   17-16. Ascaris _____ Hookworms

PHYLUM Acanthocephala   17-17. Spiny–headed worm _____

PHYLUM Rotifera
       17-18. _____ _____ "Wheel–bearing" animalcules

PHYLUM Bryozoa "Moss animals"
       17-19. Lepralia colony _____   Creeping colony _____

PHYLUM Brachiopoda
       17-20.   Lingula in burrow _____

PHYLUM Annelida
 CLASS Polychaeta
       17-21. Polychete worm, Nereis _____
             Oligochete, earthworm, Lumbricus _____
 CLASS Oligochaeta   17-22.
       Primitive annelids _____
 CLASS Hirudinea
       17-23. Leech _____

Figures on this page modified after various sources.

cylindrical animals with crown of cilia (oarlike hairs) around mouths to draw food in. Numerous in the surface waters of oceans, lakes, and ponds.

Phylum BRYOZOA. Moss animals. Live in dense colonies, clinging to rocks, wharfs, etc., each animal with a chitinous-calcareous outer skeleton. Found in fresh and salt waters.

Phylum BRACHIOPODA. Shellfish or bivalves, with the valves (curved halves) of the shell dorsal and ventral (above and below) instead of lateral as in the mollusks (true bivalves). Mainly marine.

Phylum ANNELIDA. The segmented worms (body divided into small sections).

Class I.
POLYCHAETA. Marine worms, differing from other annelids by having paired segmented appendages (parapodia or "legs"), carrying projecting bundles of chitinous rods (the setae), which grab the surface on which the worm is crawling. The highly developed head usually has sensory projections and sharp jaws for feeding. *Nereis,* clam worm.

Class II.
OLIGOCHAETA. Fresh-water and land annelids. Differ from the marine annelids by having a simple lobe-like or conical perostomian (head) without sensory feelers. The body has no appendages except setae (hair-like structures) to aid locomotion, which is done by contracting and then extending the segments to provide movement: Aquatic oligochaetes are usually very small, less than 3 cm. (1¼ in.) in length. *Diplocardia,* an earthworm.

Class III.
HIRUDINEA. Leeches. Usually flattened annelids with two suckers, one in front and one in back. No setae nor parapodia. Parasitic worms that suck the blood of mammals, including humans. Common in warm streams and ponds and swamps. *Hirudo medicinalis* (the medicinal leech, which was once used in medicine to draw blood), etc.

Phylum ONYCHOPHORA. Strange many-legged, segmented, worm-like creatures *(Peripatus),* with a pair of antennae at the head. Legs are short and conical, and clawed at the end.

Phylum ARTHROPODA. The joint-legged animals. Crabs, shrimps, scorpions, spiders, mites, ticks, sow bugs, insects, etc. All possess jointed bodies and appendages (legs), except in some of the immature stages, and have an exoskeleton (a skeleton on the outside of the body).

Class I.

CRUSTACEA. Arthropods that mostly live in the water and breathe by means of gills. Crabs, lobsters, crayfish, isopods (pill or sow bugs), ostracods (tiny shellfishlike crustacea), and barnacles belong in this class.

Class II.

CHILOPODA. Centipedes or hundred-leggers. Wormlike arthropods with laterally flattened bodies and many legs, the front pair of legs each having a poison claw. There is one pair of legs to each segment. *Lithobius*, etc.

Class III.

DIPLOPODA. Millipedes or thousand-leggers. Wormlike arthropods with two pairs of legs to each segment, the bodies not so flattened as among centipedes. *Julus*, etc.

Class IV.

INSECTA. Insects. Air-breathing arthropods with their bodies divided into head, thorax, and abdomen, and with three pairs of legs in the adults. Often there are one or two pairs of wings in the adult stage. Complete or partial metamorphosis present in most orders. Found everywhere on land and in fresh water.

Class V.

ARACHNOIDEA. Spiders, king crabs, scorpions, harvestmen, mites, ticks, etc. No antennae, no true jaws, the first pair of appendages (legs) are nippers called "chelicerae," and the body can usually be divided into an anterior part, the cephalothorax, and a posterior part, the abdomen. Usually eight or more legs present.

Phylum MOLLUSCA. Snails, slugs, clams, oysters, octopods, etc. Unsegmented animals with soft bodies, though often protected by hard shells or a leathery skin. Usually possess a single large foot for locomotion, or this may be changed into tentacles for grasping prey. Mostly marine.

Class I.

AMPHINEURA (or polyplacophora). Chitons. These strange animals have a shell of eight transverse (crosswise) calcareous plates. They live on the rocks of the seashore.

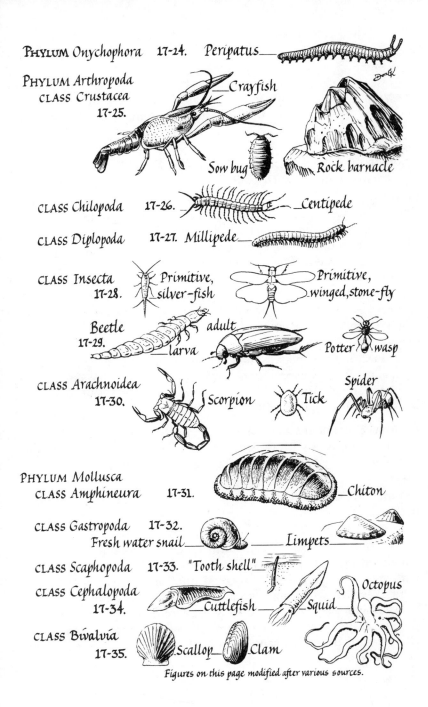

PHYLUM Onychophora   17-24.   Peripatus

PHYLUM Arthropoda
  CLASS Crustacea
    17-25.
Crayfish
Sow bug
Rock barnacle

CLASS Chilopoda   17-26.   Centipede

CLASS Diplopoda   17-27. Millipede

CLASS Insecta   Primitive, silver-fish   Primitive, winged, stone-fly
  17-28.

Beetle   adult
17-29.   larva   Potter wasp

CLASS Arachnoidea   Spider
  17-30.   Scorpion   Tick

PHYLUM Mollusca
  CLASS Amphineura   17-31.   Chiton

CLASS Gastropoda   17-32.
  Fresh water snail   Limpets

CLASS Scaphopoda   17-33.   "Tooth shell"

CLASS Cephalopoda   Octopus
  17-34.   Cuttlefish   Squid

CLASS Bivalvia
  17-35.   Scallop   Clam

Figures on this page modified after various sources.

Class II.

GASTROPODA. Snails, slugs, whelks, etc. Have a large foot used for creeping; a distinct head with eyes and tentacles. Usually a shell of one coiled piece is present. Mostly aquatic animals, though some live on land.

Class III.

SCAPHOPODA. The toothshells. Marine animals, living in tubular shells that open at both ends. *Dentalium,* etc.

Class IV.

CEPHALOPODA. Squids, devilfish, cuttlefish, octopods, and nautili. All marine animals. Have a well-developed head with large complex eyes (developed from the skin as opposed to nervous-tissue development of eyes in vertebrates). Shell found only in *Nautilus,* though some forms armed with a powerful horny beak. Part of the foot has grown around the head to form moveable, clinging tentacles, and the other part forms a muscular funnel or siphon, through which water is forced out suddenly to drive the animal through the sea.

Class V.

BIVALVIA (or Pelecypoda). The bivalve mollusks. Clams, oysters, scallops, mussels, shipworms, and cockles. Mostly marine animals with two-part shells. The foot is usually wedge-shaped and adapted for burrowing or clinging tightly to rock surfaces.

Phylum ECHINODERMATA. Starfishes, brittle stars, sea urchins, etc. Marine animals with radial symmetry (in the form of a circle with radiating arms) and a spiny skeleton. Bilateral in larvae.

Class I.

CRINOIDEA. Sea lilies and feather stars. Frondlike animals with branching arms.

Class II.

STELLEROIDEA (or Asteroidea). Starfishes and brittle stars. Adults many-armed with radial symmetry. *Subclass 1. Asteroidea.* Starfishes. Usually with five arms not sharply marked off from the center of the disk (central section). Live mostly on bivalve mollusks among the rocks of the seashore. *Asterias,* etc. Some with more than five arms. *Subclass 2. Ophiuroidea.* Brittle stars. Five arms sharply marked off from the disk. Often found buried in sand of beaches or among seaweed. *Ophiura,* etc.

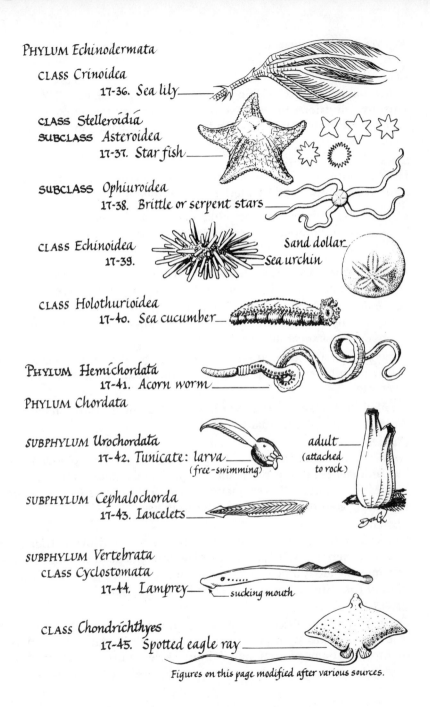

PHYLUM Echinodermata

   CLASS Crinoidea
          17-36. Sea lily

   CLASS Stelleroidia
   SUBCLASS Asteroidea
          17-37. Star fish

   SUBCLASS Ophiuroidea
          17-38. Brittle or serpent stars

   CLASS Echinoidea
          17-39.
          Sand dollar
          Sea urchin

   CLASS Holothurioidea
          17-40. Sea cucumber

PHYLUM Hemichordata
          17-41. Acorn worm

PHYLUM Chordata

SUBPHYLUM Urochordata
          17-42. Tunicate: larva
          (free-swimming)
          adult
          (attached
          to rock)

SUBPHYLUM Cephalochorda
          17-43. Lancelets

SUBPHYLUM Vertebrata
   CLASS Cyclostomata
          17-44. Lamprey
          sucking mouth

   CLASS Chondrichthyes
          17-45. Spotted eagle ray

Figures on this page modified after various sources.

Class III.

ECHINOIDEA. Sea urchins and sand dollars. Subglobular or disk-shaped with five divisions to the disk or body. The calcareous plates of the skeleton fit closely together, and are covered with movable spines. *Arbacia*, etc.

Class IV.

HOLOTHURIOIDEA. Sea cucumbers. Long and oval in shape with a muscular body wall and tentacles around the mouth. *Thyone*, etc.

Phylum HEMICHORDATA. Wormlike marine chordates with three body regions: a proboscis, a collar (around the mouth), and a trunk. *Glossobalaius, Dolichoglossus*, etc.

Phylum CHORDATA. The chordates. Animals with a nervous chord along the back, usually protected by some sort of bonelike structure.

Subphylum 1. UROCHORDATA (or Tunicata). Tunicates or sea squirts. Small marine animals with two openings at one end, body round and covered with a sheathlike tunic or test.

Subphylum 2. CEPHALOCHORDA. The lancelets. Wormlike marine animals with submarine-shaped bodies, and a caudal or tail fin. *Branchiostoma*, etc.

Subphylum 3. VERTEBRATA. Vertebrates. Mammals, birds, fishes, etc. Animals with a distinct backbone.

Class I.

AGNATHA (or Cyclostomata). Lampreys and hags. Cold-blooded, fishlike animals breathing by means of gills, but without jaws or lateral fins. Mostly marine, though many lay their eggs in freshwater streams, the young coming downstream later to the sea.

Class II.

CHONDRICHTHYES. Sharks, rays, and chimaeras. Cold-blooded, fishlike marine vertebrates with jaws, a cartilaginous (made of cartilage instead of bone) skeleton, a persistent notochord (primitive nerve chord), and placoid (primitive, flat) scales. They breathe by gills.

Class III.

OSTEICHTHYES (or Pisces). Fishes. Cold-blooded marine and fresh water vertebrates with jaws, and usually with lateral fins, supported by fin-rays (bony projections). A bony skeleton present. They breathe chiefly by gills, though lungs have been developed in a few species.

SUBPHYLUM *Vertebrata* (cont'd.)

CLASS *Pisces*
17-46.

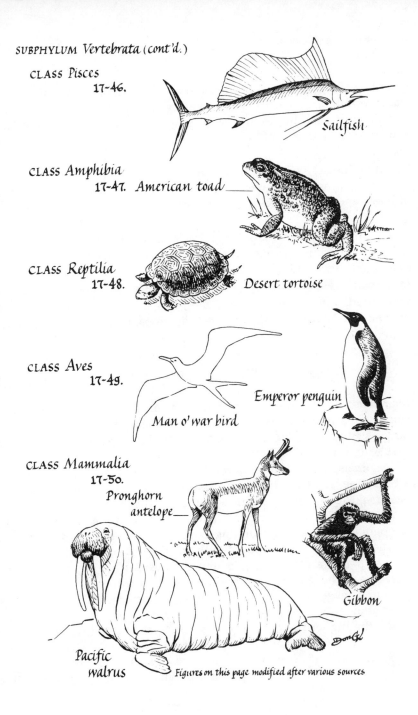

Sailfish

CLASS *Amphibia*
17-47. American toad

CLASS *Reptilia*
17-48. Desert tortoise

CLASS *Aves*
17-49.

Man o' war bird

Emperor penguin

CLASS *Mammalia*
17-50.
Pronghorn antelope

Gibbon

Pacific walrus

Figures on this page modified after various sources

Class IV.

AMPHIBIA. Frogs, toads, and salamanders. Cold-blooded, naked, fresh-water vertebrates, mostly with five-fingered limbs. Young usually aquatic and breathing by means of gills; adults usually lose the gills and breathe by means of lungs.

Class V.

REPTILIA. Turtles, sphenodons, lizards, snakes, and crocodiles. Cold-blooded marine, freshwater and land vertebrates breathing by means of lungs and usually having a hard, scaly skin.

Class VI.

AVES. Birds. Warm-blooded vertebrates, breathing with lungs, forelimbs modified into wings, and the body covered with feathers.

Class VII.

MAMMALIA. Hairy, warm-blooded vertebrates; the young are nourished (fed) after birth by their mother's milk from the mammary glands. Whales, seals, bats, rabbits, cats, dogs, monkeys, humans, etc.

LARGE LIFE ON LAND

Mammals, birds, and reptiles form the large life on land. Each, of course, is a tremendous field in itself, and this section is, therefore, only a slender introduction. Turn to the Bibliography for a list of books that go into more detail.

Mammals, birds, and reptiles are all vertebrates, that is they all have a backbone. Reptiles differ from the other two in having (at least the vast majority of them) a three-chambered heart and in being cold-blooded (their blood changes temperature with the change in the temperature of their surroundings). Also their bodies are protected by a scalelike covering as opposed to the feathers of birds and the fur and hair of mammals. Birds and mammals, besides having a four-chambered heart, have made the great advance of rearing and teaching their young, a level that only a few reptiles (some crocodiles and lizards) have attained and then only in a comparatively primitive way. Apparently, the higher the animal the less it depends upon instinct to save it from danger, and the more on teaching, brain work, and experience.

Soon after birth from its egg, a lizard or snake faces the world with a large set of instincts to help it in life. What is an instinct? An instinct is simply an automatic nervous reaction that requires no thought. To jerk your hand away from a hot iron is an instinct. You do not have to think before you do it. The lizard does not need to have a mother to teach it to run from its enemies; it is provided with the mechanism to run from enemies instinctively when it senses their presence. It also knows what to feed on and how to feed on it without being told. However, as the lizard grows older it does learn some things by experience: it learns where better feeding places are; it learns where the greatest danger is; it becomes more dexterous in catching its food. But not one of these things it has learned does it pass on to its offspring.

We can thus imagine a period of life that included more than a billion years of lost individual experience and knowledge. True, the knowledge of a species often grew in the development of its own instincts through the sheer destruction of the misfits and the survival of the fit, but it was a slow and agonizing process. The only way such animals overcame the tremendous destruction of their untaught young by enemies was by laying numerous eggs, thus assuring that at least some individuals would live to lay fresh eggs for the next generation.

Birds and mammals avoid this waste of life and talent by their ability to protect their growing young and to teach them the new tricks the grown-ups have learned. Humans went a step further when they invented writing, and so, for the first time in the history of life, made it possible for an entire species to pass on its collective knowledge to the next generation. The results are obvious.

Mammals are two steps ahead of birds. First, they overcome the unsheltered danger of eggs by giving their young a long start in life within their own bodies *before* birth. Second, they have developed mammary (or milk) glands, that wonderful adaptation that provides a readily transportable food for their young, thus enabling the babies to be under constant protection through the delicate stage of infancy.

Play is another thing that mammals have developed to a high degree. Although some birds have learned how to play, it took mammals to develop play into a truly great force for the improvement of the species. Watch a couple of puppies play, or young boys and girls; their sport helps to strengthen and prepare them for the troubles of life.

Each species of animal has developed habits and instincts peculiar to itself. Most of these are helpful to preserve its life, *but some are not.*

If too many are not, the species is liable to die off. The pronghorn antelope nearly got itself completely killed off by being too curious. Hunters would wave a red flag above a hillock and the pronghorns would come to see what it was all about, and then they would be shot. But many animals have developed new habits that are very helpful in keeping their species going. The mountain lion and the wolf, fiercely hunted by humans, have become extremely wary and cunning, traveling by night and avoiding all that smells of the human species. The lions of Central Africa have, within the last fifty years, learned to hunt the diminishing supply of game in packs instead of alone or merely in pairs as they used to do. Pack hunting has given them a great advantage over the game, as the lions have been able to spread out and then close in on a herd from all sides, thereby ensuring themselves some kills. Barn owls have so adapted themselves to humans that they take up nesting positions in many types of buildings and have even been found in abandoned attics in the midst of the largest cities.

It is this study of various habits and instincts in animals that is one of the most interesting parts of a naturalist's work, but before the naturalist can do much of such study he or she needs to know how to distinguish between various types of animals. In the Bibliography are listed books that will help you classify the birds, mammals, and reptiles of your neighborhood.

Here we have room for only a brief key to the more common mammals of the United States. However, this key (which you will find on the following pages) will serve as a sample and guide to keys in other books. Keys are indispensable to classification in zoology, and every naturalist needs to know how to use them. The key shown here has purposely been made simple so that it will serve as a stepping-stone to the use of more difficult keys. Study it carefully and you will find that it not only helps you to find the right name of an animal, but it also helps you to understand the relationship and differences between this animal and other kinds. Besides, using such a key is like working out a fascinating puzzle.

This key does not give the name and description of every mammal in the United States, but, as we have said, only the more common kinds—and often only the genus. Keeping this limitation in mind, nevertheless with the aid of this key you will be able to classify correctly at least as far as genus the great majority of mammals that are found in this country.

Let us suppose that while sitting somewhere in the country an animal comes so close to you that you are able to observe enough details about its appearance to write down the following report:

I saw a small animal, about 30 centimeters (1 foot) long, with a curved bushy tail, squat body, and fairly stout open claws. Its fur was mainly black, but with several broken white stripes down the back. The undersides were whitish. The black nose was sharp and the mouth, when opened, showed a comparatively small number of teeth, but with two strong canine (biting) teeth. It went about among some dead logs, turning the smaller branches over to nose for beetles and grubs beneath them. Once it caught a mouse.

Turn now to the key and look at the alternatives, 1 *a* and 1 *b*. The inner toe of the hind foot was "not thumblike" so far as you noticed, but the thing you are *sure* about is that the teeth were less than 50 in number. So you read on in the 1 *b* section and see that it tells you to turn to 2 for your next alternatives. You quickly see that 2 *b* is the right alternative here, because the feet of your animal are *not* "hooflike," but are "otherwise." You are told to turn to 12. The answer on this page is 12 *b*, because the forelimbs are "not modified to serve as wings." You are told to turn to 19 as your next guide. Here 19 *a* is correct because canine (biting) teeth are present, and so, as it says to, you look just below to 20. Since the animal you saw was at least 30 centimeters long, 20 *b* seems the right answer, and you are instructed by it to turn to 25; 25 *b* is definitely right, as the animal you saw had no fins, and this means you now turn to 27. It was not a dog or catlike mammal, and, while you aren't sure, you think there were 5 claws on the hind foot; so 27 *b* is probably right. This means you must turn to 36. As your animal walked on its toes instead of the whole sole of the hind foot, 36 *b* is right, and you turn to 39. The tail is not ringed with black-and-white bands; so this places your animal in the family *Mustelidae*, or weasels, coming under 40 immediately below. The tail is more than twice as long as the hind foot; so 40 *b* is the right turn here. You are told to look to 41 below. The color is black and white, as described under 41 *a*, and your trail is now definitely getting hot. So you turn to 42. As there were more than 2 stripes on the back, and the claws of the front feet were not particularly long and heavy, 42 *b* is right, and you have followed your quarry down to the last alternatives,

43 *a* and 43 *b*. There you find that 43 *b* is the end of the hunt. Your animal had more then 2 white stripes on its back and these stripes did not unite at the neck. This makes your small visitor a member of the genus *Spilogale*, a little spotted skunk.

Use this key with any American mammal you may encounter. Other keys may differ in appearance, but the fundamental idea is the same— turning to alternatives and following your answers down to the final one.

A KEY TO SOME COMMON MAMMALS
OF THE UNITED STATES

1 *a*.   Inner toe of hind foot thumblike and without a claw. Female with outside pouch on the abdomen for carrying young; 50 teeth. Order MARSUPIALIA (MARSUPIALS, pouched mammals). Family *Didelphidae*: opossums. *Didelphis virginiana*, Virginia opossum. Found over most of U.S. except far north.

1 *b*.   Inner toe of hind foot not thumblike; female without outside pouch on the abdomen; fewer teeth than 50.   **2**

2 *a*.   Feet hooflike. Order ARTIODACTYLA (hoofed mammals). **3**

2 *b*.   Feet otherwise. **12**

3 *a*.   Body form piglike. Family *Tayassuidae*. *Pecari angulatus*, collared peccary. Sharp 5 to 7.5 cm. (2 to 3″) tusks; stiff, bristly hair; musky smell; weight usually less than 34 kgs. (75 lbs.); U.S. and Mexico border lands.

3 *b*.   Body form not piglike. **4**

4 *a*.   Horns hollow and in bony sheath on the head (as in a cow). Animals not deerlike in form. Family *Bovidae*: sheep, goats, and buffalo. **5**

4 *b*.   Horns not so. Animals with deerlike form. **7**

5 *a*.   Males with spirally curved horns; horns brown or gray in color; body form sheeplike. Color brownish with white rump. Lives in mountains of the west, but not near the sea. *Ovis canadensis*, Rocky Mountain sheep.

5 *b*.   Males without spirally curved horns; horns usually black or dark gray; body form not sheeplike. **6**

6 *a*.   Horns curved; form very large and buffalo-shaped; color brown and gray. One herd in Arizona, one at Yellowstone National Park, a third at Wind Cave National Park, South Dakota. *Bison bison*, bison or American buffalo.

6 *b*. Horns black and straight; body form medium-sized but very powerful; body covered with long white hair. Lives in mountains of the West to the Pacific Coast. *Oreamnos montanus*, Rocky Mountain goat.

7 *a*. Horns, at least in males, many forked; horns not pronged or barely so. Family *Cervidae:* deer, elk, and moose. **8**

7 *b*. Horns forked once, pronglike. Family *Antilocapridae*. Color brown with light markings; rump white. Lives on western plains. *Antilocapra americana*, pronghorn antelope.

8 *a*. Adults very large animals, often as large as or larger than a horse. **9**

8 *b*. Adults not much larger than a good-sized sheep; form very slender and graceful. Genus *Odocoileus*, deer. **10**

9 *a*. Horns not flattened out and leaflike, but with narrow spikes. Powerful brown animals with white rumps. Live in western North America. *Cervus canadensis*, Wapiti, or American Elk.

9 *b*. Horns flattened out and leaflike. Color dark brown or black. Lives in forests of northern U.S., east of the Pacific Coast. *Alces americanus*, American moose.

10 *a*. Tail mostly black. Medium-sized deer; limited to Pacific Coast ranges and forests. *Odocoileus columbianus*, black-tailed deer.

10 *b*. Tail mostly white. **11**

11 *a*. Body form very slender; small or medium-sized deer. *Odocoileus virginianus*, Virginia white-tailed deer. Eastern U.S.
O. couesi, Arizona white-tailed deer. Arizona and New Mexico.

11 *b*. Body form stockier; large deer; tail tipped with black. Mountains of the West except near the sea. *Odocoileus hemionus*, Rocky Mountain mule deer.

12 *a*. Forelimbs modified to serve as wings. Order CHIROPTERA (bats). (Only commonest kinds.) **13**

12 *b*. Forelimbs not modified to serve as wings. **19**

13 *a*. Tail mostly free from the wing membrane. Family *Molossidae:* free-tailed bats. *Tadarida*, free-tailed bats. Southwest U.S.

13 *b*. Tail mostly joined to wing membrane. Family *Vespertilionidae:* most bats. **14**

14 *a*. Nose topped by a large horseshoe-shaped ridge. Color pale; ears

large. Mainly in southwestern U.S. *Antrozous*, pallid, or big-eared bats.

14 *b*. Nose not topped by a large horseshoe-shaped ridge. Color usually darker; ears usually not so large. **15**

15 *a*. Upper surface of wing membrane between hind legs partly furred. **16**

15 *b*. Upper surface of wing membrane between hind legs naked except for scattered hairs, or sometimes a little furred at the base. **18**

16 *a*. A large bat with total length more than 12.5 cm. (5″). Most of U.S. *Nycteris cinerea*, hoary bat.

16 *b*. Smaller; total length less than 12.5 cm. (5″). **17**

17 *a*. Color rufous red to yellowish-gray. Ranges over most of U.S. *Nycteris borealis*, red bat.

17 *b*. Color blackish-chocolate, often tinged with silver. Western U.S. *Lasionycteris noctivagans*, silvery-haired bat.

18 *a*. Total length more than 11 cm. (4½″). Most of U.S. *Eptesicus*, brown bats.

18 *b*. Total length less than 11 cm. (4½″). Range over most of U.S. *Myotis*, little brown bats.

19 *a*. Canine (biting) teeth present; more than 2 incisor (front) teeth in lower jaw. Meat-eaters. **20**

19 *b*. No canine teeth present; incisor teeth large and chisel-shaped; never more than 2 in lower jaw. Largely vegetarians. **47**

20 *a*. Total length of adults less than 30 cm (1′); eyes and external ears poorly developed; tail hairless or with few hairs; snout long and sharp; canine teeth little different from the other teeth. Order INSECTIVORA (insect-eaters). **21**

20 *b*. Total length of adults more than 30 cm. (1′); eyes and ears well developed; tail well haired; canine teeth large and prominent; snout not particularly long. **25**

21 *a*. Total length more than 10 cm. (4″); forefeet and claws made for digging. Family *Talpidae:* moles. **22**

21 *b*. Total length less than 10 cm. (4″); forefeet and claws small and not made for digging. Family *Soricidae:* shrews. **24**

22 *a*. With a fleshy, star-shaped protuberance on the nose. Central and eastern U.S. *Condylura*, star-nosed moles.

22 *b*. No fleshy, star-shaped protuberance on nose. **23**

23 *a*. Range west of the Sierra Nevada and Cascade Mountains; fur velvety and smooth. *Scapanus,* Western moles.

23 *b*. Range in the eastern U.S.; fur coarser and not so smooth. *Talpus,* eastern moles.

24 *a*. Body and tail slender and long; tail longer than 2.5 cm. (1″).
   (1) Hind feet broad and fringed with hair; colder parts of U.S. *Neosorex,* water shrews.
   (2) Hind feet not broad and fringed with hair. Found throughout U.S. Genus *Sorex,* long-tailed shrews.
   (3) Very tiny; eastern U.S. Genus *Microsorex,* pigmy shrews.

24 *b*. Tail short and often stout, less than 2.5 cm. (1″) long.
   (1) Range east of the Rocky Mountains. *Blarina,* short-tailed shrews.
   (2) Range in the Rocky Mountains. *Cryptotis,* Rocky Mountain short-tailed shrews.

25 *a*. Forefeet in the form of fins. Order PINNIPEDIA (seals and walruses). **26**

25 *b*. Forefeet not in the form of fins. Order CARNIVORA (land flesh-eaters). **27**

26 *a*. Small external ears, limbs long and modified for waddling on land. West Coast. Family *Otariidae:* eared seals. *Eumetopias,* Stellar sea lion; *Zalophus,* California sea lion (smaller).

26 *b*. No external ears; limbs short. Family *Phocidae:* hair seals.
   (1) Very spotted body. *Phoca vitulina,* vitulina eastern harbor or leopard seal.
   (2) Few spots on body. *P. vitulina richardi,* western spotted seal.

27 *a*. Hind foot with four claws; dog or catlike mammals. **28**

27 *b*. Hind foot with 5 claws; weasel, coon, and bearlike mammals. **36**

28 *a*. Claws sheathed and retractile (can be pulled inward). Teeth not more than 30; catlike form. Family *Felidae:* cats. **29**

28 *b*. Claws not sheathed and retractile; more than 30 teeth; dog or foxlike form. Family *Canidae:* foxes, wolves. **32**

29 *a*. Tail less than 30 cm. (1′) long. **30**

29 *b*. Tail more than 30 cm. (1′) long. **31**

30 *a*. Length of adult rarely more than 60 to 72 cm. (25 to 30″); ears with small tufts; color tawny. Most of U.S. *Lynx rufus,* bobcat or wildcat.

30 *b*. Length of adult usually over 72 cm. (30″); ears with large tufts;

color mainly white or gray. Northern and mountain forests of U.S. and Canada. *Lynx canadensis*, Canada lynx.

31 a. Color uniform, dark or tawny brown.
(1) Over 1.2 m. (4') long; ranges in mountains of the West. *Felis concolor*, mountain lion.
(2) Under 1 m. (40") long. Southwestern border of U.S. *Herpailuras cacomitli*, eyra or jaguarundi cat.

31 b. Color spotted or striped, black and tawny.
(1) Over 1.35 m. (4½') long; spotted with rosettes; southwestern U.S. *Felis hernandesii*, mexican jaguar.
(2) Under 1.2 m. (4') long; spotted and striped; southwestern U.S. *Felis pardalis*, ocelot.

32 a. Upper incisor teeth lobed; stocky animals with wolflike form; neck short and thick. **33**

32 b. Upper incisor teeth not lobed; slender animals with foxlike form; neck usually long and slender. **34**

33 a. Adults usually not more than 1.2 m. (4') long; rarely go in packs. Through much of U.S. and Canada. *Canis latrans*, plains coyote.

33 b. Adults usually more than 1.2 m. (4') long; often go in packs. Northern forests and mountains and in wild sections of western Gulf States. *Canis lycaon*, timber wolf.

34 a. Color iron gray, but some yellowish-red on sides; tail black on top edge; no white tip. Through most of U.S. *Urocyon*, gray foxes.

34 b. Color otherwise; tail more fluffy and thick. **35**

35 a. Color reddish, black, silvery, or variations of these; live in forested country through much of U.S. *Vulpes fulva*, red fox; also silver and cross foxes.

35 b. Color pale yellow or gray; tail black-tipped; inhabits deserts of the West. *Vulpes macrotus*, kit fox.

36 a. The entire sole of the hind foot, both heel and toe, put to the ground when walking. Coon and bearlike mammals. Tail with rings or very short. **37**

36 b. Entire sole of hind foot not put on the ground when walking. Tail usually long and without rings (one exception). Ring-tailed cats and weasels. **39**

37 a. Tail long and with rings. Size small; less than 10 cm. (3'). Family *Procyonidae*: raccoons. *Procyon lotor*, common raccoon. Found throughout U.S.

37 *b.* Tail very short and without rings; size large, more than 1 m. (3')
long. Family *Ursidae:* bears. **38**

38 *a.* Size of adult very large, usually more than 1.5 m. (5') long; claws
7½ cm. (3") long or more, slender and curved; a distinct hump
at the shoulders. Rocky Mountains. *Ursus horribilis,* Rocky
Mountain grizzly bear.

38 *b.* Size of adult (with few exceptions) smaller; claws less than 6.5
cm. (2½") long, usually more blunt and straight; no distinct
hump at the shoulders. Mountains and forests of U.S. *Euarctos,*
black or cinnamon bears.

39 *a.* Tail ringed with black and white bands. Family *Bassariscidae,*
southwestern U.S. and as far north as Oregon. *Bassaricus astutus,*
ring-tailed cat.

39 *b.* Tail not ringed with black and white bands. Family *Mustelidae:*
weasels. **40**

40 *a.* Tail less than twice as long as the hind foot. Animal flat in shape
with short legs; front feet built for digging. Wilder parts of the
West. *Taxidea taxus,* American badger.

40 *b.* Tail more than twice as long as the hind foot. Mostly slender
animals with the exception of the wolverine. **41**

41 *a.* Color black and white. **42**

41 *b.* Color not black and white. **44**

42 *a.* Single white stripe; long heavy claws on front feet; snoutlike
nose. Range in southwestern U.S. *Conepatus,* hog-nosed skunks.

42 *b.* Two or more white stripes on back; claws on front feet not long
and heavy; nose not snoutlike. **43**

43 *a.* Two white stripes on the back united at the neck; cheek black.
Found in most of U.S. *Mephitas,* striped skunks.

43 *b.* More than two white stripes on back, not uniting at the neck;
cheek partly white. Most of U.S. *Spilogale,* spotted skunks.

44 *a.* Body form thick and heavy; tail comparatively short; color dark
brown. Northern forests and high mountain ranges, as far south
as Mount Whitney. *Gulo,* wolverines.

44 *b.* Body form more slender. **45**

45 *a.* Hind feet webbed for swimming; tail broad and partly flattened.
Forests and rivers of North. *Lutra canadensis,* Canadian otter.

45 *b.* Hind feet not webbed for swimming; tail not broad and partly
flattened. **46**

46 *a.*   Length of adults usually over 60 cm. (2'); weight more than 1.8 kilograms (4 pounds); tail bushy. Northern forests.

   (1) Smaller, less than 75 cm. (2½') long; color reddish- or yellowish-brown. *Martes americana,* marten.

   (2) Larger, more than 75 cm. (2½') long; color dark brown. *Martes pennanti,* fisher.

46 *b.*   Length of adults usually under 60 cm. (2') (two exceptions); weight less than 1.8 kilograms (4 pounds); tail not bushy.

   (1) Length over 60 cm. (2'); color dark brown. *Mustela vison,* American mink.

   (2) Length over 60 cm. (2'); light color, black feet. Plains of West. *Mustela nigripes,* black-footed ferret.

   (3) Length under 60 cm. (2'); feet not black. Most of U.S. *Mustela,* common weasels (various species).

47 *a.*   Length of adults less than 1.5 m. (5'). **48**

47 *b.*   Length of adults more than 1.5 m. (5'). Very large mammals with finlike feet dwelling in bays and lagoons of the Florida coast. Order Sɪʀᴇɴɪᴀ (sea cows). Family *Trichechidae:* manatees. *Trichechas lat rostris,* Florida manatee.

48 *a.*   Body covered with tough plates like armor. Order Xᴇɴᴀʀᴛʜʀᴀ. Family *Dasypodidae:* armadillos. Texas. *Dasypus novemcinctus,* nine-banded armadillo.

48 *b.*   Body not covered with tough plates like armor. **49**

49 *a.*   Upper incisors 4; rabbit and harelike animals. Order Lagomorpha. **75**

49 *b.*   Upper incisors (front teeth) 2. Rat and mouselike animals. Order Rᴏᴅᴇɴᴛɪᴀ (rodents). **50**

50 *a.*   Tail completely flattened for use in swimming and dam building. Northern forests and streams. Family *Castoridae:* beavers. *Castor canadensis,* American beaver.

50 *b.*   Tail not flattened, or only partly so. **51**

51 *a.*   Hind feet partly webbed and modified for swimming; tail partly flattened. In streams and swamps over much of U.S. Genus *Ondatra,* muskrat (in family *Cricetidae:* native rats and mice).

51 *b.*   Hind feet not partly webbed; tail rounded, not flattened. **52**

52 *a.*   Body covered with sharp-pointed quills. Conif. forests. Family *Erethizontidae.* Throughout U.S. *Erethizon,* American porcupines.

52   *b.*Body not covered with sharp-pointed quills. **53**

53 *a.*   Cheek pouches present. Gophers, pocket mice, and jumping rats and mice. **54**

53 *b.*   No cheek pouches. **57**

54 *a.*   Hind legs made for jumping. Jumping rats and mice. **55**

54 *b.*   Hind legs not made for jumping. Part of Family *Geomyidae:* gophers and pocket mice. **56**

55 *a.*   Tail tufted on tip; body usually over 8.5 cm. (3½″) long; external cheek pouches. Part of Family *Geomyidae:* jumping rats. Southwestern U.S. *Dipodomys,* Kangaroo rats.

55 *b.*   Tail extremely long, not tufted; internal cheek pouches; body less than 8.5 cm. (3½″) long. Family *Zapodidae:* jumping mice. *Zapus,* common jumping mice. Southwestern U.S.

56 *a.*   Tail longer than head and body; small, mouselike mammals. Western U.S. *Perognathus,* pocket mice.

56 *b.*   Tail shorter than head and body; form stout; front feet adapted for digging. Throughout U.S. *Thomomys,* western pocket gophers and *Geomys,* eastern pocket gophers.

57 *a.*   Tailless. Guinea-piglike animals. Family *Aplodontiidae.* Redwood forests of Pacific Coast. *Aplodontia rufa,* mountain beaver.

57 *b.*   With a tail. **58**

58 *a.*   Tail bushy; more than 3 cheek teeth in each jaw. Family *Sciuridae:* squirrels and woodchucks. **59**

58 *b.*   Tail not bushy; 3 cheek teeth in each jaw. Rats and mice. **66**

59 *a.*   Form stout. **60**

59 *b.*   Form more slender. **61**

60 *a.*   Color reddish-brown to dark grayish-brown or black.
    (1) Eastern states. *Marmota monax,* common eastern woodchuck.
    (2) Western U.S. *Marmota caligata,* hoary marmot or whistler.
    (3) Western U.S. *Marmota flaviventris,* yellow-bellied marmot.

60 *b.*   Color pale yellowish-brown. Live on western plains in vast burrow colonies. *Cynomys,* prairie dogs.

61 *a.*   Mainly live on ground with homes in holes; rarely climb trees; tails not so bushy. **62**

61 *b.*   Mainly live in trees, building nests among the branches or in holes in the trunks; tails very large and bushy. **65**

62 *a.*   Color either uniform or with stripes in spotted bands. Middle West and West. *Citellus,* common ground squirrels.

62 *b*.   Color made up of regular stripes, not spotted. **63**

63 *a*.   Head and shoulders red-gold; face not white around eyes. Mountains of West. *Callospermophilus,* golden-mantled ground squirrels.

63 *b*.   Head and shoulders not golden or only partly so; white markings around the eyes. Chipmunks. **64**

64 *a*.   Tail white or whitish and upturned over back. Southwestern U.S. Genus *Ammospermophilus,* antelope chipmunks.

64 *b*.   Tail dark-colored and not upturned over back.
   (1) *Eutamias,* western chipmunks.
   (2) *Tamias,* eastern chipmunks.

65 *a*.   Skin forming broad winglike membrane between fore and hind feet. Eastern and northwestern U.S. *Glaucomys,* flying squirrels.

65 *b*.   Skin not forming broad winglike extension between fore and hind feet. In most forests of the U.S. Genus *Sciurus,* tree squirrels (red, gray, and fox squirrels).

66 *a*.   Tail usually completely naked; color a uniform gray-brown in small species; hair very coarse in larger species. All over U.S. Family *Muridae:* old world rats and mice. **67**

66 *b*.   Tail usually with some or much hair; color usually lighter on under parts; hair usually smooth, not coarse (with 2 exceptions). Family *Cricetidae:* native rats and mice. **68**

67 *a*.   Adults head and body over 17.5 cm. (7″) long; underparts white or whitish. All over U.S. near dwellings. *Rattus,* house and roof rats.

67 *b*.   Adults head and body less than 15 cm. (6″) long; underparts of body only slightly lighter than the gray-brown upper parts. *Mus musculus,* house mouse.

68 *a*.   Adults head and body over 12 cm. (5″) long; tail long and of the same color.
   (1) Smooth fur; woodlands. *Neotoma,* wood or pack rats.
   (2) Coarse fur; grasslands and marshes of southern U.S. *Oryzomys,* rice rats (some smaller than 12 cm.).
   (3) Grizzled, rough fur; grasslands of southern U.S. *Sigmodon,* cotton rats.

68 *b*.   Adults head and body usually less than 12 cm. (5″) long (exceptions are Richardson and Townsend voles, *Microtus* species, of northwest mountains and northwest Pacific Coast); tail, if long, with the color lighter on the underside. **69**

69 *a*. Tail less than 3 times as long as hind foot, and slender. **70**
69 *b*. Tail more than 3 times as long as hind foot; either thick and fleshy or slender. **71**
70 *a*. Fur fairly coarse. All over the U.S. *Microtus*, meadow mice.
70 *b*. Fur glossy and silky. Live mainly in forests in eastern U.S. *Pitmys*, pine mice.
71 *a*. Tail thick and fleshy; stout body; mainly meat eaters. Underparts very white. Western U.S. *Onychomys*, grasshopper mice.
71 *b*. Tail long and slender. **72**
72 *a*. Head blunt, color often reddish. **73**
72 *b*. Head and nose pointed, color not reddish. **74**
73 *a*. Bright reddish on back; underparts tawny; does not live in trees. Northern U.S. and Canada and high mountain ranges southward. *Evotomys*, red-backed mice.
73 *b*. Reddish color all over; lives in treetops. In redwood and Douglas fir forests of the Pacific Coast. (Other mice of this genus found in high mountains of West.) *Phenacomys longicaudus*, OREGON RUFOUS tree mouse.
74 *a*. Upper incisor teeth grooved; very delicately built and graceful mice. All over U.S. in fields. *Reithrodontomys*, harvest mice.
74 *b*. Upper incisor teeth not grooved; not so delicately built; mostly larger mice. All over U.S. in fields and forests. *Peromyscus*, white-footed mice.
75 *a*. Shaped like guinea pig; no tail, rounded head, short round ears, short legs, fluffy long coat of hair. In high mountains of West. Family *Ochotonidae:* conies. *Ochotona*, conies or pikas.
75 *b*. Hind legs long and built for leaping. Family *Leporidae:* rabbits and hares.
76 *a*. Ears broad and large, usually more than length of head in height; hind legs powerfully built for jumping. Throughout U.S. *Lepus*, hares and jack rabbits.
76 *b*. Ears narrow and smaller; usually less than length of head in height; hind legs not so powerfully developed for jumping. Throughout U.S. *Sylvilagus*, cottontail, marsh, and brush rabbits.

POND AND STREAM LIFE

Pond and stream life goes on all through the year. Even in the dead of winter, exploration under the stones of a brook will bring to view dragonfly nymphs, water pennies, and other interesting forms. This is because of the wonderful nature of water; it is not so subject to temperature change as is the air, and consequently the life within it can go on long after much of the life above has been frozen into quiescence. Since water is heaviest at a temperature of 4 degrees C. (39.2 degrees F.), the water at this temperature tends to sink to the bottom of a pond or stream and thus hold a fairly even temperature there even while the surface freezes over with the lighter ice. It is for this reason that trout and other fish, snails, worms, and even water insects manage to keep up their activities below the ice that covers them. The ice itself, queerly enough, acts as an insulator against any greater cold that may grip the neighboring land.

But it is the exploration of ponds and streams in the spring and summer that brings the greatest pleasure to the naturalist. The buoyancy of the water lends support and aid to many forms of life, while the thin film of surface tension allows water skaters and spiders to skim about upon the water in pursuit of their prey. I have even seen a web-footed Central American lizard species take advantage of this surface tension by skating across the water with tremendous speed; too fast apparently for gravity to pull them beneath the surface. This same surface tension allows mosquito larvae, beetles, and other creatures of the depths to come up for air and hang and rest on the surface film. Also there are odd, tiny, jointed animals called copepods (often visible only in a magnifying glass) that run about just under this surface film with their bodies forever upside down!

The life of a pond or stream is a world all to itself and one of the best places to study the struggle for existence. Fish, frogs, and salamanders are usually the top dogs, feeding on the larger and medium-sized water insects. However, those tigers of the depths, the hinge-jawed dragonfly larvae, lurking fiercely among the stems of the water plants, sometimes turn the tables for the insects. Both small fish and pollywogs are seized by these monsters, who have the wonderful food-catcher of an extensible mouth that can be shot suddenly an inch or so in front of their ugly heads. Wolflike water beetles dive at the armor-cased caddis worms, who have surrounded themselves with a protective shell of sticks or stones cemented together with silk. Every bit of sheltered hideaway is occupied by some form of life. Flatworms ooze along the undersides of rocks; snails crawl up the water plants; and even the mud of the bottom is filled with small life.

Collecting water animals requires some different techniques from those used on land. A *water net,* of which we have already spoken (see Figure 11-19), is necessary, and this should be very strong so that you can sweep with it through mud and underwater weeds. A *white pie-plate* or *saucer* is a great aid in observing the things you collect while they are still alive. The white bottom shows up the various kinds distinctly. Drop a netful of swept-up creatures into such a plate and you will be able to watch their actions in some detail. *Forceps,* of course, are necessary and a *hand lens* or magnifying glass comes in very handy. With the lens you can observe many kinds of life too small to be seen clearly with the unaided eye. A *pail with a cover* is necessary to bring back any specimens you may wish to study in your laboratory or put into your aquarium. Various sized *bottles* or *jars* filled with formaldehyde or alcohol are needed to bring home specimens for your collections. Water insects may be preserved and mounted as explained in Chapter Five. A *pipette* or bulb and glass tube is very useful in picking up eggs or tiny animals and plants too small or delicate to be handled in any other way. A *plankton net* (see Figure 17-51) is used for dragging through the water of a pond either from a boat or from the beach. The string at the bottom is untied and the entire contents of the fine-mesh net dropped into a jar for study. *Plankton* is simply the name for the microscopic and almost microscopic life that is found swimming through almost all bodies of water.

A handful of hay allowed to stay for several days in a glass of water is another way to collect microscopic one-celled animals. Possession of a microscope and knowledge of how to use slides and cover glasses will open an entirely new world for you. Turn to the Bibliography for

17-51. *Plankton net.*
*A cone of silk cloth, attached
to wire ring. Untie small
opening at bottom
to empty after use.*

After Morgan

a list of books that will help you in this study. Look under the heading Microscopy and Microscopic Life.

The collector who sweeps with a water net through and under water plants, along the bottom and even through the stretches of mud or ooze, is bound to get specimens of interest. Turn over rocks in streams and pools and carefully search the undersides; also look under the leaves of water plants and along their stems. But always turn rocks back!

See Chapter Twenty for an account of exploring a pond ecologically. The Bibliography lists several books to help your study of freshwater life.

LIFE IN THE SEA AND ON THE SEASHORE

The student of the sea and its shores delves into some of the richest life on the planet, for it was in the sea that the first of all life began, and it has flourished there in overwhelming numbers ever since. There is something about life in the sea that has a peculiar fascination. Perhaps it is because the animals there are so different from those on land, as if one were visiting another planet and seeing strange and outlandish beasts beyond one's imagination. Even fish take on exotic forms. I remember the thrill I got off the coast of Mexico when I leaned over the prow of our ship, the *Santa Lucia*, and saw a black form flash up from the dark depths. Demonlike it seemed, for the head was in the shape of a hammer with two great eyes on either end, yet the rest of the body had the streamlined beauty of a clipper ship. The demon whipped its narrow form through the dancing waves with the speed of a charging lion, and, after a bit of playing about the prow, leaped ahead with a still greater burst that left the finteen-knots-an-hour ship far behind. It was a hammerhead shark, a strange and grim denizen of the deep ocean.

The zones of life in the sea and on the shore are shown in Figure 17-52 for the Pacific Coast and Figure 17-53 for the Atlantic Coast. Notice how many animals on both coasts look similar and are adapted for similar ecologic niches, but are entirely different species. This is an example of parallel evolution. The acorn barnacle (Balanus) is so widespread, however, it is almost identical on both coasts. These zones, of course, are artificial, but they serve very well to give us a picture of the distribution of sea life. Remember that competition is so strong in the sea that there is a constant fight for favored localities, and some animals are forced out of places they would like and have to seek for others. Animals that live above the region of low tide have to fight constantly against the danger of drying up, as they all need to have their gills wet in order to breathe. They overcome this danger in a variety of ways, as shown below. In these zones, mainly West Coast species are described, but compare them with similar species shown in Figure 17-53.

The *splash zone* is inhabited by a relatively few animals who have their gills so well protected by armor or other means that a few splashings from the spray of the high tide waves twice a day is enough to keep them breathing. When the tide is out at its lowest they usually stay hidden deep in cracks of the rocks where the shade preserves their moisture. Such animals, the rock louse and one or two shore crabs among others, have two advantages from this kind of life. First, they avoid enemies who live in the water, and second, they get without much competition food such as dead organic material thrown up on the rocks by the breakers at high tide.

In the *high tide zone* dwell other animals that have been forced by the extreme competition of the lower zones into less crowded areas. Animals in this zone, however, cannot count on so continuous a supply of food, as the plankton (microscopic animals and plants) on which they feed is brought to them only at high tide. Furthermore they must stay sheltered in some way when the tide is down so as to preserve moisture for their gills. Such animals include various shore crabs (whose flat bodies allow them to find shelter from enemies under rocks), barnacles, some of the limpets (whose conical shells cling so tightly to the rocks that their moisture is preserved), and sea snails such as those of the genus *Tegula*.

The *middle tide zone* shows an increase in barnacles, snails, and limpets, but this zone is invaded most strongly by dense colonies of mussels. In the cracks between the mussels, numerous nereid worms, tiny crabs, and flat-bodied amphipods (see Figures 17-52 and 17-53) find perfect shelter.

The low tide zone has fewer mussels, but limpets and sea snails of deeper water forms still prevail, while the barnacles have altogether disappeared, driven to higher tide zones and wilder wave-struck rocks by the tigerlike whelks on the East Coast and, to a lesser extent, by the common starfish *(Pisaster ochraceus)* on the Pacific Coast. Oysters,

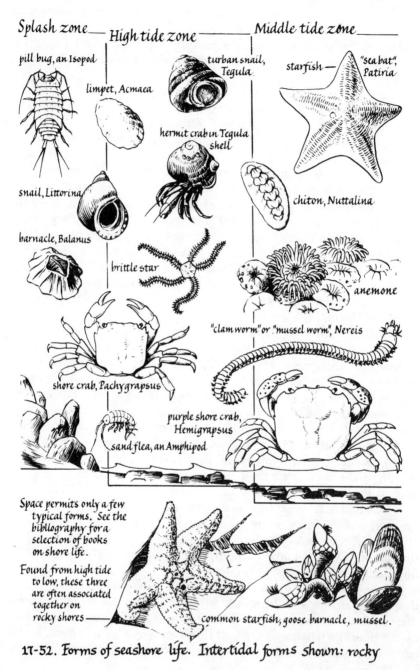

Splash zone — High tide zone — Middle tide zone —

pill bug, an Isopod

turban snail, Tegula

starfish — "sea bat", Patiria

limpet, Acmaea

hermit crab in Tegula shell

snail, Littorina

chiton, Nuttalina

barnacle, Balanus

brittle star

anemone

"clam worm" or "mussel worm", Nereis

shore crab, Pachygrapsus

purple shore crab, Hemigrapsus

sand flea, an Amphipod

Space permits only a few typical forms. See the bibliography for a selection of books on shore life.

Found from high tide to low, these three are often associated together on rocky shores —

common starfish, goose barnacle, mussel.

17-52. Forms of seashore life. Intertidal forms shown: rocky

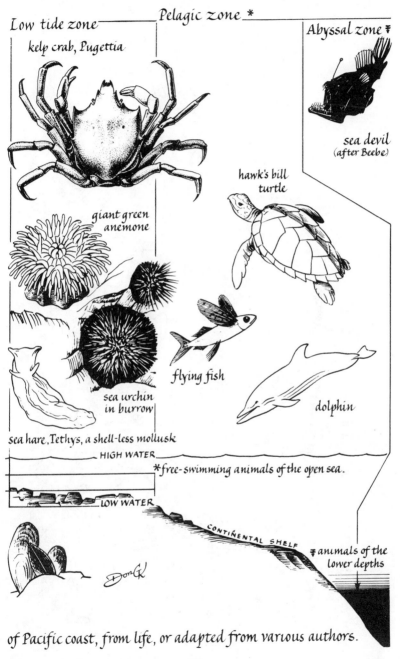

Low tide zone

Pelagic zone *

Abyssal zone ‡

kelp crab, Pugettia

sea devil
(after Beebe)

hawk's bill
turtle

giant green
anemone

flying fish

dolphin

sea urchin
in burrow

sea hare, Tethys, a shell-less mollusk

HIGH WATER

*free-swimming animals of the open sea.

LOW WATER

CONTINENTAL SHELF

‡ animals of the
lower depths

of Pacific coast, from life, or adapted from various authors.

261

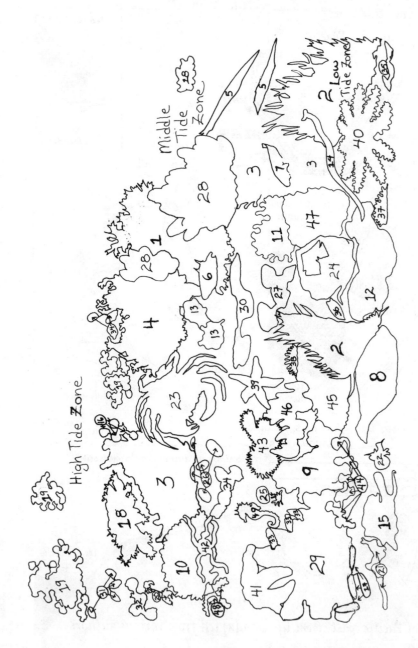

High Tide Zone

Middle Tide Zone

Low Tide Zone

262

Fig. 17-53. *Diagram of life on Atlantic Coast rocky shore. Shows animals and plants that are associated with the various zones. (Drawing by Robin Brickman.)*

clams, starfish, sea anemones, and chitons (see Figures 17-53 and 17-54) make their appearance strongly in this zone, along with shrimps and tiny fish of the tide pools.

The *pelagic zone* covers the surface and subsurface waters of the ocean and includes among its inhabitants innumerable fishes, squid, octopi, lobsters (in the East), eels, edible crabs *(Cancer)*, plankton, and so on. Below the last rays of light at about 200 meters (660 feet) lies the *abyssal zone,* which includes the bulk of the oceans and has strange forms of life rarely seen by the average naturalist.

Other places where sea life is found include: *mud flats* (see Figure 17-54), where burrowing clams, ghost shrimps, mud guppies (a kind of small fish), and mud snails find protection from their enemies; *sandy beaches* where piles of seaweed furnish dwelling places and ood for sand fleas, various amphipods, and nudibranches (sluglike shellfish or mollusks without shells); *rock pools* where sea anemones, sea cucumbers, snails, limpets, crabs, hydroid colonies, and sea urchins find food and protection in the clear green waters; and *wharf piles* where serpulid worms show their crimson and orange tentacles, amphipods and isopods (sow-bug-like creatures) crawl among the barnacles, tubeworms pile their white calcareous masses, and sea anemones of brilliant colors often form solid carpets.

The naturalist finds that the best way to study the creatures of the seashore is to place them in small tide pools where he or she can watch them leisurely in more or less natural surroundings. Taking live sea creatures home for study is usually very difficult and is certainly to be condemned if the majority brought home soon die, as they usually do. The secret of preserving such captives alive is: bring very few of them back with you, but bring lots of sea water. A ten-gallon jug full of sea water is not too much. Kept in pans or small aquaria, such sea creatures may be kept alive a week or more provided their sea water is constantly renewed from your reserve supply. But so much can actually be observed at the shore itself by the careful and patient naturalist that it is not usually worthwhile to bring much home.

Preserved specimens for collections and classification study may be fixed in one of two ways. First, you may put them in either 70 percent alcohol (this is best for delicate specimens) or a 4 percent formalin solution (large specimens put in formalin or alcohol need to have the first preservative drained off after two or three days and a fresh supply put in). Or, second, you may soak your specimens for a day or two in

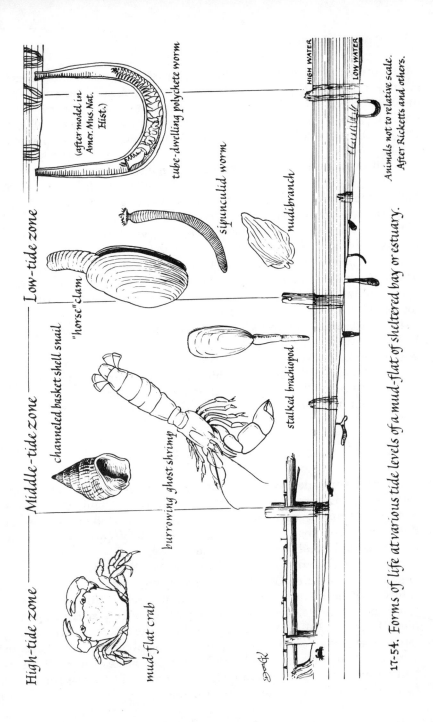

High-tide zone ——— Middle-tide zone ——— Low-tide zone

mud-flat crab

burrowing ghost shrimp

channeled basket shell snail

"horse" clam

stalked brachiopod

sipunculid worm

nudibranch

tube-dwelling polychaete worm

(after model in Amer. Mus. Nat. Hist.)

HIGH WATER

LOW WATER

17-54. Forms of life at various tide levels of a mud-flat of sheltered bay or estuary. Animals not to relative scale. After Ricketts and others.

either formalin (this may be done with starfish, and crabs, and others) or in a mixture of alcohol, glycerin, formalin, and water (best for delicate forms). After soaking, allow the specimens to dry for two or three days in the sun. Chitons should be tied tightly onto small flat boards; otherwise they will curl. Label all such specimens as explained in Chapter Five.

Shellfish, with the living animals still in the shells, should be placed in boiling water. This kills them instantly, and after a few minutes of boiling the bodies of the shellfish can be easily taken from the shells and the shells labeled and placed in your collection.

In collecting along the seashore, a *pail* for living specimens and one or more *jars* with alcohol or formalin in them are necessary. A *case knife* is needed to pry limpets and similar shellfish from rocks, although abalones need a small *crowbar*. A *long narrow spade* (best if the handle is 30 centimeters—1 foot—or more long) is excellent help in digging for deep burrowing clams and similar creatures of the mud flats.

Dried specimens of any kind must be preserved from insect pests. If kept on museum shelves, they may be sprayed from time to time with a solution of carbon bisulphide.

Good books on the seashore animals of your particular region may be found at any public library. Turn to the Bibliography (under Life of the Sea and Its Shores) for a list of those you might find useful.

INSECT LIFE

Since insects include more than half of the known kinds of animals on earth, it seems wise for us to study them. But beyond this, insects offer a field for the naturalist as fascinating as any other. Because of their small size, insects are among the easiest of creatures to study under natural conditions. Life histories with all their habits and instincts can be brought so close to our eyes that we can see every detail, and if we are quiet and careful, there is little chance that the insects will be disturbed by our watching them. Unlike the eyes of birds and mammals, the eyes of insects see us mainly as large moving blurs. If we stand still, the blur apparently merges into the surrounding territory and they pay us no attention, going about their business in a most natural manner. Their small size also makes caging them in natural surroundings comparatively simple, giving us a vast and fertile field for study right within our own homes.

Insects are six-legged, jointed animals belonging to the phylum Arthropoda (see Figures 17-28 and 17-55). Their evolution has been so successful that they are today our most serious challenge to world rulership. Their small size, their ability in many cases to fly from place to plàce, and the chiton (outer skeleton or armor) that protects them from harm have given them many advantages in the conquest of

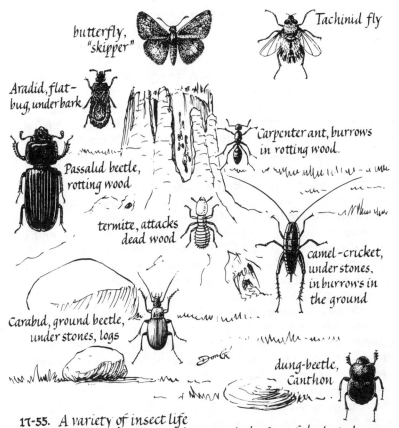

butterfly, "skipper"

Tachinid fly

Aradid, flat-bug, under bark

Carpenter ant, burrows in rotting wood.

Passalid beetle, rotting wood

termite, attacks dead wood

camel-cricket, under stones, in burrows in the ground

Carabid, ground beetle, under stones, logs

dung-beetle, Canthon

17-55. *A variety of insect life may be found almost anywhere you look. One of the best places: at the edge of a pasture and woods, where rotting stumps and logs, stones, manure, grasses, weeds, trees and shrubs provide living conditions for almost every kind of insect. A pond nearby would practically complete the picture. The picture gives only a hint. Be sure to dig in the ground for many larvae, pupae & adults.*

distance and of their enemies. The social insects—the wasp, the bee, the termite, and the ant—have evolved systems of society and communal effort that, in the world of the invertebrates, are the equivalents of human social advance above the other vertebrates. But 2,000,000 years ago, when the human ancestor was apelike, little more civilized than a gorilla, and less civilized than a beaver, ants and bees had already built their highly complex societies. (Figure 17-55 shows a variety of insect life above and below ground.)

In Figure 17-56, you see examples of four types of insects, a beetle, a wasp, a snake fly, and a plant bug, showing the main parts of their bodies.

One other great advance that most insects made over their invertebrate cousins was the development of *metamorphosis*. The meaning of this is a series of changes from one state of living to another during one lifetime. The butterfly, for instance, starts as an egg, which hatches into a caterpillar, an entirely different form of life from the butterfly. This wormlike creature feeds on leaves, whereas the fragile, winged butterfly feeds on nectar or honeydew. Actually, however, as the caterpillar grows, the way is being made ready within its body for the great change that is to come. Hidden beneath the skin of the full-grown caterpillar are the wing pads or partially grown wings that will later sweep the air for the butterfly. The caterpillar at the end of its stage finally hangs by its tail from a branch and forms itself by the aid of a cementing material from its mouth into the limp apparently lifeless chrysalid (again a different form of life) and remains in this stage until the changes that go on inside the quiet outer covering are ready. At last the chrysalid appears to wake; it wriggles vigorously until it splits down one side, and out of the lifeless covering comes gradually the completed insect, slightly weak and limp-looking at first, but surging with new-found life that swells up the wing veins with vital fluid until the wings are ready for flight. (For an example of complete metamorphosis, see Figure 5-15.)

Many insects, such as the grasshopper, the cockroach, the termite, and the dragonfly, have *partial metamorphosis*. This means that they go through two stages instead of three, and the change is more gradual. Since all insects have an outer skeleton of chiton (armor), they cannot grow in the way a mammal or bird can. Each time, when they are ready for growth, they must cast off their old skeleton and grow a new one a little larger. For instance, the dragonfly comes out of the egg (see

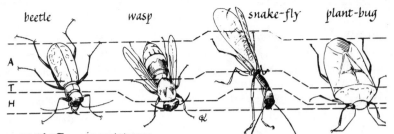

beetle   wasp   snake-fly   plant-bug

A
T
H

17-56. Four insect types
showing main body divisions : H-head ; T-thorax ; A-abdomen.
(In beetle, snake-fly and bug, abdomen is concealed under wings.)

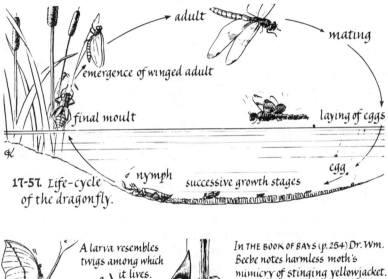

adult

mating

emergence of winged adult

final moult

laying of eggs

nymph   successive growth stages

egg

17-57. Life-cycle
of the dragonfly.

A larva resembles
twigs among which
it lives.

2

In THE BOOK OF BAYS (p.254) Dr. Wm.
Beebe notes harmless moth's
mimicry of stinging yellowjacket.

4

moth   wasp

1

Kallima butterfly
of India mimics
leaf.

3

Thorn tree hopper
at rest on thorny
stem. Hard to tell!

Adapted from Nature Magazine photographs : 1,2,3   4: Adapted from Beebe, photo

17-58. Examples of so-called "protective mimicry" in insects. Biologists
debate the question : chance or design ? Something to work on!

Figure 17-57) a very small wingless nymph, but it has six legs just like the full-grown dragonfly. This nymph goes through six or seven stages of growth, during which it again and again loses its skeleton and grows a new and larger one. As it so grows, wing pads become apparent along its back, and in the last nymph stage these are quite large. The nymph, which has spent its life so far in the water of a pond feeding on the small life there, now climbs up the stalk of a pond weed to the surface and crawls out into the air. There it loses its skeleton for the last time, the whole thing splits up the back, and out of the ugly underwater animal emerges the beautiful and graceful dragonfly, who, from then on wings the highways of the air in search of prey.

Insects have developed instinct to its highest degree. When we see a mud wasp, which has had no chance to learn any lessons from its mother about life, emerge from the chrysalid and immediately set about the complicated process of carefully building mud nests under the eaves of an old barn; then go in pursuit of spiders, which it stings exactly in the right nerve center that will cause paralysis instead of death; then carry them to the nests of mud, so that its own young (whom it will never see) may have living and harmless prey—we are amazed. Even the little motion of tamping the mud into pellets to make its nests is exactly the same as the one its ancestors made before it, and yet each such motion is passed from one generation to the next entirely by instinct.

Some of the most interesting of nature experiments can be made with instinct in insects. For instance, suppose after our mud wasp has obtained exactly the correct number of spiders for one of its nests, you come along and take all the spiders out. In spite of this loss of food for the grub to be, the poor wasp still will lay its egg in the empty nest and seal up the entrance. Instinct has thus not prepared the insect to meet such sudden emergencies. (This, however, is not necessarily always true. Some wasps have been seen to learn new habits by experience. See if you can find examples!) Ants, perhaps because their strictly ground life puts them more under the influence of "trial and error," occasionally show some ability at meeting and overcoming sudden changes in their environment. I remember watching my house in Panama being overrun by the savage driver ants of the jungle. Some of the smaller ants of the black horde got caught in a spider's web. But when the spider came out to attack them, three of the large soldier or officer ants (nearly an inch long and with great scythelike jaws) came to the small ants' rescue. These giants pulled and tugged at the cables of the spiderweb until their trapped companions were shaken out and fell to the floor.

Insects show marvelously varied methods of protecting themselves from enemies. *Protective mimicry* is shown most effectively in those forms that almost exactly mimic thorns, or leaves (many butterflies do this), or some other creature that it is dangerous to attack or poisonous to eat (see Figure 17-58 for some examples of protective mimicry). I have captured rove beetles (long, thin beetles with very short wing covers), who so violently and menacingly lashed about with their tails that they almost fooled me into thinking they would sting me. Actually, of course, they are unable to sting in the least. Other rove beetles exactly mimic the form and action of ants so that they are able to live as uninvited guests inside ant nests where they seem to act both as scavengers and, sometimes, as secret murderers in the dark.

CHAPTER
18

The Classification
and Special Study of Plants

Long ago in the violent youth of the world, seaweed and algae lived in the Archeozoic seas, but on all the vast stretch of the land there was no life. Then slowly, over millions of years, the green tide crept up out of the sea and spread over the land. Wherever life went, plants were in the vanguard preparing the way and animals came afterward when the way was made ready. First came mosslike plants and fungi; then ferns evolved through the silent struggle for existence. Cycads, those ancestors of modern trees, rose from the ranks of the ferns to wave their lacy fronds against the Paleozoic sky, and finally step by step appeared the pines and the firs, and last the beauty of the flower. (See Figure 18-1 for a picture of the evolution of the flowers.)

This slow evolution saw the differentiation into the thousands of species of plants with all the varied and complex types of growth that we see in the world today. It is an understanding of the main differences, of the differences between the large groupings that we call plant families, that we wish to reach in this chapter. But before we learn to key out the different families, we need to see the place of the family in the larger classification of all plants. Below, we have taken a section of the plant kingdom and analyzed it into its main divisions.

This partial chart of the plant kingdom shows us how each plant family fits into its particular niche in the classification system. The details of why a particular family should go where it does are too complicated for this book, but you may refer to some of the books listed under Plants in the Bibliography. In each family in turn the various genera and species have their particular places based on the structure of their forms. If you will review Chapter Twelve (Plant Study) and look over the different plant forms that are illustrated there, you will be better prepared to use and understand the key to the families of plants. Also refer to the Glossary of Plant Terms at the end of this chapter.

Figure 18-1 shows the orders of flowering plants in their evolutionary relationship. The subclass *Monocotyledonae* (see 4 *d* in key) begins

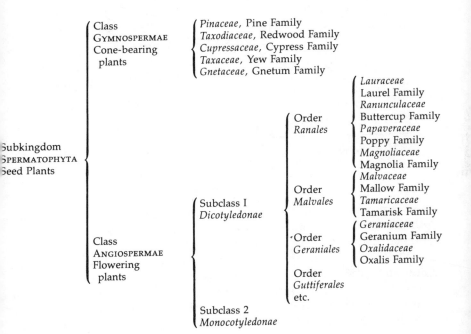

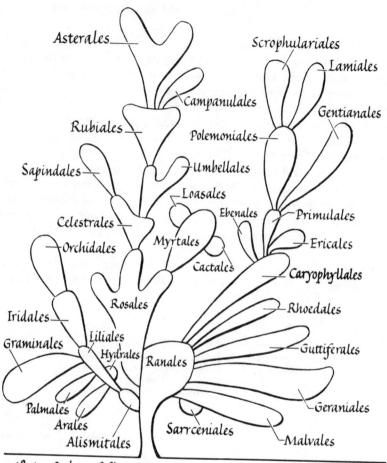

18-1. Orders of flowering plants in evolutionary relationship.

(— the author, after Bessey)

to stem away from the main trunk of evolution with the order *Alismitales* (water plantains) going to the left. As you pass up the branch of the subclass through *Liliales* (lilies) to *Iridales* (irises) to *Orchidales* (orchids), the flowers become more and more specialized and advanced. In the *Liliales* the ovary is superior (see Figure 18-4), which is the primitive state, whereas in the *Iridales* the ovary is inferior (see Figure 18-5). In *Orchidales*, the highest order in the subclass, the ovary is inferior also, but the rest of the flower is very specialized with only one or two stamens and a highly irregular perianth (see Figure 18-38), which allows only special insects to enter the flower and get its nectar.

The subclass *Dicotyledonae* splits into two main branches: first the disk flowers, and second the cone flowers. A typical disk flower is the rose (Figure 6-2); a typical cone flower is the morning glory (Figure 12-6).

The cone flowers begin with the order *Ranales* (buttercups), which are flowers with many separate pistils, petals, and stamens (a primitive condition). The branch goes with increasing complexity up through the *Caryophyllales* (pinks), which have fewer flower parts and in which the pistils are united; through the order *Primulales* (primroses) in which the petals become barely united at the base and the flower parts are still fewer in number (in fives); through the order *Polemoniales* (gilias), in which there is only one pistil and the petals are five and closely united (see Figure 12-6); and finally through the two highest orders *Lamiales* (mints and verbenas) and the *Scrophulariales* (snapdragons) in which the flower parts are very few and the corolla has the petals closely united and highly irregular.

The branch of the disk flowers starts with the order *Rosales* (roses), in which the ovary is superior and the flower parts are numerous and mostly separate from each other (see Figure 6-2). The branch goes with increasing specialization through the order *Celastrales* (lilacs, grapes, and mistletoes), in which the flower parts are fewer, the pistils are united or partly so, and the ovary is sometimes partly inferior (Figure 18-5), although the petals are still not united; through the order *Umbellales* (parsleys, and so on), in which the flower parts are still fewer and the ovary is completely inferior (Figure 18-5), although the petals are still free from each other; through the order *Rubiales* (madders and honeysuckles), in which the petals are united (Figure 18-40) and the flower parts are very few; and finally through the two highest orders of *Asterales* (sunflowers) in which the tiny flowers have their petals completely united, have inferior ovaries, and are formed into flowerlike heads (Figure 12-11B); and the *Campanulales* (bell flowers), in which the petals are united all the way to their tops (Figure 12-11A), the ovary is inferior, and the flower parts are in fives or less.

Other orders, which branched off from the main branches, have taken side developments of a less advanced nature.

On the pages that follow you will find an illustrated key to the more common families of plants. The purpose of the key is to give you a guide by which you can track down the kind of plant you have collected. You might ask: "Why use a key—why not look at pictures in a book?" Except for a few plants, pictures are not enough. They may even mislead you and make you think the plant you have is something entirely different from what it really is. This is because some plants may look very much alike in general appearance, but they may be considerably different in the exact arrangement of their parts. By using a key, and carefully studying your plant not only with your unaided eyes, but by means of a small magnifying glass as well, you learn about those real differences. You are also getting some firsthand knowledge of the wonderful nature of plants, knowledge that you can never reach by just looking at pictures.

Most botanical keys are difficult because they are intended for trained botanists and not for the general public. Nevertheless it is very important for a naturalist to try to understand these keys. The principal reason we have trouble with such keys is because of their strange scientific words, such as "perianth" and "ligule" and "dioecious." If we were as familiar with these words as we are with "petal" and "leaf" and "stem," it would not be so bad. Unfortunately, in order to understand plants we have to understand a lot of these words. The idea of the key below is to teach you the meaning of many of these words while you are using the key. To do this we use pictures. In a key, you are trying to reach the correct name for your plant by throwing aside everything it is *not,* until, by always taking the right turn, you find out what it *is.*

For instance, if your plant (we'll say it is a flower of Labrador Tea) has net-veined leaves (as you see under number 8 *a* in the key) then it belongs to the subclass *Dicotyledonae,* number 9. You look next at 9 *a,* 9 *b,* and 9 *c* and find that the corolla (circle of petals) has its petals joined together at the base as is told under 9 *c.* So you turn as you are told to number 68 where you find that, as your plant has 10 stamens, it belongs to 68 *a.* This leads you to 69, where you find that it belongs to 69 *a* and the *Ericaceae* or Heath Family, since it has a bell-shaped (campanulate) corolla, 1 stigma, 1 style, and a 4-celled ovary. In each case you had at least two choices, and you chose each time the direction that best fitted your particular plant, the choices leading you finally to the family in which it belonged. (For help with names turn to the glossary at the end of this chapter.)

Probably ninety-nine out of one hundred plants you find will key down to one of the common families in this key. For the uncommon plant that you can't place, turn to the books listed in the Bibliography under Plants. Also use these books to determine the exact genera and species of plants you have collected. (For fungi and algae, see special books on these plants in the Bibliography.)

A KEY TO SOME COMMON FAMILIES OF PLANTS

1 *a*. Without flowers or seeds, reproducing by means of spores. Fernlike plants. **2**

1 *b*. Seeds present and either flowers or cones. Seed plants. **3**

2. PTERIDOPHYTA (FERNS)

2 *a*. Stems not jointed or rushlike; mostly land plants with many much-divided leaves; sporangia (spore cases) found on the undersides of the leaves. Family *Polypodiaceae:* ferns.

2 *b*. Stems jointed or rushlike; leaves only small-toothed sheaths at each joint. Family *Equisetaceae:* horsetails.

3. SPERMATOPHYTA (SEED PLANTS)

3 *a*. Ovules attached without cover on the surface of a scale; no true flowers; cone-bearing and evergreen with needlelike leaves. (Class 1, *Gymnospermae:* conifers.) **4**

3 *b*. Ovules enclosed in a sac or ovary, which becomes the fruit and covers the seed; true flowers present. (Class 2, *Angiospermae:* flowering plants.) **8**

4–7. GYMNOSPERMAE (CONIFERS)

4 *a*. A tree with resinous sap. **5**

4 *b*. A desert shrub; sap without resin. Family *Gnetaceae:* gnetum or Mexican tea.

5 *a*. Cone woody (except in genus *Juniperus*, in which it is soft and berrylike); ovules in catkins. **6**

5 *b*.   Fruit a one-seeded berry or drupe (like a cherry); ovules solitary; leaves very narrow in flat sprays. Family *Taxaceae:* yew.

6 *a*.   Cone scales usually with either a large or small bract at the base of each (Figure 18-2a); seeds two to each scale, each bearing a thin wing; leaves needlelike. Family *Pinaceae:* pine, fir, spruce, hemlock.

6 *b*.   Cone scales without bracts (Figure 18-2b), leaves in flat sprays or scalelike and small, or, if needlelike, all around the branchlet. **7**

7 *a*.   Leaves very narrow and in two ranks of flat sprays, needle or awllike and placed all around the branchlet; cone scales without bracts; seeds 2 to 9 to each scale and not winged. Family *Taxodiaceae:* redwood.

7 *b*.   Leaves very small and scalelike, closely covering the end branchlets; cone scales without bracts and with broad flat summits, or rarely with bracts; seeds one to several to each scale and winged or wingless. Family *Cupressaceae:* cypress, juniper, cedar.

8. Angiospermae (Flowering Plants)

8 *a*.   Flower parts mostly in fours or fives; leaves usually net-veined, 2 cotyledons in the germinating plant, and the stem with vascular bundles forming a ring around a central pith (see Figure 12-9). Subclass 1, *Dicotyledonae:* net-veined plants. **9**

8 *b*.   Flower parts mostly in threes, rarely in twos, fours, or fives; parallel-veined leaves, 1 cotyledon in the germinating plant, and the stem with vascular bundles scattered irregularly through the pithlike tissue, never with rings or annual layers (see Figure 12-9). Subclass **2,** *Monocotyledonae:* parallel-veined plants. **96**

9. Dicotyleonae (Net-veined Leaves)

9 *a*.   No corolla (circle of petals), a calyx (circle of sepals) present or not present, leaflike or petallike. **10**

9 *b*.   Calyx and corolla both present; petals separate from each other or nearly so. **35**

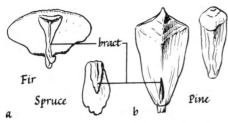

Fir

Spruce

Pine

bract

a

b

18-2. Cone scales with bracts, long or conspicuous, a, or apparently absent, b.

s

P

b Willow

s

P

a Alder
s staminate
P pistillate

18-3. Monoecious, a, and dioecious, b, flowers in catkins.

18-4.
A superior ovary.

18-5.
An inferior ovary.

18-6.
Perigynous flower.

DonGL

18-7.
Hypogynous flower.

18-8.
Flowers in umbels.
Fruit a drupe or berry-like.

Apple

18-9.
Leaf with stipules,
as in Rose family.

c

b
(sec.
of a)

a

c (sec.)

Rose

18-10.
Achene fruit;
a, calyx-tube; b, same,
cut; c, achene.

a

b

a, Utricles joined. b,
Single utricle after parting.

18-11. Utricle fruit
(achene with very
thin pericarp.)

a

b

a, Capsule.
b, Capsule split open.

18-12.
Dehiscent
capsule fruit.

(section is cut —
not naturally split)

California laurel

18-13.
Indehiscent fruit.
(example is
a drupe)

9 *c.*   Calyx and corolla both present; the corolla has the petals joined together at least at the base. **68**

10–34. Apetalous (Without a Corolla)

10 *a.*   Either perfect or unisexual flowers (with stamens or pistils only); flowers not in catkins. **11**

10 *b.*   Either monoecious (with pistils and stamens in separate flowers on the same plant) or dioecious flowers. (Figure 18-3), with one or both kinds in catkins, plant a tree or shrub. **29**

11 *a.*   Plant has a superior ovary (not attached to the calyx or circle of sepals). (See Figure 18-4.) **12**

11 *b.*   Ovary inferior (somewhat attached to the calyx) (see Figure 18-5), dioecious flowers (usually) (Figure 18-3), 3 stamens, opposite leaves, fruit a berry, parasitic on trees. Family *Loranthaceae:* mistletoe.

12 *a.*   Flowers perigynous (with the stamens rising from the calyx or a disk). (See Figure 18-6.) **13**

12 *b.*   Flower hypogynous (see Figure 18-7). **16**

13 *a.*   Flowers in a small umbel, fruit a drupe or often berrylike (see Figure 18-8). Family *Rhamnaceae:* buckthorn.

13 *b.*   Flowers in heads, or clustered, or solitary. **14**

14 *a.*   Stipules on the leaves (Figure 18-9), flowers perfect. **15**

14 *b.*   No stipules on leaves, flowers perfect, leaves alternate, 8 stamens, a 4-cleft calyx, a shrub with a drupelike fruit. Family *Thymelaeaceae:* mezereum or leatherwood.

15 *a.*   Fruit an achene (Figure 18-10), leaves alternate, a large herb or shrub. Family *Rosaceae:* rose.

15 *b.*   Fruit an utricle (Figure 18-11), leaves opposite, a small herb. Family *Caryophyllaceae:* pink.

16 *a.*   Neither calyx (circle of sepals) nor corolla (circle of petals) present; flowers monoecious and in ball-like clusters, scattered on a slender axis or stem, terrestrial (on land). Trees. Family *Plantanaceae:* plane or sycamore.

16 *b.*   A calyx present, but no corolla. **17**

17 *a.*   Pistils distinctly separated; 10 to many stamens, usually 5, sometimes 3 to 9 distinct sepals (often petallike). Family *Ranunculaceae:* buttercup.

17 *b.*   Only 1 pistil. **18**

18 *a.*   Ovary 1-celled with 1 or more styles and stigmas. **19**

18 *b.*   Ovary 2- to 5-celled. **26**

19 *a.*   Fruit a dehiscent (splitting open) capsule (Figure 18-12), opposite leaves, calyx with 5 separate or nearly separate sepals. Family *Caryophyllaceae:* pink.

19 *b.*   Fruit indehiscent (not splitting open). (Figure 18-13.) **20**

20 *a.*   Fruit fleshy (a drupe), leaves simple and alternate. **21**

20 *b.*   Fruit dry (an achene or an utricle). (See Figure 18-11.) 1 to 9 stamens. **22**

21 *a.*   6 petallike and separate sepals, 9 stamens with the anthers opening by valves (Figure 18-14), an evergreen tree. Family *Lauraceae:* laurel.

21 *b.*   Calyx 5 to 6 parted, greenish in color, 5 or 6 stamens with the anthers opening by long slits (Figure 18-15), a deciduous (leaf-losing) tree. Family *Ulmaceae:* elm.

22 *a.*   Plant not scurfy (with branlike scales on the stem or leaves). **23**

22 *b.*   Plant scurfy, living in alkaline or maritime habitats, sepals leaflike or, in unisexual flowers, the female or pistillate without sepals but surrounded by 2 bracts, alternate leaves (rarely opposite or leafless). Family *Chenopodiaceae:* saltbrush.

23 *a.*   Leaves with stinging hairs, flowers very small and monoecious (both male and female flowers on the same plant), in apparent catkins, 4 stamens and sepals, an herb. Family *Urticaceae:* nettle.

23 *b.*   Plant without stinging hairs. **24**

24 *a.*   Leaves alternate or basal, calyx not tubular. **25**

24 *b.*   Plant has opposite leaves without stipules, the calyx tubular and like a corolla, stamens 3 to 5. Family *Nyctaginaceae:* four-o'clock.

25 *a.*   Calyx scarious (thin, dry, and not green), 3 to 5 cleft or parted, 3 to 5 stamens, flowers with bractlets, no stipules, fruit an utricle (Figure 18-11). Family *Amaranthaceae:* amaranth.

25 *b.*   Flowers with a colored or green calyx, 5 or 6 cleft or parted, flowers with or without bractlets, fruit a triangular or lens-shaped achene, 4 to 9 stamens, stipules present or not (Figure 18-16). Family *Polygonaceae:* buckwheat.

18-14. *Anthers opening by valves.*

18-15. *Anthers opening by long slits.*

18-16. *Flowers with stipules.*

Fremontia

18-17. *Anthers monadelphous (united)*

Maple

18-18. *Double samara fruit*

Hazelnut

18-19. *Nut enclosed in leafy tube-shaped envelope.*

Stone-crop

18-20. *Separate pistils becoming follicles.*

Limnanthes

18-21. *Five united pistils, separating when ripe into 1-seeded carpels.*

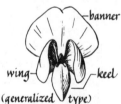

banner

wing —— —— keel

(generalized type)

18-22. *Papilionaceous flower of Pea family.*

18-23. *Violet flower. (generalized type)*

DonK

18-24. *Anthers opening by pores at top.*

a   b

18-25. *a. Follicles of Delphinium. b. one follicle, open.*

26 *a*. Flower perfect with a showy calyx and monodelphous stamens (Figure 18-17), a shrub. Genus *Fremontia* (Flannel Bush), of the family *Sterculiaceae*, sterculia.

26 *b*. Flowers dioecious or polygamous (with perfect, staminate and pistillate flowers all on the same plant), a tree or shrub. **27**

27 *a*. Fruit a drupe or samara (Figure 18-18), leaves opposite. **28**

27 *b*. Fruit a capsule (Figure 18-12), as many or twice as many styles or stigmas as there are ovary cells; leaves more often alternate than opposite. Family *Euphorbiaceae:* spurge.

28 *a*. Fruit a double samara (Figure 18-18), styles 2. Genus *Acer* (maple) of the family *Aceraceae*, maple.

28 *b*. Fruit a simple samara or drupe, 1 style. Family *Oleaceae:* ash.

29 *a*. Leaves opposite, flowers dioecious (stamens in 1 plant, pistils in another), in drooping catkins, dwells in mountainous country. Family *Garryaceae:* silk tassel.

29 *b*. Leaves alternate. **30**

30 *a*. Both pistillate and staminate flowers in catkins. **31**

30 *b*. Staminate flowers in catkins, pistillate flowers usually solitary or in clusters. **33**

31 *a*. 2 or 3 flowers to each scale or bract of plant, the calyx present, the staminate catkins long and hanging, the pistillate small, spikelike, and changing into a woody cone with small nutlets. Family *Betulaceae:* birch.

31 *b*. 1 flower to each scale or bract, no calyx. **32**

32 *a*. Fruit waxy-coated and berrylike, foliage evergreen or deciduous (falling off), flowers monoecious (male and female flowers on same plant), or dioecious (Figure 18-3). Family *Myricaceae:* sweet gale.

32 *b*. Fruit a 1-celled, many-seeded capsule, foliage deciduous, seeds with a tuft of hair, flowers dioecious. Family *Salicaceae:* willow.

33 *a*. Leaves pinnately compound (see Figure 12-8), fruit a nut with a fibrous coat. Family *Juglandaceae:* walnut.

33 *b*. Leaves simple. **34**

34 *a*. Fruit appears like a nut set in a scaly cup or bur (acorn or chestnut). Family *Fagaceae:* oak.

34 *b*. Fruit a nut enclosed in a leafy tube-shaped envelope (Figure 18-19). Family *Corylaceae:* hazel.

35–67. CHORIPETALOUS (WITH FREE PETALS)

35 *a*. Ovary superior (free from the calyx). (Figure 18-4.) **36**
35 *b*. Ovary inferior (more or less attached to the calyx). (Figure 18-5.) **62**

36 *a*. 10 or fewer hypogynous stamens (Figure 18-7). **37**
36 *b*. 10 or more hypogynous stamens, or the stamens are perigynous (Figure 18-6). **49**

37 *a*. Pistils 4 or 5 (even if these appear to be united around the central column), an herb. **38**
37 *b*. 1 pistil, though the styles or stigmas may be more than 1, a tree, shrub or herb. **40**

38 *a*. 4 or 5 distinctly separate pistils, which become follicles (dehiscent seed vessels such as a pod). (See Figure 18-20.) Family *Crassulaceae:* stonecrop.
38 *b*. 5 more or less united pistils (Figure 18-21), which are separated elastically when ripe as 1-seeded carpels. **39**

39 *a*. Stipules scarious (dry, not green), carpels (fruits) have tails made by twisted styles. Family *Geraniaceae:* geranium.
39 *b*. No stipules on leaves, carpels separate from a very short axis (stem) and not tailed. Family *Limnanthaceae:* meadow foam.

40 *a*. Corolla (circle of petals) irregularly shaped. **41**
40 *b*. Corolla regular, **43**

41 *a*. 4 petals in 2 dissimilar pairs, 6 stamens slightly united into 2 sets, 2 sepals. Family *Fumariaceae:* fumitory.
41 *b*. 5 petals. **42**

42 *a*. 10 stamens, butterflylike petals (Figure 18-22), compound leaves. Family *Leguminoseae:* bean.
42 *b*. 5 stamens, a spur on the lower petal (Figure 18-23), usually simple leaves. Family *Violaceae:* violet.

43 *a*. Ovary with more than 1 cell (Figure 18-39). **44**
43 *b*. Ovary with only 1 cell. **46**

44 *a*. Anthers of stamens open by pores at their tops (Figure 18-24), 5 petals, ovary 5-celled. Family *Ericaceae:* heath.
44 *b*. Anthers opening by long slits (Figure 18-15). **45**

45 *a*. 4 sepals and 4 petals, 4 long and 2 short stamens, ovary 2-celled (rarely 1-celled), leaves opposite or basal. Family *Cruciferae:* mustard.

45 b. 5 each of sepals and petals, 10 stamens, 5-celled ovary, alternate or basal leaves. Family *Oxalidaceae:* oxalis. See also, if in doubt, the *Geraniaceae,* in **39** *a.*

46 a. Anthers open by uplifted valves (Figure 18-14), 6 stamens, 6 petals, a capsule or berry fruit. Family *Berberidaceae:* barberry.

46 b. Anthers (tops of stamens) open by long slits (Figure 18-15), an herb. **47**

47 a. 2 distinct sepals, usually 5 stamens, a 3-valved capsule fruit. Family *Portulacaceae:* purslane.

47 b. Sepals either joined together, or 5 separate sepals. **48**

48 a. Basal leaves, a funnel-shaped calyx, 5 stamens with each opposite a petal (Figure 18-41B), fruit an achene (Figure 18-10). Family *Plumbaginaceae:* thrift.

48 b. Opposite leaves, a tubular calyx or one with distinct sepals, a central placenta (Figure 18-39B), the 5 stamens alternate with the petals (Figure 18-41A), a 3- to 10-valved or -toothed capsule, or the fruit 1-seeded and indehiscent (not splitting open). Family *Caryophyllaceae:* pink.

49 a. 10 or more hypogynous stamens (not attached to calyx, as in Figure 18-7). **50**

49 b. Perigynous (attached to the calyx or a disk) stamens (Figure 18-6), corolla regular. **55**

50 a. 2 to many simple and distinct pistils, simple leaves, entire to divided or compound, pistils becoming achenes (Figure 18-10) or follicles (Figure 18-25). Family *Ranunculaceae:* buttercup.

50 b. 1 pistil. **51**

51 a. Simple, opposite leaves, **52**

51 b. Alternate or basal leaves, **53**

52 a. Stamens arranged in 3 to 5 indistinct bunches, fruit a capsule (Figure 18-12). Family *Hypericaceae:* St.-John's-wort.

52 b. Stamens distinct, fruit capsular or separates into distinct carpels. Family *Papaveraceae:* poppy.

53 a. A 1-celled ovary, but styles or stigmas more than 1; caducous (falling off) sepals; petals 4 or 6 and twice as many as the sepals. Family *Papaveraceae:* poppy.

53 b. Ovary with more than 1 cell. **54**

54 a. Distinctly separate stamens, 5–12 sepals, 10–20 petals, an aquatic herb. Genus *Nymphaea* (pond lily) of the Family *Nymphaceae:* pond lily.

54 *b*. Numerous indistinct stamens joined into a tube around the pistil, a 5- to 30-celled ovary, flowers perfect or unisexual; rounded, palmately veined to palmately divided leaves (Figure 12-8). Family *Malvaceae:* mallow.

55 *a*. Stamens rising from the calyx (circle of sepals). **56**

55 *b*. Stamens rising from a hypogynous disk (Figure 18-26), or a disk lining the base of the calyx, a tree or shrub. **58**

56 *a*. Stipules on the leaves in most cases, 1 to several pistils, sometimes partly united to the disk, 10 to numerous stamens, leaves usually alternate and simple or compound, 5 petals. Family *Rosaceae:* rose.

56 *b*. No stipules, simple leaves, **57**

57 *a*. 1 pistil, styles or stigmas more than 1, commonly 5 (4 to 8) petals, 3 to 10 or numerous stamens. Family *Saxifragaceae:* saxifrage.

57 *b*. Many pistils, all concealed in a hollow receptacle (Figure 18-27), many stamens, many petals, a shrub with opposite leaves. Family *Calycanthaceae:* sweet shrub.

58 *a*. A double samara fruit (Figure 18-18), opposite and simple leaves, 3 to 10 stamens. Family *Aceraceae:* maple.

58 *b*. Fruit not a double samara. **59**

59 *a*. Simple, 3-foliolate or pinnately compound leaves (Figure 12-8). **60**

59 *b*. Palmately compound, opposite leaves with 5 to 7 leaflets (Figure 12-8), slightly irregular, clawed petals, 4 to 9 stamens, a 1-seeded, dehiscent (splitting open) pod fruit. Family *Sapindaceae:* buckeye.

60 *a*. As many stamens (4 to 10) as petals and opposite them (Figure 18-41B), simple, alternate (opposite in *Adolphia*) leaves, usually hooded petals, a 3- (or 2-) celled, dry fruit, which splits into 3 (or 2) one-seeded parts, or fruit like a drupe, plant a shrub. Family *Rhamnaceae:* buckthorn.

60 *b*. As many stamens (4 to 10) as petals and alternate to them (Figure 18-41A), or twice as many stamens as petals. **61**

61 *a*. Tiny stipules on the leaves, 1 style or none, leaves alternate or opposite, seeds with an aril (taillike part), fruit a capsule

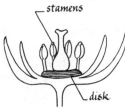

18-26.
Stamens arising from
a hypogynous disk.

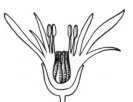

18-27. Many pistils,
concealed in a
hollow receptacle.

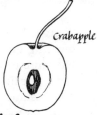

18-28.
A pome fruit.
(longitudinal section)

18-29. Flower in a
head surrounded by a
flower-like involucre.

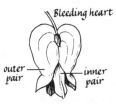

18-30. Fumitory family.
Flower with 4 petals
in 2 kinds of pairs.

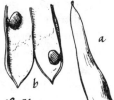

18-31.
Legume fruit.
a. pod   b. tip of
pod after splitting.

18-32.
Tendril-bearing herbs.
Gourd family.

18-33.
Fruit with two
to four nutlets.

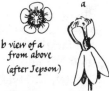

18-34.
A column of united stamens,
bearing hoodlike projections.
Milkweed.

18-35.
Capsule fruit opening
by lid. Plantain.

18-36.

Morning-glory bud with twisted folds
beginning to open.

Twining or trailing plant with
corolla plaited in folds and
these twisted in the bud.

(Figure 18-12), or follicle (Figure 18-25). Family *Celastraceae:* burning bush.

61 b. No stipules on leaves, alternate leaves, 3 to 5 styles, herbage with a resinous or acrid juice, broad leaves. Family *Anacardiaceae:* sumac.

62 a. Plant an herb. **63**

62 b. A shrub or tree. **65**

63 a. Flowers in umbels (Figure 12-11B), 5 stamens, 2 styles, petals 5 or fewer and inflexed (turned inward) at the tip, the fruit splitting into 2 (1-seeded) carpels. Family *Umbelliferae:* parsley.

63 b. Flowers not in umbels. **64**

64 a. 1 style, usually a 4-celled capsule fruit, 4 (rarely 5 or 2) each of sepals and petals, with usually twice as many stamens as petals. Family *Onagraceae:* evening primrose.

64 b. 2 to 5 styles or stigmas, petals 5, 5 to 10 stamens, a 5-lobed calyx, a 4-celled capsule fruit. Family *Saxifragaceae:* saxifrage.

65 a. 5 petals, with the stamens more numerous, alternate leaves, a pome fruit (Figure 18-28). Family *Rosaceae:* rose.

65 b. As many petals as stamens. **66**

66 a. Stamens opposite the petals (Figure 18-41B), 5 hooded petals, a 3-celled capsule with 1 seed in each cell. Genus *Ceanothus* of the family *Rhamnaceae*, buckthorn.

66 b. Stamens alternate with the petals (Figure 18-41A). **67**

67 a. 4 petals, 1 style, 4 stamens, a drupelike fruit, opposite leaves, small flowers in cymes, or, if in a head, surrounded by a showy flowerlike involucre (Figure 18-29). Family *Cornaceae:* dogwood.

67 b. 5 (sometimes 4) petals, 5 (sometimes 4) stamens, 2 styles, alternate leaves, usually with stipules, a smooth or prickly berry fruit, flowers in racemes (Figure 12-11B) or solitary. Genus *Ribes* (gooseberry and currant) of the family *Saxifragaceae*, saxifrage.

68–95. Sympetalous (Corolla with the Petals Joined)

68a. More than 5 stamens. **69**

68 b. 5 or less stamens, all rising from the corolla (circle of petals). **76**

69 a. Corolla (circle of petals) urn-shaped to tubular or campanulate (bell-shaped) (Figure 12-11A), with the stamens not or only just barely arising from it, 1 stigma, 1 style, ovary 4 to 10 (rarely 1, 2, 3) cells, anthers usually opening by a pore in the end (Figure 18-24), sometimes slit lengthwise (Figure 18-15). Family *Ericaceae:* heath.

69 *b.* Corolla not tubular or urn-shaped, petals joined only at the base. **70**

70 *a.* Ovary inferior (Figure 18-5) or slightly inferior. **71**

70 *b.* Ovary superior (Figure 18-4). **72**

71 *a.* Numerous petals and stamens, stems and leaves fleshy and spiny (Figure 12-9). Family *Cactaceae:* cactus.

71 *b.* A shrub with 4 to 8 petals, stamens about twice as many as the petals. Family *Styracaceae:* storax.

72 *a.* 10 stamens, 4 or 5 distinct pistils. Family *Crassulaceae:* stone crop.

72 *b.* 1 pistil. **73**

73 *a.* A regular corolla, a 5- to many-celled ovary, simple, roundish, nearly entire to palmately divided leaves (Figure 12-8), the numerous stamens monodelphous in a tube (Figure 18-17). Family *Malvaceae:* mallow.

73 *b.* Irregular corolla (circle of petals), a single style. **74**

74 *a.* 4 petals in 2 different kinds of pairs (Figure 18-30), 6 stamens, 2 sepals, divided leaves. Family *Fumariaceae:* fumitory.

74 *b.* Papilionaceous (butterflylike) petals (Figure 18-22). **75**

75 *a.* 3 petals, a 2-celled ovary (Figure 18-39), simple, entire leaves, a capsule fruit (Figure 18-12). Family *Polygalaceae:* polygala.

75 *b.* 5 petals, a 1-celled ovary, compound, though sometimes simple leaves, a legume fruit (Figure 18-31). Family *Leguminosae:* pea.

76 *a.* Inferior ovary (Figure 18-5). **77**

76 *b.* Superior ovary (Figure 18-4). **83**

77 *a.* Stamens united into a tube around the style (Figure 18-17). **78**

77 *b.* Distinctly separate stamens. **80**

78 *a.* Tiny flowers joined into a head surrounded by a calyxlike involucre (circle of bracts) that makes it look like a single flower (Figure 18-29), 5 or rarely 4 stamens, an achene fruit (Figure 18-10). Family *Compositae:* sunflower.

78 *b.* Flowers not in heads. **79**

79 *a.* Palmate leaves (Figure 12-8), 3 stamens, a tendril-bearing herb (Figure 18-32). Family *Cucurbitaceae:* gourd.

79 b. Narrow leaves, 5 stamens, plant an annual (growing only 1 year) herb. Family *Lobeliaceae:* lobelia.

80 a. Alternate leaves, 5 stamens, regular flowers, a 2- to 5-celled ovary, capsule fruit, an herb. Family *Campanulaceae:* bell flower.

80 b. Opposite or whorled leaves. 81

81 a. An irregular flower, 1 to 3 stamens, a 1-celled, 1-seeded fruit, an herb. Family *Valerianaceae:* valerian.

81 b. 4 or 5 (rarely 2) stamens. 82

82 a. A 2-celled ovary, the berrylike or dry fruit usually separated into 2 (1-seeded) achenelike (Figure 18-10) halves, regular flowers, simple leaves, an herb or shrub. Family *Rubiaceae:* madder.

82 b. 2- to 5-celled ovary, regular or irregular flowers, simple or compound leaves, an erect or twining shrub. Family *Caprifoliaceae:* honeysuckle.

83 a. A strongly 2-lipped to slightly irregular corolla. 84

83 b. A regular corolla. 87

84 a. A capsule fruit. 85

84 b. Fruit made up of 2 to 4 nutlets (Figure 18-33). 86

85 a. A 1-celled ovary, 4 stamens, a small nonbeaked capsule fruit, a root-parasite without green foliage. Family *Orobanchaceae:* broom-rape.

85 b. A 2-celled ovary with the placenta (tissue to which the ovules are attached) axil (central) (Figure 18-39B and Figure 18-25), wingless seeds, 2 to 4 stamens (rarely 5), alternate or opposite leaves, usually an herb. Family *Scrophulariaceae:* figwort.

86 a. A 2- to 4-celled ovary (not lobed), splitting into as many nutlets, leaves opposite, 4 stamens, 1 entire style. Family *Verbenaceae:* verbena.

86 b. A 4-lobed ovary, splitting into as many nutlets, 4 stamens, a square stem, the odor of mint, opposite leaves, 1 style (cleft at the tip). Family *Labiatae (Menthaceae):* mint.

87 a. 2 pistils (the ovaries separate, but the styles or stigmas joined), an herb with a milky juice. 88

87 b. 1 pistil. 89

88 a. Column of united stamens and stigmas bearing hoodlike appendages (projections) (Figure 18-34). Family *Asclepiadaceae:* milkweed.

88 *b*. Neither hoods nor stamens and stigmas united. Family *Apo-cynaceae:* dogbane.

89 *a*. As many stamens as lobes of the corolla (circle of petals), and opposite to them (5 to 7 stamens in *Trientalis*, star flower), a capsule fruit, 1 style. Family *Primulaceae:* primrose.

89 *b*. As many as or fewer stamens than the lobes of the corolla and alternate with them (Figure 18-41A). **90**

90 *a*. A dry-scarious (noncolored) corolla, a 2- to 4-celled ovary, 2 to 4 stamens, 1 style, a capsule fruit that opens by a lid (Figure 18-35). Family *Plantaginaceae:* plantain.

90 *b*. A colored corolla. **91**

91 *a*. A 4-celled ovary (usually 4-lobed), splitting when ripe into as many nutlets (Figure 18-33), flowers in coiled spikes or racemes, 5 stamens, 1 style. Family *Boraginaceae:* borage.

91 *b*. A 1- , 2- , or 3-celled ovary. **92**

92 *a*. A 1- to 2-celled ovary, the style not cleft, the fruit a capsule (sometimes a berry), not opening by a lid. **93**

92 *b*. A 3-celled ovary, 3-cleft style, 3-valved capsule, the rest of the flower parts in 5's. Family *Polemoniaceae:* gilia.

93 *a*. 5 distinct (or almost so) sepals, a 5-lobed corolla, 5 stamens, and a commonly 2-valved capsule. **94**

93 *b*. A 4- or 5-toothed or cleft calyx (circle of sepals), 1 entire style. **95**

94 *a*. Plant erect or spread diffusely, the corolla lobes usually over-lapping in the bud, either 2 distinct styles or 1 cleft at the apex (style 1 and entire in *Romanzoffia*), capsule few to many seeded, the flowers in coiled racemes or spikes or in heads or solitary. Family *Hydrophyllaceae:* phacelia.

94 *b*. A twining or trailing plant, corolla usually plaited in folds and these twisted in the bud (Figure 18-36), 1 or 2 styles, a 1- to 4-seeded capsule, flower groupings never coiled (Figure 12-6). Family *Convolvulaceae:* morning glory.

95 *a*. A 1-celled ovary, 4 or 5 stamens, 2 stigmas, opposite leaves, a septicidal (splitting between the valves) capsule fruit, a 4- or 5-lobed corolla (usually withering and persistent). Family *Gentianaceae:* gentian.

95 *b*. A 2-celled ovary, 5 stamens, 1 stigma (2 in *Datura*, thorn apple), alternate leaves, a many-seeded capsule or berry fruit, a 5-lobed corolla. Family *Solanaceae:* nightshade.

96–104. (Subclass 2) Monocotyledonae (Parallel-veined)

96 a. No perianth (floral envelope of petallike lobes), or this is calyxlike with scalelike parts; 1 to several carpels (pistil divisions), separate or sometimes united while young; the parts of the flower (usually) unequal in number. **97**

96 b. Perianth with parts in 2 series (rarely in 1) and often petallike (Figure 18-37), the carpels joined into a compound ovary (except in *Alismaceae*), the parts of the flower commonly equal in number. **100**

97 a. Flowers in the axils (angle between leaf and stem) of dry chafflike bracts, and arranged in spikes or spikelets. **98**

97 b. Flowers not in the axils of dry chafflike bracts; a superior ovary (Figure 18-4), an herb. **99**

98 a. Cylindrical, hollow stems, 2 rows of leaves with the sheaths usually split open opposite the blades, 2 bractlets to each flower, fruit a grain. Family *Gramineae:* grass.

98 b. A triangular and solid stem (usually), 3 rows of leaves with entire sheaths, 1 bractlet to each flower, the fruit an achene (Figure 18-10). Family *Cyperaceae:* sedge.

99 a. A leafless tiny aquatic plant with the stems looking like leaflike floating fronds. Family *Lemnaceae:* buckweed.

99 b. A leafy plant, found in marshes or rising out of water, reedlike stems with very narrow leaves, monoecious (1 sex in 1 plant) flowers, inflorescence (flower grouping) a dense cylindrical spike (Figure 12-11B). Family *Typhaceae:* cattail.

100 a. Inflorescence (flower grouping) with a spathe (a large leaflike

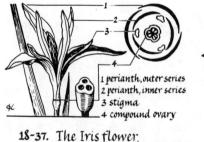

1 perianth, outer series
2 perianth, inner series
3 stigma
4 compound ovary

18-37. The Iris flower.

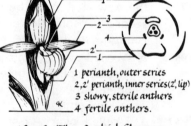

1 perianth, outer series
2,2' perianth, inner series (2', lip)
3 showy, sterile anthers
4 fertile anthers.

18-38. The Orchid flower.

bract enclosing a flower cluster), 1 pistil, the flowers on a fleshy spike (Figure 18-3B), a tree. Family *Palmaceae:* palm.

100 *b.* No spathe with the inflorescence. **101**

101 *a.* A superior ovary (Figure 18-4), a regular perianth (petallike floral envelope of flower); 6 stamens (or 3 or 4), 1 pistil. **102**

101 *b.* An inferior ovary (Figure 18-5), mostly conspicuous perfect flowers, 1 pistil, a perennial (lives 2 or more years), **103**

102 *a.* Separate green or brown perianth parts (not petallike), small or tiny flowers, rushlike. Family *Juncaceae:* rush.

102 *b.* Either separate or partly united perianth parts (at least the inner ones petallike); mostly fair-sized flowers; not rushlike. (Figure 6-1). Family *Liliaceae:* lily.

103 *a.* An irregular perianth (Figure 18-38), 1 (rarely 2) stamens, 1-celled ovary, the leaves forming sheaths or often reduced to scales. Family *Orchidaceae:* orchid.

103 *b.* A regular perianth and 3-celled ovary. **104**

104 *a.* 2-ranked swordlike and sheathing leaves, 3 stamens. (Figure 18-37). Family *Iridaceae:* iris.

104 *b.* Fleshy leaves in a basal rosette, 6 stamens. Family *Amaryllidaceae:* amaryllis.

SCIENTIFIC DRAWINGS OF PLANTS

The naturalist is not satisfied with learning how to use plant keys alone; he or she wants to reach a thorough understanding of the differences between the orders and families of plants. The greatest aid to this knowledge comes through making your own scientific plant drawings.

To draw flowers as the botanist does is not so simple. You need, first, seven tools:

1. Razor, or very sharp knife, for slicing apart delicate tissues.
2. Forceps, for pulling out or turning aside parts of a flowers.
3. Dissecting needle, made by firmly sticking a needle with the point outward into a slender, round 7.5 to 10.1 centimeter (three- or four-inch) stick; for probing apart tiny flower parts. (Also may be purchased from biological supply houses; see Chapter Five.)

4. Magnifying glass, to examine parts of plants too small to be seen very clearly with unaided eye. Magnification 8-10 times.
5. Hard lead drawing pencil (4H or 3H).
6. Good eraser.
7. Botany drawing paper.

There are three types of drawings that need to be done of each plant: (1) the picture of the flower as a whole to give an idea of its complete natural appearance, (2) a longitudinal section of the flower to give an idea of the position of the ovary in relation to the sepals, and the position of the stamens in relation to both ovary and petals, and (3) a cross section or floral design, which must show the number and arrangement of sepals, petals, stamens, and ovules, each in relation to the whole. Only by careful dissection of the flower can the facts about the last two drawings be gathered.

First, merely make a careful drawing of *the flower as a whole* (see Figure 6-1). This should show: (1) the stem and its shape, (2) the appearance and shape of the petals, including their color, (3) the appearance and shape of the sepals, (4) the appearance of either stamens or pistil if they extend beyond the corolla, and (5) the shape, size, and arrangement of the leaves on the stem.

For the *longitudinal section drawing* your main difficulty is in dissection. With the razor you must carefully cut the flower almost exactly in half, making sure that you show a longitudinal section of the ovary as it lies at the base of the pistil. For the *cross-section drawing* (Figure 18-41) cut across the middle of the base of the flower so that both the central part of the ovary and the bases of the perianth are exposed.

With the magnifying glass, you can study the inner structure of the ovary and determine whether the arrangement of the ovules is any one of the types illustrated in Figure 18-41. If the arrangement of your flower is in fives or threes (five or three petals, stamens, and so on), indicate the flower parts on one side of your drawing with heavy lines

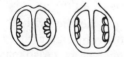

A. *Parietal placenta*   B. *Central placenta* _____ C. *Free central placenta*

18-39. *Main types of ovule arrangement.* cross-sec., left; long.sec., right

and on the other side with dotted lines (see Figure 18-40). If the stamens occur between the petals, they will show as in Figure 18-40A. If the stamens are directly in front of the petal, draw them as in Figure 18-40B.

In studying your flower to draw its cross section or floral design, you need to watch for the following:

1. Are the stamens alternate with the petals (see Figure 18-41A) or are they opposite the petals (see Figure 18-41B)?.
2. Does a horizontal section cut through the middle of the ovary show it to have any divisions (as in Figure 18-39) and, if so, how many? Use a magnifying glass to find out.)
3. Are the stamens united (see Figure 18-41C)?
4. Carefully look to see whether the petals and/or the sepals are attached together (see Figure 18-41D) or free from each other (see Figure 18-41C).

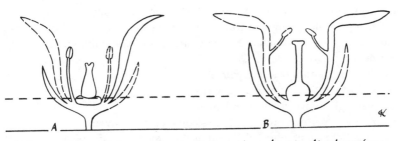

18-40. *Two types of flower, showing how to draw longitudinal sections.*

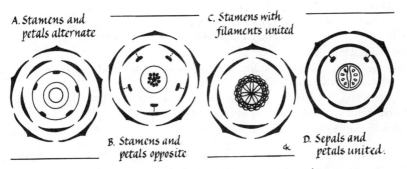

A. Stamens and petals alternate

c. Stamens with filaments united

B. Stamens and petals opposite

D. Sepals and petals united.

18-41. *Four types of floral design, cross-section diagrams.*

5. In cases where the stamens are very numerous (Figure 18-41C), try to find out how many circles of stamens there are around the center and mark these in your drawing, although you do not need to draw every stamen in such cases.

A GLOSSARY OF COMMON BOTANICAL TERMS

Below are descriptions of words commonly used in describing plants.* You are referred to pictures in the key that illustrate these terms. Getting familiar with these words will help you in using plant keys you find in other books. Study these words and their meanings carefully.

Achene: a dry indehiscent (not splitting open) one-seeded fruit (Figure 18-10).
Adherent: growing fast to, or united with, another body or organ of a different kind.
Adnate: growing fast to, or born united with, another body.
Annual: a plant flowering and fruiting in one year or season and then dying.
Anther: the sac or sacs containing the pollen at the top of the stamen.
Apetalous: without petals.
Approximate: standing close together.
Awn: a bristle (usually found in grasses).
Axil: the angle between a leaf and stem.
Banner: the upper petal in a papilionaceous, or pea, flower.
Blade: the flat part of a leaf; also said of the broad part of a petal.
Bract: the modified, usually very small and colorless leaf of a flower cluster. Among grasses it is the modified leaf that supports the base of a spikelet (grass flower).
Bur: a fruit covered with spines.
Calyx: the outer, usually green circle of lobes of the flower (the sepals).
Campanulate: bell-shaped.
Capsule: a dry dehiscent (splitting open) seed vessel made up of more than one carpel or ovary chamber.
Carpel: a simple pistil, or one of the parts of a compound pistil.
Choripetalous: petals free and not united (Figure 6-2).
Chorisepalous: sepals free and not united.

*Adapted from Willis L. Jepson, *A Manual of the Flowering Plants of California.* Berkeley: University of California Press, 1925.

Claw: the narrow base of a petal.

Cleft: with sharp lobes, reaching about to the middle.

Complete: said of a flower having sepals, petals, stamens, and pistils.

Corolla: the circle of petals in a flower.

Corymb: flowers on pedicels (stems) of unequal length (Figure 12-10B).

Cruciferous: with petals spreading in the form of a cross.

Cyme: a flower cluster in which the central flower blooms first (Figure 12-10B).

Deciduous: falling when ripe or as leaves fall in autumn.

Diadelphous: stamens united into two sets.

Dioecious: with the stamens and pistils in different flowers on different plants (Figure 18-3).

Disk: a development or swelling of the receptacle around the ovary. In *Compositae*, the sunflower family, the disk flowers are the small central flowers on the receptacle, as opposed to the large ray flowers on the outside rim.

Drupe: a fruit with a fleshy or soft outside and a stony inside; a cherry is a drupe.

Entire: said of a leaf when its edge is smooth.

Epigynous: with the flower parts as if inserted (placed) on the top of the ovary.

Foliaceous: leaflike.

Foliolate: with leaflets, as three-foliolate (with three leaflets). (Figure 12-7).

Free: not united, as when the corolla (circle of petals) is free of (not united with) the ovary.

Galea: the long or helmetlike upper lip in the mint and figwort families.

Glume: one of the two lower bracts (dry leaflets) in the spikelet (flower) of grasses.

Head: said of flowers when in a close, round cluster, often looking like a single flower (as among the sunflowers). (Figure 12-10B and Figure 18-29).

Herb: a plant without woody stems.

Hypogynous: with the corolla (circle of petals) and the stamens growing from the receptacle and free from the pistil or ovary (Figure 18-7).

Incomplete: said of a flower that is missing in one or more of its usual parts, such as stamens, pistils, petals, or sepals.

Indehiscent: said of fruits or pods that do not split open.

Inferior: growing or placed below. An inferior ovary is one attached to the calyx (circle of sepals) and corolla (circle of petals). (Figure 18-5).

Inflorescence: a flower cluster, or the manner of arrangement of the flowers in a cluster.

Involucre: a circle of bracts (colorless or colored leaflets) surrounding a flower cluster or head.

Irregular: the parts not of the same size and shape, as with the petals in a violet flower (Figure 18-23).

Keel: the two lower petals of a pea flower, which are joined together like the keel of a boat (Figure 18-22).

Leaflet: one of the divisions of a compound leaf (Figure 12-7).

Legume: a one-celled seed vessel, made up of a single carpel (pistil or pistil part), which splits both above and below into two valves (Figure 18-31).

Lemma: the lowest bract (leaflet) in a floret (tiny flower) of grasses.

Ligule: like a short ribbon or strap, such as the ray in the sunflower family. In grasses, the outside part of the hyaline (transparent) membrane lining the sheath (cover to a spikelet).

Line: two millimeters (one-half inch), used as a measurement of size for small plant parts.

Monadelphous: stamens united into one set (Figure 18-17).

Monoecious: with stamens and pistils in separate flowers on the same plant.

Node: the place on the stem where the leaf is borne.

Opposite leaves: two from each node and opposite each other.

Palea: chafflike pappus (modified calyx limb) attached to the achene (dry fruit) of the sunflower family, so as to carry it on the wind. In the grass family, the upper of two modified bracts (leaflets) below an individual flower.

Palmate: with the divisions of a leaf or its veins branching out like the fingers of a hand (Figure 12-7).

Papilionaceous: name for an irregular flower such as the pea flower, whose corolla (circle of petals) has two side petals or wings, an upper petal or banner, and two lower petals joined to form a keel (Figure 18-22).

Pappus: the modified calyx (circle of sepals) limb attached to the achene (dry fruit) of the sunflower family, usually appearing as a bristle, hair, scale, or chaff.

Pedicel: stalk or stem of a flower in a flower cluster.

Peduncle: stalk or stem of a flower or flower cluster.

Perianth: usually given as a collective name to both petals and sepals when there is no great difference between them.

Pinnate: with the leaflets arranged along both sides of a common petiole (stem). (Figure 12-7).

Prostrate: lying along the ground.

Raceme: a flower cluster in which the flowers are borne along the peduncle (main stem) on pedicels (short stems) of nearly equal length (Figure 12-10B).

Rachis: the stem or axis of a spike (Figure 12-10B) or a raceme (Figure 12-10B); the midrib of a compound leaf; in the grass family, the main axis or stem and branches of an inflorescence (flower cluster) on which the spikelets (grass flowers) are borne.

Ray: in the parsley family, one of the main branches of the umbel (Figure 12-10B); in the sunflower family, the ligule or straplike petal of the ray flower.

Receptacle: in a flower, that portion of the stem on which the pistils, stamens, petals, and sepals are borne; in an inflorescence (flower cluster), it is the base on which a flower is borne.

Samara: an indehiscent (not splitting open) winged fruit such as the key of a maple (Figure 18-18).

Scape: a leafless flower-bearing stem arising from the ground.

Shrub: a branching woody plant, smaller than a tree.

Silique: a very long, two-celled capsule, the valves splitting from the bottom.

Silicle: a short silique (see above).

Spike: a flower cluster in which the flowers are densely and closely arranged along a common peduncle (stalk). (Figure 12-10B).

Spikelet: a secondary spike; the flower cluster of grasses.

Stamen: the male organ of the flower.

Staminate: bearing or containing stamens but no pistils.

Stigma: the tip of the style of the pistil.

Stipules: small leaflike appendages of the leaf, borne in pairs at the base of the petiole or leaf stem.

Style: the slender portion of a pistil between the ovary and the stigma (top).

Sympetalous: petals more or less united together (Figure 12-5).

Synsepalous: sepals more or less united.

Umbel: branches nearly equal and starting from the same point so as to form a flat-topped flower cluster (see Figure 12-10B).

Whorl: with organs borne in a circle.

Wing: any thin expansion attached to an organ or part of a plant; the side petals in a papilionaceous flower (Figure 18-22).

THE BEHAVIOR OF PLANTS

The behavior of plants is actually a part of the ecology of plants, which will be taken up in Chapter Twenty, but here we will distinguish between plant and animal behavior and point out a few examples of particularly interesting plant behavior not discussed under ecology.

With a few exceptions, such as the slime molds and Euglena (a single-celled plant that moves about with cilia, like some of the protozoa), most animals differ from most plants in that plants are stationary. However, certain plants move their leaves to a touch, as

Acacia do, and others, like the sundew, close their petals or leaves to catch insects that they actually digest. But many plants show behavior in other ways than by visible movement, such as methods of reproduction, ways for spreading seeds, ways of attracting insects and birds to pollinate their flowers, defenses against being eaten (such as thorns and poisonous leaves), methods for resisting cold or heat, and ways of competing with other plants for space.

Be watchful when you are studying plants and carefully observe ways in which plants enhance their chances of being successful in life. Also observe the tremendous numbers of seeds and spores let out by plants, so at least some will live to carry on the species. As with animals, down through the ages natural selection has improved and changed the structure and behavior of plants, favoring the most vigorous and inventive types. The word *invent* does not imply that plants "think" when they invent, but it is evident that certain plants appear to produce over a period of time more different types to suit different habitats more often than other, more conservative plants. Inventive-type plants tend to spread over wide areas; conservative plants are often restricted to narrow niches in one or a few places and are in danger of dying out entirely if conditions change. The sundew and some of the pitcher plants are examples of inventive plants that changed dramatically over a long period of time into actual carnivores on insects.

Some of the most amazing examples of plant behavior are the various ways, several quite fantastic in complexity, that many plants have used to attract insects to their flowers so that the stigmas of the ovaries can be fertilized by pollen (or male cells) brought from neighboring plants by bees, flies, and other insects, also some by birds such as hummingbirds. How this wonderful cooperation between animals and plants started is one of the great mysteries of plant history, but it produces most of the plant food we eat today. Many plants, such as the daisy, simply attract any insects that will come, but others, such as the orchid (see Figure 18-38) and the figwort, make more certain that the right pollen will come to them by developing special kinds of openings to their flowers that only certain insects can use to obtain nectar. Thus the wisteria vine has very long peculiarly shaped flowers, which only one species of big black bumblebee seems able to penetrate, carrying with it the pollen from another wisteria plant.

In the same way, different plants have different ways of spreading their seeds. Dandelions form masses of fluffy down attached to their seeds, which allows them to be carried away long distances by the wind. Maple trees have propeller-shaped wings attached to their seeds that enable the wind to whirl them away for some distance. Other plants, such as the beggar ticks or the clot burs, have hooks attached to their seeds that clasp onto the fur of animals or the clothes of humans, allowing them to be carried off really long distances. All this helps plants to spread their species far and wide and are examples of plant behavior that you should watch for carefully when studying plants.

In defending themselves against the competition of other plants or in being aggressively competitive themselves, some plants have been very inventive indeed. In the high mountain jungles of Panama, and other areas, strangler figs not only swarm up the trunks of other trees to reach the light, but in the end strangle their hosts to death by gradual constriction until the host trees die and the figs take their places! Some plants use poisonous chemicals to keep other plants from coming too near them, as do some of the eucalyptus trees, since few other plants can stand the eucalyptus oil that this tree drops to the ground. Several desert plants do the same thing, for instance, the creosote bush of the southwestern deserts with its creosote oil droppings.

These examples give some inkling of the many ways in which plants behave. Use your eyes and your nose to investigate carefully the ways of plants in their struggle for existence with the climate, with other plants, and with animals. Often fascinating is their behavior!

CHAPTER
19

Rock and Mineral Classification

Imagine that we had a motion picture record of the long and interesting history of the earth. Fantastic as it may seem, such a record turned upon a screen with each thousand years flashing by once every second would still take at least sixteen days and four hours for the entire showing! If we could stay awake that long, what marvels of the past would unfold before our eyes! We would watch whole continents lifting in long groaning ridges from the waves; we would see a thousand volcanoes blow their tops off in a symphonic cataclysm of fire; ages of rock would be tossed into the sea in an hour of rain's erosion and river's sweeping, and then in a minute or two we would watch the underearth pressures roll the rock back up again into mighty mountains; we would see the wind blowing the desert sands of the Sahara into a thousand fertile valleys of Africa; and see once more, in a half-second's flash, the massive tidal wave that probably roared down into the valley that once was the Mediterranean before the

Atlantic Ocean forced its savage way past the Pillars of Hercules.

Unfortunately, however, we do not have such a picture to show us the true history of the earth. We can only read bits of this history from the study of rocks and minerals that coat the earth's surface. But our knowledge will be nothing unless we can first learn the names of what we see. The purpose of this chapter is to help you learn the elements of rock and mineral classification, or how to determine the real name of each specimen you find. It is too big a subject for one chapter, perhaps even for one book, but we can at least start you on your way.

The simple key to rocks and minerals you will find on the following pages will help you classify about nine out of ten rocks or minerals you are liable to find on a walk in the country. For the classification of specimens that do not appear in this key, turn to the books listed in the Bibliography. A very good book for the student is the *Field Guide to Rocks and Minerals* by Frederick Pough (Houghton Mifflin, 4th Edition).

For classifying rocks and minerals you will need the following tools:

1. *A geologic pick or hammer.* A stonemason's hammer will do. This is for breaking up rocks in the field so that you see the appearance of their unweathered surfaces.

2. *A set of the first seven hardness minerals.* (Mentioned in the glossary in this chapter.) Or use your fingernail, a penny, your knife, and a piece of quartz — all useful in measuring the hardness of minerals and rocks.

3. *A streak plate.* A piece of unglazed porcelain, to be bought from one of the scientific equipment companies in Chapter 5. Used for finding out the color of a mineral's streak when rubbed on the plate.

4. *A small bottle of weak hydrochloric acid.* This is used to determine whether there is calcite (lime) in the rock. (If there is calcite, the rock effervesces or bubbles under the touch of the acid.) A weak solution of this acid will not be dangerous provided you keep it tightly stoppered and carefully use only a small bit at a time on your rocks, never allowing it to spill on clothes or flesh. If it does spill on anybody's clothes or skin, put as much water on it as you can immediately. This will effectively stop any dangerous reaction.

Hardness is a very important aid in determining the names of minerals, as each mineral has a definite hardness. But rocks are usually made up of different minerals, and therefore hardness as an aid in classifying rocks should be used with great caution. Some rocks (such as sandstone) crumble rather than scratch when you run a knife or fingernail over them and this may be misleading. So, in classifying rocks, depend as much as possible on other characteristics. As your fingernail has a hardness of about 2.3 (see the hardness scale described in the glossary later in this chapter), you know that anything it will scratch has a hardness of around 2 or less. If a penny will scratch a mineral that your fingernail will not scratch, then, since a penny has a hardness of 3, the mineral probably has a hardness of 2.5 to 2.9. Since a good knife has a hardness of about 5.5, anything it will scratch that cannot be scratched with a penny has a hardness of around 3.1 to 3.4, depending upon how difficult it is to scratch. Quartz, with a hardness of 7, tops the list of simple hardness testers. Anything quartz will scratch that a knife will not probably has a hardness of around 5.6 to 6.9, and what quartz will not scratch, you know has a hardness of 7 or above.

Carefully study the glossary of geologic terms in this chapter before you attempt to use the key for classification. It will explain the meaning of many words used in the key. Turn back to Chapter Seventeen on animal classification for a more detailed explanation of how to use a key. Study carefully each choice in the key and test your mineral or rock in every possible way before deciding under which classification it falls. Remember that these keys are by no means complete and that if you have a rare mineral or rock, you probably will not be able to place it in the key. In such a case turn to more complete books or to an expert geologist.

For example, suppose you found a hard, dark, greenish mineral. Since you could not scratch it with a knife as stated under 1 *b*, you would turn to 40 several pages further on, where you would find that you must turn to 41 below because your mineral could be scratched by quartz. Since your mineral is green, you would next turn to 47. There you would find your specimen not a *pyrite*, so you would turn to 48. Rubbing your mineral on a porcelain streak plate would show a green streak. You would then turn as you are told to 49, where you would learn that *hornblende* and *augite* are so much alike that only by such a small difference (and difficult to be sure of) as *hornblende* having a darker green streak than *augite* would you be able to tell the difference between them. Fortunately, not all minerals are so difficult to separate.

A KEY TO SOME COMMON
ROCK-FORMING MINERALS

1 *a.* Easily scratched with a knife. **2**

1 *b.* Not easily scratched with a knife. **40**

2 *a.* Scratched with a fingernail. **3**

2 *b.* Not easily scratched with a fingernail. **19**

3 *a.* Color white or light gray. **4**

3 *b.* Color brown or black or dark gray. **8**

3 *c.* Color red, green, blue, yellow, bronze, or related color. **12**

4 *a.* Easily soluble in water, salty taste; hardness, 2.5 to 3 (sometimes can't be scratched with fingernail); luster, vitreous; sp. gr. 2.2; streak, white; fracture, shell-like or curved; structure, granular. (*Halite.*) SALT.

4 *b.* Not easily soluble in water, taste not salty. **5**

5 *a.* Feels greasy or crumbly to the touch. **6**

5 *b.* Does not feel or look greasy or crumbly. **7**

6 *a.* Heavier, specific gravity, 2.6; hardness, 1.5 to 2.5; luster, earthy to dull; streak, white; fracture, earthy; structure, massive, pearly, like soap; has a clay odor when breathed on. KAOLIN.

6 *b.* Lighter, sp. gr., 1 to 2.5; hardness, 1 to 1.5; luster, greasy or silky; streak, white; fracture, uneven to splintery; structure, foliated or bifrous. TALC.

7 *a.* Fracture, shell-like or curved; structure, massive, granular, and fibrous; hardness, 1 to 2.5; luster, pearly, vitreous, silky, or dull; specific gravity, 2.2; streak, white; 3 kinds: sheetlike is *selenite*, fibrous is *satinspar*, and massive is *alabaster*. GYPSUM.

7 *b.* Cleavage, perfect and into thin flexible sheets; structure, scale-like, transparent, elastic, and easily split; sp. gr., 2.7 to 3; luster, pearly to vitreous; streak, white. MUSCOVITE, MICA.

8 *a.* Usually feels greasy to the touch; has no brownish-yellow streak; clay odor when breathed on. See 6 *a*. (Sometimes brown.) KAOLIN.

8 *b.* Does not feel greasy; has brownish-yellow streak if crumbly or earthy. **9**

9 *a.* Luster, earthy to dull; structure, massive and earthy, sometimes with radiating nodules; looks like and often is clay; streak, brownish-yellow; cleavage, earthy; sp. gr., 3.6; hardness, 1.5 to 4 (some can't be scratched with fingernail). LIMONITE.

9 b. Luster, not earthy or dull; does not look like clay; streak other than brownish-yellow. **10**

10 a. Luster, metallic; very heavy with specific gravity, 7.5; streak, dark gray to black structure, in cubes or granular masses; cleavage, cubic and perfect; usually can be sliced and is often brittle; hardness, 2.5 (barely scratched with fingernail). GALENA.

10 b. Different from above except for hardness. **11**

11 a. Streak, white or gray; structure, scalelike but not so transparent; tough, easily split; hardness, 2. to 2.5; luster, pearly to vitreous; sp. gr., 2.7 to 3.1; cleavage, perfect and into thin flexible sheets. BIOTITE, MICA.

11 b. Streak, white; structure, scalelike, transparent, elastic. See 7 b. (Sometimes brown.) MUSCOVITE, MICA.

12 a. Dissolves easily in water; tastes salty. See 4 a. (Sometimes red, blue, or green.) SALT.

12 b. Does not dissolve easily in water or taste salty. **13**

13 a. Color, brownish-red to cherry-red; streak, dark or cherry-red; looks like red ocher clay, which it may be; luster, earthy or dull; fracture, earthy; structure, compact, earthy, granular, sometimes with nodules; specific gravity, 5; hardness, 2-6. HEMATITE.

13 b. Color not as above; streak also different; does not look like red ocher clay. **14**

14 a. Cleavage, perfect and into thin flexible sheets; structure, scalelike, easily split. **15**

14 b. Cleavage and structure not as above, more massive or earthy. **16**

15 a. Streak, white; structure scalelike, transparent, elastic. See 7 b. (Sometimes yellow.) MUSCOVITE MICA.

15 b. Streak, white or gray; structure, scalelike but not so transparent, tough, easily split. See 11 a. (Sometimes green.) BIOTITE MICA.

16 a. Streak, colored. **17**

16 b. Streak, white. **18**

17 a. Streak, pale green to gray green; color, grass-green to dark green; cleavage, basal and perfect; structure, in scaly, granular, earthy masses, flexible but not elastic, tough to brittle; hardness, 1.5 to 2.5; luster, pearly, dull, or vitreous; sp. gr., 2.8. CHLORITE.

17 *b.* Streak, brownish-yellow; color, yellow; cleavage, earthy. See 9 *a.* LIMONITE.

18 *a.* Color, light or dark green or yellow; fracture, uneven to shell-like or splintery; structure, massive, compact and fibrous, often brittle, feels smooth, sometimes greasy; luster, waxy, greasy or dull; hardness, 2.5 (some examples cannot be scratched with fingernail); sp. gr., 2.5; streak, white. SERPENTINE.

18 *b.* Color, sometimes yellow; fracture, earthy; has a clay odor when breathed on. See 6 *a.* KAOLIN.

19 *a.* Color white or light gray. **20**

19 *b.* Color brown or black or dark gray. **24**

19 *c.* Color red, green, blue, yellow, bronze, or similar color. **30**

20 *a.* Dissolves easily in water, has salty taste. See 4 *a.* (Hardness, sometimes 2.5 to 3.) SALT.

20 *b.* Does not dissolve easily in water, no salty taste. **21**

21 *a.* Effervesces (bubbles) at least a little with cold hydrochloric acid especially along a scratch. **22**

21 *b.* Does not effervesce with cold hydrochloric acid. **23**

22 *a.* Rapidly effervesces with hydrochloric acid; hardness, 3; streak, white; luster, vitreous, pearly or dull; sp. gr., 2.7; cleavage, perfect; structure, massive, granular, cleavable; found in cavities of many kinds of rocks; transparent to opaque. CALCITE.

22 *b.* Slightly effervesces in cold hydrochloric acid, especially along a scratch; hardness, 3.5 to 4; streak, white to gray; fracture, shell-like or in curves; structure, granular masses, curved, crystal faces; sp. gr., 2.9. DOLOMITE.

23 *a.* Structure, in rows or groups of prismatic crystals, compact, brittle, commonly found in limestone; heavy with a sp. gr. of 4.5; cleavage, basal, prismatic and good; luster, vitreous to pearly; hardness, 2.5 to 3.5; streak, white. BARITE.

23 *b.* Structure, granular masses; lighter with a sp. gr. of 2.9; dissolves slowly in hot hydrochloric acid. See 29 *a.* (Sometimes white.) SIDERITE.

24 *a.* Streak cherry-red or reddish-brown. **25**

24 *b.* Streak otherwise. **26**

25 *a.* Luster, resinous or vitreous; cleavage, perfect; streak, reddish-brown; structure, granular masses, crystals with rounded faces;

often found with galena; hardness, 3.5; specific gravity, 4. SPHALERITE.

25 *b*. Luster, metallic or brilliant; bright, sparkling plates or scales (*specular hematite*); cleavage, in thin plates; structure, platelike, massive, granular; streak, cherry-red or reddish-brown; hardness, 2.5 to 6.5 (sometimes cannot be scratched by a knife); sp. gr., 4.4 to 5.3. SPECULARITE.

26 *a*. Effervesces (bubbles) at least a little with cold hydrochloric acid. **27**

26 *b*. Does not effervesce with cold hydrochloric acid. **28**

27 *a*. Rapidly effervesces with hydrochloric acid; hardness, 3. See 22 *a*. (Sometimes brown.) CALCITE.

27 *b*. Slightly effervesces in cold hydrochloric acid, especially along a scratch; hardness, 3.5 to 4. See 22 *b*. (Sometimes brown.) DOLOMITE.

28 *a*. Streak, brownish-yellow; cleavage, earthy; looks like and often is clay. See 9 *a*. (Hardness sometimes 3 to 4.) LIMONITE.

28 *b*. Streak, white or gray; cleavage otherwise, does not look like clay. **29**

29 *a*. Structure, granular masses, brittle; dissolves slowly in hot hydrochloric acid: lighter with a sp. gr. of 2.9; cleavage, good, slightly curved; streak, white or gray; luster, vitreous, pearly or dull; hardness, 3.5. SIDERITE.

29 *b*. Structure, in rows or groups of prismatic crystals, compact, brittle; heavier with a sp. gr. of 4.5. See 23 *a*. (Sometimes brown.) BARITE.

30 *a*. Dissolves easily in water, has salty taste. See 4 *a*. (Sometimes red, blue, or green; hardness 2.5 to 5.) SALT.

30 *b*. Does not dissolve easily in water, no salty taste. **31**

31 *a*. Color reddish or reddish-brown. **32**

31 *b*. Color not as above. **33**

32 *a*. Streak, dark or cherry-red; luster, earthy or dull. See 13 *a*. (Hardness, 2.5 to 6.) HEMATITE.

32 *b*. Streak, reddish-brown; luster, resinous or vitreous. See 25 *a*. (Sometimes red.) SPHALERITE.

33 *a*. Effervesces (bubbles) at least a little with cold hydrochloric acid, especially along a scratch. **34**

33 *b.* Does not effervesce with cold hydrochloric acid. **35**

34 *a.* Rapidly effervesces with hydrochloric acid; hardness, 3. See 22 *a.* (Color sometimes pink, yellow, red, or green.) CALCITE.

34 *b.* Slightly effervesces with hydrochloric acid; hardness, 3.5 to 4. See 22 *b.* (Color sometimes pink.) DOLOMITE.

34 *c.* Effervesces fairly rapidly with hydrochloric acid; color bright green to dark green; streak emerald-green; hardness, 3.5 to 4; luster, vitreous, silky, or dull; sp. gr., 4; fracture, uneven or splintery; structure, fibrous, banded, grapelike, or massive; appears usually as a stain on rocks. MALACHITE.

35 *a.* Streak, brownish-yellow; looks like clay. See 9 *a.* (Color, yellow; hardness, 2.5 to 5.5) LIMONITE.

35 *b.* Streak not as above; does not look like clay. **36**

36 *a.* Streak green or greenish. **37**

36 *b.* Streak white or gray. **38**

37 *a.* Streak, greenish-gray to pale green; short, thick crystals, 8-sided in cross section, granular; hardness, 5 to 6 (sometimes cannot be scratched by knife); color, blackish-green to streaky green; luster, vitreous or submetallic; sp. gr., 3.2 to 3.6; cleavage imperfect at right angles. AUGITE.

37 *b.* Streak, green; structure, long, slender crystals, fibrous, bladed, or granular, 6-sided in cross section; hardness, 5 to 6 (sometimes cannot be scratched with knife); color, dark shades of green to black; sp. gr., 2.9 to 3.3; luster, vitreous to silky; cleavage perfect at angles of 56° and 124°. HORNBLENDE.

38 *a.* Lighter with a specific gravity of 2.9 or less. **39**

38 *b.* Heavier with a sp. gr. of 4.5 See 23 *d.* (Color sometimes yellowish or pinkish.) BARITE.

39 *a.* Feels smooth, sometimes greasy. See 18 *a.* (Color usually greenish; hardness, 2.5 to 5.) SERPENTINE.

39 *b.* Does not feel smooth or greasy. See 29 *a.* (Color sometimes yellowish.) SIDERITE.

40 *a.* Cannot, as a rule, be scratched with a good knife, but can be scratched by quartz. **41**

40 *b.* Cannot be scratched by quartz. **51**

41 *a.* Color white or light gray. (All are feldspars.) **42**

41 *b.* Color dark gray, or black, or brown. **43**

41 c. Color red, green, blue, yellow, bronze, or a similar color. **47**

42 a. Structure, short and thick crystals, granular and massive; brittle, commonly associated with quartz in granite; fracture, uneven or splintery, luster, vitreous or pearly, dull when weathered; specific gravity, 2.6; streak, white; hardness, 6; cleavage, in 2 directions at right angles; a common feldspar. ORTHOCLASE.

42 b. Structure, fine crystals, cleavable to granular masses (only the green varieties can be easily distinguished from orthoclase); cleavage, in 2 directions but not at right angles; fracture, uneven; luster, vitreous or pearly; sp. gr., 2.55; streak, white; hardness, 6 to 6.5; a common feldspar. MICROCLINE.

42 c. Structure, cleavable masses, brittle, *striated on 1 or more cleavage faces*, may show a fine play of colors: greens, reds, or blues; cleavage, in 2 directions but not at right angles; luster, vitreous or glassy; sp. gr., 2.7; streak; white; hardness, 6 to 6.5; fracture, uneven; a very common feldspar. PLAGIOCLASE. FELDSPARS. LABRADORITE, ALBITE, etc.

43 a. Luster, metallic or brilliant; bright, sparkling plates or scales *(specular hematite)*; cleavage, in thin plates. See 25 b. (Dark gray to iron black; hardness, sometimes 6 to 6.5.) SPECULARITE.

43 b. Luster not metallic or brilliant (brilliant occasionally in Labradorite); cleavage or fracture not in thin plates. **44**

44 a. Streak, green or greenish. **45**

44 b. Streak, white. **46**

45 a. Streak, greenish-gray to pale green; short, thick crystals, 8-sided in cross section, granular; luster, vitreous or submetallic. See 37 a. (Sometimes black or brown-black.) AUGITE.

45 b. Streak, green; structure, long, slender crystals, fibrous, bladed, or granular, 6-sided in cross section; luster, vitreous to silky. See 37 b. (Sometimes black or black-brown.) HORNBLENDE.

46 a. Structure, short and thick crystals, granular and massive. See 42 a. (Sometimes black or dark gray.) ORTHOCLASE FELDSPAR.

46 b. Structure, cleavable masses, brittle, striated on 1 cleavage face, may show a fine play of colors. See 42 c. (Sometimes dark gray.) PLAGIOCLASE FELDSPARS.

47 a. Quite heavy with a specific gravity of 5; luster, metallic; color, pale brass yellow; structure, cubes of 12-sided crystals in cross section, massive, granular, brittle; cubes are striated; streak, greenish-black; fracture, uneven; hardness, 6 to 6.5; found everywhere, called "fool's gold." PYRITE.

47 *b*. Lighter with a sp. gr. of 3.3 or less; luster, not metallic or only partly so; color, not brass yellow. **48**

48 *a*. Streak, green or greenish. **49**

48 *b*. Streak, white. Feldspars. **50**

49 *a*. Streak, green; structure, long, slender crystals, fibrous, bladed, or granular, 6-sided in cross section. See 37 *b*. (Hardness sometimes 6.) HORNBLENDE.

49 *b*. Streak, greenish-gray to pale green; short, thick crystals, 8-sided in cross section, granular. See 37 *a*. (Hardness sometimes 6.) AUGITE.

50 *a*. Structure, short and thick crystals, granular and massive, brittle. See 42 *a*. (Often pink, red, yellow, or green.) ORTHOCLASE.

50 *b*. Structure, fine crystals, cleavable to granular masses. See 42 *b*. (Often yellowish or green.) MICROCLINE.

50 *c*. Structure, cleavable masses, brittle, striated on 1 cleavage face, may show a fine play of colors: greens, reds, or blues. See 42 *c*. (Rarely green.) LABRADORITE.

51–55. QUARTZ MINERALS

(The following minerals are all varieties of quartz with a hardness of 7, a specific gravity of 2.6, and a white streak.)

51 *a*. Color white, light gray, or colorless. **52**

51 *b*. Color dark gray, brown, or black. **54**

51 *c*. Color red, green, blue, yellow, bronze, or similar color. **55**

52 *a*. Colorless and transparent; structure, usually as perfect 6-sided (in cross section) crystals; brittle; no cleavage; luster, vitreous to greasy. ROCK CRYSTAL.

52 *b*. Color, cloudy white, or otherwise colored. **53**

53 *a*. Color, cloudy white; luster, vitreous to greasy; structure, usually massive brittle; no cleavage; fracture, shell-like to uneven. MILKY QUARTZ.

53 *b*. Color, white, gray, blue; luster, waxy or dull; structure, always massive, tough, translucent; fracture, shell-like to uneven. CHALCEDONY.

53 *c*. Color, banded white, red, pink, brown, green; luster, dull to waxy or vitreous; structure, always massive and banded; tough, translucent. AGATE, ONYX.

54 *a*.   Color, banded brown. See 53 *c*. AGATE, ONYX.

54 *b*.   Color, red, yellow, brown; luster, dull or waxy; structure, massive and as nodules; tough, opaque. JASPER.

54 *c*.   Color dark gray to black; luster; dull or waxy; structure, massive and as nodules; tough, opaque. FLINT.

55 *a*.   Blue. See 53 *b*. CHALCEDONY.

55 *b*.   Banded red, pink, or green. See 53 *c*. AGATE, ONYX.

55 *c*.   Red or yellow. See 54 *b*. JASPER.

A KEY TO SOME COMMON ROCKS

1 *a*.   A massive rock with no signs of bands or lines. **2**

1 *b*.   A banded rock showing lines or bands of different color, different mineral composition, different grain size, or bedding planes. **20**

2–19. MASSIVE ROCKS

2 *a*.   The rock cannot be scratched with a good knife, or only with great difficulty. *Hard igneous rocks.* **3**

2 *b*.   The rock can be scratched with a good knife, but cannot be scratched with a fingernail. **10**

2 *c*.   The rock can be scratched with a fingernail. *Soft, massive, sedimentary rocks.* **16**

3 *a*.   The rock has a glassy surface. *Glassy igneous rocks.* **4**

3 *b*.   The rock is fine grained or dense (minerals not seen). *Dense igneous rocks.* **5**

3 *c*.   The rock is large grained, or with at least one type of mineral visible. *Granitoid and porphyritic igneous rocks.* **6**

4 *a*.   Color, black, red, brown, or green; luster, vitreous; fracture, shell-like or curved. OBSIDIAN.

4 *b*.   Color, usually white; luster, often satiny; brittle; very light in weight and full of tiny holes. PUMICE.

4 *c*.   Color, generally gray to black, sometimes red; luster, resinous, oily or greasy; fracture, straighter than in obsidian. PITCHSTONE.

5 *a*. Light-colored, white, red, brown, yellow, light gray, and light green; fracture, straight. FELSITE.

5 *b*. Shades of red, brown, black, and yellow; fracture, usually curved. See 12 *c*. CHERT.

5 *c*. Dark-colored, dark gray, dark green, black, etc.; fracture straight. BASALT.

6 *a*. The rock has scattered crystals (angular in shape) of 1 or more minerals in a grained, dense, or glassy rock mass. *Porphyritic igneous rocks.* **7**

6 *b*. The rock is a pumice whose holes have been filled with rounded mineral deposits. AMYGDALOID.

6 *c*. The rock is generally large grained with most of the crystals plainly visible but none especially larger than others. *Large-grained* or *granitoid igneous rocks.* **8**

7 *a*. Light-colored, white, red, brown, yellow, light gray, and light green. FELSITE-PORPHYRY.

7 *b*. Dark-colored, dark gray, dark green, or black, etc. BASALT-PORPHYRY.

8 *a*. Light-colored rocks. **9**

8 *b*. Color, usually very dark; a heavy rock composed of a pyroxene feldspar and labradorite (dark feldspar.) GABBRO.

9 *a*. Color, white, gray, pink, red, or green (usually mixed); composed of feldspar and quartz, usually with other minerals; a hard rock because of the quartz. GRANITE.

9 *b*. Color, white, gray, and shades of red; mainly feldspar, with little quartz; thus not generally as hard as granite. SYENITE.

9 *c*. Color, usually light gray; composed of hornblende and feldspar; not usually so hard as granite. DIORITE.

10 *a*. The rock effervesces (bubbles) with cold hydrochloric acid, especially along a scratch. *Limestone rocks.* **11**

10 *b*. The rock does not effervesce; is dense (not grained), and is dull or waxy in appearance. *Dense metamorphic* and *sedimentary rocks.* **12**

10 *c*. The rock does not effervesce (or only slightly) and is grained, pebbly, or fragmental. *Grained sedimentary rocks.* **13**

11 *a*. Dense to granular; shell-like to smooth fracture; hardness, 3; color, white, blue, gray, black, or red; may contain fossils. LIMESTONE.

11 b. Impure limestone with a clayey odor. ARGILLACEOUS LIMESTONE.

11 c. Composed of crystalline grains; many colors. MARBLE.

12 a. Dull or earthy in appearance; may have a clayey odor; fracture, shell-like; very common. SHALE.

12 b. Luster, dull to waxy; color, shades of green, red, or gray; fracture, smooth to splintery; feels smooth, sometimes greasy. SERPENTINE.

12 c. Luster, vitreous; color, shades of red, brown, black, and yellow (rarely green); hardness, 5-7 (when very hard cannot be scratched by knife); may be made of parts of opal, chalcedony, jasper, very fine quartz grains, serpentine, and/or clay impurities (also iron compounds). CHERT.

13 a. Made of rounded or angular pieces of rocks and minerals cemented together; pieces of different sizes. **14**

13 b. Made up of smaller more regular-sized grains cemented together. *Sandstones.* **15**

14 a. Made of rounded pieces of rock and minerals of different sizes, with clay, calcareous material or even fine sand between the pebbles. Many colors. CONGLOMERATE.

14 b. Rock fragments angular but with similar cementing material. BRECCIA.

14 c. Angular pieces of different igneous rocks and minerals cemented in a more or less fine ashlike material. Sometimes has a felsitic (dense) appearance. TUFF.

15 a. Grains round or angular, cemented with silica *(siliceous sandstone)*, or lime *(calcareous sandstone)*, or iron oxides *(ferruginous sandstone)*, or clay impurities *(argillaceous sandstone)*; grains mainly of quartz, sometimes with mica or other minerals; color, white, red, gray, brown, etc. SANDSTONE.

15 b. Similar to above; contains quartz, feldspar, and often other minerals. Grains usually larger than in sandstone. ARKOSE.

16–19. SOFT, MASSIVE, SEDIMENTARY ROCKS

16 a. A dense rock with a clayey odor, earthy in texture. **17**

16 b. A dense rock without clayey odor, occasionally earthy in texture; may crumble to powder. **18**

16 c. A grained rock without clayey odor, usually crumbles into grains when scratched. **19**

17 *a*. Soft, breakable, earthy masses; color, white, yellow, red, brown, or gray; smooth, greasy feeling when rubbed between the fingers; breaks irregularly. CLAY.

17 *b*. As above, only it effervesces (bubbles) with cold hydrochloric acid. MARL.

17 *c*. Not so soft as the above, though crumbly; fracture, shell-like. See 12 *a*. SHALE.

18 *a*. Soft, breakable earthy masses; color white, yellow, or gray; effervesces with cold hydrochloric acid. CHALK.

18 *b*. White to gray, crumbly, no effervescence. DIATOMACEOUS EARTH.

18 *c*. Color, light or dark gray, or green; the light-colored rocks sometimes show a shining surface; no cleavage; feels smooth or greasy; made chiefly of talc. SOAPSTONE.

19 *a*. Crumbly grained rock. See 15 *a*. SANDSTONE.

19 *b*. Grains cemented in fine ashlike material. See 14 *c*. TUFF.

20–27. BANDED ROCKS

20 *a*. The rock cannot be scratched with a good knife, or only with great difficulty. *Hard schists* and *gneisses (metamorphic rocks).* **21**

20 *b*. The rock can be scratched with a knife, but cannot be scratched with the fingernail. *Banded sedimentary* and *metamorphic rocks.* **22**

20 *c*. The rock can be scratched with the fingernail. *Soft, banded sedimentary* and *metamorphic rocks.* **25**

21 *a*. Scalelike rocks of very thin, scalelike layers. Where mica is present, it can be scratched. SCHIST.

21 *b*. Banded rocks in which the bands are coarser and wider than in the schists. GNEISS.

22 *a*. The rock effervesces, at least along a scratch, and the bands are either fine or not. **23**

22 *b*. The rock does not effervesce, has a dull to shiny luster, and the minerals are visible. **24**

22 *c*. The rock does not effervesce; minerals are usually visible, sometimes fiberlike, sometimes as grains. **25**

23 *a*. Effervesces easily with acid. LIMESTONE.

23 *b*. Effervesces only along a scratch; harder, heavier than limestone. DOLOMITE.

24 a. Splits off in chips, shell-like fracture, clayey odor (usually); luster, dull, earthy. SHALE.

24 b. Cleaves into thin plates that ring when struck, splintery fracture on the ends; color, gray, green, red, black, etc.; luster, dull to shiny. SLATE.

24 c. Made of parts of opal, chalcedony, jasper, very fine quartz grains, serpentine, and/or clay impurities. See 12 c. (Sometimes banded.) CHERT.

25 a. Very thin, scalelike layers. **26**

25 b. Dense rocks, or crumbly. **27**

26 a. Scalelike layers made of much mica and some quartz; cleaves irregularly; color, black, gray, green, white; the mica scales off easily. MICA SCHIST.

26 b. Scalelike layers very dark green, usually black; luster, shiny; minerals often long and fibrous; may look like a mass of needles. HORNBLENDE SCHIST.

26 c. Greenish color, greasy feeling; masses in curved bands; easily cleaves into leaves that do not bend; often translucent. TALC SCHIST.

26 d. Green to dark green; very fine grained; luster, dull to shining; feels smooth. CHLORITE SCHIST.

27 a. Made of quartz grains; the bands may be caused by different colored mineral grains in the quartz. SANDSTONE.

27 b. Made of quartz, feldspar, and mica grains; often more shining than sandstone, and with the minerals apparently larger. ARKOSE.

27 c. A dense rock, coarsely or finely banded. SHALE.

A GLOSSARY OF COMMON GEOLOGIC TERMS

Amygdaloidal: the name given to porous (spongelike) lavas when their cavities or steam holes have been filled by deposition with other minerals, such as calcite, etc.

Cleavage: a tendency found in most minerals to cleave or break along definite planes. This cleavage is not irregular, but is usually definite and characteristic in each mineral. According to how good it is, cleavage is spoken of as perfect or imperfect, distinct or indistinct, good or poor, etc.

Color: in minerals is often important in determining the name of a specimen. A metallic mineral usually has a fixed or, as it is called, *natural* color. But in nonmetallic minerals the color may be due to impurities, and these colors are called *exotic* and are not very dependable in classification.

Concretion: said of a round mass of mineral or rock deposited within a sedimentary rock. The concretion contains the original grains of the sediment inside its mass. What usually happens in the forming of a concretion is that some foreign body (such as a leaf, twig, bone, skeleton, etc.), caught in the sediment, attracts to it certain mineral solutions such as iron oxide, lime, etc., which deposit around the body in a circular manner until the concretion is formed. Thus often very valuable fossils can be found by breaking open one of these round-shaped concretions.

Crystals: see Chapter Thirteen, The Nature of Minerals.

Crystal systems: there are six crystal systems, by which is meant that there are six ways in which crystals arrange themselves as they form out of a molten magma or grow through the slow deposition of a mineral (as in a geode). Each line of arrangement is called an axis (see Figure 19-1), and there are *a*, *b*, and *c* axes, which vary in their relationship to one another to form the six systems. The figure will give the main idea of these systems, but the subject is too complex to be explained in a short space; turn for further information to the books listed in the Bibliography.

Dense or felsitic: said of rocks when the lavas that formed them cooled slowly enough so that crystals were formed, but in which the crystals remained so small as not to be visible to the unaided eye. Felsites and basalts are such rocks.

Fragmental: as applied to igneous rocks, refers to those that have resulted from explosive eruptions. Loose or consolidated (joined together) fragments may be found. Volcanic ashes are usually fragmental.

Geodes: nodules or round masses in rocks, which, when broken open, appear hollow and are lined within their cavities by one or more minerals in the form of crystals.

Glassy: said of rocks whose lavas have cooled so quickly that they show no evidence of crystallization and are very smooth. Obsidian, pitchstone are examples.

Granitoid: said of rocks whose magmas have become solid so slowly that all the minerals have crystallized, and the crystals are large enough to be easily seen. Granite, gabbro, etc.

Hardness: is told in a mineral (or rock) by scratching the specimen with something slightly harder. A set of minerals for measuring hardness can be bought from one of the scientific equipment companies listed in Chapter Five. As hardness is measured from very soft, 1, to very hard, 10, the mineral set shows the complete variation between these extremes:

1 TALC	5 APATITE	8 TOPAZ
2 GYPSUM	6 FELDSPAR	9 CORUNDUM
3 CALCITE	7 QUARTZ	10 DIAMOND
4 FLUORITE		

The first seven of these minerals are the most important in mineral classification and also are much cheaper than the last three. Softer minerals are scratched by harder, but do not mistake a streak of powder left by a soft mineral on a harder one for a scratch.

Lava: said of a magma after it flows out of a volcano. It has then lost much of its originally contained vapors or gas.

Luster: said of the appearance of the surface of a mineral under reflected light (important in classification). Luster is either called *metallic* (opaque on the thin edges of crystals), or *nonmetallic* (transparent on the thin edges). Common nonmetallic lusters are: (1) *silky*, fibrouslike silk, (2) *vitreous*,

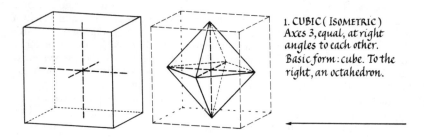

1. CUBIC (ISOMETRIC)
Axes 3, equal, at right angles to each other. Basic form: cube. To the right, an octahedron.

2. TETRAGONAL
Axes 3, 2 equal. 1 different, all at right angles to each other.
Basic form: square prism. To the right, a dodeca-hedron.

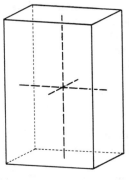

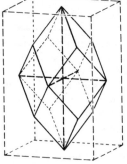

3. ORTHORHOMBIC
Axes 3, all different, at right angles to each other. Basic form: rectangular prism. To the right, an orthorhombic bisphenoid.

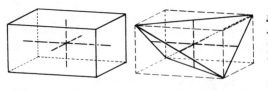

19-1. The six crystal systems. (Drawings in clinographic pro-

glassy, (3) *pearly,* like mother-of-pearl, (4) *greasy,* oily looking, (5) *resinous,* like the resin of pine trees, (6) *adamantine,* brilliant like a diamond, and (7) *dull,* chalklike.

Magma: molten rock beneath the earth's crust.

Mineral: see Chapters Six and Thirteen

Porous: said of rock that is spongelike, with many small holes.

Porphyritic: said of rocks whose magmas have cooled in such a way that one or more minerals have formed large crystals while the main part of the rock has remained dense.

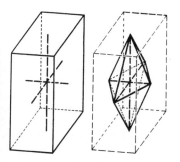

4. MONOCLINIC
Axes 3, all different. Two axes are at right angles to each other, but not to the third. Basic form: inclined rectangular prism. To the right, an octahedron.

5. TRICLINIC
Axes 3, all different, no two at right angles with each other. Most difficult system to determine, but rarest in occurance. To the right, a typical form.

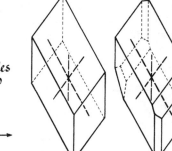

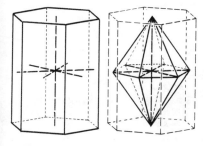

6. HEXAGONAL
Axes 4, 3 of equal length, at 60° angle to each other, different from and at right angles to the main axis. Basic form: 6-sided prism. To the right, a hexagonal bipyramid.

jection, best for study, but cubic forms appear foreshortened.)

Specific gravity: the weight of an object compared to the weight of an equal volume (amount) of water. As minerals have different specific gravities, finding the specific gravity of a mineral by carefully weighing it first in the air and then in the water (see Figure 19-2), helps determine its name. Thus:

$$Specific\ gravity = \frac{weight\ in\ air}{weight\ in\ air - weight\ in\ water}$$

Subtract the weight of the mineral in water from its weight in the air. Thus, if the weight of the mineral in the air is 5.2 grams and its weight in water is 4.1 grams, then:

$$Specific\ gravity = \frac{5.2}{5.2 - 4.1}\ or\ \frac{5.2}{1.1} = 4.73$$

And 4.73 would be the specific gravity of the mineral.

Streak: said of the color of the mineral when powdered. By rubbing a corner of the mineral on a streak plate (piece of unglazed porcelain), the color of the streak shows, and this (especially in metallic minerals) is often very important in classification.

Twinning: said of two crystals growing together as though they were placed side by side on one of their faces.

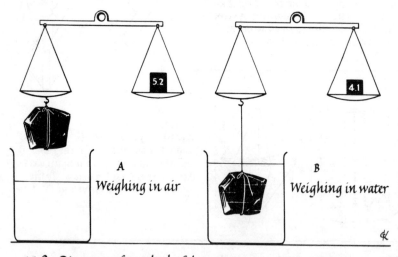

A
Weighing in air

B
Weighing in water

19-2. Diagram of method of determining specific gravity.

LAND FORMS

The naturalist and amateur geologist should be able to understand the formation of the land wherever he or she goes. This is important because such knowledge enables us to tell: (1) whether there are fossils to be found in a certain section of land, (2) whether the land is rising or sinking with consequent effect on the life that was and is found there, (3) other facts of the past history of the land that bear on the general history of life and of the rocks, and (4) what the mineral content of such a land form is likely to be. Below is a key to the common land forms of the earth. Wherever you go on field trips and hikes through the country, try to visualize the land forms about you as they fit into this key. Also collect rocks near and in such forms, labeling exactly where you got them, so that later you will be able to study and compare them in relation to the forms from which they came. Some surprising discoveries have been made by geologists through exactly similar studies. For instance the famous *theory of world glaciation* was discovered and proved through just such simple comparative studies of rocks and minerals and the land forms with which they were found associated.

A KEY TO LAND FORMS

1. Results caused by rain and stream action. **1**
2. Results caused by the action of glaciers. **2**
3. Results caused by the action of wind. **3**
4. Results caused by the action of the ocean. **4**
5. Results caused by the action of forces within the earth. **5**

1. Results caused by rain and stream action.
   a. *The erosion cycle* (see Figure 19-3).
     (1) *Youth.* A stream (after an uplift of the land) has a steep-walled canyon. Erosion is very fast.
     (2) *Maturity.* A stream has a valley with gently sloping walls. Erosion is slower.
     (3) *Old age.* A stream meanders through a wide flat valley where hills and slopes have been worn down by a million years or more of water action. Erosion is now very slow.
   b. *Deposition through stream erosion.*

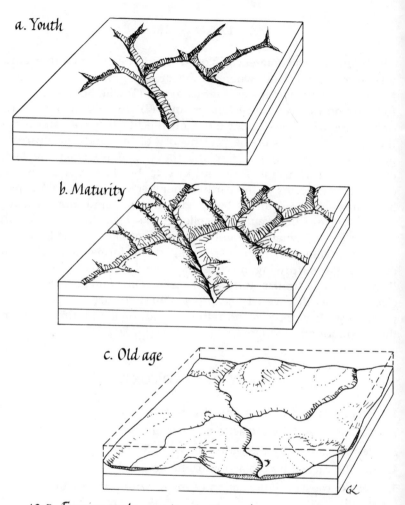

a. Youth

b. Maturity

c. Old age

19-3. Erosion cycle: results of rain and stream action on a plain.

(1) *Meanders* in a stream (see Figure 19-3c) are caused by its wearing against the side of a turn in an old-age valley until each turn is pushed out into a deep curve.
(2) A *flood plain* is the flat area around an old stream that is flooded at the time of high rainfall.
(3) A *natural levee* is the wall of dirt and gravel pushed up to either side by the action of an old stream.

19-4. *Alluvial fan: mountain stream quickly loses speed on reaching plain, deposits its sediments – which in turn absorb water.*

(4) *Alluvial fans* (see Figure 19-4) appear in desert countries where streams flood out of the mountains in the brief rainy seasons and deposit fan-shaped areas of sediment on the side of the valley or plain below.

(5) *Deltas* appear where streams enter lakes or seas and are caused by the growth of layers of sediment at the stream mouth until these layers appear above water.

c. *Groundwater.*

(1) *Wells* are caused by the water in the surrounding rock seeping toward the place of lowest pressure (the well, since water is being constantly drawn from it). (See Figure 19-5.)

(2) *Springs.* A zone of underground water usually forms along a layer of sandstone above a layer of clay or shale. Where this zone is cut (as by a fault or canyon) a spring is liable to appear (see Figure 19-5).

(3) *Artesian wells* are caused by the pressure of the rain water as it settles through soil and rock, becoming so great that it forces an underground stream to push up toward the surface if the pressure from above is released by a hole (see Figure 19-5).

(4) *Geysers* are caused by underground water coming in contact with hot rock, which causes the water to expand and boil upward through fissures in the rock above. This boiling water spouts out of the earth at intervals whenever the pressure from below becomes great enough to blow the water up the spout (see Figure 19-5.) Such geysers often deposit layers of light-colored rock called travertine.

(5) *Limestone caves* are formed whenever water goes through a thick layer of limestone and dissolves the rock, leaving a cave behind.

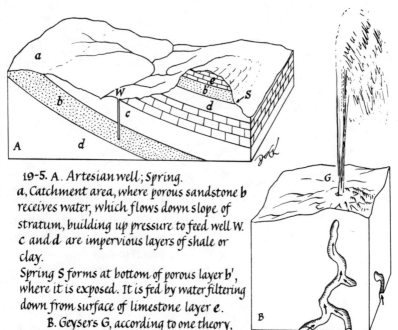

19-5. A. *Artesian well; Spring.*
a, Catchment area, where porous sandstone *b* receives water, which flows down slope of stratum, building up pressure to feed well W. *c* and *d* are impervious layers of shale or clay.

Spring S forms at bottom of porous layer *b'*, where it is exposed. It is fed by water filtering down from surface of limestone layer *e*.

B. *Geysers G*, according to one theory, result when underground water is superheated by hot rock and forced up tube or fissure with great pressure. Heat increases with depth.

2. Results caused by the action of glaciers.

a. *Icebergs* result when glaciers meet the sea and their ends break off into huge chunks of ice.

b. *Cirques* are circular depressions high on the slopes of tall mountain peaks, caused by the glacier pulling away rocks from its source by its movement down the mountain (see Figure 19-6d).

c. *Glaciers* (see Figure 19-6) are caused by so much snow falling and gradually solidifying into ice by the pressure of its own weight that eventually it forms a great mass of ice that slowly but steadily moves downhill.

d. *Hanging valleys* are caused by small tributary glaciers joining a main glacier, which, because of its greater weight, has cut a U-shaped valley deep below their points of entrance. When the glacier is melted away, the small valleys pour their streams in waterfalls into the deeper valley below. Yosemite in California provides the most perfect example of this.

e. *Perched boulders* are often a sure sign of glacial action. They occur where a melting glacier has deposited boulders carried for many miles in the ice on some rocky ledge or hill. When you find such a boulder, see if it

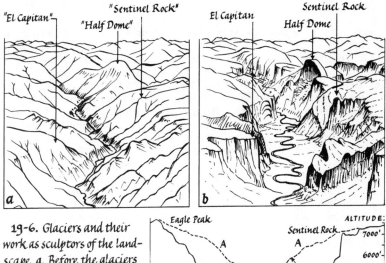

"El Capitan"   "Sentinel Rock"
    "Half Dome"

a

El Capitan   Sentinel Rock
    Half Dome

b

19-6. Glaciers and their work as sculptors of the landscape. *a.* Before the glaciers came Yosemite Valley was probably a typical V-shaped river gorge. *b.* Yosemite Valley today is the world's most celebrated work of glacier sculpture. *c.* Cross-section showing deepening and widening done by the mighty ice stream. AA. Probable profile of canyon before glacier came. BB U-shaped profile curve characteristic of glaciated valleys. CC. Present profile with river and layer of sandy sediment deposited by former Lake Yosemite – the body of water left by the melting of the glacier.

Eagle Peak   Sentinel Rock   ALTITUDE:
7000'
A   A   6000'
5000'
Merced River   1700'   1600'
1200'   4000'
c   B   C   C   B

d   CIRQUE

d. A glacier is born of high mountain snows which pack into ice and constantly feed the glacier at its head (cirque). *e.* Close-up of a glacier's "spoor": scratches, grooves and polish on rock, made by stones and gravel embedded in ice.

e   polish, grooves   scratches

(a,b,c, redrawn from Emmons & Thiel, after Matthes.)

325

isn't made of material very different from that found in nearby rock beds.

f. *Glacial polish* occurs wherever a glacier has rubbed against rock and polished its surface until it is smooth and shiny (see Figure 19-6e).

g. *Moraines* are the result of the deposition of the dirt and rock carried within and on the glacier. Material pushed along the glacier's sides becomes *lateral moraines;* that pushed in front and left when the ice melts forms *ground moraines;* that carried within or on top of the glacier and dropped when it melts becomes *ground moraines.* These heaps of dirt and rock often remain as a reminder of where glaciers have once been.

h. *Drumlins* occur where glaciers have melted so fast that they become too light to carry much of their material and so ride up over it, producing an elongated hill-like mass. Most of the islands in Massachusetts Bay are drumlins, as are many hills throughout New England.

i. *Glacial lakes and kettles.* Kettles are small depressions scooped out by glaciers and often holding lakes after the glacier has gone. Other glacial lakes are made by terminal moraines damming up a stream.

3. Results caused by the action of wind.

a. *Loess* is a deposit of yellowish-brown dust (which later may solidify into a claylike material) carried by the wind. It lodges around the roots of grasses and other plants until it may become very thick. The deepest loess deposits are found in China, but they are also common in the upper Mississippi Valley.

b. *Sand dunes* occur whenever sufficient sand is brought up by the wind to form a small hill. The steep side of the hill is always away from the direction from which the wind is coming. Common on beaches and deserts.

4. Results caused by the action of the ocean.

a. A *wave-cut terrace* is formed wherever breakers from the sea rush against rocky headlands. Storm breakers carrying rocks of many tons cut rapidly into the cliffs. Wherever such wave-cut terraces are found inland they indicate that the coast is rising or has risen (see Figure 19-7).

b. A *beach* is caused by the finer material in the ocean, particularly sand, being washed up on the shore by the waves.

c. A *barrier beach* is formed wherever the slope of the shore is so slight that the waves break far out and pile up sand and silt into a reeflike neck of land. In between the mainland and this reef lies the *lagoon*.

d. A *spit* is a small neck of land formed at the mouth of a bay when the ocean current along the shore deposits enough sediment there to bring it above the surface of the water.

e. A *bar* is a spit that extends nearly across the mouth of a bay.

5. Results caused by the action of forces within the earth.

a. *Extrusion* (eruption) of molten rock.

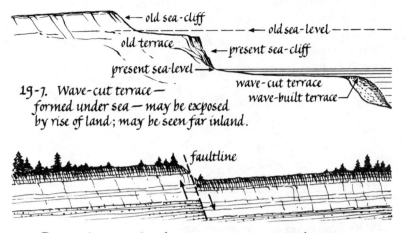

19-7. Wave-cut terrace — formed under sea — may be exposed by rise of land; may be seen far inland.

19-8. Earthquake fault. Displaced mass may move up, down, or sideways. Masses may be upthrust and downthrust simultaneously.

(1) A *volcano* (see Figure 13-4) is caused by molten magma pushing up to the surface under the influence of its gases and forming a funnel-shaped exit.

(2) A *fissure eruption* is caused by the magma welling up through a large fissure or crack in the surface of the earth and spreading liquid rock over a large area (see Chapter Thirteen).

(3) *Cinder cones* appear wherever volcanic action has thrown out a vast quantity of volcanic ash from a central point. Such cinder cones are found in Lassen Volcanic National Park in California and at the Craters of the Moon in Idaho.

(4) *Columnar structure in lavas* is caused by the contraction of exposed lava when it loses heat and gas rapidly. The lava cracks in three directions, thus forming triangular columns.

b. *Intrusion* (growth under the surface) of molten rock.

(1) *Batholiths.* A tremendous amount of molten rock may form an underground lake, which pushes up toward the surface and then hardens into igneous rock. This magma and the rock into which it turns is called a batholith. When a batholith is exposed by erosion, it usually appears as a great mass of granite or gabbro in a high mountain chain.

(2) *Dikes* (see Figure 13-4) are formed where the molten rock intrudes into a fissure and then hardens into rock without reaching the surface.

(3) *Sills and laccoliths* (see Figure 13-4) are caused by the magma moving into spaces between beds of stratified rock and there hardening. If such an intrusion is thin, it is a *sill;* if short and thick, it is a *laccolith.* Sills, laccoliths, and dikes, because of their smaller size, usually cool

327

19-9. Simple folds.
a. Anticline
b. Syncline
(Diagram also shows a type of stream erosion.)

SEDIMENTARY BEDS

19-10. Geosyncline or "earth trough" of type represented by San Joaquin Valley, California.

NOTE: This diagram not intended to represent actual topography.

19-11. Block moutains.
A. Faulted rocks, idealized.
B. Same after erosion.

a. Elevated block, "horst".
b. Depressed block, "graben".
x. Fault lines.

more rapidly than batholiths, thus forming rocks with smaller crystals, but they show a more solid form (less air holes) than most lava rocks.

c. *Results of earth movements.*

(1) *Earthquake faults* are the result of the slipping of earth blocks along a line of fracture (see Figure 19-8). The line of intersection of this plane with the surface of the earth is called the *fault line.* Such a fault line after a great earthquake will show extensive signs of movement, either vertical (up and down) or horizontal (from side to side). The San Francisco earthquake of 1906 saw fence posts moved many feet along the San Andreas fault.

(2) *Folds* in the earth's surface are caused apparently by the contraction of the size of the earth. The sides of quarries and road or railroad cuts through hills often show these folds in the rocks. A simple fold that bends upward is called an *anticline* (see Figure 19-9); a fold that bends downward is called a *syncline* (see also Figure 19-9).

(3) *Geosynclines,* or "earth troughs," are long and narrow depressions in the surface of the earth, such as the San Joaquin and Sacramento valleys of Central California. Some geosynclines are shallow seas, such as the Yellow Sea near China. Such depressions accumulate tremendous amounts of sediment over long periods of time. The weight of this sediment may press the geosyncline down while at the same time pushing up a nearby zone in the form of a mountain range. In some such way the Sierra Nevada were pushed up by the geosyncline of Central California (see Figure 19-10).

(4) *Block mountains* are caused by the dropping of earth blocks along fault lines, leaving blocks of rock higher than others. When the down faulted portion is narrow, it is called a *graben* (see Figure 19-11). Such movements also form plateaus, or large flat areas higher than the rest of the land.

(5) *Talus,* or the pile of dirt and rocks at the foot of a cliff or very steep slope, is the result of the action of gravity on material that has been loosened by weathering. Such talus often forms by pressure and depositon of cementing minerals into various rocks such as conglomerate and breccia.

CHAPTER
20

Ecology and the Ecosystem

Ecosystems can be small or large, but they usually can be thought of as complete ecologic units of associated animals and plants with a similar habitat of soils, rocks, water, and atmosphere. Understanding and studying the ecosystems—or biomes, as the larger ecosystems are called—are necessary parts of the development of a naturalist. Such study begins to give you the overall picture of life in a wide area of similar composition and shows how each element of that life influences the others. Space limits us to the study of just three ecosystems in this chapter—the deciduous forest biome of the eastern and some midwestern states, the coniferous forest biome of the Rocky Mountains and the Sierras, and the life of a pond, with which we will deal most thoroughly because ponds can be found in most any part of the country. Two other similar but wide-apart ecosystems—the rocky seashores of the Atlantic and Pacific coasts—are pictured in Figures 17-53 and 17-54, and briefly described in Chapter Seventeen. This chapter should encourage you to dig deeper into the fascinating subject of ecosystems by study, research, and field trips. (For a map of the major biomes of North America see Figure 20-1.)

THE DECIDUOUS FOREST BIOME

The Temperate Deciduous Forest Biome, as it is called by Dr. Victor Shelford in his book on North American ecology,* is far and away the most complex and varied land biome we have in North America. At the same time it is probably also one of the two most changed by human influence, the other being the Northern Temperate Grassland Biome, which includes the Great Plains and prairies of North America. (See Figure 20-2 for a cross-section diorama of a deciduous woodland in the eastern Kentucky area.) The variety and complexity of the deciduous forest biome are due to the many separate types of woodlands.

Life in these many different forest communities is vastly more affected and modified by the greater changes that deciduous trees exert on the climate and physical conditions than is true in coniferous forests. The rainfall varies between about 70 and 150 centimeters (28 to 60 inches) each year, with rainfall least in the north and west and highest to the east and south, particularly near the Gulf of Mexico. Since this rainfall (or snowfall) continues off and on through most of the year, with rarely any long dry season, these woods are comparatively free of drought and are usually able to hold enough moisture to prevent fires from becoming as serious as they do in the western and northern areas.

Most remarkable is the way these woods inhibit wind movement, cutting it down by 65 percent or more in most areas, which gives protection to many of the creatures of the forest, particularly birds and insects. The thick foliage is very helpful to such creatures on a hot summer day, cutting the number of footcandles found above the forest canopy down to less than 10 percent in the middle of the foliage and to less than 1 percent at ground level.

The complexity of life within the forest is especially illustrated by the various layer communities (see Figure 20-3). The modern deciduous

*Victor E. Shelford, *The Ecology of North America*, paper (Urbana: University of Illinois Press, 1978).

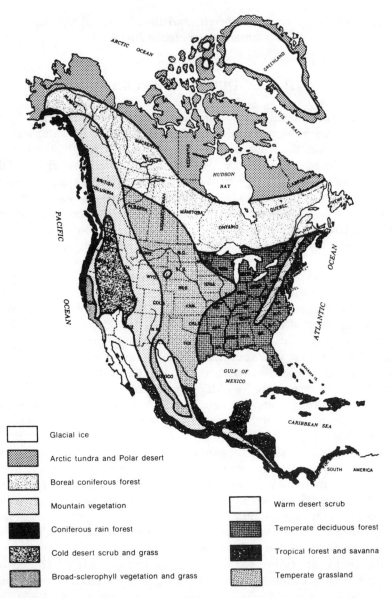

	Glacial ice
	Arctic tundra and Polar desert
	Boreal coniferous forest
	Mountain vegetation
	Coniferous rain forest
	Cold desert scrub and grass
	Broad-sclerophyll vegetation and grass

	Warm desert scrub
	Temperate deciduous forest
	Tropical forest and savanna
	Temperate grassland

Fig. 20-1. *Diagrammatic map of the major vegetational regions or biota of North America. From W. D. Billings,* Plants and the Ecosystem, *3rd ed. (Belmont, Calif.: Wadsworth Publishing, 1978), reprinted by permission of the publisher.*

forests of the biome are generally not as high as they were at the beginning of the nineteenth century; they may range from 23 to 34 meters (75 to 110 feet) in height, with tree trunks 58 to 95 centimeters (2 to 3 feet) in diameter. The canopy layer includes the bark of the limbs and upper trunk plus the higher leaves. In this area there may be as many as 1,500 invertebrates to the cubic meter (a little more than a cubic yard), all fine food for the many birds. The red-headed and downy woodpeckers, the white-breasted nuthatch, the tufted titmouse, and the barred owl both hide and nest in the many cavities in the main trunk and upper limbs of trees. So also do such mammals as the flying squirrels, the gray squirrels, and the raccoons. The competition for such hollows must often be very strong. Several other birds, such as vireos, warblers, and tanagers, nest and forage there.

Other layers include the understory tree layer of smaller trees, around 9 to 11 meters (30 to 37 feet) high, where as many as seventy-five or more invertebrates, such as caterpillars, snails, spiders, and insects, may be found on each square meter of bark. Below this in the high shrub layer (2 to 6 meters, or 7 to 20 feet), the red-eyed vireo and the eastern wood pewee are particularly common species. The principle shrub there is usually the pawpaw. The low shrub layer (1 to 2 meters, or 3 to 7 feet), of which the spice bush is a major dominant, includes also the seedlings of the larger trees. Lace bugs and tree crickets are common, and wood thrushes are common birds. The upper herb layer (15 to 100 centimeters, or 4 to 37 inches) includes the waterleaf, common nettle, jewelweed, and sanicle as dominant plants, with wedge beetles (*Anoplitis inaequalis*) and mirid bugs particularly common insects. The lower herb layer (0 to 15 centimeters, or 0 to 4 inches) has the violets and wild gingers as common plants, while millipedes, fly larvae, and predatory snails are common invertebrates. Standing and fallen tree trunks might be considered part of this layer. Both are covered by shelf fungi, with flat underbark beetles common; collembolans or springtails are also very common insects. Spiders, of course, are common through all these layers, and their relationship with the different plants and insects is practically a new field to explore. Lowest of all is the soil and root layer where gophers and moles burrow industriously, the first feeding on plants and the second mainly on insect grubs and worms. Millipedes, centipedes, and sowbugs are other common creatures of the soil found throughout this biome and its many tree mixtures.

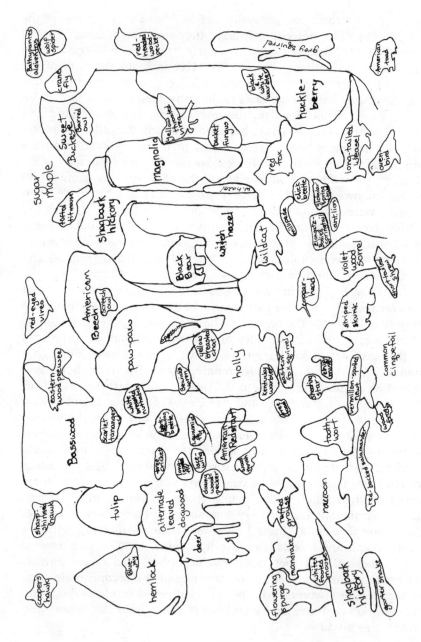

334

Fig. 20-2. Diagram of life in a mixed deciduous woodland of eastern Kentucky. Animals and plants are shown in areas they are most likely to be found. Names of animals and plants are indicated on facing page. Diagram shows some relationships of life in this forest. (Drawing by Robin Brickman.)

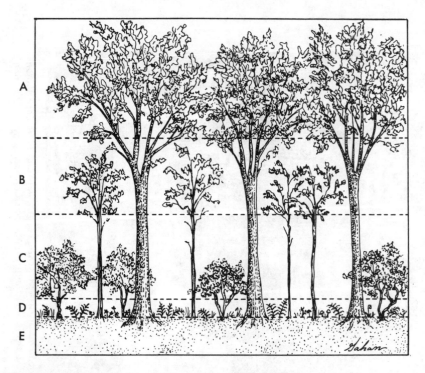

Fig. 20-3. *Stratification in a deciduous forest: (A) canopy, (B) understory, (C) shrub layer, (D) herb layer, (E) litter and soil layer. From Leon Dorfman,* The Student Biologist Explores Biology *(New York: Richard Rosen Press, 1975), by kind permission of the publisher.*

The changes brought by humans to these forests is explained by the fact that this biome was the most pleasant and fertile for occupancy and exploitation. The white hunters and settlers were ruthless in their destruction of the trees over wide areas, so that only a small percentage of the original beautiful woodlands remains today. Fortunately many abandoned farms, particularly in New England, are beginning to recreate these ancient forests, while parks and nature preserves in which they are protected have been increasing in number (see the section on conservation at the end of this chapter).

The trees that most dominate as climax species in the part of the biome shown in Figure 20-2 are the black oak, white oak, shagbark hickory, post oak, and butternut hickory. The northern red oak is a similar dominant in forests farther to the north. Dominants in the southern states are the southern red oak and laurel oak, as well as the mockernut hickory, American holly, and the redbay. Widespread but less dominant trees are the chestnut oak, black walnut, and American beech. Trees that are found in large numbers, but in special areas as along streams, are the willows and cottonwoods. Those growing up after fires include the chokecherry and the hawthorns. Other special areas with their communities include the American elm, slippery elm, red maple, tulip tree, hackberry, bur oak, swamp chestnut oak, hemlocks (in the north), and the sugarberry. Numerous vines, shrubs, and smaller understory trees add to this complex grouping, in which the number of species of mammals, birds, reptiles, amphibians, and invertebrate creatures usually far outnumber per square kilometer those found in any other biome except pond life or riparian.

The amateur naturalist should examine all these layers to get the feel, appearance, and some knowledge of the species of plants and animals found in each, particularly noting how they affect each other. It is this overall knowledge that gives you the background, and in a way the right, to make a more thorough study of an ecologic niche of a particular species of plant or animal, for you need to know its relation to the whole biome.

THE MONTANE CONIFEROUS FOREST BIOME

This biome extends through the mountains of western North America, except near the Pacific Ocean where the Pacific Coast Rainy and Foggy Coniferous Forest Biome takes over. Since the Sierra Nevada form a major block of this biome and are near large centers of population, we will touch on this area briefly.

The forests of the Sierras are divided into four major types (see Figure 20-4), according to the amount of moisture and the kinds of temperature prevalent on the slopes of different altitudes. The cold temperatures of the higher elevations form the major inhibiting factor in preventing some trees, other plants, and animal life from living there, although some animals go much higher during the summer and fall.

On the lower slopes appears the pine-oak woodland, what Merriam*

---

*C. Hart Merriam, famous California biologist and early ecologist of the late 19th and early 20th century.

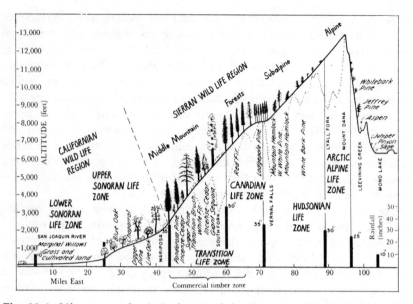

Fig. 20-4. *Life zones and principal trees of the Sierra Nevada and their foothills. After* Trees, Yearbook of Agriculture, U.S. Department of Agriculture, *1949.*

called the Upper Sonoran Life Zone, a dry and rather open wooded area of usually less than 50 centimeters (20 inches) rainfall per year, actually more a border area to the Montane Forest Biome than a part of it. Dominant plants include the blue and live oaks, the digger pine, and various chaparral brush, such as manzanita and wild lilac or ceanothus. Pocket mice, brush mice, California ground squirrels, dusky-footed woodrats, gray squirrels, and black-tailed jackrabbits are the most common animals of this area, being preyed on by the weasels, bobcats, coyotes, and gray foxes. This is often the winter range of the mule deer, who are preyed upon by mountain lion, coyote, and bear. The large stick nests of the dusky-footed woodrat are particularly noticeable under the thick areas of trees in this forest and near streams, each such nest being home also for such invertebrates as ants, beetles, fly larvae, and so on. Common birds of the area are the California jay, brown towhee, mountain quail, hairy woodpecker, Bewick's wren, vireos (in the tree tops), fox sparrow, screech owl, great horned owl, and Cooper's hawk.

The main montane forest has two major divisions, influenced almost entirely by the amount of snowfall in winter and variations in temperature. At the lower elevations where there is less snow and the temperature does not drop so low is the Ponderosa pine forest or Lower Montane Forest, of which the ponderosa pine is the most common tree, with its sweet-smelling bark. But there are also goodly numbers of white fir, incense cedar, and sugar pine, as well as, higher up, the tremendously large and impressive giant sequoias, the greatest trees on earth. Underbrush is mainly of wild lilac and manzanita, also gooseberries, which makes us note that there are much fewer layers in this forest than in the deciduous eastern forest. In the tree tops the chickaree or Douglas squirrel and the flying squirrel are common animals, hunted by the martin, a dark-furred tree weasel, while on the ground Trowbridge's shrew, the long-eared chipmunk, the white-footed mouse, and the bushy-tailed woodrat are dominant animals. Common birds are the band-tailed pigeon, pygmy owl, solitary vireo, Nashville warbler, purple finch, and winter wren. This is also a particularly good area to find the beautiful red, black, and yellow banded California mountain kingsnake, while the arboreal salamander is common in the black oaks. Several pine beetles, large brown creatures with long antennae, are deadly enemies of the pine trees.

The Upper Montane or Red Fir Forest is distinctive by being dominated almost entirely by the beautiful red firs. These trees, often perfect, rounded pyramids, grow so thickly together as to cut out almost all undergrowth and are perfectly adapted to the large amounts of snow, often up to 6 meters (20 feet) deep in winter, that gives them moisture in the ground for the whole year. Almost all bird life leaves this forest in winter because of the cold, while the mammals that stay active in the snowy times are mainly the snowshoe rabbit, mice (making tunnels under the snow), the chickaree and flying squirrel in the trees, who, with the golden-mantled ground squirrel and the chipmunks, store nuts and seeds for the winter in tree hollows or holes in the ground and come out when the weather is fair. Preying on these creatures are the martens in the trees and the weasels, red fox, and mountain coyote on the ground.

Sleeping in caves, tunnels, or under deep snow are the yellow-bellied marmots of the rocky meadows and rock slides, and the bears of the forest. Unusual is the porcupine, who wanders everywhere even in winter, well-protected by its spines from enemies and thick hair from the cold, and living mainly on bark, a food available throughout the year, holing up to sleep awhile only in the severest storms. In springtime the deer come back from the lower country along with great numbers of birds, particularly vireos, warblers, chickadees, flycatchers, woodpeckers, red- and white-breasted nuthatches, and many others. More particular to this forest, even sometimes in winter, is the Townsend's solitaire, who goes to the highest peaks in summer, as does the red cross-bill, whose ability to crack open hard pine seeds with its peculiar bill makes life easier for it in winter. In studying the trees of this forest, it is interesting to watch for the ways in which the harmful insects, such as the pine beetles, the sugar pine tortrix, and the pandora moth larvae, which can destroy whole forests if unchecked, are held under control by other creatures. Numerous larvae of these insects are destroyed by the many forest birds, who kill them to keep their own babies growing in the nests, while ground squirrels and chipmunks seek carefully for their hidden pupae in the fall. Then there are the helpful insect allies of humans, such as the parasitic wasps, cleriid beetles who attack and eat the pine beetles, and parasitic medestrus flies, as well as others.

The Subalpine Forest, which includes the timberline, has thick stands of lodgepole pines in its lower parts, with mountain hemlock and western white pine somewhat higher up, while the rugged white bark pine, often completely dead on one side of its trunk from the cold and fierce winds, struggles up in stunted growth to the beginning of the high alpine meadows. This is the tree that is famous for the history written by the weather in its tree rings, some of them going back more than 3,000 years, a few to as much as 5,000, telling us the climatic history of North America.

Even to these cold upper levels of forest and into the still higher alpine meadows, the mule deer wander in summer, feeding on grasses, herbs, and shrubs, while the extraordinary fisher, not really a fish catcher at all but an enormous weasel, armored by thick fur against the cold, can occasionally be seen. The bushy-tailed woodrat, yellow-haired porcupine, and golden-mantled ground squirrel get up that far, too, as do the coyote and the marten (killer of squirrels, but eaten by the fisher). In the rocky meadow areas surrounded by conifers, the interesting pikas or little chief conies (related to the rabbit), make their stores of hay in the rock crevices and little caves, while their shrill whistles of warning echo down the canyons. Competing with them for the meadow grass are the yellow-haired marmots, who dig deep holes under the large boulders and rush to them for protection when black bears or coyotes appear. They also whistle warnings, deeper in tone and longer. Birds common to the area include particularly the Townsend's solitaire, giving its loud warbling rambling song, the large pine grosbeak, and the beautiful gray-crowned rosy finch. Insects are limited in number by the cold, for ice can come at night at these altitudes even in summer.

In such mountains the amateur naturalist finds many tests and experiments to be made in trying to find out how the different creatures and plants adapt to each other and to the extreme cold and heavy snow that comes in winter. The varying life seen as you climb from the lower to the higher slopes is endlessly fascinating and each a part of a grand whole to which it adds its own growth, feeling, or urges. I once spent weeks in these mountains just studying the black and red ants of the forest floor and how they reacted to their predators, such as birds and lizards, but mainly the very interesting ant lion

Fig. 20-5. *The interesting life of the ant lion. From Vinson Brown,* How to Make a Miniature Zoo, *(Boston: Little, Brown, 1957), with permission of the author.*

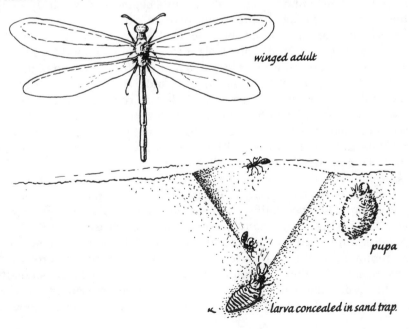

winged adult

pupa

larva concealed in sand trap.

larvae that dig their conical pits in the sandy soil and lie in wait for the ants and other forest floor insects to fall into their traps and meet death or escape from their long sickle-shaped, grooved mandiles or jaws. Each day brought a new adventure!

THE POND BIOME

In all of North America aside from the ocean shores, there is probably no ecosystem or biome with such concentrated and complex life as can be found in a good-sized pond that has developed three zones of plants along its shores but also has plenty of open water. We can loosely define a pond as a body of fresh water shallow enough to allow plant growth for most of its depth. A pond is thus usually less than 5 meters (15 feet) deep, while a lake goes deeper. It is the complex interrelations of life in a pond that make this kind of ecosystem most interesting to a naturalist. Also one does not usually have to travel far to find a pond, and studies can be confined to a small area.

Ponds, of course, are young when they are first made and have only bare dirt or rock; middle-aged when plants begin to grow thickly along their borders; old-aged when they become choked most of the way across with vegetation; and they are dead when the plants eventually turn the water into land. This is plant succession in a pond (see Figure 15-7). In this section, we will look at a pond at the beginning of middle age, and about 50 meters (165 feet) wide and 5 meters (15 feet) deep in the middle. A pond is called *lentic* (calm) as compared to a creek or river, which is *lotic* (running). But a small creek from a spring runs its waters into this pond, so we can consider that the water is being kept more aerated and thus filled with oxygen, which would not be the case in a stagnant pond with no such inflow. (See the cross section of a pond illustrated in Figure 20-6.)

Because of the complexity of life in such a pond, in this account you will grasp only a beginning picture of its total life, but enough to give you some idea of the many worlds that you can explore. First, the pond is influenced by the land and the land plants and animals that surround it. If the soil is acid, as found under normal broad-leaf woodlands, the pond surrounded by such woods will be similarly acid. Acidity and alkalinity of soils and water are measured on what is called the pH Scale, 0 to 14, with a pH of 7 being neutral, above 7 alkaline, and below 7 acidic. For comfortable life conditions, pH should generally not be lower than 4.7 or higher than 8.5, and life is much reduced in number below or above these two levels. Between pH 8 and 5, bacterial and fungi activity in the soil is quite high, meaning that organic matter (dead animals and plants) is being decayed rapidly to produce humus. In higher pH soils, snails and worms are very common; below 5 they disappear and are largely replaced by arthropods such as mites and springtails. Changes in pH also affect life in ponds, as many animals and plants can live only within relatively narrow pH limits. (A project to do in studying pH is given in the Appendix.) If brown forest soil (mainly from deciduous trees) surrounds the pond you are studying, it has a pH of 6 to 7 (slightly acidic); coniferous forest soil (podsol) is still more acidic (down to 3 pH), and chernozem, the soil found mainly in grasslands, is from 7 to 8, meaning slightly alkaline. Each would affect a pond and produce in it a similar pH. How to test for pH can be learned from any government agriculture office. Send for information.

Life in the pond is also affected by the animals that come to it from the surrounding land. The mink who dives into it and hunts for muskrats and fish under its surface brings fear wherever it goes; the ducks who come to eat many of its water plants churn up the bottom mud, and people play their part by fishing and hunting for the life that lives there. As you study the pond, seek for other outside effects.

But what is happening to the main life in the pond itself, the life that lives there all the time? If you go noisily to such a pond, it will become very quiet for some time, as the creatures there naturally fear and resent such an intrusion. If you go very quietly, however, you will soon begin to hear many of its natural sounds—the soft pop of a bubble of gas coming up from the muddy bottom, the mating calls of frogs and toads, the clear song of a yellow warbler from the willows, or the many-splendored chant of a long-tailed chat in a cottonwood tree. You may hear the sound of explosive splashes at one end of the pond where a number of frogs have jumped into the water to be sure to escape an approaching raccoon, while a splash from the middle of the pond reveals that a large-mouthed bass has just jumped for a fly. Perhaps if you are still enough for a long enough time, you can begin to sense something of the innumerable conflicts and adventures of many life forms in the pond, still invisible to you, but the swarming myriads of microscopic life that fill every cubic centimeter of clear

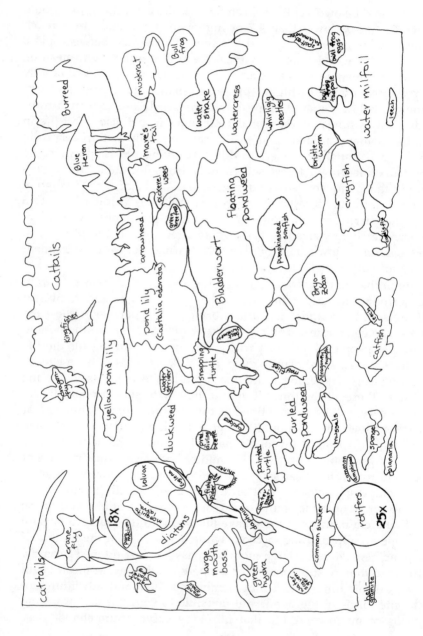

cattails

Burreed

muskrat

Bull frog

Blue Heron

mare's tail

water snake

watercress

whirligig beetles

spotted salamander

bull frog eggs

water milfoil

pickerel weed

bristle-worm

leech

green frog eggs

crayfish

arrowhead

Floating pondweed

cattails

kingfisher

pond lily (Castalia odorata)

Bladderwort

pumpkinseed sunfish

catfish

Bryo-zoan

yellow pond lily

dragonfly nymph

boat swimmer

snapping turtle

dragonfly nymph

mayflies

dragonfly nymph

water strider

duckweed

predaceous diving beetle

curled pondweed

mussels

sponge

Cyclops

planaria

crane fly

volvox

Euglena

painted turtle

fishing spider

caddis larvae

common amphipod

18x

Paramecium

mosquito larvae

diatoms

large mouth bass

Gammarus

water mite

green hydra

water flea (Daphnia)

common sucker

rotifers 25x

Hell-grammite

Fig. 20-6. *Cross-section diagram of pond life, showing common animals and plants in zones with which they are associated. Diagram on opposite facing page shows relationships of life in the pond. Note that "x" indicates magnification of circled life in relation to main illustration.(Drawing by Robin Brickman.)*

water will have to wait until you can get a microscope to explore. What you are seeing and sensing is probably less than the tip of your finger compared to your whole body!

The plant life that stretches out thickly for 5 to 7 meters (15 to 22 feet) from the shore is the dense jungle that forms all kinds of hiding places, fortresses and hunting channels and tunnels for the adventuring, feeding, and hiding of many creatures. Magnifying glasses and microscopes, dip nets (Figure 11-19), and a glass-bottomed box (Figure 20-7) are all ways you can explore this life yourself, and you can invent other methods. For now, however, let us explore this pond in our imagination, but an imagination based on many scientific facts established by explorers before us.

For practical purposes, we can divide the pond into sections or kingdoms where different kinds of life dwell, although there are always some kinds of creatures that are found in two or more of these divisions. First, we can consider three plant zones in the shallow water near the shore. Zone one is the kingdom of the emergent water plants, whose roots are underwater, but the bulk of whose stems and flowers are waving above the water where it is shallowest. The cattail is the best symbol of this zone. Next is zone two where there are many floating plants, with the bulk of their stems underwater, a small part reaching above, but most of the visible flowers and leaves floating on the surface. The water is ½ to 1 meter (1½ to 3 feet) or a little deeper. Water milfoil and pond lilies are examples of this zone. In zone three

Fig. 20-7. *Underwater observation box in pond. Watertight box with one or more 13 centimeter (½ inch) thick glass windows is secured to four posts previously driven into bottom. From Vinson Brown,* How to Explore the Secret Worlds of Nature *(Boston: Little, Brown, 1962), with permission of the author.*

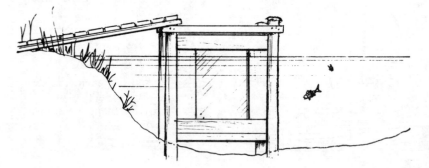

mainly completely submersed plants are found, such as eel grass and pond weeds, with most of their leaves underwater, but some floating on the surface. There the water goes down from 1 to 3 meters (3½ to 10 feet) or more. At these depths and with so many plant leaves cutting off the sunlight, the water below 2 meters is shadowy and dim, a mysterious jungle indeed where many shadows move. Aside from the plant zones zone four is the surface film, the very thin, elastic, and somewhat clinging layer, with some small life skating on top, as do the water striders, and others clinging or walking upside down on its under surface, as do some pond snails. Zone five is the open pond water where most of the large fish swim; zone six exists down in the darkness of the muck and mud at the bottom of the pond where life may be as intense as anywhere else, hidden from us and mainly felt rather than seen by the life that swarms there.

Through the emergent water plants of zone one, such as the cattail and the water plantain, wander the creatures who are most tied to shore and water in near equal amounts. A tree frog climbs up among the leaves of an arrowhead plant where its green color merges with the plant in near perfect camouflage, while below it pollywogs hide among the plant stems in the shallow water, a difficult area for even small fish to find and catch them. The frog quivers as a water snake comes coasting along the surface and through the plant jungle. As the snake lifts its head the little frog makes a great jump onto the land, and it disappears in the bushes of the shore, carrying out a great ploy of the frog, to leap ashore from water enemies and back into the water when necessary to escape attacks from land creatures. The water snake twists its blackish coils down under the water, and in two swift strikes of its head, it scoops up two of the pollywogs that were trying to hide deeper among the stems. Meanwhile deep in the stems of the cattails, where small cattail moths once laid their eggs, a whole population of little gray caterpillars dwells in safety inside the stems until the time when they are ready to emerge from their pupae and the stems to become moths.

Out in zone two where the yellow water lilies spread their immense leaves on the water surface, a huge bullfrog surveys its kingdom from the topside of the biggest leaf. The frog is a veteran of several hundred narrow escapes from death, each one a lesson teaching it to be more and more cautious, for the frog is probably the only one still alive out of thousands of eggs from one mother frog that hatched as tadpoles fifteen summers ago. Now the frog is so big that it has few enemies, but it sits very still, its colors merging with the colors of the leaf, waiting for live food to come near. Occasionally the frog's long tongue sweeps out quickly to snatch flies and other insects out of the air or where they land on the leaf surface, but they are only a minor part of the meal it needs. Nearly ½ a meter (18 inches) long when stretched out, the bullfrog is a giant of its kind, and hungry. So, when the meter-long water snake comes gliding near on the water surface, the bullfrog does not hesitate, but it leaps for the snake and seizes the head in its huge mouth. There is a great flurry of white water as the snake lashes about furiously, but the great bullfrog quickly crushes the neck and then works the whole body down its gullet by a series of heaves of its powerful throat muscles. Soon the snake disappears, and the bullfrog swims back to sit quietly on the lily pad, temporarily satisfied.

In the water below, another life-and-death struggle is in the making, but it is to be a double one. A dragonfly nymph, ugly and ferocious enough to be called a water tiger, is crawling over the mud of the bottom, sometimes dipping out of sight beneath the mud surface into the sixth or mud zone, when it sees the shadow of a large fish passing. The nymph comes up among some stems of the pond lilies and in this hiding place lies perfectly still, its ugly head with its huge dark eyes staring out like the face of a gargoyle. Its rectal gills allow it to breathe underwater, unlike its parent dragonflies, who breathe air. Suddenly it sees a young killifish, about 8 centimeters (3 inches) long, darting down after a free-swimming mayfly larva that is trying to reach shelter among the water weeds. The dragonfly nymph shoots out its hinged lower lip on which are four sharp teeth that instantly clamp onto the killifish. The fish makes violent efforts to escape, but it is held tightly and the blood is sucked out of its body until it quivers and is still. Yet now something more ferocious still is plunging toward the mud from the surface, a giant water bug, fully 7 centimeters (2⅔ inches) in length, who dashes at the preoccupied dragonfly nymph and seizes it with the powerful claws of its front legs, lunging its long (2 centimeters, or ¾ inches) daggerlike beak into the other creature's side. There is an explosion of muddy water as the dragonfly nymph tries to shoot backward with its jet propulsion to escape in the mud, but the blow to its insides soon takes all the fight out of it, and in turn the nymph is sucked of its blood.

In zone three, among the tops of the submerged water plants,

Gomphid dragonflies, the male holding the female in tandem with his rear claspers, are laying eggs. The female dips her tail now and then low to the water surface to drop her eggs so they will sink through the water to the mud below. In zone three, among such common submerged plants as the water milfoil and the quillwort, life is more dangerous for the medium-sized creatures than closer to shore, for this is a prime hunting ground of the larger fish. But a dotted fishing spider has gone as far out on the pond as it will ever go, running over the surface film (zone four) so lightly that it seems like a dancing fairy; it is only the spider's speed that keeps it from being caught by a fish. When it dives below the surface, it carries a silvery sheen of air bubbles covering its whole body, which keeps it alive below the surface for several minutes, as this spider is an air breather. But it swims to the linear leaves of a bladderwort, avoiding, from past experience, the small underwater bladders attached to the leaves that might trap it, as they trap other small creatures, by closing on the spider's legs like a door. On the stem, the dotted fishing spider becomes completely still, looking like a silvery part of the plant, but when a small and young minnow pauses for an instant in the water nearby, the spider dashes out like a torpedo and seizes the minnow with its sharp jaws, which emit a poison that stills the prey in a few seconds. The spider sucks the blood from the minnow's body and then soars toward the surface, its air bubble supply dangerously low. To break through the surface film, it uses the stem of a common pondweed for leverage, then climbs higher to be safe from water enemies. Like the frog, this fishing spider is a creature of two worlds.

Moving along the bottom below, a snapping turtle lumbers clumsily over and through the muck. More than 1/3 meter (1 foot) in length, plus being protected by a very tough horny carapace and having a very powerful horny beak capable of cutting through a person's leg almost down to the bone, this turtle is a king of the pond depths, fearing nothing in the waters except a spear- or harpoon-wielding hunter. Arriving among the stems of the submerged water weeds, the turtle first begins to chew on some of them and drag them down into its mouth, but soon decides to wait for a more meaty morsel, sinking low into the mud until it seems to be a part of that sixth zone of life, only its head and dark beady eyes visible. It senses a damselfly larva moving through the mud nearby and snaps it up with one lunge; then is quiet again. A 45-centimeter (1¼-foot) long, wide-mouthed bass, another king predator of the pond, swirls down from the surface where it has just struck at some flies. The bass comes near, but it somehow senses the turtle's presence and stays out of reach of those cutting jaws. A smaller fish, a common sucker, is now approaching, its mouth that is low on the side of its head acting like a vacuum cleaner as it dips again and again in the mud, sensitively picking out small creatures such as worms and insect larvae that are hidden in the muck. The snapper waits until the sucker comes within 15 centimeters (½ foot), then moves its head out like a striking snake. Instantly the water becomes clouded with swirling silt as the sucker convulsively struggles, and fails, to get free from those powerful jaws.

Zone five, open water, is mainly the domain of the fish. While the suckers and catfish are seen lazily moving near the bottom, finding most of their food in the mud, the bass, the killifish, the minnows, and the sunfish seek insects and other small creatures in the open water or on the surface, and the larger fish prey on the smaller. The bass that was swimming among the water-covered plants is now cruising just under the surface, rising at times to seize a struggling fly or other land bug that is helplessly caught on the surface film. This is easy catching, but when the bass tries to capture a natural denizen of zone four (the film), it finds that the water strider, skating over the surface like a world champion ice skater, is far more difficult. As the bass rises swiftly to strike, the water strider executes a soaring leap that takes it right over the opening and closing mouth of the bass, completely safe. Not deterred in the least by this episode, the water skater dashes over the surface, to which it is perfectly adapted, to where a mayfly is struggling in the film, seizes it with its front feet, and plunges its beak into the body to suck the blood.

At the same time a young sunfish, about 25 centimeters (nearly 1 foot) long, is rising to seize a bee that is buzzing on the surface. So intent is the sunfish on the insect that it does not see what looks something like a large blue and white bullet diving down from the sky. It is a kingfisher, smashing into the water and seizing the sunfish in its powerful beak. But the sunfish is almost too big for the bird, and there is a furious struggle, during which the kingfisher is even partly dragged under the water, but at last, wings beating madly, the kingfisher carries the flopping fish up to the top of a tall stump on the bank, where it breaks the back of the sunfish with a swift blow and proceeds to tear it into edible chunks. A denizen of the air who is also a capable water bird has well earned its food!

Zone six, the dark world of the mud on the pond bottom, is both a hiding place and a hunting place for a myriad of creatures. The carnivorous bristleworm (*Chaetogaster*), more ugly and fierce looking than even the dragonfly nymph, is another inhabitant of the mud zone. It moves purposefully through the mud seeking to kill and eat with its strong jaws, sharp as needles, almost anything it can find. Copepods, leeches, segmented worms, amphipods, and even the tiger flatworm, another carnivore, flee before it if they sense its presence. On it moves sinuously and sinisterly, at last trapping a snail near the surface of the mud, dragging it under, and preventing the body from being drawn back into the protective shell. It misses a couple of leeches, who seem so much a part of the mud itself and stay so still that they are not sensed. But when their fierce enemy has passed, the leaches leave the mud and climb upward on plant stems, searching no doubt for the legs of mammals, such as the muskrat or a human, to which they can attach and suck out the blood. The mud stays below them, the endless lurking place of worms.

The life of the pond is indeed a life of struggle to stay alive, to eat or be eaten, but there are peaceful times for every creature and also times of great excitement when the mating urge is being fulfilled. If we come at night to the pond in midspring, and often by day, it is loud with the "chug-a-rum" roars of the bullfrogs, or the shrill peeping of the spring peepers, the tree frogs, each species finding its special time to be noisy, calling to its mates, or to be actively mating. Many insects, such as the dragonflies and damselflies, mate several times during the warm parts of the year. Sometimes the mayflies dance over the waters in great swarms at night, dying after the eggs are laid on stems underwater and giving a feast to the fish and other carnivores.

Many indeed are the ingenious methods that different creatures use to stay alive. Giant water bugs and other aquatic insects store air under their wings, often held in place by millions of microscopic hairs. Others use tubes to come to the surface and suck air through the surface film, as do mosquito larvae. Special spines or beaks are used by still other insects to get the air that is often stored in the stems of underwater plants.

Caddis fly larvae have the most amazing varieties of protective cases glued together with their saliva, and made of tiny stones, pieces of bark, leaves, sticks, and so on, some of them marvelously and beautifully designed. Find the ecologic niches of several of these creatures and explore their life-styles. You will be given many surprises and delights in such adventures.

CONSERVATION

During the great ecological awakening of the 1960s and early 1970s, fanned by Rachel Carson's book, *Silent Spring*, when more and more people became concerned about the deterioration of the world's environments, some people, including scientists, began to fear that the human species was dooming itself and all life to total destruction. They pointed to Lake Erie and a number of other areas where pollution conditions were so bad that many felt these areas were ruined beyond recall. They pointed also to the steadily rising world population as a phenomenon that, very shortly, even within the twentieth century, could lead to a worldwide catastrophe of starvation. And they correctly pointed out the incredible danger that hovers over us because of the proliferation of atomic weapons, which have the potential to bring about perhaps complete destruction of all life on our planet.

However, some developments in the late 1970s and leading into the 1980s began to show that people could turn back the doomsday clock and make a possibly successful fight for a better and more beautiful world in harmony with life. The war of words continues between scientists who warn of the human-caused dangers and those scientists who "poo-poo" all thoughts of ecological suicide. But a growing number of other scientists are helping to develop a comeback and an intelligent realignment of ecosystems that may actually be new entities, in harmony and in balance. Even Lake Erie is getting better, and England's once extremely polluted Thames River, as well as the once-announced completely ruined James Bay in New York State, has seen a remarkable return of life with the enforcement of strict antipollution laws and the protection of wild life. Also, as world populations show strong tendencies toward slowing down their increases and leveling out, scientific advances in the betterment of domesticated plants and animals continue along with a steady movement toward biological controls over pests rather than the massive doses of chemical poisons.

People in South China have been showing the way with their marvelously well-balanced rice crop and marsh ecosystem where no chemicals are used, but the proper and scientific use of both human and animal wastes continually improves and strengthens soil values so that plants grow luxuriously and are far more resistant to pests. At the same time wildlife is encouraged by hedges and protected woodlands so there are plenty of birds to fight the necessary battles against insects. In the United States in western Texas and some other areas of the West, ranchers have learned that scientific land management, with alternation of sheep and cattle and complete prevention of overgrazing, in the long run produces far better meat crops. They have found also that where grass grows strong, water tables increase in height and creeks begin to flow again.

The rather new scientific philosophy behind these developments is well described in the following memorable passage by Dr. René Dubos:

Nature is like a great river of materials and forces that can be directed in this or that channel by human interventions. Such interventions are often needed because the natural channels are not necessarily the most desirable, either for the human species or for the Earth. Nature often creates ecosystems which are inefficient, wasteful, and destructive. By using reason and knowledge, human beings can manipulate the raw stuff of nature and shape it into ecosystems that have qualities not found in the wilderness. They can give a fuller expression to many potentialities of the Earth by entering with it in a relationship of symbiotic mutualism.

The Earth is neither an ecosystem to be preserved unchanged, nor a quarry to be exploited for selfish and short-range economic reasons, but a garden to be cultivated for the development of its own potentialities and the potentialities of the human species. The goal of this relationship is not the maintenance of the status quo but the emergence of new phenomena and new values. Millenia of experience show that, by entering into a mutualistic symbiosis with the Earth, humankind can invent and generate futures not predictable from the deterministic order of things, and thus can engage in a continuous process of creation.*

*René Dubos, *The Resilience of Ecosystems: An Ecological View of Environmental Restoration* (Boulder: Colorado Associated University Press, 1978), with permission of the author.

CHAPTER
21

Animal Behavior
or Ethology

Ethology is a science that is a part of ecology, as noted earlier. It is important for the amateur naturalist to grasp some of the basic ideas of ethology because it is one of the most interesting parts of natural science and one that the naturalist may very well become excited about investigating. Being fairly new, it is also a science with tremendous areas yet unexplored.

As more and more scientists became specialists in ethology, they tended to draw away from, and even sometimes to come into conflict with, the general line of ecologists, who, by the very nature of their science, are still involved also with animal behavior. Another group of scientists, the psychologists, also became interested in animal behavior, but they attacked it from a somewhat different angle, the study of the reactions of laboratory animals, particularly the laboratory rat (an offshoot of the common Norway rat). The very complexity of animal behavior, vastly greater than its original explorers could imagine, drew these three groups into a conflict of ideas that still exists today. It is important to realize that conflicting ideas like this can be fruitful and that eventually they may tend to be ironed out as deeper knowledge is gained. The way for all of us also, both amateur and professional scientists, is to keep an open mind and to keep seeking for the truth by continually comparing and testing all ideas with equal diligence. Human nature being what it is, this is hard for most of us to do.

It is rather interesting that the strict ecologists tend to think of ethologists as becoming so interested in animal behavior by itself as to become neglectful of the total effect of the environment on such behavior. Ethologists, on the other hand, became very critical of the animal psychologists because they seemed to pay so little attention to the behavior of wild creatures, but even more so because, in their laboratory experiments with the rat, mouse, guinea pig, monkey, and other animals, they seemed to put the whole emphasis on learned behavior, with little or no attention to the innate form of behavior we call instinct. These conflicts caused a good deal of fireworks and hard feelings in the past, but gradually the groups are starting to reconcile their opposing views. Two books—*The Behavioral Aspects of Ecology* by Peter H. Klopfer (Prentice-Hall, Inc., 1973) and *The Ecology and Evolution of Animal Behavior* by Robert A. Wallace (Goodyear Publishing Co., 1973)—help to show how this is happening and are also very informative on the whole sciences of ethology and ecology.

It is fortunate that there are some aspects of the science of animal behavior that can be approached fruitfully by the amateur naturalist and may even develop into new discoveries in science. But you should realize also that this science as a whole is becoming increasingly complex, with many elements requiring such sophisticated and expensive instruments, difficult mathematics, and elaborate techniques that the amateur naturalist would be nearly helpless unless he or she obtained sufficient college training or became part of a team directed by highly trained professionals. If you show intelligence and deep interest and can present samples of your work that are impressive, you could try through a local college or university to contact such a team and interest its leaders in your joining them to help with their projects. Some amateurs have done very well in such teams and have contributed significantly to science.

Where the amateur naturalist can shine in the science of ethology is mainly in field work, in the actual study of the behavior of a particular wild species in its natural habitat or ecologic niche. Careful day and night (with red light or even infrared light) observations can lead to new discoveries, some of which might be quite important. We have already stressed in this book that eternal vigilance in observing every action of an animal is necessary, plus its reactions to all phases of its environment, including the careful keeping of accurate and unbiased notes. By unbiased notes, we mean those in which you are careful not to put down as facts your own emotional feelings toward the animal, or, at least, when you do write this way, plainly classify your emotional reaction for what it is. Emotions can sometimes be right, but they can be dangerous if not checked carefully by continued careful research. For example, you may think one animal is acting in a helpful way toward another animal out of altruism or even love, as you as a human being might act, but you should not let this feeling cloud your judgment. Instead, keep an open mind and seek carefully for other reasons for its action, realizing that what you feel might be true, but would need considerable facts to convince a skeptical scientist.

We should note, however, that even well-known scientists are capable of making dogmatic statements based on lack of complete knowledge. For example, Dr. Robert A. Wallace of the University of California at Santa Barbara, in his book, *The Ecology and Evolution of Animal Behavior*, states categorically on page 47: "It would be extremely difficult to imagine anything as starkly humorless and unplayful as a chicken!" I, personally, feel strongly that the *unplayful* word in that statement is wrong because my wife and I have raised chickens for the last thirty years and have often observed how baby chicks are very playful, even playing something similar to hide-and-go-seek and tag in the deep grass! We have seen even adult chickens sometimes play together in a similar way. Catching a scientist making such a statement is useful in making us all realize that everyone can be fallible and that it is unlikely that any scientist is so perfect that we must take every word he or she says as gospel truth!

Ethology has grown to such vast proportions as a science that we can only briefly outline some of its meanings here, urging you to make further explorations in the field and in larger books on the subject. Following is a glossary of some of the more commonly used terms in ethology, some of which will be illustrated and all of which should be useful in understanding how to approach animal behavior as an ethologist does. Study each of the definitions carefully and see how you can apply their meanings to what you observe in forest and field.

GLOSSARY OF COMMON
ETHOLOGICAL TERMS

Action specific energy: energy is built up in the central nervous system of an animal, which is inhibited from being used until it is triggered by something in the environment that produces a releaser of the energy. Thus a flock of ducks in the Arctic feel the increasing cold of winter approaching until one day it becomes cold enough to trigger them into their migratory flight south.

Activity, displacement: appears when energy is building up, but no immediate release appears in the environment. Thus a male bear who is seeking a mate may not find one, but needs release for the buildup of his feelings and so tears with his claws at the bark of a tree, leaving his scent and marks there to warn a rival male and to attract a female.

Alarm signals: many kinds, but particularly those given inside one group of animals, as when a beaver strikes the water with the flat of its tail (Figure 21-1) to alarm other beavers of danger approaching, or, more widespread, as when a jay calls loudly to warn other life in the forest that a human is coming (see also Figure 21-9).

Ambivalent behavior: irregular behavior, as when an animal cannot choose between two instinctive drives within it, and so moves in a third way. Thus an opossum about to be attacked by a dog may not know whether to

Fig. 21-1. *Beaver gives warning signal to other beavers that danger is approaching by slapping tail loudly on water. This is an instinctive response. From Vinson Brown,* How to Understand Animal Talk *(Boston: Little, Brown, 1958), with permission of the publishers.*

attack back or to flee, so it simply stays still and plays dead (see also **displacement activity**).

Appetitive and consummatory behavior: shows how instinctive (consumnatory) behavior, such as the pounce of a cat to seize a mouse if it sees one close—something even a young kitten can do instinctively—is added to by learned (appetitive) behavior so that the adult cat, who has learned from its mother and other cats how to start hunting for a mouse and how to get into proper position by the mouse hole, does all this at least partially learned behavior first and then is ready for the consummatory act of jumping on the mouse when it appears.

Behavior patterns: each major instinct or drive, such as the hunting or reproductive instincts, has different patterns of behavior associated with it, some of which have to be learned in the higher animals. Thus the behavior of a wolf trying to join a strange pack goes through several phases in an attempt to win the favor of the pack (Figure 21-2).

Behavioral control: animal behavior is controlled by a very complex nervous system and the various connected organs in the body and the glands. To begin to understand this, scientists are using very highly evolved machines, such as electronic calculators and nerve stimulus testers, plus a combined general theory of control called *cybernetics*. Every possible phase of interaction of the animal within itself and with its environment is studied before any conclusions are reached, and even then conclusions are usually tentative because of the complexity of nervous systems. This is a subject the amateur can study in more advanced books and which he or she can probably get into only as part of a scientific team.

Fig. 21-2. *Wolf attempting to ingratiate himself into a strange pack. Tail is down in sign of submission and, if necessary, he will roll on his back like a puppy in sign of complete submission to the leader. From Vinson Brown,* How to Understand Animal Talk *(Boston: Little Brown, 1958), with permission of the publishers.*

Biological clock: rhythms in nature that govern animal behavior, such as the rhythm or biological clock of the ocean tides, which influence all life along the ocean shores. The daily twenty-four-hour (circadian) clock is another such rhythm, as well as the various rhythms of the seasons.

Biotelemetry: the use of instruments, such as miniature two-way radios, to follow the daily movements of a particular animal or bird.

Central filters: found in the nervous system where they filter out signals from the environment that are not important, allowing only the important signals to come through. Thus a bird may hear the wind and see other birds flying, but acts quickly to hide only when it sees a bird hawk approaching.

Communication, levels of: (1) inadvertent signals, as when a gull sees another gull feeding in the distance and flies over to see if it too can feed, (2) animals or birds in herds or flocks signal each other to keep together when traveling, (3) special signals are sent between one animal and another or others (see Figure 21-9), as when a sentinel crow signals its flock with a call that warns of a hawk or eagle approaching, (4) the complex signals of such intelligent animals as elephants, dolphins, and primates, which enable them to work together in difficult situations, as when dolphins, for example, are under attack by sharks and signal to each other methods of unified defense. Communications are also divided into: (1) acoustic (sounds), (2) chemical (usually smell, see **Pheromones**), (3) electric (electric fish), (4) visual (Figure 21-9), and (5) social (in animal groups).

Comparative studies: usually the close observations of the behavior of two or more related types of animals, such as the scrub jay of California and the closely related Florida jay, comparing their actions.

Competitive exclusion principle (Gause's hypothesis): describes how competing animals of similar species in the same niche cannot continue to exist together if their feeding habits are too closely alike; one (the stronger) usually drives out the other (see problem under Tests for this chapter at the back of this book).

Conditioning: a repeated action toward a particular animal will, in time, cause it to be conditioned to act in a consistent way to the same stimulus. Thus, our very agile young goat, Bonnie, has been conditioned by mild but repeated punishment, followed by the loud word NO!, not to jump over the gate in the barn! (This conditioning is not *that* perfect yet!)

Consummatory (behavior) stimulus (see also **fixed action pattern**): a stimulus that triggers what is called the final consummatory (instinctive) act in a pattern of behavior, as when a mountain lion is stimulated by a deer's closeness to leap on the deer after stalking it.

Dispersion: the spreading out of animal species into wider areas to prevent overcrowding, as baby spiders do when they travel long distances on the wind, using their silken threads like balloons.

Displacement activity: occurs when an animal cannot choose between two competitive drives, such as to attack or flee. So a gull, challenged by another gull, may pick up twigs as if making a nest, something that seems to have no value, but which may reduce the tension and prevent an attack.

Display: usually occurs in courting when a male (or sometimes a female) displays feathers (birds) or a blue belly (fence lizard), or whatever to attract a mate.

Dominance: one animal or bird (or a series) dominates others in a flock or herd, which usually prevents too much conflict among individual members.

Drive: another word for instinct, the innate reaction of an animal, inherited from its ancestors and causing it to drive toward a definite goal, such as seeking a mate or seizing a prey. Most drives are more complex than simple instincts and are reinforced by learning (see Figure 21-4).

Emitted energy orientation: said of bats when they echolocate the position of their insect prey in flight, or of electric fish who understand their environment by electric flashes or waves that show the locations of other creatures and even the kinds they are.

Ethogram: complete record of the behavior of one animal or its species.

Fixed action pattern: an action such as the striking out of a praying mantis with its spined front legs to seize a passing insect prey; an action that is stereotyped, meaning instinctively repeated in the same way.

Geographic range: each animal species usually is found in a specific geographic area, which may expand if the animal is dynamic, like the starling in America, or may contract if the creature is too conservative, as happened to the large pileated woodpecker when humans began to destroy its usual habitats.

Group selection hypothesis: explains how a successful group or community of animals is selected by its ability to avoid or overcome predators, parasites, and so on. Thus the crows, among the most intelligent of all birds, have been able to avoid humans' planned destruction of them by quickly learning how to avoid traps and people with guns.

Holistic or Gestalt nature of signs and signals: the signs and signals given by a specific species of mammal or bird should be considered as parts of the entire understanding of the animal, since understanding of the parts alone may be misleading.

Home range: the area used for gathering food by an animal or pair of mates while raising and feeding their young: often different from *territory*, which is usually a smaller area actively patrolled and defended against outsiders.

Homing: the ability found in some creatures to come back to a home base from some distance. Pigeons do this naturally for short distances, but some have been taught to become expert at long-distance homing; many sea birds, because of their long journeys over the oceans, have proved to be most adept of all.

Inhibitors: patterns of nervous control of behavior that inhibit or prevent the completion of such natural drives as hunting aggressiveness or sex. Thus a short-eared owl on its nest fluffs its feathers up and looks so big and fierce that it may inhibit a wildcat from attacking (see Figure 21-4). Our big shepherd dog, Buck, was once so ferociously attacked by a mother hen that he has been inhibited ever since from getting too near young chicks!

Fig. 21-3. *Baby robins cheep when they are hungry and gape or open their bills wide when the mother comes; these are instinctive responses to hunger. From Vinson Brown,* How to Understand Animal Talk *(Boston: Little Brown, 1958), with permission of the publishers.*

Innate perceptual mechanisms: over tens of thousands of years, natural hazards of life may select in a given species those innate drives or reactions that best help it to keep healthy and alive (see Figure 21-3). These become innate perceptual mechanisms, as when a beaver instinctively slaps water with its tail to alarm others because it has just seen an approaching lynx (see Figure 21-1).

Instinct: see Innate perceptual mechanisms (above).

Intensity of behavioral patterns: if *action specific energy* has been accumulated over a period of time for an animal, such as a buck deer who has been seeking a mate and suddenly it sees another buck approaching a doe, the chances are that this accumulated energy will cause the first buck to attack the second with intense vigor, probably driving it away from the doe (see Figure 21-4).

Isolating mechanisms, ecological: similar kinds of creatures are frequently kept from competing with each other in similar habitats by ecological isolating mechanisms, such as different types of bills in birds (allowing one species to attack insects in the cracks of bark, while another has a bill designed for catching insects on leaves), or simply one kind of bird's preference for tree tops, while another similar kind prefers the middle parts of the trees, as found among vireos (see also **sympatric**).

Kinship altruism: found mainly in social insects who fight and die to save their colonies, but also in some social birds and mammals to protect flocks or herds.

Learning ability: some creatures learn new behavior much more quickly than others (particularly mammals and birds who raise their young), but a scientist must be careful not to jump to conclusions about this until after much close observation and experiments. *Tradition learning* happens in the social groups of the more intelligent animals and birds, as when the knowledge of when and how to use good feeding grounds is passed down in a goose flock from one generation to the next (see Figure 21-5).

Multifactorial control of behavior: the idea that many kinds of patterns of behavior are controlled by more than one factor. Knowledge of this helps to guard the scientist from jumping to conclusions too soon in his or her investigations.

Natural selection: probably the most important force in animal evolution; may influence behavior as well as the anatomy and physiology of various creatures over long periods of time. Thus some moths have somehow learned to drop quickly through the air in a zigzag pattern when they hear

Fig. 21-4. *Signals of sex drive rivalry given by cats before a fight. Loud yowling occurs as cat crouches and all hairs stand on end; cat is trying to appear big and to frighten the other cat away. If this does not succeed, the male cat that feels stronger brings his tail up and charges. From Vinson Brown,* How to Understand Animal Talk *(Boston: Little, Brown, 1958), with permission of the publishers.*

Fig. 21-5. *Mother bear teaching cubs how to obey when danger threatens by driving them up a tree with growls and sometimes a blow from her paw. Such learning prepares young animals for life as adults. From Vinson Brown,* How to Understand Animal Talk *(Boston: Little, Brown, 1958), with permission of the publishers.*

the squeaking sonar of bats approaching to attack. If enough moths that use this method of escape stay alive, natural selection may make this an innate escape mechanism (an instinct) of the species.

Navigation: intimately connected with migration, but it is how birds and other creatures navigate their way when on migration that most fascinates naturalists. Navigation is likely to be made: (1) by using landmarks for short distances, (2) by using stellar objects, such as the sun or stars, for long distances, (3) by using the feel of the earth's magnetic force, also for long distances, (4) by emitted energy orientations, as when whirligig beetles guide themselves through the waters by whirling to create energy vibrations, or bats travel by echolocations, or (5) by a sense unknown as yet, such as the so-called sixth sense.

Niche, ecologic: see glossary in ecology, Chapter Fifteen.

Parental care: developed mainly among mammals and birds, but also among insects and some reptiles and fish. It is a step forward in evolution as the young are protected when helpless and are trained by their parents how to deal with the dangers and opportunities of their environment (see Figure

21-6). This also allows for much more growth of intelligence and learning than among creatures that produce large numbers of young, but leave them to themselves after the parents leave the eggs.

Perceptions, unitary and serial: young animals begin life by perceiving simple parts of units, as when a newly hatched gull chick sees at first only the red mark of the bill of its mother, which means to it "food" (see also Figure 21-3). But soon it begins to see the whole bird and later begins to perceive its surroundings as a whole (Gestalt).

Phase: part of a cycle in the biological clock (such as the twenty-four hours of a night and day, or the eleven hours of the change of a tide). The time

Fig. 21-6. *Young otters play on slide into pool while adult stands guard. Play increases strength and agility and gives training that helps young learn to cope with problems of living. From Vinson Brown,* How to Understand Animal Talk *(Boston: Little, Brown, 1958), with permission of the publishers.*

when seashore creatures feed on the animals and plants of the plankton brought in by the tide would be such a phase.

Pheromones: smell molecules in the form of chemical hormones may be deposited by ants (or some other creatures) to lead fellow ants to a new food supply, or to warn them of an impending attack by enemy ants.

Photoperiod effect: different intensities of light have different effects. Decreasing daylight in the fall, for example, will trigger a flock of ducks or geese to start their migration to the south.

Protection in groups: social animal groups band together for protection against cold weather by close crowding, as do buffalo or penguins; or against enemies, as do horses when they form a circle with their heels directed outward to fend off wolves; or to discourage an enemy as do bird flocks when they mob an owl or wildcat (see Figure 21-7).

Recognition signals: used by advanced animals to recognize their own species or group, and so exclude others who might be enemies. For example, bee moths parasitized a beehive, because the bees of the hive did not recognize them as enemies, while other hives nearby recognized the moths as enemies, because they did not give the right signal, and drove them away or killed them.

Releasers: stimulative events in the environment of a particular animal act as releasers when they cause the animal to act out instinctive drives. Thus the sex drive in a male stickleback fish is released when it sees a female with a large stomach full of eggs approaching, and it leads the female into its nest where the eggs can be fertilized (Figure 21-8).

Reproductive behavior: usually released with most creatures only at certain times of the year when climatic conditions are right and when males and females get together, but each species usually has its special way in such behavior so that individuals from other species are screened out and rejected so as to prevent cross-breeding. In some creatures, such as birds, there are definite steps taken, such as the male establishing a territory, attracting a mate, building a nest, laying eggs, and raising the young (see Figure 21-3). In most creatures below mammals and birds, the female is usually through with her participation when she is fertilized and lays her eggs, as the young, after being hatched, fend for themselves. However, there are a few exceptions, such as the stickleback fish in which the male takes care of the eggs by fanning them and even watches over the young for awhile after they have hatched, guarding them from predators.

Ritual fighting (also called tournament and ceremonial fighting): these stereotyped conflicts between males over mates usually are so programmed as to do the least harm possible to the combatants, thus helping to preserve the species. Some birds, such as robins, may execute the whole conflict with threat and posture alone, with no physical contact. Some mammals, such as the antelope, may settle the matter with a shoving contest until ones gives way.

RNA molecules: ribonucleic acid molecules, which have been shown by

Fig. 21-7. *Birds mobbing bobcat, trying to annoy it enough to drive it out of area of their nests and young. This is an unusual example of cooperation of several species, actually observed by the author. From Vinson Brown,* How to Understand Animal Talk *(Boston: Little, Brown, 1958), with permission of the publishers.*

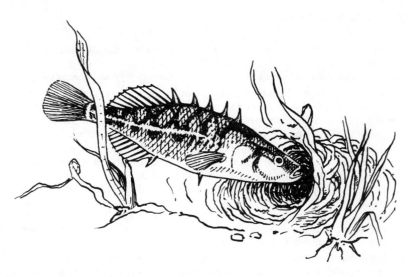

Fig. 21-8. *Brook stickleback male leading female into nest where eggs can be fertilized. From Vinson Brown,* How to Make a Miniature Zoo *(Boston: Little Brown, 1957), with permission of the author.*

experiments to control what are called "memory banks" in the central nervous system. A great deal of fascinating research lies ahead in this field.

Selection, types of: (1) directional—happens in an environment such as a forest, where lighter colored animals are caught more easily by predators, while darker colored are selected to live because they can hide more easily, (2) group—animal groups that cooperate most effectively against predators are selected to continue, while less effective groups fade away, (3) sexual— if sexual differences make the males too conspicuous and they are killed, selection may gradually make living males less conspicuous, (4) stabilizing— occurs when the more stable members of a species, neither too fearful nor too brave, for example, are selected to live, (5) territoriality—applies to species that are not strongly social but need a special territory size to protect their young and to find food for them; such creatures are selected for their success in establishing territories and so best protecting the young.

Semiotics: the coming together in cooperation of several scientific disciplines, such as mathematics, ecology, cybernetics, ethology, psychology, to be able to get a wide and more complete view of animal behavior. Such groups form scientific teams.

Sensory coding: discoveries are showing how the various sensory cells of the nervous system, such as the eye cells, cooperate with the deeper layers of cells in the brain to code and direct the reactions of the animal to stimuli, and do it very quickly. Electrophysical machines are being used by scientists to unravel this sensory coding and understand it.

Social ethology: phase of ethology, first developed by John H. Crook, in which the study of social animals is enlarged to include all conditions of the environment, all innate and learned behavior, and so on, so as to give as much as possible a complete picture of social activity in an animal species.

Social feeding (trophallaxis): usually found in social insects (also in a few bird species), where the workers transfer premasticated food to both the larvae and adults and by so doing also pass on pheromones or hormones that communicate in special ways we do not yet fully understand.

Social systems, homology or analogy of: *homology* means to be derived from a common ancestor, as kittiwake gull societies on steep cliff faces are probably derived from the first kittiwake that decided to nest on a narrow niche on a high cliff to get away from predators, which induced other kittiwakes to try the same thing. *Analogy* means when two species have a convergence of similar behavior, as when both termites and leaf-carrying ants use fungus gardens for food in their colonies, although this was not derived from a common ancestor.

Spacing behavior: found usually in territorial species, ranging from very large territories of carnivores, such as mountain lions, to quite small territories, as among small insect-eating birds or in sea bird colonies on ocean rocks.

Specific action potentiality: a later term for *reaction specific energy,* meaning specific action potential energy is stored in a reservoir in the central nervous system where it is held ready to be released by the correct outside stimulus or releaser. Thus a high and hovering sparrow hawk or kestrel suddenly sees a mouse in an exposed position below, which releases the bird's energy into a power dive on the unsuspecting prey.

Sympatric: describes different species of animals that are able to live together in a similar habitat, but at different levels, as different species of vireos may live at different levels in the same trees.

Synchronization: happens when an animal group works together in harmony, as when an antelope flashes a signal with its white rump and tail and all neighboring antelope turn in unison to run from an enemy (Figure 21-9).

Taxis: to move away from or toward an external stimulus. So an animal with a positive geotropic taxis digs down into the earth, as does a gopher. Negative phototropic taxis means to move away from light, as an owl does when it hides in a tree hollow as soon as daylight comes.

Territorialism: occurs when animals mark off a territory by smells, sounds, or visual displays. Some territories are held only during mating and nesting time, while others are continuous, as with the prairie dogs.

Tradition learning: see **learning ability.**

Vestigial behavior: occurs when an animal continues to behave in an ancestral manner that is no longer of any value to the species, as when the scavenger wasp, *Microbembix*, which deals only with dead creatures, sometimes stings them, as its ancestors used to do with live insects.

Fig. 21-9. *Antelope seeing signal flash of white rump and tail of other antelope, which means "Run, an enemy is coming!" From Vinson Brown,* How to Understand Animal Talk *(Boston: Little, Brown, 1958), with permission of the publishers.*

IV

BECOMING AN EXPLORER-NATURALIST

This is by far the shortest division in the book, covered in a very few pages. But it is also the hardest. We have taken you so far in your work as a naturalist, and now we are going to shove you off rather abruptly to work on your own.

The plain fact is that nobody can become an explorer-naturalist merely by following book directions. The word explorer *refers to a person who goes into an unknown region and finds out for him- or herself things that no one has known before. The "naturalist" also has to plan and do things that are entirely the work of his or her own brain, or the naturalist remains a mere blotter, absorbing the ideas and knowledge of others, but never adding anything fresh and unusual. This book gives you a framework on which to build, but it is you who must now do the building. That is difficult. It is easier to let somebody else do your thinking and acting for you. But it is assumed here that the reader, if he or she has come this far without faltering, has the stuff inside to carry on without support.*

It is the nature of such a book as this, which seeks to cover in the pages of one volume the whole of natural history, that it covers very lightly or not at all many things in nature. Many entire divisions of the field have been completely neglected or only barely mentioned. But it is the nature of the explorer-naturalist, once started, to learn all that he or she can of these subjects. For some subjects, there will be time to read only one or two books, but other subjects will become such necessary parts of his or her work that the naturalist will study them thoroughly. Below is a list of a few of these yet-untouched divisions, and in the Bibliography you will find listed books that tell about these and other parts of natural history in detail. Look them up and study as many as you can.

Amphibians and *Reptiles:* Herpetology.

Bacteria: Bacteriology.

Birds: Ornithology.

Cell divisions: Embryology.

Fish: Icthyology.

Fungus: Mycology.

Inheritance: Genetics.

Invertebrate life (besides insects).

Parasites: Parasitology.

Plant cells: Plant Cytology.

Reproduction. Embryology.

CHAPTER
22

The Naturalist as a Scientist

In the time of early civilization, the need to find enough food to sustain life was so urgent that the search for wild fruits and tubers, and hunting and fishing, occupied everyone's time and thought. There were no scientists then, not even people whose minds were filled with curiosity about the world and its nature.

WHAT THE SCIENTIST IS

Perhaps the first human with the beginning of a scientific mind was some disabled or otherwise handicapped person, who, by a miracle, was allowed to live on in those wild times, possibly because he or she could make good arrowheads and spearpoints out of flint. Denied the chase and the plunge of the fishing spear, this person—let us say, a young man permanently injured in a hunt—found time to look more closely at the world all around. A dawning consciousness of the innumerable unanswered questions of existence may have begun to enter his mind. Soon he was wondering at the meaning of each sight and sound and in his mind groping toward the first crude answers, answers usually wrong, but nevertheless the first timid tugging at the darkness hiding truth.

The young man watched the flight of the raven and the hawk, and in his imagination he soared with them. This queer thing of flight, how could it be? These birds had weight; he had felt their dead bodies in his hands. Could a human fly too? He dared to answer "yes." If he could fly, his wounds would no longer hold him to his place beside the cave fire; he could see the world; he could feel the mysterious texture of the white clouds that sailed through the blue, and reach and touch the snow of mountain peaks; he could sail over the green waves of the sea and find a farther shore; these and much more he could do; to these and many more questions he could find the answers.

Secretly the young man began to experiment in the woods with frameworks made of skin, and long hours he watched the birds in soaring flight and sought to learn the laws that governed their progress through the air. He endured the kicks and laughter of the strong who despised him, bearing the blows bravely because of the great secret within him. Legend tells us what happened when he tried to put his thoughts and experimental wings to actual trial (there are stories of such attempts at flight in the folklore of all peoples). He climbed a cliff and there he fastened on the clumsy wings and gazed over the valley below, seeing himself soaring across it and into the sky, on and on. The women at their skin-scraping and the men about to leave on their hunt looked up at him in amazement from the camp below. For a moment his was the glory, for they stood transfixed, thinking he actually was going to fly.

In the deep reaches of the blue, some eagle might have cried a warning, for it would be 10,000 years before humans learned the secret of the birds. But if the eagle did cry, the young man did not hear him. His was the mind that first foresaw the modern airplane; his the first mind to leap from the humdrum of daily life into the unknown; and so he leaped from the cliff. The pitiful wings could not turn back the savage demands of gravity; twice only the crude skin frameworks flapped, then they collapsed and the body plummeted with a last scream to the sharp rocks below. The people of that time left the experimenter's body to the hyenas and the vultures. What to them was the mind that soared beyond earthbound life? Mad they called him, and for 10,000 years they were to call those with similar minds mad, too.

If so, Columbus was mad, and Galileo, and Pythagoras, and La-marck, and Jane Goodall—these and a thousand other great minds; of such madness is science made.

Science is the human's way of reaching toward the stars. Never let the technicalities and hard disciplines of scientific study blind you to the warm life of the search. People who have so filled their minds with dry facts and have so relegated their research to a series of mechanical tests, who have blinded themselves to beauty, may try to tell you that they are the only true scientists and that romance is forgotten when you pass into the halls of the scientific worker. Do not believe them.

One of the greatest of natural science books, a book that enormously influenced the thought of the world—*The Origin of Species* by Charles Darwin—fairly breathes the vibrant life of forest and mountain, of desert and restless ocean. No book that does not do something of the same ever becomes a classic of science; the dry-as-dust textbooks that litter the walls of scientific libraries may give needed information, but they do not stir the mind as science is meant to do. The scientist is a man or woman who is more keenly aware of the world than most; he or she is one to whom its every color and form and motion have meaning, or, if they have no meaning, then the scientist wants to find it. In the last analysis, science is nothing more or less than the search for truth, and how can such a search, weighted as it is with the most astounding discoveries in all history, be anything but an adventure!

THE SCIENTIFIC ATTITUDE

A famous American geologist, THOMAS CHAMBERLIN (1843–1928), in-vented a system of scientific research called the *theory of multiple working hypotheses*. Actually this system has always been used by scientists; Chamberlin was merely the first to put it into words. Do not let the complex wording bother you; the theory is relatively simple. It means only that a person starting out to solve a scientific problem looks at it from every possible viewpoint that he or she can find, experiments in as many possible ways as he or she can think of, and tests every possible answer. The reason that this is a scientific attitude is simple also. It merely means that you do not allow yourself to pass up any good lead that might take you to the truth simply because you are prejudiced in another direction. This is common sense. But you will be surprised at the large number of people who are so prejudiced in favor of the various ideas they may have that they close their eyes and ears to anything else. There have also been so-called scientists with this same attitude; people who will twist every fact they find in such a way that it seems to bear out what they believe and will simply ignore or try to laugh scornfully out of existence facts that they cannot so twist. This, of course, is the exact opposite of the scientific attitude.

The scientific attitude recognizes first that truth is what is being sought; second, that no ways should be missed that might help find the truth; and, third, that what may seem to be the truth at one time may later, under the advance of new facts, prove to be something less than truth. For this reason someone with the scientific attitude withholds judgment on the final truth of a theory such as natural selection until time and facts have joined to prove it undeniably right; even then judgment should be held, by which is meant that he or she simply keeps mind and eyes open for anything new that may prove better than the old. Thus the true scientist or naturalist would not take the apparent facts shown in the experiment and the graph in Chapter Sixteen as the final answer. He or she would not be satisfied with such answers until the experiments had been carried on for many months, perhaps for years.

It is this need to work tirelessly, to try every nook and cranny of thought, to experiment on and on, that turns so many back from being scientists and naturalists, not the lack of adventure or romance in science. There is romance and adventure in plenty for those who can see their way through to the glory at the end of the long, hard trail of work. I once heard a college student complain because he had to spend two weeks observing mud-flat life for a short paper he was writing for his class in zoology. Two weeks! Darwin spent *forty years* working, experimenting, observing, and thinking before he came out with his theory of evolution. And even then he realized that he had not found the final answer. We are still working on that and may still be for a thousand years or more to come!

SOME CLASSICS OF NATURAL SCIENCE

Below is a short list of some of the famous books by great naturalists that everyone interested in natural science would do well to read. Some have changed the course of human history, but all will give you the chance to walk mentally with some of the master minds of the world. Some are more difficult to read than others; for that reason they are arranged according to difficulty, with the easiest first, but you should not look on reading them as tasks, rather as adventures of the mind. Each adventure becomes more complex than the one behind it as each mind reaches deeper into the things that it has observed. By reading these books, you may help bring your mind nearer and nearer to a deeper understanding of nature.*

1. *The Sea and the Jungle,* by H. M. Tomlinson. Really not a scientific book at all, but a fine tale of a journey across the Atlantic and up the Amazon.

2. *Jungle Days,* by William Beebe. Interesting observations on the animal life of the jungle. Norwood, 1923.

3. *Social Life in the Insect World,* by J. Henri Fabre. Fascinating studies of insect life. Gale, 1974.

4. *A Naturalist in Nicaragua,* by Thomas Belt. The stimulating observations and adventures of an amateur naturalist in Central America. Regency 1976, rep. of 1888 ed.

5. *Galápagos, World's End,* by William Beebe. About the strange and primitive animals of the Galápagos Islands on the equator.

6. *Arcturus Adventure,* by William Beebe. Experiences of a naturalist on the sea. Norwood, 1926.

7. *The Life of the Bee,* by Maurice Maeterlinck. A classic study of a famous insect.

8. *Animal Treasure,* by Ivan Sanderson. A vivid, exciting book about a naturalist's experiences in Africa.

9. *Thrills of a Naturalist's Quest,* by Raymond Ditmars. Shows the actual growth in knowledge and experience of a famous naturalist.

10. *The Malay Archipelago,* by Alfred Russel Wallace. One of the greatest naturalist travel books of all time; packed with the color, beauty, and adventure of the East Indian jungles, yet filled with fine bits of thought and theory based on innumerable observations.

11. *A Naturalist on the River Amazons,* by Henry Walter Bates. A fine

*Note: Many of these books are out-of-print, but may be found in libraries. Some may come into print again by reprint publishers such as Dover or AMS Press.

book on the natural life of the Amazon jungles. Dutton, 1969.

12. *Travels in the Interior of North America,* by Maximilian, Prince of Weid. A look at our continent in more primitive times from the eyes of a naturalist.

13. *Journal during Captain Cook's First Voyage in H.M.S. Endeavor,* by Joseph Banks. The South Seas and their nature as seen by the eyes of the first whites to explore them thoroughly.

14. *Journal of the Voyage of H.M.S. Beagle around the World,* by Charles Darwin. A book showing how Darwin got his ideas of evolution from his natural history explorations of South America in his early life.

15. *The Wonder of Life,* by J. Arthur Thomson. A famous English naturalist tells entertainingly about the natural world.

16. *Natural Selection and Tropical Nature,* by Alfred Russel Wallace. Darwin's codiscoverer of the theory of evolution explains his views.

17. *The Origin of Species,* by Charles Darwin. A famous book that changed the history of thought. Takes some mental digging. Various editions.

18. *The Seven Mysteries of Life,* by Guy Murchlie. A classic book, but vibrant and as modern as tomorrow. Houghton, 1978.

Besides increasing his or her general knowledge of these and other fields of nature, the advanced naturalist soon starts individual nature projects and experiments as a part of the great search for truth. How such projects are carried out is explained in some detail in Chapters One, Ten, and Sixteen, although these specific examples are not meant to be taken as perfect models. Actually the experiments explained in those chapters are only beginnings to the problems they tackle. The real naturalist must be prepared to go on and on, searching, thinking, and trying experiments and tests over and over, often for months without feeling that he or she has reached any final results. Your problems to tackle should be found by yourself, but below are listed some problems in various natural sciences that possibly still need to be worked out by naturalists, either amateur or professional. Perhaps they will give you ideas. Others you can find by asking experienced biologists about new fields to explore.

ZOOLOGY

1. The seed-eating habits of the various species of goldfinches, or crossbills.
2. The life histories of local species of rove beetles, or leaf hoppers.
3. The difference in the hunting and feeding habits of the weasel species of your neighborhood.
4. The consumption of and the percentage of different kinds of insect food eaten by the frogs of your neighborhood.

BOTANY

1. The types of soil preferred by any species of plant you wish to study and why it prefers them.
2. A study of the exact species differences of the genus *Grindelia*, or gum plant, or any other interesting small genus.
3. The relation between sun and shade in the distribution of the wild blackberry, or the trillium.
4. A census to determine the ten commonest plants of a given county with a study of the reasons for their success.

GEOLOGY

1. A study of local concretions, where they are found, and what they contain.
2. Local geode formation, its causes, and types.
3. Local sandstone beds, their ages, and distribution.
4. The minerals of a given county, their distribution, and the causes of their formation.

CLIMATOLOGY

1. A careful comparative record of the relation between wind direction and velocity and the approach of storms at a given weather station.

2. A comparative study of the weather records from two stations on different sides of a range of hills or mountains to determine how the barrier affects their relative climates.

ECOLOGY

1. The symbiotic and parasitic relationships within the hills of harvester ants, or any other ant species.
2. The enemies of the caddis worm and their methods of attacking it and overcoming its protective covering.
3. A study of the parasites and hyperparasites of the caterpillars of local species of the genus *Papilio*, swallowtails, or any other butterfly or moth genus.
4. The effect of oil from ships on the lives of sea creatures along a certain stretch of shore.

ETHOLOGY

1. Complete behavior study of two interacting ant species in your neighborhood.
2. Comparative study of the behavior of two species of birds of the same genus, but one found in entirely different territory than the other.
3. Comparative study of behavior of bivalves on a Pacific Coast rocky shore and an Atlantic Coast rocky shore, cooperating with another naturalist.
4. Study of the behavior of insect-eating and insect-repelling plants in your neighborhood and whether they operate successfully.

CHAPTER
23

Conclusion: The Crossroads

And now you stand at the crossroads. From here on you may no longer depend on this book; you must help yourself. If you have done your job well and thoroughly learned what the book has to teach you, then you have a sharp tool for your work as a naturalist. The satisfaction and pleasure of this work are tremendous for both amateur and professional, but beyond all this is the knowledge that what one does now, enthusiastically and thoroughly, may last on through the centuries to come as a part of human knowledge and wisdom.

"But," you say, "you haven't told me exactly what I must do to become an explorer-naturalist."

How can you be told exactly, when the explorer-naturalist is the product of his or her own special seeking, own exploration into the unknown, own development of the qualities of intelligent reasoning, of thoroughness and controlled imagination?

Have you read all this book? Have you tested yourself carefully on the knowledge you have gained from it? Have you gone on to read other books on natural science, learning to understand and use them in your work? Have you carried to successful conclusion with full written reports four or five of your own nature projects? When you have done all of this, you may deserve to be called an explorer-naturalist. But remember that just doing things in order to win an honor is not enough; you must also have the spirit.

APPENDIX
1
Nature Tests

The tests that follow are meant to help you make sure that you have benefited from the study of this book. If you prefer to make your own tests, that is fine provided they have standards equal to the ones in the tests given below and that you work them out carefully. The tests are divided into two main classifications: general and specific.

General tests are meant to test your *general understanding* of each of the main chapters in this book. They are the most important tests, and each should be done thoroughly if the maximum good is to be obtained from your study of the book.

Specific tests usually deal with special fields of nature study more or less touched upon in the text of the book. They are divided into three classifications: C class, or easy tests; B class, or medium-hard tests; and a few A class, or difficult tests. This is for your convenience so that you may start with easy tests and then work up through more difficult ones as your knowledge and training grow.

The minimum requirement for a student of this book should be the following: do each of the general tests; then, for Division I, do one C-class test for each general test; for Division II, do one C-class and one B-class test for each general test; and, for Division III, do one C-class, one B-class, and one A-class test for each general test.

The specific tests mentioned in this book are not meant to cover the field of natural science completely, but are only a small sample lot of the total number of nature tests. Make up your own tests, with those you find here as a guide.

CHAPTER FIVE: ANIMALS AND ANIMAL COLLECTING

General Animal Test. (1) Explain the 9 fundamentals to be observed in watching wild creatures, (2) know by sight and be able to describe fully at least 20 living creatures of your neighborhood, (3) explain in detail at least 6 different methods of collecting animal specimens, (4) make a collection of 10 correctly mounted and labeled specimens.

1. *Animal Observation* (C class). For at least 10 minutes, carefully and quietly watch a wild animal or wild animals and make a complete written note on what you see.

2. *Animal Skinning* (C class). Skin correctly a snake or small animal, mounting the skin spread on a board.

3. *Animal Study Skin* (B class). Mount a mouse or other small animal as explained in Chapter Four.

4. *Bone Collection* (C class). Make a mounted and labeled collection of 10 different bones.

5. *Butterfly Net* (C class). Make your own butterfly net.

6. *Insect Mounting* (C class). Demonstrate 4 ways to mount insects, making 4 correctly mounted specimens.

7. *Feather Collection* (C class). Make a mounted and labeled collection of 10 or more different bird feathers.

8. *Mounting Soft-bodied Creatures* (C class). Explain how to mount soft-bodied insects, sea animals, etc., in alcohol or 4 percent formalin, showing examples of 10 you have correctly labeled and mounted.

9. *Naming Tests* (C class). Be able to point out, describe, and name at least 4 local species of each classification of animals, such as birds, mammals, insects, sea life, amphibians and reptiles, fishes, spiders, etc.

10. *Nature Notebook* (C class). In a good notebook take down at least 4 complete nature notes on animals.

11. *Seashell Collection* (C class). Make a correctly mounted and labeled collection of 10 or more different shells.

12. *City Exploration* (C class). Take approximately a square ½ kilometer (0.3 miles) of your city and map it for those places where careful observation has shown you the existence of animal life. Write in your notebook as correctly as you can the names of such creatures observed, using various field books (see Bibliography) for identification.

CHAPTER SIX: PLANTS AND PLANT COLLECTING

General Plant Test. (1) Explain the fundamentals of plant observation, *(2)* know by sight and be able to describe fully at least 15 wild plants of your neighborhood, *(3)* explain how to collect and mount plants, *(4)* make a collection of 10 correctly mounted and labeled plants.

1. *Bark* (C class). Make a collection of 10 correctly mounted and labeled pieces of bark.

2. *Leaf Tracing* (C class). Trace 10 different types of leaves, drawing in ribs and veins.

3. *Plant Drawing* (C class). Draw correctly 3 different types of plants, showing type of leaves, stem, root, and flower.

4. *Seeds* (C class). Make a collection of 10 correctly mounted and labeled seeds.

5. *City Exploration* (C class). In the same square ½ kilometer (0.3 miles) of your city, make a map showing where different kinds of trees and other plants, particularly wild plants, are found. Through books identify as many as possible and mark them on your map by number.

If any of the plants are very common, collect them and mount them as described in Chapter Six.

CHAPTER SEVEN: ROCKS AND MINERALS AND THEIR COLLECTING

General Rock and Mineral Test. (1) Describe the 3 main kinds of rocks, (2) tell about the 8 places to look especially for rocks and minerals, (3) explain the difference between a rock and a mineral, (4) make a collection of 10 correctly labeled and mounted rocks, knowing each by name.

1. *Minerals* (C class). Make a collection of 10 different correctly mounted and labeled minerals.

2. *Pebbles* (C class). Make a collection of 10 different stream pebbles, correctly label them and mount them so that they are divided into the 3 main rock classifications.

3. *City Exploration* (C class). Find a park or a couple of vacant lots in your city that have some exposed strata of rock. Secure permission from the owners or authorities simply to photograph or draw carefully what you see, showing the lines of strata if there are any. Hold rocks in your hands for several minutes and close your eyes to get the feel of each, describing this in your notebook. Take the photographs, specimens, or drawings to your nearest museum and see if you can identify from their specimens what you have found. Remember, this is only a beginning.

CHAPTER EIGHT: CLIMATE

General Climate Test. (1) Know the 7 main laws of temperature, the 4 main laws of winds, and the 5 main laws of moisture, and be able to explain each, (2) know the 3 main types of clouds and be able to describe each.

1. *Climate Questions* (C class). Be able to answer at least 4 out of 5 questions on the facts of climate explained in this chapter.

2. *Home Climate* (C class). Study the climate of your local region in

relation to the laws of climate, reporting on how these laws influence the weather phenomena where you live.

3. *City Exploration* (C class). Investigate how the city itself affects climate by the buildings cutting down on wind, by any industries that produce quantities of heat, by pollution, and so on. Also watch for the effects of city climate on animals, birds, and plants. This is training in observation. Write a brief paper or in your notebook describing your observations.

CHAPTER NINE: BEGINNING ECOLOGY

Ecology Test. (1) Be able to explain examples of 7 major divisions of ecology listed in Chapter Nine. (2) make your own ecological study of a section of ground, keeping accurate notes over a period of a month on all ecological relationships observed and making a chart and map that illustrate your results.

1. *Animal Ecology* (A Class). Carry out a careful experiment in animal ecology, such as studying all the ecological relationships of the animals in an ant nest, or in an oak tree, part of whose trunk has turned rotten.

2. *Plant Ecology* (A class). Carry out a careful experiment in plant ecology, such as exploring and tabulating the ecological relationships of the plants on a given hillside.

3. *City Ecology* (C class). Map a 3-meter square (3.3 yards) area in your backyard or in a neighborhood park, indicating all the plants present by number—as elm (1), rose (2), etc.—and study the relationship of animal life with these plants over a 2-week period, finding those animals that are harmful to the plants and why, and those that are helpful to them. Write a report of this in your notebook or journal.

4. *Laboratory Experiment* (C class). Prepare a small terrarium (see Figure 11-13) with a simulated ecologic niche (part of a desert or a small section of grassland, for example), and place two kinds of animals in this niche, as, for example, a single species of caterpillar that feeds on some of the plants enclosed and a single species of ground beetle. Carefully watch their relationships with each other and with the plants, noting all that happens in your notebook during a 1-week or 2-week period. In your notebook explain these relationships based on your observations.

CHAPTER ELEVEN: ANIMAL STUDY

Animal Study Test. (1) Know the 6 fundamental characteristics of animal life and be able to explain each, *(2)* make a collection of 25 or more correctly mounted and labeled specimens of animals, *(3)* keep 2 or more animals alive and healthy in your own zoo for at least 3 weeks, carefully noting their behavior and food habits during this period, *(4)* be able to explain the binomial system of nomenclature as applied to animals, *(5)* dissect 1 or more of the animals described in Chapter Eleven, studying the anatomy as described and making a careful drawing of what you see, *(6)* know the main differences between the phyla of animals described in the chart at end of Chapter Eleven.

1. *Anatomy* (B class). Be able to explain the anatomy of the earthworm, the grasshopper, and the frog after you have dissected each of them and made drawings of their structures.

2. *Aquarium* (B class). Make your own properly balanced aquarium, keeping a record for at least 2 weeks of the activities of life within it.

3. *Artificial Ant Nest* (B class). Make an artificial ant nest, fill it with living ants including a queen, and keep a record for at least 2 weeks on their principal activities.

4. *The Animal Cell* (B class). Know the nature, function, and structure of the animal cell, and make 3 or more drawings of different cells seen through the microscope.

5. *Zoo* (B class). Make your own small zoo, with carefully constructed cages and all preparations for watering, cleaning, and feeding.

6. *Laboratory Project* (B class). Escape or defense abilities of animals. Most animals depend on locomotion and speed for escaping enemies or catching prey, but some use other methods. Take about 4 or 5 kinds of small animals—for example, an earthworm, a millipede, a ground beetle, a small snake, and a frog—and put each separately into a box (1 meter, 3.3 feet, long) with high sides to prevent escape. Weigh each animal on a scale and then time each for speed over the 1-meter course when they are frightened. Which are the most efficient speedsters and why? You should find 2 that don't even try to escape. Why?

7. *City Project* (B class). Propulsion of water animals. Take 4 or more

small creatures from a pond or lake edge in a city park (with permission if necessary) and place them in your aquarium. A tadpole, water beetle, water bug, dragonfly larva, and water scorpion would be good examples. Study carefully their methods of moving through the water, and compare them for speed, agility, and other qualities that would help them escape enemies or catch food. Fully describe all this in your notebook.

CHAPTER TWELVE: PLANT STUDY

Plant Study Test. (1) Grow a living plant and make careful day-by-day notes and drawings on the stages of its growth from seed on, (2) know the 6 fundamental characteristics of plant life, be able to explain each, and compare them to the fundamental characteristics of animal life, (3) know the main parts of a plant and their functions, (4) be able to point out and name in the field at least 30 wild plants of your neighborhood, (5) make a collection of 20 different properly pressed, labeled, and mounted plants, (6) know the main differences between the 5 sub-kingdoms of plants.

1. *Chemistry of Plants* (B class). Test the leaf of a plant for its manufacture of starch as described in Chapter Twelve. Write down your results and furnish mounted examples of the leaves you tested.

2. *Flower Types* (B class). Make a chart of mounted and labeled flowers and flower inflorescences, showing all the main varieties of flower types.

3. *Leaf Types* (B class). Make a chart of mounted and labeled leaves, showing most of the varieties of leaf types.

4. *Primitive plants* (B class). Make a mounted collection of 12 different primitive plants (ferns, mosses, lichens, horsetails, algae, and fungi) showing wherever possible the two forms that take place in the alternation of generations (see chart at end of Chapter Twelve).

5. *Laboratory Project* (B class). Beans are easy plants to raise in or around a home. An interesting experiment is to see how similar bean seeds grow under different conditions. Get about 8 or 10 bean seeds and try each of them in different soil (some sandy, some with much

humus, some with lime, clay, etc., and each with the same conditions of sunlight, moisture, and so on). Keep careful records of their growth in your notebook for at least 3 weeks and find out the effects of growth of the different kinds of soils. Ask questions and answer them.

6. *City Project* (B class). Find a part of your city that has very little smog and another that has much more. Arrange, perhaps with a friend, to grow plants in both of these areas, bean plants for example, giving each the same kind of soil and same amount of water, sunlight, and care, keeping a day-by-day record of growth. Keep them at least 3 or 4 weeks. At the end of this period compare results, ask questions, and answer them about the why and how of the differences in the two different areas.

CHAPTER THIRTEEN: STUDY OF ROCKS AND MINERALS

Rock and Mineral Study Test. (1) Make a chart showing the various types of crystal formation and lack of crystal formation in igneous rocks, and, below this, the evolution of sediment by pressure into sedimentary rock and this latter into metamorphic rock by heat, pressure, and chemical action (as illustrated in the chart of rock development in Chapter Thirteen) using 6 actual specimens to help illustrate your chart, (2) explain fully the nature of a mineral and the various characteristics of minerals, (3) know the 5 great eras of earth history and the main changes in the rocks and the life of each.

1. *Ancient Animals* (B class). (1) Know the ages of the earth from the beginning of the Archeozoic to the present time, and the principal animals found in each, (2) make drawings of 10 different animals of 10 different ages. (See *The Earth for Sam*, by W. Maxwell Reed, Harcourt, 1960.)

2. *History of the Rocks* (B class). Know how the different kinds of rocks were formed in the earth's history and the rock formation of each in the 5 great eras of the earth.

3. *Mineral Collection* (B class). Make a collection of at least 25 different correctly mounted and labeled minerals.

4. *Rock Collection* (B class). Make a collection of at least 25 different correctly mounted and labeled rocks.

CHAPTER FOURTEEN: CLIMATE STUDY

Climate Study Test. (1) Know by sight the 13 regular cloud forms and 5 or more of the unusual cloud forms, (2) make your own weather station and keep accurate graph and other records of the temperature variation, the rainfall, the amount of clouds and their types, the wind direction and wind force, and any other weather records you are able to make for at least 14 consecutive days, (3) know and be able to explain how to read a weather map.

1. *Storms* (B class). With the aid of weather maps from the weather bureau, chart the course and variation in intensity of at least 2 storms that pass through your neighborhood, describing also the changes in wind direction, force, and the formations of clouds as the storms come and go.

2. *Weather Symbols* (B class). Know the weather symbols and their meanings.

3. *Climate in the City* (B class). On the same day and as close as you can to the same time of day, take the temperature, the wind direction and speed, and the relative humidity, first at street level and then at the top of one of the highest buildings in the city (on the outside if possible). Compare the two and ask questions and answer them as to why and how these differences appear. What would these different effects have on animal and plant life? How do humans affect the climate most in your city?

CHAPTER FIFTEEN: THE STUDENT ECOLOGIST

General Test. (1) Give one or two examples of succession that have happened in your neighborhood or could happen there, and explain how they happened and their effects on different plant and animal species, (2) what tends to make succession so complex and varied; write your answers on one page, (3) how do humans often control or otherwise affect succession, (4) write a paper of 2 or more pages explaining what is being done about conservation in your area and what you think should be done, (5) study the glossary of ecologic terms and be able to explain at least 90 percent of them correctly when tested.

1. *Experimental Succession* (B class). Level a square meter area in a grassland or a garden down to bare mineral soil and watch what happens to this over a year's time, keeping a careful record of the plants and animals that invade the area.

2. *Conservation Project* (B class). Find where pollution of the water or destruction of the land by overgrazing or other erosion is happening and organize or join a group of people who will work to save at least part of the area. Keep a complete record in your journal of all progress and defeats until the effort is either concluded successfully or fails. Suggest at the end what could have been done to prevent the mistakes that were made.

CHAPTER SEVENTEEN: THE CLASSIFICATION AND SPECIAL STUDY OF ANIMALS

Animal Classification Test. (1) Know the names, characteristics, and typical animals of each of the main phyla described in the chart in this chapter, (2) make a mounted collection, correctly labeled and named, of at least 45 different animal specimens, of which half or more have been classified by yourself, (3) demonstrate your ability to use the mammal key in this chapter, (4) know the life zones of the seashore and the typical animals that are found in them, (5) know the general nature of pond life and some of the typical adaptations of its inhabitants, (6) know the difference between habit and instinct, and be able to give at least 5 examples of each in animals you have studied.

1. *Birds* (A class). Learn by name, sight, and call, at least 45 different birds of your neighborhood.

2. *Bird Life* (B class). Study the lives of at least 2 different kinds of birds, learning their call notes, their songs, and much about their habits and methods of raising their young. Show at least 10 pages of accurate notes taken on each species of bird.

3. *Insect Classification* (A class). Be able to classify 18 out of 20 insects

down to their correct orders. Know the main orders of insects and the differences between them.

4. *Insect Life* (B class). Study the life histories from egg to adult of at least 2 different insects and make riker mounts showing these life histories. Give full written reports.

5. *Mammal Classification* (A class). Be able to classify at least 15 different mammals correctly by the key in this chapter. Know the main orders and families of mammals and the differences between them.

6. *Pond Life* (B class). Study the life of a pond and make a drawing or chart showing the main types of life and the habitats in the pond in which they live.

7. *Pond and Stream Life* (A class). With the aid of *the New Field Book of Freshwater Life* by Elsie B. Klots (Putnam, 1966), or another good book, collect, classify, label, and mount 20 specimens of animals from ponds and streams. Make at least 2 charts showing the differences in life and the habitats of animals in ponds and streams that you have studied.

8. *Reptiles* (B class). Know at least 12 different reptiles of your neighborhood, also something about the habits of each.

9. *Seashore Life* (B class). Study the lives of at least 5 different animals of the seashore, making drawings and keeping careful notes based on your observations of at least 2 different field trips.

10. *City Project* (A class). Get a map of your city and write or phone to biology teachers at different high schools and colleges to see if they can help you, with the aid of their students, to map the distribution of bird, mammal, reptile, and amphibian life in the city by parks, school grounds, gardens, and such. When all the information is in and placed on the map and in a small booklet to accompany it, send photocopies to those who will pay for them to interested schools, colleges, universities, park offices, and museums in your city, asking for suggested corrections and improvements if the map is to be brought out again. Possibly in time it could be printed, blueprinted, or mimeographed.

11. *Laboratory Project* (A class). Barns and piles of old boards or trash in a vacant lot or field are often good places to find field or white-

footed mouse nests, with babies and mothers. A butterfly net can be used to sweep up the family; then put them into a deep cardboard box until you can provide a comfortable cage, preferably with a glass front (see Figure 11-13). Bring them grain as well as freshly caught insects, and keep a careful daily watch and record in your journal of their activities, watching particularly how the mother teaches the young ones. This is a good project also for Chapter Twenty-One on ethology.

CHAPTER EIGHTEEN: THE CLASSIFICATION AND SPECIAL STUDY OF PLANTS

Plant Classification Test. (1) Know the main branches of evolution of the orders of flowering plants and the differences between the higher and lower orders, (2) be able to classify correctly with the plant key in this chapter at least 18 out of 20 plants you find in the fields or woods, (3) make scientific drawings of typical plants from at least 7 different families, (4) make a collection, correctly mounted and labeled, of at least 45 different plants.

1. *Plant Drawing* (A class). Make scientific drawings of plants in each of the major orders of flowering plants shown in Figure 18-1. Arrange these drawings to illustrate a large chart of the orders of flowering plants.

2. *Plant Raising* (A class). Raise at least 6 different kinds of plants, keeping careful day-by-day drawings and records of their growth from seed to fruiting. Experiment with raising plants in different types of soils and with different types of fertilizers, keeping careful records of your results.

3. *Plant terms* (A class). Learn the meanings of all the plant terms given in the glossary at end of Chapter Eighteen.

4. *City Project* (A class). Observe the effect of smog on plants. Chart on a map of your city the places where there is the thickest smog and also ask the city health department to give you the scientific data on the amount and composition of smog in at least 6 city areas, 3 with bad smog and 3 with comparatively cleaner air. Choose 3 species of common plants found in waste places or parks in the city and compare the effects of smog on these plants in the 6 areas chosen. Make careful

notes of all your observations and, if possible, compare your city plants with the same plants in the country where there is no smog. Write a description of what you have learned.

5. *Laboratory Project* (A class). Take 2 different species of plants from each of the following families: Polypodiaceae (ferns), Pinaceae (pines), Ranunculaceae (buttercups), Rosaceae (roses), Cruciferae (mustards), Leguminosae (peas), Compositae (sunflowers), Gramineae (grasses), Liliaceae (lilies), and Orchidaceae (orchids), and make scientific drawings of their inner parts (see Figures 18-39, 18-40, 18-41). Using Bessey's arrangement of plants by evolutionary relationship (see Figure 18-1), arrange your plant drawings on a similar tree on a big sheet of paper, showing the development from simple to complex. When finished, get permission from a botanist at a college or university for you to bring this chart to him or her and see how close you came to putting your plants into proper relationships on the evolutionary tree.

CHAPTER NINETEEN: ROCK AND MINERAL CLASSIFICATION

Rock and Mineral Classification Test. (1) Make a mounted and correctly labeled collection of at least 20 minerals and 20 rocks, most of which you classified with the aid of the keys in this chapter, (2) know the meaning of each of the words in the glossary of geologic terms near the end of this chapter, (3) know and be able to describe most of the land forms listed at the end of the chapter.

1. *Land-Form Modeling* (A class). Make accurate clay or papier-mâché models of at least 15 of the land forms described and illustrated at the end of the chapter.

2. *Mineral Classification* (A class). Thoroughly understand all the differences between the minerals mentioned in the mineral key, and be able to pass a test on them.

3. *Rock Classification* (A class). Thoroughly understand all the differences between the rocks mentioned in the rock key, and be able to pass a test on them.

4. *City Project* (A class). On a city map mark the areas where, in

vacant lots or parks, road cuts, and so on, you find rock or earth exposed, identifying rocks, minerals, and soils that you find as best you can and making a collection of labeled specimens (if this is allowed). (For identifying soils, see books listed in the Bibliography). Locate all specimens by area found and mark on map with numbers. Show this map and your collection to a geologist and have him or her correct your work so you can learn from any errors.

CHAPTER TWENTY: ECOLOGY AND THE ECOSYSTEM

General Ecosystem Test. (1) Find a local ecosystem, such as the chaparral in California, the northern spruce-fir forest in Maine or southeast Canada, or the magnolia and tulip tree forest of a southern state, and determine the dominant plants and animals found in it, (2) study, investigate, and then describe the characters of each species that make it a dominant, (3) determine the ranges of temperature, rainfall, humidity, soil PH, predator-prey relations, and human influence that limit the types of animals and plants found in this ecosystem, (4) make diagrams or charts or both that illustrate the relationships of life in this ecosystem, such as food chains and food pyramids (see glossary and illustrations in Chapter Fifteen for examples of other relationships).

1. *Effect of Humans on an Ecosystem* (A class). Take the same or another ecosystem, such as the above, and study carefully the effects of pollution, overgrazing, tree cutting, and other human-made influences that tend to degrade or hurt the ecosystem. Write a paper describing these effects and suggest ways to improve the situation.

2. *Human-made Ecosystem in Balance and Beauty* (A class). Find, if you can, a park, ranch, farm, or other fairly large area where humans have created a new ecosystem, but one that is in harmony. If you cannot find such a system near your home, get books, articles, and such that describe such an ecosystem as the rice paddy ecosystem of South China, or any other anywhere in the world, and discover what people have done to make this kind of system work. Write a description of the ecosystem in your own words and draw diagrams and charts that help to explain what has happened.

3. *Creating a Beautiful Neighborhood* (A class). Find, develop, or join a team of scientists or conservationists who are working or would work on such a project. Keep a journal of all that happens, describing failures and victories in the work. At the end state fully what has been accomplished and what could have been accomplished.

CHAPTER TWENTY-ONE : ANIMAL BEHAVIOR OR ETHOLOGY

General Ethology Test. (1) Study carefully the glossary of terms regarding animal behavior in this chapter, then have someone test you on the meaning of each, getting at least 90 percent correct, (2) compare the difference between studying the behavior of one species of animal in the wild or in a cage or terrarium by studying each carefully for at least 12 hours, and write full descriptions of all activity in your notes, (3) select 3 of the terms described in the glossary about animal behavior and find examples in your study of wild creatures that show their meaning, writing in your notes a full description of what you observed.

1. *Ecological Isolating Mechanisms* (A class). Vireos are a good type of bird for studying these mechanisms. With binoculars, go into a woods in your neighborhood, preferably a deciduous woodland, and identify correctly all vireos you find there. Then study the ecologic niche of each species to determine how each hunts for food separately from other species, thereby eliminating too much competition. Write your observations in your notebook and explain your conclusion on how this happens.

2. *Pheromones* (A class). Study the meaning of pheromones given in the glossary, then do research on their use by various species of ants in your neighborhood, learning the names of the species by having them identified by an expert. Keep careful notes of all you observe. This can be a very fascinating bit of exploration into ant behavior.

BIOLOGICAL SCIENCES CURRICULUM STUDY

The amateur naturalist, if he or she is not aware of it already, should investigate the Biological Science Curriculum Study, P.O. Box 930, Boulder, Colorado 80306, initiated by the Biology Department of the

University of Colorado at Boulder, and the Biology Department of the University of Texas at Austin. This is the work over many years of many fine biologists, both in colleges and in high schools, on ways to teach and learn biology better in higher schools. Particularly good in some of the books and pamphlets produced are a number of laboratory experiments and field projects that would be excellent extra training for you as a naturalist and that would reinforce your basic knowledge of biology. Below is a list of a few of the more important books produced under the BSCS label. Most of these books could probably be obtained through your local library. Listings and accounts of many more books, booklets, film strips, and so forth, can be obtained by writing to the BSCS for their latest catalog.

Biological Science: An Inquiry into Life, 4th ed. (BSCS Yellow Version).

Biological Science: A Molecular Approach, 4th ed. (Blue Version).

Biological Science: An Ecological Approach, 4th ed. (Green Version). Probably the most important volume for the amateur naturalist.

Biological Science: Interactions of Experiments and Ideas, 3rd ed. An excellent help in showing you how to set up experiments, some of them fairly complex.

APPENDIX
2
Bibliography

This list of books is not meant to be complete. But in these books you will find other bibliographies that will lead you to many fine volumes of natural science literature. Listed here are guides to many of the kinds of animals, plants, rocks, and minerals that you will encounter anywhere in North America. You should be able to find many of these books in your local library, and others you can get from your state library. Many are indispensable to the naturalist and all will bear study.

Every naturalist gradually builds up his or her own library of natural history literature. This bibliography will give you an idea of some of the books you would like to buy.

GENERAL NATURE STUDY BOOKS

Adams, Richard, *Nature Through the Seasons*. New York: Simon and Schuster, 1975.

Adams, Richard, and Max Hooper, *Nature, Day and Night*. New York: Viking, 1978.

Bellamy, John, and John Sparks, *Forces of Life*. New York: Crown, 1978.

Borland, Hal, *The Golden Circle: A Book of the Months*. New York: Harper and Row, 1977.

Burton, John, and John Sparks, *World's Apart: Nature in Cities and Islands*. New York: Doubleday, 1976.

Carrigher, Sally, *Wild Heritage*. Boston: Houghton Mifflin, 1965.

Hillcourt, William, *New Field Book of Nature Activities and Hobbies*, rev. ed. New York: G. P. Putnam's, 1978.

Palmer, E. Lawrence, and H. Seymour Fowler, *Fieldbook of Natural History*, 2nd ed. New York: McGraw-Hill, 1975.

Stevens, Peter S., *Patterns in Nature*. Boston: Atlantic Monthly Press, 1974.

GENERAL BIOLOGICAL BOOKS

See also Biological Science Curriculum Study at end of Appendix I.

Allen, Robert D., *The Science of Life*. New York: Harper and Row, 1977.

Beckett, B. S., *Biology, a Modern Introduction*. Fair Lawn, N.J.: Oxford University Press, 1977.

Brown, William H., *Concepts and Inquiries in Biology*. Chicago: Education Methods, Development Systems Corp., 1978.

Dobzhansky, Theodosius, et al., *Evolutionary Biology*, 2 vols. New York: Plenum Press, 1974 & 1975.

Galbraith, D., and D. Wilson, *Biological Science, Principles and Patterns of Life*, 3rd ed. New York: Holt, 1978.

Gunstream, Stanley, *Explorations in Basic Biology*, 2nd ed. Minneapolis, Minn.: Burgess Publishing, 1978.

Headstrom, Richard, *Nature in Miniature*. New York: Knopf, 1968.

Jacques, Harry E., *Living Things, How to Know Them*, rev. ed. Dubuque, Iowa: William C. Brown, 1947. A good basic introduction.

Keys, Charles, et al., *Laboratory Explorations in General Biology*, 4th ed. Dubuque, Iowa: Kendall Hunt, 1977.

Kirk, David, et al., *Biology: The Unity and Diversity of Life*. Belmont, Calif.: Wadsworth Publishing, 1978.

MacQueen, Jean, and Ted Hanes, *Living World: Exploring Modern Biology*. Englewood Cliffs, N.J.: Prentice-Hall, Inc., 1978.

Sanderson, Isabella, and W. D. Henderson, *Dictionary of Biological Terms*, 8th ed. New York: Van Nostrand Reinhold, 1963. Excellent for understanding scientific words.

Sterling, Keir B., *Biologists and Their World*. New York: Arno Press, 1978.

Vinson and Ridgway, ed., *Biological Control by Augmentations of Natural Enemies*. New York: Plenum Press, 1977. Vital recent knowledge in the efforts to cut down or eliminate chemical pesticides.

BOOKS ON ANIMALS

Amphibians and Reptiles

Brown, Vinson, *Reptiles and Amphibians of the West.* Happy Camp, Calif.: Naturegraph Publishers, 1974.

Cochran, Doris, and Colman Goin, *The New Field Book of Reptiles and Amphibians.* New York: G. P. Putnam's, 1970.

Conant, Roger, *A Field Guide to Reptiles and Amphibians of Eastern and Central North America.* Boston: Houghton Mifflin, 1975.

Frye, Frederick, *Husbandry, Medicine and Surgery in Captive Reptiles.* Bonner Springs, Kan.: Veterinary Medicine Publishing, 1973.

Leuscher, Alfred, *Keeping Reptiles and Amphibians in Captivity.* North Pomfret, Vt.: David and Charles, 1978.

Stebbins, Robert C., *A Field Guide to Western Reptiles and Amphibians.* Boston: Houghton Mifflin, 1966. A very fine field guide.

Birds

Bendire, Charles E., *Life Histories of North American Birds: Their Breeding Habits and Eggs,* reprint. New York: Arno Press, 1974.

Bent, A.C., *Life Histories of North American Birds.* New York: Dover, 1927. In a large series of many volumes dealing with different divisions.

Brown, Vinson, et al., *Handbook of California Birds,* 3rd ed. Happy Camp, Calif.: Naturegraph Publishers, 1978.

————*Backyard Birds of California and the Pacific Northwest.* Neptune City, N.J.: TFH Publications, 1965.

————*Backyard Birds of the East and Midwest.* Neptune City, N.J.: TFH Publications, 1971.

Forbush, Edward H., *Natural History of American Birds of Eastern and Central North America.* Boston: Houghton Mifflin, 1955.

Karalus, Karl, and Allan Eckert, *The Owls of North America.* New York: Doubleday, 1975.

Lamb, Ronald, and Jerry Buzzell, *Handbook of Birds of the Pacific Northwest and Alaska.* Happy Camp, Calif.: Naturegraph Publishers, in press.

Robbins, Chandler, et al., *Birds of North America: A Guide to Field Identification.* Racine, Wis.: Western Publishing, 1966. Very good.

Peterson, Roger T., *Field Guide to the Birds,* 2nd ed. Boston: Houghton Mifflin, 1968. Eastern and midwestern birds.

————*Field Guide to the Birds of Western North America.* Boston: Houghton Mifflin, 1972.

Tyler, Hamilton, *Owls by Day and by Night.* Happy Camp, Calif.: Naturegraph Publishers, 1978. All the owls of North America in full color.

Insects, General

Borror, Donald J. and Richard H. White, *Field Guide to the Insects of America North of Mexico*. Boston: Houghton Mifflin, 1970.

Swan, Lester, and Charles Papp, *The Common Insects of North America*. New York: Harper and Row, 1972.

Beetles

Evans, M.E., *The Life of Beetles*. Riverside, N.J.: Hafner Press, 1975.

Headstrom, Richard, *The Beetles of America*. Cranbury, N.J.: A.S. Barnes, 1977.

Jacques, Harry E., *How to Know the Beetles*. Dubuque, Iowa: William C. Brown, 1951.

Butterflies and Moths

Allen, P. B., *Leaves from a Moth Hunter's Notebook*. Los Angeles: Entomological Reprint Specialists, 1977.

Ehrlich, Paul, and Anne Ehrlich, *How to Know the Butterflies*. Dubuque, Iowa: William C. Brown, 1961.

Holland, W. J., *The Moth Book*, rev. ed., A. E. Brower, ed. New York: Dover, 1968.

Howe, William H., *The Butterflies of North America*. New York: Doubleday, 1976.

Klotts, Alexander B., *A Field Guide to the Butterflies of North America, East of the Great Plains*. Boston: Houghton Mifflin, 1977.

Parenti, Umberto, *The World of Butterflies and Moths*. New York: G. P. Putnam's, 1978.

Tyler, Hamilton A., *Swallowtail Butterflies of North America*. Happy Camp, Calif.: Naturegraph Publishers, 1975.

Social Insects

Butler, Colin G., *World of the Honeybee*. New York: Taplinger, 1975.

Evans, Howard E., and Mary Eberhard, *The Wasps*. Ann Arbor: University of Michigan Press, 1970.

Goetsch, Wilhelm, *Ants*. Ann Arbor: University of Michigan Press, 1957.

House, P. E., *Termites: A Study in Social Behavior*. Atlantic Highlands, N.J.: Humanities Press, 1970.

Oster, George S., and Edward O. Wilson, *Caste and Ecology in the Social Insects*. Princeton, N.J.: Princeton University Press, 1978.

Spozczynska, Joy O., *The World of the Wasp*. New York: Crane-Russak, 1975.

INTRODUCTION

I wake up staring into the bluest blue I've ever seen. I must have fallen into a deep sleep during the short break because I need several seconds to realize that I'm looking at the sky, that the pillow beneath my head is a large clump of dirt, and that Manuel is standing over me and smiling. I pull myself to a sitting position. To my left, in the distance, a Border Patrol helicopter is hovering. To my right is Mexico, separated by only a few fields of lettuce.

"*Buenos días.*"

"How much time left?"

Manuel checks his watch. "Four minutes."

I stand up gingerly. It's only my third day in the fields, but already my thirty-year-old body is failing me. I feel like someone has dropped a log on my back. And then piled that log onto a truck with many other logs, and driven that truck over my thighs. I reach down and grab two 32-ounce bottles of Gatorade, both empty. This is nothing new: Yesterday I finished four bottles. A few people on the crew have already suggested that I see a doctor about my sweating problem.

"Let's go," I say to Manuel, trying to sound energetic. I fall in line behind him, stumbling across rows of lettuce and thinking about the five-day rule. The five-day rule, according to Manuel, is simple: Survive the first five days and you'll be fine. He's been a farmworker for almost two decades, so he should know. I'm on day three of five—the goal is within sight. Of course, another way to look at my situation is that I'm on day three of what I promised myself would be a two-month job. Or that this is only the first in a series of jobs that I hope to survive over the course of the year. But that kind of thinking doesn't benefit anyone. *Day three of five.*

"I've been thinking," Manuel calls over his shoulder. "When you showed up, I could tell right away that you had money." On the first day I was wearing jeans and a hooded sweatshirt I've had since high school, but I know what he means. I'm white, the only white person on the crew and the only white person in the fields. "So I thought maybe you were a supervisor. But you don't know what you're doing with the lettuce." He laughs. "Candelario thinks you're with immigration." He makes a dismissive gesture with his right hand and turns around, waiting for me to catch up. "But why would you be working in the fields and not stopping people at the border?"

We've nearly reached the lettuce machine, where two dozen crewmembers are putting on gloves and sharpening knives. A radio is blasting a Spanish love song and a few men and women are laughing at something; it sounds like a party.

We're late, but Manuel remains stopped in his tracks. "You're an American. But you're not a supervisor and you're not with immigration. So what are you doing?"

I shrug my shoulders. "I don't know, I just—"

"Manuel! Gabriel! Let's go!" The foreman is impatient and the question is quickly forgotten. "*¡Vámonos!*" We hustle our butts to the machine, grab our knives from a box of chlorinated water, and set up in neighboring rows, just as the machine starts moving slowly down another endless field.

"WHAT ARE YOU doing here?" Over the course of the year I would hear Manuel's question dozens of times. I'd ask it myself when things weren't going well—which was often. But because I was undercover, I couldn't explain that I was writing a book. Instead I made up a variety of responses: I was traveling and needed money to continue my journey; I enjoyed learning new skills; or, later in the year, with the economy collapsing, I needed whatever work I could find. At other times, in the middle of a shift so draining that I didn't have the energy to make something up, I would simply say, "I don't know." At those moments the answer felt honest enough.

I do know what gave me the idea for this book. In the fall of 2007 the *New York Times* published an article entitled "Crackdown Upends Slaughterhouse's Workforce." Written by labor correspondent Steven Greenhouse, the piece documented the difficulty that Smithfield Foods was having in securing a stable workforce at its massive hog slaughterhouse in North Carolina after a series of raids by immigration agents. Although the crackdown resulted in the arrest of only twenty-one undocumented immigrants, more than 1,100 Latino workers subsequently quit, leaving the 5,200-employee plant severely short staffed. Some of the workers were no doubt working without proper papers, while others simply wanted to avoid a situation in which government agents could come barging into their trailers in the middle of the night.

In response to the exodus of immigrants, Smithfield stepped up efforts to recruit U.S. citizens. Based on wages alone, this shouldn't have been overly difficult: Most of the local jobs paid minimum wage and positions at the plant averaged $12 an hour. Still, as Greenhouse reported, "The turnover rate for new workers—many find the work grueling and the smell awful—is twice what it was when Hispanics dominated the workforce . . . At the end of the shifts, many workers complain that their muscles are sore and their minds are numb."[1]

As a teenager, I relished George Orwell's accounts of going into dangerous coal mines in *The Road to Wigan Pier* and washing dishes in *Down and Out in Paris and London*, and was likewise moved by Barbara Ehrenreich's adventures scrubbing floors and waiting tables in *Nickel and Dimed*. I've always been drawn to chronicles of immersion journalism; they have a unique ability to explore fascinating and sometimes brutal worlds that are usually kept out of sight. I thought it would be exciting to try this type of reporting myself, and immediately upon finishing the *Times* article, a project formed in my head. I would enter the low-wage immigrant workforce for a year and write about it.

In many ways, this project was a natural outgrowth of my previous work. I had reported on immigrants for the past three years—mostly Latino because I speak Spanish—and I have always been interested in documenting what life looks like through the eyes of my subjects, transforming them from statistics to real people. The notion of going undercover to work alongside immigrants in the factories and fields—assuming I could actually get hired—held an immense appeal. In 2008, the Pew Hispanic Center estimated that there were 8.3 million undocumented workers in the United States, making up 5.4 percent of the workforce. The role that these low-wage workers play in our economy is, of course, a matter of much debate. But whether one believes they are a threat or a boon to the economy, the fact remains that very few of us nonimmigrants know what it's like to do the jobs they do. I wanted to find out.

I ULTIMATELY DECIDED to seek employment in three industries that depend heavily on Latino immigrants: agriculture, poultry processing, and back-of-the-house restaurant work (this refers to the people who work in the kitchen and do not interact with customers). While I could just as easily have elected to slaughter cows, work in construction, do landscaping, or clean offices, I chose farmwork, chicken factories, and restaurants mostly out of sheer curiosity; they were industries I wanted to know more about. (I've been a vegetarian since grade school, so my curiosity was tinged with apprehension when it came to poultry.) Having decided on the three jobs, it quickly became clear that my year of work would also be a year of travel. The poultry industry is concentrated in the American South, and there are few fields in need of harvesting near my apartment in Brooklyn. I planned to go west for farmwork, south in search of a chicken plant, and return home to New York to find a restaurant job. Heading to the southern states where the Latino population is growing fastest would also grant me the opportunity to report on how the region is adapting to its newest arrivals.

The neat little itinerary that I drew up in my apartment left a critical question unanswered: How in God's name would I get hired? It seemed likely that I would face skeptical looks from hiring managers, perhaps even be laughed out of an office or two. I figured that the increase in immigration enforcement might make it easier to find work—and that the sorts of jobs I was looking for would have openings due to high turnover. But ultimately, from the moment I left Brooklyn, I was operating on little more than blind faith.

I SET SEVERAL parameters for the year. When discussing my project, I learned that a fair number of Americans had some experience with farmwork. Many were similar to my father's time spent hoeing beet fields in the Red River Valley of North Dakota. As a youth he had planned to spend a summer in the fields; after just a few days—perhaps a week—he had had enough. So I set myself a goal: No matter how unpleasant, I would stay with each job for two months.

The second guideline was that while I was away from New York, I would live among the immigrants that I worked alongside. This would be the most cost-effective arrangement and would allow me to get to know my coworkers better.

STRICTLY SPEAKING, THERE is no such a thing as an "immigrant" job. There are many industries that rely heavily on Latino immigrants, but many of these also employ at least a handful of U.S.-born citizens (though not in the lettuce fields, as I discovered). Often, when workplaces offer a variety of jobs—restaurants are a good example—immigrants tend to be assigned the most strenuous, dangerous, and worst-paid positions (e.g., washing dishes and delivering food). So a book about the world of immigrant work is also one about the very poor Americans who labor with them. As I would discover, these Americans had much in common with undocumented immigrants—for one thing, they are ignored equally in the stump speeches of politicians—and despite the lack of a shared language, the drudgery of the workplace can contribute to a sense of solidarity.

SOME FINAL WORDS on what this book is and is not. It is not my attempt to get by on the wages an immigrant earns or to "walk in their shoes." Wages figure into this story, but unlike Ehrenreich in *Nickel and Dimed*, it is not an experiment to see if I can survive financially. My challenge is to keep showing up for the next shift.

Nor will I be walking in anyone's shoes but my own. In Alabama, for instance, I worked the graveyard shift at a poultry plant, often next to a man named Jesús. Many nights we spent eight hours doing identical work, tearing thousands of frigid chicken breasts in half and tossing them onto a conveyor belt. Although we both suffered frozen hands, our identities did not blend together. I was still a middle-class American citizen who spoke English and graduated from college. Jesús had fled a civil war in Guatemala at the age of fifteen and spent the majority of his life picking tomatoes in Florida and processing chickens in Alabama. I eventually left the plant behind and fill my days with reading and writing; tonight, Jesús will probably spend another eight hours tearing up chicken parts. This book was an exhausting learning experience for me; for my coworkers, it is life.

The learning began in early 2008, when I traveled to my first stop, the state of Arizona. I packed several empty notebooks, a laptop, a bottle of painkillers, and a collection of books about immigrants and labor. By the time I left, I'd read them all, but my real education was just about to begin.

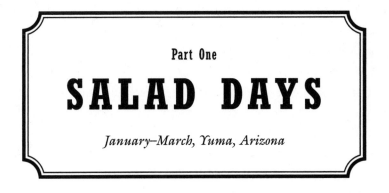

Part One

SALAD DAYS

January–March, Yuma, Arizona

GETTING THE JOB

Wedged into the corner of southwestern Arizona, the city of Yuma sits at a crossroads. Mexico is twenty miles to the south, California a stone's throw to the west, the cities of Phoenix and Tucson about a three-hour drive to the east. Yuma is a place to eat and perhaps spend an evening en route to somewhere more interesting, or at least less oppressively hot. One of the sunniest places on earth, the city receives less than four inches of rainfall a year and temperatures in July frequently exceed 107 degrees. A soldier back from Iraq—Yuma is home to a Marine Corps air base—observed that it wasn't so hard to adjust to the Arabian Desert after surviving a Yuma summer.

I relocate to Yuma on a balmy January day during the first week of 2008. Each winter Yuma's warmth attracts 90,000 retirees from Canada and the northern states, doubling the city's population and filling the local malls, restaurants, and movie theaters. Nearing

Yuma I pass a number of RV campgrounds—really just expansive slabs of black asphalt with water and electricity hookups—packed with some of the largest land vehicles I've ever seen. I pull over and take photos of what seems a distinctly American scene: the desert wilderness paved over, with folks sitting on lawn chairs under the shade created by their gas guzzlers, angled so that they can watch the cars zoom past on the highway.

By the time I enter the city limits, green fields of lettuce stretch from either side of the highway to the horizon, irrigated with water from the nearby Colorado River. Buses are parked among the fields, and I can see groups of farmworkers in the distance to my right. A California native, I've seen this scene many times while driving up and down the West Coast, a glimpse of a workforce that seems to belong to another universe entirely. This time I pull over to the shoulder and park. It's hard to see much detail—the workers are too far away—but I watch the figures for a few minutes, letting the idea sink in that in a few days, with some luck, I'll join them.

WHY BEGIN IN Yuma? It's mostly a question of timing: While doing research I learned that Yuma has been the "winter lettuce capital" of America since the early 1980s, when companies moved to the area from California's Imperial Valley. Today, there are about one hundred growers—individual contractors who are responsible for the crop until two weeks before harvest, overseeing aspects like irrigation and pest and weed management. These growers can be in charge of anywhere from 500 to 5,000 acres, and sign contracts with companies like Dole, Fresh Express, and Tamimura & Antle, who supply the laborers to harvest and pack the crop. At the height of the winter growing season, Yuma farmworkers are harvesting an astounding 12 million heads of lettuce a day.

Along with a ready supply of water from the Colorado River, Yuma's climate is a key reason the winter lettuce industry is centered in the area. When the weather turns cold in Salinas, California—

the heart of the nation's lettuce industry from the spring to the fall—temperatures in Yuma are still in the seventies and eighties. Each winter, Yuma produces virtually all of the iceberg lettuce and 90 percent of the leafy green vegetables consumed in the United States and Canada. Yuma lettuce is slapped between the buns of Big Macs, topped with anchovies in Caesar salads at posh Italian restaurants, and packed into ready-mixed bags that line grocery aisles from Monterey to Montreal. Still, the area's contribution goes unrecognized: it's a billion-dollar-a-year industry that most people outside of Arizona don't even know exists. "Companies think that customers associate quality lettuce with Salinas and California, so that is what you'll see on the labels," explains Kurt Nolte, an agriculture specialist at the University of Arizona Cooperative Extension in Yuma.

The second reason I chose Yuma is that the industry needs people like me. I've come across several articles documenting a shortage of farmworkers. They cite an aging workforce (the median age of Yuma farmworkers is forty-five); immigration crackdowns; and long delays at the border implemented after 9/11, all of which discourage many workers who have green cards and live in Mexico from commuting to the fields. American-born workers can help fill the shortage, and wages have been rising somewhat in response to the demand for laborers. But Doug Mellon, a grower interviewed by the *Arizona Republic*, scoffed at the notion that U.S. citizens would ever flock to the fields. "I don't care if you paid $40 [an hour], they'd do it about three hours and say, 'That's not for me.'"[1]

Senator John McCain, speaking to a group of union members in Washington, D.C., made the same controversial point. "I'll offer anybody here $50 an hour if you'll go pick lettuce in Yuma this season, and pick for the whole season," he said. Amid jeers, he didn't back down, telling the audience, "You can't do it, my friends." Although I don't plan on staying the entire season, if I manage to land a job I certainly hope I last longer than three hours.

AFTER MILES OF lettuce fields, the terrain turns more generic: Like any number of fast-growing cities, Yuma seems well on its way to becoming one long commercial strip. I pass several huge shopping centers and a Burger King, whose sign makes the odd boast that it has the largest indoor play area in the state. Checking into a nondescript motel, I tell the manager that I'm looking for work in the fields. She pulls out a photocopied map of the town and marks an intersection. "Mostly Mexicans in the fields, you know. But here's the Dole building—maybe you should go there. Sometimes people from Dole stay here, seem nice enough to me."

For weeks I've been digesting everything I could find on farmworkers, from documentaries and novels to investigative exposés and government reports, but I haven't given much thought to the particular company I want to work for. Dole sounds like as good a place to start as any: It's large and well known. I unload some of my possessions and head over.

Dole Fresh Vegetables, part of the company that is the largest producer of fresh fruits and vegetables in the world, is located several miles from the motel, across the street from the Marine Corps air station and down the block from a windowless Adult XXX superstore, both of which are surrounded by fences topped with concertina wire. It's an ugly area, but the narrow road leading into Dole's headquarters is grassy and lined with palm trees, like the entrance to a small college. A large sign sits next to a beige one-story building, which reads Headquarters Office—Agriculture and Harvest.

Inside, a young Latina woman is seated behind a desk. "May I help you?"

"Yes, could you tell me where I should go to apply for a job picking lettuce?"

She directs me back outside and around the corner to human resources. That she doesn't seem the least surprised by the request bolsters my confidence. I follow her directions, pushing open a door to find myself in a small office where a man is holding a telephone conversation in Spanish. When he hangs up, I repeat my request, and he switches to English.

"The fields? You want to work outside in the fields?" He smiles, like I've cracked a joke. A long moment of silence follows. "You know, maybe it would be better if you worked inside, in the plant. You could make more money and it wouldn't be so hard. That might be a better fit."

"No, I think I want to try working outside."

"Have you ever worked in the fields before?" I shake my head.

"Well, I can tell you one thing: It's not easy out there. Every year a few people come in who look like you. They last only two days, sometimes only a few hours. They get out there and realize it's not for them."

"Yeah, I know it's hard. But I'm looking for a job that I can start right away. I don't want to have to wait weeks for an interview—I just want to get started."

"You want to get started," he repeats. I fill the silence with vigorous nods. "You want to work in the fields."

"I want to work in the fields," I insist. "Are there any openings?"

He chuckles. "We can put you in the fields right away. That's not a problem." He tells me to stop by tomorrow—Friday—and fill out an application.

THE FOLLOWING AFTERNOON the skeptical man has been replaced by a middle-aged woman wearing heavy makeup and standing behind the front desk chatting in Spanish to several teenagers. I take a seat next to a cubicle wall that is covered with a poster reading We Use E-Verify. E-verify is a voluntary federal program that checks Social Security numbers against given names. Dole is using the program—which has been shown to be error prone—because three days earlier a new law went into effect. The state policy, known as the employer sanctions law, can permanently revoke

the business licenses of companies that knowingly hire undocumented workers, and was pushed by anti-immigrant forces and
signed into law in July 2007 by Democratic governor Janet Napoli-
tano (who is now the secretary of homeland security under President Obama). Using E-verify will protect Dole from legal action.
It will also protect lettuce-picking jobs for Americans like me.

After the teenagers leave she turns to me. "May I help you?"

"I hope so. I'd like a job picking lettuce." Her penciled eyebrows rise.

"*Lettuce?*" She makes the word sound ridiculously out of place.
"Yes."

"You want to cut lettuce?"*

"Yes. Are you by any chance hiring?"

"This time of year, there is always work in lettuce. But have you
done this kind of work before? Do you know what it's like in the
fields?"

"No, but I've worked construction. I like learning new things."

She nods politely and hands me an application. I imagine she
has seen this before: eager (or, more likely, financially desperate)
gringos, not knowing what they're signing up for.

"Fill this out and come back Monday morning. We'll do an orientation and you can start Tuesday, if you really want to do this."

I quickly fill out my personal information but pause when asked
to give employer references. I've spent the last three years writing
about Mexican immigrants, but this isn't something I'd like Dole
to know. They also probably don't need to know that I've completed an internship with a union, or just published a book about
community organizing. Instead, I put down the Fifth Avenue
Committee, a nonprofit organization in Brooklyn where I have
done part-time work; more importantly, I am good friends with

---

* I'll soon learn that, contrary to common terminology, no one actually
"picks" lettuce; instead, it is cut at the stem with a knife.

Artemio Guerra, the director of organizing, and I list him as a reference. I note that I did translation.

"So you speak Spanish," she says when I hand over the application. "Do you happen to know how to drive a forklift?"

"No, no idea. But anyway, I think I want to try working in the fields."

"You could even get training," she insists. "I know they've been looking for a bilingual driver. The money is much better."

I've been in this office twice and both times have been offered promotions on the spot. I have a hard time picturing myself writing an entertaining book about driving a forklift. Trying to underscore my desire to harvest lettuce and nothing else, I say, "I'm just looking for something a little simpler."

On hearing these words her posture straightens. "Oh no, cutting lettuce is *not* simple. I worked in the fields all my life, since I was sixteen. That's all I did before moving here to the office. Let me tell you, there is nothing simple about it."

I immediately regret my choice of words, but she seems more amused than insulted by my ignorance. "We don't get many Americans around here. There was one guy who came earlier this year. He was from Colorado, I think."

"Is he still around?"

"No, but he lasted two weeks. I felt really bad for him because he didn't speak Spanish and he said he got lonely in the fields. It can be very hard work. You'll learn."

"Two weeks isn't very long, is it?"

She flashes a knowing smile. "To tell you the truth, it was longer than I expected."

I USE THE weekend to search for a place to stay. I have an idea of what I should be looking for in farmworker housing: ramshackle trailer parks, or long one-story complexes, filled with bunk beds and tucked away behind corners or down dusty roads. But during hours of searching—in Yuma and the nearby towns of Somerton and San Luis—the closest thing I find to migrant housing are RV parks filled with retirees. Out of curiosity I tail a bus carrying farmworkers from the field, but after twenty minutes it pulls into a large parking lot near the border and the workers file into Mexico.

On Sunday afternoon I move into a room I found on Craigslist. The owner of the house is a gregarious elementary school teacher named Janice who lives in the western section of Yuma, just blocks from a long series of lettuce and broccoli fields. She is initially skeptical about my source of income—"You are doing what, exactly?"—but after I explain the project she seems to get a kick out of it.

On Monday, I go through a short orientation with two other employees, both female.* They both live in the Mexican border city of San Luis Río Colorado. The older of the two worked in broccoli for Dole last year but had to stop midseason when she gave birth. The younger, Rosa, is in her twenties and has harvested lettuce for other companies; we will be placed on the same crew. We are all given a thick packet of papers, covering items such as the number to call if we're going to be absent, how to file sexual harassment claims, and general safety rules. There is also, to my surprise, a section of papers that includes a collective bargaining agreement and membership application for Teamsters Local 890, based out of Salinas. The only thing I know about the Teamsters in the fields is that they undercut a number of United Farm Worker union drives in the 1960s and '70s by signing sweetheart deals with growers, but I will later learn that it was another Team-

---

* A recent University of Arizona survey found that Yuma's agricultural workforce was 40 percent female, about four times greater than the national average. I surmise that this is because many migrant farmworkers are undocumented men who travel long distances to land jobs; in Yuma, the workforce is local—living on both sides of the border—so that families remain unified and can head to the fields together.

sters local (unions are divided into locals that can pursue different agendas) that fought with the UFW. I decide to pay a $50 initiation fee and have the $24 dues taken out of my paycheck. The two women decline this option. (Because Arizona is a "right to work" state, employees who work for a union company can elect to withhold their union dues, which makes building a powerful union difficult.)

Once we've finished signing papers, our last stop is with the company nurse, for what an overweight security guard calls the "whiz quiz." I'm not worried—I'll be clean—but I'm amused to think that the first time I take a pre-employment drug test is for a job cutting lettuce. A supervisor wearing yellow gaiters and a bib drives us to and from the nurse's office; as I'm waiting for the others to take the test, I read more carefully through the wages section of the packet.

On the short drive back to human resources, I say, "The packet says that lettuce cutters make $8.37 an hour, but broccoli cutters only get $7.69. Why is that?"

"Broccoli grows higher up," the supervisor tells me. "So you can cut it higher. For lettuce you have to cut it near the ground, so you bend over more." He rubs his back and grimaces. "That's why you get paid more."

"So lettuce is the hardest?" I ask, suddenly thinking that perhaps readers will find tales of cutting broccoli more interesting.

The driver considers the question. "Well, maybe a little harder. But *trabajo es trabajo.*" It's all just work. "You have to do it and see. For people like you who haven't worked in the fields, you never know if your body can take it or not until you try."

CHAPTER 1

At 6:45 a.m. the lot behind Dole's office is empty. As instructed, I'm parked in my car waiting for bus no. 158 to pick me up. Though it is still dark, I can make out a row of portable toilets stacked on trailers to my left, and when I roll down the window a sharp smell of disinfectant seeps in.

A white truck turns into the lot at seven o'clock. It backs up to one of the restroom trailers and a man steps out, attaches it to his truck, and drives off. Over the next thirty minutes a dozen more trucks pick up toilets, but there is no sight of a bus. By now the sun is rising over the foothills, illuminating the sky: another cloud-free day in Yuma.

Just when I'm convinced that I misheard my directions, a sedan pulls up parallel to my car, driven by a woman whose face is swathed in several bandanas to protect against sun and dust. We make eye contact—using the only part of her face that's exposed. I've seen photos of female farmworkers wearing bandanas, but in person it is an intimidating sight: I half expect her to pop her trunk and toss me a rifle, ready to expand the Zapatista rebellion to U.S. soil.

Instead, she gets out of her car and pulls a pair of rubber galoshes from the backseat. "*Hola, mi hijo,*" she says in a high-pitched voice, erasing my insurrection imaginings. As she pulls on her boots we exchange good-mornings, after which she asks the inevitable question: "What are you doing here?"

I should have a stock answer prepared; instead, I give a rambling and incoherent explanation. I'm from New York. Some of my Mexican friends in New York have parents who worked in the fields. Right now I have a few free months, so I decided to try cutting lettuce. My parents live in San Jose. Most of the Mexicans in New York are from the state of Puebla. That's a long ways away. I'm thirty years old. It's hot in Yuma, isn't it?

The woman, Dalia, listens as she places various items in her backpack. "Well, this is hard work, but I enjoy it," she says when I finish my monologue. The first bus of the morning drives by and stops to pick her up; like the others I've seen around Yuma, the vehicle is an old American school bus that's received a fresh coat of white paint. After a brief phone conversation, the driver informs me that my bus, which has picked up workers at the border, will be arriving in ten minutes. "If you're here tomorrow," Dalia tells me as she boards her bus, "I'll have an extra taco for you."

Minutes later my bus roars into the lot. The driver dashes down the steps, nods at me, and jogs back to attach the portable toilets. I've been excited about this project for months, yet I am suddenly overwhelmed by a severe lack of confidence, that first-day-at-a-new-school sinking feeling. Inside the bus most of the people are asleep, their legs sprawled in the aisles and heads wedged against bundled sweatshirts. I don't see an open space but then notice Rosa from orientation seated to my right. She moves over and I sit down, scrunching my knees up against the back of the seat, which has clearly been designed for kids who have yet to hit their growth spurt.

As we drive west on the highway, I sneak glances at Rosa, who is assembling her face mask. She first pulls down a fabric that fits like a hood, followed by a bandana wrapped around the top part of her head. Another wrap—what I come to call the ninja bandana—is wound tightly above her nose and then knotted in the back. It looks like it must get awfully hot in there.

After twenty minutes we turn off the highway and head down a dirt path, parking in the middle of the same lettuce fields I stopped to observe on my initial drive into Yuma. A slender foreman greets us when we step off the bus, walking us to his truck for a field orientation. "Since you haven't worked in the fields before," he says to me, "I'll do your orientation last."

While he goes over safety issues with Rosa, I keep my eyes on the field. Men and women are rushing back and forth in front of a large contraption, which I will·later learn is simply called *la maqina*—the machine. The machine has two waist-high wings jutting out to the left and the right—at least fifty feet long from one end to the other—connected to a number of extensions. Behind the wings is an eight-wheel flatbed. While the majority of the crew fiddles with the machine, two men stand on the flatbed, stacking wooden pallets and folding boxes. A third man is tying a yellow Dole flag to two poles above the wings.

"*¡Ejercicios!*" someone shouts. The crew gathers in a circle and begins doing coordinated stretches, swinging their arms and touching their toes. Who knew farmworkers have a formal warm-up routine?

The foreman is talking louder now, and it dawns on me that Rosa has departed. I turn away from the farmworkers, now doing a series of squats. "You're switching crews," he tells me. "A guy's on his way to get you."

I turn my attention back to the field. The calisthenics wind down and the crew divides into pairs, each pair taking a single row immediately behind the machine. A radio is switched on, flooding the field with the famous voice of Mexico's Vicente Fernandez, as the tires of the machine start to slowly turn. In each row, the person farthest from the machine bends down, quickly cuts a head of lettuce with a knife, stuffs the lettuce into a bag from a packet hanging from his waist, and drops the lettuce on an extension. The second person in the row snatches the bag from the extension and packs it into a cardboard box that is resting on the machine.

I spend fifteen minutes watching the crew, made up of eighteen men and twelve women. As they move away from the road, it becomes difficult to make out the details of their activities, but one thing is quite obvious: *They move fast.* A dozen knives are stabbing and slicing and slashing, sending hundreds of leaves flying in all directions. As they march across the field they are military in their efficiency, leaving nothing behind except glistening white stumps and the occasional discarded head of rotten lettuce. The flatbed quickly fills with completed boxes, which are stacked on pallets by two barrel-chested men wearing flannel shirts. A third man, perched on a ledge of the machine directly above the rows, frantically assembles empty cardboard boxes and shoves them to his right and left to replenish the supplies. During the fifteen minutes that I observe the workers, they harvest more than 1,600 heads of lettuce.

On most crews, each cutter harvests six heads of lettuce each minute, or 360 an hour. At this pace, a farmworker earning an hourly wage of $8.37 is paid just over two cents per head; these heads are then sold in stores for about $1 apiece. Although total farm labor costs are less than one-third of grower revenue, companies argue that low wages are necessary in an industry forced to deal with unpredictable weather and shifting market demands. But Philip L. Martin, professor of agricultural economics at the University of California–Davis, has shown that even a dramatic increase in labor costs—passed fully to the consumer—would have a very modest impact on the typical American household budget, which spent $322 on fresh fruits and vegetables in 2000. Martin's detailed analysis of the agricultural industry found that a 40 percent increase in farmworker wages would increase a household's annual spending on fruits and vegetables by only $8, to $330. A single head of iceberg lettuce, selling for $1, would increase by just two to three cents.[2]

"You sure you want to do this?" asks a deep voice. I turn around to find a bronze-faced man staring at me from beneath a cowboy hat, behind the wheel of a truck.

"I think so."

"So get in. You're going to be working in Somerton," he says, referring to a town ten miles south of Yuma. On the drive over, I learn that the man has been with Dole for fifteen years. "During all those years I never saw a single white person. But this year you're the second American we've had."

"Why is that, do you think?"

"I don't know. Maybe because people know we need workers." He eases off the accelerator as a Border Patrol truck passes us on the left. "Things have become very tough here for Mexicans without papers. They can't get jobs anymore in the fields, so they leave for California or Las Vegas. Too much Border Patrol, too many problems." He points at the truck disappearing in the distance. "And so we have a lot of jobs that people like you could do, if they wanted."

We drive through Somerton and make a left at Cesar Chavez Boulevard. (Chavez, the iconic founder of the United Farm Workers, was born in 1927 near his family's farm in Yuma; he died in

San Luis, Arizona—just ten miles away—in 1993.) Turning down a dirt path, the tract homes open up into a wide field. "There's your crew," the driver tells me. "This is the first year for most of them, but you'll see they learned quickly. They won't think you're going to last, I can tell you that right now. They had the other American, and he left right away. We put you both here because the *mayordomo* [foreman] speaks English." I step out and thank him for the ride.

A chubby man—Pedro—ambles over to greet me. But when I take his outstretched hand, the soft white flesh of my palm is crunched between cement-hard calluses. This is a man made thick not from eating but from labor. And though he may speak more English than the other foremen, it's still fairly basic, so he is relieved when I interrupt his halting introduction in Spanish.

"Don't worry about anything," Pedro tells me, assuming—correctly—that I'm nervous. "Right now you are beginning, but soon you'll be cutting like a pro. The first thing you need is your equipment." I follow him to his truck.

A lettuce cutter's uniform consists of a surprising number of items, which I struggle to put on as he runs down the basic rules (no running, safety above all else, paychecks every Friday). Pedro introduces me to his assistant, Diego, who hands me large black galoshes to put over my shoes. Next comes the *gancho* (hook), a metal S-shaped bar that slips over my belt. The gancho has two metal prongs, and the packets of plastic bags have two holes at the top, so that they slide onto the gancho just like paper slides into a two-ring binder. A gray glove goes on my left hand, a white glove on my right; the gray glove, according to Pedro, offers protection from cuts. (I'm skeptical—it looks like a normal glove.) Over the cloth gloves I pull on a pair of latex gloves, then put on a black hairnet under my baseball cap, slide on a pair of protective sunglasses, and slip a leather sheath onto my belt: I'm good to go. I feel ridiculous.

"When you're going to the machine, always walk along the *camino*," Pedro explains as we head toward the crew down a narrow dirt path. Rows to our right have just been harvested and are littered with thickets of lettuce leaves.

He stops when we reach the machine, which is identical to the one I observed earlier. "This is Manuel," he says, motioning to the nearest cutter, an attractive and wiry man with brown hair, a trimmed mustache, and fair skin. Manuel pauses from his work and waves, a knife in his hand. I notice, too, that every other member of the crew has turned to stare at me. "Manuel has been cutting for many years, so watch him to see how it's done." Pedro walks away, my field instruction apparently complete.

Manuel resumes cutting. Every several seconds he bends down with the knife in his right hand, grabs the head of iceberg lettuce with his left hand as if palming a basketball, and makes a quick cut, separating the lettuce from its roots. Next, he lifts the head of lettuce in front of his stomach and makes a second cut, trimming the trunk. He shakes the lettuce to the left and right, and the outer leaves fall to the ground; the lettuce has been reduced to half its original size. With the blade still in his right hand, he brings the clean, white-and-green head of lettuce toward his stomach and the bags hanging from his gancho, and with a flick of the wrist the lettuce is bagged and on the extension. A woman standing in front of him grabs the bag, tapes it shut, and packs it in a box that sits about waist high on the machine. When the box is full she shoves it forward onto a conveyor belt, which takes it to the middle of the machine, where a tall man stacks it on the flatbed.

Manuel does this over and over again, looking bored as he explains each movement. I watch and give my assessment. "You make it look easy, but I know it's not."

"It's not so hard," he argues, and takes me through the entire movement again. "That's all it is, right there."

I watch for five more minutes, walking forward with the crew to keep up with the machine. Pedro reappears. "Gabriel, now it's your turn—come get your knife." I follow him to the end of the machine, where a metal case of chlorinated water is affixed, and reach in and grab the handle of a knife and begin walking back to Manuel's row.

"No, Gabriel," Pedro says. "Anytime you are walking with the knife, it has to be put in its sheath." I do as told, putting the eighteen-inch knife away. Lesson number one.

"Try this one." Manuel points at a head of lettuce to my right.

I bend over, noticing that most of the crew has turned to watch. I take my knife and make a tentative sawing motion where I assume the trunk to be, though I'm really just guessing, as the head is overflowing with outer leaves. Next, I secure the head with my left hand and raise it up as I straighten my back, doing my best to imitate Manuel. Only the head doesn't move; it's still securely connected to the soil—so now I'm standing up with nothing to bag.

Pedro steps in. "When you make the first cut, it is like you are stabbing the lettuce." He takes my knife and makes a quick jabbing action, then lifts the large head and turns it upside down. "You want to aim for the center of the lettuce, where the trunk is, with the front section of the blade. Then, when it's cut, you turn it and with the side of the blade you make another cut on the trunk, higher up." I watch him do as he describes, and again it looks effortless. Someone calls for Pedro, and he hands me back the knife. Manuel points out another head.

This time the lettuce comes up. I cradle the head against my chest, as if hugging it, and look for a good place to make the second cut. I make a second slice through the trunk, trying to shake the lettuce, but I lose my grip and send it to the ground. When I pick it up, it's covered in dirt.

"Make another cut," Manuel says. "There are still too many leaves." I hold the lettuce upside down and make another trim, and the dirty leaves fall. Now it's starting to look like the iceberg lettuce in the produce section of grocery stores.

"That's good, right there. Now you bag it." Manuel does another slow demonstration of bagging, which I do my best to follow. His right hand holds the lettuce and the knife. He inserts his left hand into the outermost bag hanging from the gancho, spreading his fingers to open the bag as wide as possible, and lifts it from the packet. With the bag fully open, he passes the lettuce from his right to his left hand—thereby encircling the lettuce in the bag—and with both hands grabs the top corners of the bag and twists the head over, so that it swings around. The bag is then separated from the packet and is ready to be placed on the extension. It is a complicated process, but done correctly it takes less than a second and looks quite graceful.

I need about a minute to figure out how to get the damn lettuce in the bag. The first bag rips in half. The second bag somehow expels the lettuce, which flops to the ground. On the third attempt I am finally able to massage the lettuce into the bag, flip it over correctly, and tear the bag from the gancho. Only I have somehow managed to pull the entire packet of bags off the gancho, so I'm holding a head of properly cut and bagged lettuce that is attached to another hundred bags.

"I know what's wrong," Manuel says. He takes off a plastic glove and folds it twice, lengthwise, then pulls it taut in front of me. "Make a cut over here by the end." Confused, I do as told, slicing off a section. He takes the section I have cut and opens it; it's now a wrist-sized rubber band. He slides the bags back onto my gancho and winds the band around the prongs, and now I get it: This will prevent more than one bag from tearing off at a time. I look at Manuel's gancho and see that he too has this custom-made rubber band. Lesson number two.

Ten minutes later, Pedro comes over to see how I'm progressing. I've probably cut twenty heads of lettuce so far and feel pretty accomplished. With the first stab I sometimes cut the stem correctly, though when my back tightens up, I don't stoop far enough, and my stab—instead of landing an inch above the ground—goes right through the head of lettuce, ruining it entirely. The greatest difficulty, though, is in the trimming. I had no idea that a head of lettuce was so humongous. In order to get it into a shape that can be bagged, I trim and I trim and I trim, but it's taking me upwards of a minute to do what Manuel does in several seconds.

Pedro watches me cut several heads and go about my endless trimming routine. "Act like the lettuce is a bomb," he suggests. He goes through the motions of cutting and bagging with his hands, pretending to drop the lettuce on the machine's arm before it explodes. "Imagine you've only got five seconds to get rid of it."

Surprisingly, I find that I'm able to greatly increase my speed when I keep the phrase *like a bomb* in my head. I vigorously shove the lettuce into bags, then drop the bags on the extension before they can harm anyone. "Look at me!" I want to shout at Pedro, who is several rows over, talking on his cell phone. For a minute or two I feel euphoric; I'm in the zone.

The woman packing the lettuce swivels around to face me. "Look, this lettuce is no good." I study the contents of the bag I've just handed over. She's right: I've cut the trunk too high, breaking off dozens of good leaves, which will quickly turn brown. I've also jammed the lettuce in sideways—you're supposed to bag so that the trunk sticks up toward the bag's opening—and there are a bunch of outer leaves, connected to nothing and that don't belong. I look at the three other bags I've placed on the extension. None looks very appetizing.

"Okay, sorry," I say. With her left hand she holds the bag up, and with her right she smashes it violently, making a loud pop. She turns the bag over and the massacred lettuce falls to the ground. She does the same for the three other bags I've placed on the extension.

"It's his first day," Manuel tells her. Then to me: "It's okay. She's not feeling well. You shouldn't try to go too fast when you're beginning. Take it slow." Pedro passes by, catching Manuel's comments.

"That's right," he tells me, seconding Manuel. "Make sure the cuts are precise and that you don't rush." So I am to be very careful and precise, while also treating the lettuce like a bomb that must be tossed aside after five seconds.

An hour later, when I am just starting to notice the slightest signs of improvement, the female packer stands up and walks around the wing of the machine. As I continue to cut, I can see her through the slits in the metal. She is doubled over and looks on the verge of vomiting. Manuel walks around to join her and they talk briefly before returning.

"Are you feeling okay?" I ask.

"I have a stomachache," she says, pulling her gloves back on.

"Sorry about my lettuce." She doesn't respond. "I'm impressed you come to work when you're sick," I continue, wanting to make amends. "When I'm sick I become such a baby. Even when I just have a cold, I don't get out of bed."

She turns around to face me. "Some things you do out of necessity—you don't have a choice. You, are you here for the money, or just to see what it's like?" It's not exactly a hostile question, but her tone sounds more aggressive than merely curious.

I'm a terrible liar, and I decide to abandon any prior notions of passing myself off as a down-on-my-luck, possibly alcoholic guy doing whatever he can to earn some quick cash. "I can always use the money," I say, as any struggling freelance writer can attest. "But mostly, I want to know what the work is like."

She turns around and doesn't say anything else.

DURING THE THIRTY-MINUTE lunch break, a number of people ask me why I'm there, and I give them what will become my standard response: I had a few months off and thought it would be interesting to see what farmwork was like. They ask how long I'll be staying, and I tell them until March. They don't argue, but it's obvious they don't expect me to last.

After lunch I take up my spot next to Manuel. We have a new packer, a man people call Nacho, who looks like a Vietnamese rice farmer under his giant conical straw hat.

"What happened to the other woman?" I ask Manuel as we begin to cut.

"That's my wife, Maria. She went to see the nurse. She isn't feeling well."

The rest of the day goes smoothly. I continue to cut slowly but am picking up techniques, like how to bag the lettuce. Resisting the impulse to stuff the lettuce in forcefully, I learn from watching Manuel that it requires a gentle motion: the less effort, the better. He deftly places his left hand into the bag to open it wide, uses his right hand to push the lettuce into the opening, lets it go, and with a flick of his wrists uses the momentum of the head to do the work. I even succeed in emulating the motion several times before the day is over.

It's nearly six o'clock when we finish. Following Manuel's lead, I drop my knife in the box of chlorinated water and place my remaining packet of bags in a box. Pedro gives me a ride to the office, telling me that from now on I should drive my own car. We'll be working the same field tomorrow, starting at 8:00 a.m.

As I drive home I take an inventory of my body. The most noticeable pain is in my swollen feet, but it isn't too terrible: It reminds me, if anything, of how I feel when forced to spend a day wandering in a museum. My thighs are a bit rubbery and my hands have that early-morning weakness, though they don't feel sore. By far the most remarkable development is that after completing my first day in the fields, my back doesn't ache.

It's not until the following day, when Maria doesn't show up, that I learn she won't be returning for the rest of the season. I'm her replacement. I ask one of the workers, whose name I don't yet know, how he can be so sure she won't return.

"She didn't seem like the kind of person who would quit over a stomachache."

"A stomachache?" he says. "Who told you that? She's nearly eight months pregnant."

CHAPTER 2

A woman wearing bandanas over her face—for some reason, I've noticed that only women wear the bandanas—is already leading the calisthenics when I walk up to the crew the next morning. I see Manuel and say hello as he swings his arms with the group.

"You're back?" he asks, sounding surprised.

Nacho, standing next to Manuel, gets into the act as well. "Look who returned," he tells me. I reiterate my plan to stay for two months while struggling to get the gancho locked onto my belt (the first sign that my hands are beginning to weaken; it will get much worse).

"Gabby, exercises!" yells the calisthenics woman, whose name I later learn is Adriana. (How does she know my childhood name was Gabby?) For some reason—perhaps a vestige of my lack of enthusiasm for high school gym class—I half-heartedly swing my arms. "No, better!" she calls again. "Or else you'll lead the group!" I straighten up and begin to participate, squatting and stretching and doing whatever the boss-woman says I should with maximum enthusiasm.

Once the exercises are completed, Pedro calls us in for a group huddle, something we'll do every morning for the rest of my time in the field. He explains that we will be using bags with the Dole logo this morning but might shift to another brand after lunch. "The ground is dry, but that doesn't mean that we should stop being careful," he says. "Sometimes we can get careless when it's dry, and that's when injuries often occur." (Pedro, I will learn, gives one of two speechess every morning: Be careful because the ground is wet, or be careful because the ground is dry.)

During the morning session, which runs from 8:30 to 11:30 a.m., I cut next to Manuel. While everyone else cuts two rows, I am still responsible for only half of one row at the end—selecting every other head of lettuce from one of Manuel's rows. I gradually get the hang of it and am just able to keep up the pace—although I'm clearly working harder than anyone else. Thirty minutes into the day, I'm already stripped down to a long-sleeve T-shirt, blinking burning sweat out of my eyes while the others are bundled in sweatshirts and knit beanies, trying to stay warm.

About an hour into the day, just when I'm beginning to feel my back tighten up for the first time, a tall man wearing a cowboy hat, Wrangler jeans, and a large belt buckle swaggers over to me and introduces himself as one of the supervisors. He asks me the usual question—why are you here?—and then watches me struggle through a few especially poor cuts.

"Give me your knife and watch." A second later, somehow, he's got a fully trimmed head of lettuce in his hand. "Bag this." He does it again: lightning-quick bend and stab, another lightning-quick trim. "Bag this." He spends ten minutes showing me the correct technique, explaining as he goes along.

"The most important thing is to find the head of the lettuce and grab it hard before you make the first cut. If you need to, take extra time to reach down through the leaves and search for the head—that's the part that you need. If you do that, it won't be so hard to trim it, and you'll know right away if it's a twenty-four or thirty."

"What's a twenty-four?"

"Oh, you're very new, no? Twenty-four is what we normally do—they are the bigger ones. It means twenty-four heads of lettuce will fit in the box. The smaller ones are thirty. You see how your packer has two boxes in front of him?" I look at Nacho; indeed, on the machine's rack he has a box to his left and his right. "That one on the left is for smaller lettuce, for the thirties."

A few minutes after the supervisor leaves, I reach down and cut a head of lettuce, which feels spongy and has a stem that is partially purple. "Manuel, is this one okay?" I ask, holding it up. He shakes his head.

"That one is sick, just leave it." The next, too, is purple, and the next. "That's good," he explains. "It means you get to take a break for a second."

By now I'm in need of a break. I walk to the orange cooler, which is attached to the side of the machine, and gulp down several cups of water. When I resume my cutting, Adriana comes over with a suggestion.

"Gabby, I've been watching you. After you cut the lettuce you stand up straight to bag it. It's better if you stay bent over the whole time." She shows me this method, looking like a hunchbacked grandmother shuffling down the street.

"Hmm. That looks like it might not be so good," I say quietly. "For your back, I mean."

"No, it's much easier."

I try it. Instead of straightening up, I remain slightly stooped when bagging. By the third head of lettuce, my back, already tightening up, is screaming for relief. Adriana's gone by now, so I revert to my original style. Sweat is pouring down my face so fast that I have to keep taking my cap off to mop my forehead, which causes my pace to slow. The temperature must be in the eighties. Manuel, working next to me, is talking about something, but I can't understand: Fatigue has cut my Spanish comprehension level in half. I'm about to take another trip to the cooler when Pedro calls out to take our break, and the machine halts.

I follow Manuel's lead, taking my gancho and gloves off and placing my knife in the chlorinated water. We sit with a group of others—three men and a woman—on white plastic chairs that have materialized from somewhere. I open my backpack and drain a 32-ounce bottle of Gatorade.

"The first five days are the hardest," Manuel tells me. "That's when you feel the pain the most, but then it goes away." I nod, opening my second bottle. A skinny man with dark skin, seated to my left, introduces himself as Julio. He tells me that he still remembers his first week, but now, after three years, he's accustomed to it. I nod again. I'm sure I must have a lot of questions to ask—I'm a reporter, after all—but it's all I can do to just drink and nod.

"Let's go, guys!" Pedro calls. *That* was our break? I follow the group with my chair, stack it on the back of the machine, then grab my knife and slip on my sweaty gloves, as the work resumes. Pedro comes over at one point, looking cheerful. "Save your energy for tomorrow, Gabriel. That's when you'll have your own row to cut."

The rest of the day is a blur, and it ends with the gathering darkness. When I get home I eat dinner, take a shower, and type up some quick notes before falling into a sound sleep. In what will become my frequent first line, I write: *Today was a long day.*

THERE ARE SEVERAL problems with my body the following morning, starting with my hands. Both are swollen, and my right ring finger has doubled in size. I broke it several years ago and never went to a doctor, but assumed it had healed correctly. Evidently I was wrong: It now remains hooked no matter how hard I try to straighten it, and I can actually feel my pulse in the digit.

Ambling to the bathroom, I feel like someone must have crept into my bedroom overnight and beaten me on the back with a two-by-four, then continued pounding on the soles of my feet. I swallow several painkillers and put in my contact lenses, noticing that my eyes are bright red. My neck is also crimson; I'm lathering myself with sunscreen twice a day, but it doesn't stand a chance against my overactive sweat glands. There's also a tennis-ball-size bruise on my right thigh, where the gancho jabs each time I bend. It seems impossible—simply impossible—that I can spend another day cutting lettuce.

After coffee and breakfast I feel a bit better, and less melodramatic. I tell myself that there are more than a million farmworkers in America, doing this every day, some for years. Plus, I remind myself that Manuel said the first week is the toughest.

We're back at the same field today, and as promised, Pedro has found me a special row to do all by myself, next to Julio. The first few minutes aren't promising—my hands are so weak I have a hard time holding on to the lettuce—but once the blood starts pumping through my system, I feel better. I'm starting to get a sense of the lettuce, learning more about its various shapes with each new cut. The easiest are the ones whose outer leaves are already spread away from the head, so you can immediately see what you need to cut. The hardest are the massive heads with the outer leaves wound tight; for these, I lose time peeling off each individual leaf, using what Pedro calls the "she loves me, she loves me not" method. With a single cut, more skilled cutters are able to trim these large monsters down to size, but when I attempt this I invariably cut too deep—into the good leaves that make up the head—and have to discard the lettuce.

I eat lunch with two middle-aged men, Angel and Tomás. Though they live in the same small Mexican village, Mezquital, they have different interests: The first question Angel asks is whether I am a Christian; Tomás wants to know my favorite beer. Both have worked at Dole for three years and spent many years before that in the fields. They were part of the same broccoli crew for the previous two years but were switched to lettuce this season. "Broccoli was definitely easier than lettuce," Tomás says. "But anything is better than doing farmwork in Mexico," where, he explains, he earned only one hundred pesos a day. It's a big pay increase to harvest crops on this side of the border—from about $10 a day to $8.37 an hour.

In the afternoon we switch from using Dole bags to harvesting lettuce *desnudo*, or naked. When cutting *desnudo*, we don't trim or bag the lettuce, instead placing the heads flowing with extra leaves directly on the extensions before they are crammed tightly into boxes for Sysco. It's an easier job, especially since we can dispense with the heavy packets of bags hanging from our belts, but to make sure we don't get too comfortable, Pedro speeds up the machine's pace. Before we reach the afternoon break, Pedro stops the machine and tells me to help load materials. I sheath my knife and follow the crowd to a spot in the field where a truck has dumped hundreds of flattened cardboard boxes and a dozen wooden pallets.

Crewmembers begin carrying the cargo to the machine, tossing the packets of flattened boxes to one of the three men who work as loaders. It wouldn't be too difficult a task on flat ground, but the uneven terrain—we are walking across several rows of uncut lettuce—causes one person to stumble. I grab a bundle of twenty-five boxes and lift them over my head, as I've seen others do, crossing two rows without incident before my front foot slips and I nearly plant my face into an iron bar of the machine.

"Careful!" someone shouts, too late to be of any use. I mercifully regain my balance, which leads to a series of hoots, and toss my boxes. I smile at the crew as I return for another load, too tired to be embarrassed.

During the break I join the group sitting on the ground next to an irrigation canal. I've been feeling stronger today, but as soon as I get off my feet I realize how swollen they've become. I rest them on a row that has been harvested and feel the blood draining back to my legs. People are having animated conversations, but I don't care. I close my eyes, the sun beats down, and I drift off.

I'm awakened by Diego, who is talking to Manuel. "How much more time do we have?" I ask.

"It's already been sixteen minutes."

"So what are we waiting for?" Diego doesn't know. Others are wondering as well. From this vantage point I can see that there remains only a small section of the field to cut, less than an hour's worth of work. Once we finish, we'll be done, as Pedro will have to relocate the machine to our next field. I wouldn't mind getting started so we can get out of here.

We sit for another few minutes. Pedro isn't calling us back, and the machine isn't moving—the two signals that the break is over. Eventually we begin to meander back. As we're putting on our gear, Pedro pops up from somewhere and calls for us to gather around.

"How long has it been?" he asks. "Has it been more than fifteen minutes?"

Most of the crew nods, but my head stays steady: I don't like the tone of voice Pedro has adopted.

"I just did an experiment," he continues, looking extremely pleased with himself. "I waited to see and observe how long it would take for you to finish your break and come back if I didn't say anything. You all know that the break is fifteen minutes long.

And my experiment showed that it took you more than twenty minutes to return. From now on, I want everyone to make sure that they keep an eye on time." He goes on about his experiment for another five minutes, enjoying playing the role of management genius, but I stop trying to follow. I look at Manuel as we head back to our rows, and he gives me a shrug. I roll my eyes and make that talk-talk-talk motion with my right hand, then take my knife and stab a lettuce, with a little more force than necessary.

WITH SOME EXCEPTIONS, the schedule of my first several days will be repeated throughout my time in Yuma. We arrive thirty minutes before the machine starts—me in my car, most of the others in the white agricultural bus that picks them up each morning on the U.S. side of the border. Our early arrival allows us to put on our equipment, sharpen our knives, do calisthenics, and listen to Pedro's instructions. Work begins either at 8:00 or 8:30 a.m., and we put in two or three hours before the first fifteen-minute break. After another two hours of work, we get a thirty-minute lunch. Another two hours or so, and another fifteen-minute break. Then we work until the day is over. When demand is low, we may leave the field before the afternoon break. When demand is high, we'll work until dusk. (One year, Julio told me, they frequently worked until 10:00 p.m., under bright lights connected to the machine.) Because demand fluctuates and lettuce begins to wilt the moment it's cut, there is very little planning ahead: Most mornings even Pedro doesn't know how long we'll be in the field.

We use four different types of bags: Dole, Dole Canada, King Size, and UPC (no brand with only a barcode on the bag). At times, as during my first few days, we use only one type of bag, but typically we're instructed to have two ganchos hanging from each side of our belt, one that holds bags for medium to large heads of lettuce (24s) and the other for the small (30s). There is no rule as to what goes where: In the morning, Pedro could instruct us to bag all 24s with Dole Canada and 30s with UPC; in the afternoon, Dole Canada for the 24s and regular Dole with 30s; the next morning, UPC for 24s and King Size for the 30s. (We often put the small heads of lettuce in the King Size bags, which made little sense to me.) It was a constant struggle to keep this straight in my mind as I rushed to keep pace with the machine as it moved down the field.

While cutting, one has to constantly check the quality of the lettuce. Crops like onions grow in a uniform manner and can therefore be harvested by machine; but about 20 percent of a lettuce field will be unusable, a key reason why lettuce is still harvested by hand. Some lettuce is too small (I see heads less than two inches tall); some too big (twice the size of a human head); some too light; and many get hit with infections that turn the trunks red or purple. Others have yellow leaves from sun exposure or have suffered damage from cold nights, creating unappetizing rivets in the leaves. What we do with the rejects depends on the preferences of the supervisor wandering the fields on any given day. Sometimes Pedro will tell us to turn all rejects upside down on the row; other days, we are instructed to slice up the head thoroughly and dump it in the furrow.

Several times a day a truck drives into the field to dump boxes and pallets and to pick up the lettuce we have cut, generally while we are taking a break. Each morning we complete 10 pallets of lettuce. Each pallet has 40 boxes, and each box about 25 heads of lettuce—which means that our crew cuts and packs 10,000 heads of lettuce before the first break, or nearly 800 heads a person. In a typical day we cut 30,000 heads of lettuce, enough to fill 1,200 boxes. On the longer days—the ones beginning just after sunrise and ending at dusk—we can harvest in excess of 40,000 heads.

For a cutter, that means 3,000 heads in a single shift; put two of those long days in a row, and getting out of bed at 5:30 the next morning becomes a true test of willpower.

Once the lettuce is on the truck, it heads straight to Dole's cooling plant, located next to the office where I first applied for the job. The pallets are transferred into a large vacuum tube, and within seconds the warm air is sucked out and replaced with air that is precisely 33 degrees, a temperature that extends the shelf life of lettuce to four weeks. Once the lettuce is cooled, the pallets are transferred to a refrigerated truck. A head of lettuce cut on Monday will arrive in San Francisco by Tuesday, most parts of Canada by Wednesday or Thursday, and New York City by Thursday or Friday.

In the field, it can be hard to remember that the lettuce I harvest will end up in someone's salad—perhaps tossed with walnuts and dried cranberries in a wooden bowl on a large dining room table, with family members gathered around chatting about their days. Harder still for the recipients to imagine our crew out here, with swollen hands and sweaty shirts. But as Daniel Rothenberg writes in *With These Hands: The Hidden World of Migrant Farmworkers Today*, the connection—whether acknowledged or not—is an intimate one:

> When we reach into a bin to choose an apple, orange, or plum, our hands stretch out in much the same way as a farmworker's hands—harvesting our nation's fruits and vegetables, piece by piece. While the produce may have been mechanically sorted and packed, supercooled, chemically treated, waxed, and shipped hundreds, if not thousands, of miles, often the last hand to touch the fruits and vegetables we buy was that of a migrant farmworker. Through the simple act of purchasing an orange or a head of lettuce, we are con-

nected with a hidden world of laborers, a web of intercon-
nected lives, with hands on both ends.[3]

It is an arresting image—that the next person to touch the lettuce I personally harvest will be the person who puts it in their
mouth. It's also a connection that, without coming across this passage, I would never have made. Rothenberg wants us to remember
that each time we eat food that has been harvested by hand, we
do so in the presence of strangers. I see them—my crewmembers—
knives in hands, wiping sweat off their brows, taking a break as
they hover over our plates and bowls to proudly whisper: "Enjoy.
I cut that, you know."

THE THIRTY-ONE members of my crew are divided into three
categories. Three men, the loaders, are on the flatbed of the machine, stapling and stacking the completed boxes; thirteen men,
like myself, are cutters; another thirteen—including three women,
after Maria's departure—are packers. The remaining two members
are Pedro and his assistant, Diego.

Crews at Dole work together for the entire season, but unlike an
office setting—where personalities frequently clash over an e-mail
or a comment taken the wrong way—there doesn't seem to be
much conflict in the fields. For one thing, we're not maneuvering
for advancement: Our roles and wage of $8.37 an hour will remain
the same. Equally important, we lack the extra energy needed to
gossip or hold grudges for long; our exhaustion ensures that
there's simply no time to develop the dysfunction that plagues
many work environments.

During my first week, most people remain strangers, although
a few names and personalities start to emerge. I come to think of
Tomás as the heart and soul of our crew. He is one of the older
cutters, probably in his fifties, whom others affectionately call *tío*,

or uncle. Decades of farmwork have left him with strong hands and skinny limbs, and decades of beer drinking have left him with a medicine ball under his sweatshirt. His distinguishing feature is an unruly handlebar mustache, which is always on the verge of swallowing his entire chin (one of the packers, a young man named Andrés, threatens to pull a hairnet over Tomás's entire face if he doesn't trim the growth).

Tomás speaks fast and enthusiastically. He's missing many of his teeth, so although others can understand him, I hear a lot of mumbling and only occasionally a decipherable word. Despite our inability to communicate, I enjoy hanging out with him and listening to him ramble. As I gulp down Gatorade and Clif Bars, he smokes as many cigarettes as possible. Tomás is given to belting out an enigmatic line several dozen times a day: "*Si a tu ventana llega un burro flaco,*" which translates to: "If a skinny donkey arrives at your window." I have no idea what the lyric means, and Tomás never finishes singing the song. No matter, the line gets stuck in my head whenever I hear it.

If Tomás is the crew's heart and soul, then the lithe thirty-year-old Julio is its driver, the fastest cutter who is also in charge of managing the machine's speed. He always cuts at one of the end rows, and keeps a remote control near him with buttons that he presses to speed or slow the pace (when I'm near him, I badger him to take it down a notch). Julio, like a handful of others, is originally from the state of Sinaloa, more than 500 miles from the border. He came north in search of work and found a job in a *maquiladora* (factory) before signing up with Dole three years ago. His wife, Norma, also from Sinaloa, packs the lettuce that he cuts. (I encounter a number of married couples in the field; they always work together, with the man cutting and the woman packing. During my months in the fields, I never see a female cutter. I'm not sure why this is, just as it is never adequately explained to me why men never cover their faces in bandanas. "That's just how it's always been," is how one worker explains the arrangement.)

Besides his speed, Julio attracts my attention because he never seems to tire. In the morning he is bouncing around, and in the early evening he's still chatting up a storm and laughing: Someone has clearly forgotten to tell him that this is hard work. He, like Manuel, is a good guy to cut next to because he'll always swoop in and snag a couple of my heads of lettuce when I fall behind. He can actually cut three rows without falling behind the pace of the machine.

Manuel, thirty-seven, has a workmanlike attitude. He comes, he cuts, he goes home. He's the senior cutter on our crew, with five years' experience in lettuce, and he has spent most of the past two decades in the fields, many in California. Along with lettuce he has labored in the strawberry fields of Watsonville, cut broccoli in Salinas, and picked apples and pears in the San Joaquin Valley. He even worked at a slaughterhouse in Texas. (He lasted only a month: His job was to shoot the cows in the head with an air gun all day. "That was no good.")

I was initially leery of Diego, the stocky assistant, until I learned that he earns the same pay as everyone else and does not serve as the eyes and ears of Pedro. Early on, Pedro often had me helping Diego with odd jobs, like placing plastic sheets on lettuce to prevent ice from forming overnight, and I was surprised to find that Diego spoke the best English of the group. Unfortunately, I learned this while suffering through his rendition of "Ice, Ice, Baby," followed immediately by "Hammertime." Surprisingly, Diego had not been to the United States before beginning the season (it wasn't just songs he knew; he could speak and understand enough to roughly communicate). I persisted in querying him about his English—it just seemed so odd—and he finally offered a clue toward the end of the season, when he said that he had worked for many years as a bodyguard to a Mexicali-based *narcotraficante* (drug dealer). At first I thought he was kidding, but he insisted he was telling the truth, describing the weapons he had at his disposal. He left the job after the birth of his first child, choosing to move his family to San Luis Río Colorado to get away from the scene. I came to believe his account as he wasn't given to boasting, and I gather that he picked up his English through the job.

Adriana, the strong female voice of the group, is a packer and responsible for driving the bus from the border to the fields and back. Second in command to Pedro, she is a U.S. citizen and lives in San Luis, Arizona, just across the border from Mexico. A Dole employee for decades and now in her forties, she declined an offer to become forewoman, saying she "didn't want the responsibility."* Early on she adopted me as her project—she was going to teach this gringo to work—and while I was struggling to trim a particularly annoying head of lettuce, I'd frequently hear, "Gabby, no!" directed my way. She'd grab my knife and correct my technique, all the while insisting that I was "so close" to getting it right.

It was harder to make up my mind about the foreman, Pedro. He was not abusive—I'd asked around, and everyone said that they were paid on time and never shorted wages. He stressed safety and made sure we had our proper gear, replacing it if it ripped (as the plastic gloves seemed to do daily). But he also had an aggravating tendency to come over when I was falling behind and stand really close to me. I wanted to turn around and say, "Hey, this really isn't helping," but instead I'd just keep plodding along, cursing him silently.

---

* In Yuma I came across one Dole crew that was headed by a woman. When I asked a man from the crew how he felt about his forewoman, his answer was much as I felt about Pedro: "She's *tough*."

What was most striking about the crew, after several days in the field, was how quickly they welcomed me as one of their own. I expected, and encountered, some skepticism and suspicion, but neither lasted long. Simply showing up for a second day seemed to be proof enough that I was there to work. If I took a seat on the ground alone during a break, someone would call me over to join their group, usually offering me the plastic chair they were sitting on along with a homemade taco or two. People whose names I didn't yet know would ask how I was holding up, reminding me that it would get easier as time went by. When I faltered and fell behind, hands would come across from adjacent rows to grab a head or two of my lettuce so I could catch up. On Thursday, we worked a field with another crew, and I could hear them talking about me during lunch. Tomás, sitting beside me and smoking furiously, stood up. "The white guy can work!" he shouted. I felt like I had passed some sort of test.

ON FRIDAY WE move to a new field, south of Somerton and ten miles from the Mexican border. We begin cutting in silence, until Cesar, a jolly man who has gladly shared his sharpening stone with me, calls out "*Música, maestro!*" Within seconds our workplace is filled with song.

Nearly every crew has their radio set to the same station: 104.9 FM, *Radio Campesina*. The Spanish-language station is run by the UFW, broadcasting in Arizona, California, and Washington State. It's probably the only station where a listener can hear DJs regularly say things like: "Greetings to all the farmworkers in the different crews of the many companies out in the fields today."

Much of the time, though, you wouldn't be able to distinguish the station from other commercial Spanish radio; the most popular songs—which I'll hear repeated until I want to stab myself with a fork—have titles like "I Cried" and "I Love You a Lot." But each morning we also listen to *Punto De Vista*, a call-in show hosted by Mary Martinez, who is often joined in the studio by a doctor or immigration specialist. This particular morning, a woman from Bakersfield, California, calls in worried about a growth near her stomach. She's been to a white doctor, who said they were fatty deposits and not to worry. Though she doesn't say it outright, it's clear she doesn't trust the gringo.

"That's very common, the fatty deposits," the doctor tells her in Spanish. He goes on to explain the differences between these deposits and a dangerous, cancerous growth. The relief in the woman's voice is palpable; she's been worrying herself sick.

Another caller speaks to an immigration attorney. He's been caught three times while crossing in the Yuma area (the crew hoots when they hear this), and once spent fifteen days in jail (the crew quiets down). Each time he's signed a voluntary deportation document. His girlfriend is a U.S. citizen and lives in Yuma, and they're planning on getting married. He wants to know whether his previous crossing activities will keep him from eventually gaining legal residency.

"No, not if you signed voluntary deportation papers," the attorney says.

He's happy to hear this but has another pressing question. "Is it better to get married in Mexico or in the U.S.? It would be easier for her to come here, but if I need to go there, I have to save some money for the smuggler." He has heard that even more Border Patrol agents have been massing, and he's nervous about his chances of crossing without incident.

The immigration attorney can't help chuckling. "Don't cross," he says. "You want to start following all the laws so you won't have any problems, so have her come to Mexico. And then, just so you know, be prepared to wait some time for the process to go through."

"You're gonna have to wait a long time for the fucking process," I hear someone to my left say. "A long fucking time."

Over a lunch of tortillas, eggs, rice, and beans, Mateo and Veronica talk about their newest jobs. Last April, instead of heading to Salinas to continue on the lettuce circuit, they traveled to St. Joseph, Missouri, where they had heard from a friend that they could find work at a pork processing plant. "You should go there sometime," Mateo says. "Just to hear the way they speak. Normally English doesn't sound good to me, but in Missouri they speak very beautifully, almost like singing."

He and Veronica earned a couple dollars more an hour than in the fields, and they might return once the lettuce season concludes. Their task was to slice away excess fat from the torsos of pigs that zoomed past on a belt, using an electric knife. The temperature of the plant was just above freezing, but the pace of the work kept them from getting cold.

I ask them to contrast cutting lettuce to cutting pigs. Since my next job will be poultry processing—which I imagine must be similar to pork processing—I'm interested to see how the two stack up. To my mind, no matter how nauseating a poultry plant might be, it *has* be less strenuous than cutting lettuce.

That's not what Mateo is telling me, however. "First, it's easier to learn how to cut pigs. But I would say that it is a more difficult job overall. With the pigs, they make you work so rapidly that there's never any time for rest." Despite wearing five gloves on one hand and two on the other, his hands ached terribly. "But you can't ever stop, you just keep cutting and cutting or the boss will get angry."

"The breaks are so short," adds Veronica. "They begin when the line stops moving, so you have to use five minutes of your break just to take off the gloves and equipment." Fifteen minutes after the line stops, it begins again—so almost two-thirds of the "break" is spent taking the gear off and putting it back on. "It's also depressing because you are stuck inside all day, doing the same thing," she adds.

"That's right," Mateo says. "In the field you can look at the sky, but in the plant . . ." I had wanted to hear about the plant, but as the husband and wife continue to describe the job in a manner that paints lettuce in a favorable light, I stop paying close attention.

IN MID-FEBRUARY, a new week brings a "breakthrough." Mateo casually mentions that his feet sometimes hurt more when he wears the boots over his shoes. I am reminded of this comment as I rub lotion on my aching soles one evening. Breakthrough: Of course my feet are sore—I've been wearing the boots! I leave them off for two days; at the end of the experiment, my feet are still killing me, and now my shoes are coated in mud. The pain, it turns out, is caused not by the boots but by walking along uneven ground all day and jamming my feet into the furrows. I don't waste time reflecting on these setbacks, however, because doing so would get in the way of my search for the *real* breakthroughs. The possible solutions are endless. My knife isn't sharp enough; my knife is too sharp. I should cut walking backwards, as a young man in our crew named Abel does. Why should this make anything easier? I'm not sure, but do it anyway, learning that it's difficult to see what's in front of you when you walk backwards. It's much easier, though, to fall.

A new insight hits me on a Tuesday, when for some reason Pedro has me cutting a single row for the entire day. Since my week of training I've been cutting two rows, and I now use the extra time to watch the others. Julio, as usual, seems to have ingested a fair amount of methamphetamines. He chats with Pedro and darts to his left and right, snapping up the lettuce and trimming it at a frenetic pace. When he catches me watching, he shouts out "Gabriel!" and waves, hopping up and down as if he's been stung by a wasp, and rejoins his conversation with Pedro. I like his athleticism—I *want* his athleticism—but by now I know he isn't a good model for me. Not everyone can be the star.

The temperature is in the mid-80s, but when I look over at Manuel I see that he has kept his sweatshirt on and his face is bone dry. Although he is able to cut nearly as quickly as Julio, his guiding principle is energy conservation. While Julio expends an enormous amount of effort as he careens around the field, Manuel proceeds in a daze, apparently on the verge of falling asleep. There is no anxiety on his face: He can keep up with the machine and he knows it. I watch him make the same simple motions again and again, as he stares off into space.

At one point I notice that Alfonso has lost ground to the machine and is placing bags of lettuce on the ground. A tall man with a deep voice and trimmed goatee, Alfonso is the most likely person to fall behind the machine's pace (after me, of course). I leave my row to help out, knowing that, cutting only one row, I can easily catch up. By now he is huffing and puffing, making violent thrusts at the lettuce and slamming the heads into his bag. Perspiration is streaming down his face into the lettuce—I'm glad to see another person in the crew has functional sweat glands—and his eyes have a frenzied look. I glance back at Manuel, who is stifling a yawn.

When I return to my row it hits me: I've been my own worst enemy. When I attempt to cut fast, my muscles tighten, my anxiety rises, my heart beats faster . . . but I actually cut slower. In the rush to keep up, I expend more energy and make more mistakes, which causes me to fall behind, which causes me to rush, which causes me to fall further behind. At the end of the day, I'm exhausted not only because the work is hard, but also because I've been unwittingly generating tension.

I begin to mimic Manuel, taking deep breaths and moving smoothly, and find that the precision of my cuts increases. Of course, I'm cutting only one row—so remaining relaxed isn't nearly as difficult—but I'm convinced the lesson will be equally relevant when applied to two rows. When I share this insight with Manuel at the end of the day, he nods. "You have to put your mind somewhere else," he explains. "Like the Chinese. If you concentrate right, you feel no pain." Zen and the art of lettuce cutting.

I am actually excited to come to work the following morning, so eager to show off my new knowledge. At 8:30 a.m. the machine roars to life, and I take my place between Julio and Manuel. Normally there's a knot in my stomach as I cut my first few heads of lettuce, worried that I'll fall behind. But not today. I notice that within five minutes I am being forced to reach farther to place my bags on the extension, but this doesn't rattle me. Instead of trying to increase my pace, I continue in a steady rhythm. Take it easy.

Five minutes later I'm beginning to wonder what's wrong: The machine is leaving me behind. Pedro notices and comes over. "Let's go, Gabriel!" he yells. I'm a foot away and he's yelling. I hate it when he does that.

"Pedro, I'm working like Manuel today," I say, trying to regain my equilibrium. "Very calm, so that I cut the lettuce better."

Pedro doesn't look impressed. "Let's go, Gabriel!" he shouts again. "Let's go! Let's go!"

While speaking to Pedro I've lost even more ground, and while I try to stay relaxed, I realize that this determination to stay relaxed is starting to stress me out. The machine has inched out of reach, so I put a head of lettuce on the ground, then another. The morning's first drop of sweat flies off my nose. Goddamn. I bend over quickly and stab the lettuce too high, rendering it worthless. I toss it into the furrow and vigorously stomp on it, obliterating my mistake. I take another head of lettuce and cut. I'm about to bag it when I see that there's a yellow leaf wrapped around the head. I try to grab it but can't get a hold of it. I finally peel off the leaf and bag the lettuce, dropping it on the ground, and sloppily grab for another. My left hand is wrapped around the bottom of the head, and as my blade cuts through the stem it connects with my middle finger. The pain is intense, but I'm relieved to see that when I take off my glove, though my finger is already turning purple, I didn't break the skin. I put my glove back on, now a good ten feet behind the machine, and start cutting in my typical, maximum-intensity style. Another once-cherished insight, quickly discarded.

I TAKE MY lunch sitting on the ground in a group that includes Candelario, Cesar, and Manuel. "I am dying today," I tell them as I rip open the package of my thousandth energy bar. "People said that the soreness would go away. But I don't think the soreness goes away. You just get used to it. You forget what it's like to not be sore."

Manuel considers the comment. "That's true, that's true. It always takes a few weeks at the end of the year to get back to normal, to recover. But the first week is the hardest. The first week is the week you'll always remember."

Candelario takes a long drag on his cigarette and exhales the smoke, which is taken away by a light breeze. He straightens his back and clears his throat, a professor of agriculture preparing to deliver an address. "I will tell you how it is. This is one of the hardest jobs you can do. Why? Okay, I'll tell you. You come in Monday and you're okay; Tuesday you're a little tired; Wednesday you're very tired; Thursday you can hardly walk; and Friday you're crawling. Friday, you *just want to get it over with*." Cesar, Manuel, and I are nodding: This is a very accurate description. Except that I'm crawling and it's only Wednesday.

After Candelario's comments, the lunch break shifts from a time of conversation to recuperation, as people lay back with their eyes closed or gaze without focus across the field. I finish another bar and then take inventory of my hands, which are swollen and lopsided. The middle finger of my left hand, which I banged with the knife, has ballooned at the end, and the nail has turned purple. When I touch the tip it throbs, which is inconvenient, since this is the hand that must grab each lettuce. The ring finger of my left hand is also looking more swollen than I've seen it before. I clench my right hand into a fist and open it, but my ring finger remains at a 90-degree angle—halfway open—and I have to take my left hand and manually move the finger so that it opens all the way. When I do, I hear a little pop, but no pain. I clench my fist again, and it happens again. I should really start icing it at night. I take two painkillers to get through the day.

I GO TO bed that night at 8:30 p.m. I'm exhausted, but it's a familiar exhaustion: I'm accustomed to my head hitting the pillow and my world going immediately black. If nothing else, farmwork is a medication-free solution to insomnia. What's different tonight is that lettuce invades my time of rest as well, no longer content with just dominating my waking hours.

In the first dream I am cutting lettuce as fast as I can, tossing the bags quickly onto the arms of the machine. People are working to my left and right, but their faces are nothing but blurs. The speed of the machine keeps increasing, as does my mental stress. I want to ask someone why the machine is going so fast, but when I look around I find that I'm alone. No matter how fast I cut, the machine stays just out of reach. I feel my entire body overheating, like I'm going to explode, and I come to the sensible conclusion that it's time to stop—this is just a job, after all. But in the dream I'm physically unable to stop, no matter how convinced I am that the pace is unsustainable. When I try to freeze my arms in place, they keep moving, as if I'm the puppet of a sadistic god. For whatever reason, I have to pursue the machine, I have to keep cutting, I have to catch up, I have . . .

That's how I wake up, in a state of frenzy. It takes me a few seconds to shift from dream to reality, and as the basic facts come to the surface, I feel a huge sense of relief. I'm in bed. I'm not working. It's okay to rest. I write up the dream quickly—it's not often that I dream, and I want to remember this one—and fall back asleep.

Only to have another dream, less vivid in its details but with the same frenzied quality: I'm cutting, but not fast enough. I awake from this dream in pain, with my right hand extended against the night table next to my bed. My ring finger is throbbing—I've apparently flicked my arm out, mimicking whatever motion I was making in the dream, and banged it against the drawer. I check the clock. It's 1:30 a.m.

I have two more of these dreams during the night. They also lack the details of the first, but they carry the same sense of dread that I can't keep up with the machine. The initial novelty of a lettuce dream has by now grown frustrating, and after the last two dreams I admonish my brain: Relax! Show some creativity! Take me someplace else, sitting on a beach or soaking in a hot tub. But just as I can't stop my body in the dreams, I can't stop my subconscious from returning me to the fields. The last dream wakes me up at 5:30 in the morning, again in pain: I've extended my left arm and slapped my hand against the wall—the hand with the injured middle finger. I'm mentally exhausted, both my hands are throbbing, and it's time to get up.

And that's when an idea comes to me, nursing my sore finger and staring at the ceiling: *I don't have to go to work today.* I can call in sick. This is obvious but it feels like an earth-shattering revelation. For whatever reason, until this moment, the thought never crossed my mind. I break into a grin, my schedule suddenly rearranging itself in my mind. Instead of sweating and lettuce and Pedro shouting at me, I can sleep late and drink too much coffee and read the paper. I can see a matinee! I get out of bed and go through the orientation packet, which has the number employees should call to report an absence. I leave a message on the machine, telling them my name and crew number, and fall back asleep.

This proves too easy. I finish a novel on Thursday and watch an afternoon movie, and when I wake up Friday, I'm still sore and tired. Most illnesses last at least two days, don't they? Sure they do. I call the number and leave another message, making sure to cough loudly into the receiver. With two quick calls I've created a four-day weekend.

LIKE ANY HUMAN being, after getting what I want I'm still not satisfied. Friday is filled with more reading, a trip to a museum of the old Yuma Territorial Prison, and another movie. But on Saturday I wake up and am immediately hit with a deep sense of loneliness. I've got two more days off and nothing to do; even if I thought of something, I don't know anyone to do it with.

Like many immigrants, I've settled in a new place with few connections. As is the case with many sprawling suburbs, Yuma proves to be a very difficult place to meet people, as folks emerge from their cars for only short periods—usually when walking from a parking lot to the store. If I had relatives in the area, or friends, or even friends of friends, I'd definitely call them. I leave the house, hoping to stumble across someone to hang out with. I visit a bar that's full of marines one night. I try out the local Starbucks, full of high school students. I go see movies, and I'm the only person under sixty-five. My alienation from Yuma feels complete.

On Sunday night, I receive a call from Pedro. He says that we'll be working away from Yuma tomorrow, so that I need to show up at Dole's office at 5:30 a.m. to catch the bus. This news might have caused me to groan before, but I'm eager to get back to work. That's what I'm here for, after all.

CHAPTER 5

Today should be easy. I'm rested, my fingers are opening properly, and I can walk without the soles of my feet hurting. I'm at Dole's office, waiting for the bus to come and the sun to rise, with two strong cups of coffee already in my system. I feel strong, healthy, recuperated—but no matter. It turns out to be the hardest day of my brief career in lettuce.

We're working a field near the town of Tacna, ninety minutes east of Yuma. After my two-day absence, a number of people are surprised to see me again. "I thought the lettuce killed you," Angel says, patting me on the back. "It almost killed me on Friday." It turns out I chose my vacation wisely, as the crew worked well into the evening on the days I missed.

The first notable difference in Tacna is that, for the first time, I'm actually seeing bugs in the field. When I had asked Pedro about the complete absence of insects, he responded by praising the "very good fumigation." I suppose this was true, if by good one meant effective in killing all life except that which is necessary to grow lettuce. But I was glad to finally see little black critters clinging to the heads of lettuce and wandering in the dirt. It was unnerving to be in a field with zero bug life, and for farmworkers the "very good fumigation" can be very dangerous: The EPA estimates that each year between 10,000 to 20,000 farmworkers are diagnosed with pesticide poisoning, while also admitting that the true figure is likely much higher, as many workers never visit physicians.[11]

Along with being buggy, the field in Tacna is wet, so instead of firm dirt I'm sliding around in mud. I can handle this, but there's a new challenge: The lettuce is soaked. Each time I raise a head of lettuce and trim off the leaves, I get a face full of cold water. Within the first hour my hands—the hands I believed were completely recovered—feel weaker than ever. I'm soon placing lettuce on the ground, and starting to wonder what's wrong with me. I've been doing this almost two months, I just had four days off, and I *still* can't keep up? Exhausted but aware that the morning break is still thirty minutes away, I make a drastic decision. After checking to make sure Pedro isn't looking, I forget about trimming or bagging the lettuce. Instead I cut each stem, slice through the head three of four times, drop the remnants between two rows, and nonchalantly crush them with my feet as I move forward. It's quicker and takes much less energy. Julio, working to my right, sees my new trick and dubs me the "lettuce assassin."

During the break I'm a wreck. I make no attempt to socialize, instead finding a patch of dirt to lie in away from the group. By the end of the day—a day filled with Pedro cajoling me and often taking my knife and helping me—I'm not even attempting to do two rows. Luckily, Julio is still to my right, and he doesn't seem to be having any problem handling three rows. There is something seriously wrong with this man. "Don't worry, Gabriel, I'm helping you! Three rows, *no problema!*" In between his manic encouragement, he says he and Norma left the house at 3:00 a.m. "We got up at two! To get ready! It was completely dark outside!"

I feel like I'm going to vomit from exhaustion. It's a very passive, nearly out-of-body experience; I don't feel sick but it seems that every ounce of energy is being sucked from my body, and the logical last step of this process is to release whatever is in my stomach. I keel over a few times but nothing comes out.

"*¡Ya!*" Pedro calls, signaling we're done for the day. If I could muster the energy I'd feel relieved. We track back to the bus and hop in. For a few minutes the crew is lively, but as we near the highway the bus goes quiet. I am sharing a seat with a sleeping Gloria, and I turn around to see that everyone—minus Adriana, who is driving and has a Christian rock CD cranking on the stereo—is unconscious, as if someone flipped the switch on the crew's power. Even Julio is out, collapsed against Norma with his beanie pulled down over his eyes.

When we get to the Dole office, Adriana drops me off at my car and continues on to the border. I get home after 7:00 p.m., having been away fourteen hours. Making dinner, I realize that the day I just survived was exactly what my coworkers have been going through all season. Only now, their workdays are even longer: Today they left their homes at 3:00 a.m. and will return sometime after 8:00 p.m.

The next day, also in Tacna, we work just as long. I feel good the entire day. Even my hands have a much better grip on the knife and the lettuce.

It's counterintuitive, but after talking with several coworkers who have had similar experiences, I come up with a theory. Early in the season—say, after the first week—a farmworker's body is thoroughly broken down. Legs and arms are sore, hands and feet swell up. Eventually, a tolerance for the pain is developed; the sharp aches dull but don't disappear. The weekend is just enough time for the body to recover from the trauma, but not so much that it actually starts to mend. My four-day break was actually too long; my body began to recuperate, and it wanted more time to continue. Instead, it was thrown right back in the mix, and rebelled. But the next day, I'm back to normal. (My belief in this theory will grow stronger once I quit the job and finally understand just how much time my body needs to fully recover. It takes two weeks until I feel comfortable shaking someone's hand, and an entire month before the numbness in my right foot disappears.)

We have four visitors today from the government, and they check that we are following the proper food safety procedures. It's a good thing we get a heads-up about their visit two hours before they arrive, or Dole would have been slapped with a number of violations. During every break, for example, we stuff our gloves in the packet of bags hanging from our belts. "You can't do that anymore," Pedro says, explaining that we must now lay our gloves on the machine. He's definitely nervous about the inspection. He checks to make sure everyone is wearing their hairnet (several people aren't), and tells us to make sure to eat our lunch away from the lettuce that hasn't been harvested.

After reminding us about the gloves for a third time, Pedro goes behind the machine to talk with the loaders. As I'm cutting I look over at a coworker who is chomping on a piece of iceberg lettuce as he works. Pieces of the lettuce are falling from his mouth. During breaks, we're not supposed to eat near lettuce that hasn't yet been cut, and we're definitely not supposed to eat *over* the lettuce and dribble remnants on produce that will soon be purchased by customers. "*No debes comer mientras cortas,*" I say—

don't eat—quietly enough so that Pedro won't hear. "The government is coming, remember?"

We pass our inspection with flying colors.

AFTER A WEEK of long days away from Yuma, on Monday we're back at a field outside Somerton. As I'm grabbing my knife I let Pedro know that Friday will be my last day. Manuel and Julio overhear, and the people who didn't think I'd last a week are now telling me I need to stick around until the end of the season—in two weeks—if I want to say I've actually cut lettuce. Plus, there's a bonus for people who stay till the end.

The next several days I take out my camera and snap photos, and during a lunch break convince the crew to get together for a group photo. On Tuesday I run into Dalia in the field; I haven't seen her since the first morning when I was waiting at Dole's parking lot. Her crew is working the same field, and she learned from Adriana that I'd be leaving soon. She reaches into her backpack. "Here's the taco I said I'd give you."

Later that day we learn why Roberto, who normally steers the machine and helps load boxes, is absent: His mother has passed away. Several times men from other crews have walked along our line as we worked and asked for money. "My sister died in Salinas and we need to get the body home for the burial," one man said, wearing a tattered straw hat. The wife of another died of cancer. Sometimes a few details are given. Other times there is just the simple statement that someone died and money is needed, for a flight or a funeral or even, in one case, for a headstone. Once our crew hears news about Roberto's mother, we dig into our pockets for pesos and dollars, and someone is selected to solicit funds from nearby crews.

On Wednesday something new happens. Humberto and Alfonso fall behind the machine and are forced to put their lettuce on the ground. For whatever reason, at the moment I'm cutting pretty well. Pedro, of course, makes a note of this, loudly informing the men that I'm winning the race. For a moment I take a certain joy in the experience, but it's fleeting. I've been in their shoes for the last two months, and both men—like everyone in the crew—have helped me cover my rows at various times. I hop a few rows over and cut several heads for both, until they catch up. Of course, by doing so I fall behind, so Manuel helps me catch back up: from each according to his ability, to each according to his need.

On Thursday Manuel is absent—Pedro tells us that his wife gave birth to a healthy baby girl. This is wonderful news. It also means we're short a cutter, and Pedro informs us that we've got a big order today. As the week has progressed and my impending departure nears, I've actually felt waves of nostalgia. During the last two months I've enjoyed getting to know the members of the crew, and I realize that—barring some unforeseen development—I'll never find myself in the fields again.

That sense of nostalgia is easily crushed. It's the hottest day of the year, with temperatures reaching 90 degrees, and by 10:00 a.m. I'm drenched in sweat. For the first time, so is everyone else. We work more than ten hours, with the machine going faster than usual. Diego stirs powdered Gatorade into the water to make sure no one passes out, and I gulp down four painkillers to deal with the swelling in my right foot.

By the time the sun sets we've had our most productive day of the year. Each cutter has harvested about 3,300 heads. Altogether, our crew has cut, bagged, and packed 43,222 heads of lettuce (Pedro lets me look over the day's statistics). Our harvest has filled up more than 1,700 boxes of lettuce, for a combined weight of thirty-two tons. It's dark by the time I walk through my front door. I eat a bowl of cereal, peel off my clothes, and fall asleep without showering.

The next morning I wake up before the alarm clock, buzzing with energy since it's my last day. I arrive at the field early and while parking see Manuel walking to the machine. By the time I've suited up most of the crew has surrounded him, asking questions while he passes out celebratory chocolates. His daughter was born yesterday at 10:30 a.m. with no complications, and he's already back at work, while Maria recuperates at home with friends. During an extended morning huddle, Pedro congratulates Manuel and tells us to give ourselves a round of applause for the previous day's efforts.

The morning passes quickly, and for lunch Adriana has prepared a special meal in honor of my departure. Laid out on the ground in the shade of the bus are plates full of beans and rice, chicken and tuna salads, tostadas, and tortillas. I've been a vegetarian for twenty years, but I eat everything with gusto. People with cell phone cameras snap photos, while others, leaning against the bus, share their initial impressions of me. There's a moment of confusion when Carlos tells me that at one point he believed I was a *silla*—which means "chair" in Spanish.

"No, CIA," he clarifies. "Like some secret agent."

Pedro lets us take a longer than normal lunch, and while we relax in high spirits I'm tempted to tell them about my book. I know they will like the idea of Americans learning about the grueling work of *campesinos*. Since all of them are legally authorized to work, there is no concern that my writing could result in their being deported. But I hesitate; in the end, I suppose I keep my secret because as we're sitting, eating, and reminiscing, I enjoy feeling like a member of the crew.

By the time the sun begins to set, there is still a small section of lettuce to cut. As some begin to pack up the trash, I join a group to finish harvesting. I have two rows to cut, perhaps twenty feet long. As I cut and bag each head of lettuce, I am aware that the experience is coming to an end, and so slow down. The last remaining head of lettuce is to my right, and I don't bend down quite far enough to cut it correctly, so when I lift it up I see that it's not usable. Well, that's that. I hold the lettuce in my left hand, and bring the blade down several times, chopping it to pieces. I dump the remnants of the last lettuce I'll ever kill on the ground, and step on it.

"That's it, Gabriel!" Julio, who evidently has been watching me, yells. "You are finished, finally free from lettuce!"

I turn to him and break into a goofy grin. "I killed my last lettuce!" I call out, and he laughs. Then I raise my right arm and point the knife toward the sky. The moment passes and I feel slightly silly. I put my knife back in its sheath, help break down the machine, and grab my backpack.

I turn around and see that many members of the crew are lined up waiting to say good-bye, and a sense of sadness unexpectedly overcomes me. As we shake hands, many tell me to drive safely back to San Jose, and not to forget about the *lechugeros* in Yuma. They head to the bus. Pedro is standing by the side of the machine, holding a stack of papers, calculating the number of boxes we've completed.

"Pedro, it's been a real pleasure. Thanks for taking me on and teaching me how to cut lettuce."

"No problem, no problem," he replies, extending his hand. "Now you're set for life. If you ever need a job, you know you can always cut lettuce."

I laugh and say that I'll keep that in mind, then turn and walk back to my car, waving good-bye to the bus as it pulls out of the field.

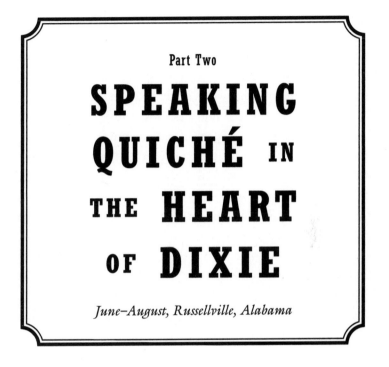

Part Two

SPEAKING QUICHÉ IN THE HEART OF DIXIE

June–August, Russellville, Alabama

GETTING THE JOB

An hour after pulling off the highway and entering Russellville, a 10,000-person town in rural Alabama, I start to think about leaving. I've checked into a motel—I'm the sole occupant—and I am wandering the streets of downtown. I know it's downtown only because a sign tells me so. I walk along the main strip, in what can fairly be called the heart of the city, which resembles a movie set for small-town America, circa 1950. There are furniture stores, bargain shops, and a local insurance company and bank. I can see two church steeples in the distance, along with a classic movie theater, the Roxy, which is shuttered. I stumble upon a coffee shop and try to enter, but the door is locked. A Spanish-language bookstore is next door, also locked. Although it's a Wednesday afternoon, most of the establishments are closed and the few that are open don't appear to have any customers. I spend fifteen minutes exploring downtown on foot without seeing another living creature. It's unbelievably hot. This could be a long summer.

I get back in my car and find a desolate Mexican restaurant on the outskirts of town. The Spanish-speaking waitress doesn't know of anyone with a room for rent, or whether the chicken plant is hiring. I eat my enchiladas, consult the map, pay the bill, and drive to the plant, located several miles outside Russellville's city limits. I'm the only car on a two-lane road, littered with chicken feathers, that winds through fields of corn and grazing cattle. A few ranch houses dot the countryside, but the main sign of human habitation is tumbledown trailer parks.

I already know from online research that the plant, owned by Pilgrim's Pride, can kill and process nearly 1.5 million chickens a week, but I'm still surprised by its size. The white and mostly windowless structure is as long as a city block and about thirty feet tall, with all the charm of a large cement box. On one side of the plant is a large parking lot filled with hundreds of cars, whose windshields shimmer in the heat; on the other, three trucks loaded with crates of live chickens are waiting at a checkpoint. I take the middle entrance and drive up to a security booth. An obese man with pale skin steps out.

"I'm looking for work—is there someone I can speak to?"

"Nope." He walks back into the booth and returns with an application. "Just bring it back to me when you're ready."

"You happen to know if they're hiring?" I ask.

"Nope."

This is not a promising beginning. I was hoping it would be like Dole: Show up and get hired on the spot. My anxiety grows as I look over the application. Pilgrim's Pride wants to know every job I've had in the last ten years, and promises to check my employer references. They also want three personal references, along with the jobs my references currently hold. For the first time, I begin to worry about whether they'll actually hire me. My driver's license is from New York, and Russellville isn't the kind of place that draws a lot of outsiders—except migrants from countries south of the border. If the company is suspicious about potential "salts"—covert union organizers who get a job to organize from within—I'm probably a likely candidate.

About the only thing I have in my defense is my work at Dole, a reference that clearly suggests dire financial straits. Again I put down Artemio, this time identifying him as the owner of a construction firm where I worked for many years.

The process of filling out two work references helps me come up with a cover story, which I hope I won't need. Unless I'm questioned in detail, I plan on keeping it vague: something along the lines of "I'm traveling for awhile," or the less plausible "I've always wanted to visit Alabama." If that's not enough, I'll offer what to me seems like the most believable story from my limited options: I left my construction job in New York over the winter eager to leave the cold behind and see the country. I started in the Southwest, harvesting lettuce in Yuma until I saved enough money to continue. While visiting a friend in Montgomery and low on funds, I learned that there were chicken plants in this part of the state, and figured I could find work and live cheaply. That night I actually practice in front of a mirror, preparing for an interview.

Early the next morning I drop off my application with the guard and head into the city of Decatur, fifty miles east, to check out another poultry plant, this one owned by Wayne Farms. I'm less interested in this plant as I would prefer a completely rural experience, but since I'll be giving up my rental car soon—I have enough funds to cover only a week's use, after which I'll be relying on my bike for transportation—I want to make certain I explore every option.

The Wayne Farms plant is in an industrial area crowded with big rigs. The plant is surrounded by a high fence, and next to the security booth is a large sign that reads: Our Team Has Worked 934,380 Hours Without a Lost Time Accident. This is meant to be a statement of pride and integrity, but to me it raises questions about creative record keeping. Nearly one million hours of repetitive work with sharp knives, and not a single employee has suffered an accident causing them to miss a shift?

Inside the office my luck doesn't improve. "We don't have any jobs right now," a woman in human resources tells me. "But we'll keep your application on file." I walk out the door increasingly convinced this experiment is destined for failure. The only other poultry plant I know of is more than a hundred miles away.

Heading back to my car I pass three African American men seated at a picnic table wearing blue hairnets. "The woman in the office told me the plant is full," I say. "If I come back in a few days, do you think I'll get hired? Do people quit a lot?"

The man sitting nearest to me takes a long drag on his cigarette. "Sheeyiit," he says in a five-second exhalation of smoke. "Two people just quit. They're laying down over there right now." He points across the parking lot. Two men are stretched out on the ground next to an old sedan in the shade provided by a row of trees. "They had the easiest job in the plant, not doing nothing but mopping up the damn floor. They walked out an hour ago, rather be taking a nap enjoying the day." He flicks his cigarette. "You come on back, you'll get yourself a job."

I look again at the two figures. One is lying on his back with his arms and legs spread out, as if frozen in the act of making a snow angel. The other is facedown, with his right cheek pressed hard against the gravel. They don't look like they're taking a nap—they look like someone dropped a bowling ball on their heads. I thank the men and head out.

Not yet ready to stare at the walls of my motel room, I decide to swing by the Russellville plant again. This time, coming from a different direction, I notice a small white building at a quiet intersection not far from the highway. A faded sign reads: Mama's Kitchen Country Cookin. Painted in yellow across the window are various specials, including *huevos rancheros* and *ricos tacos de tripe y lengua* (tasty tripe and tongue tacos). Looks like Mama's been changing up her country cookin'.

I step into a bazaar of Latino products ranging from Mexican soccer jerseys and Lucha Libre masks to Guatemalan flags and international calling cards. As I sit down an attractive woman with fair skin steps out, smiling politely. I explain in Spanish that I'm looking for a place to stay for a few months. She looks at me with undisguised curiosity and takes a seat across the table. For twenty minutes I answer her skeptical questions—What am I doing here? Where did I learn Spanish? Why do I want to work in the plant?—but we finally find common ground when I learn that Sabrina is from the Mexican state of Guerrero, which I've visited.

"Before I opened this restaurant I worked in *la pollera* for two years," she says, referring to the plant. "I don't know why you would want to work there."

"Just for awhile, so I can save some money and practice my Spanish. But right now what I'm looking for is a place to stay."

She begins to say something, pauses, then starts again. "Well, I have a trailer that is empty since my sister moved out. It's close, near the plant. But I don't want to rent it to a single person for only two months."

"How much did she pay?"

"$300 a month."

"If I get the job, how about I pay you $600 up front?" Sabrina considers the proposition. I can see that she is conflicted. On the one hand: Who the hell am I? On the other: I'm familiar with parts of Mexico and she's impressed that I speak Spanish. She eventually concludes that while I may be odd, I also seem harmless, and nods her assent.

I CALL PILGRIM'S PRIDE the next morning, a Friday, and leave a message. Next I check in with Wayne Farms, and am told to call back on Monday. By now it's 11:00 a.m. and I'm sitting in a motel with nothing to do. Bored, I go on the Internet, searching for items related to immigrants and Russellville and find an article about a Ku Klux Klan march that was held in the town in 2006. This links to a white supremacist site called Stormfront.com, and a group called the Council of Conservative Citizens (CCC), which is the reincarnation of the White Citizens' Council, formed in the 1950s to fight desegregation. Not surprisingly, they have added the threat of a "Mexican invasion" to their list of concerns. But I really start paying attention when I read a posting about their annual conference, which is being held *right now* in Sheffield, Alabama, only twenty miles away. Though the CCC doesn't disclose where the meeting will take place— only that it will be in a hotel—I figure I can drive around town and find it without a problem. If nothing else, it'll give me something to do.

It takes me twenty minutes of driving around Sheffield before I come across a large hotel and conference center off the highway with a scrolling electronic sign that reads: Welcome to the Council of Conservative Citizens. I park my car next to a row of large trucks with confederate flag bumper stickers and walk inside, following the posted flyers for the CCC straight past the welcome desk. I'm hoping to project an image of confidence.

Down the corridor burly white men with shaved heads are standing in front of two doors that open into a conference room. They are wearing camouflage pants, with handguns strapped to their belts. Not what I was expecting. I seek refuge in a nearby men's room. While I'm doing my business a man steps up to my left. I can't help but notice the large handgun hanging on his right hip, just inches from my left thigh. I turn and walk right out of the hotel, get in my car, and drive away.

Which is when I start feeling stupid. If there is a day in which I can fairly say I have nothing to do, this is it. What are they going to do, shoot me? (A quiet voice in my head, which I try to suffocate, answers: "Perhaps.") I turn around, drive back to the hotel, and park. Now there are a dozen men standing outside the door, all armed, athletic, and (to my mind) angry. I take a deep breath and ask one of the men—trying hard to keep my voice from cracking—if he's here for the CCC meeting.

"Nah, they're next door. We're the NRA." I let out a deep sigh of relief—the National Rifle Association, how moderate!—and push through the double doors into a room whose occupants are focused on an older speaker behind the podium. A young white man wearing a suit dashes across the room, apparently quite excited about my presence. I play it straight, introducing myself as a journalist who writes about immigrants, and ask if I can sit in.

"Immigrants, of course!" He ushers me to an open seat near the back. There are about seventy-five white people in the audience, a larger turnout than I expected.

The first speaker I hear is an elderly man named Drue Lackey, whose head of soft white hair resembles two cumulus clouds. His lecture is called "Civil Rights in Alabama," which ought to be interesting. Lackey begins with a caveat: "There are some things I can't talk about because the statute of limitations hasn't run out yet." It turns out that Lackey was the police officer who fingerprinted Rosa Parks in Montgomery after her arrest, an iconic image of the civil rights movement. He spent twenty-two years in law enforcement, retiring as the chief of police for Montgomery in 1970, and recently self-published a book on the era. In his first anecdote, Lackey speaks about the firebombing of four churches and the homes of Martin Luther King Jr. and Ralph Abernathy. While investigating one of the incidents, Lackey noticed a car slowly driving by. "This is something that for some reason criminals like to do, to revisit the scene of the crime," he comments. His police instincts turned out to be correct: He pulled the car over and won a confession from the men, who led him to a stash of explosives that they were planning to use in the future.

"We had an all-white jury on that case," he continues. "They deliberated for forty-five minutes, and they returned a 'not guilty' verdict on all counts." The people sitting at my table start to clap. Others join in, some standing, until the room fills with applause. Lackey looks heartened by the response. He explains that one of the reasons he wrote his book was to tell the "other side" of the Montgomery Bus Boycott. In his rendering, "The communist Rosa Parks refused to give up her seat to an elderly, feeble man," and "Martin 'Lootin' King was a traitor to his country." Presumably the only journalist in the room, I take notes nervously, expecting someone to chase me out of this movement-building meeting.

I needn't have worried. Over the two-day conference, I hear a number of wildly racist claims, and no one seems to mind that I'm writing them all down. "We're witnessing the demise of the greatest race in the history of the world," thunders Paul Fromm, who I later learn is Canada's leading white supremacist. A speaker named Joel LeFever argues that the recent "pro-sodomite marriage" ruling in California can be traced back to the disastrous legalization of mixed-race marriages. Roan Garcia Quintana, a Cuban American who is quick to point out that his ancestors are from Spain, laments the "invasion of aliens" from Mexico, who "bring diseases and don't know how to use the toilet."

What's shocking to me, as the day goes on, isn't just that this white power group has granted me entrance even after I've identified myself as a journalist, but that a politician is proudly participating. Alabama state senator Charles Bishop, who represents a district near Russellville, speaks during a buffet luncheon (catered by African American women who are in and out of the room too quickly to glean what the conference is about). Bishop's rant about the critical need to reject "Mohammed" Obama is followed by a presentation that delivers a biblical defense of slavery. As speakers compete to see who can make the most incendiary remarks, I keep waiting for someone to take offense. No one does.

Judging from the presenters, the group's mission has evolved as the demographics of the South have changed, and the influx of Latino immigrants has drawn at least some of the members to the conference. A man from Russellville pulls me aside when he hears where I'm staying. "We've now got more Mexicans than niggers," he spits. The implication is clear enough: There's a new target in town. Nearly everyone I talk to mentions the imaginary *Reconquista* plot whereby immigrating Mexicans are motivated by a desire to recapture the Southwest. "They're not coming to be good little immigrants; they're coming to take over!" thunders Fromm.

The rhetoric about immigrants is offensive, with frequent complaints about "Mexicans bringing leprosy" and an "illegal alien crime wave," but what leaves the biggest impression on me is the still-raging hatred of blacks. No one expresses that hatred more vehemently than Fromm, in a talk entitled "Immigration." A more accurate title would be something like "Let the Blacks Die."

I hang in as long as possible—writing notes, trying to keep my face expressionless, adopting the posture of a passive sponge— but by Saturday afternoon I quietly make my exit. Driving back to Russellville, I feel like the rental car has become my personal time-traveling machine. I step into the car, the year is 2008; I drive twenty miles north and emerge in a year that could be 1950, or 1900, or even 1860 (minus the electric lights and air-conditioning). Liberal Yankee goes south and is taken aback by racist rednecks: I realize this is a trope. And the CCC is very low-hanging fruit: This is a cuckoo group consisting of mainly very old white men who were on the wrong side of history fifty years ago and have been nurturing their sense of victimhood ever since. I also acknowledge that what I've seen does not represent "the South."

But there are two things that stay with me. The first, which reflects very poorly on the political culture of Alabama, is that a state senator addressed the group and spoke highly of their work. It's not everywhere that an elected official feels comfortable speaking to an openly white supremacist organization. The second—and this is due to my own agenda—are the words of the Russellville man: "We've now got more Mexicans than niggers." I wonder how much more of that sort of talk I'll come across.

ON MONDAY AFTERNOON I receive a call from Pilgrim's Pride. A perky woman tells me they have an opening in the debone department. It'd be from 11:00 p.m. to 8:00 a.m. Am I still interested? "Of course!" I tell her, doing my best to contain my excitement so as to not come off as too eager. She's glad to hear that I want the job, and tells me to come by the office the following afternoon.

At Mama's Kitchen I hand over a check and Sabrina writes up a crude lease and gives me the keys to the trailer. I head into town and have the city turn on the electricity and water, then drive to my new home. It sits about a mile south of Mama's Kitchen on Highway 75, which is really just a two-lane street. I pass dozens of trailers and a few houses before the grasslands open into a large field; my trailer is the last one on the right, sitting alone down a long gravel path. One of the windows to a small shed attached to the trailer is broken, and a spare tire rests against the front wall. It looks abandoned.

I push the door open and find a kitchen table with three wooden chairs; a washer and dryer; a flimsy child's desk; a broken refrigerator; and two air conditioners. Small bedrooms, each with a tiny bathroom, are at either end; the space between them is taken up by the living room and kitchen. Every drawer is crawling with spiders, which is okay because I like spiders. I also like the kitchen floor, which consists of a sheet of plastic faux tiles. The rest of the trailer's floor is covered in blue carpet and littered with spider webs, dead insects, and nails. It will take me a few days to sweep all the debris into the trash.

The trailer has two quirky touches. There are ten mirrors in the living room. Every time I walk into the living room from the kitchen, I see ten different versions of myself.

The second oddity is a circular bar that is in one corner of the living room. There are two cabinets below the bar—also claimed by spiders—and the exterior is covered in padded purple vinyl. A bar situated in a county where alcohol hasn't been sold since Prohibition might not be the most practical piece of built-in furniture, but it pleases me nonetheless.

The trailer's major drawback is that it resembles "living in a hot tin can," as one of my neighbors pointedly observes. After taking a quick tour of my new home, every inch of my skin is coated in sweat. I open the windows in the living room, but as they are north and south facing, and the wind seem to be flowing east, it's hard to notice any difference. The trailer's only west-facing window is in the bathroom and a foot wide. Still, despite the small size of the window, the bathroom quickly becomes the coolest area (and the place I go to watch afternoon storms march toward me across the grasslands). But it's not large enough to comfortably hang out in, and there's also a large swatch of black mold climbing up one wall.

To combat the humidity, I try leaving the trailer's two doors open, which leads me to an important discovery: a nearby wasp's nest. The space quickly fills with the large black beasts, so I shut the doors—neither has a screen—and go about smashing them with my shoe. With both doors shut, the trailer soon feels like a parked car sitting in the sun. It doesn't take long to realize that, with wasps as neighbors, I'm going to keep the air conditioners running pretty much all the time. I drive into Russellville and spend $30 on a fan, which, along with the two AC window units, keeps the place livable. As I turn into the driveway with the fan in the backseat, I look across the field and realize that I can clearly see the chicken plant to my left. I've lucked into the perfect location. If I want, I can even walk to work.

PILGRIM'S PRIDE HIRES me the next day. "Your app looks great," a blond-haired woman in human resources tells me, struggling to hide a yawn. "It shows that you are very patient and don't mind doing hard work." I assume the hard work comment relates to my lettuce cutting. I'm not sure how she determines I'm patient, but I'm glad she thinks so. During the thirty-minute interview she never asks me how I ended up in Russellville, even when I hand over my New York driver's license. They need workers, I can work: end of story.

There are three different shifts at the plant. The first shift is from 8:00 a.m. to 5:00 p.m.; second shift, which follows immediately after, is sanitation. "During sanitation we have workers come in and take everything apart and hose it down with bleach and chemicals," she says. After sanitation is the third shift, which begins at 11:00 p.m. and concludes at 8:00 a.m. the next morning. "All we have right now are jobs in the third shift."

She has several positions that she thinks I would enjoy. All of them pay $8.05 an hour, but if I arrive on time every day, I'll earn $8.80 an hour for the week. After sixty days the base rate will increase to $8.80, with the perfect attendance bonus reaching $9.45. If an employee makes it to the year mark, he will earn $8.95 an hour with a bonus of $9.70. The various numbers can make it seem complicated, but the basic truth is this: You could work at the plant for ten years, without missing a minute of a single shift, and never see your wage reach $10 an hour. (The one exception is a job in "live hang and killing," where workers are paid extra because they are in a department that is called *live hang and killing*. Their pay scale maxes out at $10.75 an hour. "We don't have any openings in that," she tells me. Not a problem, I assure her.)

There are jobs available in packing chicken into boxes, loading boxes onto trucks, or adding marinades to chicken in the "further-processing" department. What I want, though, is a line job in debone. Artemio, originally from Mexico, briefly worked in a Georgia poultry plant, and told me that all of the debone workers were immigrants, while the few American citizens were supervisors or performed less strenuous jobs.

"You said something about debone, right?"

"Yes, we have that too. Now, deboning is just what it sounds like. Each person has a place on the line and makes a certain cut. The chicken just sits there, stuck on a cone, passing by like this." She sticks out her tongue and smiles, apparently doing her dead-chicken-on-a-cone impression.

"After cutting lettuce, my back could really use a break, so I'd rather not be loading anything. If it's open, I think I'll go with debone."

"Because your application is so strong, I'm going to offer you the job right now," she says, handing me papers to sign while explaining the attendance policy. Pilgrim's Pride doesn't have sick days or personal days. Instead, employees accumulate points based on days missed: Every time we are absent for an entire shift, we are given one point; if we leave early or arrive late, we earn half a point. A point is erased six months from the date it is issued, and if we accumulate more than seven points we're fired. Seems simple enough.

"You'll be working Sunday through Thursday nights, but you first have to take an orientation class. You should show up Thursday for orientation, and then you'll begin Sunday night. Just one more thing before we're all set. It looks like your Social Security card was issued in Oregon. Can you tell me why you don't have a work history there?"

"We moved when I was in preschool."

She smiles and writes something down. "Sorry, we just have to ask. Homeland Security is really cracking down. They want to know about things like that."

At the nurse's station I pee into a cup and blow into a Breathalyzer. Since I don't do drugs and managed to come to the interview sober, I've cleared the last hurdle. I've got a new job.

CHAPTER 6

Pilgrim's Pride gets its name not from the group that came over on the *Mayflower*, and whose image serves as the company logo, but from its founder and chairman Lonnie "Bo" Pilgrim. During an eight-hour orientation that largely consists of receiving many handouts and then signing papers to acknowledge we received many handouts, that fact is one of the nuggets of data I retain. In fact, our ability to remain awake during the onslaught of papers and extended PowerPoint presentations actually seems to be part of a test. "You won't remember all of what we go over today," promises the African American woman who conducts the training. "But whatever you do, don't fall asleep." That's rule number one at Pilgrim's Pride.

Our trainer tries to project an aura of corporate cheeriness with a series of awkwardly timed smiles, but it's plain to see that she is tired and bored. Although she buries us with an amazing amount of eminently forgettable material—"We are a customer-focused organization committed to continuous improvement"—she's managed to memorize nearly everything. "This one here has one hundred and three slides," she warns us before dimming the lights and rattling off information so quickly it becomes one long word. High turnover makes it a challenge to keep the plant sufficiently staffed, forcing the people in human resources to give four of these orientations every week. A former employee who spent many years at the plant told me that over the course of a single week, 150 new people were hired. That's about one-tenth of the plant's entire work-force. It wasn't quite enough: During the week, 175 people quit.

The nine others in my orientation are mostly recent high school graduates or dropouts, though several people are in their thirties. Orientations are conducted in either Spanish or English; my English-speaking group consists of eight whites and two blacks. We'll all be working the third shift. Several in the group have worked at the plant before, and the black woman seated to my right has another job caring for people with dementia from 2:00 to 10:00 p.m. I've been wondering how I'll adapt to sleeping dur-ing the day; I wonder how she'll adapt to not sleeping. "I'll get along fine," she tells me. "You get used to it." She will arrive home from the plant just as her daughter is leaving for school, enjoy her four hours of "down time" until 1:00 p.m., take a shower, and head back out the door.

Christianity plays a big role in the company. A friendly, portly man tells us about the "Pilgrim's Cares" program, which is pro-vided through a group called Marketplace Chaplains USA. "We have white, black, and Hispanic chaplains who can listen to you and pray with you," he says. Now that I'm an employee, I have the option of calling upon any one of the six plant chaplains, who will make hospital visits, plan weddings, even offer premarital coun-seling. The speaker worked for thirteen years in the live hang and killing department—"People told me I sure do kill a lot for a chap-lain," he chuckles—and believes that our arrival at Pilgrim's Pride is sure to prove a blessing. He offers us free Bibles, which several people accept, and passes out a daily devotional. (Today's theme: "To be anxious about nothing, pray about everything.") After he leaves we're handed a brochure about the "Pride Line," which is a confidential number we can call to report any unethical behavior in the workplace. The front of the brochure features a photograph of a white-haired Bo Pilgrim with a Bible in his hands.*

Safety is discussed by a man who I am convinced has his bottom lip stuffed with chewing tobacco. He lays out his vision for the plant: that we "leave with the same number of fingers and toes as when we arrived." I'm new to Russellville but know that not everyone is so lucky: I've already bumped into one woman in town whose son lost part of his foot when it was crushed by plant machinery.

After the safety director leaves, our trainer explains that we will be in pain even if we follow every safety precaution. "You'll be using muscles and nerves and tendons all the time that you normally don't use. Remember, thirty-eight birds are going by every minute on the debone line. It's fast and it's hard and your hands are gonna swell and ache. That's why the nurses say it's best to take ibuprofen every four hours." I'll soon discover that alongside the vending machines selling candy and soda in the break room is an entire section stocked with various brands of painkillers.

We are offered other advice to make the job less painful. One PowerPoint slide argues that in order to prevent repetitive damage,

---

* In 2008, Bo Pilgrim received an award from the American Bible Society for "25 Years of Workplace Evangelism," and he has been called a "crusader for Christ." For Pilgrim, being a titan in the poultry industry isn't just a job—it's his calling. "There's no doubt that God wanted me to exemplify being a Christian businessman," he told one reporter, and his religiosity seeps into many areas that appear quite secular. "I want to thank Jesus Christ for our new Hawker 800 XP airplane," he wrote in the company newsletter after purchasing a second corporate jet for $12 million in 1999. "Another Bible has been added to the new airplane, thanking Jesus," he continued. "We are now operating both airplanes for our company which always praises Jesus."

it is necessary to "organize your daily activities," suggesting that a supervisor will present us with a variety of work options at the beginning of each shift. (They won't: Work at a chicken plant consists of doing one thing over and over again.) Another tip, "Take micro breaks," sounds more helpful, but I never hear anyone mention it on the processing floor, and several attempts to implement the strategy do not go over well with my supervisors.

One notable omission from the orientation curriculum is the topic of animal welfare. This is especially surprising in light of video footage released in 2004 by the People for the Ethical Treatment of Animals (PETA) that was taken inside a Pilgrim's Pride plant in Moorefield, West Virginia. The video shows workers stomping on live chickens and smashing them against the wall. Eyewitness testimony also included accounts of workers "ripping birds' beaks off, spray-painting their faces, twisting their heads off, spitting tobacco into their mouths and eyes and breaking them in half—all while the birds are still alive."

Pilgrim's Pride and one of its major partners, KFC, were hit with a firestorm of negative publicity following the video's release. One op-ed in the *Los Angeles Times*, written by animal rights activists Peter Singer and Karen Dawn, was entitled "Echoes of Abu Ghraib in Chicken Slaughterhouse." They argued that in any environment in which "humans have unchecked power over those they see as inferior, they may abuse it."[1] In fact, there was a very loud echo that the authors didn't yet realize: Lynddie England, the female soldier giving the thumbs-up in many of the Abu Ghraib photos, had worked at the Moorefield plant for seven months. She left, she says, after her complaints to a supervisor about "discolored and diseased-looking" chicken meat getting through were ignored. "People were doing bad things," she said about the plant. "Management didn't care."[2] But while Pilgrim's Pride fired eleven people after the video surfaced and pledged to "re-educate" their employees about animal welfare, I don't recall those words even being spoken during orientation.

The final segment of the orientation deals with the company's belief that "remaining union-free" is a key to making sure workers are "proud to be identified with the company." The trainer turns on the television and slips in a tape. "The union has tried to organize here three times before," she says. "Here is the company's view on that."

We are greeted by an attractive black man with a mustache, while a curious message is pasted across the top half of the screen: Not for Employee Viewing or Training.

"There are some things that we sign that can be very valuable," he begins. "Credit card charges, checks, loan applications—it's your signature that makes them valuable. Here's another example: union authorization cards, or multi-signature petitions." Be careful, the man advises, because "your autograph may mean you just agreed to become"—his voice deepens, forecasting doom—"a *union member.*"

Surprisingly, he praises earlier unions. "Back in the forties, unions weren't short of members—one out of three workers were union. And back then, unions did have good laws passed. Laws that put a stop to child labor, set up a minimum wage, improved workplace safety."

After these achievements, however, "The union's job was done. Over with. Nobody needed them!" The man celebrates, as should we all. Everyone in the room, it bears remembering, has been blessed: We're about to become members of a low-wage poultry plant, where employees make thousands of cuts a day with sharp knives. What could be less relevant than notions like workplace safety and higher wages? We turned that corner after the Depression.

The screen cuts to a series of painfully acted mini-dramas. In one scene, union organizers circle around a reluctant worker and tell her to sign the card because "everyone else is doing it." (Remember how well that argument worked in junior high?) Nearly all of the actors are white, and judging by their attire they apparently spend their days pushing papers around an office. When organizers aren't attempting to crush workers under the weight of peer pressure, the narrator continues, they might "put up notices about union meetings" or even "give out handbills!" We watch as a man stands next to a truck, speaking to a worker through the window. "Hey, brother, you've heard about our union, haven't you?" Cars are honking in the distance; the organizer is keeping honest workers from going home. "Listen, here's my card. Gimme a call sometime and I'll let you know all that the union can do for you."

"Yeah, I'll call you," the worker says, as the drama reaches a fevered pitch. Two young guys seated to my left are flicking a piece of paper back and forth.

The video concludes with more rousing advice from the narrator. "Keep the union out—do it! Don't get hustled into something that could hurt you. So think about it. Give a rip about being treated as an individual, and not a number." I've kept a straight face up until now, but at the "give a rip" line—which company executive wrote this script?—the audio recorder I'm holding under the table captures my giggle.

The video concludes our orientation. Since we're getting paid, I've just completed my first day of work.

I RETURN MY rental car to Huntsville Airport the next day. Unable to find any safe roads for cycling—the highways here don't have consistent shoulders—I'm forced to pay a taxi driver $100 to drop me off at my trailer. The driver is an older black man who's never heard of Russellville; when we pull up to my trailer he says, "Um . . . huh. Must be nice and quiet out here at least, right?"

I wake up early Sunday morning and bike over to Mama's Kitchen for breakfast. Sabrina is in the kitchen, and I call out a greeting and order *huevos a la mexicana*. Since I'm the only customer, she brings out the food and joins me at a table. Pouring salsa over the eggs, I ask how she ended up in Alabama.

"It started with a visit from my aunt," she says. When Sabrina was a young girl, her aunt returned home with an American husband. They were in a brand-new truck, towing a brand-new boat; the truck was full of toys for Sabrina and her eight siblings. "In my mind, the United States became a place where everything was good, where you could have anything you wanted." By comparison, the village of San Tomás offered nothing; it was so insignificant that it didn't even show up on maps.

Sabrina didn't begin school until the age of ten; because she was older, the other students called her a *burra*. Although she laughs now at being called a donkey, it wasn't funny at the time, and she dropped out of third grade at thirteen. Three years later her family moved to Mexico City to live with an uncle, and she started cleaning houses. "Mexico City is beautiful," she says, staring out the window. "That is where I opened my eyes for the first time. It is a place that will either smash you down or that will make you stand up and wake up."

In Mexico City she met her future husband, Cruz, and in 1992 gave birth to her daughter, Malena. Two years later Sabrina and Cruz crossed into the United States, leaving Malena with Sabrina's mother. It was a painful crossing. "The same day I crossed I also nursed Malena," she says, looking near tears. "I felt like I was losing my life, my daughter, but I also felt like I had to do it. During the entire crossing I was sick with a fever and a chest full of milk." At first they lived with a cousin in Washington State and picked apples, and a year later moved to Russellville, where another cousin had found work at the plant.

Sabrina's parents and daughter arrived in Russellville the following year. Cruz was hired at a nearby mobile home factory, and she took a job working nights at the chicken plant, then owned by Gold Kist. She was in the evisceration department, accompanying inspectors from the United States Department of Agriculture (USDA). "It was a good job for the plant," she admits. On the weekends, she began cooking batches of Mexican specialties like *pan dulce*, which she delivered to the homes of coworkers who yearned for familiar food. The two income streams from the plant and the weekend food business eventually netted her enough money to purchase the land where my trailer sits. She quit her job at the plant and began cooking full-time, hoping she could build a restaurant on the land one day.

In 2003, coming back from church, she saw that Mama's Kitchen had a closed sign. A neighbor told her that the owner was sick and hoping to sell. Sabrina toured the restaurant that evening. It seemed perfect. The only problem was money: The owner was selling for $37,000 and wanted a down payment of $5,000. Sabrina stands up and pulls out her empty pockets. "That's how much money I had. But my head was going crazy—I wanted that restaurant!"

On Monday morning she raced over to Franklin Community Bank, where she'd been a member for five years. At first they didn't want to give her a loan. "I almost started crying right there in the office," she says, but she returned later that day and obtained a $2,500 loan. She spent the rest of the day borrowing money from everyone she knew, mostly in $100 increments. By nightfall, she had another $2,500. The next day she paid the owner and signed papers in the courthouse; on Wednesday she was cooking in the kitchen of her new business. She didn't know anything about running a restaurant, but she printed up flyers announcing the change of ownership and spread word among her existing customers.

"Some days I didn't even make a hundred dollars, and lots of people told me that it was going to fail. I even started to doubt myself sometimes. But I never thought I was a loser, because the people that lose are cowards. Why do they lose?" she asks. "Because, Gabriel, they pass their lives lamenting what they might have done. What you *might* do doesn't exist." She brings her right fist down on the table three times, seeming to say *I might have started from nothing, but I will bend the world until it's in a shape I can use.*

The restaurant gamble eventually paid off. Business picked up, she added a small store, and she and Cruz purchased a mobile home equipped for cooking—dubbed Mama's Kitchen II—that he staffed in town. (They have recently separated, and he owns the truck, which he operates at a downtown intersection.) She has an employee to help with the cooking and was able to buy the house across the street.

"Enough about me," she says. "How is work?" I tell her that I survived orientation and start this evening. The look on her face is easy to read: She finds me perplexing. She's living proof that the American dream, if you're lucky and willing to take risks, can be attained. A third-grade dropout from Mexico who refused to be smashed down owns her own restaurant. So why would I be heading backwards, into the plant that she left?

I TRY TO sleep that afternoon but eventually give up after hours of staring at the ceiling. Thirty minutes before my shift is to begin I'm standing at the end of the driveway with my bike and backpack. It seemed a lucky break to find a trailer so near the plant— just a five-minute bike ride away—but I hadn't considered how dark the journey would be. With neither streetlights nor moonlight, I find myself pedaling slowly along the two-lane road, my small headlight pointed at the ground so I can dodge any rocks or roadkill.

All is quiet except for the thwacking of large insects against my chest until I near a bend in the road and hear a growing rumble from behind. I turn my head to stare directly into the headlights of a honking semi truck. I turn back around and veer to my right, tugging on the brakes as my tires hit gravel. I'm able to keep from falling and feel a large whoosh of air slam into me as the big rig careens past. Several seconds later, the truck a good fifty feet away, the smell hits. To say I smelled live chickens and their waste would be accurate, but incomplete. The sensation was more akin, I imagine, to soaking a rug in chicken urine and smearing it with feces, and tightly wrapping that rug around my face. In the future, whenever a chicken truck passes me I'll remember to breathe through my mouth, or not at all.

I make it to the plant without further incident, swipe my photo ID to pass through a revolving gate, and sit in the orientation room with the rest of the new hires. Various supervisors come in and collect their workers, but it seems that the three of us set for debone aren't needed (a fourth from orientation hasn't shown up—the first in what will be a long line of casualties among my orientation class). After thirty minutes of confusion, the nighttime head of human resources, a man named Bill, tells us that we're being transferred to a department called DSI. "No one really wants to go to debone," he says. Middle-aged with a round face and balding head, Bill smiles. "Y'all just got really lucky."

The others don't seem to care one way or another, but I've actually been looking forward to the debone line, primarily because I figured—correctly, as it turns out—that the department would be made up primarily of immigrants.

"If it's possible, I'd still like to do debone," I say. "I just finished a job cutting lettuce, and my back is sore. I was told in the interview that in debone I wouldn't have to lift anything." Bill doesn't seem to be listening, though he finally nods before leaving the room.

When he returns, he repeats that we're being transferred to DSI, and I decide to drop the issue for the moment. "How many of you worked nights before?" Bill asks. None of us. "Nights are great 'cause you can get stuff done during the day." He mentions that the schedule has allowed him to attend minister school in the afternoons. "And of course I have time to go to church on Sundays. It's not for me to say, but I hope all of you go to church." I agree: It's not for him to say. The three other workers are nodding, though, so I stay silent.

During the next twenty minutes of aimless waiting I strike up a conversation with my two new coworkers. Seated next to me is an eighteen-year-old named Ben. He keeps his blond hair military-short and must weigh at least 250 pounds, but Big Ben turns out to be a gentle giant, answering my questions in a soft voice that is barely audible. With a baby face, red cheeks, and small circular-framed glasses, he strikes me as a cross between an overstuffed teddy bear and Harry Potter's giant brother. He lives near Haleyville, about twenty-five miles south of Russellville, and graduated from high school two months ago. He pulls from his wallet a shrunken copy of his diploma, displaying it proudly. "This is gonna be my first job, but my mom worked in debone and so she told me some stuff about it."

"What are the other people from school up to?" I ask.

"I only keep in touch with three people. One guy is here at the plant. Another is at Wal-Mart, and one is at Jack's." Jack's is a fast-food chain that began in Alabama.

Sitting next to Ben is a twenty-three-year-old woman named Diane, who graduated from Russellville High School and is the mother of a two-year-old. She hasn't worked since giving birth and is anxious to earn a paycheck. With cartoonishly large blue eyes, long blond hair, and a waiflike build, she looks more like a southern belle than chicken worker. "The only reason I'm here is because I couldn't find any other job," she explains. "I put in applications all over, but no one is hiring right now. My ma says I won't last two weeks, but I know I can do it."

A new man enters the room, wearing a white overcoat and blue hard hat. He introduces himself as Lonnie, the plant's night manager, and tells us to follow him. We shuffle clumsily through the break room as if across a frozen lake, sliding over a floor made slick with chicken fat. Lockers line the walls, two of which have UNION NO stickers slapped on them. A corridor opens up into a smock room, where we are given a week's supply of white hairnets, a pair of white cotton gloves, earplugs, and rubber overshoes, which provide much better traction. "Okay, let's go," Lonnie says once we're suited up. We follow him dutifully in a single-file formation.

SUPERHERO COMICS AREN'T complete without an evil genius. Often he seeks to construct the ultimate weapon to hold the world hostage; if he's really deranged he simply wants to use it to end human civilization. Since the construction of the weapon must be clandestine, work goes on belowground or behind hidden doors. Walk through the door and an immense world of nameless and undoubtedly evil scientists are at work, tinkering with mysterious equipment while wearing smocks and continuously checking devices.

That's the image that immediately comes to mind when I push through the double doors that separate the break room from the plant floor. This isn't a workplace: This is an underground lair. In the first room, workers scurry around in plastic blue smocks akin to a surgeon's, carrying buckets of chicken pieces. Others lean over a long conveyor belt that moves a continuous stream of meat, their feet planted as they arrange the pieces in a line. We weave our way around large metal machinery and step through a frothy puddle of foam that spews from a thick hose on the cement floor. The smell is a mixture of strong industrial cleaner and fresh meat. To my left is a chest-high cylinder filled to the brim with chicken bits; while it captures my attention, I step on what feels like a sponge and lift my foot to find a piece of pink meat, now flattened. Up ahead, I can see from the puffs of condensation coming from his mouth that Lonnie is saying something to our group—the temperature is frigid, probably in the low forties—but I can't hear anything. I remove my earplugs and am greeted by the roar of machinery. It's not a piercing noise, more of a loud, all-encompassing rumble: Think of the sound you hear when putting your ear to a seashell and multiply by a hundred. I put my earplugs back in.

We walk beneath a doorway and the full scale of the processing floor is revealed. I see no walls in front of me, just open space filled with workers standing in various areas without moving their feet. Hundreds of dead and featherless chickens are hanging upside down from stainless steel hooks, moving rapidly across my field of vision. I hear a beeping sound and step aside for a man driving a scooter-like contraption, which is carrying a container of steaming chicken meat (the contraption turns out to be a pallet truck, and the steam is actually from dry ice). As we cross the plant floor we pass beneath a line of chickens, whirling along more steel hooks; liquid falls from their carcasses and lands with chilly plops on my scalp. Hopefully water. In front of us dozens of workers are slicing up chickens—the debone department—but we proceed further, until we're standing aside a blond-haired woman in her forties who, like Lonnie, is wearing a hard hat.

"This is your supervisor, Barbara," Lonnie tells us, "but she won't be needing you tonight." He tells Ben and Diane to follow him and motions for me to stay put. When he returns he leads me through another doorway. "You're going to work in a different department today, but check in with DSI tomorrow," he says. Lonnie deposits me at the end of a line where boxes are being stacked.

The nearest person is a skinny white man with the hood of his Alabama football sweatshirt pulled tight over his head. I stay quiet, feeling slightly intimidated by my new coworker, who has deep lines cutting across his gaunt face and is missing a few front teeth. But when he turns to me he flashes a friendly smile. "How long you been here?" he asks.

"About five minutes."

He lets loose a squeaking chuckle, his shoulders bouncing up and down. "I've only been here two weeks." Kyle, it turns out, is my neighbor. He lives in a trailer with his wife and two kids about half a mile from where I'm staying. "Been right at that trailer for eighteen years, on land that was my granddaddy's. I worked in the plant four years, then quit. Now I'm back . . . don't know exactly why."*

Kyle normally works in DSI, but he says that today they're short people in the IQF department, another mysterious trio of initials. In IQF, bags of chicken wings are stuffed into boxes, taped, and shoved down on rollers to us. Our task is to stack the forty-pound

---

* A note here on accents. Kyle, like many native Alabamans at the plant, speaks in a very heavy and melodic drawl. It was beautiful to hear, but that beauty soon becomes distracting when I attempt to render it accurately on the page. For example, when he told me had been at the trailer for eighteen years, it sounded to my ears like: "Been rahht at tha-yat trawla' for eightee-yin years." For the sake of readability, I will not try to capture every nuance of the local dialect. One final point to illustrate the strength of the country accent: It took me a week of hanging out with Kyle before I finally realized that his name wasn't, in fact, Kyle. It was Gil. Later, when I listened repeatedly to a message he left on my cell phone, I realized that it wasn't Gil, but another name entirely. Here, he will remain Kyle.

boxes onto pallets. Once a pallet is stacked with forty-nine boxes—seven boxes to a row, seven rows high—a pallet driver whisks it away and we start loading up another. This is almost identical to the stacking of lettuce boxes completed by loaders on the machine, except that the pace here is much slower. I help Kyle do this for twenty minutes, until the machine at the front of the line breaks. A black woman with short blond hair, who has been taping the boxes shut, lets out a good-natured curse. It takes several minutes for a group of men to fix the machine; several minutes later it breaks down again. Over the coming month, I'll occasionally be asked to help out in IQF, and during almost every shift the machine breaks down—hourly. For this reason alone, it's considered a good place to work (as one of the "good" jobs, it also doesn't have a single immigrant working in the department).

With nothing to do, Kyle and I take a seat on the rollers. "You ever work in debone?" I ask him.

"Way back when I started, they tried to get me on there. Stayed a month. They told me I couldn't work fast enough so they shifted me out. I made sure I wasn't working fast enough too. Run you like slaves over there. I already knew how they did, though, 'cause my old lady was on the debone line for years." Now, he tells me, she's working at Wal-Mart.

"It looked like they mostly got Mexicans working in debone," I say.

"That's good, that's where they should be. Most of them are illegal anyways. Didn't have no Mexicans around before the plant opened. Now, I look out my front window I could throw a rock in any direction and hit one of them."

The machine is finally fixed and we return to stacking boxes. After thirty minutes the black woman who was cursing the contraption asks me to come up and tape boxes. I'm happy for the change in scenery, but this task soon becomes tedious. My job is to shake the box so that the bags lie flat, then pull the two top flaps together and shove it through a machine that tapes it shut. Cutting lettuce confirmed in my mind that much of what we call "low-skilled labor" is in fact quite difficult. But at the chicken plant, I'm already learning, many of the jobs are designed so that a person off the street, with minimal instruction, can do them correctly the very first time. I'm sure this is considered a "breakthrough" by the managerial class, but all it does is leave me bored within fifteen minutes.

SOMETIME AFTER 2:00 a.m., I'm told to take a break. I hang up my gloves and white smock on a hook and walk away from IQF. A minute later I've pushed through one swinging door and walked beneath two other doorways, and I'm watching an endless line of carved-up carcasses fall into a large container. I have no idea where I am. To my left, dozens of immigrant men and women are cutting up chickens with knives and scissors. I approach one woman, who can't be much taller than four feet, and ask her in Spanish if she can tell me how to get to the break room. She looks at me and shakes her head.

"She doesn't speak Spanish," another woman says, in Spanish. "You go straight down that row and make a left." I hear the two speak in what sounds like an Indian dialect, thank them both, and follow her directions.

The break room is mostly empty, but I notice Ben sitting alone in a corner booth. We're both struck by how disorganized everything seems to be. Like me, Ben has been hired for one department (debone), transferred to another (DSI), and then relocated once more, with unclear instructions along the way. He doesn't even know the name of the department that he's in. "Whatever it is, they have me standing and watching chickens go by."

"That's it?" I ask. "Are you supposed to *do* anything?"

"Uh, I think like maybe they said to look for mold."

"Mold? The chickens have mold?"

"Not yet anyway. I haven't seen any. I'm looking for green stuff."

"And if they have mold, what do you do?"

"I dunno." Ben pushes his sliding glasses up, beginning to look concerned. "I hope that's what I heard. I'm pretty sure somebody said something about mold." He looks at his watch and stands up. "I gotta go."

By now there are perhaps fifty people sitting in nearby booths, with about an equal number of whites, blacks, and Latinos, who are mostly gathered in self-segregated groups. One wall is plastered with what are meant to be inspiring corporate messages in Spanish and English, illustrated with geometric shapes and arrows. The "Cornerstones of Continuous Improvement" are written at each point of a large triangle: "Quality, Process Improvement, Teamwork." Next to this diagram is a more detailed "14 Points of Continuous Improvement," which include quizzical tips like "Drive Out Fear." Workers pass these grand pronouncements without pause, but they take note of a yellow flyer taped to the wall that reads "Taco Soup Wednesday Night."

I'm joined a few minutes later by a white man in a flannel coat who tells me that he's been on the debone line for five months. He snorts when I tell him that I'm impressed he's lasted so long.

"It's work release," he says. "The only reason I'm here is 'cause they locked my ass up." I don't ask what landed him in prison, but he does reveal that after the death of his father, he went on a number of epic alcohol binges. "Can't do that anymore 'cause I'm locked up and got myself a bleeding ulcer. But I'll tell you one thing," he says before I depart, "once I'm free you ain't never gonna see me step foot inside a chicken plant again."

I use the bathroom and manage to find my way back to Kyle and the boxes. He is seated on the rollers, hood pulled even lower on his head to ward off the cold, while a mechanic tries to get the machine back up and working.

LATE IN THE shift, a stocky nineteen-year-old with Popeye forearms joins IQF to cover for Kyle while he takes his break. Though I haven't asked, Popeye relates his recent history to me as we alternate the stacking of boxes. He's been on parole since he was fifteen, for breaking and entering a mobile home. Since then he's spent much of his free time smoking crack and snorting crystal meth. He has a son, which he admits is unfortunate for the son. He hit a cop once—never a good idea—and was promptly arrested. He was found to be carrying a pistol and three ounces of cocaine.

"I'm never going to have drugs or a piece on me if I'm going to be fucking up a cop." I nod as I grab another box of chicken. That seems a wise course to follow.

"So what the fuck are you doing this bullshit work for?" he asks. I tell him I'm traveling and need money to keep going. "Hey, I'm getting myself a good job making fifteen bucks an hour building churches. I'm not staying doing this shit. You should come with me, since you like to travel." I nod again, my eyes focused elsewhere. "They say that we'll be going to Tennessee and Maryland. Maybe some other places after that, if it turns out to be the shit. They even pay for us to stay in motels." He stacks a box and stands up straight, turning around to face me.

"You want to go? I can tell this guy I know, and we can be partners."

I stay quiet, wondering how I got myself into this mess.

"It's like, why *wouldn't* you want to go?" His voice has become serious, and there's a hint of potential aggression.

"Fuck," I say. I know I don't make an impressive tough guy, so when forced to pretend my only real hope is to curse. "Sounds like a good idea. Only thing is that I just paid two months' rent here. But otherwise, I'd be on it in a fucking second." There, that seemed okay.

He seems to accept it. "Fair enough—I get you." We finish up the shift without further discussion. He lasts a few more days at the plant; my last interaction with him is in the break room before the start of a shift. He tells me that he's getting ready to hit the road, and I gently say again that I'm going to stay. I put down the Elmore Leonard mystery I've been reading and wish him good luck.

"What the fuck?!" he yells. I'm not sure how to respond.

"What the fuck, what?"

"What the fuck are you reading a book for, Yankee?"

FOR REASONS THAT aren't explained, IQF is released earlier than other departments. As I walk toward the break room at 7:40 a.m., I meet a stream of men and women heading in the other direction, getting ready to begin the day shift. I swipe my ID card to sign out, am hit by the bright sunshine of another scorching day, hop on my bike, and pedal home. Kyle has agreed to pick me up tonight, so I don't have to worry about getting run over by a chicken truck. Back in my trailer I eat a quick breakfast of cereal and a peanut butter and jelly sandwich, type up my notes, and lay down. The sun is streaming through the window, my trailer shakes each time a truck loaded with live chickens passes, and my neighbor's roosters are engaged with a dog in some sort of noise competition. I can't be bothered; I fall asleep instantly.

CHAPTER 7

In 1989, the announcement that a poultry plant would be coming to town was cause for celebration. Russellville and its surrounding communities were desperate for jobs, with the county's unemployment rate holding steady at about 10 percent. Dozens of jubilant stories were filed in the *Franklin County Times*, the local newspaper. Six hundred processing jobs would need to be filled; 300 chicken farmers would be contracted to raise birds; an estimated $40 million would be infused into the economy. "This just may be the shot in the arm our economy has been needing," noted one reporter. A member of the economic development board that helped attract Gold Kist described poultry plant work as "the finest type industry," before adding that many employees would earn $4.35 an hour. Two months later, speaking at the plant's groundbreaking ceremony, Governor Gay Hunt heralded it as a watershed moment for economic development. "Alabama has become a pro-business and pro-jobs state. When we have people working together like you have here, our children won't have to leave the state to find jobs."

Russellville had been in competition with other poor towns, and in order to attract "the finest type industry," taxpayers had to sweeten the pot. The local water, gas, and electric boards made sizable contributions toward the $100,000 used to subsidize the purchase of the land for Gold Kist, and the water board invested another $200,000 in piping to supply the facility. State funds, too, were committed: More than half a million dollars were allocated to upgrade roads leading to the plant and hatchery.[3] Such is the model for much of the economic development that occurs in the American South: Poor regions make large concessions to corporations and are rewarded with minimum-wage jobs in return.[4]

In the late 1990s, with the poultry industry booming, Gold Kist expanded the plant and added another 750 workers. But when VF Jeanswear, maker of Lee Jeans, announced in 2001 that it was shuttering three local plants—resulting in a loss of 1,300 jobs—it became clear that the story of economic development in Franklin County was less about adding jobs than replacing them. Workers at Lee were unionized, earned wages that averaged between $10 and $11 an hour, and had free medical insurance: It was an occupation on which one could build a stable life. Indeed, the loyalty of Lee's workforce put any poultry plant to shame. Nearly a third of the workers at Lee's Russellville plant, which opened in 1972, had been with the company for more than a decade; one in five had been there at least twenty years. "This is a dark day in Franklin Country," remarked a representative of the chamber of commerce. "I can't remember anything this bad happening to us as a community. There are not that many jobs in Franklin County to replace these jobs."[5]

I arrived in town eighteen years after the surge of optimism that followed the opening of the poultry plant. The county's unemployment rate still stood at over 8 percent, and the dream of high-quality jobs had vanished: Poultry processing was soon discovered to be punishing work for poverty wages. Claims of a new day dawning no longer held water, as parents who had stepped foot inside the plant certainly didn't hope their children would one day join them. But while the early hype had died quickly, the plant jobs were still "better than nothing," as one local told me.

As the most important industry in an impoverished region, the chicken company wielded significant power; this was most evident in the positive press it received. Over the years, the *Franklin County Times* ran upbeat articles that profiled the chicken industry, interviewed a few satisfied chicken farmers (obviously hand-picked by the company), and included feel-good statements by plant managers. Most of the articles looked like little more than company press releases. Searching through the paper's archives, I wasn't able to find many attempts to tell the story from the bottom up, through the voices of ordinary workers. On the drive over to the plant on my second night of work, Kyle offers up his perspective on poultry work.

"It's a fucking struggle every night just to get my ass in," he says, the glowing lights of the plant illuminating the cloudy sky. "And when I worked here before, it was the same thing: four years of forcing myself to come in. I don't know how I lasted that long. I was always one point away from getting fired."

"Why'd you quit?" I ask. (After a few more days of work I realize this is the sort of question a poultry plant worker never needs to ask.)

"I just got to a point one night when I couldn't take it. How long can you do work that a trained monkey could do? I didn't even tell my supervisor I was going to the bathroom or nothing. I was stacking boxes: I put a box down and walked out of the plant, right on home in the dark. Had to bang on the door 'cause

Cindy was asleep and I didn't have keys. But she was real cool about it. She said, 'We'll make it through. I don't know how, but we'll make it.'"

During the two-year stretch away from the plant, he collected unemployment and twice worked at Wal-Mart, earning minimum wage. (He is not alone: Many people—like his wife—bounce back and forth between the town's two dead-end jobs.) Though he found Wal-Mart less depressing than the plant, he soon soured on that experience as well. About the mega-retailer he says, "I don't care if they call us 'associates,' they still treat their people like shit. They never gave me enough hours or any regular schedule." So now he was back working with chicken—"for how long, I couldn't tell you." He opens the car door; we are parked in the lot, watching two dozen inmates on work release step out of a department of corrections bus and head into the plant. "Alright, I s'pose we should be heading in. Don't want to, but got to."

TONIGHT I'M AGAIN transferred out of DSI. Barbara tells me that I'll be "making combos," which explains nothing. I follow her to a large room out of sight of DSI and am introduced to a black man who tells me his name is Squirrel. He shows me a completed combo, which turns out to be a chest-high octagonal box made of stiff cardboard that is open at the top—the perfect size for a child to construct a makeshift fort. Here, I learn, they are used for a much less fun purpose: Placed at the end of various lines throughout the plant, they collect everything from chicken nuggets and breasts to skeletal remains.

Combos arrive flat, so the first task is to open the box and seal the bottom by pressing and locking the flaps together. Once this is complete, I take the combo and place it upside down on the cement floor and grab a wooden pallet and toss it on top. Dizziness becomes a factor at this point, because the pallet needs to be con-

nected to the box through the use of enough plastic wrap to im-
mobilize a giant elephant. I walk around the combo in a tight circle a dozen times, holding the tube of wrap in my hands and
winding it around the combo, then the pallet, and around the
combo again. It's not a particularly hard job, but it does induce
vertigo. Each time I complete a combo I need a few seconds to
regain my balance before starting another. For the first few hours,
as soon as I finish a combo, there is someone who drags it away,
so I have no time to rest.

After a few hours of making combos as quickly as dizziness allows, demand slows. I take a seat on a cardboard box and lean back
against the cement wall. Sweat has soaked through my T-shirt and
is beginning to saturate the cloak that Squirrel has given me to
wear. The temperature in the room is much warmer than at IQF,
and walking in circles seems to be burning off a decent amount
of calories.

For the first time I'm able to take in my surroundings. To my
right is the re-hang area. It is called re-hang because it is the second time the birds are hung up: The first is in "live hang," where
workers grab live chickens that have been delivered by truck and
hang them upside down on metal hooks. Once attached, the heads
of the live birds pass through a tank of electrified water, rendering
them immobile. They are then beheaded by a mechanical blade
and submerged in boiling water to remove their feathers.

When the process works correctly, the chicken becomes unconscious upon hitting the electrified water and is killed by the blades.
But, as anyone who has worked in a chicken plant knows, the scale
and pace of the operation means that the system rarely operates
perfectly. When the water isn't sufficiently charged, the birds remain conscious for the beheading phase. When the mechanical
blades miss the chickens' necks, a group of workers known as "kill
room attendants" or "backup killers" are on hand to manually slit

the birds' throats. Still, each year millions of birds somehow survive the bath and various blades and are boiled alive.[6]

Now dead and de-feathered, the chickens enter the evisceration phase. One way to envision what happens in evisceration (or "Evis," as it is called at the plant) is to read through the job titles, which range from neck breaker and oil sack cutter to giblet harvester and lung vacuumer. Workers stand one next to the other as the birds fly past, each doing their part until, by the end of the line, the result is a disemboweled carcass that moves on to re-hang.

Evisceration is out of my line of sight, but I have a clear view of re-hang, and it looks like a particularly unpleasant job. At present there are twelve men in re-hang, all Latinos except for one African American. (Although the plant workforce is diverse, with roughly an equal number of whites, blacks, and Latinos, it's becoming clear that immigrants dominate the most arduous jobs.) The men stand shoulder to shoulder on an elevated platform in a U-shaped design, facing a waist-high metal moat that is overflowing with featherless chickens. The chickens look like what you'd find in a butcher shop, except for the presence of long spinal cords, which give them a particularly macabre look. The workers stick their hands into the pile of moist chickens, grabbing carcasses by the legs, and slide what I guess are the chicken's ankles through metal hangers that pass quickly at forehead level. After one bird is hung, they immediately stick their hands in the pile of chicken for another; in re-hang there is no time for breaks.

Squirrel has been at the plant for many years and previously worked in re-hang. He's glad to be out. "You have to hang twenty-eight birds a minute," he says, joining me on a nearby cardboard box. "They will stand by you with a stopwatch to make sure. When you first start, it tires out your shoulders, until you get used to it." Indeed, at the moment there is a supervisor's assistant—identifiable by his blue hairnet—walking back and forth in front of the workers, pausing occasionally to assess an individual's output.*

When I tire of watching re-hang, my attention turns to an area that Squirrel tells me is called leg quarters, located in the same rectangular room where we assemble combos. Here the bottom half of a chicken, still hanging from hooks ten feet in the air, is sliced down the middle by a circular saw. Once cut, the legs fall into a funnel-like contraption. Boxes travel along a conveyor belt below the funnel, and every few minutes, the funnel opens and shoots out the legs in a movement that resembles violent defecation. Most of the plant's chicken is sold in the United States, but the dark meat of leg quarters is shipped to Russia and China. (China is also the market for the plant's "Paw" department—chicken feet—a cuisine that hasn't yet developed a following in the States.)

Once the funnel shoots out a load of legs, the full box is weighed, taped, labeled, and stacked on pallets to be loaded onto trucks. My attention turns to a man standing directly in front of me, about twenty feet away. He is white, probably in his fifties, and wearing a flannel coat, tattered work boots, and large red headphones to keep out the noise.

His role is to place lids on the boxes that pass by. There is simply no way to describe his task in a manner that is interesting. He grabs lids that are on a platform running at eye level and puts them on the boxes that pass by at waist level. He does this over and over again, without shifting his gaze. Other people on the line are out of earshot, so he has no one to talk to. As the lull in demand for combos continues, I remain seated on my cardboard box and enter a sort of twilight zone, transfixed by the man's repetitive

---

* The hairnets (*mayas* in Spanish) are color-coded: white for regular workers, red for cleanup workers, and blue for assistant supervisors. Supervisors wear blue hard hats.

motions. Grab a lid, put it on. Grab a lid, put it on. How long do I watch him? I have no idea. Long enough to see him put on hundreds of lids, without pausing or even shuffling his feet. Leaning forward so my elbows rest on my knees, I start dipping my head with each lid. The spell is finally broken when a woman comes to pick up three combos, and I rise to replenish my stock.

I'VE DONE A number of less-than-glamorous jobs in my life, from delivering pizzas and filing papers to selling electronics at K-Mart and installing drywall. Still, none of those low-wage jobs are adequate preparation for what I've just witnessed. For people who have never worked at a fast-paced, low-skilled factory job, it is difficult to communicate through words the weight of the endeavor. The usual adjectives—*monotonous* or *boring* or *endless*—point in the general direction, but are much too mild.

Paradoxically it's the mindlessness of the jobs that can make them so difficult. Think of a task you can complete with minimal concentration. As I later reflected on the man placing lids on boxes, the task that came to mind involved a giant arithmetic workbook. Imagine that your job is to complete the workbook, which is full of simple addition problems like $8 + 6 =$ ___ or $3 + 9 =$ ___. Perhaps there are fifty such problems on each page and 500 pages in the workbook. The first few minutes might be fun—it feels good to be able to breeze through the pages—but the problems quickly start to repeat. There is muted satisfaction in finishing the first workbook, but it is short-lived: Another takes its place. In no time the game has grown old, you're tired and bored, and you never want to be asked the sum of $2 + 3$ again.

Which is too bad, because if you're stuck in a place like Russellville, you just might spend the next twenty years of your life in a job whose primary task is as meaningful and challenging as noting that $2 + 3 = 5$. I'm not arguing that people in the plant would prefer work that is physically or mentally taxing. But we all like to learn new things, find some purpose in what we do, and be at least occasionally challenged. This is an elementary observation, but it's easy to forget how many people never get that chance. Early on, Kyle asked me what my father did for a living. I told him that he runs his own nonprofit organization working to improve youth sports. "You know, that sounds interesting," Kyle said. "Does he like it?"

"He loves it."

Kyle got a dreamlike look, as if I was describing something exotic, like the contours of the planet Mars. "Huh. I always wondered what that would be like, you know, to enjoy what you do. Never did like what I was doing. Don't know nobody else who does, neither."

I GET MY first taste of true line-work monotony the following evening, when I'm told to stay in DSI. Since DSI deals directly with fresh chicken meat—unlike IQF or the combo department— for the first time I put on the standard plant uniform: a cheap blue plastic smock no thicker than a single piece of paper, a pair of cotton gloves under a pair of plastic ones, and a white hairnet.

At this point DSI remains a mystery. I don't know what the acronym stands for, or what it does. I do see two lines running parallel to each other, with workers standing on either side. Since keeping workers totally in the dark seems to be part of the business model at Pilgrim's Pride, I'm not surprised when Barbara tells me to follow her without explanation. We leave the twenty or so other DSI workers and walk up a low platform, where another short belt runs at waist level. I'm now standing above the workers.

"You————————-before?" Barbara asks. There are words in between that I can't hear. I pull out my earplugs and the noise of the plant rushes in.

"What's that?" I shout.

"I said, you ever tear chicken breasts?" She's now shouting too.

"Not really."

"Okay, good. Stay here and when the breasts come by, tear them in half."

Tear them in half? With my hands? I turn around in time to see her walking away and I put my plugs back in. This should be interesting.

I stand at the perch for several minutes, waiting nervously for chicken breasts. From this angle I have a view of a large section of the plant floor, looking out on both DSI and debone, but it's just too complex to make sense of. I realize that while workers are slaving away on the ground, an intricate system of machinery is constantly churning above us. I am reminded of those plastic marble sets of childhood, in which you placed a marble and then followed its progress along a circuitous path until it eventually landed at the bottom. Wherever I look I see chicken meat flying off belts, spinning around gears, dropping from one moving plane to another.

"What's going on, Gabriel?" Kyle ambles up the steps, wearing his hooded Alabama sweatshirt. "Looks like we're fixin' to be partners."

"You know what we're doing here?"

"Chicken breasts. You tear them in half, they come to me, and I put them in boxes."

Just as Kyle takes a position to my right, the first few chicken breasts begin dropping from a belt ten feet in the air. They land on another belt with a plop and travel directly past my station.

The breasts are pink, slippery, heart-shaped, and much larger than I expected.* A line of sinew connects the two halves of each

---

* Industrial chickens, I later learn, are selectively bred to develop outsized breasts. This artificial tinkering is profitable for companies like Pilgrim's Pride; less so for the chickens. Along with suffering from broken

UNLIKE MEATPACKING, WHICH has its origins in northern cities like Chicago, and where for a time militant labor activism carved middle-class jobs out of the carving of meat, poultry has always been a poor person's occupation. The first chicken farmers emerged in the 1920s in the Delmarva Peninsula (the combined eastern shores of Delaware, Maryland, and Virginia); chickens were seen as a means for hardscrabble farmers to hedge their bets in case of a poor vegetable season, and were delivered live to markets in cities like New York and Philadelphia.

Government intervention during World War II dramatically increased the amount of chicken consumed in the country, while shifting its center from Delmarva to the South. Beef was rationed; the source of protein was seen as something best saved for the troops. "Raising and eating chicken were now patriotic duties and a matter of national security," writes Steve Striffler in *Chicken*, his book about the industry. At the same time, the government commandeered the entire supply of chicken meat from the Delmarva Peninsula for federal food programs. "This wartime policy," notes Striffler, "effectively meant that the premier poultry-producing region in the country, a region that produced over half of the country's commercial broilers, was suddenly removed from the market."[11]

Southern entrepreneurs like John Tyson of Arkansas stepped in to fill the vacuum, and the South has been the center of the poultry industry ever since. It has two key advantages: an unorganized workforce and low labor costs, along with a ready supply of desperately poor farmers eager to switch to raising chickens. Eventually the model became one of vertical integration, with large companies like Pilgrim's Pride controlling everything from the hatcheries to the feed to the processing plants. The one aspect they left "independent" was the growers—the farmers—who signed contracts, were given chicks, and expected to deliver slaughter-weight birds.

Keeping the growers as independent contractors ensured that companies weren't responsible for investing the capital to build the growing sheds. As a result, growers took on debt and were especially vulnerable to market forces, as well as the dictates of the company, since without a contract their sheds became worthless.

Poultry officially entered the modern era in 1983, when McDonald's introduced the Chicken McNugget. Chicken lost its identity as a bird and became a deep-fried industrial creation. Over the following decade, American consumption of chicken outpaced beef. Today, the average American consumes eighty-six pounds of chicken a year, the equivalent of 262 chicken breasts. Originally touted for its health benefits, much of this chicken is consumed as nuggets, strips, and patties in a "further processed" form—fried in oil and breaded—resulting in a product that could be twice as fatty as a hamburger.

IT TAKES LESS than a month for my body to start breaking down under the strain of feeding America's appetite for chicken. As in Yuma, the pain is primarily focused in my hands and wrists, though the lifting of tubs is starting to wear on my forearms and back as well. I dealt with the pain early on by taking ibuprofen before and during each shift—two pills at 10:30 p.m., two more at 2:30 a.m.—but now I start taking painkillers even when I'm not working. Jars of pasta sauce are becoming difficult to open, and the throbbing in my hands is starting to wake me up when I'm sleeping.

From what I can tell, the most common method of dealing with pain is to quit. One person has already left tub dumping after two months, and Ben, whose hands hurt when he opens and closes them, will depart in a matter of weeks. I have no doubt that despite being a healthy thirty-year-old, something in my body—my hands or my back—would most certainly give out within the year.

By the time Kyle's wife, Cindy, departed the debone line, she tells me that she was having problems even holding on to a glass of water, an indicator of carpal tunnel syndrome. It took some time to recover, but she did; the real damage occurs when an employee perseveres and attempts to work through the pain.

One worker whose hands were destroyed by line work is Roxanne, a middle-aged woman who lives in a modest house near the plant. When I interview her over the telephone, she tells me that she spent twelve years in various departments, including four years on the debone line, and along with increasingly painful arthritis, she saw the joint in her left thumb deteriorate. In 2006, her doctor recommended surgery. He also recommended that she not set foot again in the plant, and so she quit and paid for the surgery out of her pocket. "The workman's comp over there is rotten—if you have surgery one day, they expect you to come back the next," she says in a hushed voice. "The doctor told me that the joint in my thumb was almost completely worn away, so they took an extra vein in my leg that I didn't need and wrapped it around my thumb. Over time that's supposed to form a gristle." In effect, the vein will eventually replace the cartilage of the thumb joint.

"My hand still hurts; they say it will never be like it was. But it wasn't just me—everybody on the line had hand problems. When you work over there, I guess you have to accept that you're gonna hurt. But if you tell them that you're hurting, all they say is to take more Tylenol and go home." (In a passing comment, a human resources employee at Pilgrim's Pride later tells me, "Everyone on the debone line complains about their hands.")

Sabrina's mother worked four years in the evisceration department and has three surgeries to show for it, each paid for by the plant. Each shift she made thousands of cutting and squeezing motions, causing the tendons in both her wrists to become inflamed;

one wrist had to be operated on twice. After the last surgery she returned to work for a few months, but when her wrists started hurting again, her husband convinced her to quit. Even years later, Sabrina says that her mother's hands "still aren't normal," pointing to a recent attempt to make tamales that was cut short by wrist pain.

Dr. Don Beach, whose office is in the town of Moulton, about thirty miles east of Russellville, sees a lot of poultry workers. His patients come from three states—Alabama, Mississippi, and Tennessee—traveling considerable distances because Dr. Beach speaks Spanish. He's been a doctor in the area for sixteen years and nearly one-fifth of his patients are immigrants. "The most common problem for line workers that I see—especially the debone workers— is carpal tunnel," he tells me when I visit his office.

But during breaks people don't often talk about ailments, and most of the positions on DSI place much less stress on the hands than debone. Although line workers are using their hands, many of the tasks in DSI—lining up breasts on a belt or snatching sections of nuggets and strips—are easier than the thousands of cuts debone workers make with knives and scissors. During breaks I see men and women from debone flexing their hands and massaging their wrists as they sit in booths, but it seems like folks deal with the pain in the same way that Ben does: privately, without complaint, and with painkillers.

OFFICIAL GOVERNMENT STATISTICS paint a very different picture of working in the poultry industry. According to the Labor Department, it is very unlikely that a poultry plant worker will develop a musculoskeletal disorder (MSD) such as carpal tunnel or tendonitis. In 2006, only 20.8 of every 10,000 poultry workers missed work due to an MSD. By comparison, toy store employees were more than twice as likely to miss work due to an MSD.

To account for the low incidence of MSDs, which were four times higher for poultry workers a decade ago, the industry points to improvements like more ergonomic workstations, the rotation of jobs, and the introduction of machinery to replace some line workers. In the words of Richard Lobb, the National Chicken Council spokesperson, "Workplace safety is a key objective and core value for all poultry processing companies."

But this "core value" and government statistics are called into question by recent reports. A Duke University study, published in 2007, interviewed nearly 300 female workers at two poultry plants in North Carolina. They found that 43 percent reported symptoms of MSDs. The study blamed the high rate of MSDs in part on the lack of workplace safety regulation. The maximum line speed, for example, is set by the USDA—and takes into consideration only food safety, without worrying about whether such speeds are safe for workers.

"Since the USDA began setting line speeds in 1968, the pace has increased from less than 20 birds a minute to the current maximum of 91 birds a minute," says Hester Lipscomb, an associate professor of occupational and environmental medicine at Duke and the study's senior author. Lipscomb believes that the women didn't complain or seek treatment for their injuries because they were worried about losing their jobs. (It's worth mentioning that these weren't undocumented immigrants; all the women in the study were African American.)[12]

In 2008, the *Charlotte Observer* published "The Cruelest Cuts," a weeklong series on the poultry industry.[13] During a twenty-two-month investigation, they interviewed workers from thirteen plants and various companies, focusing especially on the House of Raeford, a chicken and turkey processor with seven plants in the Carolinas. On paper, House of Raeford was an extremely safe place to work: Over a four-year period at their 800-employee plant in West Columbia, South Carolina, not a single worker suffered from an MSD, while another of their plants had a five-year streak without a lost time accident.

But these statistics contradicted what reporters heard from doctors and workers. "I don't know a single worker who doesn't have some sort of pain in their hand," Dr. Jorge Garcia, who has seen an estimated 1,000 poultry workers in South Carolina, told the paper. The *Observer* interviewed more than 130 workers who said they had been injured on the job; three-fourths of these injuries were to their hands and wrists. Some complained they were denied a request to see doctors; others contended that they were fired after being injured. The *Observer* eventually obtained internal injury log reports for three House of Raeford plants, and soon discovered the reason for the company's stellar safety streak: They failed to report more than half the injuries to OSHA. When they did record injuries, they often rushed workers back to the plant floor just hours after surgery so that they wouldn't have to report a missed day.

Bob Whitmore, who has directed OSHA's record-keeping system for twenty years, was presented with the *Observer*'s findings—most backed up by medical documents from injured workers—along with the injury log reports. He concluded that House of Raeford brazenly broke workplace laws, and went on the record to admit that the injury rates for poultry processors are likely two to three times higher than official government figures indicate.

In response to the series, North Carolina's Occupational Safety and Health division launched an investigation that found 49 serious safety violations at one of the company's plants and proposed $178,000 in fines. The federal government also indicted a plant manager and a head of human resources, along with about a dozen supervisors, for knowingly hiring undocumented workers.

Unfortunately for many of the workers, they also raided one of the plants and arrested more than 330 immigrants. Most were deported, while dozens are serving prison time for using false documents or reentering the country illegally.

The *Observer* also found that OSHA inspections of poultry plants were at a fifteen-year low and that federal guidelines written in 2002 made it easier for companies to hide MSDs in the injury logs (when they bothered to report injuries). It was a neat feedback loop: Weakened federal guidelines and enforcement allowed companies to underreport injuries; a company that reported low injury rates was less likely to be inspected. Companies saved money. Poultry plants were safer than toy stores. The only people not prospering from the arrangement were the people it was putatively designed to protect: workers.

I'VE STOPPED BY human resources twice to ask Bill, the overnight HR manager, about a transfer to debone, so I figure this persistence has paid off when Barbara tells me at the beginning of the week that I'm needed elsewhere. Instead, I'm told to make combos again. This time I am working with a partner. David is a recent high school graduate from Haleyville who has been at the plant less than a month, and judging by his physique could be training for a triathlon. As we're waiting for the combo supplies to be delivered, I comment on the size of his arms. "Been working out?"

"Lifting weights every day." He looks at me with curiosity. "You don't talk like you're from around here. Mind if I ask what you're doing?" I tell him my story about liking to travel, and he nods his head. "I'm the same way. I want more than what I can get in Haleyville. That's why I'm going to sign up for the air force." He hopes to join the special forces and teach fighting and survival skills, which would mean, according to what he's heard, that he wouldn't be deployed anywhere "unless it gets real bad." I think of Iraq and Afghanistan but say nothing.

With two people doing what I previously did alone, we work for only about three hours the first night. Most of the time we sit around on boxes, David chewing his Grizzly wintergreen tobacco and me staring at the same man placing the same lids on the same boxes. It's a wonder he hasn't gone crazy.

Day two is even slower. The plant just isn't using that many combos right now, and once we've got a dozen made, the area becomes crowded, so we have to wait for them to be picked up. It feels like we're doing something wrong by sitting around, so I try to keep busy, but there's really not much to do. I sweep up a little—totally unnecessary—and engage in a host of pointless tasks like polishing the handles of a scissor with my shirtsleeve. I also start making the combos very deliberately, walking around the cardboard containers with the plastic wrap as slowly as possible. I usually walk around the combos in a counterclockwise direction but start switching this up: This counts as my entertainment for the night.

By the third evening I don't even try to look busy. I want to transfer out of here; I want a supervisor to realize that Pilgrim's Pride is wasting money and put me into debone, or DSI, or anywhere that actually has something for me to do. In a plant that pushes its workers to keep up a fast pace, I've somehow found the one job in which I can literally do nothing. It may seem strange to complain, but the truth is that a night of sitting around and freezing my ass off passes a lot more slowly than one in which I'm actually doing something. Ever have a day at the office where you didn't have a single thing to do? Remember how long that day lasted? That's how I'm feeling, except my office doesn't have an Internet connection and is located in a walk-in freezer, so I'm also shivering like mad and tapping out songs on my knees and occasionally jumping up and down.

So I start walking around. Not to be rebellious or for journalistic purposes—I've already seen most areas of the plant—but simply because I need something to do. I walk circles around DSI, I stroll past the debone line, I make repeated and unnecessary trips to the bathroom. I say hi to Kyle as he shovels ice into combos, I check in on Mario and Jesús, I observe Ben struggling with a few heavy tubs. But it's cold just standing around and gawking, so I saunter around the much warmer break room and then figure what the hell and buy a coffee and drink it in a booth. It's not break time but no one says anything, so I put my head down and fall asleep for who knows how long, then walk back to my station and see that we still have thirteen combos waiting to be picked up. David is sitting on a box staring at the ground. When he sees me, he shrugs then spits tobacco juice into a bottle he has tucked away in a shirt pocket. So I make another round. By Thursday, workers in rehang, who have watched me do very little as they keep up a frantic pace, make a sign of rubbing their fingers with their thumb when I pass: easy money.

"*Dinero fácil,*" Mario tells me during break, echoing their sentiments. Maybe so, but I can't take this much longer. I complain to Barbara that I have nothing to do, but she says that I'm to stay put. I stop by the HR office but Bill isn't around. Finally, on one of my strolls I try to circumvent the bureaucracy by asking the debone supervisor, a Mexican immigrant named Carlos, if he needs any help. He looks at me, confused for a moment, but says he'll see what he can do. I would bet quite a bit of money this is the first time a worker has requested a transfer to his department.

On the last night of work for the week, I meet Fernando, a Guatemalan in the rehang department. I've seen him give me the easy money gesture a number of times, and during a break he calls me over. He's sitting alone in his booth, and is surprised to learn I speak Spanish and have traveled through Guatemala. He tells me that he never went to school—not even grade school—and harvested sugar cane as a kid. He was eighteen when he came to the United States in 1999. For some reason he seems to trust me instantly, and without prodding reveals that he spent five months on the border in Nogales, Mexico, working in construction to earn money to pay a smuggler to guide him across.

"But how did you get a job here?" I ask. "They checked out my Social Security number and everything." This is something I've been curious about but afraid to ask.

He smiles. "It's a real number; it just belongs to someone else. I paid for it after I came here." He doesn't know the owner of the number and doesn't appear particularly interested in finding out.

"Supposedly he's Puerto Rican. Where are you staying?" I describe my trailer's location. "I know that trailer. I live nearby. If you want sometime you could go to church with me. Do you go to church?"

"No, not normally. But I'd go with you." As people start heading back we exchange phone numbers.

"I go to services on Saturday night," he says. "If you want to go, give me a call and I'll pick you up."

RELIGION IS VERY important in Russellville, and a more determined reporter would already have spent his weekends visiting different congregations instead of camped out in the library. Even though I have yet to step inside a church, I've nonetheless been struck by the degree to which they dominate the landscape. On one of my walking tours of downtown, the first place of worship I noticed was Faith Outreach Mission, its name freshly emblazoned in a bright red font over a modern black façade. Two red-and-orange flame decals were affixed to its glass windows, along with an image of Jesus, a crown of thorns atop his head. The effect was dramatic and aggressive.

Next door I noticed the Church of God, which was within sight of My Father's House Church, which was near Iglesia Pentecostes.

Storefronts on the next block included The Church on the Street, Ministerio Emmanuel, and Igelsia Bethel del Congreso. The string of churches was broken up by a Spanish bookstore and the Eagle's Nest Youth Center. In the bookstore, every title was about Jesus; the youth center was a space for teenagers "where living for Jesus is cool." One block north was the First United Baptist Church, followed by the First United Methodist Church, which was across the street from the Church of Christ, which was near the Casa del Padre, which sat directly opposite the New Beginning Worship Center (which was looking for musicians to join its praise and worship team).

I call Fernando on Saturday afternoon and a few hours later he pulls into my driveway, his eighteen-month-old son, Ricky, in a car seat in the back. Fernando's evangelical church is located in the eastern section of Russellville, not far from the highway, and when we enter, thirty people are already seated on folding chairs and singing. The crowd seems to be entirely Guatemalan except for a bearded white man named Jimmy, who doesn't speak Spanish but later says that he enjoys the energy of the group.

And there is a lot of energy: The church's amplification system seems more appropriate for a large hall with hundreds of congregants. We take seats in the fourth row, about twenty feet from the stage, where eight speakers are lined up, each five feet tall. A guitarist strums one chord repeatedly, the bassist plucks two notes, and a drummer keeps up a steady four-beat rhythm. None of their efforts are easy to hear, as they are drowned out by the cacophony created by two very enthusiastic men on keyboards. While they occasionally tap out simple melodies, the pair prefers the dizzying number of special effects generated by their machines, and at times the results sound less like music than a fireworks display. "Jesus Christ is everywhere!" Ba-boom! "From Guatemala to Alabama!" Ba-da-boom! I'm not much of a singer, but it doesn't take long for me to get into the act, standing and clapping with the group.

As the singing continues the audience grows livelier. In the pauses between words, people start shouting "Hallelujah!" and "*¡Cristo vive!*" (Christ lives). We keep this up for sixty minutes until the guest pastor—a short man with dark skin and a white double-breasted suit—takes the microphone. His sermon emphasizes the idea that if we follow Jesus we will meet him in heaven.

Once he has finished speaking, we reach a period called free time, which I assumed was set aside for mingling and drinking coffee. Instead it is a chance for members to come up and share their stories. Tonight's speaker is a solidly built Guatemalan man dressed in jeans and a flannel shirt, by far the least formally attired person present (many of the congregants are wearing suits and dresses). He speaks eloquently about coming to the United States as a teenager to better his life and then succumbing to alcohol. It is a brutally honest account—he mentions visiting prostitutes while working in the fields of California and "doing other things that I knew I shouldn't do, but that I didn't seem able to stop." In Russellville he has sobered up, found God, and "become more honest and less ashamed." By the time he finishes, tears are streaming down his face. The audience stands and applauds loudly, then begins another song.

Once the service concludes, we move to another room for a quick meal of tortillas, rice, and chicken. On the way home, Fernando tells me that he too had a problem with alcohol when he arrived. Like many American teenagers, it seems that he started drinking out of boredom. He didn't know very many people, he was away from his family, and there wasn't a whole lot to do in Russellville. Like Dagoberto, the rally organizer, and the man who made the church presentation, Fernando credits church with helping him swear off alcohol, because "at the church you have people who look after you and care for you."

When I was young, I remember church as a sterile place where I had to sit down and stay quiet, but in Russellville the institution appears to play an opposite role, providing a space where people can let their guards down. Walking around downtown, the immigrants I pass often look serious and even apprehensive. Church, on the other hand, is a forum where folks can talk and laugh and sing, a place where they can share the many stresses that come with being an immigrant in a new land and receive critical moral support. I later attend an overflowing crowd at Good Shepherd Catholic Church, where I recognize dozens of faces from the plant. The mood at Good Shepherd, like Fernando's church, is celebratory.

"When I arrived they held a great welcoming party for me," says Father Jim Hedderman. Hedderman, who stands 6 foot 3 inches tall and weighs "255 pounds and going down," recently arrived in town from Huntsville. Known as Father Jaime, he is a jolly presence who takes a more lighthearted approach to Catholicism: He describes his perspective as, "No guilt, no guilt—we've had enough guilt already!" With a church of 400 families—350 of them immigrant—he loves the new assignment. "It is so *fun*," he says, laughing. "We have a soccer field behind the church, people playing all sorts of games—there's a spirit of youth and energy here." He speaks Spanish but also hears confessions in various indigenous languages like Quiché and Q'anjob'al.

"You don't find as much isolation among the Hispanic culture as you do among Anglos," he tells me. Along with strong family ties, it is the church that plays the central role in creating a sense of community. Although many of his immigrant parishioners are earning poverty wages, they usually have large support systems of friends and relatives. "The majority of people coming to the church for financial assistance are whites," he says. "They are the ones who can feel very alone."

CHAPTER 10

On Sunday night a debone supervisor stands in our path as we head onto the processing floor. "Everybody stop and wash your hands!" she shouts, motioning to a long sink against the wall that is typically ignored. I am walking in with Ben, and like everyone else we grumble and wonder what's going on, but do as we're told. Already waiting at DSI, Kyle has heard a rumor that "the Russians are coming." Apparently one of the company's Russian clients will be inspecting the plant before renewing a leg meat contract, and so for a few days we are to put on a show and act as if we always wash our hands at this station. "This happens every time someone important comes," Kyle says.

The news about the Russians provides a momentary distraction from what is usually the most punishing night of the week. Sundays are the hardest for me—and many others—because we've returned to a normal sleep schedule over the weekend. This wasn't my original plan; I figured that I would become a night owl and maintain a daytime sleeping schedule even on my days off. But after a week of fitful sleep, I find that I need the weekend to recharge, and often sleep twelve hours a night.

During the first break I put my head down but am awakened by a tap on the shoulder. "You eat hot dogs?" Kyle asks. I shake my head. Cindy has packed him a lunch of franks but he's no longer hungry: He just spent three hours in a department called MSC (mechanically separated chicken). "They take the chicken skeletons and grind them up in a machine," he says. "They come out the other side like franks in this brown paste. I sit there looking for foreign objects in the bones before they are ground up." He shivers.

"Foreign objects like what?"

"Anything, I guess. Plastic, pieces of tape. I've been finding tape—found maybe fifteen so far."

"And if you miss one?"

"Then I guess someone will be eating tape in their hot dog. I saw a chicken eye pass by, didn't touch that. You want my hot dogs?"

"Nope."

"Maybe if I worked here for a couple of weeks I'd get used to it. But I don't think I can eat these right now." I mentally add a walk-through of MSC to my list of areas I want to visit before I leave the plant; my agenda already includes a tour of the live hang floor and paw (chicken feet) department, where I hope to surreptitiously snap a couple of photos. I'm saving this mission for my last week of work—I have two left—just in case a supervisor catches me and asks what the hell I'm doing.

There is some amusement tonight on the line, thanks to Debbie. After the break, while I am dumping for Mario, he slows the pace in which he places the breasts on the line.

"*¿Qué pasa?*" I shout.

"It's not cutting right," Mario says. He points at the spot where the first slice is made to lop off the top. "If I go quicker the machine won't be able to keep up." I can't see what he is referring to, but am happy nonetheless: The slower pace means I don't have to dump as many tubs. After a few minutes he stops entirely. "It's not working."

Debbie passes by, pauses at the bin, and shouts, "*¡Ándale, Mario!*" Mario looks at her and points to the machine, starting to say something. "Hurry, Mario. *¡Ándale!*" With Debbie still hovering, he shrugs and starts throwing the breasts on the belt, trying to hide a growing smile. Satisfied, she walks away.

"Stop! Mario, stop!" Less than a minute later the machine has jammed, incorrectly cutting a bunch of breasts that will now be discarded. Mario, usually sober-faced, is grinning widely. We pull off our gloves and wait for the mechanics. One of the women lining up the breasts calls me over angrily.

"Who told you to start up again?"

"Debbie."

"Aaargh! I knew it! She doesn't have a clue. If I—"

"Hey, what's wrong?" Debbie has popped out from behind the slicing contraption. "You doing okay?"

The woman grabs her back. "Oh, nothing. Just my back is hurting."

Standing next to the bin with Mario, I say, "You should be a supervisor. You know more than her, for sure."

"I can't. You need a GED." If that's true, it's nonsense—though it might explain why, in a plant where at least one-third of the workers are immigrants, there is only one Latino supervisor, the Mexican immigrant in the debone department whom I spoke to about transferring.

I rest for a few more moments and then join Ben in dumping tubs for the other line, which is running smoothly. As always, his cheeks are bright red and sweat is pouring down his face. "What's up, loser?" he asks, glad for the help. Five minutes later, Barbara yells for us to stop this line, as well.

For the next thirty minutes no one is doing anything. Jesús goes to the bathroom; Ben leans against the wall, recuperating and flexing his right wrist, still with a brace around it; the six women who line up breasts are talking to each other. I toss a few pieces of ice at Kyle, who is standing across the line and leaning on the shovel he uses to deposit dry ice in combos. My throws sail wide and he doesn't notice: He's in another animated conversation with someone about the prospects of the University of Alabama's football team this year. The only people not enjoying the break are Debbie and Barbara, who are staring at the machine while the mechanics go to work, probably with no better understanding of what is wrong than we have, though making a point of scrunching up their faces as if in deep concentration. Debbie in particular seems distraught by the malfunctions, and walks back and forth along the line in agitation.

"She's pissed that we're resting," I say to Mario.

"She always gets upset when the machine breaks. One time she even started crying."

I ponder this as I join Ben in leaning against the wall. In my mind, Debbie has grown to embody everything that is wrong with bosses: all-powerful, demanding, condescending. I've even started to think of her as some sort of big shot that needs to be taken down a level. But she cried when the machine broke down? Imagining tears streaking down her face as she pounds the machine in frustration triggers a realization: She isn't too high above us. A typical plant worker earns less than $17,000 a year; I doubt Debbie makes more than $25,000. Sure, her work is less dangerous and less repetitive, but she's earning working-class wages. And unlike many of my coworkers and me, she is very emotionally invested in the work. I resolve to try and think nicer thoughts about her.

Ah, but how quickly sympathy disappears! Once the line is back up and running, she comes over as I'm lifting an eighty-pound tub. "I don't want Mario taking any breaks," she says. "You need to make sure the tub is always completely full so that he doesn't have to reach. *No reaching.*" I grunt as I raise the tub to my chest and dump the meat over the lip of the bin. When Mario works quickly, he can sometimes clear out the section of the bin nearest him, and so he reaches across to pull breasts stacked on the other side. Over the course of an eight-hour shift, there is no way that this movement could use more than a minute's time.

"No breaks, Mario," she says as she walks away. "*Ándale.*"

I tell Mario about the no reaching rule, and he scoffs. "She thinks this is easy, but I'd like to see her come do it," he says. "It's very easy when all you have to do is talk."

At 7:40 a.m., when I've dumped the last tub and Mario is finishing up, Debbie walks over, evidently concerned that she hasn't caused enough trouble. "*Ándale*, Mario!" After a long shift and several visits from Debbie, Mario has finally reached the limits of his tolerance, and he does the unthinkable: He begins to slow his pace. The message is obvious—get out of my face and let me do my work—but a smiling Debbie doesn't seem to get it. "Come on, Mario!" Mario keeps up the slower pace until he places the last chicken breast on the belt, all the while listening to Debbie's encouragement. Once the tub is empty she actually starts clapping.

I SLEEP UNTIL noon and wake up both restless and groggy. It is a testament to the vertiginous nature of the night shift at a chicken plant that, entering my second month, I simultaneously feel as if my time in Alabama is rushing past in a blur, creating few distinct memories while hidden within every blurry day are stubborn hours that refuse to pass normally, stretching so long as to nearly stand still. Add the intense daytime heat and humidity with the frigid nighttime temperatures of the processing plant—along with varying degrees of sleep deprivation—and the most precise description of my state of mind is discombobulated.

I tell myself that I should get out more during the day. With two weeks left, I am growing convinced that I need to augment my work experiences with more traditional reporting. Up to this point I have purposely kept a low profile so as not to attract undue attention, and I have told only a few select people about my book. I've been in Russellville for seven weeks and I've settled in nicely—now is the time to start exploring. And I already know my first goal. I want somehow to gain access to the inside of a chicken farm.

Hundreds of thousands of live chickens are trucked in every day to be slaughtered and processed, many passing within a hundred feet of my trailer. But though I watch the birds on their journey, and help turn them into fattening finger food, I know about only the last hour of their life. I want to walk through a factory farm where the chickens spend about six miserable weeks before reaching slaughter weight (fifty years ago, without the benefit of growth-enhancing drugs or high doses of antibiotics, this "growing" process took more than three months). I've read horror stories about these farms, where tens of thousands of birds are stuffed into cramped sheds reeking of ammonia from chicken shit, frequently collapse on broken legs that can't support their enormous breasts, and see the light of day only when they make their short trip to the slaughterhouse. But during my bike rides around the countryside, I have yet to see a single farm.

Ironically, McDonald's is the only place in Russellville that I've found with public Internet access, aside from a Christian bookstore that keeps irregular hours. After some online exploring, I'm able to download a list of factory farms in Alabama from the Environmental Protection Agency. There are dozens in Franklin County, and I select one of the nearest, which looks to be about ten miles east of my trailer.

The following afternoon I head out to the chicken farm, cycling past Mama's Kitchen and turning east. The ride takes me through miles of hilly countryside occasionally interrupted by collapsing farmhouses and trailers, which are set back from the narrow road and often obscured by brush. Some of the structures are evidently still inhabited, as twice I find—with no warning barks—a large canine sprinting several paces behind me, trying to tear off my ankles.*

I arrive at my destination—an impressive two-story brick house—in forty-five minutes, without passing a single car. Six long and low buildings are off to the left, down a dirt path: These are the sheds where the chickens are kept. I expected them to be noisy, but I don't even hear the proverbial peep. At the head of the dirt path is a sign with the Pilgrim's Pride logo, and another with some sort of bio-safety emblem and a warning not to trespass. A truck is in the driveway and as I approach the door of the house, I prepare my rap. I need to explain who I am and what I am doing as concisely and innocently as possible. I can't imagine the farmer has many unannounced visitors, and I'm probably the first adult who has ever biked up to his house to say hello. I'm also from out of town, and a journalist, and covered in sweat. I sop up the moisture from my forehead with the sleeve of my T-shirt. I hear someone approaching and take a deep breath.

---

* This is a recurring event—it happens nearly every time I ride into Russellville—that never fails to deliver at least several seconds of sheer terror. There is nothing quite like cycling through peaceful pastures, only to be set upon by a rabid-looking dog gnashing its teeth as it tries to pull you from your bike and, presumably, devour you.

A slender blond-haired woman, probably in her forties, opens the door. "Hello?"

"Hi, how are you doing?" I introduce myself as a journalist from New York City who is writing about the poultry industry. "I was riding by and saw the sign for Pilgrim's Pride and thought maybe you all raised chickens here." As I talk I do my best to read her face but find it hard to know what she is thinking. If anything, she looks skeptical.

"It's my husband that takes care of that," she says, "and he's not here."

I immediately fill the awkward silence that follows her declarative statement with talk. Friendly talk; ingratiating talk. I explain that I decided to move to Russellville for two months in order to complete a book that deals, in part, with the poultry industry. "I'm hoping to learn as much as possible—about how chickens are raised and killed and processed. I already know it's one of those industries that we all depend on but that very few people really know anything about." Still nothing—I keep talking. "So I've been working for a while at the plant and have learned how hard that work can be. But I thought it would be good to also tour a farm and interview a farmer, you know, 'cause the work they do, I'm sure, is just as hard, and I want to be able to explain that side of things."

As I'm rambling her face seems to soften. "I'm sure my husband wouldn't mind showing you around," she eventually says. "He feeds the chickens every morning at 8:30. You can stop by then if you want." I thank her and say I'll be by in the morning, then decide to give her my name and phone number so that her husband can call if anything comes up. And indeed, while I'm taking a nap that evening, he leaves me a message on my cell phone. Though he'd like to help me out, he can't give me a tour.

He tells me that as a chicken farmer he's too concerned about bio-safety; I might have a cold and pass the germs along to his chickens.

I'm frustrated, but at least I still have a long list of farms within biking distance that I can check out. Eventually I'll get lucky.

But the following day is simply too hot, so instead of going in search of another farm I decide to eat lunch at Mama's Kitchen. With my time winding down, I have been meaning to stop by and tell Sabrina that I'm a journalist. I know she won't blow my cover, and she'll probably get a kick out of the project. Also, there is something in me that wants to divulge my secret, to explain my project to other people.

Thus far in Alabama, when I've told someone that I'm a reporter—which I consider to be very important news—they are completely unmoved. But Sabrina's reaction is dramatic. Standing behind the store's counter, she lets out a relieved sigh and breaks into a wide grin. I stand there proudly: She is evidently impressed that I've written books and articles.

"Gabriel, I was sure you were immigration."

The pride turns to shock. She believed I was an undercover federal agent with Immigration and Customs Enforcement (ICE).

"I thought you were here to get a job and investigate and deport the workers. You're a journalist? I have to tell my friend!" She goes into the kitchen and returns with a newspaper clipping about a new deportation scheme by the U.S. government, speaking into her phone rapidly. I hear her tell the person on the other end about me. "He works with the union—he's in Postville right now," she says after hanging up. Three months earlier, ICE conducted a massive raid at Agriprocessors Inc.'s kosher slaughterhouse in Postville, Iowa, and arrested 389 undocumented immigrants. About 300 of the immigrants, primarily from Guatemala, were convicted of identity fraud in speedy trials and sentenced to five months in federal prison, in what was the largest immigration enforcement operation at a single workplace. (Later that year, in August, an even larger raid in Laurel, Mississippi, would result in the arrest of 595 undocumented immigrants working at a Howard Industries transformer plant.)

In retrospect, the fact that I might have been an immigration agent was an obvious possibility. I knew that in April 2008, while I was planning out the details of the trip, ICE had raided five Pilgrim's Pride plants—in Arkansas, Tennessee, Florida, West Virginia, and Texas—and took 400 workers into custody. Although they hadn't targeted Russellville, workers had undoubtedly been following the news closely. But I naively figured that once I started speaking Spanish and displaying my sympathies, people would trust me.

Sabrina evidently did trust me, at the outset—at least enough to rent me her trailer. But I learn that she started wondering about me and speaking to her friends, and became convinced I had an ulterior motive (which I did—just not to deport immigrants). Why else would an American citizen who spoke perfect English and passable Spanish—and who lived in New York City—wind up renting a broken-down trailer and working the graveyard shift? I recall, too, her exact words when describing the trailer:

"You should know that there are only Mexicans and Guatemalans living around it."

And my reaction: "*Perfecto.*"

For weeks now, Sabrina, an ardent defender of immigrants, believed that she was renting a trailer to an immigration agent. Earlier, she had invited me to her daughter's fifteenth-birthday celebration—her *quinceanera*. Now I understand why she had retracted the invitation: She figured it was an intelligence-gathering activity.

Biking back to the trailer, I feel like a fool. Do most of the immigrants at the plant think I'm with immigration? Does Jesús? Or Mario? I was certain that I had a rapport with both of them, but I was certain that Sabrina and I had a rapport too. I'm the friendly white guy who speaks Spanish and is interested in hearing details about the lives of immigrants. What sounded innocent now seems pretty damn suspicious. I decide to tell Jesús and Mario tonight about my book.

AS I'M TIEING on my smock and noticing a long tear down one side, Barbara comes up to me.

"HR says they want to see you."

"About what?"

"Don't know. They just said for me to bring you." After more than a month of requesting a move to debone, maybe they're finally taking me up on the offer. I'm glad, but also annoyed, since I'm eager to divulge my secret to Mario and Jesús. I suppose it doesn't matter; I can tell them during break.

I follow Barbara back through the plant and down a series of offices. We turn into one room, where a white man with wispy brown hair is seated behind a desk. He looks to be in his late thirties. A younger Latina woman is perched on a chair to his right.

"You don't need me, right?" Barbara asks before heading back.

"Have a seat. I'm Eric," the man behind the desk says. He explains that he is the head of human resources for the plant. I have the first flash of anxiety. "This is a complicated story, and we have a lot of questions, but we should probably start first at one point and then go backward. We've been speaking to corporate and our lawyers, and we decided that in today's environment, we're going to have to let you go."

I hear the words clearly, but they seem far away. "Let me go?"

"We got a call from one of our farmers. He said a journalist wanted to get a tour of the farm, and that he was working at the plant. So we pulled your file. We went on your Web site and read your writings."

The pace of events has exceeded my ability to make sense of them, as if someone has smothered my brain with a pillow. "Uhhh . . . oh?" I look up to see Bill, the HR night manager, standing in the doorway.

"Hey, Bill, you know Gabriel, right?" He nods a hello and steps into the room. Eric tells me that he's been given a list of items from the attorneys of Pilgrim's Pride that he has to go through. If I've taken photographs or video in the plant, I need to turn in the footage. (I haven't done either, as I was saving any documentation for next week.) Eric has me surrender my ID card—which I had hoped to save as a memento—and explains that had I contacted Pilgrim's Pride as a journalist, perhaps something could have been worked out in terms of me working at the plant. There's no reason to argue the point, though it's obviously false. Pilgrim's Pride wouldn't have acceded to my request to work at the plant with knowledge that I was a journalist for the same reason they are now firing me.*

"Okay, I think that's everything the lawyers wanted me to say," Eric says, sounding relieved. "This has gone much better than we expected." Thus far I've listened quietly. Did they anticipate that

---

* The following week, Trevor Stokes, a reporter with the *Times Daily*, a paper out of the nearby town of Florence, visited the plant in an attempt to get a comment for a story he was writing about immigration in Franklin County. His brief "interview" went poorly: The plant manager ushered him off the property and refused even to give her name. So I think it is safe to say that the company would not have "worked something out" with me had I been up front about my identity and project.

I would jump up and angrily denounce my firing? "Now that that's out of the way," Eric continues, "I'm hoping we can just talk. We've all been scratching our heads over here since we found out. I mean, I've only been here three weeks, and I find out there's a guy here from Brooklyn, and this is how I have to meet him?" It turns out Eric is a new hire, having arrived not long after me, and is originally from upstate New York.

Since receiving the farmer's phone call, Eric has read a number of my articles and ordered both of my books from Amazon. "I'm fascinated by what you've been writing," he tells me. "I almost signed up for your newsletter, but I figured that would be strange to do before we met. Can you tell us what exactly you're doing?" By now I'm mentally caught up with what's happening, so I'm able to give my five-minute marketing pitch: I'm writing about immigrant work by actually doing jobs alongside immigrants.

"I'm sorry I never got you a job in debone," Bill says once I'm finished, sounding like he means it.

"That's okay—dumping tubs was hard enough. I didn't want to push too much, 'cause I knew it was a strange request."

The Latina woman, whose name I don't catch, laughs. "That's right—no one wants to be transferred to debone." Like Eric, she's been reading my articles. "I really admire the work that you're doing," she says. This is getting weird, but I'm starting to enjoy it: I've got a mini fan club in human resources. On later reflection, I realize that I've probably provided some intrigue and relief from a job that—like the processing work—must get pretty monotonous and mind-numbing: endless orientations and worker interviews and everything else that constitutes the constant struggle to keep a poultry plant staffed. I would have imagined that this scene—being caught and fired—would be more hostile, but instead the room has a feeling of camaraderie.

And so, fifteen minutes after the firing business has been completed, I'm sitting in the same chair, feeling quite comfortable and chatting it up with the trio. Eric asks if I've read *The Omnivore's Dilemma* by Michael Pollan—I have—and points out the book on a shelf. It's not a title I'd expect to find in a plant of the largest poultry company in the world, but Eric tells me that his old job was at Petaluma Poultry, the organic chicken company that Pollan profiles. (It's not a very positive portrayal: Pollan finds 20,000 "free range" chickens crowded into a shed with very little room to move—much like factory-farmed chickens.)

I tell them my next stop on the immigrant work circuit will be New York City. "Let me know if you need a reference," Eric jokes, before the others file out and he gives me a ride to my trailer. I type up the notes of what happened and call my parents to tell them the news. "Can they just do that?" my mom asks. "Is it legal for them to fire you?" In the heat of the moment the question hadn't occurred to me. Either way, I explain that with my cover blown, I didn't feel like sticking around. I wanted to know what it was like to work at a poultry plant, which required that the company not know I was a journalist. (I later learn that since I was an "at will" employee, Pilgrim's Pride could legally fire me without cause.)

"You don't sound too upset," my father says. He's right. It took several minutes to recover from the initial shock of being discovered. Once I did, I was able to enjoy what should have been an awkward and unpleasant post-firing interview. Instead, it turned into a nice little chat—cheery even. While I was doing my best to remember each line that was said, in order to report it as accurately as possible, I was also distracted by a thought that kept surfacing every few minutes. With each repetition, a wave of relief washed over me: This means I don't have to dump tubs tonight. This means I don't have to dump tubs tonight.

Kyle stops by my trailer the next morning. "Where'd they put you last night? I didn't see you at break and couldn't find you when we got out." He listens to my story about being fired and about my real occupation. He is quiet and interested.

Finally, he says: "Gabriel, you're one slick motherfucker." It's one of the best compliments I've ever received.*

---

* Although clearly false: A slick motherfucker wouldn't get caught and fired.

Part Three

FLOWERS AND FOOD

October–December, New York, New York

GETTING THE JOB

In October I'm ready to begin searching for work in my place of residence, New York City. Yuma and Russellville made the selection of work easy: Each had one major industry in town, and I just hoped they'd hire me. Here, one of my difficulties is deciding what type of work to seek out. New York is a city of immigrants: They clean our clothes and care for our children; build our homes and vacuum our offices; drive the taxis we hail; and cook the food we order. With 36 percent of New York City's residents foreign-born, one would be hard-pressed to find an industry that wasn't in some way dependent on their labor. So what should I aim for?

This question is tied up with another challenge of my project's new locale: Many low-wage immigrants find work in the city's sprawling underground economy. Here, employers are generally much smaller than Dole or Pilgrim's Pride—they might be a one-man construction company or a single, non-chain restaurant. Almost none of the dozens of undocumented immigrants I've known, either through my organizing work or as a journalist, had what we would call a traditional work arrangement. Instead, they are paid off the books, usually in cash, with no overtime and frequently earning less than the minimum wage. Many find jobs through informal references—someone tells a boss that their sister needs work—or unlicensed labor agencies. Manual laborers gather on corners hoping to be picked up for a day's work. I don't stand a chance on the corners, I'm likely to elicit suspicion if I entered a labor agency in an immigrant neighborhood, and I don't have any Mexican siblings to vouch for my dependability to their boss.

The third complication is that many workplaces are segregated by ethnicity. A construction foreman might want only Mexican workers; the head of a dry cleaner could prefer Chinese employees. At root, the informal referral systems and segregated workforces are a direct result of an employer's preference for a docile workforce. The bosses are breaking the law, day after day after day. They hope to find undocumented workers that they can exploit by paying sub-minimum wages and avoiding overtime.* "How do

---

* In response, some immigrants who are legally authorized to work instead present their employer with obviously forged immigration papers they have purchased on the black market. Because they know that the boss prefers to hire undocumented workers, their status as a legal immigrant, in such situations, becomes a guarded secret.

you plan on getting someone to hire you?" one of my friends asks, to which I have no real answer.

I'M PUZZLING OVER this riddle in my study when I hear snippets of Spanish. I prop open a window and lean out from the fourth floor. A crew of Ecuadorian workers, installing new windows, is perched precariously on wooden scaffolding held up by a primitive-looking system of ropes and pulleys. I ask about work and they tell me to speak to their Indian boss, who can be found at a midtown Manhattan worksite early each weekday morning. He pays cash, $100 a day.

I'm not able to track down the boss, but while cycling through Manhattan I nearly collide with a restaurant delivery worker who is blasting down Sixth Avenue against traffic. He apologizes to me for nearly ending my life, but the episode, and the sheer number of immigrant delivery workers I encounter on the street, leads me to spend the next week trying for a restaurant job, especially as I have read several stories about construction work drying up with the downswing in the economy. Without being able to think of a better strategy, I spend my days pedaling up to delivery workers to ask if they know whether their restaurant is hiring, explaining that I'm hoping for a job in dishwashing or delivery. This tactic surprises a few people; one older man, when I turn to ask my question as we're coasting up Eighth Avenue, flinches so dramatically that he nearly falls over. I decide to approach people at red lights.

A handful of men tell me that their restaurants are short delivery workers. When I show up, however, the bosses—who thus far are white, Latino, or Asian—look at me skeptically and tell me the position has just been filled. I don't believe them. I finally come close to being hired at a trendy Asian fusion restaurant near Union

Square, after spending ten minutes doing my best to convince a young Thai manager that I can handle delivery.

"But it's very, very hard," he says, arguing that I should consider a waiter position instead. "The Mexicans do the delivery, and you're not Mexican."

This is hard to refute. He finally hands me a card and tells me to stop by the next week. "Maybe the Mexicans will say yes, we'll see," he says, as if the delivery workers make the hiring decisions.

I inquire about jobs at twenty or so other restaurants over the next two days, without success. One morning, as I'm biking up a busy avenue in Chelsea to check out a few eateries near Central Park, I'm forced to slam on my brakes. A virtual forest has been planted in the bike lane. Hundreds of long branches, tied together with twine, are leaning against each other. Next to the branches are buckets of colorful flowers, and next to the flowers are potted plants that are overflowing into the traffic.

Cars are zipping by on my right at thirty miles per hour. As I'm standing over my bike, impatiently waiting for traffic to thin, I notice that two Latino men are frantically tossing bales of branches into the back of a large white commercial truck. Three other men, who are speaking Spanish to each other, come out of a storefront and join in. It slowly dawns on me that I've just entered New York's flower district.

"*¿Su jefe necesita gente? Estoy buscando trabajo.*" I ask the men if their boss needs any help.

One of them turns toward me; he is wearing a Guns 'N Roses *Appetite for Destruction* T-shirt. I take this as a good omen. "I don't know. You should go talk to the Greek inside."

I lock up my bike and walk into a storefront jammed with plants and trees. I squeeze through a narrow pathway to the back, where I find the "Greek," a man named Tony, sitting on a wooden stool and talking rapidly into a telephone. He is wearing jeans and a stained short-sleeve shirt with a drooping collar, and while his gray hair is thinning on the top, there is still enough on the sides to be unruly, giving the impression that he recently rolled out of bed. "Yes, beautiful maple, sir, best maple you can find," he says. "Come pick it up. Yes, sir, yes . . . okay." He hangs up.

"How can I help you, young man?"

"I'm looking for work."

"What kind of work?"

"Anything."

"Good, that's good, young man," he says approvingly; I almost expect him to pat me on the head. He writes down my name and phone number and sticks it on the wall. "The woman is out right now but I'll talk to her. Come back tomorrow. Maybe we can get you something." This feels very old-school, very mom-and-pop. It could provide a nice contrast to my last two jobs, both within multinational corporations.

"I have a really good feeling about the job," I tell my partner, Daniella, that night. "For some reason it feels like home to me."

I stop by the following day, but "the woman" is still out. "Come back tomorrow, young man," Tony tells me between phone calls. While I observe him during these brief interactions, he strikes me as the quintessential New Yorker: fast-moving, gruff, no-nonsense. Outside the shop I chat with one of the workers, Lucas, who keeps his long black hair in a ponytail and is wearing a blue tank top that reveals powerful arms. He's confused when I explain that I'm looking for work, thinking instead that I'm searching for a certain kind of plant.

"Oh, if you want a job, he [Tony] won't help you. He doesn't make any decisions. The real person in charge is Helen."

"That's what Tony told me. He said to come back tomorrow."

"But you don't want a job here."

"Sure I do. Why not? At least I can practice my Spanish."

"Well, maybe. But I don't think you'll like it."

"Is it that hard?" I ask.

"A little," is what I think I hear him say. Later I'll wonder about that, because *un poco* (a little) sounds similar to *es loco* (it's crazy).

I MAKE TWO more trips to the shop until I finally meet "the woman." Helen appears to be in her fifties and has blond hair; when she looks me over, her face—already tense—becomes even more pinched and pointed. I'm guessing it's been a long time since she's taken a deep breath.

"Where are you working now?" she asks. I tell her I'm unemployed.

"Where have you worked before?"

"I've done a lot of work. I've cut lettuce, construction, delivered pizzas—"

"What's the problem, you can't keep a job?"

"A lot of the jobs are seasonal, like lettuce. So they have work for only a few months."

"Where do you live?"

"Crown Heights, Brooklyn."

"Do you have a car?"

"No."

"How much rent do you pay?" A weird question, but I tell her.

"Who do you live with?"

There is no way this can be a legal question to ask a potential employee. Still, I comply: I want the job.

"What does your girlfriend do?"

A few more questions like this and she finally focuses her glare on something other than my face. She shrugs at Tony. "Okay, come by tomorrow at five in the morning. We'll see how you work."

"Before I leave, could you tell me, like, what I'll be doing or how much you pay?"

"You do whatever Tony tells you to do," she snaps. "I can't tell you money. We'll try you for a week and see what we think, then we talk about money."

CHAPTER 11

My alarm wakes me at 3:45 a.m. Thirty minutes and a shot of espresso later, I'm out the door. New York City at this hour is a magical place: deserted, quiet, manageable. It feels like my private metropolis as I cruise through downtown Brooklyn and across the Manhattan Bridge.

Lucas is in the shop with a white woman I haven't yet met; she writes up a time card for me and tells me to do whatever Lucas does. "The first thing we do is move all this stuff outside," he says. The storefront is even more claustrophobic than I remember, and as I follow Lucas deeper into the store, we have to push our way through branches as if we're bushwhacking. We spend the first fifteen minutes carrying bales of oak and maple branches outside, leaning them against the store's front window. Several other immigrant workers sleepily punch in and join us.

It's a pretty calm work environment until Tony arrives. I'm in the process of dragging two bales of birch through the front door.

"Morning," I say.

"Look at all those leaves, mister." I turn in the direction he is pointing, my early-morning brain still foggy. Leaves are strewn around the sidewalk. "Clean that up, mister. Get string and tie it up. Throw it away!" He dashes into the store.

It's not clear what I'm supposed to do. Tie up leaves with string? I tell Lucas, who is rushing past with a large plant, what Tony has said. "*Su abuelito es loco*," he replies. He's saying that Tony, whom he's calling my grandfather evidently because we're both white, is crazy.

After a few minutes of searching I finally come across a ball of twine and scissors. Tony is on the phone taking an order, so I don't bother him with questions. I cut several sections of twine and head back outside. As I'm looking at the leaves, still trying to formulate a plan, Tony rushes up to me.

"Mister!" he yells into my face. He hasn't brushed his teeth. "Mister, take the pear and put it in the corner." He points north, in the general direction of a white truck, and is off.

I stick the twine in my pocket, wondering what the branches of a pear tree might look like. Have I missed some sort of orientation? By now there are dozens of bales leaning against the store-front window. I stare at them for several seconds, until another worker passes by and points out the pear. I pick up the bale and hoist it over my right shoulder. "Put it in the corner," Tony has told me. I assume he means in the corner of the truck. I walk to the truck and am about to heave it in when I decide that it wouldn't hurt to double-check. I turn back and see Tony standing outside the store, staring at me.

"You want it in the corner of the truck?" I yell. He doesn't respond. "You want it here, in the corner of the truck?" Again, nothing. I'm sure he can hear me. Okay. I toss the pear bale in the truck. Tony walks over quickly.

"Mister, what are you doing? Mister, why didn't you listen to me? I said put it *in the corner*." I look at him blankly.

"Forget it. Hand it to me." I step inside the truck and pass him the branches. "In the corner, in the corner. That's what I told you, mister. You need to use common sense." He mutters to himself as he carries the branches up the street to the corner, dumping them in the middle of the sidewalk. Apparently someone is coming to pick them up. "Common sense, mister," he tells me when he returns. "In. The. Corner."

I WILL FOREVER remember the next five hours as being one of the most stressful periods in my life. If there is a system to the organization of the shop, I can't discern it. Tony paces back and forth, his faded jeans drooping low and the grimace on his face indicating the likelihood of cardiac arrest. His managerial style combines maximum intensity—just being in his presence causes my shirt to become soaked in sweat—with a reliance on enigmatic instructions. There is nothing here that should be so difficult: We are moving bales of branches outside, arranging plant and flower displays on the sidewalk for customers to peruse, and loading and unloading trucks. But with Tony as my boss, even the simplest task becomes damn near impossible to understand.

"We're looking sloppy out there!" he shouts in my face as I'm carrying two bales of oak, one over each shoulder. I nod. We cross paths again. This time, I'm lugging a massive pumpkin, which must weigh at least sixty pounds. Halloween is approaching. "Mister, we're looking really sloppy out there!" I have absolutely no idea what he is talking about.

Seeing my confusion, Lucas explains that when Tony shouts, "We're looking really sloppy out there!" he is actually instructing me to grab a broom and sweep the sidewalk. My task explained, I dig out a broom that is wedged between bales of magnolia. As I'm sweeping the leaves into a pile, Tony shouts from behind, "Wake up!" I turn around just in time to prevent a bale of branches from falling on me. "Wake up, mister! Put these in the truck. Gotta stay awake." I grab the branches, which have red berries hanging from them, to discover they are covered in thorns. (Later in the day I ask Lucas about gloves. "If you want them you have to buy them," he explains.)

Within an hour I'm alternating between waves of paranoia and fury. No matter what activity I am engaged in, Tony finds time to come up and make comments like, "Mister, what are you *doing*?" Often I am doing exactly what he had instructed me to do not five minutes earlier. I come to realize, after this happens a dozen times within twenty minutes, that he doesn't even seem aware that he is asking a question. Instead, he has developed two verbal tics. The first is to address everyone, incessantly, as mister. This is maddening enough; it is made worse by the fact that some of the other workers have picked up the habit. The second is that anytime he comes across workers—a frequent occurrence, as we are in a tight space—he automatically asks us what we're doing. As the boss, it would appear, his job is to accuse.

"You can't let your grandfather bother you," Lucas tells me at 9:00 a.m. We're standing behind the truck stripping leaves from birch branches, out of Tony's line of sight. "He's always like this. No one knows what he's talking about."

A tall white guy, who apparently knows Lucas, shouts out, "You've got a new guy!" Lucas nods.

"Just started," I say.

"Welcome to the jungle!" the man yells. "You learn quick enough it's crazy here."

As the morning wears on, I am relieved to see that Tony isn't singling me out; it's a jungle for everyone. By now I am working with four others, all immigrants: Lucas, Israel, and Carlos, in their late thirties or early forties, are from southern Mexico; and Antonio, a powerfully built twenty-seven-year-old, is from Honduras. None is safe from Tony's tirades, but though they make faces to each other when Tony isn't looking, they seem to be taking it in stride.

They have grown accustomed to a workday in which nothing is ever sufficiently explained, in which they are expected to jump from one random activity to another whenever Tony opens his mouth. I realize that I'm going to need to develop thick skin, and quickly.

"Right now it's good, because he can't see us," Lucas says as we continue to pull leaves from birch branches. "But the secret is to stay busy. Don't forget—they are always watching." He opens his eyes wide and moves his head back and forth, mimicking Big Brother. "If you don't know what to do, grab the broom. If they see that you are a good worker," he flexes his large right bicep, "then you shouldn't have any problems."

"Any idea how much money they will pay me?"

When he started, Lucas explains, he made between $300 and $350 a week for sixty hours of work—Sunday is the only day off. That comes to about $5 an hour. "But like I said, if they see you're a good worker they might pay more." At home that night I do the calculations. New York's minimum wage is $7.15 an hour. Factor in twenty hours of overtime, and an employer like Tony— if he's interested in complying with U.S. labor laws—owes each worker $500 before taxes.

As I'm moving goods back and forth between the store and the sidewalk, customers browse through our selection. It doesn't take long to learn to identify the basic branches: oak, maple, curly willow, birch, pear, and magnolia. My least favorite is the Washington hawthorn, with its red berries and sharp thorns. The customers, who seem mostly to be interior decorators, are of the sleek and skinny sort with spiked hair and too-tan skin; they could have walked directly into the shop from an MTV set. Some are quite nice, but a few are pushy and whiny and make no effort to get out of our way when we're balancing heavy loads. Twice I spin ever so slightly after passing customers of this type, giving a gentle tap to their heads with the back end of whatever I'm carrying over my shoulder.

RELIEF FINALLY COMES at 1:00 p.m., when Tony tells me to hop in a truck to make deliveries. The driver, Hector, is from Puerto Rico and has been working for the company for years. "How's it going, Junior?" he asks as we pull away. "This is your first day, right?"

"Yeah. This place is a little crazy."

"Don't worry about it. You can't let Tony bother you—he's always like this."

Over the next ninety minutes we make a half-dozen deliveries. Several smaller loads are for boutique flower shops; the others are large deliveries of branches for private parties ($750, for example, for magnolia and maple branches for the Union Club on the Upper East Side). The final stop is a residence near the Museum of Modern Art, where I use three different service elevators to bring a bale of pear and magnolia to an apartment on the forty-sixth floor. I'm in and out in a hurry but glimpse enough of a massive living room with a sweeping view to realize I am bringing branches to a very wealthy man (I later see a listing for a three-bedroom apartment in the building for $8.9 million).

As we're driving back to the shop, I ask Hector about the origin of the branches. He tells me that Tony has land in New Jersey where many of the trees are grown, and that a group of workers are responsible for cutting and loading the branches each day. Like lettuce, a bale of branches begins to die immediately after being cut, and so the product must be moved quickly in order to arrive looking like something you'd want to gaze on as you're sipping wine and discussing the most recent issue of the *New Yorker*.

"You getting hungry?" Hector asks.

"Yeah, was thinking about taking my break when we get back." I've been going nonstop for nearly nine hours now.

"Break?" He laughs. "They don't give you any breaks here, Junior. But if you're doing a delivery, you can grab something. Just make sure to finish it before we get back." We stop at a pizza joint and I gobble up two slices. It's 2:30 p.m. by the time we arrive back at the shop and the day is winding down—the flower district opens very early and is largely shuttered by the afternoon. After an hour of moving branches inside and sweeping up, I'm dismissed.

THE NEXT DAY I spend most of the morning hours making deliveries around the flower district—one dozen bales of various branches to G. Page Wholesale Flowers, a large shop located in the heart of the district on Twenty-eighth Street; large pumpkins to an advertising agency on Twenty-sixth Street; a collection of flowers for a nearby floral stylist.

I was too busy yesterday to get much of a sense of the flower district, though I had done some reading overnight and learned that the once sprawling region has been shrinking. In the 1960s the district was home to more than a hundred wholesalers, but today there are only about two dozen running along Twenty-eighth Street from Seventh Avenue to Broadway. (When it was formed in the mid-1890s, the district's borders went from Twenty-sixth Street to Twenty-ninth). Still, these two blocks are unlike anywhere else in the city; the urban bustle remains, but pedestrians pass beneath archways of ferns, forming single-file lines as they snake through endless rows of cut flowers and potted plants.

The main threat to the flower district has been real estate, especially since the 1990s, when the area was rezoned to make it easier to build residential buildings. As luxury buildings and hotels have displaced merchants, some advocated relocating the district to a cheaper neighborhood. A couple of years ago, the Flower Market Association—headed by Gary Page of G. Page Wholesale Flowers—believed they had enough support to move to Queens, but some merchants refused, forcing the association to scuttle the plan. As a result, Chelsea still has a couple of blocks left that remain interesting and eccentric, a reminder of what the city was like before the proliferation of generic luxury developments.

When I make my first delivery to G. Page Wholesale Flowers, it's not yet 6:00 a.m., but already dozens of Latino workers—mostly men—are frantically arranging bouquets and wrapping up flowers for customers. I make my way toward the rear with two bales of maple, passing rows of flowers bursting with color. (I am not a flower person, but I later log on to the G. Page Web site, which testifies to the global economy of cut flowers: They sell hydrangeas from Colombia, echeveria from New Zealand, roses from Ecuador, and orchids from Vietnam and Malaysia. The workforce is also geographically diverse: I speak briefly with men from Mexico, Ecuador, and Guatemala.)

Once I've completed the deliveries it's back to the same routine of trying to decipher Tony's orders. Around 10:00 a.m. one of the commercial trucks pulls in, driven by Helen, who shouts at Lucas and me to begin unloading. I walk to the back with Lucas, who pulls the rear door open. "Stay here and I'll hand the bales to you," he says.

Five seconds later, as Lucas is climbing into the truck, Helen rushes up. "What are you doing?" she shrieks at me. "Grab these, grab these!" She pulls out two bales, nearly tripping up Lucas, who is now standing in the truck, and slams them over my shoulder. "Go! Go!" I turn around and notice a black man standing several feet from me, waiting to cross the street.

"Whoa," he says softly. "What's up with her?"

I wonder the same question the rest of the day. As tiresome as Tony can be, he is no match for the sheer meanness of Helen. After we've unloaded the truck as quickly as humanly possible, I carry two bales of maple into the walk-in cooler in the back of the store.

"You need to take the trash out of the cooler," she orders as I pass.

I drop the maple in the cooler, step into the very back—and into three inches of icy water—and grab two soaked bags of trash. As I'm carrying the bags to the front, Carlos, who is standing on one of the wooden tables to my right, asks me to take a bale of magnolia that he is holding.

I place the bags of trash to my side so I don't completely block the only pathway through the store, a movement that takes anywhere from one to two seconds. I mention the elapsed time because such details are necessary to appreciate the extent to which Helen monitors our activity. "Wake up and help!" she yells, upset at the fraction of a second that I needed to position the heavy bags of sopping trash. As I'm carrying the magnolia out I hear her repeat the call for me to "wake up!" I wonder if she is on speed.

In the afternoon I feel fortunate when Helen orders me to accompany Lucas on a large walking delivery to a store on Twenty-eighth Street. The delivery includes boxes of lemon leaves and moss and bales of magnolia, which we place on a large dolly. The dolly, however, keeps wanting to swerve right—into oncoming traffic—so we have to walk slowly, and when we arrive at the building we're forced to wait several minutes for the service elevator.

As we're walking back we find Helen angrily pacing toward us. "Where have you been?" she roars, coming at us with frightening speed. I half expect her to clock Lucas and me in the face. "It took you thirty minutes to make a delivery!" It hasn't been anywhere near thirty minutes. I could also mention the broken dolly and the elevator delay, but instead follow Lucas's lead and stay silent. She turns and, now nearly running, heads back to the store. Lucas curses her in Spanish.

"He's crazy . . . she's crazy. I don't know why you want to work here. If I was an American—if I had papers—I would move on to something else." He's been at the shop for several years and, like the other Latino workers, he is undocumented.

I have to admit that the possibility of a quick exit has already entered my mind. Yesterday evening, as I lay exhausted on the couch and recounted the day, Daniella said that she didn't see how I'd last one month—much less the two months I set as my goal for each occupation. I was starting to wonder that myself. By now I knew that I could handle hard physical labor and had learned to put my head down and grit through tough shifts. But what I wasn't accustomed to was the relentless verbal harassment *while* I worked. This was an entirely new experience, and it left me drained and feeling defeated.

BY 4:00 P.M. the store is closed and the workers have gathered inside, drinking Coronas and trying to figure out what to do on this Friday afternoon. After an eleven-hour day without a break I'm exhausted and ready to head home, but I'm waiting in the doorway of the office. Helen is sitting in the cramped space with another woman, evidently the bookkeeper. At Helen's desk is a checkbook, in her hand a pen. "I'm having a problem because we didn't decide on how much to pay you." She sighs, grimaces, and sighs again, as if this is a burden I ungraciously placed on her shoulders. I've been standing in the doorway for at least two minutes, watching her agonize over my payment.

"A lot of the time you look lost, like you don't know what to do." She continues to finger the checkbook. Finally she writes out $150 for my 21.5 hours. That's less than $7 an hour; minimum wage in New York is $7.15. "Maybe if it was the summertime . . ."

I start to realize that I'm being fired. "I'm all set to come in tomorrow, just tell me what time," I say, trying to change the direction of the dialogue. "I'm still learning, but I'm getting it."

"But I can tell that you are not made for this work." Helen looks over at the bookkeeper as if for assurance. "You're like a happy chicken out there. Always smiling."

What the fuck is a happy chicken? I leave the question unasked. "That's just how I am. It doesn't matter what I'm doing, I'm going to try and enjoy it." She shakes her head slowly.

"If it was summertime and slower maybe we could use you."

Now I'm shifting from shock to anger. "How am I supposed to know everything? It might seem like common sense to you and Tony but I've been here only two days. When I started I didn't even know what a magnolia tree looked like."

She shakes her head again. "It's not just the magnolia trees. If you don't know something, you should ask Tony."

Hysterical. What world is this woman living in? I quickly learned that asking Tony a question—any question—was useless. He ignored my questions; only once did he actually answer. Yesterday afternoon he told me to sweep trash into a bag. I did, and then made the mistake of asking where he wanted the trash placed.

"What should you do with the trash?" he asked. "You should call UPS and have them pick it up. Come on, mister—common sense!"

"You must know that Tony doesn't answer questions," I tell Helen. I consider reciting a list of the responses Tony has given me—beginning with the UPS anecdote—but can already sense the futility of arguing with her.

"You just don't fit in here. You can call Tony tomorrow and see what he says." I stand up, wanting to curse her out. Instead I walk away, tell the workers I've been fired—they are all equally incredulous—and bike home. I call Tony the next day and plead to be rehired, but he doesn't budge.

OVER THE WEEKEND I process the two-day experience. After surviving in lettuce fields and a poultry plant, I certainly didn't expect to be fired from a flower shop of all places. It was difficult to explain the firing to friends. Why, they wondered, would this store—in violation of so many labor laws—even hire

me? And once they decided to hire me, and saw that I was a dili-
gent employee, why let me go so soon? It would have been one
thing had I loafed or talked back. But I worked *hard* in the shop.
I held my tongue when yelled at; I learned to remain silent and
keep my eyes down when Tony or Helen went off. I didn't even
complain about not having a lunch break, or ask for gloves to
protect my hands. When I was given a task I did it, as quickly as
possible. On my second day another new worker showed up,
from Ecuador. I helped him out as much as I could, but he was
having an even more difficult time than I in keeping up. This
man, I later learned, kept the job.

The issue, I came to believe, wasn't about "work ethics" or "following instructions" or any other concrete criticism a boss might
make. It was about power and submission. Tony and Helen, the
rulers of their little fiefdom, had a very particular notion of how a
worker ought to comport themselves. They should hang their
heads, look miserable, and extract very little enjoyment out of the
experience. In my case, they were mostly successful: I hated being
at the shop. But I still did my best to keep up a friendly banter with
coworkers and maintain an incongruous smile on my face throughout much of the day. It was a means to mentally distance myself
from the place, to assert some small measure of levity into an environment that felt like a sweatshop. While I was on the clock they
owned me—as they did everyone else—but my "happy chicken"
antics evidently made this sense of ownership less secure. What if
the other workers started smiling? That could be dangerous.

IN 2007 THE Brennan Center for Justice, a progressive think
tank, published a report on the unregulated economy in New York
City. Although the underground economy is vast, they wrote, it
is "a world of work that lies outside the experience and imagination of many Americans":

It is a world where jobs pay less than the minimum wage, and sometimes nothing at all; where employers do not pay overtime for 60-hour weeks, and deny meal breaks that are required by law; where vital health and safety regulations are routinely ignored, even after injuries occur; and where workers are subject to blatant discrimination, and retaliated against for speaking up or trying to organize.[1]

I found low wages and grueling conditions in Yuma and Russellville, and judging the work by degree of difficulty alone, the flower shop was an "easier" job. I wasn't stooped over in the sun or lifting and dumping tons of chicken breasts. But there is something qualitatively different about my short-lived stint in the flower district. They didn't pay overtime or grant lunch breaks—and paid me less than the minimum wage—but these are not the abuses I will remember. What leaves a lasting impression is the incessant string of accusatory comments, the assumption that we, as workers, merited zero respect. In sum, I will remember being in an environment where the workers were treated as chattel—a more difficult phenomenon to quantify with statistics than wages, but a key component of the work experience for many undocumented immigrants. Just as certain occupations are physically unsafe, certain workplaces are psychologically unhealthy (often, of course, they are both). On some level, then, I ought to be grateful to Tony and Helen for granting me direct access to a world hidden to most Americans—if only for a brief period. But gratitude isn't the first word that springs to mind.

And either way, Tony and Helen are now behind me. I've been fired twice in the last three months, and I'm back where I started: in need of a job.

CHAPTER 12

Less than a week after getting fired at the flower shop, I'm sitting in the lounge of a Mexican restaurant that I'll call Azteca, flipping through the most recent issue of *Portfolio*. The magazine's placement on the table is clearly a status signifier: Azteca aims to be the kind of place that people who read *Portfolio* go to eat, the sorts of folks who, even in an economic downturn, will gladly shell out $14 for an order of guacamole.

After a weekend spent recovering from the flower shop, I spent the first part of the week visiting another half-dozen restaurants, leaving my name and number with noncommittal managers. Azteca holds some promise, because Daniella saw a listing on Craigslist for various positions, including dishwashers and delivery workers. A manager named Greg, wearing a sleek dark suit, invites me to join him at a table in the bar area. Six feet tall and with closely cropped gray hair, he gives a cursory glance over my application and offers me a job in delivery. "We're adding more workers now 'cause we're going to get slammed soon, once we sign up for Seamless Web." Seamless Web, he explains, will allow customers to place delivery orders online.

"I could see you becoming the delivery team leader," he tells me. Thus far, I've shaken his hand and said hello.

"Thanks," I say, not knowing how else to respond.

He nods. "It will be nice to have someone who speaks English. I try to tell people things and they can't understand me." Ah, there's my leadership quality.

Greg doesn't ask many questions during the short interview, or seem surprised that I am interested in doing a job that is normally done by immigrants. He asks briefly about my work experience, and I tell him that I'm coming from a nearby flower shop—"It didn't work out so well"—and have done a variety of nonprofit work for my trusty reference, Artemio. Neither seems to raise any red flags. In fact, once I've accepted the job, Greg is too distracted to focus on the interview; his eyes dart around the mostly empty restaurant, giving the sense that he's got important work left undone. He tells me to come back tomorrow with my Social Security card and driver's license. "Once we get that, you will have a day-long orientation and trail a person for two days." Like the flower shop, there is no discussion of pay, although they do check my license and Social Security card.

The following day Greg is out, but a young Latina at the hostess station is expecting me. I follow her through the double doors of the kitchen, where a handful of people are chopping vegetables, and down a flight of stairs to a small office. She copies my documents and hands me an orientation packet, which includes photos of the thirty or so meals that Azteca delivers. I'm to bring the packet for my first shift, and show up wearing all black. While in training I'll earn $7.50 an hour but won't get to keep any tips. After the training is over, my pay will be $4.60 an hour and I'll split the tips with the other workers. This sounds low to me, even for a position that receives tips, but that evening I learn it is New York's minimum wage for delivery workers.

"Greg mentioned I was supposed to go to an orientation some-where," I tell her before leaving. Orientations, as I learned in Russellville, can be inadvertently instructive. "Do you know anything about that?"

"He said that?" She shrugs and picks up the phone. "I don't think the delivery boys have to go to the orientation, because you're just . . . the delivery boys." She's on the phone for a few minutes. "No, you don't have to go. Greg says come back tomorrow at five to start your training."

ON THE MORNING that I am to begin work, the *New York Times* publishes another article by Steven Greenhouse that catches my eye: "For $2-an-Hour Restaurant Deliverymen, a $4.6 Million Judgment."

The story involves a group of workers from Saigon Grill, a Vietnamese restaurant with locations on the Upper West Side and in the West Village (the West Village location is not far from Azteca). I already knew that there had been a boycott of the restaurant—complete with noisy protests that certainly scared away a few customers—along with a lawsuit against its owners, Simon and Michelle Nget. The *Times* reported that a federal judge, Michael H. Dolinger, had ruled in favor of thirty-six workers—all Chinese immigrants—finding that over an eight-year period they regularly worked thirteen-hour days, six days a week, for less than $2 an hour. Along with back pay, the judge awarded the deliverymen substantial damages, citing the fact that they were illegally fined up to $200 by the restaurant for such crimes as letting the door slam behind them as they rushed out. "At a minimum, Simon

Nget and Michelle Nget showed no regard whatsoever for legal requirements in connection with their wage policies," Dolinger concluded.

As a result of the lawsuit, a woman with Justice Will Be Served, a group that organizes restaurant workers, said that some businesses, fearful of another high-profile boycott, had already increased wages. It was a remarkable ruling: From earning $2 an hour, a number of the deliverymen were awarded more than $300,000 apiece. One of the workers, Yu Guan Ke, said that the first thing he would do with the money was purchase health insurance for his family. "It was worth the fight because we were treated badly for so long," he said. "I never imagined we would receive so much money."

When I arrive at Azteca, Greg shows me how to clock in using a computer touch screen—my ID number is 6905—and gives me a quick tour of the kitchen. The delivery area includes a counter space and sink, and is on the immediate right after walking through the swinging doors from the restaurant floor. A short man with spiky black hair stands at the counter making guacamole in a stone bowl. His left arm ends at the elbow, an apparent birth defect, but the lightning-quick speed with which he slices the avocado and stirs in spoonfuls of tomatoes and onions is truly impressive. "This is Guillermo," Greg says, introducing me to the senior delivery worker, whose name is not, in fact, Guillermo. (Names are a challenge for Greg; he will call me "Gable" for the first several weeks. Here in the book I'll follow Greg's lead and stick with Guillermo.)

The kitchen is pretty quiet at the moment, as it's too early for dinner. A long grill and stovetop run along the rear wall, where two cooks stand and chat in Spanish. In the far corner is the dishwashing station, where I can see the outline of a man behind a wall of steam. Opposite the delivery counter is the dessert and salad area. As I take in the scene, Greg rattles off a list of things to know while waving his arms about the kitchen—hang jackets here, get sodas from there, receipts print downstairs—at a pace that seems designed to confuse.

I follow Greg past the food preparation counters to the exit door, which leads down a corridor and onto the street that runs behind Azteca. This is how I am to come and go from deliveries. Near the exit is a set of stairs that leads to a small storage room. Leaning against the stairs is a large black bike with a basket attached to the handlebars, which Greg says I'm to use; another mountain bike, whose paint has been partially stripped, is propped against a wall. "The very first thing you do when you arrive is make sure you're stocked up on containers for the night," Greg explains. "All the containers you'll need are up these stairs. Once you've got the containers stocked, fill up at least ten bags of chips. You'll be fucked if you don't get those ready before the rush."

Back at the station, Greg hands over a set of keys for the bike lock. "Your main tasks tonight are to watch how the kitchen works and study the menu," he says.

"Excuse me, *niñas*," says a stocky man, balancing a tray of food over his head with one hand and grabbing a collapsible stand leaning against the counter. He just called Greg and me girls. The man, with a shaved head and puffy nose, brushes past us and sends the double doors flying open with a vigorous front kick. I make a mental note to enter the kitchen carefully.

"Fucking asshole," Greg says. "Okay, you're set. Any questions, ask Guillermo." He leaves, following the trail of the karate kid.

There's another person standing next to Guillermo. Rafael is also in training—this is his third day—and at six feet he towers over most of the kitchen workers. He grew up in the Bronx and is of Dominican descent. "Didn't ever think I'd be doing this," he tells me. The economic slowdown caused his employer, a marketing firm, to slash his hours, and he came across the opening on Craigslist as well. "I told myself that I'd give this two weeks," he says, sounding doubtful. "It was the only job I could find. Getting really hard to make an honest dollar out here—be so much easier to just sell drugs."

"Delivery!" yells a heavyset white woman—the only non-Latino in the kitchen besides me. Guillermo walks over to her and grabs the ticket.

"Since it's your first night, let me give you a word of warning about Greg's bike—the black one," Rafael says. "I call that thing the catapult. First night I was here, take out my very first delivery. Food is in the basket and I hit this little pothole and the containers go flying into the street. Had to come back and take out another order. If you're riding the catapult, make sure to hold the food in the basket with one hand."

Guillermo waves me over. The delivery is for chicken tacos, mole enchiladas, and guacamole. Stacks of containers are on a shelf above the delivery counter; he grabs a container with three compartments for the tacos and a circular one for the enchiladas, placing them on a shelf near the cooks. "You have to watch to make sure they're cooking your order," he instructs. "They like to forget our orders. If it's taking too long you have to tell Becky." He motions to the white woman.

Now that the delivery containers are ready for the cooks, Guillermo grabs two plastic bowls and heads to a station to dish out rice and beans, adding a sprinkling of white cheese onto the beans and cilantro atop the rice. "Enchiladas always get a side of *arroz y frijoles*," he says. "If you forget that, people will call and complain. They'll complain too if you forget tortillas." He puts the rice and beans on the delivery counter and grabs a piece of tin-foil. I follow him across the kitchen to a grill, where two women are making tortillas by hand. "Each order of tacos comes with four tortillas—and four more for the guacamole." He reaches for a metal cylinder that contains a stack of steaming tortillas. One of the tortilla women turns and lightly smacks his hand.

"Don't you rob me!"

Smiling, Guillermo snatches the tortillas. "They're mine now." He crinkles the foil around them. "For the guacamole you need red and green salsas—those are in the fridge over there—and a bag of chips."

Once I've grabbed the salsas from the fridge and a bag of chips from below the counter, Rafael walks me through a guacamole tutorial. On the counter, four small glass bowls sit in a metal pan filled with ice; the bowls contain chopped jalapeño peppers, onions, cilantro, and tomatoes. Next to the pan is a ceramic bowl of salt and a cylinder that holds several knives and spatulas. Rafael grabs a *molcajete* and *tejolote* from a sink—a traditional Mexican stone version of the mortar and pestle—and adds a small scoop of jalapeños along with a spoonful of onions and cilantro and a teaspoon of salt. "Now the fun part." He grinds the mix with the pestle until it forms a green paste, then cuts an avocado in half and places the pit to the side. "Hold on to that—we put it in the guacamole at the end. Supposedly it keeps it fresh." He slices up the avocado, scoops the pieces into the molcajete with a spoon, and adds more salt, onions, and cilantro, along with two scoops of tomatoes. Once it's mixed together he dumps the guacamole into a plastic bowl, plops the pit into the middle of the serving, and snaps on a lid. "That's it. One avocado, fourteen bucks."

By now the tacos and enchilada are ready. Guillermo shows me how to pack the order: tacos on the bottom, then the enchilada, then rice and beans, then guacamole and tortillas and salsa, and finally the bag of chips is stuffed down one side to keep things from moving around. I'm starting to realize how easy it could be to overlook an item: This isn't even a big order.

Rafael volunteers to take the food out, asking and receiving permission to use Guillermo's mountain bike instead of the catapult. He returns fifteen minutes later with scraped hands. "This fucking asshole was walking across the street with a red light," he tells me as he hangs up his jacket. "I know he saw me, but he just kept walking—didn't even try to move." Rafael tugged too hard on the front brake and went face first over the handlebars. Luckily he had already made the delivery and only scraped his hands. He heads to the bathroom to clean up.

"Delivery!" This time I pick up the ticket from Becky: tacos with baby goat meat and an order of guacamole. With Guillermo's guidance I fumble through my first guacamole experiment. He packs the meal and I'm off on my first delivery, to Seventh Avenue and Twenty-seventh Street.

DESPITE INITIALLY STRIKING me as a decent guy, I quickly identify two reasons to believe that Greg wants his deliverymen to be killed. The first is the uniform. I am wearing, as ordered: black socks, black shoes, black pants, black T-shirt, black button-up long-sleeve shirt, and a black windbreaker (the windbreaker is provided by the restaurant). This all-black ensemble makes Azteca's by far the coolest, most quintessentially New York delivery team in Manhattan. At night, it also makes us nearly invisible. On my first trip out I notice that many deliverymen from other restaurants have been given florescent yellow vests, with reflective tape stitched across the front and back. Some even have front lights and bells, as required by law. Safer, sure, but not nearly as sophisticated.

The second dangerous item is the bike itself, a Raleigh that on closer inspection turns out to be a beach cruiser. I stick the bag of food into the basket and walk the bike down a ramp to the street. As soon as I slide onto the seat I realize that I'm in for a completely new experience, despite having cycled throughout New York City for years. It is easily the heaviest bike I've ever ridden—probably weighing more than fifty pounds—and has chopper-style handle-bars that are three feet wide, completely erasing a bike's normal mobility advantage. As I wobble down the street in the bike lane, cars feel like they're inches away. Nearing the first intersection I hit a slight bump and the catapult leaps into action, launching the bag into the air; thankfully the order lands back in the basket. Choosing to steer with one hand while holding the food down in the basket, I come to a red light and press back on the pedals—the bike is equipped with only coaster brakes. Unaccustomed to the distance needed to halt such a boat, I skid through the cross-walk, narrowly dodging a pedestrian who shoots me an angry look. Two minutes on the catapult and I already understand why, of the thousands of crappy delivery bikes I have seen crowding Manhattan's streets, I have never seen anyone, anywhere, rolling along on a beach cruiser.*

Using my own bike, I could easily have made the trip in five minutes, but the girth of the catapult forces me to wait several times with the traffic on Sixth Avenue, as I'm unable to wind around cars crowding the bike lane. More than ten minutes after leaving the restaurant I finally arrive at the corner building and lock the bike to a scaffolding post. What seems to be an unremark-able structure transforms as I pass beneath an archway and enter a long courtyard. I initially believe that the gentle sounds of splashing water are being piped in to induce a sense of peace, until I notice that the entire right wall is an illuminated waterfall. Inside the lobby—which feels like it belongs to a hotel—a large Jackson Pollack–inspired painting hangs on the wall, and I get in

---

* I later look up the bike on the Internet, hoping to learn its weight. While that fact is not revealed, I discover that the bike is called the "Special." The company writes, "Cruising on one of these, you can't help but feel exceptional." Perhaps on a boardwalk; in New York City, it only feels exceptionally stupid.

line behind three other deliverymen at the security desk. When it's my turn I give the guard the apartment number, he makes a call, and I'm allowed up.

A woman who looks to be in her early twenties, evidently a frequent customer, answers the door. "New delivery guy?"

"Yeah, just started." I hand over the food. She signs the bill and closes the door. On the way down I check the tip—$5. Not too bad for a $30 meal. It's official: I'm a deliveryman.

When I arrive back at the kitchen, Guillermo and Rafael are standing at the delivery counter with their hands in their pockets. "Slooow," Rafael says. "It's been like this every night I've been here."

By now the action in the kitchen has picked up. Becky, who I learn is playing the role of expediter, stands in the center of the storm, next to a machine that prints out the orders. Her primary task as expediter is to make sure the cooks know what the orders are, which she does by yelling, and to coordinate large orders so that they are served simultaneously. Three stocky men stand alongside Becky; these are the "runners," who ladle out sides of rice and beans, wipe the edges of the plates clean, and carry out the orders on trays—some quite massive—without breaking a sweat. I find the runners intimidating: One has a large scar running across his face, another calls us "*niñas*" each time he passes, and the third has a habit of hitting Guillermo in the shoulder whenever he gets the chance. Each time they leave for the front of the restaurant, they snatch up one of the folding stands—which they call *burros*, or donkeys—that are leaning against the delivery counter. As a result, we're frequently in their way. All seem to take special pleasure in kicking the double doors with unnecessary force as they exit the kitchen.

While dodging the runners I focus my attention on the cooks. Two men grill meat while two women, farther down the line, heat food in pans over a stovetop. When the food is ready they slide the dish on a shelf running above the counter, where it is kept warm by heat lamps. To the left of the cooks is another stovetop— the tortilla station—where two women roll corn meal into balls, flatten the balls with a metal presser, and place, flip, and remove the tortillas by hand over the heat.

"You getting all this?" Rafael asks.

"Kinda. I think."

"It's hard for me to remember everything 'cause of the stress— already forgot tortillas for one delivery. Too many people running around shouting."

"Yeah, I can see that." It's true that the kitchen has become a beehive of activity. Becky is yelling out orders and cooks are yelling back questions and waiters are wandering in complaining about customers ("Is it just me or was she a total *bitch*?") and burly guys are streaming past while warning us *niñas* to get out of the way. Still, it seems like a manageable place to work. Of course, I'm fresh from the flower shop, so just about anything seems preferable to the constant nagging of Tony and Helen.

"Delivery!" I grab the ticket from Becky: enchiladas, tuna salad, and guacamole. Fifth Avenue between Twenty-sixth and Twenty-seventh. I place the enchilada container on the shelf and dish out rice and beans while Rafael starts mashing the ingredients in the molcajete. Ten minutes later I'm out the door. Ten minutes after that, I'm back at the station with a $4 tip in my pocket. This isn't too bad.

By the end of the five-hour shift, I've made only three deliveries, for a grand total of $13 in tips. The slow night doesn't much matter to me, since I don't keep any tips during training. "Use this time to learn as much as you can," Greg says as I'm preparing to leave. "Once we get Seamless Web hooked up, you won't have any time to stand around."

WHEN I ARRIVE at work the next evening, Greg is engaged in an animated conversation with Guillermo, laying out his vision for Seamless Web. I overhear Greg mention that we're going to have a computer, printer, and fax machine so that orders will come up at our station. "That way it prints right up—bam!—and you can just grab the containers and get moving," he says excitedly. "The fax machine will be used only if for some reason the Web isn't working—that way people can send us a fax directly with the order."

It was my impression that Guillermo, who told me he came to the United States from Mexico about six years ago, didn't speak much English. Indeed, as soon as Greg walks away he turns to me. "What did he say?" I do my best to explain the backup function of the fax machine. Guillermo looks nonplussed, saying, "I don't know how to use a computer, but it will be good if it means more deliveries."

Tonight, again, begins slowly. We stand at the counter for fifteen minutes, waiting for a delivery, until a man wearing a white apron and camouflage pants—who worked the grill yesterday—introduces himself as Armando, one of the head chefs. I ask how he rose through the ranks so quickly, as he looks young.

"I'm only twenty-five." He smiles. "Started as a grill cook, then sous-chef." (Totally ignorant about restaurant jobs and titles, I have to look up sous-chef to learn it is the assistant chef.) He tells me he's from Mexico City, which concludes our time for small talk: He orders us to measure out shredded cheese in the prep area.

The assignment—we fill small bags with 2.5 ounces of shredded cheese—is the sort of mindless work that leads to rambling conversations. I learn that Guillermo, who rents a room in the Queens neighborhood of Astoria, worked for five years at a large restaurant not far from his home, mostly as a prep cook. A fire has temporarily shut down the restaurant, but it's set to reopen next week; Guillermo will then work both jobs. He hopes to return to his regular schedule in Queens, working from six in the morning to five in the afternoon, which will allow him to arrive at Azteca by six o'clock.

"Do you think the other place needs people?" Ideally, I'd like more hours; I'm scheduled to work six nights a week at Azteca, but that comes out to only about thirty hours. He shakes his head. Out of curiosity, I ask how much they pay.

"Three hundred a week, cash. That's pretty good, no?" Pretty good works out to roughly $5 an hour, well below the minimum wage—and doesn't include overtime (as a prep cook, the minimum wage is $7.15, not the $4.60 of deliverymen).

"I know," he says when I point this out. "They have signs up that show the minimum wage." This is a new one: a workplace that posts labor laws while breaking them.

Long after we've finished weighing the cheese, two orders finally come in. Both have guacamole, which I prepare. Guillermo says I can borrow his bike—I'm done experimenting with the catapult—and I string the bags on either handlebar and set off (I can't use my own bike, because its drop-style handlebars don't allow for the hanging of bags).

Guillermo's bike, despite being adjusted for someone about half a foot shorter than me, is a much more pleasant ride. With his narrow handlebars I'm able to weave around traffic, and when I pull on the brakes I actually find myself immediately slowing down. Still, as I'm pedaling down Broadway, I can tell that I'll need time before I feel completely comfortable riding with food.

Both deliveries go to what I will learn are typical buildings for Azteca customers: brightly lit awnings, spotless lobbies complete with flat-screen televisions, doormen, and security desks. Also typical is that very few words are exchanged at the apartment doors.

"How's it going tonight?" I ask. "Good, and you?" "Good." "Good." "How much is it?" "Forty-five eighty-six." "Here you go, keep the change." "Thanks, have a good night." "You too."

Back in the kitchen I wander over to the tortilla ladies and introduce myself to Gloria, who has been at Azteca for several months and makes $8 an hour. She stands over the stovetop the entire shift, churning out thousands of handmade tortillas each night. "This is exactly how I made them in Mexico," she says, showing me how to roll the corn meal into small balls that she then flattens with a metal press. "I just didn't have to do it all day."

A compact woman with long hair and a ready laugh, Gloria grew up in Cuautla, Morelos, just a few blocks from what was once the home of Emiliano Zapata. She came to the United States six months ago—her first time north of the border—at the age of forty-six. Soon after arriving she paid $100 to an employment agency in Washington Heights, near the apartment she's sharing with her boyfriend, and was placed in a job cleaning houses. "The boss said he'd pay me $7 an hour, but only gave me 6," she says, so she went back to the agency and was sent to Azteca. She knows very little about New York, beyond the subway route she takes to and from work, and her only contact is her boyfriend, whom she met in Cuautla.

In Cuautla, Gloria—a sweet-looking grandmother who may be *just* five feet—worked as a security guard for a hospital, earning two thousand pesos a month while sporting a .22 pistol on her waist. "It was such a pretty little thing," she says about the handgun in her high-pitched voice. She eventually became a cook at the hospital, but decided in early 2008—with encouragement from her boyfriend, who had already emigrated to New York—to come and join him. She flew from Mexico City to the border and endured an eight-day trek through Arizona, anticipating a glorious reunion. Instead, she's starting to wonder if she wouldn't have been better off staying put.

"He's acting strange," is how she describes her boyfriend's behavior. Eventually she clarifies the statement: He's seeing other women and drinking too much. She can't imagine a future with the man he has become, but doesn't feel like she's in a position to break it off, as he's the only contact she has in the city. She has friends in the United States, but they all ended up in Los Angeles. "Maybe I'll go there," she says. "If someone would tell me where it is."

By the end of the shift I've made only five deliveries and rolled several hundred balls of corn meal for tortillas. My back isn't sore; my hands are perfectly functional. I could get used to this.

AND THEN COMES Saturday night, marking the official end of my honeymoon with delivery work. The first bad omen occurs before I even arrive at the restaurant. As I'm biking from my apartment it begins to drizzle and swiftly turns into a downpour. I haven't biked in the rain for some time—since Russellville, actually—and I've apparently forgotten that wet ground means slow down, because as I'm veering onto the sidewalk near the Manhattan Bridge, my tires slide out. I slam the right side of my body into the pavement but thankfully discover, once I recover from the accident, that I have avoided doing any serious damage to my body or bike.

Guillermo and Rafael are already at the kitchen when I arrive, with two delivery tickets hanging from the shelf and a third packed and ready to go. I clock in, do my best to wipe the dirt from my pants, and grab the three orders from the counter. Just as I'm walking out the door, Claudia, who takes the delivery orders over the phone, stops me. "The credit card didn't go through for the guy on Irving Place," she says. "Make sure he calls back while you're there." I scribble a note on the ticket and head back into the rain.

In my eight years of cycling around New York City, my general strategy in dealing with cars is to avoid making direct contact. If someone cuts me off, I'll slam on the brakes and mutter to myself. If a driver is moving into the bike lane, I'll slow down and let him take it over. But when one spends five or six hours a night pedaling back and forth in a very congested area, there quickly comes a time when passivity and avoidance are no longer sufficient if one hopes to survive. This is when being a deliveryman becomes a contact sport.

I hit that point riding down the right side of Third Avenue with the three orders of food. A black town car, driving at the same speed that I'm cycling, starts edging into my path. The driver either doesn't see me through the rain or sees me and considers my presence a trivial matter. In response, I drift slightly rightward; moments later, so does the car. By now I can't move any more to the right without launching my body into a row of parked cars. I glance backwards, preparing to slow down, and see a yellow cab bearing down from behind, ready to make a turn at the upcoming light. As the town car continues to list right, I take the only appropriate action and slap the palm of my hand on the passenger-side window. The driver looks over and gives a slight nod of the head, moving several inches back into the lane, as if this is his normal means of determining correct driving position: Wait for the frantic strike. Although the encounter speeds up my heart rate, it also gives me an odd sense of confidence and control. I can slap these cars around if they get out of line.

The first order, on Third Avenue, is for $55. The building is a fourth-floor walk-up, and since I've got two more deliveries to make, I take the steps two at a time. By the time I knock on the door I'm panting and soaking wet. A man comes to the door. "It's raining, huh?" Behind him a movie is playing on a massive flat-screen TV.

"Yep, just started coming down pretty hard." He signs the credit card bill and hands it back to me, which I pocket without looking. As I'm huffing back down the stairs I take out the bill. He's left me a $2 tip.

My next stop is at 1 Irving Place. According to the ticket, it is near Fifteenth Street. I ride down Irving until it ends at Fourteenth Street, but don't see the address, so backtrack to Sixteenth Street. Nothing. Because it's raining, there aren't many people on the street, but I eventually stop a woman walking her dog, who points to a large awning halfway down Fifteenth Street. As I get closer I can see that it's the address I'm looking for.

One Irving Place is by far the largest building I've delivered to thus far. I take one elevator that runs to the seventh floor, then walk through a long hallway, passing a number of people wearing workout gear—the building has a pool and health club—and take another elevator up one of four towers. The man who answers the door has short gray hair, is wearing a suit, and continues speaking rapidly into his cell phone about what sounds like some sort of business deal. I explain politely over his conversation about the credit card number not going through.

"I knew that idiot on the phone would mess up," he snarls. "Look at this"—he holds the bill up to my face—"She didn't even spell my name right! Fucking idiot. No, not you," he says into his phone. "I've got a delivery here. Hold on." He puts the phone into his pocket.

"Sorry about that, sir. Could you just call her back and give—"

"Forget it, I'll pay cash. How much?" I tell him. "Okay, here's the money. Give yourself a five-dollar tip out of it."

"Thanks. I think this is right." I hand over his change. He flips through the bills.

"*Hey*, someone graduated high school," he says before closing the door.

Next up after Mr. Dickhead is a penthouse apartment on Eleventh Street. I check my watch—I've got six minutes to go if I want to make the forty-five-minute window that Greg has said is our goal. I ride east along a congested Fourteenth Street, take a left on Fifth Avenue, and am standing at the door of the penthouse with a minute to spare. The man who answers has a friendly smile, and I can hear his wife in the background, yelling to the kids that dinner is ready. He leaves me a $12 tip, my largest so far.

Back at the kitchen, three more bags are packed near the exit door and ready to be delivered. I snatch them up, noticing that the catapult is gone—poor Rafael—and am off. Since the buildings are nearby, I'm back within twenty minutes. "I forgot tortillas at Eleventh Street," Guillermo tells me, handing over a small bag. "Can you run them over?"

"Anything else to take?"

"No, not right now."

When I ring the buzzer at Eleventh Street, a woman's voice shouts angrily at me through the intercom. "It's too late! We've already finished our meal—*thank* you!" Since I haven't even said anything, I realize that the building must have a hidden camera (good to know: wouldn't want to be picking my nose at the door). By now I'm ready for a quick break and a few tortillas, and take a seat on steps beneath the awning of a nearby building. I open the bag and discover that, in apology, the restaurant has included a large piece of cheesecake (value: $8.50) along with the tortillas. While the rain falls around me and people scurry for shelter, I combine the two items, enjoying four cheesecake tacos.

By the end of the night we've completed twenty-three deliveries. Rafael, riding the slow catapult, took six; Guillermo, responsible for packing, took one; I dropped off sixteen. Together we make nearly $100 in tips, which Guillermo splits evenly with Rafael and me, even though, since this is my last day of training, I'm not supposed to see any of it.

CHAPTER 13

I've worked in two restaurants before coming to Azteca. The first was a relaxed pizza joint in San Jose, California, where I made deliveries in the company pickup. The second was a line cook position at a ski resort in Jackson Hole, Wyoming, where the general goal of the staff, most in their early twenties and with zero interest in things culinary, was to have a good time (my coworkers and even one manager were often drunk, or stoned, or both). Over holiday breaks the lodge could become very busy, but the hectic pace was leavened by the fact that we lacked proper supervision and so could often do as we pleased. One friend, after receiving a complaint that he had overcooked a hamburger, reached over the grill, grabbed the patty from the customer's plate, and slung it against a wall.

Neither experience was especially good training for the culture of a busy, upscale restaurant. Picture the atmosphere of a rush-hour subway station in New York City, late July: Folks are dashing around, muttering to themselves or yelling at others, oozing sweat and stress and in no mood for pleasantries. I've seen a few episodes of those reality cooking shows, where celebrity chefs berate the cooks and the cooks soon turn on each other, acting as if lives hang in the balance. I figured they were over-the-top. They're not.

One night, during a busy stretch, an Ecuadorian waiter named José comes to Becky with a question. Becky, playing the role of expediter, is busy. So Becky says, "José, get the fuck out of my face." José stays put, hoping to get a word in. "I need a tuna salad, *now*!" Becky screams. "*¡Atún!*" (Becky has picked up some Spanish while in the kitchen.) "I need tuna!" shouts the salad preparer in Spanish; the salad is already on a plate, awaiting a grilled tuna from a cook. "The tuna is fucking coming!" yells a cook, standing over a grill jammed with chicken, skewers of shrimp, salmon, and—yes—a tuna steak. Becky turns to grab a bottle of sour cream from the fridge to squeeze onto an enchilada, in the process bumping into José. "José, I can't take your shit right now! Where the fuck is my tuna salad? I need tuna!"

The stress level reaches its highest point when the restaurant hosts large parties, which is often. This is when the screaming and fighting that goes on between cooks and the expediter, or servers and cooks, or runners and servers, or—when there's a true crisis—between just about everyone at the same time, sounds like it will erupt into a full-scale brawl. The beads of sweat, always present on foreheads, start rolling down cheeks. Faces usually pink from the heat turn crimson. But once the rush passes, after the fourteen house salads and five tortilla soups and sixteen racks of lamb have been sorted out and served, the people in the kitchen quickly put the conflict behind them. There is an understanding, it seems, that at rush hour the kitchen is a war zone, and that people behave differently in war zones—so don't take it personally. It's definitely not an environment for everyone, but there's something attractive about the lack of pretense and brutally direct communication. Of course, my ability to enjoy the environment is certainly helped by the fact that as a delivery worker, I'm usually not a target.

Most nights Becky plays expediter, setting the emotional tone of the kitchen. Becky is fun to be around. She has perhaps the foulest mouth I've ever encountered, shares my interest in 1980s punk music, and tells me that she can't stand *Top Chef* because it's "full of pretentious assholes." In her late twenties, she dropped out of culinary school and works between sixty and seventy hours a week while raising a young son. In the kitchen she is fearless: She gets into shouting matches with managers, grill cooks, even the executive chef. One night Azteca has a VIP customer—a vice president of operations for the restaurant chain, or some such title. "We have some feedback," the general manager, a woman given to wearing skintight dresses, tells Becky. "He says it's too salty."

"Fuck that!" Becky shouts. She tastes the sauce. "There's hardly any fucking salt in it! What a fucking dick!" It's hard not to enjoy watching her work.

The one person who seems completely unaffected by the environment is Pancho, a thirty-four-year-old runner from the state of Puebla who has long black hair tied back in a ponytail.* "He says he's from Mexico, but he seems like a total California surfer dude," is how one of the servers puts it to me. Even at the height of kitchen craziness, Pancho always seems to be playing practical jokes. He'll pat Guillermo in a friendly manner, leaving a sticker on his back that stays on through an entire shift, or he'll drop an avocado into the hood of my windbreaker, which I'll discover when I flip it up as I head out the door. When I return from a delivery with a story of

---

* After working in lettuce fields and a chicken plant, where every employee—even the completely bald—was ordered to wear hairnets, it is curious to see that in restaurants, which serve food directly to consumers, plenty of long hair is allowed to dangle over plates.

avocados falling from the sky, he scrunches up his face in determination and says, "You know what, I'll look into who did that."

Across the kitchen from the unflappable Pancho is his polar opposite, a lanky nineteen-year-old cook who left Mexico, he tells me, because his hometown in Guerrero had grown too dangerous due to the drug trade. Called Flaco (skinny) by the other workers, his face seems to have frozen some time ago into a petulant scowl. It doesn't matter what Flaco is doing—grilling up an order of chicken, sucking down a Coke through a straw—he retains the same "what the fuck are you looking at?" expression. When he walks to get a pan of beans, he struts slowly; when someone criticizes something he does, he looks like he's going to explode. Like many young men, he hopes to project an image of toughness, but what comes across instead is a very vulnerable and sensitive boy, far from home and making his way in a foreign country. It also doesn't help that he weighs about 130 pounds and looks like he could be in junior high.

During my second week a stocky white man wearing remarkably unattractive black-and-white pants replaces Becky as expediter.

"What the fuck is this?" the man shouts at Flaco. He's holding a plate of food. "Is this how we do rice, *niño*?" Flaco shoots him a look of total disgust and shrugs, remaining silent. "What? What!" The man walks over. "I said, is *this* how we do rice, *niño*?" He dumps the yellow rice back into a metal container. After several more seconds of uncomfortable staring, Flaco finally stirs a bunch of greens into the container of rice—perhaps cilantro, I'm not sure—and puts a serving on the plate. "I will stop calling you *niño* when you start acting like a man," the man with the piebald pants says.

I turn to Guillermo. "What was that about?"

"He's the head chef." Guillermo looks pleased; he often complains to me that Flaco purposely forgets delivery orders, waiting until Becky reminds him.

I'm able to stand around observing the goings-on in the kitchen because after the rush of Saturday the next few shifts are unbelievably slow—so slow that I wonder if Greg has made a mistake in hiring me. With Guillermo coming from his second job in Queens, I'm now arriving an hour before him, so it's my responsibility to set up the station. For the first twenty minutes I fill bags of tortilla chips, replenish the avocado supply from downstairs, fill the glass bowls with tomatoes, jalapeños, cilantro, and onions from the walk-in fridge, and stock needed containers from upstairs. By 5:30 p.m. I'm ready with no place to go.

I soon learn that standing at the delivery counter ensures that I'll keep bumping into the runners as they move in and out of the kitchen. Aside from Pancho, whose lighthearted demeanor I appreciate, my general desire is to steer clear of the runners whenever possible. Felix, who has a prominent facial scar and gravelly voice, is impossible to read. Sometimes he seems to be joking when he tells me to "move it," but other times I'm not so sure; I figure the less he tells me to move it, the better. And Isaac, a broad-shouldered man who refers to everyone on the delivery staff as little girls, is definitely someone I don't want to annoy.

Another reason to give room and respect to the runners is their propensity to purposefully punch people, usually each other. The first time I witnessed this I was convinced that Pancho, who was hit in the ribs by Isaac while hoisting a large tray over his head with one arm, would drop the order. But he simply proceeded onto the restaurant floor as if nothing had happened, and returned the favor to Isaac a few minutes later. On Pancho's prodding, I try to balance a tray holding only two plates overhead and barely get it back on the stand without the food sliding onto the floor. Yet the runners can literally *run* through a crowded kitchen with a full tray balanced high above their heads—often using only their fingertips—while absorbing body shots.

TO FILL THE downtime during the slow week—I make only fourteen deliveries over a three-day period—I take on a variety of jobs in the kitchen, from helping the dishwashers toss out the trash to pulling chicken meat from drumsticks and rolling tortilla balls. While assisting the back-of-the-house staff—all Latino immigrants—it doesn't take long to realize that Azteca suffers from a turnover rate that rivals the poultry plant, at least for the positions that don't receive tips.

Most of the prep cooks and dishwashers have paid storefront referral agencies in immigrant neighborhoods anywhere from $100 to $200 for the job, a common practice within the restaurant industry in staffing the less desirable positions. In recent years, the state attorney general has launched dozens of investigations into employment agencies, often finding that they violate laws by referring immigrant workers to jobs that pay less than the minimum wage. Some of the referred workers have been at Azteca for a few weeks, some a few months, but no one I speak to has a year under his or her belt, and many aren't planning on sticking around much longer. By far, the most disgruntled workers are the dishwashers. "They don't pay enough," says Alvaro, a middle-aged dishwasher from the Galapagos Islands, as we're rolling a heavy dumpster to the curb. Earning $7.50 an hour, he has taken another low-paying job washing dishes at a restaurant called Chop't, and frequently works fourteen-hour days. "They have me running around all night, doing work that should be done by two people," he says. Sweat is trickling down his wide cheeks and his black mustache glistens under the streetlight. "And for what? At the end of the night I have earned almost nothing."

One of Alvaro's dishwashing partners, Antonio, also plans to leave soon. When I ask Antonio how much he makes, he tells me, "No good, no good." One night at the end of the shift I see him staring in concentration at his paycheck.

"Something wrong?"

"I'm missing hours." He tells me that he worked forty-four hours last week, but received payment for only forty hours. "They did that the week before, too," he mutters quietly. Hour shaving is a widespread practice in the restaurant industry; of the more than 500 workers surveyed by the Restaurant Opportunities Center of New York (ROC-NY), for its study "Behind the Kitchen Door," 59 percent reported not being paid overtime hours.[2]

"You should go downstairs and tell a manager," I say. He nods halfheartedly. "Really—if you worked forty-four hours then they should pay you for forty-four. I could even go down there and tell them in English."

He shakes his head. "I'm going to wait and see," he says before leaving. I hope to check in on the situation, but a few days later Alvaro informs me that Antonio quit. A new man takes his place, from a town near Mexico City. He paid a labor agency in Queens $100; thus far, no one has told him how much he'll be making at Azteca. When he learns that Alvaro earns less than $8 an hour, he tells me that he'll probably be gone soon. A week later, I strike up a conversation with a third dishwasher, Javier, in the locker room downstairs as we're changing. He also reports that he's being shorted hours each week, and though he says he might switch jobs, he would rather not complain directly to management, despite being one of the few back-of-the-kitchen staff I've met who has their immigration papers in order.* "If I need to, I'll just switch jobs," he tells me. "That's easier than starting a fight."

Which brings me to something else: There is a certain perversity to the wage scale of restaurant workers. The people earning the

---

* I later learn that this dishwasher is the uncle of Enrique, a friend of mine whose life I chronicled in my first book, *There's No José Here*. When I called Enrique, who worked as a dishwasher when he first arrived in New York, and told him about his uncle's payment problems, he scoffed. "Of course they don't pay all the hours," he said. "I worked sixty hours a week but was paid forty. That is nothing new."

least are the dishwashers, and they have the hardest jobs. They are stationed at one end of the kitchen, obscured behind an always-present wall of steam, coated in sweat and smeared with leftovers. When they emerge from the humidity, pushing heavy carts of clean dishes, they often receive glares, as they inevitably clog up the passageways as they unload plates and bowls. If restaurant kitchens are filled with people who are invisible to the general public, dishwashers are the most invisible. While servers and cooks and delivery people banter amongst themselves and call each other by name, the only time anyone notices the dishwashers is when they're in the way.

On the opposite end of the earning scale are the servers. In less expensive restaurants a server takes an order and returns to the table with the food. But at Azteca, as with most upscale restaurants, a server doesn't usually *serve* anything: They describe the specials, write down the orders, and plug the orders into a touchscreen computer. The task of serving falls on the shoulders of the runners. For this, servers can earn hundreds of dollars a night. Meanwhile, the people who prepare the food, cook the food, and clean the dishes make somewhere between $7.50 and $10.00 an hour. The wide gap in earnings between these two extremes is filled by the restaurant's "middle class," the runners, bussers, and baristas, who are tipped out by servers and seem to average anywhere from $70 to well over $100 a night. As a deliveryman, I suppose I'm part of the lower-middle class, earning more than dishwashers but much less than other tipped positions, while dealing with inclement weather and the dangers of the road.

At Azteca, the servers are generally a nice and funny crew, and in contrast to many upscale restaurants, they are quite diverse.*

---

* Azteca's diverse server staff is unusual for fine-dining establishments in New York City, which are usually segregated by race, with the high-paying positions of servers and bartenders filled almost exclusively by whites. In 2009, the Restaurant Opportunities Center of New

There are white and black and Latino servers, servers born in Ecuador and servers born in Queens. I have no bone to pick with servers; what I find confounding is the system of payment that exists throughout the restaurant industry. By what logic do servers receive tips, and runners receive tips, but not dishwashers or grill cooks? Each job is of comparable importance—whether or not the customer sees the face of the person performing it—as anyone who has received a dirty dish or undercooked meat can attest.

IT'S A RELIEF on slow nights when deliveries finally start rolling in sometime after seven o'clock and I'm able to escape the heat of the kitchen. By now Guillermo and I have reached a working agreement: He packs the orders and I make the deliveries using his bike. I'm glad to hand off the packing responsibilities, because even though my training ended some time ago, I still tend to forget obvious items.

On the streets I'm starting to spot trouble early in what can be a dangerous profession. A 2006 report published by the city found that an average of 23 cyclists were killed each year, with another 400 left seriously injured (the data lumps all cyclists together, and so precise figures on delivery workers aren't available). One of the most frequent dangers occurs when a passenger swings open a car door without looking. When this happens and a cyclist is passing within close range, he plows into the door at full speed, an experience called getting "doored." It happens to just about everyone who spends enough time on a bike—I've been doored twice—and

---

York published the results of a study in which equally qualified applicants—one white and one of color—applied for server positions at more than a hundred Manhattan restaurants. The white applicants were nearly twice as likely to receive a job offer. The report, "The Great Service Divide," is available online (as of April 30, 2009) at www.rocunited.org/files/greatservicedivide.pdf.

it is as unpleasant as it sounds. The worst offenders are taxi passengers: People entering and leaving cabs can be very dangerous, behaving as if they are protected by a force field and not in the middle of a very busy street.

Being doored is one of the predictable dangers; what makes each delivery an adventure are the threats that pop up without warning. Riding along a dark stretch of Nineteenth Street, I hit a huge and invisible pothole. It's nearly as jarring as slamming into a curb, and though I'm able to avoid tumbling over the handlebars, the two orders I'm carrying rip through the bottom of the paper bags and go flying into the street. Containers of shrimp salad and goat tacos and duck breast and guacamole explode, ruining $150 worth of food and ensuring that I'll be making two late deliveries to two upset customers.

Yet another danger to deliverymen, ironically but not surprisingly, are other deliverymen. Many have had little cycling experience before landing the job, and riding around Manhattan on a rickety bike loaded with food is a baptism by fire. Rafael, for instance, had never ridden in the city, and when I went out with him on an early delivery, it was plain that he had no idea what he was doing: He rode against traffic, ventured onto the sidewalk for no apparent reason, and nearly ran into two pedestrians. Of course, Rafael received zero training: Like all deliverymen, he was given an ungainly bike and an address and told to hurry up and go. "It's not rocket science," is how Greg described the work to me one night, with a flippancy that would be erased if he ever tried to make a delivery himself.

Rafael eventually becomes a safer cyclist, but with such a high turnover, there are always beginners on the streets, and over two months I hit three deliverymen who are riding the wrong way and have a handful of extremely close calls. The blogger BikeSnob NYC is exaggerating, but not by much, when he writes about certain rogue deliverymen:

I don't mean to begrudge anybody making a living by bike, and I certainly respect someone who makes a living in a manner as difficult as this. But the fact is, some of these guys are incredibly dangerous and will come at you in ways you'd never expect: from between parked cars; flying off curbs; head-on between two lanes of traffic; and leaping from rooftops and swinging from power lines like Paul Reubens did in *Pee-wee's Big Adventure* during the climactic Warner Brothers studio rampage scene.[3]

But while I'm occasionally spooked by someone pedaling at me like mad from the opposite direction, more often I feel a sense of camaraderie. At some intersections, waiting for the light to change, a team of four or five deliverymen, Latino and Asian, will gather (for whatever reason, it seems to be an entirely male occupation). Some wear rectangular heat-retaining backpacks, some hold pizzas in their baskets, but most use the low-tech method of dangling bags from the handlebars. As we stand and wait, it can feel like I'm a member of a biker gang, and when we zoom off, there are times, especially cruising down Broadway, that our numbers give us the confidence to take over two lanes, at least for a short while.

Now that I'm delivering food, I discover that it's very easy to strike up conversations with fellow deliverymen. Once when I worked on an article for which I needed to interview a deliveryman, I had approached dozens of people in the streets, but after I identified myself as a journalist, they were very hesitant to speak. It took several weeks to find an individual willing to share details about wages and working conditions. Now, whenever I bump into someone, whether we're taking the same elevator or waiting in a lobby, I find that people readily share information, and ask the same questions of me. (My conversations are only with Latino workers; I try conversing with several Asian men but none speaks English.)

What I learn, as far as deliverymen go, is that my minimum wage of $4.60 an hour puts me in the highest income bracket. One Mexican man delivers for an Indian restaurant, and is paid $25 in cash for a twelve-hour shift, which he works six days a week. On a good day he makes $50 in tips. Another, who cooks and delivers for a pizza joint, gets $4 an hour in cash and takes home between $30 and $40 in tips. He also works twelve-hour shifts, six days a week. A nineteen-year-old Ecuadorian I meet while locking up my bike just started at a Thai restaurant; at the end of each day he's given $20 in cash, and earns an additional $40 or so from tips. When I ask how they're able to survive on their income, the answer is always the same: They live in a small apartment with many others.

It quickly becomes obvious that I don't need to "investigate" the prevalence of illegal wages in the food delivery business: That's all there is. The "Behind the Kitchen Door" study of restaurant workers by ROC-NY found that 13 percent of respondents earned less than the minimum wage. For deliverymen, I'm willing to bet that number is more like 95 percent. Over the two months that I deliver food, I speak to perhaps fifty deliverymen about wages, and never meet another person who matches my princely wage of $4.60 an hour, which runs counter to the claim that restaurants increased wages in response to the Saigon Grill decision. That Azteca has decided to comply with minimum-wage laws probably explains why they were willing to hire me. In terms of understanding why Azteca was willing to pay the minimum wage in the first place, the best I could figure was that since it is part of a small corporate chain operating in multiple states, they are more centralized, professionalized, and potentially vulnerable to large-scale lawsuits by workers.

ON THE JOB, I enter buildings that I would never otherwise set foot in, including many in the posh neighborhood of Gramercy

Park. They have doormen and security desks and sign-in proto-cols. Some require that I wear an ID badge around my neck (Hello, my name is FOOD DELIVERY). At times, guards accompany me into the elevator, even follow me to the resident's door to ensure nothing untoward happens during the transaction. Others tell me to leave the lobby and enter the building around the corner. "*You* use the service elevator"—as if my presence might somehow lower property values.

The city the residents have chosen to live in is noisy, dirty, and rowdy. Their apartment buildings are closely guarded refuges, offering multiple barriers to the unwashed masses, even small children. During the week leading up to Halloween, I see notices posted in various buildings that read something along the lines of: "Halloween is just around the corner! Happy Halloween! If you have people that you would like to allow up to knock on your door for treats, please inform the security desk within three days so we can put their names on our list!"

ON HALLOWEEN, as I set up the delivery station, Azteca's bar back, who assists the bartender, stops by to say hello. Raimundo is stocky and exceedingly polite—he calls me *caballero* (gentleman) instead of *güe* (sort of like dude)—and worked his way up from delivery. "Last year deliveries on Halloween were very slow," he says.

Greg stops in, and, as usual, his mind is on Seamless Web. "It's going to be up next Tuesday," he says.

My first delivery, which normally should take about ten minutes, is to an apartment on Thirteenth Street between Sixth and Seventh Avenues. As I cruise toward Sixth Avenue, the street becomes increasingly congested with foot traffic, all heading in the direction I'm pedaling. This should tell me something, but I keep plowing forward as the density increases, winding between groups of revelers decked out in costume. I manage to swerve around Fred Flintstone before finally dismounting and walking with the throng. I push my way to the front only to realize that the street is blocked off by barricades and police officers.

"Sorry, can't get across Sixth here," an officer tells me, sounding sympathetic to my situation: With two bags of food hanging from my handlebars, I must look pretty helpless. "I'd like to let you through, but if I do then I'm gonna have a hundred assholes screaming that they want across too." He tells me that because of the Halloween parade, Sixth Avenue is blocked all the way up to Twenty-third Street. To get to the apartment I have to go up ten blocks, west two blocks, and south ten blocks. Then, to get back to Azteca, I have to do the entire loop in reverse.

It would be a long detour on any night—I'm cycling an additional forty-four blocks—but when I turn around I am faced with thousands of people streaming to get close to the barricades so they can watch the parade. I begin to pick my way through the crowd, cursing myself for not remembering the parade (I'd watched it once before, after all). "It's a delivery guy!" a woman yells at me, impressed with her powers of observation. Other people join in. "Hey, delivery guy!" someone shouts to my left. I turn and look at the man, who is dressed as a marshmallow. *Hello, idiot.* "That's my delivery!" The marshmallow's buddies laugh hysterically at this witticism. "Watcha got for us?"

I finally make it through the dense throng and hop back on my bike, pedaling through a group of mimes playing tennis. I normally depend on Sixth Avenue to travel north, but since it's shut down, the only way to Twenty-third Street is to go against traffic on Fifth Avenue for ten blocks. I have a rule of thumb about going the wrong way—I'll do it for a maximum of three blocks; otherwise I'll schlep over to another avenue—but tonight I have little choice.

It proves to be an especially bad time to break my rule, because Fifth Avenue is a madhouse. The cars are bumper to bumper and

Contents

Preface

*A*n American born late in the eighteenth century and blessed to live past the midpoint of the next would have witnessed a series of changes, by turns heady and bewildering, to the world of her youth. Between 1800 and 1850, twenty-one new states were admitted to the Union, for a total of thirty-four; the national population exploded, going from around 4 million to 31.5 million, in part due to rapidly increasing numbers of immigrants, from 5,000 in 1790 to 600,000 in the 1830s and 2.6 million in the 1850s; the nation launched its first imperialistic adventures, in Central America and the Caribbean; the national legislature paved the way for the extension of slavery into new territories in the South and the West; and the economy swiftly modernized and expanded as a result of the advent of water- and steam-powered manufacture and the construction of roads, canals, and railways that linked distant producers and consumers.

Other changes marked the era in less visible and quantifiable ways. The invention and dissemination of steam power, telegraphy, photography, and other new technologies changed people's perception of time and space, while the widespread religious upheavals of the period and the fracture of American Christianity into scores of denominations placed many believers in new relations to God and to one another. Late in his career, as Ralph Waldo Emerson recalled this religious tumult, he identified what was to him the defining transformation of the age: by 1850 "the mind had become aware of itself." He wrote that beginning in the 1830s, there arose "a new consciousness" based in the belief that "the individual is the world." This perception cut like "a sword . . . never drawn before" and led to an age "of severance, of dissociation, of freedom, of analysis, of detachment." The youth were "born with knives in their brain [*sic*], a tendency to introversion, self-dissection, anatomizing of motives."[1]

The trajectory Emerson hinted at can be fleshed out. In the late eighteenth century, most Americans lived in a world defined primarily by an individual's relation to divine otherness. A quarter century later, the reigning notion was that of free will, though the expectation that the individual would conform to agreed-upon religious and social models still prevailed. In the two decades preceding the Civil War, another shift occurred, this time toward the self-consciousness that Emerson recognized. Cultural commentators less optimistic than he, pining for a world and way of life that was fast slipping away, saw not freedom but solipsism in this latest turn.[2]

Not incidentally, the first American novels appeared at the start of this transformation, and both reflected and helped make possible the movement toward free will and then Emersonian self-consciousness and self-reliance. A narrative form imported from Europe, the novel took on a distinctively American cast in the hands of native writers. Owing to the fundamental religiosity of American life and to a fractured spiritual landscape, the early novel was often an author's means for articulating her theological position and her prescriptions for her fellow citizens. But, especially deeper into the century, many novelists began to espouse areligious and even antireligious ideas. The novel was frequently a proselytizing tool, but not always for religious ends. In the 1850s, a reviewer for Philadelphia's *Graham's Magazine*, intending merely to comment on the ubiquity and variety of the novel, revealed the contemporary assumption that most novels had such a purpose. He wrote that there are "political novels, representing every variety of political opinion—religious novels, to push the doctrines of every religious sect—philanthropic novels, devoted to the championship of every reform—socialist novels . . . philosophical novels, metaphysical novels, even railway novels [that is, those suited, in topic or length, to be read as one rode the rails]."[3] In the same decade, a reviewer in *Putnam's Monthly Magazine* wrote, "Novels are one of the features of our age . . . we would not know what we would do without them."[4]

To understand how religion determined the nature of the early American novel, we need look no further than the eighteenth-century theologian Jonathan Edwards. On May 30, 1850, the Reverend Edwards Amasa Park addressed the Convention of Congregational Ministers of Massachusetts in the venerable Brattle Street Meeting House in Boston. The assembly was eager to hear an important member of the influential group known as Consistent Calvinists—those who preserved and refined Jonathan Edwards's theology.[5] Yet Park's sermon, titled "The Theology of the Intellect and the Theology of the Feelings," only fanned a controversy smoldering within American Christianity since Edwards's time. No religious address since Emerson's at the Harvard Divinity School fourteen years earlier had so captured the public's attention.[6]

Park asked the question of the era: Were the great truths of Christianity apprehended through the head or the heart? Put another way, were men's actions motivated by rational analysis or emotional impulse? In 1790 the answer had been uncontroversial: by the power of man's reason. But by 1850 some theologians had started to question the divine origin of the Bible, and to argue that the truth of Christian doctrine should be felt rather than understood. The German theologian Friedrich Schleiermacher, who declared that true religion consisted of "feeling" rather than "knowing," was particularly influential in American religious circles. To the chagrin of conservative theologians, Schleiermacher's ideas, at first confined to radical religions such as Transcendentalism, began to spread more widely, so that one's emotional life—how one was affected—often took precedence over what one thought.[7]

Park, drawing on a lesser-known aspect of Edwards's thought, had his own ideas about how one should interpret Scripture. His premise was simple: The theology of the intellect and that of the feelings both had a role to play. He saw that his namesake had recognized the value of the theology of the feelings, a fact de-emphasized by Edwards's logic-chopping acolytes. "In order to reach all the hiding-places of emotion," Park explained, great theologians occasionally had to strain a word "to its utmost significancy," and in so doing seemingly contradicted other parts of their theological system. Such had been the case with Edwards. He was not "a mere mathematician" but gave "his feelings a full, easy, and various play."[8] Because his writings on what he termed "the religious affections" lent themselves to the nineteenth century's understanding of the theology of the feelings, Edwards remained relevant through the antebellum period.[9] Between 1800 and 1860 his hortatory volumes, particularly his narratives of the eighteenth-century revivals, *A Treatise Concerning the Religious Affections* and *The Life of David Brainerd*, were among the most frequently reprinted American books; their primary competition was Benjamin Franklin's *Autobiography*.[10]

Edwards's insistence on both the religious affections and the mind greatly influenced a number of the best-known early novelists. In his *Pierre; or, The Ambiguities* (1852), Herman Melville opined, in a way that Edwards and Park would have understood, that God's truth was one thing and man's conception of it another, yet "by their very contradictions they are made to correspond."[11] Harriet Beecher Stowe, daughter of the Edwardsian clergyman Lyman Beecher, recalled that when she was a child, Edwards's works were still "discussed by every farmer, in intervals of plough and hoe, by every woman and girl, at loom, spinning wheel, or wash-tub."[12] In *The Minister's Wooing* (1859), she used one of Edwards's chief disciples, Samuel Hopkins (who famously argued that a Christian should be willing to be damned for the glory of God), as a sounding board for her characters' conflicting religious views. Stowe's brother Henry Ward Beecher, the most famous and highest-paid preacher in post–Civil War America, wrote in his historical novel of New England, *Norwood; or, Village Life in New England* (1867), "I think we owe everything to her theologians, and most to the doctrinal."[13]

* * *

If the arc from traditional religion to self-consciousness helps us understand how the early novel evolved, the contest between civic duty and individualism, the most consistent trope of the early novel, religious, blasphemous, agnostic, or otherwise, shows that in important ways the novel retained certain features throughout the period. Moreover, this contest was more often than not embedded in the sentimental genre, which traces its origins to Great Britain—to Laurence Sterne's *A Sentimental Journey* (1768) and Henry Mackenzie's *The Man of Feeling* (1771). A reaction to the neoclassical values of restraint and order, the sentimental novel, like Parks's theology, made room for the emotions alongside rational analysis. It took as its primary concern the feelings of its characters, tended to focus on moral behavior, and featured weaker, neglected members of society—women struggling for acknowledgment and self-determination as well as orphans and the poor.

With these constants in mind, let us explore some of the many ideas, settings, and forms that characterized the early novel. Around the turn of the century, William Hill Brown and Charles Brockden Brown (no relation) explored the limits of rationality, emphasizing the random irruption of the irrational into even the most settled lives; their target was the young nation's emergent ethos of liberal individualism. Beginning in the 1820s, some novelists, inspired by the fiftieth anniversary of American independence as well as the bicentennial of New England's settlement, began to write historical fiction, evincing a concern for the public good; in novels by James Fenimore Cooper, William Gilmore Simms, and others, readers encountered characters whose altruistic behavior signaled not only their virtue but also the success of the country's democratic experiment.

Less remembered but just as significant were Catharine Maria Sedgwick and Lydia Maria Child, who questioned the legacy of their Puritan forefathers in light of newer liberal religious denominations, like the Quakers or Unitarians. Moved by debates over the controversy of Indian removal—particularly the expulsion of the Cherokees, Seminoles, and others from their ancestral lands in the Southeast—as well as the budding abolitionist movement, they and other writers approached race in startlingly complex and progressive ways. The Philadelphia novelist Robert Montgomery Bird's *Nick of the Woods* (1837) later pushed this liberal religious bent to its limit with a main character who was both an exemplary Christian and a cold-blooded killer. There were also novelists—the incomparable John Neal most memorably—who questioned the very efficacy of historical knowledge to inform behavior in a time of transformative change. Neal's proselytism was about the form of the novel itself; he thought that novelists who truly confronted contemporary challenges had to conceive of new kinds of narratives, as he did throughout the 1820s.

Neal was ahead of his time; most novelists remained firmly within a religious and sentimental mode. Countering centuries-old narratives that presented humankind as fallen, sinful creatures, they held optimistic views of man's capabilities and believed that no matter what one's circumstances, rather than awaiting religious conversion he or she could achieve moral perfection through self-sacrifice and the power of individual will. For many writers, concern for humanity thus replaced Scripture as the standard against which to judge godliness. As a result, their characters, often beset by severe hardships, struggled against ironclad doctrine in order to fully realize nondenominational piety. In America such fiction reached its apogee in works like Susan Warner's *The Wide, Wide World* (1850) and Maria Cummins's *The Lamplighter* (1854), whose main character, Gerty, inspired millions of readers to emulate her Christian humility.

Yet other authors had already begun to reject what they viewed as the sentimental novelists' shallow assessments of character and motivation. They derided the emergent middle-class consensus about how to be and do good by turning for inspiration to European gothic novels. George Lippard and George Thompson shocked readers with graphic depictions of the violence and sexuality of the city. For them, the formation of Christian character was hardly the issue. They questioned not only the economic system that created flagrant social inequity but also whether in such an environment individuals could maintain any sense of communal responsibility.

Still, the sentimental mode, more malleable than is often recognized, proved enduringly useful. American novelists set sentimental novels in mill villages, for instance. An alternative to working in the city, the mill village provided another opportunity for people seeking wage labor. But life in these communities often was as impersonal as city life; company-owned tenements threw together young, unattached people from different communities, and work spaces filled with the deafening noise of gears, wheels, and belts, as well as health hazards like insidious cotton or wool fibers that lodged in the lungs, and poisonous dyes. Novelists endeavored to draw attention to the plight of the worker, in their estimation a major social problem, through wrenchingly emotional stories.

Accelerating economic and territorial expansion in the 1840s and 1850s brought slavery to the fore, and here, too, American novelists deployed sentimental tropes in new and significant ways, particularly to illustrate the humanity of the enslaved. Slavery in the South spawned a literature of social reform in the North, and by the 1850s African American novelists, including some runaway slaves, added their own testimony to that offered by Stowe and a host of other white antislavery writers who gave dignity and agency to a population that novelists had previously disregarded. Notably, among black novelists there were dissenters from abolitionism. Frank J. Webb questioned the intent of whites who crusaded for emancipation but could not abide living or working alongside a free black, while Martin R. Delany variously advocated revolution and repatriation to Africa or Cuba.

A small number of novelists of utopian fiction created plots that centered on an even more radical reorganization of American society,

North and South. These writers portrayed ideal communities, often based on the socialist ideas of the early-nineteenth-century French utopian thinker Charles Fourier (1772–1837), who was widely read at the time for his vision of a harmonious world devoid of social and economic competition, where gratification of one's passions was assured. Others imagined faraway kingdoms untouched by the corruption of European or American civilization and so offered yet different models of the good society.

By the 1850s novelists had begun to write as much about the individual's consciousness of his behavior as of the behavior itself. They followed the lead of Continental Romantics, who believed that self-examination was central to one's humanity. But they fused secular ideas with the language and concerns of American religion, which now included the ultra-liberal, virtually post–Christian Transcendentalism promulgated by Emerson and his disciples, whose ideas of self-reliance, the primacy of mind over the material world, and the centrality of conscience in directing morality had begun to permeate many aspects of American thought. Even evangelical religion did not escape the influence of the Romantic belief in the limitless power of the mind. The famous revivalist Charles Grandison Finney, for example, a key figure in the Second Great Awakening and an example of Romanticism's reconfiguration of the American religious landscape, accounted for his conversion as follows: "I had no where to go but directly to the Bible, and to the philosophy or workings of my own mind as they were revealed in consciousness."[14]

How to convey such views of mind and personality became the project not only of such well-known novelists as Nathaniel Hawthorne in *The Blithedale Romance* (1852) and Melville in *Moby-Dick* (1851) and *Pierre* (1852), but also of Donald G. Mitchell ("Ik Marvel") in his immensely popular *Reveries of a Bachelor* (1850), Lillie Devereux Blake in *Southwold* (1859), and Elizabeth Stoddard in *The Morgesons* (1862). In these mid-nineteenth-century novelists one sees the halting emergence of a style that in 1890 William James would call a "stream of thought, of consciousness." The novel had entered a new phase, and as subjectivity gradually replaced sentiment as the novelist's donnée, we soon arrive at the doorstep of William's brother Henry and literary modernism.

Just as certain novelists began to represent the mysteries of the interior life, however, some of their contemporaries challenged hyperindividualism as a threat to the nation. The new self-indulgence needed its own counterweight, one provided by a reaffirmation of the nation's demo-cratic bases, the supposed willingness of individuals to live for the com-monwealth. In Rebecca Harding Davis's work, particularly *Margret Howth: A Story of To-Day* (1862), and in several of Elizabeth Stuart Phelps's novels of the 1870s, self-indulgence is the chief reason for the country's moral decline. Self-knowledge, Davis believed, should end not in self-absorption but rather in the realization of the nation's founding principles. Hers was one of the first secular arguments for civic duty over individualism to appear in the American novel.

* * *

This book is organized more or less chronologically, moving from the late eighteenth century to the early 1870s, ending with novels written shortly after the war years but not indelibly affected by the cataclysm, which, as a number of historians have argued, American writers took years to assimi-late.[15] The emphasis is on the period after 1820, when the publishing in-dustry modernized and expanded, making possible the novel's emergence as the country's most popular literary form. I attempt as much as possible to put every novelist in his or her historical and biographical context, though some remain insufficiently knowable to us. The focus is on authors whose works marked significant turning points for the novel. By my lights, the most popular novelists at the time were not always the most influential, and the work for which an author was best known was not necessarily the most significant in her œuvre.

Three debts make the goals of this book clear. The title is borrowed from Melville's last work, *Billy Budd, Sailor (An Inside Narrative)* (1891). Late in this novella, Melville admits that his narration of Billy's story is not as "finished" as readers might hope, because "Truth uncompromis-ingly told will always have its ragged edges." I take him to mean that it is difficult to comprehend, let alone write of, truth in any fullness be-cause of its complexity and ultimate ambiguity. My reading of early American fiction is attentive to authors who made an honest attempt to capture that fullness.

My subtitle is likewise borrowed, though not, as is surely evident, from a novel. Alexander Cowie's 1948 history *The Rise of the American Novel* still remains, along with Richard Chase's 1957 classic *The American Novel and Its Tradition*, one of the most thorough and well-regarded studies of its kind. Though I review my book as a revival of a dormant tradition, I hope to recapture only the earlier books' ambition, not their content. After all, much has changed since Cowie and Chase's time. The rediscovery of writers forgotten or ignored because of their gender or race has upended the history of the novel, and stands as an important thread in the rewriting of early American history over the past few decades to make it more inclusive and attentive to the powerless members of society. My hope is that bringing women and African American novelists into the discussion will result in the fullest understanding yet of the early American novel.

The final and greatest debt is to the late Alan Heimert, for the approach to the history of ideas I learned from his work early in my career. As he put it, "An understanding of the significance of any idea, or of a constellation of ideas, requires an awareness of the context of institutions and events out of which thought emerged, and with which it strove to come to terms." But full comprehension, he continued, "depends finally on reading, not between the lines but, as it were, beyond and through them."[16] My intent is to read beyond and through the lines of early novels, to find and examine the constellation of ideas that defined American life in the first half of the nineteenth century and that drove citizens to pick up their quills and write fiction.

PART I } 1789–1850

I } Beginnings

Historians of the English novel point to John Bunyan's *Pilgrim's Progress* (1678) as a progenitor of the form. The American version of this tale is Joseph Morgan's *History of the Kingdom of Basaruah* (1715), a minister's allegory of the Calvinist view of man's fall and redemption.[1] Though uninspired, the book is a testament to the centrality of Christian allegories in eighteenth-century British North America.[2] But with the circulation in the newly independent United States of popular English novels like Samuel Richardson's *Pamela* (1740) and *Clarissa* (1747–48), Laurence Sterne's *A Sentimental Journey* (1768), and Henry Mackenzie's *The Man of Feeling* (1771), novelists began to revise and sometimes challenge allegorical narratives of the pious Christian life. Rather than provide road maps through the Delectable Mountains, they heralded the triumph of individual virtue and urged the cultivation of sentiment in contemporary settings readers would recognize. They often based their novels on the kinds of stories heard from neighbors or read in the weekly newspapers—tales, in other words, populated not by pasteboard archetypes but by real people. Appropriate for earlier times, accounts of a pilgrim's progress lacked the texture and complexity of everyday experience in the late-eighteenth-century United States and particularly its moral ambiguity.

Fictional works that directed an individual through this sinful world emerged first as handmaidens and then as rivals to the sermons, religious allegories, and wonder tales that hitherto had dominated native literature. In his *Algerine Captive* (1797), one of the earliest American novels, Royall Tyler, Vermont superior court judge, playwright, poet, and novelist, noted this shift. His character Updike Underhill, following six years of captivity in the Barbary States, remarks how on his return from his forced absence from the United States he "found a surprising alteration in public taste," for now everyone read novels. "The worthy farmer no longer fatigued himself with Bunyan's Pilgrim up the 'hill of difficulty,' or through the 'slough of despond,'" and "Dolly, the dairy maid, and Jonathan, the hired man, threw aside the ballad of the cruel stepmother, over which they had so often wept."[3] A character in another early American work commented on the same shift in reading habits. "We fly from the laboured precepts of the essayists," he observed, "to the sprightly narrative of the novelist."[4]

This comment appears in what is widely recognized as the first bona fide American novel, William Hill Brown's *The Power of Sympathy*.[5] Brown (1765–1793) was born in Boston, the son of a prominent clockmaker.[6] Educated locally, he displayed a penchant for classical and English literature and by his early twenties was publishing patriotic poetry, thereby contributing to the city's nascent cultural nationalism. In one poem, "Shays to Shattuck: An Epistle," Brown imagines a conversation in prison between a despondent Daniel Shays, fomenter of Shays's Rebellion, and one of his foot soldiers, in which the former tries to justify his rebellion. In another, "Yankee Song," Brown celebrates the state's recent ratification of the Federal Constitution. The poem contains the refrain "Yankee Doodle keep it up, Yankee Doodle dandy" and upon republication the following year carried the now-familiar title "Yankee Doodle." In his early twenties, Brown came to the attention of the prominent printer and publisher Isaiah Thomas, who encouraged regional authors by publishing them in his newspapers and a periodical titled *The Massachusetts Magazine* (1789–1796), whose contributors eventually included Benjamin Franklin, the New Hampshire essayist Joseph Dennie, the poet Sarah Wentworth Apthorp Morton, and the early women's rights advocate Judith Sargent Murray. Thomas was not particularly interested in publishing native fiction, however, finding children's books and almanacs, as well as reprints of popular English titles, more lucrative. But his good nose for profit led him in 1789 to publish Brown's *The Power of Sympathy*, no doubt thinking that its thinly veiled references to recent sensational events in Boston guaranteed its success.[7]

For almost a century this novel was mistakenly attributed—Thomas had issued it anonymously—to another Boston writer, the poet Sarah

Wentworth Apthorp Morton, because she was intimately involved in the scandal that had inspired it. This sordid tale unfolded in two of Boston's most prominent families. Sarah Apthorp married Perez Morton, a prominent state politician who counted the Revolutionary patriot James Otis among his friends. The Mortons graciously allowed Sarah's unmarried sister Frances (Fanny) to live with them in their Beacon Hill home, but she proved too tempting to Perez; a surreptitious affair led to the birth of their child. Sarah and Fanny's father, James Apthorp, was outraged and demanded that Morton openly acknowledge the baby girl. Morton refused, and just before a meeting at which Apthorp planned to press his demand even more forcefully, Fanny poisoned herself and died.[8]

"THIS TYRANT CUSTOM"
Brown used the scandal to explore the vagaries of human passion in a young republic that extolled free will. *The Power of Sympathy*, an epistolary novel, alternates between scenes of overt moralizing and outright melodrama. It begins in a way familiar to contemporary readers, with Thomas Harrington writing to his friend Jack Worthy about his attraction to Harriot Fawcet, whom he plans to seduce. But she successfully resists his intentions, whereupon Brown includes his first surprise: Harrington, now admiring her virtue as well as her beauty, eventually falls in love with her, and she with him. However, some in their circle disapprove of their marriage plans. In particular, Mrs. Holmes, a family friend, urges another of Harrington's friends to dissuade him. Before long, the secret comes out: the couple cannot marry because they are siblings. Harriot is the result of Harrington's father's illicit affair sixteen years earlier with a young woman, Maria. When Harrington's father learned that his mistress was pregnant, his interest cooled, and he abandoned Maria to her fate. The Reverend and Mrs. Holmes took her in, and the family soon included Maria's young daughter, Harriot; Maria revealed the identity of the girl's father to her benefactors. After Maria becomes gravely ill and dies, the Holmeses, to protect their friend Harrington's reputation, place young Harriot out to service. The news of her early years shocks and dismays both Harrington and her, and before long she dies of sorrow and despair. Learning of her death, Harrington shoots himself, an end that borrows from Goethe's book *The Sorrows of Young Werther* (1774).

Much of the novel consists of secondary characters moralizing on this tragic course of events. Worthy's epistles, for example, and those of Mr. and Mrs. Holmes read like didactic essays or sermons on character formation in young women, the dangers of reading fiction, and proper republican marriage. But the characters also punctuate their moral lessons by alluding to other events at least as troubling as the dilemma in which the Harringtons and Harriot find themselves. One subplot concerns a young man, Henry, who after his lover, Fidelia, is kidnapped just before their marriage, takes his own life. Her abductors release her; but on hearing of Henry's fate, she despairs and becomes deranged. Another tangential tale, again centering on the vagaries of passion, details the affair of the senior Mr. Harrington and the young Maria. And in a brief textual reference and lengthy footnote, Brown alludes to yet another contemporary story making the rounds in New England. Elizabeth Whitman, a Connecticut clergyman's unmarried daughter, had died alone in childbirth at a tavern near Boston, the baby's father unknown, a scandal that later became the basis of another early American novel, Hannah Webster Foster's *The Coquette* (1798).

As these stories indicate, in *The Power of Sympathy* Brown was chiefly interested in the wages of excessive passion, both socially approved and illicit. Henry's love for Fidelia is so great that once she is abducted, he kills himself because he cannot imagine life without her. Ophelia and Maria are unable to resist the advances of men who they believe are willing to marry them but in fact are rakes. Harrington and Harriot's affection is so deep that the impossibility of their marrying leads to one's suicide and the other's premature death. Brown implies that love, hatred, and fear cannot be easily controlled and often push one to irrationality. Recounting Ophelia's story, Brown writes that when Martin turned on her, "she awoke from her dream of insensibility, she was like one . . . deluded by an *ignis fatuus* to the brink of a precipice, . . . abandoned . . . to contemplate the horrours of the sea beneath him, into which he was about to plunge."[9]

That terrifying moment, standing at the edge of an abyss and peering over, fascinated Brown, as it did other early American writers. Famously, it became the subject of Edgar Allan Poe's story "The Imp of the Perverse," his name for the impulse to look over the edge, fascinated by the thought of one's extinction. In *The Power of Sympathy*, Harrington and Harriot continue to feel more than familial love even after they realize that their love is illicit. He wonders why "this transport" is a crime, for his affection for Harriot is "most pure, the most holy . . . Here," Harrington exclaims upon learning his dilemma, "was all the horrour of conflicting passions."[10] What precisely *does* one do about such a love? The rational Mrs. Holmes cannot help them. "GREAT God!" she cries to Harrington's sister, Myra. "Of what materials has thou compounded the hearts of thy creatures! Admire, o my friend, the operation of NATURE—and the power of SYMPATHY!"[11] Even the elder Harrington is at a loss to comprehend his son's and Harriot's plight. He asks the Reverend Holmes, "How shall we pretend to investigate the great springs by which we are actuated, or account for the operation of SYMPATHY?" His son, he continues, had "accidentally seen [Harriot], and to complete THE TRIUMPH OF NATURE—has loved her."[12]

Brown, too, stands at the verge of such an abyss but refuses the plunge. He does not pretend to know why such things as Harrington's and Harriot's love occur and ends his novel the "easy" way, with the death of one of the lovers. Harriot's demise drives Harrington to despair, even as his suicide serves a higher purpose: soon he will join her in heaven, where their love "will not be a crime," although the reader never learns why not.[13] In their earthly lives, the problem resides in society's arbitrary rules, in particular an insistence on the supremacy of reason over passion. "Why did I love [this] Harriot?" Harrington ruefully asks. "Curse on this tyrant custom that dooms such helpless children to oblivion and infamy!"[14]

Brown's characters' failings indicated his allegiance to the ideals of republican virtue, selfishness at odds with their privileged position in society. The elder Harrington's dalliance with Maria, his inferior in social class, betrays a social hierarchy that exists even in a supposedly democratic nation. "I am not so much a republican," the younger Harrington tells Worthy early in the novel, "as formally to wed any person of this class. How laughable," he thinks, openly to acknowledge as his wife a "daughter of the democratick empire of virtue."[15] To his surprise, "the power of sympathy" prevails, for he does fall in love. But once the couple's true relationship is known, to formalize it would only fray, if not sever, the still-fragile bonds of republican virtue. Brown thus postpones their happiness until heaven.

SUSANNA ROWSON'S EMERGENCE

The revolutionary nature of the U.S. government was not explicit in *The Power of Sympathy* but in various degrees was the focus of other early

American novels, particularly Hugh Henry Brackenridge's *Modern Chivalry* (1792–1815), set in western Pennsylvania after the disruption of the Whiskey Rebellion, and Tyler's *Algerine Captive*, which drew on the United States' conflict with the Barbary States. These are loose and baggy picaresque novels that through satire probe the country's new social order, in particular the still-uncomfortable notion that the most plebeian citizen should be afforded the same respect as a person of wealth and influence. Thomas Jefferson voiced this ideal when he famously wrote John Adams in 1813 that there is a natural aristocracy among men based in virtue and talent that should trump any inherited or honorary rank.

But these picaresque novels were never as popular as other contemporary novels, such as *The Power of Sympathy*, that center on the vagaries of human passion, typified by seemingly omnipresent tales of seduction. One historian attributes this genre's popularity in part to the "dramatic slackening" of laws against moral offenses like prostitution and adultery. In this climate women "began to experience unprecedented social and sexual freedom," even as didactic novels and other moralistic literature warned of the dangers of female sexuality.[16] Perennially the most popular novel of passion was Susanna Rowson's *Charlotte: A Tale of Truth*, first published to an indifferent reception in England in 1791 by William Lane at his Minerva Press and issued in Philadelphia three years later. In the United States, however, *Charlotte Temple*, as it was retitled in 1797, became one of the bestselling novels before Harriet Beecher Stowe's *Uncle Tom's Cabin* (1852), appearing in scores of editions, most commonly as *Charlotte Temple: A Tale of Truth*. What was its appeal to an American readership?

One answer lies in the way Rowson's biography gave the book an air of undeniable veracity, for just as William Hill Brown's life was brief and relatively uneventful, Rowson's was the stuff of contemporary fiction.[17] She was born Susanna Musgrove Haswell in 1762 in Portsmouth, England, the daughter of William Haswell, a career naval officer, and Susanna Musgrove Haswell, who died when her daughter was only ten days old. When Rowson was a year old, the English navy sent Haswell on assignment to New England as a customs official, and relatives in England cared for her until he brought her over in 1767. Having landed in Boston Harbor on a frigid and stormy midwinter day (a scene she later re-created in her novel *Rebecca; or, The Fille de Chambre* [1792]), Rowson found a new home at nearby Nantasket, a peninsula just south of the city. There she faced many adjustments, for she had to live not only with a parent she hardly knew but also with a stepmother, whom Haswell had married two years earlier. Although Susanna never warmed to Rachel Woodward Haswell, she later looked back fondly on these years, filled as they were with seaside and country walks and fine literature from her father's library, not to mention spirited conversation with the future patriot James Otis, who gave her, according to one early biographer's account, "particular notice and favor."[18]

But the 1760s and 1770s were increasingly difficult times for the Crown's officers. As the imperial crisis escalated, Haswell attempted to stay neutral, but his situation grew tenuous. Finally, in 1775, he and his family were placed under house arrest and relocated, first to nearby Hingham and then inland to Abington, this second move occurring because none other than Perez Morton had accused Haswell of "frequently making such false representations among the inhabitants, as tend to cause divisions, to strengthen our enemies, to intimidate and weaken our friends."[19] During these difficult years Susanna played a large role in staving off the family's privation, often securing food and other necessities from sympathetic friends, both English and American. The family was finally able to return to London in 1778, after Haswell requested an exchange for an American prisoner, a trade completed in Halifax, Nova Scotia, between British and American authorities.

But in England the family's economic difficulties only mounted. After a succession of unremarkable jobs, Rowson found her way to the stage and then, after a modicum of success, began a prolific career as a songwriter, playwright, and novelist. In 1786 she published *Victoria*, and three more novels followed. None, however, drew much attention. During this period she married William Rowson, a hardware merchant, handyman on theater sets, and occasional actor and musician who brought an illegitimate son to the union. William Rowson never attained anything like his wife's success and reputedly was a drunk, but the two remained together until her death in 1824.

In the early 1790s Rowson caught the attention of the prominent American actor and playwright Thomas Wignell, who enticed her across the Atlantic to work in his New Theater in Philadelphia. Arriving at the end of the great yellow fever epidemic of 1793, the family decamped to Baltimore almost immediately. When it was safe to return to Philadelphia, Rowson resumed acting, filling important secondary roles in several of Wignell's productions. She tried her hand at playwriting, penning the relatively popular *Slaves in Algiers; or, A Struggle for Freedom* (1794). She also convinced the city's major publisher, Matthew Carey, to reissue *Charlotte*, the last of the quartet of novels she had written in England in the 1780s. Its publication proved a better business decision for him than it had for Lane, and he issued three subsequent editions in the next few years. But frustrated because on the stage she remained in the shadows of more prominent leading ladies, in 1796 Rowson moved to the Federal Street Theatre in Boston, where her two stepbrothers lived. There she briefly continued her acting career and then, recalling the difficulties of her own teenage years, reinvented herself one more time, as the preceptor of a female academy. She abandoned fiction altogether upon completion of the ambitious but not overly popular historical novel *Reuben and Rachel* (1798). For the next twenty-five years Rowson devoted herself to her Young Ladies' Academy.

SEDUCTION AND BETRAYAL

Rowson's career was transatlantic in scope and achievement, yet surprisingly she is mainly remembered for *Charlotte Temple*. The book's plot is straightforward and, to a late-eighteenth-century reader, would have been familiar. Charlotte is an attractive fifteen-year-old at an English boarding school, placed there by loving parents who have done little to prepare her for adulthood's trials. On one of her walks, she catches the eye of John Montraville, an English officer who is about to go to America and who, after losing interest in marrying the girl when he learns that she has no great wealth, decides he still wants her as his lover.

In the brief dalliance that ensues, Mademoiselle La Rue, a French teacher at the school who herself plans to elope with Montraville's associate Belcour, convinces Charlotte to see the lieutenant one last time before he leaves the country. Told by Madame Du Pont, the preceptor, that her parents soon will arrive to take her home for her birthday, Charlotte has one last chance to turn from her folly. "The irrevocable step is not taken" yet, she reasons; "it is not too late to recede from the brink of a precipice, from which I can only behold the dark abyss of ruin, shame, and remorse!"[20] But La Rue convinces her that it would be cruel not to see Montraville a last time, and caught between love and reason, Charlotte capitulates. Montraville sweeps her into a waiting carriage and seals her fate. Immediately remorseful, Charlotte writes to her parents to alert them to her whereabouts, but Montraville, who has promised to mail her letter, instead destroys it. As their ship embarks for New York, the abductors show their true colors. The fortune hunter La Rue, realizing that Belcour has no money, instead sets her eyes on one Colonel Crayton, a wealthy but simple soul who quickly succumbs to her wiles. For his part, Belcour, aware that Montraville does not intend to marry Charlotte, decides to woo her as soon as opportunity permits.

After disembarking in New York, where Montraville is stationed, he installs Charlotte, now pregnant, in a small home just outside the city. His increasingly infrequent visits do little to alleviate her growing depression, as she finally understands the severity of her plight, as well as the pain her precipitous behavior has caused her parents. Still looking for marriage to a lady of means, Montraville begins to court Julia Franklin, a wealthy heiress. Though he seems genuinely guilty about his treatment of Charlotte, he jumps at an excuse to break with her, an opportunity that arises when Belcour (still trying to advance his prospects with her) convinces him that Charlotte has been with other men, including himself. Having discovered Belcour with her in a deceptively compromising situation (of Belcour's contrivance), Montraville marries Julia but leaves Belcour money for Charlotte and her unborn child. Despondent, she again writes to her parents. Her health continues to decline, and Belcour, too, loses interest in her, stops his visits, keeps the money Montraville earmarked for her, and marries a wealthy farmer's daughter.

Charlotte's only happiness comes when her father, having received her missive, travels to the United States and finds her on her deathbed. She begs his forgiveness and makes him promise to care for her recently born daughter, Lucy. Distraught after he has made a visit to the cottage and not found Charlotte, Montraville frantically searches for her and comes upon her funeral. Meeting Mr. Temple, he confesses his part in his daughter's downfall; he will go on to lead a melancholic life punctuated by frequent visits to his former lover's grave. Mr. Temple and little Lucy return to England. Ten years later Temple and his wife find on their doorstep a destitute woman, none other than La Rue. Separated from her husband for seven years and mired in vice and misery, she asks forgiveness for her part in the family's tragedy. Ever compassionate, the Temples place her in a nearby hospital, where a few weeks later she dies, completing the wreckage begun at the girls' school years earlier.

Charlotte Temple thus has all the markings of a morality tale that warns young women of seduction. But what is one to make of its wildly different reception in England and the United States? Did its subject matter resonate differently because of the younger nation's distinctive political and social ideals? The answer lies not in the reader's sympathy for Charlotte but in Rowson's carefully wrought depictions of other characters' reactions to her plight.

"THE IMPULSE OF A YOUTHFUL PASSION"

Belcour is the novel's only truly unrepentant soul and presumably ends the tale enjoying his gentleman's life in the country. Rowson makes clear that he is a villain and from the outset distinguishes him from Montraville, who is "generous in his disposition, liberal in his opinions, and good-natured almost to a fault." In contrast, Belcour "paid little regard to moral duties, and less to religious ones," and did not think twice about the misery he inflicted on others. In short, "Self, darling self, was the idol he worshiped."[21] So why does Montraville seduce and abandon Charlotte? It is because he lacks virtuous friends who could point out the cruelty of his actions. He is oblivious of the consequences of his unchecked passion: infamy and misery for her and his own "never-ceasing remorse." Had someone informed Montraville of what lay ahead, Rowson writes, "the humanity of his nature would have urged him to give up the pursuit."[22] Instead, Belcour, his ostensible friend who is lost to selfishness, only made the situation worse.

La Rue's story is more complex. Early in her life she is placed in a French convent, from which she elopes with a young military officer, the first of many lovers. In England she continues her debauchery, living with several different men "in open defiance of all moral and religious duties."[23] With La Rue, Rowson, an avowed Federalist, confirms her contemporaries' suspicion that the French Revolution, which while taking its inspiration from the American, descended into what most Federalists believed to be anarchy and madness and has spawned an attendant libertinism. The result, as the Yale president Timothy Dwight warned in a lecture on infidelity to the college's students: "its great object is to unsettle every thing moral and obligatory, and to settle nothing."[24] Rowson's book spoke directly to such fears that in the United States, where the effects of its own revolution were not yet completed, such transgressions as Charlotte's would become all too common.

After another lover abandons La Rue and she is "reduced to the most abject want," she gets a chance at rehabilitation. An acquaintance of Du Pont's generously takes her in, and after La Rue displays what her benefactress takes as sincere penitence, she brings her to the preceptor's attention. La Rue did, after all, have "a pleasing person and insinuating address," as well as "liberal education and the manners of a gentlewoman." But she could not govern herself and had "too much of the spirit of intrigue to remain long without adventures."[25] Unlike Belcour, though, La Rue finally cannot live with herself and finds her way to the Temples to ask for forgiveness. "I am the viper that stung your peace," she exclaims. "I am the woman who turned the poor Charlotte out to perish in the street."[26]

Rowson intended *Charlotte Temple* as a guide or even a warning. She addresses the "young, volatile reader," who she guesses is bored at her novel's frequent depictions of "fainting, tears, and distress." "I must request your patience," she writes. "I am writing a tale of the truth" and intend to "write it to the heart." Do not throw the novel aside, she pleads, "till you have perused the whole."[27] Such perusal, however, does not bring the reader to a simple moral but to Montraville's and Charlotte's welter of conflicting emotions. Uncertainty and remorse complicate the novel; with a little more maturity, Montraville might have made a worthy match.

The message of *Charlotte Temple* is that capitulation to one's feelings without proper rational reflection could lead not only to personal tragedy but to a breakdown of social mores of the sort that Federalists believed had followed the Reign of Terror in France and that would visit the United States if Jefferson were elected president. Once again Timothy Dwight, along with the Charlestown, Massachusetts, minister Jedediah Morse, most typified the hysterical alarm among conservatives. Dwight opined that if Americans did not combat France's infidelity, "those morals which protect our lives from the knife of the assassin, which guard the chastity of our wives and daughters from seduction and violence, defend our property from plunder and devastation and shield our religion from contempt and profanation" would be trampled upon, and "our wives and daughters [would become] the victims of legal prostitution."[28] Charlotte's melancholy death after her abandonment by those whom she, in her naiveté, thought trustworthy was a political as well as a moral lesson for the new nation.

The only American book to approach *Charlotte Temple* in popularity was another tale of seduction and betrayal, Hannah Webster Foster's *The Coquette*, a complex work that, like *The Power of Sympathy*, emerged from the ideas and mores of post-Revolutionary Boston. Although upon publication it did not sell as rapidly as Rowson's novel, it was reprinted throughout the nineteenth century, including a remarkable eight times from 1824 to 1828.

We know less about *The Coquette*'s author than we do of Rowson or Brown. Foster was born in 1758 in Salisbury, Massachusetts, the daughter of a prominent merchant, Grant Webster, and Hannah Wainwright Webster, after whose death four years later the widower sent his young daughter to a women's academy. In 1785 she married John Foster, a young Dartmouth College graduate and minister of the Congregational church in Brighton, Massachusetts. They had six children, three sons and three daughters, two of whom themselves became notable writers.[29] During this busy period Hannah Foster found time to publish two books, *The Coquette; or, The History of Eliza Wharton: a Novel Founded on Fact* (1797), whose title page identified her only as "A Lady of Massachusetts"; and *The Boarding School; or, Lessons of a Preceptress to Her Pupils* (1798), based in part on her own experiences. Aside from some anonymous essays published a decade later in *The Monthly Anthology or Magazine of Polite Literature* (later the *North American Review*), Foster left no other writings, in large part because of her deep engagement in Brighton's religious and social life, which accompanied her station as a minister's wife.[30] After her husband's death in 1829, Foster moved to Montreal to live with her daughter Elizabeth (known as Eliza), the wife of Dr. Frederick Cushing, a physician in that city, where Foster died in 1840.

Like Brown, Foster based her most popular work on a widely discussed current event first reported in the *Salem* (Massachusetts) *Mercury* for July 29, 1788. It was an account of the death four days earlier of a young woman at the Bell Tavern in nearby Danvers, shortly after she had delivered a stillborn child under circumstances to "excite curiosity, and interest [one's] feelings." Someone engaged for the purpose had brought her there in a chaise and then left. The woman's demeanor marked her as from "a respectable family and good education," the report continued, but she "was averse to being interrogated concerning herself or [her] connexions" and kept mainly to herself, anxiously awaiting the arrival of someone (presumably, the father of her child). After her child's and her deaths, kindly townspeople gave them a decent burial.

Within days other papers copied the story, and soon it was the talk of the region, particularly after the woman was identified as Elizabeth Whitman, the daughter of the Reverend Elnathan Whitman, a prominent Hartford clergyman.[31] Though the story was not in itself extraordinary—after the Revolution rates of illegitimate births skyrocketed—the fact that a prominent person had met so sad and mysterious an end caught the public's interest and led many to ask why she had been at the tavern and for whom she had been waiting. A decade after these events, Foster published her novel based on them, changing Elizabeth Whitman's name to Eliza Wharton.

In 1855 Jane E. Locke introduced a new edition of *The Coquette* with a lengthy biographical introduction that included significant new information about Whitman, her family, and the stillborn child's father. Although all of Locke's facts cannot be verified, she did at least help the reader understand just how Foster transformed Whitman's tragic tale for her own purposes.

Elizabeth Whitman had an impeccable New England pedigree. Her great-grandfather had married one of the daughters of Solomon Stoddard, a prominent minister in the Massachusetts Bay Colony and the grandfather of Jonathan Edwards. She seemed destined to unite with a clergyman, and when she was still quite young, such a match was proposed—arranged, really—with one Joseph Howe, minister to Norwich, Connecticut. A considerably older man, Howe died suddenly. At some point in the next few years Whitman, a society belle, entertained another offer, from a recent Harvard graduate, Joseph Stevens Buckminster, minister to an important church in Portsmouth, New Hampshire, and one of the most prominent young "liberal Christians" of the day. But Whitman rejected him and, remaining single, eventually met the untimely death described in the newspapers. Locke offered a crucial but unsubstantiated fact: the father of Elizabeth's child was none other than the Honorable Pierpont Edwards, Jonathan Edwards's youngest, wayward son and thus her second cousin.[32]

Locke intended her biography to rehabilitate Whitman's image. Exceedingly beautiful, highly intelligent, and accomplished, Whitman was always the center of attention. She was extraordinary in other ways, too: very moody, "as the truly gifted ever are, and of a wild incomprehensible nature, little understood by those who should have known her best." In Pierpont Edwards she met someone who presumably understood her and could satisfy her emotional needs. Between them there was "a close affinity of spirit," a "marriage of the soul . . . that overshadows sin." Then the bombshell: the two lovers had not only such a marriage of spirits but also "one [that], though secret, [was] actually sanctified by the law of the land," a fact Whitman was "known to have declared" prior to her death.[33]

Why, then, was she left alone at the tavern to die? Locke repeats the story of Whitman's lonely isolation as she waited in her room, passing the time writing and occasionally playing a guitar, "the only companion of her solitude." Then, one night after about two weeks, a chaise appeared. Someone got out, paused at the door as though looking for something but, evidently not finding what he sought, drove away. In daylight, one could see, in chalk over the lintel at which he had peered, the scrawled letters "E. W.," too faint to see in darkness. Pierpont Edwards, Locke believed, had returned for Whitman, only to miss the agreed-upon symbol by which she marked her location.[34]

More than *The Power of Sympathy* or *Charlotte Temple*, *The Coquette* places the reader in a world in which what passed as moral rectitude conflicted with the national belief in individual freedom. *The Coquette* begins with Eliza's scarcely disguised relief at the death of the Reverend Haly (Howe), an older clergyman whom her parents approved of as an ideal spouse. Free to enjoy more time in genteel society, Eliza draws the attention first of Boyer (Buckminster), who is soon to be installed as the minister over an important church and who thinks that she will make an ideal spouse, and then of Peter Sanford (Edwards), an attractive and self-centered rake who wishes to seduce but not marry her. Boyer presses his suit, but Eliza, unwilling to give up her newfound freedom, asks for time. Boyer grows increasingly impatient because Eliza sees more and more of Sanford, even after friends pointedly warn her of his promiscuity. So pressured, she finally decides to marry Boyer, but because she promised Sanford first to inform him of her decision, she agrees to meet him. By chance, Boyer stumbles on the two in the Whartons' garden and precipitously breaks off the engagement. Sanford is now free to pursue his pleasure. Eliza is mortified at the misunderstanding.

Sanford, who views Eliza as a coquette, knows that he now has the advantage. To prolong his titillation, he announces a lengthy business trip to the South. Genuinely distraught over the breakup with Boyer,

Eliza has no outlet for her affection. After a year, Sanford still has not returned, and she writes Boyer to confess her shortsightedness and to ask if despite her faults, he still might accept her. But he is about to marry his friend Selby's sister, whose personality and character he believes more suited to the sober and important career on which he has embarked. Though still fairly young, Eliza has no more suitors, presumably because they, too, question her judgment and consider her a mere flirt. She falls into a deep melancholy.

Sanford returns to the area married to a wealthy woman, yet Eliza more and more depends on him for attention. He craftily (and perversely) establishes a friendship between his wife and her, so he can regularly see his old amour. Then, as his finances and marriage begin to fail, almost in desperation he again pursues Eliza, needing her attention as much as she does his. He persists, and a dalliance becomes outright seduction. When Eliza realizes that she is pregnant, Sanford deposits her at a tavern, promising to return. Delivering a child that dies after only a few hours, Eliza, too, perishes, leaving her friends and family (and Sanford) in despair. As in *Charlotte Temple*, the wreckage is complete.

"THE VERY SOUL OF PLEASURE"

The Coquette is more than a retelling of the Elizabeth Whitman story. The reader would have sympathized with Eliza very differently than she would have with Whitman or Charlotte Temple. For one, Foster's narration takes a sophisticated epistolary form, with central episodes retold from various points of view. Eliza corresponds most often with her friend Lucy Freeman; Boyer, with his friend Selby; and Sanford, with his friend Charles Deighton. There are also letters among Eliza's friends Lucy Freeman Sumner and Julia Granby, the Richmans, and Mrs. Wharton.

More to the point, Eliza is complex. Unlike the immature and insipid Charlotte Temple, she is attractive and prepossessing. Her unwillingness to abide by conventional norms and to engage in the self-regulation demanded by society tears her apart psychologically. Foster registers how attributes that should be regarded as Eliza's strengths—her honest self-scrutiny and fierce independence—instead cause confusion and depression. Attentive contemporary readers of *The Coquette* would not have merely condemned her folly but rather would have considered the nature and consequence of her desire to exercise her free will.

Part of Eliza's appeal is her willingness to say what she thinks and to declare who she is. Writing to Lucy after the untimely death of the Reverend Haly, she does not hide how she welcomes the opportunity to again indulge her "accustomed vivacity" and playfully complains that she disagrees with Lucy's deeming her ways "coquettish." They deserve "a softer appellation," she argues, because they proceed from "an innocent heart, and are the effusions of a youthful, and cheerful mind."[35] Having escaped what from her standpoint clearly would have been a loveless marriage to an older man, all Eliza wants is "that freedom which [she] so highly prize[s]."[36]

Her dilemma is clear: she does not yet want to marry, even if an acceptable suitor appears and even though her parents and friends think that in this she is dangerously bucking common sense as well as morality. Eliza notes the Richmans' insular and private happiness. It saddens her that "[t]hey have no satisfaction to look for beyond each other."[37] Eliza seeks something else, "some amusement" beyond what she can supply by herself, by which she means attendance at the social occasions at which she is the center of attention.[38] Sanford, who prides himself in his judgment of women, notes her "agreeable person, polished manners, and refined talents," all of which make her "the toast of the country around." He registers as well, however, her tendency to flirtation. This makes him want to "avenge [his] sex, by retaliating the mischiefs she meditates" against men. At this point, he has no "ill designs" but wishes only "to play off her own artillery."[39]

What young woman, beginning to entertain thoughts of the other sex, would not identify with Eliza or wish to emulate her freedom and savoir-faire? Or fantasize about companionship with such a man as Sanford, "a professed libertine" who already had "but too successfully practiced the arts of seduction"? Not ready to accept a comfortable but staid life with Boyer, or wanting to become "an avowed prude at once," she continues to flirt with Sanford, who can easily distinguish between "a forbidding, and an encouraging reception." "His person, his manners, his situation, all combine to charm my fancy," she tells Lucy.[40] But although Sanford is lured to the table, he has more experience at the game. "I am," he tells Deighton, a "Proteus, and can assume any shape that will best answer my purpose."[41]

After Lucy reminds Eliza of Sanford's reputation as a rake, she adds that no person of Eliza's "delicacy and refinement" should ever consider connection to such a man and so believes that Eliza must only wish to exhibit "a few more girlish airs" before she "turn[s] matron."[42] Urging Eliza to accept Boyer, Lucy advises that it is time to "lay aside those co-quettish airs which you sometimes put on." But Eliza bristles at Boyer for continuing to press his suit before she is ready to make a decision and recoils "at the thought of immediately forming a connection, which must confine [her] to the duties of domesticity." "You must either quit the subject, or leave me to the exercise of my free will," she tells him emphati-cally, wanting to claim in the sphere of personal behavior the kind of personal freedom to choose that theologians offered in the religious.[43] Trapped in a culture in which marriage was normative, many readers identified with Eliza's frustrating dilemma as a young woman simply "too volatile for a confinement to domestic avocations" yet having no socially sanctioned alternative.[44]

Even Sanford is surprised at Eliza's continued attention. Knowing that her "sagatious [sic] friends have undoubtedly given her a detail of [his] vices," he asks, "[w]hy does she not act consistently, and refuse at once to associate with a man whose character she cannot esteem?"[45] Still, unable to help himself, Sanford takes every opportunity to point out to Eliza the dissimilarity of her disposition and Boyer's, knowing that if he can sepa-rate them, he will be more likely to succeed in his "plan." "Not that I have any thoughts of marrying her myself," he writes Deighton; he simply de-sires Eliza too much "to see her connected with another for life." In fact, Sanford thinks so much of her that he has not yet even decided to seduce her, although "with all her pretensions to virtue," he certainly thinks it possible. "She is," after all, "the very soul of pleasure," he notes.[46]

Thus, Boyer and Sanford seek to entrap Eliza, whose only refuge is to remain single, disapproved of by friends and family. When Lucy marries George Sumner, Eliza does not partake of the general happiness. Why? The idea "of an alienation of affection, by means of entire devotion to another," appalls her.[47] To Eliza, the sacred bond of matrimony promises too short a tether.

After Sanford leaves town to make his fortune, Boyer marries, and at-tention from other suitors ends, Eliza tumbles into depression. "Health, placid serenity, and every domestic pleasure, are the lot of my friend," she writes to Lucy, while she, "who once possessed the means of each, and the capacity of tasting them, has been tossed upon the waves of folly" until "shipwrecked on the shoals of despair! . . . What have I now to console me?" Eliza exclaims. "My bloom is decreasing; my health is sensibly impaired," and all those talents "with the possession of which I have been flattered" were "of little avail when unsupported by respectability of character!"[48] Lucy's retort stings: "Where is that fund of sense, and sentiment[,] which once animated your engaging form? Whence that strength of mind, that independence of soul, that alacrity and sprightliness of deportment, which formerly raised you superior to every adverse occurrence?"[49] Eliza cannot explain it, and to her other close friend, Julia, she can only invoke the imp of the perverse. "In many instances," she writes, "I have been ready to suppose that some evil genius presided over my actions, which has directed them contrary to the sober dictates of my own judgment."[50]

Sanford's return momentarily delivers Eliza from her melancholia. He renews their flirtation, confessing that his has been a marriage of convenience. Soon enough after his renewed attentions, her friends notice a change in Eliza, a rapid return to her "former cheerfulness," her taste for "company and amusements" again evident. But they believe these only "indications of a mind not perfectly right," as is her irrational defense of Sanford.[51] She tells her friends that she has forgiven his past. To Lucy, who warns her against any reinvolvement because "the world would make unfavorable remarks upon any appearance of intimacy" between her and Sanford, she replies coldly, "I care not for that." It is, she continues, "an ill-natured, misjudging world; and I am not obliged to sacrifice my friends to its opinion."[52] Even at the age of thirty-seven, she rejects social convention and particularly Lucy's notion that "we are dependent beings" and "must feel the force of that dependence."[53]

Eliza's mother expands on the same sentiment, at one point counseling her daughter that we "are all links in the great chain of society, some more, some less important, but each upheld by others, throughout the confederated whole."[54] Here Foster locates one pole of what in the new nation has become a central problem: the relation between individual freedom and social obligation. Mrs. Wharton continues to believe in a reciprocal relation between these two duties, even as her daughter wishes to claim a personal liberty and attendant self-fulfillment that to some was not only morally problematic but also unpatriotic, detrimental to the good of the commonwealth that the Revolutionary generation enshrined as the greatest good. Could it be, Foster asks, that liberal democracy thus contains the seed of that which might destroy common purpose?

Eliza's end comes quickly, narrated by Julia Granby in a letter to Lucy. One night, staying with her friend, Julia awakens to see a man stealing from the house, after which she hears Eliza's footsteps on the stair. Soon enough, Eliza becomes pregnant. Sanford installs her at the tavern, and readers of the many newspaper articles about Elizabeth Whitman knew the rest.

The Coquette is not a simple morality tale like *Charlotte Temple*. It depicts an attractive, intelligent, independent woman meeting an end she does not deserve. For all the patriotic rhetoric and talk of freedom in the air in 1798, many of the country's citizens—women in particular—remained fettered. Eliza Wharton, like others who bristled under such restrictions, learned the length of her chain, and readers registered this as much as Sanford's perfidy.

The Coquette thus explores the national mind-set roiled by inflated notions of freedom and equality beginning to circulate in the late eighteenth century. The novel's continuous republication during the 1820s, when the New Haven theologian Nathaniel William Taylor famously championed free will and thereby fueled much theological bickering, is understandable. But its popularity depended as well on its trenchant presentation of what were becoming more and more complex questions. What was the Revolution's legacy in the realm of personal behavior? When did the pursuit of individual happiness, guaranteed as much as life and liberty, conflict with the greater good of the social organism? Or should the latter even be considered as more than its individual constituents? Foster had transformed a sad tale of frailty and human sorrow into a parable about democracy and its incipient discontents.

A FEMALE QUIXOTE

One of Foster's implicit laments is that a man's sexual transgressions are often excused or forgotten, while a woman's stay with her for life. "It has ever been my opinion," Sukey Vickery, another novelist from this period, wrote, "that the world has been too rigid, much too rigid, as respects the female sex."[55] Other writers noticed such inequalities but handled them differently, sometimes with humor or satire. Such was the case with Tabitha Tenney, author of the popular *Female Quixotism, Exhibited in the Romantic Opinions and Extravagant Adventures of Dorcasina Sheldon* (1801), the title of which, a conflation of Miguel de Cervantes's *Don*

PART II } The 1850s

4 } The Conventions of Sentiment

In the spring of 1849 George Palmer Putnam received a hefty manuscript from Henry Warner, a prominent New York attorney who had fallen on hard times during the Panic of 1837. Warner already had shown the manuscript to two other publishers, but both had passed on it. Putnam was not immediately convinced of its merit. He took it to his summer home on Staten Island, where his mother was visiting. Putnam asked her opinion, and the next day she told him: "If you never publish another book, publish this."[1] He put the book into production and invited Susan Warner to stay at his home through the summer and early autumn to correct the proof. She and her family—her father, Henry, and her younger sister, Anna, who had come up with the novel's title, *The Wide, Wide World*—eagerly awaited the published book, her first literary effort, which finally arrived in mid-December and carried on its title page her pseudonym, Elizabeth Wetherell.

Sales started slowly. Putnam's mother remained confident and reminded him that "the book was so good, she was sure that Providence would aid him in the sale of it."[2] She was right. By February the first edition of fifteen hundred copies had almost sold out. In April Putnam printed another thousand copies and told the author that "your book has been received with remarkable interest in various quarters, and I consider it . . . 'a hit' in a special and emphatic sense of the word."[3] Indeed it was, for within two years *The Wide, Wide World* was in its fourteenth edition. It eclipsed Lippard's *Quaker City* as the most popular book in the nation, a position it held until the publication of Harriet Beecher Stowe's *Uncle Tom's Cabin* in 1852, and it remained in print into the early twentieth century. Other authors envied this success. Nathaniel Hawthorne wrote his publisher, William Ticknor, that "America is now wholly given over to a d[amne]d mob of scribbling women, and I should have no chance of success while the public is occupied with their trash." A bit disingenuously he added, "and should be ashamed of myself if I did succeed in the same way."[4]

Warner's book changed the dynamic of the publishing industry. Publishers began to search for the next bestseller. In trying to re-create *The Wide, Wide World*'s financial success, they began to invest large sums in advertising campaigns in papers and periodicals with large circulations. And often women wrote these books. The popularity of Warner's novel inaugurated an era when women writers, following Warner's formula, dominated the publishing world.

Two aspects of Warner's novel made it a distinctively American example of the novel of sentiment. The first was its basis in, and evocation of, Christian life. *The Wide, Wide World* descended from religious tracts and the stories and novels of Sarah Savage and Catharine Maria Sedgwick. What set it apart from its predecessors was that it embodied the larger shift in American religious life from the soul-searching and theological basis of earlier works to ideals of Christian behavior and service.[5] It proposed that a woman's character and life were now up to her and not divinely ordained at creation—that she should align her behavior as much as possible with the virtues exemplified by Christ.[6]

The implications of this idea suggest the second aspect. *The Wide, Wide World* was empowering. Because women were still excluded from politics and the market, they had to turn elsewhere to exercise their will and intellect.[7] While their fathers, husbands, and brothers were out of the home, building reputations and adding to their worldly gains, women remained in the home, becoming adept at conquering themselves with the goal of entering the kingdom of heaven. Hence they found ways of exercising that vaunted American value: free will. From invisibility to prominence, from disregard to respect, from religious tract to lengthy fiction, women writers made enormous strides during the 1850s through the sentimental novel.

SUSAN WARNER

Warner was born in 1819 in New York, the second of five children, three of whom died in childhood; she was close to the other survivor, her sister,

Anna, born in 1827. Their father, Henry, a New England farm boy who made good, had graduated from Union College, studied law with a well-known New York attorney, established his own practice in the city, and married Anna Marsh Bartlett, stepdaughter of a wealthy and prominent New Yorker. She died in 1828, and his sister Frances—beloved maiden Aunt Fanny—moved in to help her brother care for his young children.

For the first twenty years of her life, Susan lived comfortably. The family resided at first in Brooklyn and, after 1830, on Broome Street, near Broadway, in Manhattan, then at St. Mark's Place, one of the best addresses in the booming city. During this period Henry Warner purchased Constitution Island, a square mile of land in the Hudson River across from West Point, as a picturesque location for a future country home. In 1836, the Warners were well on their way to becoming one of New York's most fashionable families, one of the city's "upper ten," as George Lippard would soon put it.

But the Panic of 1837 crushed Henry Warner as it did countless others. He had to sell the home on St. Mark's Place as well as all the family's furniture and many other belongings. He was able to keep Constitution Island, where the family now spent summers, but during the rest of the year he was relegated to renting only a few rooms in Manhattan. He tried unsuccessfully to reestablish his law practice. As he got older, he and his two daughters, neither of whom married, moved permanently to the island, where he unfortunately got involved in costly lawsuits with neighbors when he tried to drain some marshland on the riverbank. He almost lost the property to foreclosure. Fortunately, a friend stepped in and assumed the mortgage until Warner could pay it off.

In an attempt to stave off that financial crisis, in 1849 Susan began writing *The Wide, Wide World*, and thereafter, she and Anna (who also wrote fiction) supported the family through their novels and stories. After Henry's death, the sisters spent the rest of their lives together in the old farmhouse, still writing novels—Susan a remarkable twenty-seven and Anna four—along with four coauthored books. Still, they struggled to remain solvent, often transferring the copyright to their work outright rather than wait for royalties. Susan died in 1885, but Anna stayed on, selling the island with stipulations that she be allowed to live the rest of her life on it and that it eventually be given to the federal government (it was made part of West Point). During the last years of her life, Anna wrote a memoir of her beloved sister that remains the best source of information about her.

The Wide, Wide World tells the story of Ellen Montgomery, a young girl who grows up in comfortable circumstances in New York until her father, an attorney, loses an important lawsuit. The family's fortunes spiral downward. Montgomery accepts a job in Europe and asks his wife, already in poor health, to accompany him, thinking that the climate will be conducive to her recovery. Because her mother is too weak to care for Ellen, her parents send her to live with her aunt, Miss Fortune Emerson, who lives in Thirlwall, in the country, and is not pleased to have to take charge of a presumably spoiled city girl who knows nothing of farm life. Ellen's separation from her mother is terribly painful, though both submit to Mr. Montgomery's will, which they treat as an extension of God's. This is Ellen's first lesson in female resignation.

Subsequent lessons come at Miss Fortune's, where she suffers indignities and humiliations because of her "fancy" upbringing. Her aunt, for example, dyes all her expensive white stockings a drab color more suitable to farm life and withholds Mrs. Montgomery's letters to Ellen until her behavior "improves." Again someone absolutely controls Ellen, just as her father did. Her recourse is to her faith and the belief that God intends her suffering for some good, a lesson whose logic derived from the eighteenth-century theologian Samuel Hopkins's controversial notion that one must be willing to be damned for the glory of God.

Finding little solace in this harsh doctrine, Ellen becomes resentful, angry, and dispirited, until a woman named Alice Humphreys befriends her. Alice, a minister's daughter, instills in Ellen the ethic, not doctrine, of Christian love and urges her to fill her new household with it. Ellen tries sincerely. She pays more attention to her grandmother (whom Miss Fortune neglects) and obeys her aunt to a fault, until she has no reason to berate or belittle her niece. Ellen also learns the worth of honesty and hard work when Aunt Fortune and Bram van Brunt (a neighbor who tends the farm during Fortune's illness and whom she later marries) assign her various household tasks that earlier would have baffled her.

After her marriage, Miss Fortune allows Ellen to board at the Humphreyses' home, enlivened by the return of Alice's brother, John, who is studying for the ministry. This happy time for Ellen soon ends, however, because of first Alice's untimely death and then that of her father in

Europe. Unhappily acceding to the last of her father's demands, Ellen moves to Scotland to live with her mother's family, the Lindsays. They are strict but more in a social than a religious sense; they are aristocratic types who "know" what is right and try to mold their ward. Again Ellen submits, even though she yearns for independence and to return to America and John Humphreys, thus to be independent of her family's influence. At one point Mr. Lindsay takes away a book that John has sent Ellen, prompting her to exclaim, "But it is mine." Her uncle's chilling rejoinder sums up a nineteenth-century woman's plight: "And you are mine."[8] A visit from John gives Ellen the will to endure until she is of age, and the novel ends with the reader believing that soon enough Ellen will be rewarded with marriage to John Humphreys, who will not "own" her in the way others have, even if she must love and obey him.

ONLY SUBMISSION MAKES ONE FREE

Anna knew something of Susan's own religious struggle, and in her invaluable reminiscences, she relates much about the solace she and her sister found in Christianity, especially after 1836, when Henry Warner purchased a pew in the Mercer Street Presbyterian Church, near the family's home on St. Mark's Place. Administered by the Reverend Thomas Harvey Skinner, a theologian of some note and later a founder of Union Theological Seminary, the church became a haven for the Warner sisters, with Skinner's sermons the highlight of their week. In April 1841, Anna and Susan were admitted to church membership and devoted themselves to good works. Susan's writing was a part of this effort.

Skinner was prominent in New School Presbyterianism and counted as close friends Albert Barnes and Edward Beecher, both of whom in the 1830s were tried by the General Assembly of the Presbyterian Church for heresy. The trials ended in acquittal but also in a severely split denomination, with opposing parties debating the importance of revivalism to faith. Skinner's New School welcomed and encouraged a congregant's emotional reinvigoration through revivalism, a theology of the feelings; the Old School emphasized a probationer's strict adherence to doctrine and the central role of sacraments, a theology of the intellect that reinforced the clergy's rather than the church member's responsibility in salvation. Even the parishioner Henry Warner weighed in on the debate. In 1838 he published *An Inquiry into the Moral and Religious Character of the American Government*, an anti-Jacksonian tract in which he looked to those of strong religious faith to resist the Democrats' descent into folly and evil, exemplified by, among other developments, Jackson's insistence on Sunday mail delivery. Warner thought the Whigs, many of whom strongly supported Skinner's kind of evangelical fervor, measured up to his own standards.

In Skinner's thought, conversion did not always come instantly and overwhelmingly, as it did to Saul on the road to Damascus, but was an individual's choice. Conversion was "an intelligent, voluntary, invisible act of the mind, in which it ceases to rebel against God, submits to his authority, and accepts his mercy."[9] In a passage that derived from Jonathan Edwards's notion of true benevolence (Skinner had trained at Princeton Theological Seminary, where Edwards's works still informed the curriculum), Skinner defined the effects of such conversion. "The offering up of prayer and praise," he wrote in *The Religion of the Bible* (1838), "meditation on the Scriptures, attendance upon ordinances, liberality toward the poor, the utmost exactness and irreproachableness of life"—none of these meets the requirements of "spiritual religion" unless there is "a correspondent sensibility in the heart." There must be "a feeling of the divine Presence" and a "relishing of the Divine excellence." "God must be enjoyed," he concluded, "or there will be disquietude of soul."[10] A Christian need not master the intricacies of Protestant theology. He ought only to study the Bible and align himself with Christ's teachings. This is what Ellen Montgomery does in the course of *The Wide, Wide World*.

Another famous theologian, in this case a Congregationalist, also influenced Susan Warner's novel. In 1846, Horace Bushnell (1802–1876), pastor of a church in Hartford, Connecticut, published his highly controversial but influential *Christian Nurture*, a book that, like the trials of Barnes and Beecher, rocked American theology. Even more than Skinner, Bushnell downplayed the significance of conversion and argued instead that an individual becomes a Christian over time through strong religious education, particularly in the family. If religious virtue is to prevail, parents have to inculcate it in their children by teaching and through the example they set. The family unit is the key to Christianity's power: "How trivial, unnatural, weak, and, at the same time, violent, in comparison, is that overdone scheme of individualism, which knows the race only as mere units of will and personal action." "Our over-intense individualism," he continued, "carries with it an immense loss of feeling, affection, sentiment, which hardens the aspect of every thing, and dries away the sweet charities and tender affections." Individualism thus "makes the church a mere gathering of adult atoms."[11]

Parallels with *The Wide, Wide World* are many, for Bushnell's notion of a young person's growth toward grace fits Ellen precisely. Christian education, he wrote, "is not to break, but to bend rather, to draw the will down, or away from self-assertion toward self-devotion, to teach it the way of submitting to wise limitations."[12] Thus Ellen cares for Aunt Fortune, even though this relative treats her harshly, because she knows that it is right. Likewise, she endures (though with many tears) her time with the Lindsays, unsympathetic and unsentimental Scots Calvinists (as well as prissy aristocrats) to the core. As the reader learns in what Warner intended as the novel's final, though originally unpublished, chapter, Ellen will be indeed rewarded by marriage to John Humphreys.

John S. Hart, in his pioneering *Women Prose Writers of America* (1852), wrote that *The Wide, Wide World* was the only novel in which religion as understood by "Evangelical Christians" was "exhibited with truth." He also marveled at the novel's rapid rise to prominence. Its "readers soon began to multiply," he wrote, "and every one who read the book, talked about it, and urged its reading upon his neighbors, until, within a year from the time of its publication, it had reached a circulation almost unprecedented." Perhaps even more unusual, this occurred without advertising by the book's publisher. "It was one of the most signal instances in recent times," Hart wrote, "of a popularity reaching almost to fame, and springing up spontaneously, and entirely in advance of all the usual organs of public opinion."[13]

The most interesting notice of the novel appeared in a remarkable nineteen-page review in the *North American Review* by another successful woman novelist, Caroline Kirkland (1801–1864), who had moved from New York to the wilds of Michigan. Her first work, *A New Home, Who'll Follow?* (1839), based on her experiences after her relocation, made her so well known that Wiley and Putnam issued her second work, *Western Clearings* (1845), in its Library of American Books. In her lengthy essay Kirkland reviewed not only *The Wide, Wide World* but also Warner's more recent *Queechy* (1852), set in early-nineteenth-century New York and based in part on the experiences of her parents' generation; and Anna Warner's *Dollars and Cents* (1853), a novel set in Philadelphia that, like her sister's first book, deals with a wealthy family's difficulties after the father's ill-considered investments.

Kirkland's essay was a lament about the current state of the American novel, which she divided into two main types: "the philosophical, political, sectarian, or philanthropic novels" and those "which are essentially essays on the condition of the poor, with hardly a fiction to soften the sharp outline."[14] Nowadays, she wrote, "There is no truth but literal truth," and "heroes, who do not interest themselves in political economy and the condition of the masses, are unworthy of good fortune."[15] As a result, the novel had become "a *quatrième état* [fourth estate]; something considerable in government; a power formidable to evildoers; but not particularly lovely or cheering to those who resort to it merely to delight or exalt the imagination, suggestive of possibilities of happiness, or as counteragent to the disenchanting tendencies of our wayward, blundering experience."[16]

But *The Wide, Wide World* was something new. The book, originally "bought to be presented to nice little girls, by parents and friends who desired to set a pleasant example of docility and self-command before those happy beginners," soon found mothers, fathers, and older brothers and was even "under the pillows of sober bachelors," who read it with tears in their eyes.[17] Kirkland believed that the Warner sisters, though they had not so intended, had created "new rules" for the novel, moving it beyond the didactic religious tract. Their books had a "character of their own—humane, religious, *piquant*, natural, national," for they paint "human nature in American type"—that is, they reflected the country's democratic promise—and "appeal to universal human sympathy." Above all, they recognize the heart as "the strong-hold of character and religion as the ruling element of life; religion—no *ism*, however specious or popular" but defined as being of "one mind with Christ" and thus ecumenical, not bound to the restrictive dogma of any one denomination. Kirkland knew "of no prototype of such books" except for the Bible.[18]

GERTY'S PLIGHT

Susan Warner's *Queechy*, the name of a fictional country village based on Canaan, Connecticut (where Warner's Aunt Fanny had lived), appeared in 1852 and was well received, though not as well as its predecessor. The novel was about life among New York's fashionable citizens in the 1820s and 1830s, before the panic, so had neither the immediacy of *The Wide, Wide World* nor an appealing universal character like Ellen Montgomery. Two years later another runaway bestseller, Maria Cummins's *The Lamplighter*, eclipsed Warner's first novel. The book sold forty thousand copies in its first two months of publication and seventy thousand in its first year.[19] Cummins achieved not only popular success but also a kind of literary celebrity that Warner never experienced.

Cummins was born in 1827 in Salem, Massachusetts, into a prosperous family. When she was small, her father, David, became the judge of the court of common pleas of Norfolk County, and the family moved to Dorchester, a few miles from Boston. He took a strong interest in her education and, when she was a teenager, sent her to Mrs. Charles Sedgwick's Young Ladies School, in Lenox, Massachusetts, overseen by Catharine Sedgwick's sister-in-law. The writer herself was a frequent visitor. Sedgwick's effect on the young woman is unknown, but *The Lamplighter* was thematically similar to *A New-England Tale*, and Cummins, like Sedgwick, never married. Also like Sedgwick—and unlike Warner—Cummins never wrote from financial need. She did not have much in common with the heroine of her novel.

The Lamplighter opens in the kind of squalid urban setting made vivid by Lippard. The reader meets eight-year-old Gerty, an orphan living with Nan Grant, who is cruel to her young charge, the child of her husband's friend, who is presumed drowned at sea. At one point Nan drops Gerty's pet kitten, her only joy, into a pot of boiling water, prompting the young child to throw a piece of firewood at her. At another, she locks Gerty in her garret when she learns the child is afraid of the dark.

After several fights, Nan throws Gerty out of the house, and soon enough the aptly named Trueman Flint, an old "lamplighter" whose job it is to illuminate the city's gas streetlights, takes Gerty under his wing. In his tenement Gerty meets Mrs. Sullivan, a kind woman caring for her elderly father, and her son, Willie, who is five years older than Gerty and boards with a city pharmacist to learn his trade. Trueman introduces Gerty to someone called "God" and a thing called "prayer." The two Sullivans educate Gerty in more prosaic ways. Mrs. Sullivan teaches her how to keep house, and soon Gerty has cleaned and rearranged Trueman's room, making it a place of comfort and love.

Through Trueman, Gerty meets Emily Graham, a young blind woman.

Trueman worked for Emily's wealthy father until he sustained a serious injury that reduced him to his current job. Because of his misfortune, Emily feels obliged to help Trueman whenever she can, even though he holds no grudge and is thankful for whatever odd jobs Mr. Graham provides. Emily assumes responsibility for Gerty's Christian education. Her first task is to tame the young girl's furious temper and to replace it with an ethic of patient love. Emily's own life offers the strongest argument for such a change: although blinded several years earlier—the reader does not learn how until late in the novel—she bears the tragedy without bitterness and ministers to those in need.

Gerty is tested often during her transformation. Trueman suffers a stroke from which he never recovers; Gerty, twelve years old, nurses him through his final illness but harbors no anger at a God who could allow her friend to die in such a manner. Later, while living at Emily's family's home, she finds herself persecuted by Mrs. Ellis, the Grahams' housekeeper of many years, who resents the addition of another family member. Emily counsels that Gerty must "learn to bear even injustice, without losing [her] self-control."[20] Soon enough, Willie Sullivan goes to India for several years to pursue a career in the merchant trade, leaving Gerty at the mercy of Mrs. Ellis. Gerty decides to leave the household to assume a teaching position in the city, hoping to move in with Mrs. Sullivan to care for her and her father, both of whom are ill. But when the two die, Gerty moves to a city boardinghouse.

Within a month she is back in Mr. Graham's country home, for Mr. Graham has married a fashion-hungry widow who brings along two insufferable daughters, Isabel (known as Belle) and Kitty, and Emily needs Gerty by her side. With their mother's tacit approval, both stepdaughters, but especially Belle, treat Emily with indifference and are overtly cruel to Gertrude (as she now is called), who has blossomed into an attractive young woman. Emily's example finally takes hold in Gertrude. Boiling with anger over another slight, in a moment of startling self-consciousness she looks out the window at nature's beauty and is transformed. "A delicious composure" steals into her heart, extinguishing any desire for revenge. "She had conquered; she had achieved the greatest of earth's victories, a victory over herself."[21]

The trials do not end, however. Emily's health begins to fail, while Willie Sullivan returns. He seems infatuated with Belle, a lapse in judgment that makes Gertrude question her high opinion and continued affection for him. Now a stoic Christian, she keeps her composure and accepts this disappointment. Complicating matters is the appearance of an older man named Mr. Phillips, who accompanies the Grahams on a tour along the Hudson River. He seems particularly interested to hear as much about Gerty's early life as she can remember.

On this trip, Gertrude makes what readers at the time would have understood as the ultimate Christian sacrifice. In a steamboat accident and fire, with Belle in mortal danger, Gertrude risks her own life to rescue her tormentor. Both survive, and Gertrude's good deed is rewarded. Mr. Phillips turns out to be Philip Amory, not only her long-lost father but also Emily's onetime lover, who had accidentally blinded her after her father banished him. The novel concludes with the reconstitution of Gertrude's family. Amory and Emily marry, as do Gertrude and Willie.

The complexity of its characters and plot sets *The Lamplighter* apart from *The Wide, Wide World* and many other sentimental novels. Like Warner's novel, it instructs the reader to acquiesce rather than to resist, yet Gertrude never resigns herself to her fate. She begins in combativeness and self-consciously transforms herself into a Christian but never relinquishes her powerful personality. Empowering rather than passive, Cummins's ideal of womanhood grew from her religion, which, unlike Warner's, did not involve submission.

Like Sedgwick (and perhaps as a result of her influence), Cummins joined a Unitarian church. *The Lamplighter* reflects that denomination's broadly ecumenical stance as well as its emphasis on Christ as the only necessary moral exemplar, another way Cummins's religious views differed from Warner's. As opposed to Bushnell's doctrine of self-abnegation, Cummins's Unitarianism emphasized self-realization. Gertrude controls her own life in ways that Ellen does not. She has the courage to stand up to Mr. Graham, for instance, when after she tells him that she is going to return to the city to work, he virtually orders her to remain at Emily's side. As she mulls over his outburst, she wonders if he considered "that my freedom is to be the price of my education, and I am no longer able to say yes or no."[22] Independence and grace go hand in hand. Cummins's emphasis on a woman's free will accounts in part for the appeal of *The Lamplighter*, for it shows that however divorced a woman might be from political and economic life, she can retain her agency and self-worth.

Gertrude, like Ellen, settles into marriage, but surely Willie's and her relationship becomes one between equals rather than protector and protected.

MILL GIRLS

Of course, the harshness of Ellen Montgomery's and Gerty's early lives might have appeared less so in comparison to the drudgery of factory life. Alongside the rise of the modern city, the opening of lands west of the Mississippi River, and the proliferation of railroad track and telegraph wire, the development of large-scale industries was one of the period's most significant economic and demographic developments. Sarah Savage's *The Factory Girl* (1814) was just the first of many novels set in this new environment.

When Charles Dickens made his American tour in 1842, he stopped at the great factories in Lowell, Massachusetts, which seemed to be one of the seven wonders of the modern world. He was struck by Lowell's newness; factories, churches, merchants' shops, roads, hotels: all seemed to have sprung up the day before he arrived. He was also surprised at the appearance of both the workers and their workplaces. Well dressed and clean, the female workers "had the manners and deportment" of "young women," not "degraded brutes of burden." In the factories' well-organized and clean workrooms he was amazed to see plants "trained to shade the glass" from excessive sunlight. He found the city's boardinghouses, segregated according to sex, similarly neat. He noted that the landlords looked after their charges' morals.

Dickens also marveled at the "joint-stock pianos" in many of the boardinghouses, the fact that most of the young ladies belonged to circulating libraries, and, most amazingly, that they issued their own literary magazine, *The Lowell Offering*. The contrast with the squalor, poverty, and ignorance of the Manchester mills in England was stark. Dickens attributed the better conditions in America to the young nation's seemingly endless opportunities for economic opportunity and, hence, geographic mobility. "Many of the circumstances whose strong influence has been at work for years in our manufacturing towns have not arisen here," he observed, because Lowell's workers did not constitute a permanent population. "These girls," he wrote, primarily the "daughters of small farmers," come from other places, "remain a few years in the mills" to earn their wages, "and then go home for good."[23]

American observers offered less enthusiastic takes on factory work. A story in *The Lowell Offering* of a mill girl's introduction to her work did little to entice others to follow her:

She went into the Mill; and the sight of so many bands, and wheels, and springs, in constant motion was very frightful. She felt afraid to touch the loom, and she was almost sure that she could never learn to weave . . . the day appeared as long as a month at home . . . There was a dull pain in her head, and a sharp pain in her ankles; every bone was aching; and there was in her ears a strange noise, as of crickets, frogs, and jewsharps [Jew's harps] all mingling together, and she felt gloomy and sick at heart.[24]

A writer for the *Olive Leaf and New England Operative* found the constant din the most oppressive aspect of the mills. When the heavy waterwheels began to turn and move other wheels in the building, she wrote, the sound "deepen[ed] at every revolution, until the confused hum of spindles and the discordant clang of looms filled the air, and the very earth seemed to tremble under the combined operations of these giant powers."[25] Lucy Larcom, who had worked in the mills in the 1840s and who became one of the factory world's most articulate chroniclers, thought it ironic that "hours passed in the midst of monotonous noise, which drowned the sound of human voices, brought with them a sense of isolation as one feels in the loneliest wilderness."[26]

Whatever the physical or psychological effects of factory work, however, Americans unsurprisingly focused on its moral consequences. One mill girl's lament brimmed with moral anxiety: "Thrown into company with all sorts and descriptions of mind, dispositions and intellects, without counselor or friend to advise, and surrounded on all sides with the vain ostentation of fashion, vanity and light frivolity—beset with temptations without, and the carnal prosperities of nature within, what *must*, what will be the natural, rational result?"[27] In his introduction to Dorus Clarke's *Lectures to Young People in Manufacturing Villages*, which typified many such books published in the 1830s and 1840s for the new laboring population, the Lowell, Massachusetts, minister Amos Blanchard similarly observed that just as "a new direction has been given to a large amount of American genius, capital, and labor" and "every village of New England resounds with the din of machinery," so "a corresponding change has come over the character and habits of a large portion of the people."

Multitudes, especially the youth, once scattered "among the farms and smaller workshops of the country," now were "congregated in compact masses" and subject to "all the influences, good and evil, which attend a dense and busy population." The once-pervasive influence of family, "restraining from vice and stimulating to good behavior with all the secret magic of a charm," had virtually disappeared.[28]

Novelists took up the task of re-creating and commenting on factory life as well. Aside from Savage's work, Catharine Williams's *Fall River: An Authentic Narrative* (1833) was one of the earliest and most narratively distinctive examples.[29] Williams retells the tale of the murder in the factory city of Fall River, Massachusetts, of the young millworker Sarah Maria Cornell, purportedly by the Methodist minister Ephraim Kingsbury Avery. Several months pregnant, she was found hanged from a farmer's haystack roof in a nearby town shortly after she had met with Avery; other marks on her body and the type of knot used on the rope suggested foul play rather than suicide, and Avery was apprehended and indicted. The trial played out over several months, captivating public attention, and Avery finally was acquitted. Williams, author of several other books, clearly thought the judgment erroneous and tried to recover as much of Cornell's story, sad as it was, as she could. Using published accounts of the trial as well as other primary materials (including some of Cornell's letters), Williams created a hybrid narrative, half fact, half conjecture or outright fiction. *Fall River* spoke to Cornell's hardships as a poor weaver in the new industrial economy, with much about the tenor of life in factory villages.

The book did not immediately produce many imitators. Within months of Lippard's success with *The Quaker City*, however, city mysteries set in the new factory environment quickly appeared: titles like Bradbury Osgood's *Mysteries of Lowell* (1844) and the anonymous *The Mysteries of Nashua; or, Revenge Punished and Constancy Rewarded* (1844). In these novels, unscrupulous millowners, agents, and overseers replaced Lippard's corrupt and depraved attorneys, bankers, and clergy.

Warner's and Cummins's formulas lent themselves to the same setting. Tales of girls who leave behind the comfort and virtues of home to test their independence in the factories became common. Ariel Cummings's *The Factory Girl; or, Gardez la Coeur* (1847) was a typical sentimental mill novel. Calliste Barton leaves her country home for "the City of Spindles" to make money to send her brother to college. Once at the factory, she must avoid such frivolous entertainments as dancing school and cotillions, which only abet temptation. Raised a good Christian, Calliste resists sin and, after she has put her brother through divinity school, returns to the country to marry her local swain, now a doctor.

The eponymous and impressionable heroine of a novel by "Miss J.A.B.," *Mary Bean, the Factory Girl* (1850), meets a different fate. A good country girl, she is swayed by the attention of George Hamilton, who pretends to be wealthy and, telling Mary that he loves her, convinces her to go with him to the mill city of Manchester, New Hampshire. Once there, installing her in a women's boardinghouse, he promises to marry her. Hamilton confesses that he is impecunious, and she, still infatuated, vows to work in the mills to support them. Worse than poor, though, he turns out to be a villain. He gets her pregnant, commits robbery and murder, and leaves her for another mill city, Saco, Maine. Mary tracks him down; they reconcile and go to Boston, where she once again begins to work in a factory. Because her pregnancy is now apparent, Hamilton sends her to a doctor for an abortion; she dies during the procedure. Indignities continue, for her lover dumps her body in a millstream, and after it is recovered, her loving sister returns it to the country and erects a marble tablet on Mary's grave. *Mary Bean* reads like *Charlotte Temple* updated for the factory world.

Pointing out the abyss was one thing; proposing an alternative required greater imagination and resolve. Of novels from the 1850s devoted to the worker's plight, Martha W. Tyler's *A Book Without a Title: or, Thrilling Events in the Life of Mira Dana* (1855), a plea for the rights of women as well as the first American novel to depict a labor strike, stands out.

The novel's first section details the title character's experiences in Lowell, where her brother Warner, a boardinghouse supervisor, secures her a job as a factory worker, even though she is only sixteen years old. A country girl, a tomboy whose family nicknames her Dick, Mira is the "wildest, merriest being, that ever rambled over clover meadows, or danced gypsy-like" through the woods.[30] For her, going to Lowell is part of growing up, for she has a "wild vague yearning for education and fame, that ever sweeps over the soul of the young and hopeful."[31] Although she finds the city a "perfect heap of houses, and people, too," and is surprised that she has to sleep with seven other girls in a room in one of the company's boardinghouses, Warner tells her that she will soon get used to the change and must strive to "tame down that high, wild spirit."[32] Because she does not want a life of mere "selfishness and ease" like many of her coworkers but instead to help "lift the pall" of suffering she sees in the world, rechanneling her exuberance is not difficult. She resolves not to be swayed by frivolity and "to lay aside a sum of money for the purpose of attending school" when she leaves the mills.[33]

A natural leader, attractive, articulate, and brave, Mira emerges as the organizer of a "turn out," or strike, after the company cuts its employees' wages. Urging her coworkers to stick together, Mira leads four thousand young women out of the city. She stays behind to make sure that the paymasters honor the wages already owed and becomes the target of retaliation by the company's agents and overseers. The strike is widely reported in regional papers, bringing Mira to the attention of an American ship captain in Europe, who, fascinated by news of the remarkable young woman, decides he wants to marry her after he returns to the United States.

Mira does marry the captain; even Tyler could not envision her heroine's remaining single. The author thus shifts her focus from factory life to family life and then from the joys of this first marriage to the trials of a second. Mira hints at her domestic troubles. She asks why if crime demands a "retributive act," one should not build a "scaffold for the hanging of men's reputations, and suspend them before the public gaze [as] a warning to others to follow in their footsteps."[34] The subject of her anger is Edward Tyrell, her abusive second husband (her first, happy marriage ends when her spouse dies at sea). "If this little book should be instrumental in saving a single sister from sorrows like those which befell the heroine of these pages, then my labor is not in vain, and I shall hear contentedly the fault-finding of the critic, and the murmur of dissenting voices."[35]

Mira becomes so desperate for financial independence that she decides to write a book about her trials. She shows it to a publisher in Boston, who offers her a thousand dollars for the manuscript, but she wisely holds out for more. The novel ends with her achieving her independence from Tyrell and buying a cottage for her family, which now includes her aged mother. Her anger in the preface seems much justified, even as she feels blessed to have fulfilled her youthful promise and ambition.

Within a year, Tyler self-published a second edition of her book, with telling revisions. In her preface she admitted that the story's ending had been "merely imaginative" because Mira (Tyler?) did not regain custody of her children. Moreover, she described the unenthusiastic response to the book. Her readers were not as sympathetic as she had hoped. Tyler's heroine, who takes charge in the factory as well as in her family life, may have been too radical for readers accustomed to the more biddable heroines of Warner and Cummins.

FANNY FERN'S DYSFUNCTIONAL FAMILY

Or perhaps Tyler's prose, rather than her main character's radicalism, was the problem, for a similar character in another novel from the time became a cultural sensation. She was Ruth Hall, the thinly fictionalized alter ego of Sara Payson Willis Parton, popularly known as Fanny Fern. Parton's stories and first novel, *Ruth Hall: A Domestic Tale of the Present Time* (1854), made her one of the most widely read authors of the 1850s. In some ways she hewed to the formulas of the sentimental novel but at the same time challenged the foundations of the American version of the genre, foremost in her avoidance of Christian didacticism—and of Christianity altogether, for that matter. Her bold self-assertion at a time when submission of one kind or another was expected of women appealed to readers, many of whom found her work salutary and inspirational.

Parton was born in Portland, Maine, in 1811, the fifth of Nathaniel Willis and Hannah Parker Willis's nine children. Her father was a printer and editor, first of the *Eastern Argus*, a Portland newspaper, and later, in Boston, where the family moved a few weeks after Sara's birth, of both a religious paper, the *Boston Recorder*, and a children's paper, the highly successful *Youth's Companion*. Her parents sent her to female academies, including Catharine Beecher's Hartford Female Seminary. There she met Sedgwick and the popular poet Lydia Sigourney, the "sweet singer of Hartford." She also encountered Catharine's sister, Harriet Beecher Stowe, who remembered her as "a bright laughing witch of half saint half sinner," a girl with "a head of light crêpe curls—with a jaunty little bonnet tipped to one side, & laughing light blue eyes," who excelled at writing compositions and hated arithmetic.[36]

In 1831 Parton returned to Boston and began to work for her father. In 1837 she married Charles Eldridge, a Boston bank cashier with whom she had three daughters, the first of whom died in 1845. The next year tragedy struck again: her husband died of typhoid fever, leaving her with two young children, little cash, and considerable debt. Neither Charles's parents nor hers offered to support her in any significant way; instead, they urged her to remarry. She did so in 1849, to Samuel P. Farrington, a widower with two daughters of his own. The match was a disaster. Farrington was jealous and abusive, and two years into the marriage Sara took her daughters and left him. Farrington spread ugly rumors about why she had gone and, two years later, obtained a divorce from her for "abandonment." Influenced by these false rumors, her parents and parents-in-law again refused her any significant aid.

Sara found it difficult to find work and so to support her family. She tried unsuccessfully to get into teaching and worked as a seamstress for pitiful wages until, recalling how some women made money from publishing in newspapers and journals, decided to see if she could sell some of her writings. She asked her brother, Nathaniel Parker Willis, one of the best-known New York writers and editors, if he would publish her, a reasonable request given that in his *Home Journal* he regularly included the work of Lydia Sigourney, Lydia Maria Child, "Grace Greenwood" (Sara Jane Clarke Lippincott), and "Fanny Forrester" (Emily Chubbuck), among the country's most popular women writers. Unsettled by the rumors surrounding her second marriage, though, he refused. Reminding his sister that every day brought in the work of "dozens of starving writers" trying to make it in New York, he told Parton that her writings showed "talent" but "overstrain[ed] the pathetic," while her humor "[ran] into dreadful vulgarity sometimes." He was embarrassed that other editors might know that his own sister had even written such things, for "in one or two cases they trench very close on indecency." He saw "no chance" for her.[37]

Such a cruel response would have crushed a less independent woman. But it only fueled Parton's ambition. She sold some work to the *Olive Branch* and William Moulton's popular *True Flag*, and by the end of 1851, having adopted the pseudonym Fanny Fern, her work—trenchant commentary on city life and personal relationships—was appearing in many other city papers and journals (including her brother's) as readers speculated about their author. Moulton's subscriptions picked up, too, but he continued to pay her next to nothing. In September 1852, Oliver Dyer, editor of the *Musical World and Times*, approached her with a lucrative offer to write exclusively for his paper, which she accepted.

An enterprising publisher, James Derby, of the firm Derby & Miller, published a book-length collection of Parton's articles that appeared in 1853 as *Fern Leaves from Fanny's Portfolio*. Within a year the book sold close to seventy thousand copies in the United States and a remarkable twenty-nine thousand more in England. Later that year Derby published a collection of her writings for children, *Little Ferns for Fanny's Little Friends*, and a year later, *Fern Leaves, Second Series*. By then Sara Willis Parton was making enough money to support herself and her daughters quite comfortably.

Early in 1854 Mason Brothers, a relative newcomer in New York's publishing circles, convinced her to sign a contract for a novel that included the unusual stipulation that she not publish anything else until the book appeared. This proved to be a brilliant public relations ploy, for while her audience clamored for more of her short pieces, Mason Brothers filled newspapers and journals with announcements of the forthcoming novel. When *Ruth Hall* finally appeared late in 1854 (it carries an 1855 publication date), it was an instant hit, reportedly selling seventy thousand copies in its first year, fewer than Cummins's *The Lamplighter* and Stowe's phenomenally successful *Uncle Tom's Cabin* (1852) but still enough to make waves in the literary world.

Within the year Parton followed with *Rose Clark* (1855), which did not do as well as *Ruth Hall* but still added to her reputation as a writer. She also signed another exclusive contract, with Robert Bonner, to write weekly columns for his *New York Ledger*, as she did until her death. In 1856, at the age of forty-four, she married the editor and writer James Parton, best known as Horace Greeley's biographer, and together they kept one of New York's best-known literary salons. The Partons' marriage was happy. Interestingly, though, at Sara's request, the two had signed a prenuptial agreement, guaranteeing her the income from her books and articles should she choose to remarry; by statute law, the income was his. Fortunately, she never had to invoke the clause. The couple remained together until her death in 1870 from cancer.

Parton used the autobiographical *Ruth Hall* to settle scores with her unsympathetic parents and in-laws, her brother, and the New York editors who had grown rich from her work while paying her little. One of the earliest reviews, a negative one in *The New York Times*, labeled Fern's style "masculine," a telling remark. "If Fanny Fern were a man," the reviewer wrote, "a man who believed that gratification of revenge were a proper occupation for one who has been abused, and that those who have injured us are fair game, *Ruth Hall* would be a natural and excusable book." But, he continued, "[w]e cannot understand how a delicate, suffering woman can hunt down even her persecutors so remorselessly."[38]

Hawthorne made an observation in the same vein in response to Parton's astonishing success, which he envied. Early in 1855 he wrote his publisher, William Ticknor, that he had been reading *Ruth Hall* and wished to except it from his blanket condemnation of other women writers. "I must say I enjoyed [the novel] a good deal," he told Ticknor. "This woman," he continued, "writes as if the devil was in her; and that is the only condition under which a woman ever writes anything worth reading . . . Generally, women write like emasculated men, and are only to be distinguished from male authors by greater feebleness and folly." But when they "throw off the restraints of decency, and come before the public stark naked, as it were—then their books are sure to possess character and value." He ended by asking if Ticknor knew anything about Parton and requested that if the publisher ever met her, to "let her know how much I admire her book."[39]

What about Parton's writing made Hawthorne separate her from the novels written by that "damned mob of scribbling women" that he despised? In her preface Fern noted that her book would undoubtedly puzzle some, for it was "entirely at variance with all set rules for novel-writing," having no "intricate plot," "startling developments," or "hair-raising escapes." She noted its verbal economy, for she had "compressed into one volume" what she could have expanded "into two or three," a skill honed on her short stories and essays. Finally, she admitted that in the novel she had "entered[,] unceremoniously and unannounced, into people's houses, without stopping to ring the bell."[40]

"THE DEVIL WAS IN HER"

At the start of *Ruth Hall*, its title character seems to be a typical domestic heroine. Parton skims through Ruth's early life in a chapter. The second chapter, less than a page long, recounts her wedding to the good Harry Hall, the only child of a rural doctor and his termagant wife. The newly-weds start life together and try to avoid Harry's prying and hypercritical parents, who regard Fanny as a spoiled young girl and an incompetent housekeeper. Parton's tone is genial and facetious as she writes of Ruth's giving birth to a young girl she and Harry name Daisy.[41]

The book takes a dark turn when one winter little Daisy falls ill with the croup. After putting off a visit to the ailing child, Dr. Hall, Harry's father, finally appears and pronounces matter-of-factly that "the child is struck with death." He counsels the shocked parents to "let her drop off quietly" and to refrain from seeking a second opinion, which would be a waste of money.[42] Daisy dies within the day. Ruth's depression following her child's death is only partially relieved by the arrival several years later of two more daughters, Katy and then Nettie.

Eight years later Harry, summering with his wife and daughters at a northeastern beach resort, falls ill with typhus and dies, but not before Daisy's deathbed scene is essentially repeated: Dr. and Mrs. Hall arrive before the end, and the former informs Ruth, "It is all up with [Harry]; he's in the last stage of the complaint; he won't live two days."[43] Parton paints an equally vicious portrait of Ruth's family. When her foppish brother Hyacinth Ellet appears at the hotel after Harry's death, all he thinks of is how unkempt his sister, who has just fainted, looks. "It is really quite dreadful to see her in this way," he says. "It is really quite dreadful. Somebody ought to tell her, when she comes to, that her hair is parted unevenly and needs brushing sadly."[44]

The Halls and Mr. Ellet (Ruth's mother is deceased) bicker after they realize that Harry recently lost money in a poor business deal and has left his wife and child with virtually nothing; neither party wants to extend help. Instead, each family wants to take one of the little girls, but Ruth insists that she will find work instead to support them. The Halls consent to providing a pittance only after they learn that some of their fellow parishioners are talking about how stingy they are. Mr. Ellet follows suit, agreeing only to support his daughter and grandchildren for a limited time.

With her children, Ruth moves to a truly hellish environment: New York City. As they enter the city, they meet people out of George Lippard's world: "a low-browed, pig-faced, thick-lipped fellow, with a flashy neck-tie over a vest," says of Ruth, "prettyish, is n't she?" "Deuced nice form," his friend replies, as he lights a "cheap cigar." "I should n't mind kissing her."[45] Parton's description of the boardinghouse district, which replaces the idyllic country cottage in which the family once lived so happily, similarly recalls Lippard and Thompson:

In a dark narrow street, in one of those heterogeneous boardinghouses abounding in the city, where clerks, market-boys, apprentices, and sewing-girls, bolt their meals with railroad velocity; where the maid-of-all-work, with red arms, frowzy head, and leathern lungs, screams in the entry for any boarder who happens to be inquired for at the door; where one plate suffices for fish, flesh, fowl, and dessert; where soiled table-cloths, sticky crockery, oily cookery, and bad grammar, predominate; where greasy cards are shuffled, and bad cigars smoked of an evening...

At the summer resort, Ruth met a despairing woman named Mrs. Leon, who warned her never to allow one of her daughters to marry someone whom she did not truly love, for she herself had made that fateful error. Now, as Ruth, Katy, and Nettie pass an insane asylum in the city, Ruth hears that Mrs. Leon has just perished inside, her husband having committed her. She and the children are led past chained inmates to Mrs. Leon's corpse, while the cries of "maniacs over [Ruth's] head echoed through the stillness of that cold, gloomy vault." The attendant hands Ruth a letter that Mrs. Leon addressed to her in her last days but never sent. "I am not crazy, Ruth, no, no—but I shall be; the air of this place stifles me; I grow weaker—weaker. I cannot die here; for the love of heaven, dear Ruth, come and take me away."[46]

Pressured by Harry's parents, Ruth consents to let Katy visit them, without realizing that they intend to keep her. Further reduced to desperation by her failure to find a livable wage, Ruth finally decides to try the literary world and encounters the disapproving Hyacinth. Just as Parton's brother had done to Sara, he dismisses her and her abilities. Yet in the very issue of his journal, he pleads "for public favor for a young actress, whom he said had been driven from the sheltered privacy of home, to earn her subsistence upon the stage" and whose acting he believes should have received a better welcome. Ruth must take her writing elsewhere, but how, she thinks, "can I ask of strangers a favor which a brother's heart has so coldly refused?"[47]

Soon enough, Ruth is a regular contributor to the story papers under the pen name Floy, whom everyone is discussing. There are all sorts of rumors about her identity—for example, that she is a man, "because she had the courage to call things by their right names, and the independence to express herself boldly on subjects which to the timid and clique-serving were tabooed." Others think she is "a disappointed old maid," a "designing widow," a "moon-struck girl," or a "nondescript." Some try to imitate her and, "failing in this, abused and maligned her." The "hypocritical denounced the sacrilegious fingers which had dared to touch the Ark," and the "fashionist [*sic*] voted her a vulgar, plebeian thing"; "the earnest and sorrowing," however, "to whose burdened hearts she had given voice, cried God speed her."[48]

Floy becomes a literary celebrity. Fan letters start to arrive at her editor's office. Some ask for advice; others are marriage proposals. A college professor writes her to complain about her violation of "all established rules of composition," for in her writing she was "as lawless and erratic as a comet."[49] The composer Louis Jullien publishes "The Ruth Hall Schottische," sheet music whose cover pictures a young woman representing Ruth. Another enterprising musician, G. F. Wurzel, issues a popular song, "Little Daisy." Underneath the veneer of fame, though, lurks discontent. Nettie asks her mother, "When I get to be a woman shall I write books, mamma?" "God forbid," Ruth replies. "No happy woman ever writes. From Harry's grave sprang 'Floy.'"[50]

Hyacinth is livid, for he has learned Floy's identity. He forbids any of his sister's articles from appearing in his paper and refuses to read positive reviews of her book. Still, he pathetically clings to her success. He points out to a friend a steamboat on the Hudson River named *Floy* and admits that it is named after his sister, but when the friend wonders how it could be so, for he has heard that Floy was "in very destitute circumstances" and wandered "from one editorial office to another in search of employment," Hyacinth becomes apoplectic.[51] Mr. Ellet is less ambivalent about claiming a role in Ruth's phenomenal ascent. He self-servingly tells a friend that he just had been reading some of his own daughter's sketches and "thinking what a great thing it is for a child to have a good father."[52]

The novel ends with Ruth's assuring her permanent financial security through her purchase of a bond for one hundred shares in the Seton Bank, a document that Parton reproduces in the book as a tangible symbol of Ruth's (and her own) remarkable diligence and talent. In the last chapter, Ruth, her children, and her beloved editor, Mr. Walter, visit Harry's grave. As they turn away, a bird "trilled forth a song as sweet and clear as the lark's at heaven's own blessed gate." "Accept the omen, dear Ruth," Mr. Walter says. "Life has much of harmony yet in store for you."[53]

Ruth Hall had indeed made Parton wealthy, but reviewers differed on what she had accomplished. The harshest notice came from the *Southern Quarterly Review*, in which the reviewer used the occasion to assess Parton's readership. "The almost universal ability to read," he wrote, "and the consequent love of reading, have developed in this nation of readers especially, an immense middle class of ordinary readers of average intelligence." He then speculated on what precisely this audience sought in novels. "Flat insipidity is not tolerated even by the middle class," he noted. "Until the advent of 'Ruth Hall,'" no writer "had hit the nail precisely on the head; the small intelligences were yet without a pet book." Parton had written a book for the great, unwashed middle-class readership, for *Ruth Hall* was, in this reviewer's snide opinion, "a miracle of *inspired mediocrity*." He went on in this condescending tone, explaining that a typical middle-class reader like "Nancy" never wanted to go "beyond her depth. She is quick and sensitive too," he added sarcastically. "She knows that Hawthorne's Psychology was never meant for her," for when she encounters it, she has "a disagreeable sense of insecurity," presumably of the sort with which she has plenty of experience in her own restricted role as wife and mother.[54]

The reviewer for *The Pioneer; or, California Monthly Magazine* attacked the novel on different grounds. He pilloried the cult of celebrity and all "those false enthusiasts who gather autographs, portraits and anecdotes without any idea of the worth and character of the objects of admiration." Gossipmongers were even worse. "Why should the world care about anything" in writers, except "what is really uncommon? What have we to do with their private lives, petty sins, or family quarrels?"[55]

"You have perverted the good your covert hints of reform might have accomplished," he wrote, addressing Parton and the high quality of her previous writing. He accused her of a "petty, vindictive spirit," something "sprung from a malignant heart," and was outraged at Parton's attack on domesticity. "The family circle had always been considered sacred," but Parton had exposed to the entire world what should have been kept private. She had "violated the sanctity of the fireside." And to what end? The book was nothing less than Parton's "glorification of herself."[56] *The Knickerbocker* agreed with this last judgment. "There is one thing that militates against the idea that [*Ruth Hall*] is an entirely authentic and veritable history," its reviewer noted: "the praise that she is all the while awarding the heroine."[57]

Writing in the early feminist journal *The Una*, Elizabeth Cady Stanton, one of the country's foremost advocates of women's rights, understood that the novel was a breakthrough. Its great lesson "is that God has given to woman sufficient brain and muscle to work out her own destiny unaided and alone." Further, with regard to the depiction of an unloving family, Stanton thought that "the censure more justly belong[ed] to the living subjects," not to Ruth herself.[58]

In *Ruth Hall*, Parton worked through and beyond the conventions of the sentimental novel. The novel is about family, domesticity, and womanhood, but Parton had little interest in Christian submission and morality. Like the heroines in other sentimental novels, Ruth endures one defeat after another and the cruelty of those who should be protecting her. But she never resigns herself to her fate. Rather, Ruth fights for herself and her children at every turn, succeeding in a man's world without much help at all. She becomes wealthy and famous because of her innate talents and ambition. The latter, notably, grew in part out of her desire for revenge. The novel simultaneously fought against the pervasive sexism of American society and exemplified American values—namely, individualism and self-reliance. No wonder it upset so many critics.

Not insignificantly, Parton created an unorthodox, fragmentary style for *Ruth Hall* that was perfectly suited to her subject. Her ninety chapters are often very brief—some less than a page—and consist of evocative vignettes, rapid shifts in scene, and overheard conversations, as though the reader were walking Manhattan's streets and piecing together what she could of Ruth's story as it unfolded. Some readers would find the same experience in Whitman's contemporaneous long poem *Leaves of Grass* (1855). The reader observes Ruth's growing self-consciousness, and Parton comes close to revealing the workings of consciousness itself.

BREAKING THE MOLD

Parton was not alone among women novelists at the time who came up with new ways of presenting character and selfhood in their fiction. Among the most innovative was Caroline Chesebro'. Born in 1825 in Canandaigua, New York, she was the daughter of Nicholas Cheseborough, a hatter, wool merchant, and postmaster, and Betsey Kimball

Cheseborough. Her father acquired some notoriety when, with two other Freemasons, he was charged in the kidnapping and disappearance of William Morgan, who had planned to publish a book revealing Masonic secrets. Cheseborough and his coconspirators served a year in jail, but because Morgan's body was never positively identified, he escaped further punishment.

Cheseborough sent his daughter to the local Canandaigua Seminary. A few years later she began to write stories for *Graham's Magazine* and *Holden's Dollar Magazine*—she shortened her family name at this time— which were later collected in her first book, *Dream-land by Daylight* (1851). Encouraged by positive reviews—one reviewer found in its stories "unmistakable evidence of originality of mind"—she wrote her first novel, *Isa, a Pilgrimage* (1852).[59] Next came *The Children of Light* (1853), the story of two strong women, Asia Phillips and Vesta Maderon, who, when they are rejected by the men they love, move together to the city, where Vesta fulfills her ideal of service by supporting Asia in her budding acting career. Like Sedgwick in *Married or Single?*, Chesebro' bemoaned the indignities suffered by women in heterosexual relationships. Unlike Sedgwick, she ventured an alternative.

Chesebro' followed *Children of Light* with a long, sprawling novel, *Getting Along: A Book of Illustrations* (1855), focused on various couples' relationships. Assuming marriage as the norm, Chesebro' judges the soundness of each marriage by the partners' fidelity to their original commitment. The novel is about the varied and complex nature of commitment and is proof that the search for a suitable spouse was just as compelling a fictional trope as it had been in *The Coquette* fifty years earlier. Finally, in 1863, Chesebro' published *Peter Carradine; or, The Martindale Pastoral* (1863), an innovative novel, about three heroines and their differing versions of the same events. For reasons unknown, she then abandoned writing, even though *The Knickerbocker* had opined that "among the numerous candidates for literary same," Chesebro' had "few or no superiors."[60] She took a position teaching English composition at the Packer Collegiate Institute in Brooklyn, where she remained until she moved to Piermont, on the Hudson River, to live with her brothers. She died there in 1873 and was buried next to her parents in Canandaigua.

Chesebro' was interested in the plasticity of gender roles—she had an expansive view of womanhood—and this interest sets her novels apart. Her heroines are not trapped by society's expectations, but rather experience more of themselves and the world as they challenge the limits of propriety. This approach found a memorable expression in her first novel, *Isa*, which Chesebro' dedicated to Grace Greenwood (1823–1904), the pen name of Sarah Jane Lippincott. The choice is significant, for by 1852 Greenwood, who had started out writing children's stories and poetry, was well known not only as an author and editor but as an outspoken advocate of women's rights and abolition. Given the plot, characters, and politics of *Isa*, Greenwood was the proper muse.

The novel relates Isa Lee's story, which begins in conventional sentimental fashion. She is raised in a poorhouse but is rescued by Mrs. Dugganne and her son, Weare, who, on a charitable mission to the house, recognize that she possesses intelligence and spirit. Isa flourishes in their home, a place of love and stability. She is deeply impressed by Mrs. Dugganne's kindness and forbearance, particularly during the periodic visits of her husband, an alcoholic. She admires Weare, in all respects Mr. Dugganne's opposite, who is a strongly moral and religious young man (of orthodox faith); the reader learns that he had his clerical education in Richmond, presumably at the Presbyterian seminary in that Virginia city.[61] Isa grows remarkably, soon surpassing Weare, the divinity student, in knowledge and ability.

Isa's studies open new vistas, and she begins to write philosophical essays on the power of the human will. As Weare describes her unorthodox belief, "Will, human will, is next to, it leans up close against God—God first—yes, he is the first of all powers, and mortal will next."[62] Her essays so impress Mr. Warren, the owner of *The Guardian*, that he invites her to live with him and his wife and to work as an assistant to his editor, Alanthus Stuart. Isa accepts, even though it means leaving Weare, but soon enough she begins to delight in the company of Stuart, also an author, "though neither a popular nor even an acknowledged one," because his views are too "transcendental" and "demand too much of a reader's thought and investigation." When she learns his nom de plume, though, she realizes that he is the author of a book that she admires but that Weare has banished from the family library for its supposed theological radicalism.[63]

When Mrs. Dugganne falls ill, Isa returns to her home but, after the benevolent old woman recovers, leaves once again feeling that her ideas about religion, morality, and woman's place in society have made her incompatible with the people who raised her. Debating Weare about God's sovereignty, for instance, she shocks him by declaring that belief in it is "cowardly" at best, for "there is no limit given but that which our own will regulates. No other voice," Isa writes, "than man's mental capacity, ever said, *thus far, no farther.*"[64] It also dawns on her that Alanthus Stuart is her intellectual match, and after Mr. Warren sells *The Guardian*, the two turn exclusively to their writing. Isa's works are "curious and powerful" and "singular enough to enchain attention" so that "it became a fashion to read them, and for a time, among certain classes, those who longed and labored for the progress and advancement of their kind, to praise them."[65]

Isa receives a proposal of marriage from an older man, General S., with whom she discussed women's rights at one of Mr. Warren's soirees. He offers her "his name, his fame, his fortune." Isa refuses, for she wants no restrictions in her life. She and Alanthus move to Europe, where they can live together unmarried without breaking societal taboos. Isa reveres his "originality, daring, and power," while Alanthus admires her confidence, for that was the "keystone of Power, Love, and Knowledge."[66] He beholds in her nothing less than "the completion of himself."[67]

They have a child, who tragically dies young. Isa then becomes gravely ill, and in her last days, as her sickness becomes widely known, Weare Dugganne visits her. "Do you anticipate annihilation?" her husband asks in front of Weare. No, she replies, "THERE IS NO ANNIHILATION. I have never for a moment imagined that there is. I am going within the veil—and you will follow me."[68] To Dugganne's horror and despair, Isa dies without returning to the Christian faith, and he curses Stuart for "ruining" her immortal soul. But she dies peacefully, having wagered that if there is an afterlife, Stuart will meet her there.

In *Isa*, Chesebro' broached subjects few other American novelists at the time, men or women, dared to: the relationship between orthodox religious faith and personal fulfillment, between the demands of the soul and the demands of society, and between love and marriage as well as the possibility of living a life of the mind, inhabited by radical philosophical and political ideas. *The American Whig Review* took notice. "Somebody has remarked that this is an age of skepticism" in which there is a tendency to "mistrust all old faith and creeds, to disregard the old landmarks in almost every thing." But "amid the Babel of creeds and beliefs," the male reviewer asked, "is there one that in any measure does or can compensate for those so perseveringly sought to be overturned?" And can "the new fill and take the place of the old in the human mind?" *Isa* is "the embodiment of these questions," the reviewer continued, but he criticized the eponymous heroine's progress toward what he thought of as "self-deception." The fault of the novel is that "Isa makes her self-will, her intellectual progress, and her ambition, a three-fold deity."[69] In this sense, Chesebro' had not surpassed traditional religious belief; she had merely fashioned a personal religion out of secular values and ideas.

The reviewer for *Harper's New Monthly Magazine* similarly pointed out Chesebro's skepticism but thought that her novel left the reader bewildered. Instead of proposing a coherent religious or intellectual alternative to traditional Christianity, the novel exemplified "the perils of entire freedom of thought" during "the state of intellectual transition between attachment to tradition and the supremacy of individual conviction."[70] The author's thought was in fact coherent, though it was rooted in a variety of contemporary (and secular or at least non-Christian) ideas: Emerson's Transcendental idealism; Margaret Fuller's pathbreaking *Woman in the Nineteenth Century* (1845); and the women's rights movement, particularly Elizabeth Cady Stanton's Declaration of Rights and Sentiments, issued at the Seneca Falls Convention of 1848 (an event that occurred not far from Canandaigua). Fuller's trajectory was not so different from Isa's, in fact. The former went to Europe as a correspondent for Horace Greeley's *New-York Tribune* and there conceived a child out of wedlock; like Isa, she could not find emotional comfort in her own country.

Significantly, the reviewer did praise the interiority of the author's approach. "The scene is laid in the interior world—the world of consciousness, of reflection, of passion. In this twilight region, so often peopled with monstrous shapes, and spectral phantasms," Chesebro' trod "with great firmness of step." When Isa discovers a volume of essays that "canvassed without mercy, without reverence, even mock-reverence . . . the belief of Christians, the laws of society, the standard of morality, the principles of duty," she was most taken by the author's treatment, "wholly, or principally," of the internal life.[71] "With rare subtlety of discrimination," Chesebro' brings "hidden springs of action to light, untwisting the tangled webs of experience," as she reveals "some of the darkest and most fearful depths of the human heart."[72] This was the thread connecting Chesebro' to Charles Brockden Brown and George Lippard, who likewise plumbed the depths of human motivation, as well as to her contemporaries Hawthorne and Melville, who, like she, "risked the uncertain chances of success in resting a popular tale upon a purely psychological foundation."[73]

"AN INFINITESIMAL OUTBIRTH OF THE INFINITE"

Isa was reformist and feminist fiction, in which Chesebro' advocated allegiance to the voice within over the demands of traditional faith. Another important novelist, reformer, and feminist, Mary Gove Nichols (1810–1884) was a restless believer and seeker of truth who championed such causes as dietary reform, enlightened physiology, hydropathy or the water cure, and free love. Nichols was born in 1810 in Goffstown, New Hampshire, a small town in the southern part of the state. Her parents, William Neal, who farmed the area's rich river bottom, and Rebecca Neal, held unusual religious views. William was an avowed freethinker and atheist while Rebecca was his opposite, a professing Christian who insisted that parents should curb children's willfulness. More influenced by her father, Mary was not broken by her mother's discipline or attracted to her religion; she found her way to Quakerism, through an uncle. She met a fellow believer, the thirty-one-year-old bachelor Hiram Gove, who fell in love with her, eleven years younger than he was.

Mary realized that she did not love Gove but, yielding to social pressure, accepted his proposal. To make matters worse, during her engagement she did fall in love, with another Quaker about her own age. Gove discovered their dalliance and was enraged, prophesying that if Mary did not marry him, she would burn in hell. Confused, she went through with the nuptials, only to realize very quickly that she had made a terrible decision. For all his outward piety Gove was a possessive, cruel, and unscrupulous man, always bending her will to his, and so paranoid and violent that to Mary his lovemaking came to seem like rape. She remained in this horrific situation for years. Finally, when she was thirty-one, she left him, taking their daughter, Elma, with her (she had lost several other children to miscarriage or stillbirth). Because state law mandated that only men could initiate divorce proceedings, technically she remained Gove's wife.

During the years she suffered with Gove, Mary was the main breadwinner, lecturing and teaching classes as a public advocate for various health reforms. She advocated dietary reform, influenced by the vegetarianism of Sylvester Graham (of graham cracker fame) and then by the new

ecration and contempt."[56] Three deaths punctuate the novel's final passages. On his deathbed, the Irishman McCloskey confesses that Stevens ordered Mr. Garie killed, and Stevens's fear of exposure and trial drives him to suicide. And even though the children's patrimony is restored to them, Clarence, humiliated and without any future prospects, moves in with his sister, Emily, and soon thereafter dies of consumption.[57]

The Garies and Their Friends was startlingly ahead of its time. The Garies, Ellises, and Mr. Walters care less about slavery than they do about class. When Mrs. Ellis tells Mr. Walters that they plan to put their son, Charlie, out "to service," Walters argues against it, for "it begets a feeling of dependence to place a boy in such a situation" and would spoil him for any more meaningful or lucrative work. Where, he asks, "would I or Ellis have been had we been hired out all our lives at so much a month?"[58] Yet as Walters realizes, the white people whom he surpasses in wealth will never accept him. No black character mentions that a few years before the events in the first part of the novel, Pennsylvania passed a law disenfranchising black men, a privilege they long had enjoyed.

A comparison between Webb and Lippard is instructive. Both wrote of Philadelphia and its problem, but they did so in quite different modes. Lippard was a vicious satirist; Webb, an anatomist. In *The Quaker City*, the reader learns little of Lippard's Devil Bug; he is less a character than a symbol. It's never apparent how he thinks of himself as a free black among whites. In contrast, Webb's characters exhibit a liberating but also problematic self-knowledge. They choose their own lives, but when a light-skinned black decides to "pass" as white, the result is confusion and despair. If Lippard wanted to shock readers into recognizing the immorality of the American city, Webb wanted to prod readers, white and black, toward a new self-consciousness about race and American values. And since his cause was not abolition, Webb's *The Garies* best comparison is not the novels of Stowe or Brown, but the African American literature during Reconstruction and under Jim Crow, of which Frances Ellen Watkins Harper's *Iola Leroy* (1892) is perhaps the most powerful example.

THE LURE OF REPATRIATION

Like Webb's *The Garies*, the white sentimental novelist Sarah Josepha Hale's *Liberia; or, Mr. Peyton's Experiments* (1853) and the black radical Martin R. Delany's *Blake; or, The Huts of America; A Tale of the Mississippi Valley, the Southern United States, and Cuba* (1859–1862) explored black self-consciousness, but in settings farther afield. Both novels are about black emigration, to Liberia and Cuba, respectively. The novels could not have been more different. Hale believed that blacks were inferior and therefore could not be peacefully or fruitfully integrated into white society; Delany, that the continued dilution of the black race through miscegenation sapped its inherent power and beauty.

Hale (1788–1879), a New Englander, headed the *Ladies' Magazine* of Boston for two years before becoming the inaugural editor of *Godey's Lady's Book*, a monthly Philadelphia journal whose popularity soared during the antebellum period. In this position she sought only unpublished work and avoided controversial topics; more than any other periodical, hers became a widely recognized emblem of sentimental culture. Although Hale supported abolition, her views of blacks were like those of many northerners (including Stowe)—that is, she believed that they were human beings deserving of respect, but at the same time that they were inferior to whites. Hale supported the American Colonization Society's plans to repatriate blacks in the West African region that became Liberia, an effort that had begun in earnest in the mid-1820s, when the first shiploads of free blacks left the United States, bound for the region south of Sierra Leone.

In 1853 Harper & Brothers published Hale's *Liberia*, the only American novel of the period to treat this episode in African American history. No doubt influenced by the widespread interest in utopian schemes like Charles Fourier's, Mr. Peyton, a Virginia plantation owner, attempts to ameliorate the conditions of his slaves by establishing a quasi-socialist collective. His effort fails because of a lack of interest and commitment on the part of the slaves, and Mr. Peyton sees "that matters could not be much worse" and would improve only "when each one felt himself individually responsible."[59] Peyton next considers resettling his slaves in Canada, a project that he finally rejects when he realizes that the kinds of prejudice free blacks encounter from American whites would likely be present there, too, and that in a remote settlement there would be little opportunity for the regular religious instruction of his former slaves.

This leaves Liberia, which he learns of at a meeting of a "Colonization Society." The second half of the book is set in the new African nation, as black emigrants try to convert the native tribes not only to Christianity but also to American principles of self-government. For the settlers, this is not a return to African roots but a neocolonialist enterprise. Hale depicts the settlers' economic, political, and social institutions, foreign relations with European powers bent on enlightening the "dark continent," and combat with indigenous tribes who sell captives to the traders in West African ports. Hale sincerely believed that Liberia had a transforming effect on those who emigrated. "I can tell a man that's been raised in Liberia from America as soon as I see him," Nathan, a repatriated black, tells his friend Ben. "Why, they seem more like men. You know, Ben, you never felt like a man in America." "No," Ben replies. "I used to try mighty hard, but I could never feel like anything but a nigger."[60] Because the Africans are so benighted, American blacks cannot help feeling superior. Hale concludes the book with documents that support her observations, as Stowe had done in *A Key to Uncle Tom's Cabin.*

Martin Delany was less sanguine about the Liberia enterprise. From his reading—particularly William Nesbit's damning *Four Months in Liberia* (1855), for which he provided an introduction—he believed that Liberia was doomed, for two reasons: first, because the settlement project was undertaken by American blacks who thought of Africans as inferior, and second, because many of the settlers were of mixed, not pure, black heritage. Oddly, Delany himself was not pure, though he claimed to be descended from African chieftains. He was born in Charleston, (West) Virginia, in 1812, to a slave father, Samuel Delany, and a free mother, Pati, who traced her heritage to what is now Angola. Early on his mother moved the family to Chambersburg, Pennsylvania, supposedly to protest a Virginia law prohibiting blacks from learning to read. At nineteen Delany went to Pittsburgh, where he married Catherine Richards, daughter of a merchant, and devoted himself to newspaper editing and the cause of abolition; his *The Mystery* (1843–1847) was one of the earliest black newspapers. From 1847 to 1849 he coedited *The North Star* with Frederick Douglass and often lectured for the antislavery cause.

In 1850, having studied medicine with several doctors in Pittsburgh who provided testimonials to his education and ability, Delany was admitted to Harvard Medical School, along with two other blacks. They were the first African Americans to be admitted, but administrators dismissed all three a few months later after white students complained of their presence. Infuriated by the experience and others like it, in 1852 Delany published *The Condition, Elevation, Emigration, and Destiny of the Colored People of the United States, Politically Considered,* a powerful polemic in which he challenged the economic and social discrimination he found rampant even in liberal northern circles. In these years, he also began to advocate black emigration to Central or South America.

Delany soon began to look across the Atlantic as well. In 1859, he traveled to Africa to assess the possibilities for repatriation. He and Robert Campbell, a Jamaican who had been teaching school in Philadelphia, went to Lagos and then Abeokuta (both now in Nigeria), where they signed a treaty with local (Yoruba) chiefs for a parcel of land that later was abrogated because of tribal infighting, ending Delany's dream of a black republic there. The journey inspired him, however, for during this period he wrote and published serially in *The Anglo-African Magazine* and then in *The Weekly Anglo-African* pieces that were republished as *Blake; or, The Huts of America*. The work dealt with blacks in the Caribbean and Africa as well as in the United States. Unfortunately, because key weekly issues of the latter paper have not yet been located, there is no complete version of the novel (about six chapters are missing).

With one exception, the first half of *Blake* follows a trajectory familiar to readers of slave narratives. It tells the story of Henry Holland (later Blake), a pure black West Indian stolen and sold to one of Louisiana's Red River plantations, the same region where Uncle Tom meets his death. Henry "marries" another slave, Maggie, but while he is absent on business for his master, Stephen Franks, Franks sells her to a northerner who takes her to Cuba. Henry then escapes and travels through the South as a fugitive, spreading—and here is where *Blake* deviates from the usual narrative—his dream of slave rebellion wherever he goes.

The second part of *Blake* takes place in Cuba and Africa. Henry travels to the Caribbean island as a servant of American filibusters intent on annexing Cuba to the United States.[61] Henry is fortunate enough to locate his wife, and he purchases her freedom. He is here transformed into "Blake," the "Commander in Chief of the Army of Emancipation," the leader of black insurgents whose goal is the overthrow of the Spanish-backed Cuban government and the establishment of a black state based on an economy of cotton production that would rival the South's (Delany believed that political economy was inextricably linked to black liberation). His army seeks to repel the incursions of American filibusters who want to make the island another slave state and who fear that any liberalization of legal codes against blacks might lead to their eventual supremacy.

In Cuba, the liberation poet Placido gives Blake and his followers advice and inspiration. Through him Delany champions black pan-nationalism. "Colored persons," Placido says at one meeting of the conspirators, "whatever their complexion, can only obtain an equality with whites by the descendants of Africa of unmixed blood." He explains his logic. "The instant that an equality of the blacks and whites is admitted, we, being the descendants of the two, must be acknowledged the equal of both."[62] Unlike Webb, who doubted the final efficacy of amalgamation, Delany saw true revolution as possible only through those who took pride in every drop of their black blood. But the latter could be trusted in the all-important work of nation building only if they became self-reliant and independent, free of the subservience that too often marked their lives among whites. With the overthrow of their Spanish rulers and the foiling of filibusters' plans to annex their land, Cuba's blacks would set an example for the rest of those enslaved in the Americas. "I am for war," Blake declares at one point, "war upon the whites."[63]

But Placido also understands Africa's place in this grand project: it is where blacks can build an economy that will lead to true political and psychological independence. After another central African character among the revolutionaries, Madame Cordora, hears Placido extol the virtues of Africa, she says, "I never before felt as proud of my black as I did of my white blood." Now she sees that "blacks compose an important element in the commercial and social relations of the world."[64] For such a revolution to succeed, enlightened leaders like Blake had to take the lead so that "the more ignorant slaves" who returned to Africa would "have greater confidence in, and more respect for, their headmen and leaders."[65] As one of the nation's leading black intellectuals, Delany believed that he was destined to fill such a role.

And fill it Delany did, but in ways that he did not anticipate, for the revolution he sought never occurred. During the Civil War he led efforts to recruit black soldiers and was commissioned as a major, the highest military rank attained by an African American. He served in the Freedmen's Bureau on Hilton Head in South Carolina before being mustered out of the army in 1865. He subsequently held appointments as a judge and ran, unsuccessfully, for political office in South Carolina. Later in life he worked as a doctor in Charleston. He continued to write political pamphlets and completed his ambitious *Principia of Ethnology: The Origin of Races and Color, with an Archaeological Compendium of Ethiopian and Egyptian Civilization, from Years of Careful Examination and Inquiry,* published in 1879, in which he argued that since time immemorial there had been original, uncorrupted races that had to be preserved, a position that pitted him against "assimilationists" like Douglass. When Delany died of tuberculosis in Wilberforce, Ohio, in 1885, his dream of a racially pure society was farther from reality than ever.

LIVING "FREE" IN NEW HAMPSHIRE

Even more unusual in the history and development of the American novel than Delany's work was Harriet E. Wilson's *Our Nig; or, Sketches from the Life of a Free Black, in a Two-Story White House, North by "Our Nig"* (1859), which appeared in the same year Delany began to serialize *Blake*. Like Jacobs's *Incidents*, it is largely autobiographical; and like Webb's *The Garies and Their Friends*, *Our Nig* was written by a free black but, in this case, one from New England and a much lower economic stratum.

Scholarly detective work has filled in the rough outlines of Wilson's difficult but remarkable life, to add to what is known from the testimonial letters appended to her novel. She was born Harriet Adams, a free black, in the small town of Milford, New Hampshire, in 1825. At an early age she was orphaned and put out to service with local families. She led a harsh existence, her friend Margaretta Thorn recounted in one of the appended letters, "both in the house and field," and "was indeed a slave, in every sense of the word."[66] Another letter, from "Allida," reports that Adams was rescued from this fate by "an itinerant colored lecturer" who brought her to an "ancient" town in central Massachusetts (probably Worcester), where she lived with a Mrs. Walker and made palm-leaf hats, popular in the period.[67]

Through the "colored lecturer," Adams then met a fugitive slave, "young, well-formed, and every handsome." After a brief courtship, in 1851 Adams took her beau, Thomas Wilson of Virginia, back to New Hampshire, where they married. It was not a good choice, for within a year he left to go to sea and never returned to her. In mid-1852 their son, George Mason Wilson, was born, in nearby Goffstown, and, weak in health, Harriet Wilson had to take her child "to the county farm, because she could not pay his board every week."[68] This presumably was Goffstown's "Hillsborough County Farm," a "poor farm," which a family or supervisor, reimbursed by the town, would run for the indigent. This institution was quite large, and according to local histories, it was overcrowded and rife with disease.[69]

Here Wilson's story takes an unusual turn, testifying ironically to the promise of American opportunity and initiative. One day a stranger, "moved by compassion" for her and her child, "bestowed" on her "a recipe for restoring gray hair to its former color." Wilson promptly began to manufacture the product and sell it in southern New Hampshire and northeastern Massachusetts as Mrs. Wilson's Hair Regenerator. This business did well, but ill health continued to plague her, and to support herself and her son, she penned *Our Nig*. In the summer of 1859, she registered the copyright at the District Clerk's Office in Boston, where she was then living, and enlisted the printers Rand & Avery to print the book "for the author."

Our Nig was a mendicant's tract, not a slave narrative. Such works were common in the period and often played on a distinctive trait of their authors. (A book in the same genre, for example, was *Life of Maj. Joseph Howard, an American Dwarf, Thirty-eight Years of Age, Thirty-six Inches High, and Seventy-two Pounds in Weight, Written by Himself* [1855].) "Deserted by kindred," Wilson explained in her preface, "disabled by failing health," she had no choice but to write a book. She appealed not to sympathetic whites but to her "colored brethren universally for patronage, hoping they will not condemn this attempt of their sister to be erudite, but rally around me a faithful band of supporters and defenders." She realized that her description of the northern treatment of blacks might work against the abolitionist cause, and she did not wish in any way to "palliate slavery at the South." Toward this end, she had "purposely omitted what would most provoke shame in our good anti-slavery friends at home."[70]

Wilson probably sold her book as she peddled her hair restorative, but *Our Nig* did not sell well; it went unnoticed in the abolitionist press. It thus did little to alter her financial situation, and her son, George, died in Milford of a "fever" within six months of its appearance. Wilson continued to sell her hair product. By 1867 she was living in East Cambridge, and she later moved to Boston's South End. She had changed her profession; she was now Hattie Wilson, a trance medium and spiritual healer. She was also active as a public lecturer on such topics as labor reform, human brotherhood, and the threat of the "money power." She even appeared onstage with the celebrated women's rights advocate Victoria Woodhull and on one occasion reportedly spoke before an audience of sixteen thousand. Her life came to an end in 1900 in Quincy, Massachusetts, where she died at the age of seventy-five.

A WHITE HOUSE, NORTH

In *Our Nig*, Wilson tells the story of Frado, a mulatto child, and under-
cuts the conventions of the sentimental novel on every page. As the story
opens, the reader learns of Mag Smith, an orphan who, "early deprived of
parental guardianship, far removed from relatives," is left to "guide her
tiny boat over life's surges alone and inexperienced."[71] Trusting and naive,
she falls in love with someone of higher social standing, believing he will
change her life. After "she surrendered to him a priceless gem," however,
"which he promptly garnered as a trophy, with those of other victims,"
the wily seducer leaves her to face the condemnation of her community.[72]
For years she lives as an outcast in a hovel on the edge of town, doing low-
paying work, for which "foreigners who cheapened toil and clamored for
a livelihood, competed with her ... Every year her melancholy increased"
as her means diminished.[73] These opening passages are unusual because
despite the impression given by the book's title, Mag is white.

No one cares for Mag, except "a kind-hearted African" named Jim.
Eventually, Jim begins to wish that she will marry him, for "she'd be as
much of a prize to me as she'd fall short of coming up to the mark of white
folks."[74] He musters the courage to propose. He "knew well what were
her objections." "You's had the trial of white folks, any how," he says. "They
run off and left ye, none of come to see if you's dead or alive," he reminds
her. Demonstrating the power of racism to warp its targets, Jim subcon-
sciously inverts the idea of "passing" in white society when he states, "I's
black outside, I know, but I's got a white heart inside." Jim prevails, and
they marry; Mag descends another step down "the ladder of infamy" and
has "sundered another bond which held her to her fellows." "You can
philosophize, gentle reader," the narrator observes, "upon the impro-
priety of such unions, and preach dozens of sermons on the evils of
amalgamation."[75]

The couple has two "pretty mulattos," but Jim falls ill of consumption
and dies. Mag returns to her hovel and struggles to make ends meet.
Then, with no other recourse, she begins to live with Seth, Jim's black
partner, and "enter[s] the darkness of perpetual infamy" because the
union is not blessed by "civilization or Christianity." Mag and Seth become so desperate they decide that if they are to find decent work, they
must move and leave behind their children. At the age of six, Frado, "a
beautiful mulatto, with long, curly black hair, and handsome roguish
eyes, sparkling with an exuberance of spirit almost beyond restraint," is

left at the doorstep of the Bellmonts, a well-to-do white family who live in the "large, old-fashioned, two-story white house" of the novel's subtitle and whose mistress is widely known as a bigoted shrew.[76] During the family's walk to the Bellmonts' house, a dozen children chant as they pass by, "Black, white and yeller [yellow]."[77]

In the Bellmont family, the daughter, Mary, wants to "send her [Frado] to the County House," but the son Jack says to keep her because "she's real handsome and bright and not very black, either." They begin to call her "*our* nig."[78] Mrs. Bellmont accepts her as free labor, and within a year Frado is "quite indispensable" to the family. When school approaches, they argue about whether she should go, the mother thinking "people of color" are "incapable of elevation," but Jack counters that his little favorite should have the opportunity.[79] Mr. Bellmont sides with his son, even though Mary is upset that she will have to attend the same school and is ashamed to be seen "walking with a nigger."[80] After the teacher berates her charges for making fun of Frado, their attitudes change, and, owing to Frado's wit and good nature, she becomes the school favorite.[81]

Jealous of Frado's popularity, Mary finds every opportunity to persecute her. When Mary dirties her dress crossing a stream, she blames Frado for causing her to fall, and when Frado denies it, Mrs. Bellmont, always siding with her daughter, props open her young servant's mouth with a stick for "lying."[82] The abuse escalates, with Mrs. Bellmont brutally kicking Frado for not following an order precisely enough.[83] Occasionally, Frado finds solace with Aunt Abby, Mr. Bellmont's sister, and an older son, James, who, working elsewhere, occasionally visits his family home. Jack continues to side with Frado, writing his brother about the "pretty little nig" in the house.[84] Mrs. Bellmont reacts to the attention her family members bestow on Frado by selling her dog, Fido, one of Frado's few joys, and then cutting off Frado's beautiful hair.[85]

Aunt Abby cares enough about Frado to bring her to religious meetings, even though Mrs. Bellmont, sharing the opinion of most of her neighbors, thinks it a waste of time. Abby, though, believes that Frado has a soul like anyone else and is distressed to hear the child sobbing, "Why was I made? Why can't I die? Oh, what have I to live for? No one cares for me only to get my work." Frado continues, "No mother, father, brother or sister to care for me, and then it is, You lazy nigger, lazy nigger— all because I am black! Oh, if I could die!"[86]

As when the still-enslaved Frederick Douglass sits on the shores of

Chesapeake Bay and watches the boats skimming freely over the water, prompting a remarkable address to the liberty for which he yearns, at this moment Frado becomes fully aware of herself. There are echoes, too, of *Uncle Tom's Cabin*, for when James, one of Frado's strongest supporters, falls ill, she heeds a clergyman's injunction to accept a compassionate savior and has a religious experience similar to Tom's. "Come to Christ," the minister urges. "All, young or old, white or black, bond or free, come all to Christ for pardon."[87] Frado begins to avidly read a Bible that Abby has given her, prompting Mrs. Bellmont to tell her sister-in-law that she has "caught" Frado reading it "as though she expected to turn pious nigger, and preach to white folks."[88] In a scene reminiscent of Little Eva's death, on his deathbed James urges Frado to believe as he does so that she, too, will have "a *heavenly* home" to replace the terrible one in which she finds herself.[89]

Following a talk with Mr. Bellmont, who assures Frado that she does not deserve the punishments his wife inflicts, Frado stands up to her mistress when threatened with another beating. "Stop," she shouts; "strike me, and I'll never work a mite more for you," as she stands "like one who feels the stirring of free and independent thoughts."[90] Remarkably, Mrs. Bellmont, rather than fly into a rage, drops her "weapon" and carries out the task she had set for Frado.

Frado completes her service to the Bellmonts and begins work for another local family. But soon she requires a doctor, who pronounces her very ill. Frado is put out at public expense, going to the home of "two maidens, (old,) who had principle enough to be willing to earn the money a charitable public disburses."[91] Frado remains there three years but never fully recovers. She then is placed with the less solicitous Mrs. Hoggs and gets even sicker. When she finally rebounds, she makes a semblance of a living with her skillful sewing, until she hears of an opportunity to move to a central Massachusetts town where the girls make straw bonnets, setting in motion the next phase of her life.

In the town there often appeared "professed fugitives from slavery, who recounted their personal experiences in homely phrase" to win recalcitrant northerners to the antislavery side. Wilson's use of "professed" was meant to suggest that some of these speakers were impostors or, at the least, would embroider their tales to meet their audience's expectations. Frado meets Samuel, "a fine, straight negro, whose back showed no marks of the lash, erect as if it never crouched under a burden," who nevertheless styles himself an escaped slave. In her infatuation, Frado, like many a sentimental heroine, is blind to his lie and plunges ahead, marrying him. Samuel often leaves to "lecture" for weeks at a time and has "little spare money." Eventually, "he left her to her fate—embarked at sea, with the disclosure that he had never seen the South, and that his illiterate harangues were humbugs for hungry abolitionists." He also leaves her pregnant. The story ends with a friend's giving her the "recipe, from which she might herself manufacture a useful article for her maintenance."[92] As we know from Wilson's life, illness compelled her to write in the hopes of alms. Frado "has felt herself obliged," her friend Allida says, "to resort to another method of procuring her bread—that of writing an Autobiography."

Our Nig is less about a woman betrayed by her heart than it is about the determinative power of culture. The novel challenges the sentimental novel's correspondence with reality or, at least, with the reality of black Americans. In one sense, at least, the novel is firmly sentimental: it is in part about how religion builds self-worth and provides a blueprint for surviving intolerable conditions. But its lesson is that, among free blacks, there is little hope for a better life, even through religion. Mag went with her first "love" because she was poor and took another step downward when out of dire economic need she married a black man. Though aware that her revelations of northern white prejudice could hurt the antislavery cause, Wilson wanted the reader to understand that ending slavery would do little for northern blacks, who would continue to be the victims of discrimination that kept them poor and hopeless.

Stowe was essential to the rise of African American literature; *Uncle Tom's Cabin* made a novel featuring black characters a viable proposition for publishing houses. A fervent reformer, she envisioned a better world for blacks after the end of slavery. Douglass described the prejudice of white workers with whom, on free soil, he competed for jobs, but his criticism was tempered by the generally upward trajectory of his *Narrative*. In *Our Nig*, however, there is no better world on the horizon, for Frado is subject to the vagaries of the free black's life. Brown, Jacobs, Webb, Delany, and Wilson, perhaps most of all, saw little hope for blacks in America. Contingency, not hope, is the primary theme of their works. For all the noble causes that spurred Americans to write novels in the first half of the nineteenth century, it is worth pointing out that Wilson did not write hers to counter prejudice but to merely stave off poverty.

6 } Discovering Self-Consciousness

In 1854 *Putnam's Monthly Magazine* ran a lengthy article on "Novels: Their Meaning and Mission," in which the writer observed that the last quarter century had "had the effect of completely revolutionizing" the form. While some attributed the changes in the genre to a single writer—William Godwin, whose *Caleb Williams* had so large an influence on Charles Brockden Brown, or Henry Fielding—"the true secret of the new impulse" was "with greater probability the more profoundly earnest spirit of the age," the movement toward "a radically stronger and nobler theorem of life and literature in all their departments—by a deeper theosophy and a more transcendent philosophy."[1]

By "transcendent" the writer gestured to the German idealism that had fertilized the American Transcendentalist movement.[2] He observed that the philosophy responsible for the new novel had already given us Emerson, Carlyle, Goethe, and Schiller, part of the splendid "fabric" woven by Kant, Fichte, Novalis, and Jean Paul Richter. An influence on all areas of thought at the time, the "idea" of the transcendent now had "taken possession of the field of imaginative writing—of novels," a product of an "era when there is such a fecundity and . . . overflowing of mental and psychological life."[3]

One of Transcendental philosophy's effects was (as Emerson put it so well) to make the mind aware of itself. In fiction this meant attention to the "deeper psychology" that Henry James appreciated in Hawthorne.[4] *Putnam's* essayist wrote that because "the domain of the novel ranges over the entire field of the real and the ideal," it "touches every point of man's consciousness."[5] In the 1850s, such interest in consciousness, particularly self-consciousness—the relation of the "me" to the "Not-Me" that Emerson had written about in his seminal *Nature* (1836)—began to inform fiction in a variety of ways. As sentimental novelists replaced piety with moralism, other novelists, influenced by their interest in the "transcendent," moved toward a faith based in internalized religious experience. Neither adherence toward a faith of abstract doctrine nor good works satisfied their characters' spiritual hunger, and thus they imagined a close relationship to God and particularly to Christ. In this private space, one discovered the true self. But because of the way such faith was conceived and realized, it was not easily accessible to others and could encourage solipsism.[6]

THE ETERNAL BACHELOR

Donald G. Mitchell's pseudonymously issued *Reveries of a Bachelor; or, A Book of the Heart* (1850) was the most popular example of the new self-consciousness of American fiction, even though in some ways it still epitomized the culture of sentiment in its portrayal of a bachelor yearning for the domestic life. Mitchell's novel consisted of extended "reveries" that together paint a portrait of a young, aimless bachelor, the author and Mitchell's alter ego, Ik Marvel (from two of Mitchell's favorite English authors, Isaac Walton and Andrew Marvell). Within a year of its publication, *Reveries* had sold fourteen thousand copies, and each year thereafter it enjoyed a "steady and widely extended circulation." It was quickly translated into French and German and into many more languages later in the nineteenth century.[7]

Mitchell never expected such success and later lamented that for the rest of his life, no matter what else he wrote, he would always be the dreamy bachelor Ik Marvel. Born in 1822, Mitchell was the son of a rural Connecticut minister who died when Mitchell was eight. In the following decade, he lost his mother and several siblings to tuberculosis, which he also contracted but survived. After his father's death Mitchell was placed in a boarding school in Ellington, Connecticut, and thus knew little of family life; that may explain his obsession with it that marks his immersion in the sentimental. In 1837, the year of the country's first major depression, he entered Yale College, where several relatives had matriculated and where he flourished, particularly enjoying his work on *The Yale Literary Magazine*. He graduated as valedictorian of his class and, to satisfy his relatives' wish that he soon find a profession, chose to read the law, even though his heart was not in it.

Through the good offices of a family friend, in 1844 Mitchell went to Liverpool as secretary to the U.S. consul in that city. The damp climate did not help his delicate lungs, and he spent much time wandering through France and Italy, seeking drier air and gathering material for a series of travel sketches. On his return to the United States, Mitchell placed some of these in the *American Whig Review*. Using the name Ik Marvel for the first time, he wrote more satiric sketches about Washington, D.C., where he had spent two months, for the New York *Courier and Enquirer*. Hearing of the democratic revolutions in Europe, Mitchell returned and witnessed some of the violent events in Paris in 1848. Back in America, he published *The Battle Summer* (1849), based on his firsthand observations of the upheavals.

In 1849 Mitchell published "A Bachelor's Reverie" in *The Southern Literary Messenger*. *Harper's New Monthly Magazine* reprinted it a few months later, to considerable praise. Mitchell then proposed a volume of such "daydreams" to Charles Scribner, who published *Reveries of a Bachelor* in late 1850. "Ik Marvel" was soon the talk of the literary world, and Mitchell brought out a sequel, *Dream Life: A Fable of the Seasons* (1851), which also sold well. A year later, *Harper's New Monthly Magazine* offered him a regular column on miscellaneous topics of his choice, and Mitchell thereafter sat for two years in what became the famed "Editor's Easy Chair" at the magazine.

Given his continuing financial success, Mitchell made plans to realize his dream of owning and cultivating a farm, which finally came to fruition in 1855 with his purchase of Edgewood, not far from New Haven. In the interim, he married Mary Pringle, the daughter of a South Carolina rice planter, and accepted a post as consul to Venice, which he secured with the help of Nathaniel Hawthorne, who had written a presidential campaign biography for his college classmate, the Democrat Franklin Pierce, then president.

On their return from Venice, Mitchell and his wife took up residence at Edgewood. Settling into life as an amateur agriculturalist and landscape gardener, he began to write what he called "rural" essays, although, as some scholars have pointed out, such writing is more accurately termed "suburban," for Mitchell, like Andrew Jackson Downing, among others, articulated a landscape and lifestyle halfway between the city and the country.[8] Mitchell collected some of these essays in *Rural Studies, with Hints for Country Places* (1867), a volume that typifies the incorporation of the kinds of sentimental tropes about spouses, children, and the home itself in such rural, idyllic settings.

He also began to write less autobiographical fiction. His major effort, first serialized in *The Atlantic Monthly*, was *Dr. Johns: Being a Narrative of Certain Events in the Life of an Orthodox Minister* (1866), which bears comparison to Stowe's *Oldtown Folks* (1869) as an evocation of New England life half a century earlier but which met with little success. In 1883 Mitchell revisited his popular works, writing new prefaces for *Reveries* and *Dream Life*, even though he considered these inferior to his later writing. Still widely known as Ik Marvel, Mitchell lived out his days at his beloved Edgefield, where he died in 1908, but not before he saw the beautiful fifteen-volume "Edgefield" edition of his works that Scribner published in 1906, which ensured that future generations also would enjoy *Reveries of a Bachelor*.

DAGUERREOTYPING THE HEART
Why did readers find *Reveries* so delightful and enthralling? A reviewer for *The American Whig Review* wrote that the key to the book's success was "the very ingenious form into which [the book] is thrown."[9] As another put it, in *Reveries* "all is vague, sliding, unfinished," its chapters "limpid, pellucid streams of thought."[10] The book was written in a style that was later called stream of consciousness. In his preface Mitchell called his work "a collection of those floating Reveries which have, from time to time, drifted across my brain." If he had imposed on them "more unity of design," he continued, he "might have made a respectable novel." He chose instead "the honester [*sic*] way of setting them down as they came seething from [his] thought, with all their crudities and contrasts, uncovered."[11]

Putnam's compared Mitchell's prose to one of the era's technological wonders, photography. Mitchell's book succeeded because "his nature is, as it were, iodised [*sic*], and registers, with the sensitive accuracy of a daguerreotype, every passing light and shade" of whatever comes into "his sphere."[12] That reviewer paid Mitchell another compliment by saying that in *Reveries* he had also succeeded in capturing the *interior* of his subject: it was a "book of the heart," just as the daguerreotype memorably recorded the exterior. Indeed, the reader shares Marvel's deepest secrets.

The book comprises four interrelated "reveries" or parts, each in a different way dealing with two of the standard topics of the sentimental:

love and marriage. The opening reveries find Ik musing on the desirable and undesirable aspects of marriage. On the negative side, he worries about giving up his independence. "Shall a man who has been free to chase his fancies over the wide world, without lett [obstruction] or hindrance, shut himself up to the marriage-ship, within four walls called Home, that are to claim him, his time, his trouble, and his fears, thenceforward forever more, without doubts thick, and coming to Smoke?"[13] Eliza Wharton had considered the same thing, but a half century earlier life without marriage, for a man or a woman, had been socially unacceptable. In 1850, however, a single *man*, while still raising an occasional eyebrow, was more common, although Ik's questioning of the worth of "Home," a central idea in the culture of sentiment, would have immediately seized the reader's attention.[14]

Ik considers the joy and satisfaction of having a wife always at your side and caring for you, a "sweet-faced girl" "suffer[ing] your fingers to play idly with those curls that escape down the neck," providing sympathy when family or friends die, comforting you should you fall ill, and at your bed as your last moment approaches.[15] But then comes the thought that the joy is transient. Inevitably, the fire burns down until "there was nothing but a bed of glowing embers, over which the white ashes gathered fast." Ik "was alone, with only [his] dog for company."[16] He thinks of tasting such ashes if a child should die or his wife should pass away. He imagines tending to his beloved through her last illness and enduring her funeral and grows almost hysterical at the prospect of such a loss and the loneliness that would follow. Finally, he decides that a wife is better than a coquette, even though he cannot help admitting his attraction to and fascination with the latter.

The final and longest reverie, titled "Morning, Noon, and Evening," features a different voice—he calls himself Paul—speaking directly to the reader as he relates a melancholy series of events in his own experience of love. He thinks back to his paradisiacal youth on a farm with his cousin Bella, three years younger. "Morning brings back to me the Past," Paul says, and "the past brings up not only its actualities, not only its events, and memories, but—stranger still,—what might have been."[17] He leaves Bella behind when he goes to college and then to Europe, where Carry, whom he has met on the ship and then reencounters in the bucolic English countryside, catches his interest. Then he is on to Rome, where he meets Enrica, the beautiful teenage daughter of his housekeeper, who is home after time spent in a convent. She clearly finds the American attractive and immediately goes out of her way to please him: when introduced, "she steals up behind, and passes her arm around me, with a quick electric motion, and a gentle pressure of welcome—that tells more than a thousand words."[18] But he finally realizes what a friend tells him, that her "southern nature with all its passion" is not suited to his, and he leaves her, and Rome, behind.

Later Paul meditates on the relation between past and present and wonders what has become of all the people whom he has known and loved. He returns to the farm and then decides to inquire after Bella. He trembles as he goes to her family's door, "for it flashed on [him], that perhaps,—Isabel was married." The news is worse. "Bella is dead," he learns.[19] Moreover, he finds when he reads through her unsent letters that she never lost her feelings for him. These heartfelt missives lead to an epiphany for Paul: "I loved Bella. I know not how I loved her,—whether as a lover, or as a husband loves a wife; I only know this,—I always loved her." He had shared everything else with her, he realizes, but had "never told her how much I loved her."[20] This regret haunts him like nothing else he has experienced.

But the letters also reveal something else remarkable: Bella and Carry had been intimate schoolmates. With the former gone, Carry means even more to Paul. He has to find her, for she is "doubly dear" to him, now "that she is joined with [his] sorrow for the lost Isabel."[21] Five years later, by chance he encounters Carry on a train. After they part, he writes her proposing marriage. Her reply is not what he had hoped, for her parents have already arranged for her to marry her godfather's ward, Laurence. Paul is despondent, but the hand of fate intervenes. Traveling in Europe, Laurence falls in love with another woman, and Carry's godfather finally permits him to break his betrothal to Carry, freeing her to marry Paul. A last turn of fate's windlass: on their wedding trip to Europe, they meet Laurence and find him married to—Enrica! The families end up living near each other, close to the farm where Paul and Bella had played, enacting the idyll of which Paul had often dreamed.

Mitchell's reliance on the tropes of the sentimental novel might seem to counteract his innovative style. But his ambitions were different. Toward the end of *Reveries*, Paul makes his way back to the old farmhouse and recounts, "I dreamed pleasant dreams that night for I dreamed that my Reverie was real."[22] In other words, it *all* has been a dream. Paul is the same lonely bachelor whom the reader met on the first page of the book, even though Mitchell led the reader to believe that this final "reverie" was in fact no reverie at all, but a remembrance. All along, Paul was living a dream life, trying to escape his loneliness. Sentiment informed Paul's dreams, yet one lesson of *Reveries* is that the escapism offered by the sentimental mode can have the pernicious effect of prolonging an individual's youthful unhappiness.

It should not be surprising that Emily Dickinson and her family read *Reveries* with pleasure, for Mitchell's willingness to "tell the truth but tell it slant," as she put it, can account for the book's popularity even among such sophisticated readers. *Reveries* appeared when Dickinson was an impressionable nineteen years old, and as her letters to her sister Susan and others indicate, it was a favorite. Indeed, it is possible that she acquired her love for her trademark dashes from Mitchell's compulsive use of them, for in his eddying prose as well as in her elliptic verse, this diacritical mark indicates spontaneity and helps capture the flow of consciousness.[23] And like Marvel, she, too, would work within and beyond the boundaries of the culture of sentiment in which they both thrived.

"THE OBSCUREST MAN OF LETTERS IN AMERICA"
By 1850 another writer was being lauded for writing fiction—to that point, short stories—that similarly probed his characters' hearts and minds. In that year, James T. Fields, the junior partner in the ambitious Boston publishing firm of Ticknor and Fields, solicited the work of a reclusive Salem, Massachusetts, author, Nathaniel Hawthorne, some of whose stories he had read. He showed Ticknor a lengthy short story, and he encouraged Hawthorne to turn it into a novel. The aspiring author did just that, adding, among other things, a lengthy autobiographical preface about his recent stint as a customshouse inspector in his native port city. The resulting novel was *The Scarlet Letter* (1850), which, while not a financial success compared with that year's bestsellers, Susan Warner's *The Wide, Wide World* and Mitchell's *Reveries of a Bachelor*, quickly sold out its first printing of twenty-five hundred copies and was immediately reprinted. Reviewers—admittedly, some of whom were friends of the publisher—promptly anointed Hawthorne the country's most important novelist and its best prose stylist since Irving.

But Hawthorne's road to acclaim had not been as direct as this brief summary suggests. His ship captain father, Nathaniel Hathorne, had died on a voyage to Surinam (Dutch Guiana) when his son was only four, prompting his widow and their children to move in with her family, the Mannings, in Salem. When Hawthorne was in his teens, the family settled in what was still wilderness in Raymond, Maine, where the Mannings had land; but a year later he returned to Salem, to prepare for college under the guardianship of his uncle. He entered Bowdoin College in Brunswick, Maine, in 1821; his classmates included Horatio Bridge, a future naval officer, Franklin Pierce, a future president; and, in the class behind him, Henry Wadsworth Longfellow, the future poet, translator, and professor.

After graduation in 1825 Hawthorne again returned to Salem, without a set goal but interested in the new profession of authorship. In his preface to *The Scarlet Letter* he humorously alludes to the low status of such ambition when he imagines his Puritan forebearers learning that their descendant is "a writer of storybooks." "What kind of business in life," a dour relative exclaims, "what mode of glorifying God, or being serviceable to mankind in his day and generation,—may that be?"[24] But Hawthorne was nothing if not persistent. He had completed some short stories while at Bowdoin and worked on a novel, *Fanshawe*, which he published anonymously and at his own expense in 1828. It went virtually unnoticed, however, one reviewer calling it evidently "the first effort of a Collegian," and another summarizing it pithily, if a tad sarcastically, as a "love story," which, "like ten thousand others, [has] a mystery, an elopement, a villain, a father, a tavern, almost a duel, a horrible death, and—Heaven save the mark!—an end."[25] The novel's reception so embarrassed Hawthorne that he burned many of the unsold copies. (Around this time, too, he added the *w* to his family name.) He had trouble getting noticed beyond Salem and Boston and claimed that he had the "distinction" of being, "for a good number of years, the obscurest man of letters in America."[26]

In 1831 Hawthorne began to publish stories anonymously in a popular Boston gift book annual called *The Token*. Several years later he collected these, many based in New England's colonial history, as *Twice-Told Tales* (1837) and put his name on the title page. He republished the tales in 1842, and in 1846 brought out another collection, *Mosses from an Old Manse*. This book met critical, if not popular, success. Some reviewers suggested that he was a potential successor to Irving, Cooper, and Sedgwick, a writer who could finally bring respectability to American literature.

One reviewer who believed that was his old schoolmate Henry Wadsworth Longfellow, who lavishly praised *Twice-Told Tales.* "When a new star rises in the heavens," Longfellow wrote, "people gaze after it for a season with the naked eye, and with such telescopes as they may find. In the stream of thought, which flows so peacefully deep and clear through the pages of this book, we see the bright reflection of a spiritual star, after which all men will be fain to gaze 'with the naked eye, and with the spy-glasses of criticism.'" The book could have come only "from the hand of a man of genius."[27]

Other early notices similarly enhanced Hawthorne's reputation. Some reviewers latched on to the unusual serenity and inwardness of Hawthorne's fiction. Poe claimed that the prominent feature of the stories was what a painter would term "*repose*," for "all is quiet, thoughtful, subdued," and "we are soothed as we read."[28] In *The Knickerbocker*, Lewis Gaylord Clark observed that Hawthorne had no superior "as a quiet yet acute observer and most faithful limner of Nature. His mind," Clark wrote, using the same metaphor applied to Mitchell's works, "reflects her images like the plates of the Daguerreotype."[29] Nathan Hale, Jr., observed that Hawthorne's tales never contained much "external action." Rather, he unveiled "the movements of the inner man, and the growth of motive and reflection."[30]

The young author's next collection, *Mosses from an Old Manse*, while again well received, also elicited some telling criticism. Poe, perhaps seeing no improvement or growth in Hawthorne's work, wrote that he was "peculiar" but also predictable; there was "sameness" and a "monotone" to Hawthorne's works, which too often inclined toward allegory that would keep him from both true greatness and wide popularity.[31] Hawthorne himself recognized as much when, in his introduction to "Rappaccini's Daughter," he deprecatingly described an alter ego, M. de l'Aubépine (the hawthorn tree, in French), as occupying

> an unfortunate position between the transcendentalists . . . and the great body of pen-and-ink men who address the intellect and sympathies of the multitude. If not too refined, at all events too remote, too shadowy and unsubstantial . . . to suit the taste of the latter class, and yet too popular to satisfy the spiritual or metaphysical requisitions of the former, he must necessarily find himself without an audience.[32]

In the *Democratic Review* in 1845 Duyckinck alighted on the quality that Poe and perhaps even Hawthorne himself could not explain: "a power of fascination which is exercised over the mind by the occasional gloom and pale glimpses as it were of fiends starting up on the page." For him, the "novel and original element" in Hawthorne was "the shadow which Sin and Death in their twin flights are forever casting upon the world; shadows which fall alike upon the so-called evil and the good, which darken all that is pure, and defile all that is sacred, but not more than in actual life."[33] Melville later called this Hawthorne's "power of blackness ten times black."[34] Hawthorne was content to rest among these shadows, and his reticence prevented him from imagining the kind of spiritual freedom Transcendentalists promised their followers.

If he did not seek to dispel gloom in his fiction, Hawthorne did at least try to do so in his life, as one of the original participants in George Ripley's communitarian experiment at Brook Farm. He had become engaged to Sophia Peabody—sister of Elizabeth, a spinster Transcendentalist, and Mary, a teacher who married the educational reformer Horace Mann—and intended to bring her to Brook Farm after their marriage. Hawthorne curtailed his stay, however, returning to Boston in November 1841, after about seven months; the environment, for a variety of reasons, had not been as conducive to his writing as he had hoped.[35] The experience was not fruitless, though; it was to provide the background to his third novel, *The Blithedale Romance* (1852).

Hawthorne and Peabody were married in July 1842 and took up residence in Concord at the bucolic "Old Manse," previously the home of the Reverend Ezra Ripley, where his grandson Ralph Waldo Emerson had written *Nature*. In 1845 the couple, now with a young daughter, returned to Salem to live with Hawthorne's mother, and the following year, with the help of his old classmate Pierce, now president, Hawthorne assumed the position of surveyor at the Salem Custom House, where he conceived *The Scarlet Letter*.

"A TALE OF HUMAN FRAILTY AND SORROW"

Like the earliest American novels, *The Scarlet Letter* deals with seduction, but the event—the climax in works like *The Coquette* and its progeny—occurs prior to the novel's action proper. In Hawthorne's depiction of Hester Prynne's desperate attempt to keep her daughter, Pearl, when the magistrates threaten to make her a ward, and in Pearl's desire to hold the hands of both her mother and her father in daylight and so to be acknowledged as their child, it similarly draws on sentimental tropes, particularly the idea of the sanctity of family bonds. The novel's innovation lies elsewhere, in its psychological dissection of the emotional lives of its three central characters, Hester; the Reverend Arthur Dimmesdale, her lover; and Roger Chillingworth, her husband. With the novel Hawthorne finally broke allegory's hold on his imagination.

The Scarlet Letter was widely reviewed. One of its most trenchant evaluations appeared in *The Universalist Quarterly and General Review*, where the minister Amory Dwight Mayo recognized the acuteness of Hawthorne's characterizations but in the service of what he considered a flawed religious vision.[36] Mayo related the novel to one of the most hotly debated theological propositions of the age: whether the mind was "free, acting from volitions self-suggested or voluntarily adopted," or was "subject to influences which encompass it and insinuate themselves into its structure." The former view, affirming free will, assumed in man "a definite individuality" that allowed him to stand "apart from nature, or other souls, or the Deity," and by "sheer will and energy" to create a world of his own, a position that in its extreme form ended in the subjectivism that Emerson championed. The latter view posited that God, "in some way inexplicable to man, lives in his universe, and causes his will to be done through all modes and qualities of finite action." In this view, "individuality has less distinctness of outline" and is less significant, for man is subject to the same unswerving force and aware of forces that "circumscribe his activity and interfere with the assumption of his omnipotent individuality."[37]

There are times in every man's life, Mayo argued, when this riddle of freedom and fate becomes painfully manifest and his natural reaction is to deny his cosmic dependence. "Now and then," though, a man is born who can "look straight down into the spirit without searing his eyeballs, witness this conflict of law and will, trace its results," and "not lose his balance of mind." Hawthorne was one of these, Mayo asserted, for he concentrated the reader's interest upon the raging battle between human will and spiritual law.[38] Unlike Emerson, however, who posited a healthy balance between an individual's "Power" and divinely established "Fate," Hawthorne dwelled so much on the latter that he became "an unfit medium" for the proper interpretation of man's relation to God. Thus, in *The Scarlet Letter*, powerful as it was, Mayo found a "certain ghastliness about the people," a result of the author's obsession with sin. "No puritan city ever held such a throng as stalks" through the book, Mayo observed, and "even in a well conducted madhouse, life is not so lurid and intense."[39] In portraying the cosmic battle in each individual and deciding its outcome in favor of the gods, Hawthorne, Mayo believed, lost the real flesh and blood that drove narrative.

ON MONUMENT MOUNTAIN

The critical and relative popular success of *The Scarlet Letter* ushered in a very creative period in Hawthorne's life, to which his chance meeting with another successful young author, Herman Melville, contributed. In the spring of 1850, flush from the excitement of publishing *The Scarlet Letter*, Hawthorne had moved his family to a cottage in the town of Lenox, Massachusetts, in the Berkshire Mountains, overlooking the beautiful lake known as the Stockbridge Bowl.

That August David Dudley Field, a Berkshire County historian, issued invitations for a climb of and picnic on nearby Monument Mountain. In addition to Field and his daughter Jenny, the party consisted of a number of friends and visitors: James T. Fields, Hawthorne's publisher, and his wife; Evert Duyckinck; Cornelius Mathews; Henry Sedgwick, a student of Longfellow's at Harvard; Oliver Wendell Holmes; and Herman Melville, a young novelist riding a wave of success since his first work, *Typee*, and now at work on his sixth, about the sperm whale fishery. A sudden thunderstorm overtook the group, forcing them to take cover under a ledge, where they drank iced champagne and listened to Mathews recite William Cullen Bryant's poem "Monument Mountain." When they attained the summit, there were more antics. Melville ventured on a high ledge to show how sailors hauled in canvas, and even Hawthorne entered the fun, playing at looking for "the great carbuncle," the subject of one of his best-known stories.[40] It was a memorable and spirited day.

Melville was staying at his cousin Robert Melvill's summer boarding-house in Pittsfield and by September had decided to buy Arrowhead, a farm in the same town, a purchase made possible by a loan from his father-in-law. Before long he moved his family—his wife, Elizabeth, their son, Malcolm, his mother, and three unmarried sisters—to Arrowhead, where he started renovations and continued to toil at what became *Moby-Dick* (1851). Hawthorne's presence was exhilarating, and his influence on Melville pivotal. The two visited each other as family and work schedules allowed, usually at Melville's instigation but never seemingly often enough to satisfy him. Within two weeks of their meeting, Melville published in Duyckinck's *Literary World* a deeply appreciative essay titled "Hawthorne and His Mosses," in which he announced that Hawthorne was nothing less than Shakespeare's equal and that his new friend had "dropped germinous [*sic*] seeds" deep into his soul.

The chief product of Hawthorne's Berkshire County sojourn was *The House of the Seven Gables*. Because it followed so closely on the heels of *The Scarlet Letter*, reviewers welcomed it as a less gloomy and relentless depiction of sin and guilt. The Boston writer Henry T. Tuckerman stressed Hawthorne's appeal to "consciousness" and observed that what the use of lenses in the telescope and microscope had done for the scientist "the psychological writer does in relation to our own nature," using stories to make the reader aware of "mysteries within and around individual life." If one were obliged to describe Hawthorne's writing in a single word, Tuckerman ventured, it would be "metaphysical" or "soulful." As the earth and sky blend at the horizon, the reviewer concluded, where "things seen and unseen, the actual and the spiritual, mind and matter, what is within and what is without our consciousness, have a line of union," there Hawthorne "delights to hover."[41]

But Duyckinck thought that the novel was a step backward, for it was too "semi-allegorical," the house of the seven gables itself—"one [gable] for each deadly sin"—an "adumbration of the corrupted soul of man."[42] For all of its detailed depiction of such genuine New England characters as Hepzibah, Clifford, and Jaffrey Pyncheon, said another reviewer, the book "did not have the same force, precision, and certainty of handling" of *The Scarlet Letter*. Hawthorne's "intensely meditative cast of mind[,]" by which he views persons in relation to general laws," clotted the prose and caused him to "lose his hold upon characters."[43]

THE REVERIES OF MILES COVERDALE

After the publication of *The House of the Seven Gables*, Ticknor asked Hawthorne for another volume of stories, and he obliged with *The Snow-Image and Other Twice-Told Tales* (1852). He also completed a collection of retellings of classical myths for children, *A Wonder-Book for Girls and Boys* (1852), but he had another novel in mind. To his friend Horatio Bridge he wrote in the summer of 1851, "I know not what I will write next," but "should it be a romance," he continued, he meant "to put an extra touch of the devil in it."[44] The result was salutary, for some critics declared this next work, *The Blithedale Romance*, Hawthorne's "*chef-d'œuvre*," as a reviewer in the well-regarded *North British Review* put it, "the best novel of America, and one of the best of the present age."[45] Among novels published in the early 1850s, a time of great experimentation within the form, *The Blithedale Romance* is indeed a seminal work because of the ways in which Hawthorne, influenced by his friends and neighbors among the Transcendentalists, examined the interior life in a character remarkably similar to Ik Marvel, though one whose reveries brought him beyond melancholy.

Despite his pointed disclaimer in the book's preface, Hawthorne drew much from his several months' stay in 1841 at Brook Farm. In the novel, Hawthorne explored the individual's obligations to self and society. As sentimental authors like Warner and Cummins promulgated an ethic of self-regulation or self-negation—the development of character for the benefit of something larger than the self—Hawthorne, even as he borrowed some conventions from the sentimental genre, addressed the inevitable conflict between this ethos and one that celebrated the uniqueness of personality and, by extension, the self-centeredness that Transcendentalism implicitly encouraged. His *Blithedale Romance* was one of the best examples of this growing tendency, for the novel is about both psychology and sociology. Setting his fiction at a socialist community, Hawthorne confronted the reasons why such utopian experiments were established on this side of the Atlantic—that for all its rhetoric of equality, the United States was not yet a true democracy. In so doing, he also presented a memorably inventive portrait of the interior life.

Hawthorne accurately represented Ripley's original intentions for Brook Farm, particularly his attempt to level differences among different classes and engender in each member a concern for the whole. For once, the narrator, Miles Coverdale, explains, "we had divorced ourselves from Pride, and were striving to supply its place with familiar love," in an attempt to eliminate the social conflict endemic to free market capitalism. The reformers also wished "to lessen the laboring man's toil, by performing our due share of it," as intellectuals took turns in the fields and at various crafts, demonstrating that labor was not something performed only by the lower classes. They sought their profit "by mutual aid, instead of wresting it by the strong hand from an enemy, or filching it craftily from those less shrewd than ourselves, . . . or winning it by selfish competition with a neighbor." In short, Coverdale concluded, "we purposed to offer up the earnest toil of our bodies, as a prayer, no less than an effort, for the advancement of our race."[46]

At Blithedale, however, the chief characters, noble as their original intentions are, quickly succumb to the very "Pride" that the community was established to eradicate. At the outset, the reader incongruously finds the beautiful, magnetic women's rights advocate, Zenobia, in domestic work, acting as the gracious hostess the first evening at the farm. And when she soon shows herself to be imperious, rash, and willing to sacrifice the community, it is for another domestic ideal: a man's love.

The object of her affection, Hollingsworth, a blacksmith turned social reformer, appears at the farmhouse door in a snowstorm carrying a teenage girl, Priscilla, who needs their protection, and thus seems the epitome of the man of feeling. But he soon shows his true self, too; for him, Blithedale is only a stepping-stone to establish a new kind of reformatory for criminals.

Coverdale, a bachelor who "once had faith and force enough to form generous hopes of the world's destiny," says he is willing to do what he can for the greater good. But he qualifies his commitment. If going to Blithedale means "quitting a warm fireside, flinging away a freshly lighted cigar, and travelling far beyond the strike of the city-clocks, through a drifting snowstorm," he is on board, but his elision of anything more taxing suggests that he has given little consideration to the sacrifice Ripley had in mind.[47] When psychological tensions increase, Coverdale simply leaves Blithedale, retreating to bachelor's rooms in Boston, too selfish to realize that he might do something to avert impending tragedy. Despite Coverdale's assertion that he has made "but a poor and dim figure in [his] own narrative, establishing no separate interest," he becomes Hawthorne's main focus, just as Ik Marvel was Mitchell's. Or rather, the vexed relation between Coverdale's mind and will is Hawthorne's main focus. The entire book is Coverdale's attempt to recover and understand events that happened twelve years earlier—events filtered through not only his consciousness but also his memory—and what to do about them now.

Hawthorne, sensitive to his competitors and the market, may have wished to capitalize on *The Reveries of a Bachelor*'s considerable success. Coverdale is a twenty-six-year-old bachelor when the action begins and remains a bachelor at thirty-eight, when he narrates his story. Even more striking, Hawthorne constantly evokes fireplaces, their dancing flames or dying embers signaling Coverdale's varying moods. He begins his story with the memory of the "cheery blaze upon the heart" that he found at Blithedale after he trudged there through a mid-April snowstorm. "Vividly does that fireside recreate itself," Coverdale writes, "as I rake away the ashes from the embers in my memory, and blow them up with a sigh, for lack of more inspiring breath." The fire burns vividly but only for an instant, its oak logs long ago spent. Their "genial glow must be represented by the merest phosphoric glimmer, like that which eludes, rather than shines, from the damp fragments of decayed trees, deluding the benighted wanderer through a forest."[48]

This is the reader's first warning of Coverdale's potential unreliability; conjuring his memories before an artificial fire, he sees through a glass darkly. Try as he might—"the pleasant firelight! I must keep harping on it," he says a few pages later—all that has happened at Blithedale still is not clear to him.[49] Later, after he has left the farm because of a conflict with Hollingsworth, he sits quietly in his hotel room "in the laziest manner possible, in a rocking chair, inhaling the fragrance of a series of cigars," refusing just yet to plunge again "into the muddy tide of human activity and pastime" that has ruffled his serenity.[50]

Like Mitchell, Hawthorne explores why his main character has remained a bachelor. Coverdale fears the potential pitfalls and tragedy that can beset a married man and so is unable to act on his half-acknowledged desires. Thus, an almost pathological aversion to personal risk compounds his neurotic self-doubt. His insecurity takes its most tragicomic form in his relations with Zenobia, whom he cannot keep his eyes off of. From the moment he first sees her, he is struck by her "bloom, health, and vigor, which she possesse[s] in such overflow that a man might well have fallen in love with her for their sake only."[51] When Zenobia subsequently jokes that its being so cold in the group's newly founded paradise she could not assume "the garb of Eden" until spring, Coverdale can hardly control his thoughts. "Assuredly, Zenobia could not have intended it," he writes, and thus "the fault must have been entirely in my imagination—but these last words, together with something in her manner, irresistibly brought up a picture of that fine, perfectly developed figure, in Eve's earliest garment. I almost fancied myself," Coverdale recalls, "actually beholding it."[52]

No stranger to men's attention, Zenobia avers that she has "been exposed to a great deal of eye-shot in the few years of [her] mixing in the world" but never of the kind Coverdale casts on her. "What are you seeking to discover in me?" she asks him. Caught off guard, Coverdale blurts out, "The mystery of your life. And you will never tell me." Zenobia calls his bluff. Bending her head toward his, she looks into his eyes, as if challenging Coverdale to drop "a plummet-line" into the depths of her consciousness. "I see nothing," he says, closing his eyes, "unless it be the face of a sprite, laughing at me from the bottom of a deep well." Coverdale is afraid to look directly at the source of her attraction, her blatant sexuality. The whole episode so upsets him that he begins to wish that she would leave him alone. Suppressing his carnal feelings, he declares petulantly, like a boy whistling in the dark, that he would not have fallen in love with her "under any circumstances."[53]

Frightened by Zenobia's passion, Coverdale falls in love with her opposite, the unthreatening, adolescent Priscilla. His tragedy is that he cannot speak this love, either, for more than a decade passes after the final events at Blithedale before he is able to mention it publicly. Early on, however, Hawthorne alerts the reader to the growing infatuation that leads to Coverdale's "writing" the whole book. Coverdale mentions that as time passes, "Priscilla had grown to be a very pretty girl, and still kept budding and blossoming, and daily putting on some new charm," as though "Nature [were] shaping out a woman before our very eyes." Her "imperfections and shortcomings" affected him with "a kind of playful pathos which was as absolutely bewitching a sensation as ever I experienced," a reverie worthy of Ik Marvel.[54]

But there is yet another whom Coverdale "loves": Hollingsworth, four years older, "a tenderness in his voice, eyes, and mouth, in his gesture, in every indescribable manifestation, which few men could resist and no women."[55] When Coverdale is ill, Hollingsworth provides "more than brotherly attendance," for there is "something of the woman molded into [his] great stalwart frame."[56] "I loved Hollingsworth," Coverdale later says, and Hollingsworth returns the affection.[57] He asks Coverdale to join his enterprise, offering "what you have told me, over and over again, that you most need"—a purpose in life "worthy of the extremest self-devotion." Tears come to Hollingsworth's eyes as he murmurs to Coverdale, "[T]here is not the man in this wide world, whom I can love as I could you. Do not forsake me!" As Coverdale remembers this scene "through the coldness and dimness" of the twelve years since it occurred, he still has the sensation "as if Hollingsworth had caught hold of my heart, and were pulling it towards him with an almost irresistible force . . .

Had I but touched his extended hand, Hollingsworth's magnetism would perhaps have penetrated me with his own conception of all these matters."[58] Coverdale refuses and "never said the word—and certainly can never have it to say, hereafter—that cost me a thousandth part so hard an effort as that one syllable."[59] If Coverdale's behavior had not affected others, his constitutional reticence would be excusable; but his actions, even though he does not fully realize it, contribute to the confusion and tragedy that strike those who genuinely are his friends.

FROM SELF-CONSCIOUSNESS TO SELFISHNESS

Hawthorne's use of an unreliable first-person narrator grew out of one of his preoccupations: the problem of selfishness. Blithedale's population, for example, was comprised of "persons of marked individuality, crooked sticks . . . not exactly the easiest to bind up into a faggot." So Coverdale opines that the bond at Blithedale "was not affirmative, but negative," for each in the past had found "one thing or another to quarrel with" in his or her life, even as he or she could not agree on anything but the "inexpediency of lumbering along with the old system any farther."[60] Further, like Zenobia and Coverdale, many early members were not economically dependent on the enterprise, and the fact that they had it within their power to leave when they wished could not but lessen their commitment. At one point Coverdale realizes that although they "saw fit to drink [their] tea out of earthen cups to-night, in earthen company, it was at [their] option to use pictured porcelain and handle silver forks again, tomorrow."[61]

Tellingly, the perversion of love by possessiveness that Fourier deemed a major failing in modern society brings tragedy—and an end—to the Blithedale experiment. Hollingsworth correctly argues that Fourier based his system on the gratification of each individual's needs; but at Blithedale he, Zenobia, and Coverdale all deny or repress what truly attracts them, poisoning their behavior. Hollingsworth pretends that he loves Zenobia to acquire her money; in so doing, he initially denies his true feelings for Priscilla. Zenobia suppresses her beliefs in women's equality and throws herself at the feet of a chauvinist, then, brokenhearted, kills herself. Coverdale hides any acknowledgment of his love for Priscilla, first from fear of rejection and later, for twelve lonely years, from disappointment and embarrassment. Zenobia's severe judgment of Hollingsworth when she learns the truth about whom he loves indicts them all. "It is all self!" she screams. "Nothing else; nothing but self, self, self!" His "disguise" with her is finally "a self-deception." In denying his love for Priscilla, Hollingsworth has "stifled down" his "inmost consciousness" and done a "deadly wrong" to his heart.[62] In the end, Zenobia dismisses the Blithedale experiment. She tells Coverdale,

> I am weary of this place, and sick to death of playing at philanthropy and progress. Of all varieties of mock-life, we have surely blundered into the very emptiest mockery, in our effort to establish the one true system . . . It was, indeed, a foolish dream! Yet it gave us some pleasant summer days, and bright hopes, while they lasted.[63]

Eight years were to pass before Hawthorne's next and final novel, *The Marble Faun; or, The Romance of Monte Beni* (1860). Benefiting from his friendship with President Pierce, from 1853 to 1857 he served as the U.S. consul to Liverpool, like Mitchell, and then to Manchester. Relinquishing this position in 1858, Hawthorne traveled through France to Italy, where he lived for a year before returning to England. In Italy he wrote *The Marble Faun*, another story of the psychological wages of sin and guilt but one that suffers from both excessive length and Hawthorne's revived interest in allegory.

In these same years Hawthorne also worked on another manuscript he had begun in Italy, his "English" novel, but abandoned what was published posthumously as *Dr. Grimshawe's Secret* (1883). He then started a historical romance set at the time of the American Revolution. This, too, he failed to complete; it was published after his death as *Septimus Felton* (1872). Traveling through New Hampshire with his old classmate Pierce, whose party had abandoned him after one term and so had his own failures to consider, Hawthorne died at the Pemigewasset House in Plymouth in 1864. Another unfinished work, *The Dolliver Romance* (1876), about someone seeking the elixir of life, was among his papers.

TYPEE MAKES GOOD

Hawthorne exerted a decided, if wholly unplanned, influence upon Herman Melville. The latter's journey to that fateful day on Monument Mountain was circuitous. He was born in New York City in 1819, the son of the merchant Allan Melvill and Maria Gansevoort Melville, daughter of Peter Gansevoort, a Revolutionary War general. When Melville was eleven, his father's business failed, prompting the family to move to

Albany, the Gansevoorts' hometown. Two years later his father died, leaving the family in considerable debt. Although the young Melville attended Albany Academy for a year, college never seemed to be a real possibility. Between 1835 and 1837 he worked as a bookkeeper and clerk in Albany, and he also tried teaching. Lacking steady work and family money, at the age of twenty he followed the path of many in comparable straits: he went to sea. In the early summer of 1839 he left New York as a crew member on a London-bound merchant ship, an experience he later drew on in writing *Redburn* (1849).

In Bedford in the spring of 1841 he signed on to a whaling vessel, the *Acushnet*, bound for the largely unexplored South Seas. Disliking his captain, Melville and his friend Richard Tobias (Toby) Greene jumped ship at Nuku Hiva, the largest of the Marquesas Islands (in what now is French Polynesia). The two remained in the lush Taipi Valley for a month and then boarded an Australian whaler sailing for Tahiti, where the captain remanded them for mutiny. Melville escaped, worked on Tahiti, and in the autumn of 1842 boarded a Nantucket-based whaler. Then came a stint in the U.S. Navy aboard the frigate *United States*, which docked in Boston in the fall of 1844, finally returning Melville to his home country after four years of sailing the most exotic parts of the globe.

Before going to sea, Melville had published a few prose sketches in local papers and on his return decided to write a book-length novel based on his adventures in the Marquesas, hoping to repeat the success of Richard Henry Dana Jr.'s *Two Years Before the Mast* (1840). He worked on the manuscript through 1845, and after Harper & Brothers had rejected it because the editors doubted its veracity, through the good offices of his brother Gansevoort, a member of the American legation in London, Melville placed it with the English house of John Murray. Early in 1846 it appeared as *Narrative of a Four Months' Residence Among the Natives of a Valley of the Marquesas Islands*; a few months later the enterprising Wiley & Putnam issued it in New York as *Typee: A Peep at Polynesian Life*, part of its new series of American literature.

Presented as fiction but supposedly based on the author's own travels, *Typee* became a sensation and went through a second printing in late summer, albeit without passages critical of the work of Christian missionaries that some readers found offensive. Scenes like those in which the island's beautiful bare-breasted nymphs greeted the land- (and sex-) starved sailors also raised a few eyebrows but probably sold copies.

Despite the fact that its owners were strongly Methodist and supported their denomination's missionary activity, the next year Harper & Brothers snapped up *Typee*'s sequel, *Omoo*, though like its predecessor, it first appeared in London. There Murray included it in his Home and Colonial Library, guaranteeing sales throughout the British Empire. In *Omoo* Melville drew on his time on Tahiti. As with *Typee*, the novel was aimed at satisfying the public's yearning for first-person accounts of exotic regions just opened to European and American exploration.

By 1847, even though his books sold only a couple of thousand copies each and a few thousand more in their English editions, Melville was one of the country's brightest literary lights, widely and appreciatively reviewed. His personal life, too, appeared to take a turn for the better. In August, Melville married the well-to-do Elizabeth Shaw, daughter of the Massachusetts supreme court chief justice Lemuel Shaw. The Melvilles took up residence in a house on Fourth Avenue in Manhattan.

Because of his involvement in Young America, Melville spent much time with Evert Duyckinck and Cornelius Mathews and attending New York's literary salons. He heard constant calls for a pathbreaking American novel beyond what Cooper, Simms, Sedgwick, or Mathews had produced. He also read voraciously, buying a subscription to the New York Society Library, borrowing from Duyckinck's personal collection, and frequenting the city's secondhand bookstalls. He read Shakespeare, Montaigne, Rabelais, Sir Thomas Browne, Dante, Coleridge, and others. All this could not but affect the new book he was writing about his South Seas adventures, one, he told John Murray, that would "enter into scenes altogether new" and that would "possess more interest than the former [two novels]; which treated of subjects comparatively trite."[64] At twenty-eight, Melville had begun to entertain thoughts not just of commercial success but of literary greatness.

His irritation that his first two novels had not been regarded as based in fact also influenced this new work. Tired of "the reiterated imputation of being a romancer in disguise," this book would "show those who may take an interest in the matter, that a real romance of mine is no Typee or Omoo, & is made of different stuff altogether." This work was "no dish water nor its model borrowed from the Circulating Library," he explained to Murray. "It is something new I assure you, & original, if nothing more." He added, "Forbear to prejudge it," for while "it opens like a true narrative," the "romance & poetry of the thing thence grow continuously, till it becomes a story wild enough" but "with a meaning too."[65]

Murray passed, however, and Melville made arrangements to publish *Mardi: And a Voyage Thither* with Murray's chief rival, Richard Bentley, with Harper & Brothers again bringing out the American edition. The novel is ostensibly the story of Taji, who jumps ship in the archipelago of Mardi and becomes obsessed with finding the beautiful maiden Yillah. But this is only one strand of what is an abstruse political allegory, inspired by Melville's interest in national and European affairs that Young America had nurtured. With revolutionary fervor sweeping Europe and with the continuing debate over the United States' war with Mexico, Melville portrayed the islands in Mardi as representations of European nations and various states in the Union.

Reviewers were mystified. An English reviewer put it bluntly: the novel is "a 3 vol. metaphor into the applications of which we can only now and then catch a glimpse . . . We never," he continued in a telling phrase, "saw a book so like a kaleidoscope."[66] Some traced its stylistic lineage to Europe, with Jonathan Swift's *Gulliver's Travels* frequently mentioned, as well as the works of Sir Thomas Browne, Robert Burton, and Rabelais. Others invoked Transcendentalism, one writer noting wryly that Melville had been "drinking at the well of the 'English bewitched' of which Mr. Carlyle and Mr. Emerson are the priests."[67] An English journal termed *Mardi* "a compound of 'Robinson Crusoe' and 'Gulliver's Travels,' seasoned throughout with German metaphysics of the most transcendental school."[68]

Several reviewers, however, thought that even with its failings *Mardi* should be lauded for its ambition. Its purpose was "no less than the reconciling of the mind to the creation of an Utopia in the unknown latitudes of Pacific, to call into existence imaginary tribes and nations, to describe fabulous manners, and to glass them so distinctly in the fancy that they will appear to have been implanted there by memory," claimed one attentive reader.[69] The predictably sympathetic *United States Magazine and Democratic Review* chided skeptical readers for forgetting that *Mardi* might be the latest in a line of books that had changed the world. "Pilgrims Progress [*sic*] and Gulliver's Travels were written so long ago, that they seem to have dropped through the memory of critics," who have ceased "to think any reproduction or improvement of that sort of thing possible . . . Portions of Mardi are written with . . . divine impulse, and they thrill through every fibre of the reader with an electric force."[70]

But even if it provided glimpses of ambition and imagination not yet fully realized, *Mardi* was not Melville's breakout book. Most reviewers agreed with George Ripley, now working for Horace Greeley's *New-York Tribune*: Melville should have stayed in his "sphere, which is that of graphic, poetical narration" rather than launch "into the dim, shadowy, spectral, Mardian region of mystic speculation and wizard fancies . . . Let the author return to the transparent narration of his own adventures," and he will be "everywhere welcomed as one of the most delightful of American writers."[71] Melville got the message, disappointed though he was to hear it. With a family to feed, he temporarily set aside his grand ambitions and within a year churned out two more novels, in the autobiographical vein that had made him famous.

By his own admission, Melville wrote *Redburn: His First Voyage* in less than two months, drawing on his first sea voyage, to Liverpool and London, a decade earlier. In *White-Jacket; or, The World in a Man-of-War* (1850), which took merely another two months, he re-created his fourteen months' experience in the U.S. Navy. He thought little of either novel, writing his father-in-law, "No reputation that is gratifying to me, can possibly be achieved by either of these books." They were, he continued to Chief Justice Shaw, "two *jobs*, which I have done for money—being forced to it as other men are to sawing wood."[72] *Redburn* and *White-Jacket* sold well as expected but also drew at least one prescient notice. "Keep your eye on Herman Melville," a critic wrote in a review of *White-Jacket*. "There is a humor, and sparkle of rhetoric in his writings, which, if he lives to be the man equal in years to Irving, Cooper, and Paulding, will rank as high on the chock-notch of fame as they."[73]

"A WICKED BOOK"

After returning from a trip to London to negotiate with Bentley for the English edition of *White-Jacket*, Melville mulled over his whaling voyage on the *Acushnet*, the one experience he had not yet used in his novels. In May 1850, he wrote to Richard Henry Dana that he was about "half way" into the "whaling voyage" story, which would make "a strange sort of a book . . . blubber is blubber you know; tho' you may get oil out of it, the poetry runs as hard as sap from a forest maple tree;—& to cook the thing up, one must needs throw in a little fancy."[74]

The "fancy" came from many sources besides his visceral memories of his time in the whaling industry. His preliminary "Extracts" to the novel indicate his immersion in books about whales and whaling, but there were new chief literary and stylistic influences as well: the Old Testament, Shakespeare's *King Lear* and other plays, Milton's *Paradise Lost* and *Prometheus Bound*, Virgil's *Aeneid*, Laurence Sterne's *Tristram Shandy*, Robert Burton's *The Anatomy of Melancholy*, Pierre Bayle's *Dictionary*, Montaigne's *Essays*, as well as more recent works like William Beckford's *Vathek: An Arabian Tale*, Mary Shelley's *Frankenstein*, Carlyle's *Sartor Resartus* and *Heroes and Hero-Worship*, and De Quincey's *Confessions of an Opium-Eater*. As Melville told Hawthorne as he was completing *Moby-Dick*, "Until I was twenty-five, I had no development at all. From my twenty-fifth year I date my life. Three weeks have scarcely passed, at any time between then and now, that I have not unfolded within myself."[75]

In the same letter, however, Melville expressed a worry that he continued to be "pulled hither and thither by circumstances . . . Dollars damn me," he lamented. "What I feel most moved to write, that is banned,—it will not pay. Yet, altogether, write the *other* way I cannot. So the product is a final hash."[76] To another friend, he issued this warning about the book: "Don't you buy it—don't you read it, when it does come out, because it is by no means the sort of book for you . . . It is not a piece of fine feminine Spitalfields silk . . . but it is of the horrible texture of a fabric that should be woven of ships' cables & hausers [*sic*] . . . Warn all gentle fastidious people from so much as peeping into the book."[77] "I have written a wicked book," he wrote Hawthorne after his friend had read and praised it, "and feel spotless as the lamb."[78]

Moby-Dick's themes have been explored to near exhaustion: the nature of good and evil, the personal and general havoc wrought by hubristic behavior, the failure of good intentions to halt ongoing tragedy, the ambiguity of symbol, the relativism this ambiguity breeds, and many others. Melville's use of Romantic notions of the self-willed personality has been less commented on. Struggling to explain Captain Ahab's obsession with vengeance on what his first mate, Starbuck, calls "a dumb brute . . . that simply smote thee from blindest instinct," Melville created new ways of presenting the complexity of self-knowledge and warned of the dangers of self-absorption that by then were seemingly an inextricable part of American national character.[79]

Because Ishmael narrates the story, his spiritual and psychological growth best indicates Melville's purpose. Much of Ishmael's soul-searching comes from his watching, listening, and trying to fathom Captain Ahab, who, from his first appearance on the quarterdeck, is the novel's magnetic center, drawing all toward him, no matter how fierce their initial resistance. Ishmael, presented from the first page as a seeker, succumbs like the rest to his captain's spell. The hunt for Moby Dick forces Ishmael into experiences of sympathetic identity, not unlike Sheppard Lee's metempsychotic travels. Ishmael enters the lives of many individuals, from a son of South Seas royalty from the island Kokovoko like Queequeg; to a monomaniac Nantucket Quaker of "greatly superior natural force, with a globular brain and a ponderous heart," named after a biblical king whose blood the dogs licked as had been prophesied; to an African American cabin boy frightened out of his wits by the sea's immensity.[80]

For a young man, Ishmael also has a precocious sense of the perils of self-absorption. In the first chapter, drawing on the story of Narcissus, he declares that humanity sees itself "in all rivers and oceans," and what is mirrored there "is the image of the ungraspable phantom of life": this is "the key to it all."[81] Ahab, by contrast, believes that he has seen and touched that phantom and as a result is arrogance and free will personified. Successful in swaying the crew to his purpose, Ahab declares, "What I've dared, I've willed, and what I've willed I'll do!" His hubris knows no bounds. Yes, he has lost his leg according to a prophecy, but he now prophesies that he will "dismember" his "dismemberer." "Now, then, be the prophet and the fulfiller one. That's more than ye, ye great gods, ever were!"[82]

A short while later, as Ishmael ponders the white whale, he begins to comprehend the crazed old man. After his injury, the captain, who had "been in colleges, as well as 'mong the cannibals," has linked the creature not only to "all his bodily woes, but all his intellectual and spiritual exasperations," the "monomaniac incarnation of all those malicious agencies which some deep men feel eating at them."[83] And yet Ishmael understands that knowing this, he has only begun to plumb Ahab's self. "This is much," he concludes, "yet Ahab's larger, darker, deeper part remains unknown."[84] Why, for example, did the crew so readily respond "to the old man's ire"? By what evil magic did he possess their souls, "so that at times his hate seemed almost theirs"?[85] The reason, Ishmael begins to understand, lies in the fact that Ahab's quest is also humanity's, and the young crewman struggles not to be driven mad by it. Ishmael meditates on the safety of land and the danger of the immense, unknowable sea and perceives "a strange analogy" to something in man. "For as the appalling ocean surrounds the verdant land, so in the soul of man there lies one insular Tahiti, full of peace and joy, but encompassed by all the horrors of the half known life . . . Push not off from that isle; thou canst never return!"[86] Ahab, for one, has pushed off to challenge the gods, and he has taken an entire ship's crew with him.

The central question Ahab's behavior poses for Ishmael was the same that occupied many contemporary theologians as well as Melville's new friend Hawthorne: the extent of man's free will. Ishmael's meditation while weaving rattan mats with Queequeg suggests his still-unfinished answer. He describes their work as reminding him of "the Loom of Time" and himself as a shuttle "mechanically weaving and weaving away at the Fates." The fixed threads of the warp, just loose enough to "admit the crosswise interblending of other threads with its own," seemed "necessity," or fate. In his own hand Ishmael held the shuttle, the woof, and wove his destiny "into these unalterable threads." Meanwhile, Queequeg used a wooden "sword" to hit the woof and tighten it; he did this "slantingly, or crookedly, or weakly, as the case might be," and by this difference gave the weave its final shape. Queequeg thus represents "chance." "Aye," Ishmael concludes, "chance, free will, and necessity—no wise incompatible—all interweavingly working together."

> The straight warp of necessity, not to be swerved from its ultimate course—its every alternating vibration, indeed, only tending to that; free will still free to ply her shuttle between the threads; and chance, though restrained in its play within the right lines of necessity, and sideways in its motions modified by free will, though thus prescribed to by both, chance by turn rules either, and has the last featuring blow at events.[87]

Acknowledging divine Providence, granting man free will to make choices within his sphere of action, yet allowing for the fickle goddess Fortuna: this is Ishmael's understanding of man's destiny, a formulation tested by Ahab's insistence on the utter supremacy of free will.

Ahab wants the impossible: to know what Providence intends for him, a knowledge Melville associates with the unfathomable depths of the sea.

When one of the captured sperm whales has been butchered and Ahab sees its head hanging from the hawsers, he addresses it: "Speak, mighty head, and tell us the secret thing that is in thee. Of all divers, thou hast dived the deepest . . . O head! Thou hast seen enough to split the planets and make an infidel of Abraham, and not one syllable is thine!"[88] The "Sphinx" remains silent, and Ahab hastens to his appointed meeting with his fate.

One person on board knows these metaphorical depths, however, and is marked forever. Several times the African American cabin boy, Pip, frightened by being so close to a whale, jumps from the whaleboat. Finally, in the heat of a chase, his mates forget him, and Pip is left behind, a mile from any craft. They eventually retrieve him, but fearing that he is forever lost, Pip has experienced the "intense concentration of self in the middle of such a heartless immensity" and "an awful lonesomeness." After Pip is among the crew again, he prattles on incoherently. They think that he has lost his mind, for "the sea had jeeringly kept his finite body up, but drowned the infinite of his soul." He has been carried down alive, "to wondrous depths, where strange shapes of the unwarped primal world glided to and fro before his passive eyes." Pip has seen "God's foot upon the treadle of the loom, and spake [hailed] it," and therefore his "shipmates called him mad." Pondering the poor boy, Ishmael concludes, "So man's insanity is heaven's sense . . . wandering from all mortal reason, man comes at last to that celestial thought, which, to reason, is absurd and frantic."[89] To learn what Pip now knows is to accept, without wish or will to change, God's plan. But this knowledge demands a radical alienation.

The subsequent chapter provides the alternative to Pip's story and shows that such alienation can be countered through selfless love. Ishmael, Queequeg, and others sit around a tub of ambergris, an aromatic and valuable substance produced in the digestive tracts of whales and used in perfumery, and squeeze the soft globules to release their liquid. This simple labor, akin to crushing grapes to make wine, leads Ishmael to forget the oath that he had sworn to Ahab.

Squeeze! Squeeze! Squeeze! All the morning long; I squeezed that sperm till I myself almost melted into it; I squeezed that sperm till a strange sort of insanity came over me; and I found myself unwittingly squeezing my co-laborers' hands in it, mistaking their hands for the gentle globules. Such an abounding, affectionate, friendly, loving feeling did this avocation beget; that at last I was continually squeezing their hands, and looking up into their eyes sentimentally; as much as to say—Oh! my dear fellow beings, why should we any longer cherish any social acerbities, or know the slightest ill-humor or envy! Come; let us squeeze hands all round; nay, let us all squeeze ourselves into each other; let us squeeze ourselves universally into the very milk and sperm of human kindness.[90]

This scene of subconscious affection, itself the mark of a striking utopian vision, has the power to break Ahab's satanic oath. In the middle of that "heartless immensity," Pip loses human contact; Ishmael's mystical vision of brotherhood is the antidote to Ahab's hubris and self-absorption.

Even Ahab eventually becomes aware of the transformative power of affection, and ironically, this knowledge comes through Pip. When a crew member tries to shoo the boy from some of the sailors' work, Ahab explodes: "Hands off that holiness!" Pip then breaks into one of his nonsensical monologues, and Ahab realizes that he speaks this way as a result of his having seen the secrets of the deep. The captain decides to adopt him, telling Pip that now he will stay with him in his quarters. "Thou touchest my inmost centre, boy," Ahab says; "thou are tied to me by chords woven of my heart-strings." Pip then touches Ahab's hand. "What's this?" Pip asks. "Here's velvet shark-skin . . . Ah, now, had poor Pip but felt so kind a thing as this, perhaps he had ne'er been lost! This seems to me, sir, as a man-rope, something that weak souls may hold by."[91] This powerful, reciprocal relationship soon threatens to negate the hatred Ahab feels for Moby Dick. He tells Pip that when it is time to hunt the white whale, he must remain on the ship. "There is that in thee, poor lad, which I feel too curing to my malady . . . Do thou abide here below," he insists, "where they shall serve thee, as if thou wert the captain."[92]

Affection later surfaces again. One beautiful peaceful morning, Ahab asks Starbuck to stand closer to him. "Let me look into a human eye; it is better than to gaze into sea or sky, better than to gaze upon God . . . This is the magic glass [mirror], man; I see my wife and my child in thine eye." He then tells Starbuck that he, too, must not man a boat for the dangerous whale because he has a family back in Nantucket. Moved, Starbuck begs him to turn the ship and head for port, so that they both can see their wives and children; but Ahab, against all love and reason, refuses.

What is it, what nameless, inscrutable, unearthly thing is it; what cozening, hidden lord and master, and cruel, remorseless emperor commands me; that against all natural lovings and longings, I so keep pushing, and crowding, and jamming myself on all the time; recklessly making me ready to do what in my own proper, natural heart, I durst not so much as dare? Is Ahab, Ahab? Is it I, God, or who, that lifts this arm? . . . how then can this one small heart beat; this one small brain think thoughts; unless God does that beating, does that thinking, does that living, and not I. By heaven, man, we are turned round and round in this world, like yonder windlass, and Fate is the handspike."[93]

It is a crucial turning point. Ahab now understands that he can do nothing to stop himself because as he says after the second day of the chase, "This whole act's immutably decreed. 'T was rehearsed by thee and me a billion years before this ocean rolled. Fool! I am the Fates' lieutenant. I act under orders."[94] Again, as in so many early American novels from *Wieland* on, free will is negated.

Why does Ishmael alone escape to tell the tale? Though he has sworn to Ahab's oath, he embraces sympathy and brotherhood. His close association with Queequeg, a man of a different race yet a member, as Ishmael tells the dubious Captain Peleg, of "the great and everlasting First Congregation of this whole worshipping world," to which all humanity belongs, saves him.[95] As Ishmael comes to know Queequeg, he feels "a melting" in himself. "No more my splintered heart and maddened hand were against the wolfish world," for "this savage had redeemed it."[96]

Later, with Queequeg safely tied to him by a "monkey-rope" as he descends to cut into the whale, Ishmael realizes that his destiny is linked to his friend's, for "usage and honor" demanded that if Queequeg slipped, his belayer must not cut the cord but go down with him. "So strongly and metaphysically" did Ishmael conceive this that he "seemed distinctly to perceive that [his] own individuality was now merged in a joint stock company of two," that his "free will had received a mortal blow." In contrast, when Ahab's ivory leg splinters and he has to ask the ship's carpenter to fashion a new one, he exclaims, "Here I am, proud as a Greek god, and yet standing debtor to this blockhead for a bone to stand on! Cursed

ate camps; the malignant personal hatreds wearing patriotic masks, and glutted by burning homes and outraged women; the chances in it for brutish men to grow more brutish, and for honorable men to degenerate into thieves and sots.

The Transcendentalists she encountered, blinded by their idealism, had no sense of "the actual war."[108]

Davis also lamented how Emerson allowed himself to become the object of hero-worship. "There were vast outlying provinces of intelligence where he reigned," she wrote, "as absolutely as does the unseen Grand Llama over his adoring votaries." New England swarmed "with weak-brained, imitative folk" who had studied books with "more or less zeal, and who knew nothing of actual life . . . They had revolted from Puritanism, not to enter any other live church, but to fall into a dull disgust, a nausea with all religion" that they cured by going to Concord. "To them came this new prophet with his discovery of the God within themselves," and they hailed him and his ideas with "acclamation."[109]

While not completely rejecting Transcendentalism—when she met Emerson, her "body literally grew stiff and [her] tongue dry with awe"—Davis found its best expression in such outer-directed members of the group as George Ripley and Theodore Parker. Her intellectual foundation, too, was in German philosophy; she had been tutored in it by her brother Wilse. Like Ripley, whose disenchantment with the organization of labor pushed him to found Brook Farm, and Parker, who fought incessantly for society's disenfranchised—the impoverished, the enslaved, the incarcerated—Davis challenged readers to acknowledge and lessen the suffering of others. If Melville, Stoddard, and others had brought subjectivity into the American novel, she wanted to make sure that selves in the aggregate nevertheless remained the novelist's chief subject.

"THIS VULGAR AMERICAN LIFE"

Davis was born in 1831 in Washington, Pennsylvania, just south of the booming new city of Pittsburgh. Soon after her birth she moved with her parents, Richard W. Harding, a recent emigrant from England, and Rachel Leet Wilson, to Big Springs (now Huntsville), Alabama, an area of large cotton plantations. The family moved again when she was five, to Wheeling, Virginia, a town on the Ohio River and a transportation hub between North and South that became, in 1863, part of a new free state, West

Virginia. In these same years, industry, particularly steel manufacturing, developed in Wheeling. Richard Harding entered several (not very successful) business partnerships and was actively involved in the growing city's civic life.

At fourteen Davis began to attend Washington Female Seminary in the town where she was born and where many members of her mother's family lived. Having graduated as valedictorian, she returned to Wheeling and began to assist her mother with domestic chores. Always an avid reader and an eager student, she soon began to write reviews, poems, and editorials for a local paper. At twenty-nine, she sent a story titled "Life in the Iron Mills" to Fields at *The Atlantic Monthly*. A month later she opened his reply, which included a fifty-dollar check; the story appeared in the April 1861 issue and launched her career.

The Atlantic Monthly's readers were likely unprepared for Davis's grim story of the plight of Hugh Wolfe. An impoverished Irish immigrant and ironworker, Wolfe and his cousin Deb live in a fictitious town based on the Wheeling of thirty years earlier, when owners of the mills were building their fortunes on the backs of immigrant laborers with no concern for their welfare. Years later the novelist Elizabeth Stuart Phelps, by that time better known than Davis, recalled the story's impact. Encountering it "was a distinct crisis at the point where intellect and the moral nature meet." After reading "Life in the Iron Mills," "one could never say again that one did not understand" the difficult lives of the working class.[110]

Addressing her genteel readers in a deliberately ironic style, Davis opened the story with these lines: "I want you to hear this story. There is a secret down here, in this nightmare fog, that has lain dumb for centuries: I want to make it a real thing for you. You, Egoist, Pantheist, or Arminian, busy in making straight paths for your feet in the hills, do not see it clearly,—this terrible question which men here have gone mad and died trying to answer."[111] The story that follows is essentially a description of the physical and psychological toll of working in an iron mill. Davis's is the language of suffering so common to earlier sentimental fiction, but she deployed it to spur her readers to anger and political action, rather than sympathetic tears.

Hugh has a remarkable artistic gift for sculpting human forms from korl, an end product of the smelting process. But unable to rise from his impoverishment, he turns to drinking. Imprisoned after Deb steals money for him from a wealthy visitor to the mill, Hugh dies from consumption he contracted at the mill, and his great gift perishes with him. At the end, the narrator, looking at one of Hugh's remarkable works, says, "Its pale lips seem to tremble with a terrible question. 'Is this the end?' they say, 'nothing beyond?—no more?'"[112] For the next three decades, in a variety of fictions that featured factory workers, freed slaves, immigrants, and others trapped at society's lower rungs, Davis continued to ask such difficult questions.

She did so most powerfully in *Margret Howth: A Story of To-Day*, her first novel, published the same year as *The Morgesons*. It could not have been more different from Stoddard's novel and signaled another crucial turn in American fiction. Rather than end in the hyperindividuality of Pierre Glendenning or Cassandra Morgeson, Davis's characters turn toward social awareness and commitment. In *Margret Howth*, self-consciousness leads to connections to other people across class, racial, and gender lines. Further, Davis eschews the sensationalism of Lippard, Thompson, or even Stowe, for she saw that the evils on which the social and economic systems are built are most often found in quotidian aspects of life—the paltry meal and pint of beer of the ironworker, for example—rather than just in the exceptional and lurid.

Margret Howth began as a short story. After the publication of "Life in the Iron Mills," Fields asked for more contributions. She sent him one titled "A Story of To-Day," a long fiction that he asked her to revise because he found it too "gloomy" for readers already depressed over the course of the war. She went back and forth about how precisely to change things, asking at one point if he had any objection to her characterization of Stephen Holmes, who in her story perverts Emersonian self-reliance into mere self-interest. "Would the character of Holmes be distasteful," Davis writes, "to your readers? I mean—the development of a common vulgar life of the Fichtian [*sic*] philosophy and its effect upon a self made man, as I view it?" She was alluding to the German philosopher Johann Gottlieb Fichte's insistence that the perpetual striving for self-development is the essential truth of human existence, an idea that influenced many Transcendentalists.[113] Still unsure of herself as a writer, Davis acquiesced to his suggestions and made alterations, particularly to the ending of *Margret Howth*, that resulted in a more optimistic book but that to some degree compromised the larger message toward which its earlier pages pushed the reader.

When she finally sent Fields a new version of "A Story of To-Day," he serialized it. Before gathering together its parts to publish as a novel, he toyed with it more, calling it *Margret Howth: A Story of To-Day*, a change he made without consultation. Davis pointedly told him that she did not like the title because Margret "is the completest [*sic*] failure in the story, beside *not* being the nucleus of it." Rather, at its center is Holmes, the consummate subjective idealist.[114] In the novel itself Davis responded to Fields's observation that the story lacked an easily discernible moral. Fiction no longer should be written as it had been a century earlier, the narrator explains, when people had no trouble "in seeing which were sheep and which were goats." By now there was no longer any use for didactic plots and representative characters. "I only mean to say I was never there [that is, alive at an earlier time]." She lived now, "in the commonplace," and had never seen "a full-blooded saint or sinner in [her] life."[115] The reader expects to see "idylls delicately tinted; passion-veined hearts, cut bare for curious eyes; prophetic utterances, concrete and clear," something to lift him from "this crowded, tobacco-stained commonplace." But "I want you to dig into the commonplace," the narrator explains, "this vulgar American life, and see what it is."[116]

Davis set *Margret Howth* in an Indiana factory town in December 1860, with the Civil War on the horizon. On her twentieth birthday the eponymous character has started a job as a bookkeeper in a factory owned by Dr. Knowles, "an old man, overgrown, looking like a huge misshapen mass of flesh," and an idealist who hopes to help the poor by creating a new community based on Charles Fourier's socialist theories. To finance his projected utopian community, he plans to sell the factory to Stephen Holmes, a very different type of idealist, who once was in love with Margret. Holmes threw her over, though, for a rich woman whose fortune will enable him to buy the factory. Margret's family lacks such means. Her father is a schoolteacher who can no longer work because of failing eyesight. One of his few joys is debating philosophy and history with Knowles; old Howth often baits Knowles by presenting himself as a skeptic of social reform.

Industry has brought many changes to the town. "Progress" is transforming the rural landscape; when Margret walks home after her first day on the job, she sees "trade everywhere—on the earth and under it." The river has been diverted to power the mills, the hills have been stripped of wood and grass, and along the road gape "the black mouths of coal pits."[117] Meanwhile, Mr. Howth ridicules Knowles's idealistic plans to base a community on truly democratic principles, given that to which the matters have come. "The world's a failure," he exclaims. "All the great old dreams are dead. Your own phantom, your Republic, your experiment to prove that all men are born free and equal—what is it to-day? . . . You talk of To-Day . . . Here is its type and history," he says, lifting a newspaper. "A fair type, with its cant, and bigotry, and weight of uncomprehended fact." And at the heart of the corrupt system there is only one thing: "Bargain and sale, it taints our religion, our brains, our flags."[118]

Another major character is an African American, Lois Yare, the "crippled" daughter of Joe Yare, who worked in the mill until he was imprisoned for a felony. After Yare serves his time, Knowles gives him another chance and finds that he is "as ready a stoker as any on the furnace-rooms."[119] Lois, who has a "child's face" on an "old and stunted body," sells produce from the countryside in town and is loved for her goodness and buoyant spirit. She has worked in the mill, too, starting when she was only seven and already suffering from rickets, and she remained until she was sixteen, while the disease ravaged her body.[120] She tells Margret that she thinks the factory is the cause of her deformity. "Over the years it seemed to me like I was part o' th' engines somehow," she says. "Th' air used to be thick in my mouth, black wi' smoke 'n' wool 'n' smells." Margret "listened, waked reluctantly to the sense of a different pain in the world from her own,—lower deeps from which women like herself draw delicately back, lifting their gauzy dresses."[121] Because of Margret's capacity for empathy, Knowles has long planned to include her in his work with the poor; but that now seems out of the question, for the pittance that she earns at the factory is all her family has.

As the negotiations between Knowles and Holmes proceed, the townspeople learn of Knowles's utopian vision. They are skeptical of his "Communist fraternity," having heard of the failure of similar schemes. "There's two ways for 'em to end," offers one citizen. "If they're made out of the top of society, they get so refined, so idealized, that every particle flies off on its own special path to the sun [as at Blithedale], and the Community's broke." And "if they're made of the lower mud [as Knowles's will be], they keep going down, down together,—they live to drink and eat, and make themselves as near the brutes as they can."[122] A farmer ridicules the doctor's plans:

He spends his days now hunting out the gallows-birds out of the dens [slumlike neighborhoods] in town here, and they're all to be transported into the country to start a new Arcadia. A few men and women like himself, but the bulk is from the dens, I tell you. All start fair, level ground, perpetual celibacy, mutual trust, honour, rise according to the stuff that's in them,—pah! It makes me sick![123]

Another man offers an explanation for why Knowles ventures such absurdities: "Blood, Sir. His mother was a half-blood Creek."[124] What rationale does Davis provide? Like Melville's Ahab, Knowles is "sick in soul from some pain that I dare not tell you of," for he had "looked into the depths of human loss with a mad desire to set it right."[125]

On the day before the property transfer is to occur, Holmes and Knowles meet in the countryside to look over the contract one final time. They have a philosophical discussion about Lois. The "self" in such people, Knowles offers, is "starved and humbled" but is still able to see God clearly. Holmes, drawing on Fichte, disagrees: the self is "so starved and blind that it cannot recognize itself as God." "So that's your creed!" Knowles replies. "Not Pantheism" but *Ego sum* [I am]." "And this wretched huckster [Lois] carries her deity about her . . . ? How, in God's name, is her life to be set free?" Even though he is wed to socialism, Knowles insists that "there *is* a God higher than we" and that thinking only of himself as he does, Holmes will learn this the hard way: "You'll find the Something above yourself, if it's only to curse Him and die."[126]

Later Holmes thinks about how he has "set apart the coming three or four years of his life to make money in," even though "money, or place, or even power, was nothing to him"; all this work was toward "the development of himself." "To tell the truth," the narrator says, "you will find no fairer exponent than this Stephen Holmes of the great idea of American sociology,—that the object of life is *to grow* . . . All men around him were doing the same—thrusting and jostling and struggling, up, up. It was the American motto, Go ahead" that fathers taught to their children. But Holmes's goal was to "lift this self up into a higher range of being when it had done with the uses of this."[127]

Such a man has no use for compromise, and soon enough a friend, Mr. Cox, asks him to do just that. Joe Yare is back at work but out of desperation has committed a forgery. Cox tells Holmes but asks him to keep it quiet, for if revealed, Joe will be sent back to prison for life. "He's old, and he's tryin'," Cox says, to which Holmes replies, smiling, "We did n't make the law he broke. Justice before mercy."[128] To complicate matters, the same day Holmes sees Margret, to whom he admits that he really does not love Miss Herne, his fiancée, whose father will sign the factory papers with him. "Her money," he explains, "will help me to become what I ought to be." He states, "There is no such thing as love in real life," to Margret, who loves him deeply.[129]

That evening Knowles takes Margret to the poorer area of town, to try to recruit her for his new work. "I want to show you a bit of hell," he tells her. He claims to be the inhabitants' "minister," because the regular clergy are too busy "measuring God's truth by the States-Rights doctrine"— that is, arguing whether southern states have the right to secede.[130] He asks her to consider that the loss of "that mass of selfishness" Holmes is nothing compared with what she will see. "Go back, will you, and drone out your life whimpering over your lost dream, and go to Shakespeare for your tragedy when you want it? Tragedy! Come hear,—let me hear what you call this."[131] He takes her into a room crowded with slatternly and drunken women. "Women as fair and pure as you have come into dens like this,—and never gone away. Does it make your delicate breath faint?" he asks sarcastically. "And you a follower of the meek and lowly Jesus!" In the back of one room he shows her "a heap of half-clothed blacks," on their way to Canada on the Underground Railroad. "Did I call it a bit of hell? It's only a glimpse of the underlife of America,—God help us!— where all men are born free and equal."[132] "Give yourself to these people," he implores her. "God calls you to it. There is none to help them."[133]

Things unravel quickly. Holmes encounters Joe and Lois, and Joe brings up Holmes's knowledge of his recent crime. "Have done with this," Holmes replies. "Whoever breaks law abides by it. It is no affair of mine."[134] He tells Joe that he will see him the next day and that he should not try to escape. That evening, after Holmes returns to the mill to sleep, Joe sets fire to the building, intending to kill Holmes. Lois comes upon the result of her father's act: "a live monster now,—in one swift instant, alive with fire,—quick, greedy fire, leaping like serpents' tongues out of its hundred jaws, hungry sheets of flame maddening and writhing to-wards her, and under a dull and hollow roar that shook the night." [135] Lois saves Holmes from the blaze but is now slowly dying from the burning copperas she inhaled. Still, she visits Holmes every day as he slowly recuperates.

Holmes has encountered circumstances that contest, and best, his self-reliance. As Knowles puts it, trying to forget his disappointment over the loss of his factory, where is "the strength of [Holmes's] self-existent soul now? . . . stopped in its growth by chance, this omnipotent deity,— the chance burning of a mill!"[136] Indeed, Holmes experiences a conversion after the fire. On Christmas Day, when he is released from the hospital, he visits Lois at her home and encounters Joe, who tearfully tells him that he set fire to the factory so that he could remain with his daughter. Holmes, knowing how ill Lois is, washes his hands of the "old scoundrel." "Have I his life in my hands?" he asks Lois rhetorically. "I put it into yours,—so, child."[137] Although he does not yet realize it, someday he will "know the subtile [*sic*] instincts" that drew him out of his self-reliance "by the hand of the child that loved him to the Love beyond, that was man and died for him, as well as she."[138]

Knowles, having lost his factory before the sale was finalized, plans to move to the poorer section of town to establish a "House of Refuge." Margret consents to work with him for five years. Davis's editor, Fields, heavily influenced the conclusion of the novel. Visiting Margret, Holmes admits, "When you loved me long ago, selfish, erring as I was, you fulfilled the law of your nature," but when "you put that love out of your heart, you make your duty a tawdry sham, and your life a lie." In her anger and disappointment, Margret realizes that "casing herself in her pride, her conscious righteousness, hugging her new-found philanthropy close, [she] had sunk to a depth of niggardly selfishness."[139] In the story's original version, Davis had Holmes killed on the bloody fields at Manassas.[140] Yet Fields prevailed on her to go with a happy ending, and in the published novel Holmes and Margret marry. Even more surprising, given Davis's animus against industry, the Howths' slave Joel discovers oil on their property. Was this meant to be God's reward to Margret for her finally realizing Holmes's love for her? The ending that her editor, Fields, thus urged on Davis mitigates Margret's commitment to the larger good, but the wholesale criticism of the nation's rampant acquisitiveness remains.

Margret Howth is precisely the kind of transitional fiction that one would expect at the onset of the Civil War. Like Cary, Blake, and Stoddard, Davis had not quite relinquished the sentimental mode, but all four authors brought a new and robust skepticism of religion and the market to American fiction a few decades before their male peers moved in similar directions. As women, barred from the clergy and the pursuit of wealth, they were in a perfect position to do so. Their critiques of American life were as trenchant as those of Hawthorne and Melville, but as self-conscious as their fiction often was, they did not succumb to allegory or to gloomy, self-absorbed nihilism. Rather, in showing the obstacles that real women routinely faced, they suggested an alternative to the status quo. And in their critique of selfishness, they offered as alternatives love for family and community, though not necessarily based in religion. In *Margret Howth*, Holmes's move from amoral, destructive hyperindividualism to love exemplifies a comparable shift in the trajectory of the American novel, from a Transcendentalist-infused liberalism ascendant since the 1820s to an ethic of fellow feeling. But as the nation entered the Gilded Age, the question was whether the former had already won.

8 } From a Theology of the Feelings to an Ethic of Love

On every Sunday in 1865, three thousand people crammed into the Plymouth Congregational Church in Brooklyn Heights for the weekly service. Visitors had to arrive more than an hour early to have any hope of gallery seating; the floor was reserved for pew-holding members. This middle-class congregation had formed in 1847 to accommodate the many businessmen and their families who found Brooklyn's environment more welcoming than the metropolis across the East River, to which many men traveled to work daily on the Fulton Ferry. In 1847, this church, influenced by the merchants and philanthropists Henry C. Bowen and W. T. Cutter, called as its first minister a young New Englander then preaching in Indianapolis. He accepted a generous of-fer of fifteen hundred dollars for his first year and received periodic increases until in 1870 he was making an astonish-ing twenty thousand dollars a year. This clergyman made Plymouth Church the best-known church in the country and became the nation's most famous minister.

As a preacher Henry Ward Beecher, Harriet Beecher Stowe's brother, was an iconoclast.[1] He never dressed the part, eschewing ties and appearing in open-necked shirts that resembled Walt Whitman (whom he knew and ad-mired), dressing like his working-class friends. Beecher's preaching, though, was overwhelming, "like the Falls of Niagara," reported one listener. It was electrifying, ani-mated, extemporaneous, based in his experiences and com-mon sense rather than in book learning, all of which made Beecher the polar opposite of ministers like Nathaniel William Taylor, who spent his career splitting the meta-physical hairs of the New Divinity. Rather than scholasticism and elitism, Beecher was given to dramatic gestures; not for nothing was he termed "the Shakespeare of the pulpit." Once he appeared with the chains that he claimed had held John Brown, rattling and slamming them to the floor to make his case for abolition. On another occasion, he brought to his service an enslaved child whom he "sold" to the congregation—that is, the congregation purchased her freedom.

An aesthete who patronized classical music and art, Beecher kept jewels in his pocket and stuffed hummingbirds in his study for inspiration. Although not handsome, with his large frame and thick lips he radiated a sensuality that women parishioners found irresistible. Master of the straight-faced joke, he wanted to (and often did) please everyone, taking as much time with neighborhood children or visitors who crossed the river on the so-called Beecher boats to hear his sermons as with his pew-renting congregants. Nor did his considerable gifts benefit only Plymouth Church. For several decades, Beecher was a regular on the lyceum circuit and a frequent columnist for papers like Robert Bonner's *New York Ledger* and Bowen's *Independent*. At the height of his career in the 1860s, Beecher's income from lecturing and writing added fifteen thousand dollars per year to his clerical salary. Never quite eclipsing his sister Harriet's fame, he still was an extraordinary individual, a veritable force of nature for religious and social reform.

Born, like Harriet, in Litchfield, Connecticut, Beecher was not an overly promising student and so was sent first to Mount Pleasant Academy in Amherst, Massachusetts, and then to Amherst College rather than to Yale, where his brothers matriculated. Lyman Beecher, his own generation's best-known clergyman, thought that Henry might do better at the smaller, less competitive but still religiously conservative school. He was correct, for while there, although undistinguished as a scholar, Henry flourished, particularly after he discovered his oratorical gifts in debating and acting. After graduation he accompanied his parents and a number of his siblings (including Harriet) to Cincinnati, where Lyman had become president of the new Lane Theological Seminary. He decided to follow in his parent's footsteps as a minister; his father and Harriet's husband, Calvin Stowe, ordained the young man. Beecher's first pastorate was in Lawrenceburgh, Indiana, but he soon moved to a larger church in Indianapolis, where he stayed for eight years. W. T. Cutter, a Brooklyn businessman there on business, heard him preach and came away very much impressed.

Around the same time as Cutter's visit in 1846, Beecher broke from

Calvinism and moved toward what Edwards Amasa Park called a theology of the feelings, which historians later termed evangelical liberalism.[2] Beecher's timing was propitious, for his new religion, based, as it was, in an affective response to Scripture, was precisely what Americans were looking for. Like his sisters Harriet and Catharine, he dismissed calls for religious revival, believing that rather than instantaneous, miraculous conversion, people needed something akin to what Horace Bushnell, in a book by the title, called Christian nurture.

After arriving at Plymouth Church, Beecher's writing began to appear in Bonner's *New York Ledger*. Beecher collected and issued his columns in such popular books as *Star Papers; or, Experiences of Art and Nature* (1856) and *Eyes and Ears* (1862). In the spring of 1865 Bonner, the *New York Ledger*'s savvy editor, decided to take a chance similar to the one he had taken with Fanny Fern: he offered Beecher twenty-four thousand dollars to write a serial novel, for later publication as a book. In need of cash to support his conspicuous consumption, which included the purchase of a summer home outside the city, Beecher accepted. The first installment of the work appeared in May 1867, and later that year Bonner issued the whole book. He also contributed his usual advertising blitz, whipping up so much excitement that one enterprising dramatist, Augustin Daly, brought the novel to the stage before it even hit stores.[3]

The novel's title, *Norwood; or, Village Life in New England*, does not serve it well, for it is not a conventional reminiscence. "I propose to make a story," he told Bonner, "which shall turn not so much on outward action" as on "certain mental or inward questions."[4] Surprisingly for a first-time novelist, Beecher produced precisely that: a full-blown philosophical novel that became a bestseller.

He set the novel in a small New England town much like Litchfield or Lenox, Massachusetts, where in the mid-1850s he had purchased Blossom Farm, the summer home where he and his family escaped the city's heat. Structurally, the book is uncomplicated, for as Beecher promised, the clash of ideas constitutes the drama. *Norwood* begins with the genealogy of several families—the Cathcarts, the Wentworths, the Buells, and the Davises. The story proper centers on the young college graduate Basil Cathcart, the son of hardworking middle-class farmers, who has had his faith shaken and tries to regain it. As it was beginning to do to so many other Christians, his exposure to the evolutionary science presented in Charles Darwin's *Origin of Species* (1859) initiates a crisis of faith.

Cathcart courts Rose, the daughter of Reuben Wentworth, the town's Boston-born, Harvard-educated, European-trained doctor. Despite Rose's pedigree, however, she resembles a sophisticated version of Sylvester Judd's Margaret, her spiritual life originating in her relation to the natural world and extending to Christ's gospel of love. Basil knows that he must regain confidence in his faith before he can hope to win the pious Rose, who is also being courted by two others: Frank Esel, a spoiled, spendthrift artist, and Tom Haywood, a southerner. Before the story's end all three suitors will be caught up in the Civil War.

Beecher drives his narrative through theological and philosophical discussion. Dr. Wentworth debates with Judge Bacon, the town's skeptical rationalist, and Parson Buell, a Yale-educated clergyman whose beliefs bear a strong likeness to Beecher's. At a crucial point, the young Cathcart experiences a moment of spiritual transcendence in the natural world and visits Dr. Wentworth to discuss its implications for his Christian faith. Wentworth delivers Cathcart to the doorstep of the evangelical liberalism that was becoming a major force in American Protestantism.

The debates have their drama and irony. For all his intelligence, for example, Judge Bacon, a hardened cynic, offers little beyond an emotionless, scientific understanding of the world. He has no use for religion because it is scientifically unverifiable. As Wentworth puts it, the judge has "no *ideality*."[5] Likewise Parson Buell offers Cathcart little comfort, for he has been trained in the logic chopping that characterized Yale under the influence first of Lyman Beecher's colleague Timothy Dwight and later of Nathaniel William Taylor and his phalanx of New Divinity men. Buell's knowledge of Scripture, deep as it flows, has never truly warmed his heart. He apprehends the distant logic of the gospel plan and each soul's part in it—a theology of the intellect—but he is a stranger to the theology of the feelings.

In short, both Bacon and Buell, different as they seem, are united by their belief in the supremacy of logic. As Dr. Wentworth puts it, addressing Buell, each of you "may differ in regard to facts and convictions," yet both of you "insist upon reducing all truth to some material equivalent before you are subject to conviction." To Bacon and Buell, "a truth that does not admit of a logical statement" seems a fantasy. "You believe not upon any evidence in your spirit," Wentworth continues, "but upon the semi-material form which language and philosophical statements give to thought." "Imagination," the doctor declares to the doubting Bacon, "is the very marrow of faith."[6] "Man does not live in a book." Rather, his savior is "in Nature, in human life, in my own experiences as well as in the recorded fragments of His history."[7]

Dr. Wentworth lifts Cathcart's gloom by counseling a faith based in experience and imagination, one that essentially combines Emerson's *Nature* (1836) with the metaphoric understanding of the Gospels that Bushnell championed in *God in Christ* (1849). Thus, Wentworth begins to ground his religious belief in his experience of nature, which he believes mirrors the spiritual world. In a crucial passage, he asks Buell to look at some beautiful hollyhocks as light falls on them. "They are transfigured!" he exclaims, for "the light seems to palpitate upon them, and on the crimson blossom it fairly trembles! Is that materialism? Is there no moral ground in them?" He thinks of the questions as rhetorical, but Buell thinks them heretical. "You don't mean," Buell says, "that a hollyhock is a moral and accountable being?" Wentworth does. "Does it not send sheets of light to my eyes?"

> Does not that raise up a thousand fancies and yearnings? Do I not, in its exquisite effects, almost see through matter and onto the other life? And is not that clump [of flowers], with its atmosphere of light, the instrument producing such effects? And when God created light and flowers, did he not know what power it was possible that they could exert upon human souls, and design that they should do it?

"They have a moral function," he concludes, "even if they have no moral nature."[8]

In his account of Cathcart's struggle with doubt, Beecher also invokes Emerson's notion that one needs to leave behind the past in order to move forward with self-reliance. As Emerson puts it, "Why should not we also enjoy an original relation to the universe? Why should not we have a poetry and philosophy of insight and not of tradition, and a religion by revelation to us, and not the history of theirs?"[9] The echoes in *Norwood* are direct. For Cathcart, that past is most present in his inherited religion, the religion of Buell that no longer makes sense to the young graduate. Like Wentworth, he feels a spiritual attachment to nature. Cathcart responds to the natural world with both his understanding (the logical, ratiocinative faculty) and his reason (the spiritual, intuitive faculty). As he progresses in his studies, Cathcart's "[r]eason was asserting its sovereignty." "Should he believe," he wonders, "because his parents and teachers did? ... Was a man to be superscribed by his parents, like a letter, and sent to this or that church?"[10]

Soon enough he realizes that God is in the universe around him, not in Scripture or the church; this makes him a stronger Christian, not a skeptical deist. For Beecher, a direct, experiential relation with God no longer meant, as it had when he began preaching, that the deity had broken through the natural order of things. Rather, grace meant awareness of or insight into the world in all its beauty and led one instinctively to right moral action. Rose, whom Wentworth has raised to understand nature's grammar and poetry, is the lovely fruit of his beliefs.

Thus, the inconsistencies in the Bible pointed out by the higher critics do not affect the larger truth it contains, what the Transcendentalist minister Theodore Parker terms the difference between the "transient" and the "permanent" in Christianity.[11] The Bible is not composed of logical arguments on points of doctrine but of imaginative language that has to be interpreted symbolically, as Bushnell argues in his "Preliminary Dissertation on Language" preface to *God in Christ*. So Wentworth patiently tells Buell that "[t]he Bible cannot contain the truth itself, only the *word-forms*, the lettered symbols" of divine truth. Words themselves have no signification, he explains. They "mean whatever they have the power to make us think of when we look on them," a function, that is, of experience and imagination.[12]

Beecher also brought to judgment another pillar of his father's religion, belief in a wrathful God. American Protestants had gradually been moving toward a God of love. As adumbrated in *Christian Nurture* (1847), *God in Christ*, and *The Vicarious Sacrifice* (1866), Bushnell's theology tended in this direction, as did Edwards Amasa Park's notion (borrowed from Friedrich Schleiermacher) of religion as an affectionate response to the world's beauty. In *Norwood*, Beecher explores love's many incarnations, including man's love for woman, a mother's love for her family, and God's love for mankind. "That mystic Law with which God has bound to himself his infinite realm," Beecher calls it, "the law of Love!"[13]

Cathcart comes to understand the law of love at his moment of conversion, which here derives from Wentworth's counsel on how to understand and appreciate the natural world. Cathcart recalls falling "into one of those balanced states of mind" that eventuate in a remarkable "calm." Hearing a robin call for its mate, Cathcart says, "a call of loneliness for company, of love *for* love ... I almost ceased to be conscious of my body ... I did not *think*. It was *seeing*[,] rather," that the heavens were full of "ineffable gentleness," an echo of Emerson's famous characterization of himself as a "transparent eyeball" who could see "all" when he experienced transcendence. For the first time in his life, Cathcart had "a conception of *infinite* love."[14]

The beauty of Beecher's faith—like that of Judd in his utopian Mons Christi—was that it did not require overturning society in order to renovate it. People could go about their business just as they always had, as long as they expressed their affection for everyone else in their world, from ragamuffins at their doors in Brooklyn Heights to shackled slaves on a Carolina plantation. Ever the reformer, Beecher wanted Americans to embrace this ethic to knit together a torn nation. His faith-based love would end the hatred between North and South; lessen the isolation of men locked in faceless economic combat; combat the natural selfishness of people living in a liberal society; mitigate the feelings of helplessness that resulted from scientific inquiry; and promise the reform of corrupt politics. Love was what a shell-shocked country needed, and Beecher became wealthy and famous proclaiming it.

And shell-shocked it was, which explains Beecher's inclusion of the war in his narrative. Although in the preface to *Norwood* he claimed to have never studied "the mystery of [fiction's] construction"—"plot and counterplot, the due proportion of parts, the whole machinery of a novel"—he holds the reader's attention by showing how none of the chief characters could escape the national conflagration. The Virginian Haywood, a supporter of the southern right to nullification, is present at South Carolina's attack on Fort Sumter and killed on the fields of Gettysburg. Cathcart, having quickly risen to a position of command in the Union army, is severely wounded in the same battle, captured by the Confederates, but eventually reunited with Rose, who received word that he had died. Rose and Cathcart's sister Alice, who loves Haywood and sees his body amid the carnage at Gettysburg, serve as nurses at the front. Even Dr. Wentworth is pulled into the fray, serving as a surgeon for the Union.

A combination of current events and national soul-searching over a suitable faith for the postwar nation, *Norwood* was very popular, even though the reviews were mixed. In *The Atlantic Monthly* Howells wrote that he abhorred "the ruthlessness with which the author preaches."[15]

Orestes Brownson, by now immersed wholly in the Church of Rome, aimed his barbs at what he took as Beecher's dilution of Christianity. Not accepting that Wentworth's understanding of nature leads back to Christ, "Beecherism," he huffed, only reduces "the Christian law of perfection into the natural law of the physicists . . . The persons and personages of his book are only so many points in the arguments which he is carrying on against Calvinistic orthodoxy for pure naturalism."[16] With a new century's perspective, though, the historian of American religion William McLoughlin draws an accurate bead on the novel. *Norwood*, he argues, is the "first fully developed statement of Liberal Protestantism to appear in book form," a "long-neglected key to a significant transition in the American religious mind."[17]

AMATIVENESS RUN AMOK

By 1870 word had spread that Beecher was applying his ethic of love a little too indiscriminately, in ways that could embarrass his ministry and perhaps even end it. People began to notice that he and his parishioner Elizabeth Tilton were spending a lot of time together, particularly during the months he was writing *Norwood*, for which, his most recent biographer claims, she served as something of muse.[18] Elizabeth was the wife of Theodore Tilton, before the Civil War Bowen's right-hand man at the *Independent*. During Reconstruction he became its editor as well as a major player in reformist politics, particularly as an advocate of women's rights.

Bowen had heard rumors of Beecher's infidelity, and not only with Mrs. Tilton. For his part, Tilton had long suspected an affair, but Elizabeth usually was able to explain away his accusations, even when evidence of the liaison seemed quite convincing; moreover, he admired Beecher and spent much time with him, even transcribing his lecture notes for publication as the "Star" columns for the *New York Ledger*. Eventually, worn down by innuendo and guilt, Elizabeth confessed, telling her husband that her minister had convinced her that "their love was proper and not wrong, therefore it followed that any expression of that love, whether by the shake of a hand or the kiss of the lips, or even bodily intercourse" was not only perfectly understandable but right.

Tilton tried to forgive her and control his outrage, but paranoia ensued. He accused Elizabeth of seeing other men, began to believe that one of their four children was not his, and spread ugly rumors about her infidelity to family and friends. At Bowen's urging, he demanded the minister's resignation. After much hand-wringing, Beecher convinced Tilton to keep the mess quiet; but after he became embroiled with the notorious free love advocate Victoria Woodhull, and she (without his permission) broke the story in her *Woodhull & Claflin's Weekly* at the same time that Beecher was celebrating his twenty-fifth anniversary at the Plymouth congregation, all hell broke loose.

Accusations flew in public. After a church committee, before which Beecher had confessed errors in judgment but not outright seduction, found insufficient reason to dismiss him, Tilton sued Beecher in civil court, for "criminal conversation." The trial was a media circus, with newspapers from all over the country sending correspondents to file daily reports; the proceedings occupied the nation for six months. But the jury deadlocked (with a sizable majority supporting Beecher), and the unfortunate result of Beecher's broad interpretation of Christian love was Elizabeth Tilton's excommunication from the Plymouth Church, for slandering her pastor, even as Beecher was exonerated.

One fact about Beecher may help explain, though not excuse, his behavior. Since college he had been a strong believer in and advocate of the "science" of phrenology, which posited that an individual's character could be determined by analyzing the bumps and indentations of his or her head.[19] Particularly before the Civil War, phrenology fitted with America's optative mood, for the accurate identification of one's traits and propensities might serve as a starting point on the path to personal betterment. Once the patient understood his traits, he could cultivate and improve those that were positive and rein in any with potentially negative consequences, thereby achieving harmony. Phrenology thus jibed with the age's belief in individual free will and in nurture over nature.

The traits a phrenologist examined included ideality, ambition, sociability, modesty, anger, and firmness, as well as "amativeness" and "adhesiveness." Amativeness is sexual feeling between men and women; adhesiveness is more akin to deep friendship and can occur with someone of the same sex. Beecher thus could rationalize and excuse his indiscretions with Elizabeth Tilton as owing to his "enlarged" propensity toward amativeness. He embraced phrenology because he believed it helped him understand himself, particularly his habits and obsessions, as well as his passions. Although he does not mention phrenology directly in *Norwood*, he viewed it as another of those sharp "knives" that one could use to dissect self-consciousness and thus a way to learn about the unexplored corners of the mind that had been a focus of American fiction since Charles Brockden Brown's *Wieland*.

But phrenology was not everyone's tool of choice for exploring the mind. Oliver Wendell Holmes, Sr., progenitor of the "genteel tradition" and responsible for terming Boston "the hub of the universe," was a medical doctor who dismissed phrenology as balderdash. He had different notions of motivation and explored them in *Elsie Venner: A Romance of Destiny* (1861).

In particular, he understood that the triumph of Darwin's principles of evolution and natural selection could not help but affect an individual's understanding of good citizenship, for in Darwin's amoral world, a person's obligations to his fellow men and women came into question. This was particularly true for those who adopted the sociologist Herbert Spencer's notion of the survival of the fittest to describe competition between individuals for limited resources. Social Darwinism, as this was sometimes erroneously termed, thus became the perfect faith for those who espoused the laissez-faire capitalism that exploded in the post–Civil War years, affecting all aspects of American life.[20]

In *Elsie Venner*, Bernard Langdon, a young medical student turned schoolmaster, is caught between science and religion. He encounters an odd, aloof, yet magnetically attractive seventeen-year-old student, Elsie Venner, the only child of the wealthy Dudley Venner. From her youngest years, she has been happiest in nature, often wandering off to roam through fields and woods, returning with "a nest, a flower, or even a more questionable trophy of her ramble."[21] Elsie's moods change with the weather and the seasons. She luxuriates in the noonday July heat, when she is at her most attractive but also quick to anger, and she becomes torpid and withdrawn in the depths of winter. Strange and private as she is, this young woman becomes interested in Langdon, signaling her attention through disconcerting stares and then surreptitiously placing in one of his books a rare flower from the crags on The Mountain, where she has a retreat. Fascinated by her, Langdon decides to find her remote playground in the mountains but gets into trouble. Entering a cave where he hopes to find her, he instead encounters a huge rattlesnake, about to strike. Luckily, Elsie arrives and stares into the snake's eyes, which surprisingly "shrunk [*sic*] and faded under the stronger enchantment of her own."[22] The deadly reptile slithers away.

After this terrifying experience, Langdon interrogates the town physician, Dr. Kittredge, about Elsie's seeming power over the wild creature. Kittredge hems and haws and finally cryptically explains that only love can save Elsie from her destructive urges. At the same time, when he hears that Elsie seems drawn to Langdon, Kittredge warns him away from her. Undeterred, Langdon seeks to learn about her past from her nurse, Old Sophy, an African American whose mother was a slave in the family and who has been with the young woman since her birth. He learns that, much like another insufficiently socialized woman, Isabel Banford in *Pierre*, Elsie has difficulty putting her thoughts into words. One day, however, she tells Sophy the reason for her despair. "Nobody loves me. I cannot love anybody. What is love, Sophy?" she asks her plaintively.[23]

Elsie's infatuation with Langdon persists, and in a crucial moment, she asks him to love her. When he tells her that he loves Ellen Darley, his fellow instructor at the academy, and can treat Elsie only as a friend, her health begins to decline. While ministering to her, Ellen learns her secret from Old Sophy. When Elsie's mother was pregnant, a rattlesnake bit her, and she perished a month later from complications from the wound. Strangely Elsie was born with a birthmark in the same spot where her mother was bitten, which she always covers with a golden necklace. Old Sophy believes, as does Dudley Venner, that the snake's venom transferred the creature's traits to the baby, accounting for her alternating moods, seemingly controlled by the warmth or cold of the seasons.

As Elsie languishes, surrounded by her father, Old Sophy, and Ellen, her nature becomes gentler, her visage more like her mother's than ever seemed possible. Before she dies, she tells her father that she loves him, and later, when Sophy prepares the body for burial, she sees that the birthmark has disappeared. Could Langdon have "saved" her with his love? If he was so attracted to her beauty and vitality, why did he eventually choose another, safer love, Miss Letty, Wentworth's granddaughter?

Holmes, like Beecher in *Norwood*, has a range of New England characters discuss philosophical and theological matters, in this case, the mysterious girl's implications for traditional belief. The debaters include Langdon; the conservative minister Reverend Pierrepont Honeywood; the liberal minister Reverend Chauncy Fairweather; the village physician Kittredge, who has been studying Elsie since her birth; and Langdon's medical school professor.

After his experience in the cave, the young man asks this last: "Do you think there may be predispositions, inherited or ingrafted, but at any rate constitutional, which shall take out certain apparently voluntary determinations from the control of the will, and leave them as free from moral responsibility as the instincts of the lower animals?" More simply: "Do you not think there may be a crime which is not a sin?"[24] Such questions, his mentor replies, "belong to that middle region between science and poetry"—as Hawthorne might say, a region where the "Actual" and the "Imaginary" meet and influence each other.[25]

The professor states his belief that no one, except the phrenologists, has ever properly studied the thorny question of the will, "the limits of human responsibility." Although overall a pseudoscience, phrenology had the virtue of having "melted the world's conscience in its crucible, and cast it in a new mould" by its proof that "there are fixed relations between organization and mind and character."[26] That said, in his judgment, "nine tenths" of people's "perversity" still derived from the environment in which they had been raised or still live—"outside influences, drunken ancestors, abuse in childhood, [and] bad company."[27] Nurture, in other words, trumped nature, the same lesson Beecher wished to teach.

Like his predecessors, Holmes was trying to ascertain the relationship between fate, free will, and the wages of sin. In his preface he wrote that through the "disguise of fiction," he wished to present for consideration "a grave scientific doctrine"—the possible inheritance of traits that mark one as evil—without pledging absolute belief in it. He had adopted the notion "as a convenient medium of truth rather than as an accepted scientific conclusion" and wanted readers to consider it, too, particularly as it affected their notions of free will and culpability.[28] The critical difference between Holmes and his predecessors and a sign of how far the American novel—and American culture generally—had come was that he answered such inquiries through science rather than Scripture.

To discover more about Elsie's condition, Langdon writes his medical school professor, who cites various authorities going back to Aetius and Paulus (on the cognate subject of lycanthropy—that is, men acting as wolves), the seventeenth-century savant Sir Kenelm Digby, the homoeopathist Dr. Hering of Surinam, the orientalist Claude-Étienne Savary in his *Letters on Egypt*, and even John Keats's *Lamia*.[29] Theological explanations—most obviously, the inheritance of sin from Adam—hover in the background, while Langdon puts most trust in experimentation and observation, going so far as to observe rattlesnakes in captivity for clues to the girl's condition.[30] Holmes's world is Charles Darwin's, and he, unlike many orthodox clergymen, was not afraid of what he might find.

"LIFE IS MORAL RESPONSIBILITY"

In her autobiography, published late in life, Elizabeth Stuart Phelps (1844–1911) defended her belief that fiction of any merit ought to have an ethical purpose. "Fear less to seem 'Puritan' than to be inadequate. Fear more to be superficial than to seem 'deep,'" for where "'the taste' is developed at the expense of 'the conscience,' the artist is incomplete." In a word, she continued, "the province of the artist is to portray life as it is; and life is moral responsibility."[31] No wonder that her idol was Harriet Beecher Stowe and that she claimed help from angels in writing her runaway bestseller *The Gates Ajar* (1868). As she saw it, the United States was engaged in a great moral struggle, and she would not shirk her part in it.

Phelps was born to the clerical purple. Her maternal grandfather was none other than Moses Stuart (1780–1852), the redoubtable professor of sacred literature at Andover Theological Seminary, bastion of Calvinist orthodoxy, where he taught for more than forty years and she spent much of her girlhood. He died when his granddaughter was only eight, but she felt his influence for years. Her mother, Elizabeth Stuart's oldest daughter and a writer in her own right, married Austin Phelps, a Congregational minister and son of the Reverend Eliakim Phelps, who in addition to pastoral duties devoted much time to the movement for Sunday schools and later served as secretary of the American Education Society, which trained pious men for the ministry. Austin, too, proved an important scholar and eventually became the professor of sacred rhetoric and homiletics at Andover. Before that, he worked at Boston's Pine Street Church, where the family's first daughter, Mary Gray (later renamed Elizabeth Stuart in honor of her mother) lived for the first six years of her life.

Phelps did not reject her orthodox Protestant upbringing as forcefully as the Beecher children did, even though she was exposed to English Romantics as well as to German philosophers and theologians whose works gave fits to the Andover faculty. She did gravitate toward a more liberal faith but never gave up her belief in the historical Jesus. Like the liberal Unitarians whom Andover was founded to combat, she believed that each individual was a personification of the divine and that each life was a voyage of self-development and fulfillment. This was especially so for women, who for too long had been prevented from pursuing intellectual and spiritual growth. She devoted her novels like *Hedged In* (1870), *The Silent Partner* (1871), and *The Story of Avis* (1877), as well as much in her voluminous short fiction, to this premise, even as she understood that a woman's place in society was inextricably linked to economics.[32]

A true polymath, and convinced of the existence of a spirit world by personal experiences with hypnotism, séances, and the like, Phelps was enamored with spiritualism. In 1889, she addressed the subject of paranormal experience in an essay titled "The Psychical Opportunity." Praising the newly formed Society of Psychical Research in London, which aimed to investigate "mesmeric, psychical, and spiritualistic" phenomena, Phelps welcomed the scientific community's interest in that "which is hidden, not in desert islands, or in cuneiform inscriptions, but in human experience."[33] Scientists needed to address the question of such spiritual manifestations with the same seriousness with which they investigated geology or evolution, to establish "the scientific basis of thought and action."[34] Beginning to map the physical attributes of the brain, they now had to explore the nature of consciousness itself. "The Darwin of the science of soul," she wrote, "is yet to be."[35]

One of the seminal early explorers was William James, whose *The Principles of Psychology* (1890) almost single-handedly invented the science for which Phelps called. Indeed, James brought a novelist's feel for language and experience to his *The Varieties of Religious Experience* (1902). In a sense, James, who coined the term "stream of thought" or "consciousness," bridged fiction and science, and not only because of his supple prose style. Starting in the 1850s, American novelists had begun to depict rich and distinctive human personalities. James did the same in his own writing, but his subjects (including, famously, himself) were actual people. If science followed fiction in taking up the study of interiority, it never took it over. Within two decades, modernist novelists—James Joyce, Virginia Woolf, and Marcel Proust among the Europeans, Henry James, Gertrude Stein, and William Faulkner among the Americans—began to embody consciousness in an array of new and startling ways.

Phelps's work represented another significant strain of postbellum fiction, though, for Darwin was not the only giant stalking the intellectual and cultural landscape of the late nineteenth century. He shared the stage with the French scientist and philosopher Auguste Comte, who in his writings on positivism developed a systematic and predictive science of society, focusing on groups rather than on the individual. His influence on nineteenth-century thinkers like Karl Marx, John Stuart Mill, and Herbert Spencer was immense. Like Comte, Phelps and her contemporary Rebecca Harding Davis saw where the West's culture of individualism and self-reliance led. Instead of focusing on the idiosyncrasies of individuals, they took a broader view of human life and saw mostly trouble—specifically, a sickness of the soul resulting from the conditions of modern life. The remedy lay where it had at least since the 1790s, in brotherhood and selfless commitment to the commonwealth that in ways both explicit and subtle had informed the development of the American novel.

CODA

From the late eighteenth century through 1870 many American novelists made a conversation about the nation's values the subject of their work. This conversation began and ended in religious sensibility, specifically with the implications in a new century (and then after the Civil War) of the still-influential synthesis of Jonathan Edwards's theology. The question of the nature of true virtue that Edwards had explored so brilliantly in the mid-eighteenth century took on new meaning, for the democratic ideals that the colonial patriots unleashed could not help but affect moral behavior as well as religious belief, as the nation became defined more and more by an individualistic ethos and a rapidly expanding market economy. The cultural synthesis that emerged in the early nineteenth century included a belief that good citizenship entailed sympathetic identification with those in need, be they orphans, the working poor, chattel slaves, or women economically, legally, and psychologically enchained in a patriarchy from which there seemed little hope of escape.

The country's deification of individualism led to significant shifts in theological reasoning as well as in civic behavior, the result most visible in a virtually wholesale acceptance of personal agency as well as in the momentous shift from a theology of intellect to one of feeling. Methodist itinerants, Presbyterian revivalists, Freewill Baptist proselytizers—these and others embraced free will and a religion of the heart, with emotion the centerpiece of faith. Their emphasis on self-development—and its corollary, self-control toward that end—received an added boost from the selective adoption of European Romantic thought by influential intellectual groups like the New England Transcendentalists, who championed the notion of self-reliant individuals who believed, as Emerson counseled, that they could build their own worlds.

Some, however, novelists and readers both, began to question these forces of political and cultural liberalism, realizing how they frequently led to callousness about the fate of others and thus to an unhealthy division between individual well-being and the good of society as a whole. Many American novelists creatively addressed this growing bifurcation, first evident in the merger of Protestant evangelicalism with a culture of sentiment. They pointed out the sin of egotism and the self-serving nature of the self-regulation counseled by religious groups like the Methodists and others. In doing so, these writers also addressed the nation's failures of sympathetic identification: its seemingly blind eye to the persistence of slavery and racism, the denial of equal rights to women, exploitation of the laboring classes, the hypocrisy and tribalism of religion.

Crucially, some writers also offered alternative visions of the good society. Dissecting individual character and motivation and often placing them in religious or philosophical frameworks, through their novels they contributed to a particular dialectic that subsequently marked American culture and, more specifically, the response to what came to be called modernism. This dialectic led not only to William James's "stream of thought" and his philosophical pragmatism but also to Walter Rauschenberg's and Washington Gladden's Social Gospel; to John Dewey's concern with society's influence on the development of personality; to Jacob Riis's and Lincoln Steffens's "muckraking" investigations of the country's labor and financial institutions; and to Jane Addams's redemptive work at Hull-House.

American novelists in the first half of the nineteenth century, many of them still little known, produced remarkable, and remarkably complex, fiction. But the harsh truth is that even after the cataclysm of the Civil War, the United States remained unique among countries in a schizophrenic emphasis on the individual and his feelings as well as on the commonwealth and one's obligation to it. That Americans still debate precisely the relation of the individual to society does not imply that these writers failed to frame the debate properly or to argue their positions cogently, but that despite their searching criticism and moral correctives, the nation continues to believe in the virtue of democratic liberalism, even in view of its often destructive results.

Yet the ghost of Jonathan Edwards and his conception of the nature of true virtue will not be put to rest. Making the mind aware of itself is not enough; it must become aware of and concerned with others. Trying to encourage such awareness and concern was the burden of American fiction in its first century. It remains ours.

Notes

Acknowledgments

Index

Notes

PREFACE

1. This crucial period has been the subject of recent synthetic histories. See Charles Sellers, *The Market Revolution: Jacksonian America, 1815–1846* (New York: Oxford University Press, 1991); Sean Wilentz, *The Rise of American Democracy: Jefferson to Lincoln* (New York: W. W. Norton, 2005); Daniel Walker Howe, *What Hath God Wrought: The Transformation of America, 1815–1848* (New York: Oxford University Press, 2007); and David Reynolds, *Waking Giant: America in the Age of Jackson* (New York: HarperCollins, 2008). In addition, this period saw a flowering of American literature, particularly of the novel, in which these momentous changes were treated as constitutive of a new kind of democratic selfhood. In the first half of the twentieth century, some scholars sought to assess the period's impact on and in American literature as well as on evolving American democracy. Lewis Mumford's *The Golden Day: A Study in American Experience and Culture* (New York: Boni and Liveright, 1926), Vernon Louis Parrington's *Main Currents in American Thought: An Interpretation in American Literature from the Beginnings to 1920*, 3 vols. (New York: Harcourt Brace, 1927–1930), and F. O. Matthiessen's *American Renaissance: Art and Expression in the Age of Melville and Whitman* (New York: Oxford University Press, 1941) immediately come to mind. Matthiessen's work is very selective. A broad study of American fiction on the scale of the recent work is Alexander Cowie, *The Rise of the American Novel* (New York: American Book Company, 1948), and one even more influential, Richard Chase's *The American Novel and Its Tradition* (Garden City, NY: Doubleday, 1957). Emerson's quotation is from his "Historic Notes of Life and Letters in New England," *Works of Ralph Waldo Emerson*, 14 vols. (Boston: Houghton, Mifflin and Company, 1883), 10:308.

2. I take this movement from Richard Rabinowitz's seminal *The Spiritual Self in Everyday Life: The Transformation of Religious Experience in Nineteenth-Century New England* (Boston: Northeastern University Press, 1989). Rabinowitz restricts his study to the praxis of religious experience but suggests that such shifts in consciousness indelibly stamped the antebellum years. "More than the ink and paper" that American writers used, he says, "[more than] the publishers and audiences they needed, or even the sources of their stories they told," writers drew on "the common language of religious life among their contemporaries" (30).

3. *Graham's Magazine* 44 (April 1854), 452.

4. *Putnam's Monthly Magazine* 3 (October 1854), 396.

5. Hugh Frank Foster, *The Life of Edwards Amasa Park* (New York: Fleming H. Revell Co., 1911); Anthony C. Cecil, Jr., *The Theological Development of Edwards Amasa Park: Last of the "Consistent Calvinists"* (Missoula, MT: American Academy of Religion and Scholars' Press, Dissertation Series no. 1, 1974); and Joseph Conforti, "The Creation and Collapse of the New England Theology: Edwards A. Park and Andover Seminary, 1840–1881," in *Jonathan Edwards, Religious Tradition, and American Culture* (Chapel Hill: University of North Carolina Press, 1995), 108–44.

6. See Philip F. Gura, *American Transcendentalism: A History* (New York: Hill and Wang, 2007), 101–16.

7. Schleiermacher particularly influenced John Weiss, one of Theodore Parker's acolytes; see Gura, *American Transcendentalism*, 277–80. As early as the 1820s, Park's colleague Moses Stuart, Professor of Sacred Literature, introduced his students to the new "higher criticism" of Scripture. He used it to defend conservative Trinitarian views, but some students found his conclusions inconsistent and their faith shaken.

8. Edwards Amasa Park, *The Theology of the Intellect and That of the Feelings* (Boston: Perkins and Whipple, 1850), 8.

9. Edwards's words, in one historian's assessment, gave nothing less than "a new and powerful pulse, which continued to be felt for almost a century"—one powered, however, in good measure by an understanding not just of logic but also of the affective nature of doctrine. See Joseph Haroutunian, *Piety Versus Moralism: The Passing of the New England Theology* (New York: H. Holt and Co., 1932), xxii.

10. See Conforti, *Jonathan Edwards, Religious Tradition, and American Culture*, 62–86.

11. Herman Melville, *Pierre; or, The Ambiguities* ([1852] Evanston, IL: Northwestern University Press, 1971), 212.

12. Harriet Beecher Stowe, *The Minister's Wooing*, in *Three Novels* (New York: Library of America, 1991), 728.

13. Henry Ward Beecher, *Norwood; or, Village Life in New England* ([1867] New York: Fords, Howard and Hulbert, 1887), 133–34. Until about 1820, as the literary historian Ann Douglas has noted, this complex Edwardsian theological tradition was "a chief, perhaps the chief, vehicle of intellectual and cultural activity in American life" (*The Feminization of American Culture* [New York: Knopf, 1977], 6). The literary critic Lawrence Buell agrees, adding that we should envisage nothing less than an intricate and extensive "network of Calvinist literary culture" right to the Civil War (*New England Literary Culture from Revolution Through Renaissance* [New York: Cambridge University Press, 1986], 50).

14. Charles G. Finney, *The Memoirs of Charles G. Finney [1868]: The Complete Restored Text*, ed. Garth M. Tosell and Richard A. G. Dupuis (Grand Rapids, MI: Zondervan Publishing House, 1989), 57.

15. Edmund Wilson, *Patriotic Gore: Studies in the Literature of the American Civil War* (New York: Oxford University Press, 1962), and Daniel Aaron, *The Unwritten War: American Writers and the Civil War* (New York: Knopf, 1973).

16. Alan Heimert, *Religion and the American Mind, from the Great Awakening to the Revolution* (Cambridge: Harvard University Press, 1966), 11.

1. BEGINNINGS

1. Richard Schlatter reprinted it in 1946, hyperbolically calling the book "the best allegory written in colonial America, or even in America before the days of Hawthorne and Melville." Joseph Morgan, *History of the Kingdom of Basaruah* (Cambridge: Harvard University Press, 1946), 42.

2. As David D. Hall has pointed out, such allegories (as well as "Providence tales" that

revealed God's will at work in the world) were the kinds of stories most Christians knew and recited for centuries. As he puts it, these texts tell a common story: the progress of the soul to Christ. It was, he continues, "a story rich in dramatic possibilities, as in the terrifying moments when the soul seemed on the 'brink of hell' or the Devil beckoned with a tempting offer of release from sin." Reading and relating to such stories that were as much a part of folk tradition as of Christian history, seventeenth-century colonists "learned that no matter how routine or humble someone's situation seemed, the real meaning of existence was far greater." See *Worlds of Wonder, Days of Judgment: Popular Religious Belief in Early New England* (New York: Knopf, 1986), 120–21.

3. Royall Tyler, *The Algerine Captive; or, The Life and Adventures of Doctor Updike Underhill* (Walpole, NH: D. Carlisle, 1797), preface.

4. William Hill Brown, *The Power of Sympathy* ([1789] New York: Penguin, 1986), 53.

5. Cathy S. Davidson, for one, so argues, for the book was "written in America, by an author born in America, published first in America, set in America, concerned with issues that are specifically grounded in the new country" (*Revolution and the Word: The Rise of the Novel in America* [New York: Oxford University Press, 1984], 85). Admittedly, a few lengthy fictions had appeared previously in American periodicals. The New Hampshire historian Jeremy Belknap, for example, issued his *The Foresters*, a political satire, in *The Columbian Magazine* from 1787 to 1788 but did not publish it separately until 1792. Similarly, Anna Eliza Bleeker wrote *The History of Maria Kittle*, the earliest fiction based on Indian captivity, in 1779, first published it in *The New-York Magazine* in 1790 and 1791, but only issued it separately in 1797. Brown's work thus rightly claims a certain priority as the first book-length fiction by an American published in that format.

6. For biographical details, see Henri Petter, *The Early American Novel* (Columbus: Ohio State University Press, 1971), 243–51, and Carla Mulford's introduction to the 1986 Penguin edition.

7. The same year, for example, Thomas also published Brown's play *The Better Sort; or, The Girl of Spirit*, which mockingly alluded to the same Boston scandal.

8. *Herald of Freedom*, October 9, 1788. The scandal rocked proper Bostonians, but they soon closed ranks to protect their own. The future president John Adams and the former governor of Massachusetts James Bowdoin, who reviewed an investigation by a "Jury of Inquiry" into the "late unhappy event," concluded that the accusations against Apthorp were not "in any degree supported," so that there was "just ground for the restoration of peace and harmony" between the parties.

9. Brown, *Power of Sympathy*, 39.

10. Ibid., 86.

11. Ibid., 63.

12. Ibid., 77.

13. Ibid., 89.

14. Ibid., 92.

15. Ibid., 11.

16. Gordon S. Wood, *The Radicalism of the American Revolution* (New York: Knopf, 1992), 341.

17. Biographical information gleaned from Elias Nason, *A Memoir of Mrs. Susanna Rowson, with Elegant and Illustrative Extracts from Her Writing in Prose and Poetry* (Albany, NY: Joel Munsell, 1870); Patricia Parker, *Susanna Rowson* (Boston: Twayne Publishers, 1986); Dorothy Weil, *In Defense of Women: Susanna Rowson* (State College: Pennsylvania State University Press, 1976); and Marion Rust, *Charlotte Temple: Authoritative Text, Contexts, and Criticism* (New York: W. W. Norton, 2011) and *Prodigal Daughters: Susanna Rowson's Early American Women* (Chapel Hill: University of North Carolina Press, 2008).

18. "Obituary Notice of Mrs. Rowson," *Boston Commercial Gazette,* March 11, 1824, 2.

19. Peter Force, *American Archives,* 4th series (Washington, D.C.: M. St. Clair Clarke and Peter Force, 1834), 4:1282.

20. Susanna Rowson, *Charlotte Temple and Lucy Temple,* ed. Ann Douglas (New York: Penguin, 1991), 46.

21. Rowson, *Charlotte Temple,* 36.

22. Ibid., 37.

23. Ibid., 23.

24. Timothy Dwight, *The Nature and Danger of Infidel Philosophy* (New Haven: George Bunce, 1798), 50.

25. Rowson, *Charlotte Temple,* 23.

26. Ibid., 132.

27. Ibid., 108.

28. Timothy Dwight, *The Duty of Americans, at the Present Crisis* (New Haven: Thomas and Samuel Green, 1798), 20–21.

29. Eliza Lanesford Cushing wrote *Saratoga: A Tale of the Revolution* (1824) and *Yorktown: An Historical Romance* (1826) and also coedited the annual *The Literary Garland.* Harriet Vaughan Cheney authored *A Peep at the Pilgrims in 1636* (1824) and *The Rivals of Acadia* (1827).

30. Foster's position as the town's doyenne, however, eventually became vexed, for soon after the disestablishment of the Congregational Church in Massachusetts in 1826, the Brighton church split into two separate congregations, the First Parish Church and the Evangelical Congregational Society. This ecclesiastical fracture took an emotional toll on Foster's husband, who resigned shortly thereafter.

31. William B. Sprague, *Annals of the American Pulpit,* 9 vols. (New York: Robert Carter & Brothers, 1857–1865), 1:315.

32. Although some do not accept the identification, during the late eighteenth and nineteenth centuries Pierpont was generally thought the villain. For those who do, his rejection to be seated in the Congress of 1790 after winning a seat during a heated campaign suggests embarrassment about what was coming out about his past. The term "adulterer" was in fact then used against him, even though at the time of the purported affair he was married with eleven children.

33. Hannah W. Foster, *The Coquette,* ed. Jane E. Locke (Ithaca, NY: Mack, Andrus, and Co., 1855), 10, 12–16.

34. Ibid., 19–20.

35. Hannah W. Foster, *The Coquette*, ed. Cathy S. Davidson (New York: Oxford University Press, 1986), 7.

36. Ibid., 13.

37. Ibid., 14.

38. Ibid., 15.

39. Ibid., 18.

40. Ibid., 20.

41. Ibid., 22.

42. Ibid., 26.

43. Ibid., 26, 28.

44. Ibid., 53.

45. Ibid., 55.

46. Ibid., 56.

47. Ibid., 70.

48. Ibid., 105–106.

49. Ibid., 107.

50. Ibid., 108.

51. Ibid., 121.

52. Ibid., 123.

53. Ibid., 133.

54. Ibid., 40.

55. Sukey Vickery, *Edith Hamilton* ([1803] Lincoln: University of Nebraska Press, 2009), 97–98.

56. Evert A. and George L. Duyckinck, *Cyclopedia of American Literature*, 2 vols. (New York: Scribner, 1855), 1:504.

57. Tabitha Tenney, *Female Quixotism, Exhibited in the Romantic Opinions and Extravagant Adventures of Dorcasina Sheldon*, eds. Jean Nienkamp and Andrea Collins ([1801] New York: Oxford University Press, 1992), preface.

58. Ibid., 325.

59. Such tropes, Karen Weyler argues, "indicate loci of cultural anxiety and energy, heuristics developed by and within the early novel as a means of mapping and reforming social relations" (*Intricate Relations: Sexual and Economic Desire in American Fiction, 1789–1814* [Iowa City: University of Iowa Press, 2004], 2).

60. John Adams to William Cunningham, Quincy, Massachusetts, March 15, 1804.

61. Margaret Fuller, "American Literature: Its Position in the Present Time, and Prospects for the Future," *Papers on Literature and Art, Part II* (New York: Wiley and Putnam, 1846), 146–50.

62. Anon., "Memoir of Charles Brockden Brown," in *The Novels of Charles Brockden Brown: Wieland, Ormond, Arthur Mervyn, Edgar Huntly, Clara Howard, Jane Talbot*, 6 vols. (Boston: S. G. Goodrich, 1827), 1:xii–xiii.

63. John Neal, *American Writers: A Series of Papers Contributed to Blackwood's Magazine (1824–1825)*, ed. Fred Louis Patee (Durham, NC: Duke University Press, 1937), 65–66. The most thorough early biography is William Dunlap, *The Life of Charles Brockden Brown:*

Together with Selections from the Rarest of His Printed Works, from His Original Letters, and from His Manuscripts Before Unpublished, 2 vols. (Philadelphia: James P. Parks, 1815).

64. William H. Prescott, "Life of Charles Brockden Brown," *Library of American Biography*, ed. Jared Sparks (Boston: Hilliard Gray & Co., 1834), 131.

65. *American Daily Advertiser*, February 27, 1810.

66. The publication of Dunlap's *Life of Brown* initiated a second wave of notices. A reviewer in the weighty *North American Review* presciently described what continues to hold the twenty-first-century reader's attention. Brown, he wrote, "selects minds that are strangely gifted or influenced, as if for the pleasure of exploring some secret principles of our nature, disclosing new motives of conduct, or old ones operating in a new direction . . . as if he had discovered springs of action which could not be understood in the usual way." Brown's novels, he continued, show "the mind's perfect consciousness of all that is passing within" but not merely toward the end of some obvious moral lesson, as most contemporary novelists did. Rather, the author was "perfectly satisfied 'n such analysis itself. Finally, this reviewer thought that although Brown was "chiefly occupied with the mind," for him the question was not "how much of this has happened or is about to happen" but "how is it felt" (Anon., "The Life of Charles Brockden Brown," 24 and 58–77 passim. One of the most interesting appraisals appeared in 1824 in *Blackwood's Edinburgh Magazine*. There John Neal, in one of a series of essays on "American Writers," opined that Brown's work had no poetry, no pathos, no wit, no humor, no pleasantry, no playfulness, no passion, little of no eloquence, and no imagination. Yet, Neal admitted, Brown had the remarkable facility "to impress his pictures upon the human heart with such unexampled vivacity, that no time can obliterate them; and withal, to fasten himself with such tremendous power, upon a common incident, as to hold the spectator breathless." *Wieland* particularly struck Neal, for it left the reader "in a tense—a sort of uncomfortable, fidgeting, angry perplexity—ashamed of the concern that [he has] shown—and quite in a huff with him—very much as if [he] had been running [himself to death]—in a hot wind—after a catastrophe—with the tail soaped" (Anon., "On the Writings of Charles Brockden Brown and Washington Irving," *Blackwood's Edinburgh Magazine* [February 1820], 554–55). Reprinted in Neal, *American Writers*.

67. *The New-York Weekly Magazine; or Miscellaneous Repository* 2 (July 20): 20 and (July 27): 28 (1796).

68. Charles Brockden Brown, *Wieland*, ed. Jay Fliegelman ([1798] New York: Penguin, 1991), 14.

69. Ibid., 20.

70. Ibid., 21.

71. Ibid., 29.

72. Ibid., 36–37.

73. Ibid., 39.

74. Ibid., 52.

75. Ibid., 57–59.

76. Ibid., 174–75, 123.

77. Ibid., 223–24.

78. Ibid., 235.

79. Ibid., 249.

80. Ibid., 261–62.

81. Ibid., 278.

82. Ibid., 3–4.

83. On these groups, see Stephen A. Marini, *Revolutionary Sects of Revolutionary New England* (Cambridge: Harvard University Press, 1982).

84. Brown, *Wieland*, 23.

85. Ibid., 24.

86. Ibid., 96.

87. Ibid., 99.

88. Ibid., 99.

89. Ibid., 101.

90. Ibid., 5, 167.

91. Ibid., 204–205.

92. Ibid., 214.

93. Prescott, "Life of Brown," 176.

2. GLIMMERINGS OF CHANGE

1. See, for example, Nathan O. Hatch, *The Democratization of American Christianity* (New Haven: Yale University Press, 1989), passim. Neal finally is getting some modern attention; see the essays in Edward Watts and David J. Carlson, eds., *John Neal and Nineteenth-Century American Literature and Culture* (Lewisburg, PA: Bucknell University Press, 2012).

2. James Brooks, "Letters from the East—John Neal," *New-York Mirror* 11 (1833–1834): 69.

3. John Neal, *American Writers: A Series of Papers Contributed to Blackwood's Magazine (1824–1825)*, ed. Fred Louis Patee (Durham, NC: Duke University Press, 1937), 29.

4. Ibid., 63.

5. Ibid., 68.

6. Ibid., 70, 208.

7. Ibid.,167–68; Walt Whitman, *American Primer* (Boston: Small, Maynard and Co., 1904), 4.

8. John Neal tells the reader that is what he was going to call it. *Keep Cool: Written in Hot Weather* (Baltimore: Joseph Cushing, 1817), 31.

9. Neal, *American Writers*, 169.

10. Benjamin Lease, *That Wild Fellow John Neal and the American Literary Revolution* (Chicago: University of Chicago Press, 1972), 41, from *The Columbian Observer*, clipping in Neal scrapbook.

11. John Neal, *Wandering Recollections of a Somewhat Busy Life* (Boston: Roberts Brothers, 1869), 229.

12. John Neal, *Errata; or, The Works of Will. Adams, a Tale*, 2 vols. (New York: For the Proprietors, 1823), 1:265–67.

13. Edgar Allan Poe, *Marginalia* (1849), in *Poe: Essays and Reviews* (New York: Library

of America, 1984), 1448. Poe thought enough of the writer to dedicate the poem "Tamerlane" to him when he republished it in a collection in 1829.

14. Nathaniel Hawthorne, "P's Correspondence," in Hawthorne, *Tales and Sketches* (New York: Library of America, 1982), 1020.

15. Julian Hawthorne, *Nathaniel Hawthorne and His Wife*, 2 vols. (Boston: J. R. Osgood, 1885), 1:145.

16. See Hatch, *Democratization*, passim.

17. David Paul Nord, *Faith in Reading: Religious Publishing and the Birth of Mass Media in America* (New York: Oxford University Press, 2004), 7.

18. See Thomas B. Lovell, "Separate Spheres and Extensive Circles: Sarah Savage's *The Factory Girl* and the Celebration of Industry in Early Nineteenth-Century America," *Early American Literature*, 31 (1996): 1–24, and Margaret B. Moore, "Sarah Savage of Salem: A Forgotten Writer," *Essex Institute Historical Collections*, 127 (1991): 240–59. Also Sylvia Jenkins Cook, *Working Women, Literary Ladies: The Industrial Revolution and Female Aspiration* (New York: Oxford University Press, 2008), chap. 1.

19. [Sarah Savage], *Trial and Self-Discipline* (Boston and Cambridge: James Munroe and Co., 1835), 67.

20. There is no full-scale modern biography of Sedgwick, but see Edward Halsey Foster, *Catharine Maria Sedgwick* (New York: Twayne Publishers, 1974) and [Catharine Maria Sedgwick], *The Power of Her Sympathy: The Autobiography and Journal of Catharine Maria Sedgwick*, ed. with intro. by Mary Kelley (Boston: Massachusetts Historical Society, 1993). Still invaluable is Mary E. Dewey, ed., *Life and Letters of Catharine M. Sedgwick* (New York: Harpers, 1872).

21. *Power of Her Sympathy*, ed. Kelley, 36–37.

22. Dewey, ed., *Life and Letters*, 150–51, 153.

23. Catharine Maria Sedgwick, *A New-England Tale; or, Sketches of New-England Characters and Manners*, ed. Victoria Clements ([1822] New York: Oxford University Press, 1995), 7.

24. Ibid., 131.

25. Catharine Maria Sedgwick, *Redwood: A Tale* ([1824] New York: George P. Putnam, 1850), vii, ix.

26. Dewey, ed., *Life and Letters*, 172.

27. Sedgwick, *Redwood*, ix.

28. Dewey, ed., *Life and Letters*, 168–69.

29. *North American Review* 20 (April 1825): 245–46.

30. Dewey, ed., *Life and Letters*, 187.

31. Caroline Karcher, "Introduction" to Catharine Maria Sedgwick, *Hope Leslie* ([1827] New York: Penguin, 1998), ix.

32. Dewey, ed., *Life and Letters*, 129–30.

33. Sedgwick, *Hope Leslie*, 49–51.

34. Ibid., 52–53.

35. Ibid., 55.

36. Ibid., 359.

37. Ibid., 349.

38. Ibid., 292.

39. Bryant's encomium at the end of his lengthy notice in the *North American Review* can stand for the whole. "We pray [Sedgwick] to go on in the path in which she must excel and has excelled, and which she ought to make her peculiar one," he wrote. "We pray her to go on soon . . . for the public's sake, and for the honor of our youthful literature." William Cullen Bryant, *North American Review*, 26 (April 1828): 420.

40. Review of John Lothrop Motley, "Merry-Mount," *North American Review*, 68 (January 1849): 205.

41. Donald Grant Mitchell, *American Lands and Letters* (New York: Chas. Scribner's Sons, 1899), 254.

42. In the winter of 1834 Ware wrote her to see if she would contribute to a new project he was sponsoring, "a series of narratives, between a formal tale and a common tract," to illustrate "the practical character and influences of Christianity." Dewey, ed., *Life and Letters*, 239.

43. Catharine Maria Sedgwick, *Married or Single?* (New York: Harper, 1857), vi.

44. *Cooper Memorial,* 70.

45. Poe, "William Gilmore Simms" (1846), in *Poe: Essays and Reviews*, 904.

46. See, for example, Daniel Cohen, *Pillars of Salt, Monuments of Grace: New England Crime Literature and the Origins of American Popular Culture, 1674–1860* (New York: Oxford University Press, 1993).

47. William Gilmore Simms, *Martin Faber: The Story of a Criminal* ([1833] Fayetteville: University of Arkansas Press, 2005), 1–3.

48. Ibid., 24–25.

49. Ibid., 40.

50. *Arcturus* 1, no. 28 (January 1841): 90.

51. On Kennedy, see Charles H. Bohner, *John Pendleton Kennedy: Gentleman from Baltimore* (Baltimore: Johns Hopkins University Press, 1961).

52. This ancient belief, the transmigration of souls as a means of purification and penance, had gained currency in the late-eighteenth- and early-nineteenth-century Western world with the translation of Hindu sacred texts into German, French, and eventually English. It also derived in part from ancient Greek belief, primarily through Pythagoras, who adopted it into his philosophy. Plotinus, in particular, believed that heavenly souls passed not only into earthly bodies but also from earthly bodies to other ones. Its presence in nineteenth-century American literature is attested to particularly in the works of Poe, whose tales of lost love, "Ligeia" and "Morella," depend on it.

53. John Pendleton Kennedy, *Sheppard Lee, Written by Himself* ([1836] New York: New York Review of Books, 2008), 7.

54. Ibid., 7.

55. Ibid., 8–9.

56. Ibid., 9–10.

57. Ibid., 11.

58. Ibid., 22–24.

59. Ibid., 47.

60. Ibid., 50–52.

61. Ibid., 415.

62. Ibid., 344.

63. Ibid., 341.

3. PREPARING THE GROUND

1. See Michael Winship, "Manufacturing and Book Production," in *A History of the Book in America: The Industrial Book, 1840–1880*, eds. Scott Casper et al. (Chapel Hill: University of North Carolina Press, 2007), 40–69, and "Distribution and the Trade," ibid., 117–29.

2. See Edward L. Widmer, *Young America: The Flowering of Democracy in New York City* (New York: Oxford University Press, 1999), 104, and Ezra Greenspan, *George Palmer Putnam: Representative American Publisher* (University Park: Pennsylvania State University Press, 2000), 111. "I had long," Putnam later wrote, "had an eye on the trade and written many schemes for them on the empty air when Mr[.] Wiley applied to me for counsel—so the apple had not ripened in a day though it was ready for shaking." Greenspan, "A Publisher's Legacy: The George Palmer Putnam Correspondence at Princeton," *Princeton University Library Chronicle* 40, no. 1 (Autumn 1992): 50.

3. Widmer, *Young America*, 105.

4. Nathaniel Hawthorne to George Duyckinck, July 1, 1845, in Hawthorne, *Letters, 1843–1853* (Columbus: Ohio State University Press, 1985), 106.

5. See Perry Miller, *The Raven and the Whale: The War of Works and Wits in the Era of Poe and Melville* (New York: Harcourt, Brace, 1956), passim.

6. David Dowling, *The Business of Literary Circles in Nineteenth-Century America* (New York and London: Palgrave Macmillan, 2011).

7. As one historian puts it, these New Yorkers "lived in a hyperpolitical time, when every question was probed for its relevance to the great party struggle taking place" (Widmer, *Young America,* 26).

8. Miller, *Raven and the Whale*, 12.

9. Widmer, *Young America*, 62.

10. Ibid., 40–41. "O'Sullivan's conception of democracy as a 'creed' not only lent it a spiritual hue, but more specifically, invested it with a collective sense of philanthropy, a disinterested benevolence toward all humankind, in contrast to the Whig philosophy of individual self-betterment." Further, in championing "America," he encouraged a very large understanding of the term, to include Canada, South and Central America, and even the period of pre-Columbian settlement.

11. *Democratic Review*, 1 (October 1837): 14.

12. Miller, *Raven and the Whale*, 80, where Miller notes that Mathews was someone who "excited among his contemporaries a frenzy of loathing beyond the limits of rationality."

13. Keeping to a higher road than most competitors, *Arcturus* was well regarded and even considered remarkable during its three years of existence. Poe thought it "decidedly the very best magazine in many respects ever published in the United States" (Edgar Allan Poe, "The

Literati of New York City" (1846) in *Poe: Essays and Reviews* [New York: Library of America, 1984], 1161). James Russell Lowell, who eventually grew to dislike Mathews's arrogance, paid it a backhanded compliment by saying that it was "as transcendental as Gotham can be." James Russell Lowell, *The Letters of James Russell Lowell*, 2 vols. (New York: Harper and Brothers, 1894), 1:62.

14. Cornelius Mathews, *The True Aims of Life* (New York: Wiley and Putnam, 1839), 23, 37–38.

15. *Arcturus* 2, no. 12 (November 1844): 366–67.

16. On Lippard, see David S. Reynolds, *George Lippard* (New York: Twayne Publishers, 1982).

17. Charles Chauncey Burr, introduction to George Lippard, *Washington and His Generals; or, Legends of the Revolution* (Philadelphia: G. B. Ziever and Co., 1847), vi.

18. See Samuel Otter, *Philadelphia Stories: America's Literature of Race and Freedom* (New York: Oxford University Press, 2010), 170.

19. Published as an epilogue to George Lippard's *Herbert Tracy; or, The Legend of the Black Rangers* (Philadelphia: R. G. Berford, 1844).

20. *Quaker City Weekly* (October 29, 1849), 1.

21. The brotherhood, one historian notes, synthesized various causes in which Lippard long had had an interest: "land reform, Fourierism, co-operation, election reform, and subversive anticapitalism." See George Lippard, *The Quaker City; or, The Monks of Monk Hall: A Romance of Philadelphia Life, Mystery, and Crime*, ed. David S. Reynolds ([1844] Amherst: University of Massachusetts Press, 1995), 20.

22. Ibid.

23. Ibid., 21. The editor and author Burr wrote in 1847 that Lippard had a "determinate, unmovable self-reliance." Moreover, he was "not a pipe for Fortune's finger (or anyone else's finger) to play what stop she pleases on; if it come to the matter of playing, he will be likely to play his own tunes, to his own time." Burr, in Lippard, *Washington and His Generals*, xxv.

24. Theodore Parker, *Massachusetts Quarterly Review* 1, no. 1 (December 1847): 125.

25. George Lippard, "The Heart-Broken," *The Nineteenth-Century* (1848), in *George Lippard, Prophet of Protest: Writings of an American Radical, 1822–1854*, ed. David S. Reynolds (New York: Peter Lang, 1986), 270.

26. *Quaker City Weekly* (June 2, 1849), ibid., 279.

27. Lippard, *Quaker City*, 84.

28. Ibid., 305–306.

29. *Quaker City Weekly* (March 16, 1850), in *George Lippard, Prophet of Protest*, ed. Reynolds, 47.

30. George Lippard, *New York: Its Upper Ten and Lower Million* (1853), ibid., 46.

31. *Quaker City Weekly* (July 21, 1849), ibid., 173, 175.

32. Lippard, *Quaker City*, vii.

33. Burr in Lippard, *Washington and His Generals*, xiv.

34. See Donna Dennis, *Licentious Gotham: Erotic Publishing in Nineteenth-Century New York* (Cambridge: Harvard University Press, 2009).

35. George Thompson, *Venus in Boston and Other Tales of Nineteenth-Century Life*, eds. David S. Reynolds and Kimberly R. Gladman (Amherst: University of Massachusetts Press, 2002), 47.

36. Ibid., 37.

37. Ibid., 3.

38. Edwin Percy Whipple, "The Romance of Rascality," *Essays and Reviews*, 2 vols. (Boston: Ticknor and Fields, 1848), 2:107.

39. Writing approvingly of Sue's work, Greeley criticized those in the United States who censored passages that indicated his reformist zeal. "To chronicle the horrors and suppress their moral," he wrote, to "omit the very passages that can alone excuse such exhibition—is the wrong way entirely" (*New-York Tribune*, November 24, 1843). In the 1850s Thompson's novels, pornographic by contemporary definition, ran afoul of the law. A series of prosecutions in New York against the publishers of the sporting papers drove such literature underground; see Dennis, *Licentious Gotham* and Patricia Cline Cohen et al., eds., *The Flash Press: Sporting Male Weeklies in 1840s New York* (Chicago: University of Chicago Press, 2008).

40. Arethusa Hall, *Life and Character of the Rev. Sylvester Judd* (Boston: Crosby, Nichols and Co., 1854), 74, 77–78. Also see Richard D. Hathaway, *Sylvester Judd's New England* (University Park: Pennsylvania State University Press, 1981).

41. Hall, *Judd*, 80–103.

42. Ibid., 354.

43. Margaret Fuller, *Writings from the New-York Tribune 1844–1846* (New York: Columbia University Press, 2000), 210, 335–36.

44. *Christian Examiner*, 39 (November 1845): 418–20.

45. James Russell Lowell, in *National Anti-Slavery Standard* 10, no. 35 (January 24, 1850).

46. George Ripley, in Perry Miller, *The Transcendentalists: An Anthology* (Cambridge: Harvard University Press, 1950), 152.

47. On Fourier's American disciples and implementations of his utopian scheme, see Carl Guarneri, *The Utopian Alternative: Fourierism in Nineteenth-Century America* (Ithaca, NY: Cornell University Press, 1991).

48. [Anonymous], *Henry Russell; or, The Year of Our Lord Two Thousand* (New York: William Graham, 1846), 37. Also see "Radical Freelance," *The Philosophers of Foufouville* (New York: G. W. Carleton, 1868), based at the North American Phalanx in Red Bank, New Jersey.

49. Ibid.

50. George Lippard, *New York: Its Upper Ten and Lower Million* ([1853] New York: Ranney, 1854), 284.

51. W. S. Mayo, *Kaloolah; or, The Journeyings to the Djébel Kumri: An Autobiography of Jonathan Romer* (New York: Putnam's, 1849), 461–65.

52. Ibid., 465–66.

53. Ibid., 465.

54. Ibid., 420–21.

55. He wrote three novels that treated this agitation: *The Chainbearers* (1845), *Satanstoe* (1845), and *The Redskins* (1846), known as the "Littlepage Trilogy."

56. James Fenimore Cooper, *The Crater; or Vulcan's Peak*, ed. Thomas Philbrick ([1847]; Cambridge: Harvard University Press, 1962), 139.

57. Ibid., 233.

58. Ibid., 299–300.

59. Ibid., 431.

60. Ibid., 438.

61. Ibid., 387.

62. Ibid., 455–56.

63. Ibid., 459.

4. THE CONVENTIONS OF SENTIMENT

1. Anna Warner, *Susan Warner ("Elizabeth Wetherell")* (New York: G. P. Putnam's, 1909), 283. This biography of Susan remains the most useful. Also see Olivia Stokes, *Life and Memories of Susan and Anna Bartlett Warner* (New York: G. P. Putnam's, 1925).

2. J. C. Derby, *Fifty Years Among Authors, Books and Publishers* (New York: G. W. Carleton and Co., 1884), 304–305.

3. Warner, *Susan Warner*, 305. Nina Baym, who has done more than any other to make available and help the modern reader make sense of early American women's writing, has argued that "if critics ever permit the woman's novel to join the main body of 'American literature,' then all our theories about American fiction . . . will have to be radically revised" (*Woman's Fiction: A Guide to Novels by and About Women, 1820–1870* [Urbana: University of Illinois Press, 1993], 36–37).

4. Nathaniel Hawthorne to William D. Ticknor, January 19, 1855, in Nathaniel Hawthorne, *Letters, 1853–1856* (Columbus: Ohio State University Press, 1987), 304.

5. On the sentimental and the American novel, see especially Elizabeth Barnes, *States of Sympathy: Seduction and Democracy in the American Novel* (New York: Columbia University Press, 1997); Julia Stern, *The Plight of Feeling: Sympathy and Dissent in the American Novel* (Chicago: University of Chicago Press, 1997); and Shirley Samuels, ed., *The Culture of Sentiment: Race, Gender, and Sentimentality in Nineteenth-Century America* (New York: Oxford University Press, 1992).

6. See Richard Rabinowitz, *The Spiritual Self in Everyday Life: The Transformation of Religious Experience in Nineteenth-Century New England* (Boston: Northeastern University Press, 1989), 85–137.

7. For as literary critic Jane Tompkins has argued, modern readers too often have failed to perceive what to Warner's contemporaries was everywhere apparent: that "the great subject" of sentimental fiction was "preeminently . . . the nature of power," a topic all the more significant because women novelists like Warner "lived in a society that celebrated free enterprise and democratic government" yet had as central characters in their novels women excluded from participating in these and other of the age's defining institutions (*Sensational Designs: The Cultural Work of American Fiction, 1790–1860* [New York: Oxford University Press, 1986], 160).

8. Elizabeth Wetherell (Susan Warner), *The Wide, Wide World* (Leipzig: Tauchnitz, 1854), 509.

9. Thomas Harvey Skinner and Edward Beecher, *Hints, Designed to Aid Christians in Their Efforts to Convert to God* (Philadelphia: French and Perkins, 1832), 42.

10. Thomas Harvey Skinner, *The Religion of the Bible, in Select Discourses* (New York: John S. Taylor, 1839), 14–15.

11. Ibid., 183, 185.

12. Horace Bushnell, *Christian Nurture*, ([1847] New Haven: Yale University Press, 1916), 208.

13. John S. Hart, *Female Prose Writers of America* ([1852] Philadelphia: E. H. Butler and Co., 1866), 421. A reviewer in *Holden's Dollar Magazine* (so named because a dollar purchased a year's subscription), although complaining of Ellen's "incessant blubbering" and counseling Warner to make her next book contain "less dry logic and more dry land," still found it "wholly and unmistakably good" as "moral and religious instruction," emphasizing, as many reviewers did, its importance as a religious text (March 8, 1851, 136–37).

14. Caroline Kirkland, "Novels and Novelists," *North American Review* 76 (January 1853): 104.

15. Ibid., 105.

16. Ibid., 106.

17. Ibid., 112–13.

18. Ibid., 121–22.

19. As the southern novelist Virginia Terhune put it, within a year *The Lamplighter* "was in every home, and gossip of the personality [it was published pseudonymously] of the author was seized upon greedily by press and readers" ([Virginia Terhune,] *Marion Harland's Autobiography: The Story of a Long Life* [New York: Harper & Brothers, 1910], 285).

20. Maria Cummins, *The Lamplighter*, ed. Nina Baym ([1854] New Brunswick, NJ: Rutgers University Press, 1988), 99.

21. Ibid., 117.

22. Ibid., 143.

23. Charles Dickens, *American Notes for General Circulation* (New York: Wilson and Company, 1842), 26–29.

24. *Lowell Offering* 1 (August 1841), 169–70.

25. *Olive Leaf and New England Operative* 1 (September 2, 1843).

26. Lucy Larcom, *A New England Girlhood, Outlined from Memory* (Boston: Houghton, Mifflin and Company, 1889), 181–82.

27. Factory Tracts #1, in Philip Foner, ed., *The Factory Girls* (Urbana: University of Illinois Press, 1977), 133–34.

28. Amos Blanchard, "Introduction," in Dorus Clarke, *Lectures to Young People in Manufacturing Villages* (Boston: Perkins and Marvin, 1836), ix–xi.

29. See Patricia Caldwell's modern edition of *Fall River* ([1834] New York: Oxford University Press, 1993), with its brief but informative introduction.

30. Martha W. Tyler, *A Book Without a Title: or, Thrilling Events in the Life of Mira Dana* (Boston, MA: Printed for the Author, 1855), 9.

31. Ibid., 13.

32. Ibid., 15.

33. Ibid., 18.

34. Ibid., v.

35. Ibid., vi.

36. Harriet Beecher Stowe, in Fanny Fern, *Ruth Hall and Other Writings*, ed. Joyce W. Warren (New Brunswick, NJ: Rutgers University Press, 1986), xii, from Stowe's letters at the Sophia Smith Collection, Smith College.

37. Cited in Joyce W. Warren, *Fanny Fern: An Independent Woman* (New Brunswick, NJ: Rutgers University Press, 1992), 93. This is the standard biography.

38. "Notices of New Books," *New York Times*, December 20, 1854.

39. Susan Belasco Smith, in Fanny Fern (Sara Willis Parton), *Ruth Hall*, ed. Susan Belaso Smith ([1854] New York: Penguin, 1997), xxxv.

40. Ibid., "To the Reader."

41. Ibid., 19.

42. Ibid., 47.

43. Ibid., 63.

44. Ibid., 66.

45. Ibid., 87.

46. Ibid., 141.

47. Ibid., 155.

48. Ibid., 170.

49. Ibid., 213.

50. Ibid., 225.

51. Ibid., 227.

52. Ibid., 264.

53. Ibid., 272.

54. *Southern Quarterly Review* 22 (April 1855): 438–50.

55. *The Pioneer* 3, no. 6 (June 1855): 363.

56. Ibid.

57. *The Knickerbocker* 45, no. 1 (January 1855): 84.

58. *The Una* 3 (February 1855): 29–30.

59. From *Harper's New Monthly Magazine*, cited in Hart, *Female Prose Writers*, 512. The best modern assessment of her is James Machor, *Reading Fiction in Antebellum America: Informed Responses and Reception Histories, 1820–1865* (Baltimore: Johns Hopkins University Press, 2011), 256–98. Also see his *Reading Fiction in Antebellum America: Informed Response and Reception Histories, 1820–1865* (Baltimore: Johns Hopkins University Press, 2011).

60. *The Knickerbocker* 44 (September 1856): 303.

61. Caroline Chesebro', *Isa, a Pilgrimage* (New York: Redfield, 1852), 35.

62. Ibid., 44.

63. Ibid., 131.

64. Ibid., 46.

65. Ibid., 294.

66. Ibid., 132–33.

67. Ibid., 219–20.

68. Ibid., 317.

69. *American Whig Review* 16.1 (July 1852): 94.

70. From *Harper's New Monthly Magazine*, in Hart, *Female Prose Writers*, 512.

71. Chesebro', *Isa*, 112.

72. Hart, *Female Prose Writers*, 513.

73. George Ripley, *New-York Tribune*, April 17, 1852.

74. Jean L. Silver-Isenstadt, *Shameless: The Visionary Life of Mary Gove Nichols* (Baltimore: Johns Hopkins University Press, 1992), 139.

75. Mary Gove Nichols, *Mary Lyndon; or Revelations of a Life: An Autobiography* (New York: Stringer and Townsend, 1855), 14.

76. Ibid., 119.

77. Ibid., 135.

78. Ibid., 166–67.

79. Ibid., 188–89.

80. Ibid., 200.

81. Ibid., 198.

82. Ibid., 204–208.

83. Ibid., 312.

84. Ibid., 385.

5. ON THE COLOR LINE

1. Henry James, *A Small Boy and Others* (New York: Scribners, 1913), 158–59.

2. See David S. Reynolds, *Mightier than the Sword: "Uncle Tom's Cabin" and the Battle for America* (New York: W. W. Norton, 2011) for a description of the book's remarkable influence.

3. The story may be apocryphal but was first published by Annie Fields in *The Atlantic Monthly* 78 (August 1896): 148. It also appeared in Fields's biography of Stowe, published a year later, making Fields the first Stowe biographer to print Lincoln's greeting. Annie T. Fields, *The Life and Letters of Harriet Beecher Stowe* (Boston: Houghton, Mifflin and Company, 1897), 269.

4. Joan Hedrick, *Harriet Beecher Stowe: A Life* (New York: Oxford University Press, 1994) is now the standard biography.

5. See Emily Noyes Vanderpoel, *Chronicles of a Pioneer School from 1792 to 1833, Being the History of Miss Sarah Pierce and Her Litchfield School* (Cambridge, MA: The University Press, 1903).

6. See Marian C. McKenna, *Tapping Reeve and the Litchfield Law School* (New York: Oceana, 1986).

7. On the Second Great Awakening, see David Kling, *A Field of Divine Wonders: The New Divinity and Village Revivals in Northwestern Connecticut, 1792–1822* (State College: Pennsylvania State University Press, 1993).

8. Isabella Beecher, cited in Hedrick, *Stowe*, 145.

9. An 1879 edition. This was not some sort of evangelical hubris, for others concurred in its purportedly divine sanction. Delegates to the Colored National Convention in Rochester, New York, in 1853, for example, hailed the novel as nothing less than "a work plainly marked by the finger of God." "Proceedings of the Colored National Convention Held in

Rochester, July 6th, 7th, and 8th, 1853," in Howard Holman Bell, ed., *Minutes of the National Negro Conventions, 1830–1864* (New York: Arno Press, 1969), 40.

10. *New York Daily Times*, September 18, 1852.

11. Thus, the literary critic Jane Tompkins's designation of *Uncle Tom's Cabin* as "the *summa theologica* of America's religion of domesticity" is apt (*Sensational Designs: The Cultural Work of American Fiction* [New York: Oxford University Press, 1986], 125).

12. Harriet Beecher Stowe, *Uncle Tom's Cabin*, ed. Ann Douglas ([1852] New York: Penguin, 1986), 290.

13. Ibid., 261.

14. Ibid., 388–89.

15. Ibid., 392.

16. Ibid., 412.

17. This did not necessarily detract from her characterizations' power, however, for as the literary critic Philip Fisher has observed, "The political content of sentimentality is democratic in that it experiments with the extension of full and complete humanity to classes of figures from whom it has been socially withheld" (*Hard Facts: Setting and Form in the American Novel* [New York: Oxford University Press, 1985], 99).

18. William Edward Farrison, *William Wells Brown: Author and Reformer* (Chicago: University of Chicago Press, 1969) is the standard biography.

19. Ibid., 112–13.

20. William Wells Brown, *Clotel; or, The President's Daughter: A Narrative of Slave Life in the United States* ([1853]; New York: Carol Publishing Group, 1995), 46.

21. Ibid., 46–47.

22. Ibid., 46.

23. *Literary Gazette and Journal of Belles Lettres, Arts, and Sciences* (December 31, 1853): 1263.

24. *The Athenaeum: Journal of Literature, Science, and the Fine Arts* (January 21, 1854): 86.

25. Farrison, *Brown*, 220.

26. Grace Greenwood (Sarah Jane Lippincott), *Poems* (Boston: Ticknor and Fields: 1851), 80–82.

27. Farrison, *Brown*, 222.

28. A runaway slave advertisement that Norcom placed in the Norfolk, Virginia, *Daily Beacon* (ironically, on July 4, 1835) provides a detailed portrait of her. She was "a light mulatto, 21 years of age," he wrote, "about 5 feet four inches high, of a thick and corpulent habit, having on her head a thick covering of black hair that curls naturally but which can be easily combed straight. She speaks easily and fluently," he continued, "and has an agreeable carriage and address." She "has been accustomed to dress well," he added, "has a variety of fine clothes, made in the prevailing fashion, and will probably appear, if abroad, tricked out in gay and fashionable finery."

29. Child's role was minimal, for by that time Jacobs was an accomplished writer. Child explained, "I abridged, and struck out superfluous words sometimes" but did not alter "fifty words in the whole volume." See Jane Fagan Yellin, "Introduction," Harriet Jacobs, *Incidents in the Life of a Slave Girl* ([1861]; Cambridge: Harvard University Press, 2000), xii.

30. Child solicited the Boston firm Thayer and Eldridge, which offered Jacobs a 10 percent royalty. Because Child also assured the firm that the Anti-Slavery Society was going to

peddle the volume, Thayer and Eldridge took the unusual step, for a new author, of having the plates stereotyped, so that more copies than the two thousand planned could be printed on short notice. After Thayer and Eldridge had the plates made, however, it fell into financial difficulties and went bankrupt. Presumably with the aid of others, Jacobs bought the stereotyped plates and contracted with a Boston printer to issue the book "for the author," marking it a commodity with less prestige than one backed by a prominent publishing house. There is no record of how many copies Jacobs initially had printed.

31. *The Liberator* (February 8, 1861).

32. *National Anti-Slavery Standard* (February 16, 1861).

33. Jacobs, *Incidents*, 27.

34. Ibid., 53.

35. Ibid., 154–55.

36. Ibid., 55.

37. Harriet Jacobs to Amy Post, June 21, [1857], cited in Yellin, "Introduction," xiii.

38. Webb later indicated that his wife was from New Bedford, Massachusetts, the daughter of a runaway full-blooded African slave woman from Virginia and "a Spanish gentleman of wealth" who tried (unsuccessfully) to buy his "wife" and who continued to support the mother and child. See Frank J. Webb, "Biographical Sketch of Mary E. Webb," in Frank J. Webb, *Fiction, Essays, Poetry*, ed. Werner Sollors (New Milford, CT: Toby, 2004), 425.

39. Ibid., 427.

40. Sollors, in Webb, *Fiction*, 2.

41. *Frederick Douglass' Paper* (December 1857).

42. Webb, "Biographical Sketch," 426, 428.

43. Harriet Beecher Stowe, in Frank J. Webb, *The Garies and Their Friends* ([1857] New York: Arno Press, 1969), v.

44. Samuel Otter, *Philadelphia Stories: America's Literature of Race and Freedom* (New York: Oxford University Press, 2010), 240.

45. Webb, *The Garies*, 14.

46. Ibid., 41.

47. Ibid., 121–22.

48. Ibid., 133.

49. Ibid., 129, 137.

50. Ibid., 166.

51. Ibid., 229.

52. Ibid., 226.

53. Ibid., 233.

54. Ibid., 260.

55. Ibid., 275–76.

56. Ibid., 354.

57. Ibid., 378.

58. Ibid., 63.

59. Sarah Josepha Hale, *Liberia, or, Mr. Peyton's Experiments* (New York: Harper & Brothers, 1853), 67.

60. Ibid., 224.

61. See Charles Henry Brown, *Agents of Manifest Destiny: The Lives and Times of the Filibusters* (Chapel Hill: University of North Carolina Press, 1980) and Amy S. Greenberg, *Manifest Manhood and the Antebellum American Empire* (New York: Cambridge University Press, 2005).

62. Martin Robison Delany, *Blake; or, the Huts of America, a Novel* (Boston: Beacon Press, 1970), 260–61.

63. Ibid., 290.

64. Ibid., 262.

65. Ibid., 126.

66. Harriet E. Wilson, *Our Nig; or, Sketches from the Life of a Free Black*, ed. Henry Louis Gates ([1859] New York: Vintage, 2002), 138–39. Subsequent citations in the text are to this edition.

67. Ibid., 133.

68. Ibid., 139.

69. Henry Louis Gates, "Introduction," ibid., xxiv.

70. Wilson, ibid., 3.

71. Ibid., 5.

72. Ibid., 6.

73. Ibid., 8–9.

74. Ibid., 11.

75. Ibid., 13.

76. Ibid., 16.

77. Ibid., 21.

78. Ibid., 25–26.

79. Ibid., 30.

80. Ibid., 31.

81. Ibid., 41.

82. Ibid., 35.

83. Ibid., 33–34.

84. Ibid., 47.

85. Ibid., 61, 68.

86. Ibid., 74–75.

87. Ibid., 86.

88. Ibid., 88.

89. Ibid., 95.

90. Ibid., 105.

91. Ibid., 122.

92. Ibid., 129.

6. DISCOVERING SELF-CONSCIOUSNESS

1. "Novels: Their Meaning and Mission," *Putnam's Monthly Magazine* 4, no. 2 (October 1854): 395.

2. Philip F. Gura, *American Transcendentalism: A History* (New York: Hill & Wang, 2007), 46–69.

3. "Novels," 396.

4. Henry James, *Hawthorne* ([1879] Ithaca: Cornell University Press, 1997), 51.

5. "Novels," 391.

6. Here I am indebted to Richard Rabinowitz's *The Spiritual Self in Everyday Life: The Transformation of Religious Experience in Nineteenth-Century New England* (Boston: Northeastern University Press, 1989), especially 166–77.

7. Waldo Hilary Dunn, *Life of Donald G. Mitchell, Ik Marvel* (New York: Scribner's, 1922), 225, 232. This is the standard biography, but see also Wayne R. Kime, *Donald G. Mitchell* (Boston: Twayne, 1985).

8. See, for example, Maura D'Amore, "'A Man's Sense of Domesticity': Donald Grant Mitchell's Suburban Vision," *ESQ: A Journal of the American Renaissance* 56, no. 2 (2010): 135–62.

9. *American Whig Review* 13, no. 37 (January 1851): 74.

10. "Our Young Authors," *Putnam's Monthly Magazine* 1, no. 1 (January 1853): 74.

11. Ik Marvel (Donald G. Mitchell), *Reveries of a Bachelor; or, A Book of the Heart* (New York: Baker and Scribner, 1850), in Paul C. Gutjahr, *Popular American Literature of the Nineteenth Century* (New York: Oxford University Press, 2001), v.

12. "Our Young Authors," 77.

13. Marvel, *Reveries*, 478.

14. See Vincent J. Bertolini, "The Erotics of Sentimental Bachelorhood in the 1850s," in *Sentimental Men: Masculinity and the Politics of Affect in American Culture*, ed. Mary Chapman and Glenn Hendler (Berkeley: University of California Press, 1999), 19–42, and passim.

15. Marvel, *Reveries*, 482.

16. Ibid., 484.

17. Ibid., 527.

18. Ibid., 551.

19. Ibid., 557.

20. Ibid., 564.

21. Ibid., 567.

22. Ibid., 584.

23. Emily Dickinson to Susan Gilbert, October 9, 1851, in *The Letters of Emily Dickinson*, ed. Thomas H. Johnson, 3 vols. (Cambridge: Harvard University Press, 1965), 1:144.

24. Nathaniel Hawthorne, *The Scarlet Letter* ([1850]; New York, Penguin, 1983), 13.

25. *Boston Weekly Messenger* 18 (November 13, 1828); [J. T. Buckingham], *The New-England Galaxy* 9, no. 577 (October 31, 1828).

26. Nathaniel Hawthorne, *Tales and Sketches* (New York: Library of America, 1982), 1150.

27. *North American Review* 45 (July 1837): 59.

28. Edgar Allan Poe, "Twice-Told Tales" (1842), in *Poe: Essays and Reviews* (New York: Library of America, 1984), 570.

29. *The Knickerbocker* 19 (March 1842): 282.

30. *Boston Miscellany* 1 (1842): 92.

31. *Godey's Lady's Book* 35 (November 1847), 252–56.

32. Nathaniel Hawthorne, "Rappaccini's Daughter" (1844), in *Hawthorne: Tales and Sketches* (New York: Library of America, 1982), 975.

33. *Democratic Review* 16 (April 1845): 380.

34. Herman Melville, "Hawthorne and His Mosses," *Literary World* (August 17 and 24, 1850).

35. Sterling F. Delano, *Brook Farm: The Dark Side of Utopia* (Cambridge: Harvard University Press, 2004) is the standard history.

36. Amory Dwight Mayo, "Nathaniel Hawthorne," *Universalist Quarterly and General Review* 7 (July 1851): 272–93.

37. Ibid., 276, 278.

38. Ibid., 276.

39. Ibid., 290.

40. See the description in Hershel Parker, *Herman Melville: A Biography, 1819–1851* (Baltimore: Johns Hopkins University Press, 1996), 745–48.

41. Henry T. Tuckerman, "Nathaniel Hawthorne," *Southern Literary Messenger* 17 (June 1851): 344, 346, 349.

42. Evert Duyckinck, "The House of the Seven Gables," *Literary World* 8 (April 26, 1851): 333.

43. Edwin Percy Whipple, "Review of New Books," *Graham's Magazine* 38 (May 1851): 467.

44. Nathaniel Hawthorne to Horatio Bridge, July 22, 1851, in Hawthorne, *Letters, 1843–1853*, 461–62.

45. *North British Review* 20, no. 39 (1853–1854): 49, 52.

46. Nathaniel Hawthorne, *The Blithedale Romance*, ed. Annette Kolodry [1852] in *Hawthorne: Novels* (New York: Library of America, 1995), 648.

47. Ibid., 641.

48. Ibid., 639.

49. Ibid., 652.

50. Ibid., 760–61.

51. Ibid., 645.

52. Ibid., 646.

53. Ibid., 672.

54. Ibid., 695.

55. Ibid., 656–57.

56. Ibid., 667.

57. Ibid., 692.

58. Ibid., 749–50.

59. Ibid., 751.

60. Ibid., 686.

61. Ibid., 653.

62. Ibid., 822–23.

63. Ibid., 830.

64. Melville to John Murray, October 29, 1847, Herman Melville, *Correspondence* (Evanston, IL: Northwestern University Press, 1993), 98.

65. Melville to John Murray, March 25, 1848, ibid., 106.

66. [London] *Literary Gazette*, March 24, 1849, in Parker, *Melville*, vol. 1, 628.

67. *Athenaeum*, March 24, 1849, in Brian Higgins and Hershel Parker, *Herman Melville: The Contemporary Reviews* (Cambridge: Cambridge University Press, 1995), 193.

68. [London] *Atlas*, March 24, 1849, in Higgins and Parker, *Reviews*, 194.

69. *Bentley's Magazine* 25 (April 1849), ibid., 201.

70. *United States Magazine and Democratic Review* 25 (July 1849), in ibid., 238.

71. *New-York Tribune*, May 10, 1849, in ibid., 226.

72. Melville to Lemuel Shaw, October 6, 1849, in Melville, *Correspondence*, 138.

73. [New Orleans] *Commercial Bulletin*, April 9, 1850, in Higgins and Parker, *Reviews*, 319.

74. Melville to Richard Henry Dana, Jr., May 1, 1850, in Melville, *Correspondence*, 162.

75. Melville to Nathaniel Hawthorne, [June 1?] 1851, ibid., 193.

76. Ibid., 191.

77. Melville to Sarah Huyler Morewood, September [12 or 19], 1851, ibid., 206. Morewood was a neighbor who, with her husband, had bought Robert Melvill's farmhouse in Pittsfield, Massachusetts, known as "Broadhall."

78. Melville to Nathaniel Hawthorne, November [17], 1851, in Melville, ibid., 212.

79. Herman Melville, *Moby-Dick*, ed. Andrew Delbanco ([1851] New York: Penguin, 1992), 178.

80. Ibid., 82.

81. Ibid., 5.

82. Ibid., 183.

83. Ibid., 88.

84. Ibid., 201–203.

85. Ibid., 203.

86. Ibid., 299.

87. Ibid., 233–34.

88. Ibid., 339–40.

89. Ibid., 453–54.

90. Ibid., 455–56.

91. Ibid., 567–68.

92. Ibid., 380.

93. Ibid., 591–92.

94. Ibid., 611.

95. Ibid., 97.

96. Ibid., 57.

97. Ibid., 512.

98. Ibid., 475.

99. *John-Bull*, October 25, 1851, in Higgins and Parker, *Reviews*, 357–58.

100. *News of the World*, November 2, 1851, ibid., 365.

101. *Independent*, November 20, 1851, ibid., 380.

102. *United States Magazine and Democratic Review*, January 30, 1852, ibid., 410.

103. *Southern Quarterly Review*, new series 5, January 5, 1852, ibid., 412.

104. *National Intelligencer*, December 16, 1851, ibid., 399–400.

105. *New-York Tribune*, November 22, 1851, ibid., 383–84.

106. Melville to Sophia Hawthorne, January 8, 1852, in Melville, *Correspondence*, 219; and Melville to Nathaniel Hawthorne, [17?] November 1851, ibid., 213.

107. [New York] *Day Book* 7 (September 1852), in Higgins and Parker, *Reviews*, 436.

108. *Boston Daily Times,* August 5, 1852, ibid., 422.

109. *Southern Literary Messenger* 18 (September 1852), 574, ibid., 434.

110. *American Whig Review* 16 (November 1852), 446–54, ibid., 448.

111. *Godey's Lady's Book* 45 (October 1852), 390, ibid., 440.

112. *Hartford Courant* 4 (August 1852), ibid., 420.

113. *Philadelphia Evening Post*, August 14, 1852, ibid., 425.

114. *New York Home Journal*, September 4, 1852, ibid., 436.

115. *Literary World* 290 (August 21, 1852), ibid., 430.

116. Herman Melville, *The Confidence Man: His Masquerade*, ed. John Bryant ([1857] New York: Penguin, 1991), 155.

117. Ibid., 160–61.

118. Ibid., 84.

119. Ibid., 85–86.

120. Ibid., 217–18.

121. Ibid., 282. Drummond light—limelight—was used in theaters in Melville's day for spotlighting.

122. Ibid., 35.

123. Ibid., 21.

124. Ibid., 298.

125. [Springfield (MA)] *Republican*, May 16, 1857, in Higgins and Parker, *Reviews*, 501.

7. A NEGLECTED TRADITION

1. See Ellery Sedgwick, *The "Atlantic Monthly," 1857–1909: Yankee Humanism at High Tide and Ebb* (Amherst: University of Massachusetts Press, 1994), chap. 1 and 2.

2. "A Literary Whim," *Appleton's Journal* 6 (October 14, 1871): 441.

3. Mary Clemmer, *A Memorial of Alice and Phoebe Cary* (Boston: Houghton, Mifflin and Company, 1872), 19.

4. Ibid., 32–34, 59–69.

5. Ibid., 71.

6. Ibid., 122.

7. *The Una* 1 (May 2, 1853).

8. Judith Fetterley, "Introduction," Alice Cary, *Clovernook Sketches and Other Stories* (New Brunswick, NJ: Rutgers University Press, 1987), xx. Nina Baym, *Woman's Fiction: A Guide to Novels by and About Women, 1820–1870* (Urbana: University of Illinois Press, 1978), 262.

9. Alice Cary, *Hagar: A Tale of To-day* (New York: Redfield, 1852), 255.

10. Ibid., 25.

11. Ibid., 27.

12. Ibid., 29.

13. Ibid., 256.

14. Ibid., 263.

15. Ibid., 256–57.

16. Ibid., 260.

17. *The Una* 1 (May 2, 1853).

18. Carey, *Hagar*, 299–300.

19. Ibid., 300.

20. Ibid., 74.

21. Ibid., 172.

22. Ibid., 173.

23. Ibid., 93.

24. Ibid., 210.

25. Clemmer, *Memorial*, 79.

26. Biographical details are from Grace Farrell's indispensable *Lillie Devereux Blake: Retracing a Life Erased* (Amherst: University of Massachusetts Press, 2002) and Katherine Devereux Blake, *Champion of Women: A Life of Lillie Devereux Blake* (New York: Fleming Revell, [1943]).

27. Cited in Farrell, *Blake*, 41.

28. "The Social Condition of Woman," *The Knickerbocker* 61 (May 1863): 23.

29. Lillie Devereux Blake, *Southwold: A Novel* (New York: Rudd & Carleton, 1859), 10.

30. Ibid., 18.

31. Ibid., 47.

32. Ibid., 86.

33. Ibid., 105.

34. Ibid., 194–95.

35. Ibid., 257.

36. Ibid., 80.

37. Ibid., 191.

38. Ibid., 192.

39. Ibid., 172–73.

40. Lillie Devereux Blake, *Rockford* (New York: Rudd & Carleton, 1862), 204.

41. Richard Henry Stoddard, *Recollections, Personal and Literary* (New York: A. S. Barnes and Co., 1903) offers glimpses of their married life. See particularly 106–15.

42. See the section on Taylor in Larzer Ziff, *Return Passages: Great American Travel Writing, 1780–1919* (New Haven: Yale University Press, 2000), 118–69.

43. *Daily Alta California*, October 8, 1854.

44. Ibid., July 19, 1856.

45. Ibid., January 29, 1855.

46. Ibid., December 3, 1856.

47. Elizabeth Stoddard to James Russell Lowell, May 5, 1859, in James Matlack, "The Literary Career of Elizabeth Barstow Stoddard" (Ph.D. dissertation, Yale University, 1968), 185.

48. Elizabeth Stoddard to Clarence Stedman, May 21, 1860, in ibid., 185a.

49. Ibid.

50. Elizabeth Stoddard to Clarence Stedman, June 22, 1862, ibid., 216.

51. *New York World*, July 4, 1862. If Stoddard errs, the reviewer continues, she does so "on the side of economy and paucity of language. No word is superfluous," even as this sometimes causes the reader to lose "a thread of development from the lack of fullness of expression or the exceeding condensation or reticence of speech and style." The remedy, he urges, is to read more carefully, for quite simply, "there is nothing to skip."

52. Alfred Habegger, *Henry James and the "Woman Business"* (New York: Cambridge University Press, 1989), 96.

53. "Personal," *The Round Table* 2 (October 7, 1865): 70.

54. Elizabeth Stoddard, *The Morgesons*, eds. *Lawrence Buell and Sandra Zagarell* ([1862] New York: Penguin, 1997), 1.

55. In the few changes she made to later editions of the book, she omitted this phrase but still left enough clues for the reader to suppose Ben's drinking killed him.

56. Richard Stoddard to Manton Marble, June 26, 1862, quoting a review in the New York *Transcript*, cited in Matlack, *Stoddard*, 219.

57. *New York World*, July 4, 1862.

58. [Philadelphia] *North American and United States Gazette*, June 28, 1862.

59. [Philadelphia] *Evening Bulletin*, June 24, 1862.

60. *New-York Tribune*, July 19, 1862.

61. Stoddard, *The Morgesons*, 34.

62. Ibid., 97.

63. Ibid., 13.

64. Ibid., 17.

65. Ibid., 23.

66. Ibid., 37.

67. Ibid., 40–41.

68. Ibid., 137.

69. Ibid., 245.

70. Ibid., 58–59.

71. Ibid., 74.

72. Ibid., 86.

73. Ibid., 109.

74. Ibid., 123.

75. Lillian Woodman Aldrich, *Crowding Memories* (Boston: Houghton, Mifflin and Company, 1922), 14–15.

76. Elizabeth Stoddard: *Two Men* ([1865] Lincoln: University of Nebraska Press, 2008), 3.

77. Ibid., 2.

78. Ibid., 21.

79. Ibid., 51.

80. Ibid., 33.

81. Ibid., 90–91.

82. Ibid., 96–97.

83. Ibid., 97.

84. Ibid., 130.

85. Ibid., 110.

86. Ibid., 114.

87. Ibid., 125.

88. Ibid., 124.

89. Ibid., 125.

90. Ibid., 150.

91. Ibid., 161.

92. Ibid., 191.

93. Ibid., 200.

94. Ibid., 261.

95. *New York Post*, October 17, 1865.

96. *The Nation* 1 (October 26, 1865): 537.

97. *New-York Tribune*, November 16, 1865.

98. Stoddard, *Two Men*, 172.

99. William Dean Howells, *Literary Friends and Acquaintances: A Personal Retrospect of American Authorship* (New York: Harper & Brothers, 1900), 87.

100. Thomas Wentworth Higginson, "To Mary Channing Higginson," n.d., letter 342a, *The Letters of Emily Dickinson*, 3 vols., ed. Thomas H. Johnson (Cambridge: Harvard University Press, 1958), 2: 473–76.

101. Stoddard, *Two Men*, 64.

102. *The Bookman* 16, no. 3 (November 1902): 260.

103. *New-York Tribune*, January 27, 1868.

104. Elizabeth Stoddard to Margaret Sweat, April 14, [1852], cited in Anne E. Boyd, *Writing for Immortality: Women and the Emergence of High Literary Culture in America* (Baltimore: Johns Hopkins University Press, 2004), 23.

105. William B. Greene, *Transcendentalism* (West Brookfield, MA: O. S. Cooke, 1849), 12–14.

106. Elizabeth Palmer Peabody, *Reminiscences of the Rev. William Ellery Channing, D.D.* (Boston: Roberts Brothers, 1980), 373, and "Egotheism, The Atheism of To-day" (1858), reprinted in *Last Evening with Allston and Other Papers* (Boston: D. Lothrop, 1886), 245.

107. Rebecca Harding Davis, *Bits of Gossip* (New York: Houghton, Mifflin and Company, 1904), 36.

108. Ibid., 36.

109. Ibid., 45–46.

110. Elizabeth Stuart Phelps, "Stories that Stay," *The Century* 81 (1910): 120.

111. Rebecca Harding Davis, "Life in the Iron Mills" (1861), in *Norton Anthology of American Literature*, 8th ed., ed. Nina Baym et al. (New York: W. W. Norton, 2012), B: 1707.

112. Ibid., 1732.

113. Stoddard to James T. Fields, cited in Sharon M. Harris, *Rebecca Harding Davis and American Realism* (Philadelphia: University of Pennsylvania Press, 1991), 62. On Fichte, see J. D. Morrell, *An Historical and Critical View of Modern Philosophy in Europe* (New York: Robert Carter and Brothers, 1872), 490 ff.

114. Cited in Harris, *Rebecca Harding Davis*, 64. This and Jean Pfaelzer's *Parlor Radical: Rebecca Harding Davis and the Beginnings of American Social Realism* (Pittsburgh: University of Pittsburgh Press, 1996) are the best modern studies.

115. Rebecca Harding Davis, *Margret Howth: A Story of To-day* (Boston: Ticknor and Fields, 1862), 101–102.

116. Ibid., 6.

117. Ibid., 18.

118. Ibid., 34–35.

119. Ibid., 57.

120. Ibid., 68.

121. Ibid., 70–71.

122. Ibid., 83–84.

123. Ibid., 84–85.

124. Ibid., 84–85.

125. Ibid., 90.

126. Ibid., 111–13.

127. Ibid., 120–21.

128. Ibid., 131–32.

129. Ibid., 142–43.

130. Ibid., 150.

131. Ibid., 152.

132. Ibid., 151–52.

133. Ibid., 154.

134. Ibid., 165.

135. Ibid., 171.

136. Ibid., 184.

137. Ibid., 211.

138. Ibid., 212.

139. Ibid., 233.

140. See Pfaelzer, *Parlor Radical*, 74, quoting from the James T. Fields and Rebecca Harding Davis correspondence.

8. FROM A THEOLOGY OF THE FEELINGS TO AN ETHIC OF LOVE

1. Debbie Applegate, *The Most Famous Man in America: The Biography of Henry Ward Beecher* (New York: Doubleday, 2006) is the best biography.

2. See Clifford E. Clark, Jr., *Henry Ward Beecher: Spokesman for a Middle-Class America* (Urbana: University of Illinois Press, 1978), 187–94.

3. Marvin Felheim, "Two Views of the State, or the Theory and Practice of Henry Ward Beecher," *New England Quarterly* 25 (September 1951): 314–26.

4. Letter published in preface to Henry Ward Beecher, *Norwood* ([1867] New York: Fords, Howard, 1887).

5. Henry Ward Beecher, *Norwood; or, Village Life in New England* ([1867] New York: Scribner, 1868), 52.

6. Ibid., 51–52.

7. Ibid., 59–60.

8. Ibid., 53.

9. Ralph Waldo Emerson, *Nature* (1836), in *Essays and Lectures* (New York: Library of America, 1983), 7.

10. Beecher, *Norwood*, 266.

11. See Philip F. Gura, *American Transcendentalism: A History* (New York: Hill & Wang, 2007), 145–49.

12. Beecher, *Norwood*, 59.

13. Ibid., 10.

14. Ibid., 272.

15. [William Dean Howells] *The Atlantic Monthly* 21 (June 1868): 761–64.

16. *The Nation* 6 (April 2, 1868): 274–75; *Catholic World* 10, no. 57 (1869): 399–400.

17. William G. McLoughlin, *The Meaning of Henry Ward Beecher: An Essay on the Shifting Values of Mid-Victorian America, 1840–1870* (New York: Knopf, 1970), 56, 63.

18. The story is best told in Richard Wightman Fox, *Trials of Intimacy: Love and Loss in the Beecher-Tilton Scandal* (Chicago: University of Chicago Press, 1999).

19. See John Davies, *Phrenology: Fad and Science; a Nineteenth-Century Crusade* (New Haven: Yale University Press, 1955) and Charles Colbert, *A Measure of Perfection: Phrenology and the Fine Arts in America* (Chapel Hill: University of North Carolina Press, 1998).

20. See Richard Hofstadter, *Social Darwinism in American Thought* (Philadelphia: University of Pennsylvania Press, 1944).

21. Oliver Wendell Holmes, *Elsie Venner: A Romance of Destiny* ([1861] New York: Doubleday and Company, [no date]), 128–29.

22. Ibid., 165.

23. Ibid., 343.

24. Ibid., 188.

25. Nathaniel Hawthorne, *The Scarlet Letter* ([1850] New York: Penguin, 1983), 35.

26. Holmes, *Elsie Venner*, 193.

27. Ibid., 194.

28. Ibid., 7.

29. Ibid., 190–92.

30. Ibid., 177–79.

31. Elizabeth Stuart Phelps, *Chapters from a Life* (Boston: Houghton, Mifflin and Company, 1896), 262–63.

32. See, for example, Charlotte Perkins Gilman, *Women and Economics: A Study of the Economic Relation Between Men and Women as a Factor in Social Evolution* (Boston: Small, Maynard, 1900).

33. Elizabeth Stuart Phelps, *The Struggle for Immortality* (Boston: Houghton, Mifflin and Company, 1889), 199–200.

34. Ibid., 206.

35. Ibid., 222.

Acknowledgments

Like my previous book on American Transcendentalism, this one derives from decades of thinking and teaching its subject; but again like the former, it owes much, though I did not realize it until later in my career, to Warner Berthoff. For years at Harvard he offered a course in what one might call neglected American novels from the entire nineteenth century. It included not only the "secondary" works of, say, Cooper and Melville but also the fiction of John Pendleton Kennedy and Robert Montgomery Bird from the antebellum years and John Hay's *The Breadwinners*, Henry Adams's *Democracy*, and Louisa May Alcott's *Work* and *Moods*. His suggested reading list comprised two single-spaced, typed pages, from which each student could pick and choose on which novels to write. The course was a revelation, as is Professor Berthoff's example as an elegant stylist.

At the urging of my mentor and constant inspiration (as I write, the centenarian) Daniel Aaron, I explored most of his good friend Edmund Wilson's work and here have been influenced particularly by *Patriotic Gore*. The economy and justness of his writing most strikes me, as does his ability to capture in a trenchant essay the entire life and œuvre of each subject. The chapters therein on Mary Chesnutt and General Grant epitomize his labor and his gift. I have striven, admittedly without his success, at a comparable economy in my descriptions of this book's subjects and their work.

The long shadow of Perry Miller hangs over this work, as it does over most of what I have written. His Ahab-like will to know and understand each of the subjects with which he grappled has been a constant challenge. Like many others, I am not satisfied with *The Raven and the Whale*, and here one sees part of my engagement with it. But also important to me is his unfinished *The Life of the Mind in America*, with its insistence that, along with law and science, religion remained formative in nineteenth-century American literature and culture. When I consider that I now am older than he was when he died in 1963, his work incomplete and yet so much more enduring and significant than mine, or that of most of my contemporaries, I am humbled.

I thank Ellen Dunlap, president of the American Antiquarian Society, for supporting me in the initial stages of this work and the Society's entire staff for their unflinching dedication to the preservation and dissemination of America's printed archive. As usual, too, I am greatly indebted to the inspiration of my friend David D. Hall, whom I got to know under the Society's "generous dome."

At Farrar, Straus and Giroux, Thomas LeBien first encouraged my ambitious project, and Daniel Gerstle did heroic service to put the manuscript in order. My thanks to both.

Finally, the book's dedication to longtime friend Lawrence Buell bespeaks my acknowledgment of both his mastery of one of my chosen fields and the strength of his moral example to attempt to correct what is wrong in the often strange and unsettling world of academia. I offer this work to him as a gift on his retirement after an exemplary career at Oberlin and Harvard.

Index

abolition, xv, xvi, 37, 69, 71, 79, 133, 144–47, 150, 154, 159, 162, 163, 168, 169, 173, 177, 220, 247, 248, 266; William Wells Brown on, 151–57; press, 159, 160, 173; Harriet Beecher Stowe on, 143–51; Frank J. Webb on, 161–67. *See also* antislavery movement; *specific abolitionists*

abortion, 121

Adams, John, 8, 24, 61

Addams, Jane, 280

advertising, 76, 237, 267

Africa, xvi, 99–101; black emigration to, 167–71

African American novelists, xvi, xix, 144, 147, 151–77; William Wells Brown, 151–57; Martin Delany, 169–72; free northern blacks, 161–67, 172–77; fugitive slave narratives, 149, 150, 151–61; Harriet Jacobs, 157–62; publishing industry and, 157–58, 159; Frank J. Webb, 161–67; Harriet E. Wilson, 172–77. *See also specific authors and works*

African Americans, xvi, 71, 86, 143–77, 203, 205, 259–61, 275; 1850s novels on, 143–77; 1860s novels on, 247–51; free, 145, 158, 161–77, 247–51; interracial relationships, 154–68, 172–77, 248–52; lynching, 152; Northern, 161–67, 172–77; press, 169; soldiers, 171; vote, 167. *See also* abolition; African American novelists; slavery

Albany, New York, 198

alcohol, 87, 241, 242

Alcott, Louisa May, 220, 254

Aldrich, Thomas Bailey, 238, 247

Alsop, Richard, 26

American novel, xi–xix; of 1810s–1830s, 39–73; of 1840s, 64, 73, 75–104; of 1850s, 105–215, 217–35; of 1860s, 235–63; turn of

the century, 3–37. *See also specific authors, works, genres, and themes*

American Revolution, 7–8, 21, 22, 37, 39, 61, 62, 64, 71, 85, 102, 197, 213

American Sunday School Union, 47, 89, 90

American Tract Society, 47, 89

American Whig Review, The, 134, 181, 182

Anglo-African Magazine, The, 170

Anthony, Susan B., 223, 231

Antirent War, 102

Anti-Slavery Advocate, The, 157

antislavery movement, 146–47, 151–53, 156–59, 169, 173, 176, 177; press, 159, 160; transatlantic, 146, 151. *See also* abolition; African Americans

Apthorp, Fanny, 5

Apthorp, James, 5

Arcturus, 66, 76, 78, 79, 81–83

Aristocracy, 8

Atlantic Monthly, The, 182, 220, 223, 231, 239, 252, 254, 256, 271

Avery, Ephraim Kingsbury, 120

Baltimore, 41, 44

Balzac, Honoré de, 79, 81

Baptists, 33, 103, 279

Banes, Albert, 111, 112

Barnum, P. T., 223

Barrett Browning, Elizabeth, 221

Baym, Nina, 224

Beecher, Catharine, 123, 144, 146, 267

Beecher, Charles, 144

Beecher, Edward, 111, 112, 144

Beecher, Henry Ward, xiv, 145, 147, 265–74; background of, 265–67; *Norwood*, xiv, 267–73, 275; reviews on, 271–72

Beecher, Isabella, 144, 145

Caritat, Hocquet, 27

Carlyle, Thomas, 95, 179, 200, 202

Cary, Alice, 221–28, 238, 262; background of, 222–23; *Clovernook*, 223, 224; *Hagar*, 223–28, 244

Cassell and Company, 253

Catholics, 84, 138

Century Club, The, 87

Cervantes, Miguel de, *Don Quixote*, 21–22

Channing, William Ellery, 50

Chase, Richard, *The American Novel and Its Tradition*, xviii–xix

Cherokees, xv, 58, 73

Cheseborough, Nicholas, 131–32

Chesebro', Caroline, 131–36, 141; background of, 131–32; *Isa, a Pilgrimage*, 132, 133–36; reviews on, 132, 134–36; *The Children of Light*, 132; *Dream-land by Daylight*, 132; *Getting Along: A Book of Illustrations*, 132; *Peter Carradine*, 132

Child, Lydia Maria, xv, 55, 94, 104, 124, 159; *Hobomok: A Tale of Early Times*, 55; *Philothea: A Romance*, 94; "The Quadroons," 157

Christian Examiner, 78, 96

Christianity, xi–xiv, xv–xvi, xvii, 3, 47, 55–57, 72, 73, 94–96, 103, 104, 108–14, 168, 270–72, 279–80; democratization of, 47; of 1850s, 108–18, 123, 131, 135, 149, 154, 176–77, 235; of 1860s, 243–46, 253–54, 265–74; tract societies, 46–49. *See also* religion; *specific denominations*

Chubbuck, Emily, 124

Cilley, Jonathan, 46

Cincinnati, 144–45, 152, 224, 266

Citizen Soldier, The, 84–85

city life, xvi, 60–61, 66, 94, 118; boardinghouses, 116, 121, 122, 127–28, 211, 222, 225–26, 246; Maria Cummins on, 115–16; of 1810s–1830s, 60–61, 66; of 1840s, 82–90; of 1850s, 115–16, 121–22, 124–31, 161–67, 222–23; Fanny Fern on, 124–31; free northern blacks, 161–67; George Lippard on, 85–90; George

Thompson on, 90–93. *See also specific cities*

civic duty, xiv, xviii, 60, 63, 279

Civil War, xii, 78, 138, 143, 152, 160, 171, 220, 231, 240, 247, 254, 258, 262, 268, 271, 279, 280

Clark, Lewis Gaylord, 78–79, 81, 82, 187

Clark, William, 78

Clarke, Dorus, *Lectures to Young People in Manufacturing Villages*, 119

Coates (Henry T.) & Co., 253

Coleridge, Samuel, 95, 199

Compromise of 1850, 145

Comte, Auguste, 279

Concord, Massachusetts, 188, 254, 255

Congregationalists, 112

Congress, U.S., 22, 146

Connecticut, 26, 55, 112, 114, 144, 181, 228–30, 266

Constitution, U.S., 163

consumerism, 60, 96

Cooke, Rose Terry, 220

Cooper, James Fenimore, xv, 37, 39–40, 42, 43, 45, 46, 49, 62–64, 67, 72, 73, 79, 81, 93, 102–104, 186; *The Bravo*, 63; *The Crater*, 39, 102–104; *The Deerslayer*, 43, 64; *The Headsman*, 63; *The Heidenmauer*, 63; *Home as Found*, 39, 60, 63–64; *Homeward Bound*, 63–64; *The Last of the Mohicans*, 43–44, 54; "Leatherstocking Tales," 39–40; *Lionel Lincoln*, 62–63; *The Pilot*, 63; *The Pioneers*, 39, 42, 44, 63; *The Prairie*, 63; *The Red Rover*, 63; *The Sea*, 39; Sedgwick v., 54–57, 63–64; *The Spy*, 37, 39, 61, 63; utopian fiction by, 102–104; *The Water-Witch*, 63; *The Ways of the Hour*, 39; *The Wept of Wish-Ton-Wish*, 63

Cooper, William, 40, 64

Cooperstown, New York, 39, 40, 63

Cornell, Sarah Maria, 120

counterfeiting, 24, 36, 87

Cowie, Alexander, *The Rise of the American Novel*, xviii, xix

mendicant's tracts, 173–77

metempsychosis, 67–68

Methodists, 33, 83, 84, 103, 279, 280

Mexico, 85, 200

Miller, Perry, 81

Milton, John, 202

Minerva Press, 8

Mississippi River, 118, 148, 213

Mitchell, Donald G., 60, 180–85, 192, 193, 194, 215; background of, 180–82; *Dream Life*, 181, 182; *Dr. Johns*, 182; *Reveries of a Bachelor*, xvii, 180, 181, 182–85, 193; *Rural Studies*, 181–82

Mitchell, Isaac, *The Asylum*, 25

modernism, xvii, 278, 280

Modern Times, 138

Monk Hall, 87–88

Montaigne, Michel de, 199, 202

Monthly Anthology or Magazine of Polite Literature, The, 14

Monthly Magazine and American Review, The, 26

morality, xiv, xv, 8, 10–13, 21, 37, 60, 66, 180, 239; Charles Brockden Brown on, 27–37; of 1810s–1830s, 47–64; of 1840s, 86–104; of 1850s, 107–14, 135; Hannah Webster Foster on, 14–21; George Lippard on, 85–90; Elizabeth Stuart Phelps on, 277–79; Susanna Rowson on, 10–13; Sarah Savage on, 47–49; Catharine Maria Sedgwick on, 49–64; turn of the century, 14–21, 27–37; utopian fiction and, 93–104; Susan Warner on, 107–14

More, Hannah, 48

Morgan, Joseph, *History of the Kingdom of Basaruah*, 3

Morse, Jedediah, 13

Morton, Perez, 5

Morton, Sarah Wentworth Apthorp, 4, 5

Morton, Thomas, 59

Moss, Mary, 253

Motley, John Lothrop, *Merry-Mount*, 59

Moulton, William, 124

Murray, John, 198, 199, 200

Murray, Judith Sargent, 4

Musical World and Times, 125

Mysteries of Nashua, The, 120

Mystery, The, 169

Natchez Free Trader, 157

Nation, The, 220, 251

National Anti-Slavery Standard, The, 159

National Era, The, 146, 222

Native Americans, xv, 29, 40, 54–59, 82, 86, 161, 254; Robert Montgomery Bird on, 72–73; James Fenimore Cooper on, 43–44, 63; myth of "vanishing Indian," 59; John Neal on, 43–44, 46; removal of, xv, 37, 73; Catharine Maria Sedgwick on, 54–59, 62, 64; violence, 44, 56, 72

Neal, John, xv, 35, 40–46, 49, 73, 81, 88, 93; background of, 40–41; *Brother Jonathan*, 45; *Errata*, 43, 45; *Keep Cool: A Novel Written in Hot Weather*, 40, 43; *Logan*, 43–44; pseudonymous essays, 41–42; *Rachel Dyer*, 45; *Randolph*, 42, 43, 44–45; *Seventy-six*, 61

Nesbit, William, *Four Months in Liberia*, 169

New England, xv, 6, 8, 15, 45, 49, 52, 77, 94, 147, 182, 220, 235, 241, 244, 251, 252, 275, 280; Henry Ward Beecher on, 267–72; factory girls, 47–48, 118–23; Catharine Maria Sedgwick on, 52–59. *See also specific states, cities, and authors*

New England Anti-Slavery Convention (1849), 153

New Era, 162

New Hampshire, 172–77

New Orleans, 152, 156

New York City, 26, 27, 39, 50, 60–61, 64, 109, 211, 265; of 1810s–1830s, 60–61, 114–15; of 1840s, 75, 77–83; of 1850s, 125, 127, 131, 137, 199, 222–24, 230, 238; literary salons, 199, 223, 238; politics, 77–83

New York *Day Book*, 211

Prescott, William Hickling, 26

press, xii, 4, 26, 27, 54, 75, 161–62; abolitionist, 159, 160, 173; black, 169; of 1840s, 75–76, 84; of 1850s, 159, 208, 219–20. *See also* journals, literary; reviews, book; *specific publications*

prostitution, 8

Protestants, 33, 268, 270, 272, 277, 280

Proust, Marcel, 278

psychological novels, 179–263; by Lillie Devereux Blake, 228–37; by Alice Cary, 221–28; by Rebecca Harding Davis, 254–63; of 1850s, 179–235; of 1860s, 235–63; by Nathaniel Hawthorne, 185–97; by Herman Melville, 197–215; by Donald G. Mitchell, 180–85; by Elizabeth Stoddard, 237–53

publishing industry, xviii, 4; African American authors and, 157–59; of 1810s–1830s, 46–49, 64–65; of 1840s, 75–77, 78–83, 95, 99; of 1850s, 108, 124–25, 146, 157–59, 177, 181, 185, 198–200, 208–10, 219–20, 230; of 1860s, 240, 253, 267; religious tracts, 46–49, 51; turn of the century, 8, 10, 27. *See also specific publishers*

Puritanism, xv, 54–59, 186, 189; Catharine Maria Sedgwick on, 54–59

Putnam, George Palmer, 99, 107

Putnam's Monthly Magazine, xii, 76, 179, 213, 219–20

Quaker City Weekly, The, 85

Quakers, xv, 25, 52, 69, 72, 103, 136, 152, 159

Quincy, Edmund, 153

Rabelais, François, 199, 200

race, xv, xvi, 73, 143–77, 280; African American novelists on, 151–77; Robert Montgomery Bird on, 67–73; black emigration, 167–72; William Wells

Brown on, 151–57; Rebecca Harding Davis on, 259–61; Martin Delany on, 169–72; 1850s novels on, 143–77; Sarah Josepha Hale on, 167–69; interracial relationships, 43–44, 46, 55–59, 154–68, 172–77, 248–52; Harriet Jacobs on, 157–61; John Neal on, 43–44, 46; Catharine Maria Sedgwick on, 54–59; Elizabeth Stoddard on, 247–53; Harriet Beecher Stowe on, 143–51; Frank J. Webb on, 161–67; Harriet E. Wilson on, 172–77

Radcliffe, Ann, *The Mysteries of Udolpho*, 37

railroads, xi, 47, 75, 89, 118

rape, 44, 87, 157, 158

rationality, xiii, xiv, 7

Rauschenberg, Walter, 280

Reconstruction, 167, 272

Relf, Samuel, *Infidelity*, 24

religion, xi–xiv, xv–xvi, xvii, 3, 47, 180, 279–80; Henry Ward Beecher on, 265–74; Charles Brockden Brown on, 27–37; Alice Cary on, 227–28; Caroline Chesebro' on, 133–35; James Fenimore Cooper on, 102–104; Maria Cummins on, 115–18; of 1810s–1830s, 46–64, 72, 73; of 1840s, 78, 86, 87, 89–90, 94–97, 104; of 1850s, 107–14, 123, 131, 133–35, 141, 147, 154, 176–77, 180, 188–90, 221, 227–28, 235; of 1860s, 243, 245–46, 253–54, 262, 265–80; Nathaniel Hawthorne on, 188–90; Sylvester Judd on, 94–97; Mary Gove Nichols on, 136, 139; Sarah Savage on, 47–49; Catharine Maria Sedgwick on, 49–64; Elizabeth Stoddard on, 245–46; Harriet Beecher Stowe on, 147–51; tract societies, 46–49, 51, 61; turn of the society, 3, 27–37; utopian fiction and, 93–104; Susan Warner on, 107–14. *See also specific religions*

religious tract societies, literature of, 46–49, 51, 61

Mitchell, 180–85; by Mary Gove Nichols, 136–41; by Harriet Beecher Stowe, 143–51; turn of the century, 3–37; by Harriet E. Wilson, 172–77

sex, xvi, 8; Lillie Devereux Blake on, 228–37; William Hill Brown on, 4–8; Alice Cary on, 223–28; of 1810s–1830s, 43–46; of 1840s, 87–93; of 1850s, 121, 137, 138, 155, 158, 228–37; of 1860s, 239–51; Hannah Webster Foster on, 14–21; free love, 138, 273; Nathaniel Hawthorne on, 188–90, 195; interracial, 154–68, 172–77, 248–52; George Lippard on, 87–90; John Neal on, 43–46; Susanna Rowson on, 10–13; Elizabeth Stoddard on, 239–51; George Thompson on, 91–93; turn of the century, 4–24, 27–37

Shakers, 33, 53–54

Shakespeare, William, 199, 202

Shaw, Lemuel, 199, 201

Shays, Daniel, 4

Shelley, Mary, 25, 202

Shelley, Percy Bysshe, 25

Sigourney, Lydia, 123, 124

Simms, William Gilmore, xv, 64–66, 73, 104, 212; *Martin Faber: The Story of a Criminal*, 65–66; *The Partisan*, 64; *Views and Reviews in American Literature, History and Fiction*, 65, 77; *The Wigwam and the Cabin*, 77; *The Yemassee*, 64

sin and guilt, Hawthorne on, 185–97

Skinner, Thomas Harvey, 111–12; *The Religion of the Bible*, 111–12

slavery, xi, xvi, 36, 102, 247, 249, 266, 279, 280; Robert Montgomery Bird on, 67–73; border wars, 146–47; William Wells Brown on, 151–57; Martin Delany on, 169–72; end of, 162, 177; fugitive slave narratives, 144, 150, 151–61; Sarah Josepha Hale on, 167–69; Harriet Jacobs on, 157–61; Kansas/Nebraska Act, 146, 152; rebellions, 147, 156; runaway slaves, xvi, 147–61; Harriet Beecher Stowe on, 143–51; trade, 36, 152, 154–56; violence, 69–70, 147, 149, 156; Frank J. Webb on, 161–67

Smith, Elihu Hubbard, 26

Social Darwinism, 274–77

social realism, 254; by Rebecca Harding Davis, 254–63

society, 90, 104; of 1810s–1830s, 39–73; of 1840s, 75–104; of 1850s, 105–235; of 1860s, 235–74; turn of the century, 3–37; utopian, 93–104. *See also specific groups and concerns*

Society of Psychical Research, 278

somnambulism, 36

Sorosis, 228

South, xi, xvi, xvii, 146, 160; sectional crisis, 66; slavery, 96, 147–51. *See also specific states and cities*

South Carolina, 171

Southern Literary Messenger, The, 181, 212

Southern Quarterly Review, 130, 209

Southworth, E.D.E.N., 221

Spencer, Herbert, 274, 279

Spirit of the Times, The, 84

spiritualism, 278–79

Spofford, Mary Prescott, 147, 220

sporting magazines, 90–91

Staël, Madame de, 221

Stanton, Elizabeth Cady, 131, 135, 223, 231

steam power, xi, 47, 75, 89, 117, 152

Stedman, Edmund Clarence, 240, 243, 251, 253

Steffens, Lincoln, 280

Stein, Gertrude, 278

Stephens, Uriah S., 85

Sterne, Laurence, 45; *A Sentimental Journey*, xiv, 3; *Tristam Shandy*, 45, 202

Stockbridge, Massachusetts, 49–50

Stoddard, Elizabeth Barstow, 220, 221, 223, 237–53, 262; background of, 237–39; *The Morgesons*, xvii, 237, 240–47, 253, 254, 257; reviews on, 239, 240, 243–44, 251–53; *Temple House*, 237, 253; *Two Men*, 247–53

women novelists (*cont.*)
Susanna Rowson, 8–13; Sarah Savage, 47–49; Catharine Maria Sedgwick, 49–64; Elizabeth Stoddard, 237–53; Harriet Beecher Stowe, 143–51; Tabitha Tenney, 21–24; turn of the century, 8–24; Susan Warner, 107–15; Harriet E. Wilson, 172–77. *See also specific authors and works*
women's rights, 4, 62, 86, 133, 135, 173, 220–21, 231, 237, 272, 280; Lillie Devereux Blake on, 228–37; Declaration of Rights and Sentiments, 135; of 1850s–1860s, 121, 131–41, 145, 220–21, 223, 228–37, 238; feminist fiction, 131–41; suffrage movement, 144, 231

Wood, Sally, *Dorval*, 24
Woodhull, Victoria, 173, 231, 273
Woolf, Virginia, 278
Woolsey, Theodore Dwight, 230
Wordsworth, William, 79

Yale Literary Magazine, The, 180
Yale University, 12, 94, 144, 180, 228–30, 266, 268
yellow fever, 9, 26, 155
Young America, 66, 81–83, 200
Youth's Companion, 123

Zola, Émile, 254